Extending Macromedia Flash MX 2004

Complete Guide and Reference to JavaScript Flash

Keith Peters
Todd Yard

Extending Macromedia Flash MX 2004: Complete Guide and Reference to JavaScript Flash

Copyright © 2004 by Keith Peters and Todd Yard

All rights reserved. No part of this work may be reproduced or transmitted in any form or by any means, electronic or mechanical, including photocopying, recording, or by any information storage or retrieval system, without the prior written permission of the copyright owner and the publisher.

ISBN (pbk): 1-59059-304-9

Printed and bound in the United States of America

12345678910

Trademarked names may appear in this book. Rather than use a trademark symbol with every occurrence of a trademarked name, we use the names only in an editorial fashion and to the benefit of the trademark owner, with no intention of infringement of the trademark.

Distributed to the book trade in the United States by Springer-Verlag New York, Inc., 175 Fifth Avenue, New York, NY 10010 and outside the United States by Springer-Verlag GmbH & Co. KG, Tiergartenstr. 17, 69112 Heidelberg, Germany.

In the United States: phone 1-800-SPRINGER, email orders@springer-ny.com, or visit http://www.springer-ny.com. Outside the United States: fax +49 6221 345229, email orders@springer.de, or visit http://www.springer.de.

For information on translations, please contact Apress directly at 2560 Ninth Street, Suite 219, Berkeley, CA 94710. Phone 510-549-5930, fax 510-549-5939, email info@apress.com, or visit http://www.apress.com.

The information in this book is distributed on an "as is" basis, without warranty. Although every precaution has been taken in the preparation of this work, neither the author(s) nor Apress shall have any liability to any person or entity with respect to any loss or damage caused or alleged to be caused directly or indirectly by the information contained in this work.

The source code for this book is freely available to readers at http://www.flashextensibility.com in the Downloads section.

Credits

Technical Editor
Steve Rycroft

Technical Reviewer
Peter Elst

Editorial Board
Steve Anglin, Dan Appleman, Gary Cornell, James Cox, Tony Davis, John Franklin, Chris Mills, Steven Rycroft, Dominic Shakeshaft, Julian Skinner, Martin Streicher, Jim Sumser, Karen Watterson, Gavin Wray, John Zukowski

Assistant Publisher
Grace Wong

Project Manager
Tracy Brown Collins

Copy Editor
Ami Knox

Production Manager
Kari Brooks

Compositor
Dina Quan

Proofreader
Linda Seifert

Indexer
Michael Brinkman

Production Editor
Laura Cheu

Cover Designers
Corné van Dooren and Kurt Krames

Manufacturing Manager
Tom Debolski

CONTENTS AT A GLANCE

CONTENTS

FOREWORD

If I were to tell you that the latest version of Flash can and will increase your productivity levels by speeding up the development process and eradicating all those tedious, repetitive tasks that you waste valuable development time on, over and over again, I would imagine that you would be interested in hearing a little more about it. If you find yourself craving the lowdown on these new and exciting capabilities, then you have opened the right book.

How long does it take for you to add a stop action to each of one or more frames in a timeline? Or how long does it take for you to convert a few graphic symbols into movie clip symbols? There isn't really a definitive answer, but what I am getting at is that it takes too long, or longer than it should. It is boring and nobody enjoys doing it, but developers all do it regularly without even thinking about it—these are the mundane and repetitive tasks that you often encounter when building any Flash movie. These activities and many more account for a lot of the time you spend developing or designing; you don't spend enough time doing the kind of work you enjoy.

The key feature that sold Macromedia Flash MX 2004 to me and my employer has to be the fact that by utilizing the new extensibility layer in Flash MX 2004 it is possible to build or record macro-like scripts that will perform a particular sequence of interactions—a task. You can then play back this task, at a later date with the click of a button, to automatically repeat that sequence of interactions. But that's not all you can do; we've barely scratched the surface . . .

In the relatively short time I have had Flash MX 2004, it has allowed me to reduce the amount of time I spend doing the boring, tedious stuff in my day-to-day work, and increase the amount of time I have to work on the more interesting and challenging tasks.

Recently, my company was developing an interactive world map for one of our clients. They wanted users to be able to roll over each country and have its name appear in a tooltip. They provided us with a vector world map, so we imported it into Flash, and split each country onto a separate layer, giving the layer the name of the country.

We then wrote a command that would go through this Flash movie, select the shape on each layer, convert it into a button, and add a rollover state to that button, which simply changed the color of the country. The command then added a little bit of ActionScript to activate the tooltip and display the name of the country on rollover.

With Flash MX 2004, we were then able run this command on the entire project, and within five minutes our world map was finished, leaving me free to start work on my next project, get a haircut, walk the dog, wash the car, and build a sandcastle! Can you imagine how much longer it would have taken to do this manually? Not to mention how boring it would have been to select each of the 192 countries and convert them all into buttons, adding a rollover state and the required ActionScript to each one. It'd probably easily take the best part of a full working day!

As if this weren't enough to get excited about, there's more. If you put what you learn from this book into practice, and develop an extension that you feel can be utilized by your peers, then you now, as a Flash developer, have a new commercial avenue—packaging an extension and selling it to the world. I have jumped on this opportunity and plan to release a Flash extension that adds auto-saving capabilities to Flash MX 2004 in the very near future. Developing this extension was a breeze using the new scripting language and other enhancements that the new extensibility layer provides. There is nothing stopping you doing the same.

This book will take you, step by step, through each of the various types of Flash extensions—Timeline Effects, commands, custom tools, and Flash panels, giving you all the gory details in a clear and jargon-free manner. Starting off with the basics and steadily working up to the more complex tools and techniques, *Extending Flash MX 2004: Complete Guide and Reference to JavaScript Flash* is loaded with practical examples and code snippets to help you along the way. And the latter part of the book consists of a complete reference to the JavaScript API, which you can rely on when you head off and start to build and distribute your own Flash extensions.

I applaud the authors—both experienced developers—who have managed to cover such an immense subject very accurately and concisely, creating the only book you will ever need at your desk when creating Flash extensions. I for one am very excited at the thought of all the crazy new features that Flash users will be distributing throughout the Flash community in the not-so-distant future, after reading this book.

I wish you luck and happy reading!

Guy Watson, a.k.a. FlashGuru

`www.flashguru.co.uk`

ABOUT THE AUTHORS

Keith Peters lives in the vicinity of Boston, MA, in the USA with his wife, Kazumi, and their new daughter, Kristine. He has been working with Flash since 1999, and has coauthored many books for friends of ED, including *Macromedia Flash MX Studio, Flash MX Most Wanted: Effects and Movies,* and the groundbreaking *Flash Math Creativity*. In 2001, Keith started the experimental Flash site `www.bit-101.com`, on which he regularly posts new cutting-edge, open source experiments. The site recently won an award at the Flashforward 2003 Flash Film Festival in the Experimental category. In addition to the experiments on the site, there are several highly regarded Flash tutorials that have been translated into many languages and are now posted on web sites throughout the world. Keith is currently working full time doing Flash development and various writing projects.

Todd Yard studied acting at London's Mountview Theatre School and performed in New York, Los Angeles, and on tour nationally before settling in New York to pursue graphic design and web application programming full time. Since 1999, Todd has taught classes in Photoshop, Illustrator, and Flash, contributed as an author to eight friends of ED Flash books including *Macromedia Flash MX Studio* and *Flash MX Application and Interface Design,* served as technical editor for *Flash MX 2004 Games Most Wanted,* and has written more than a few Flash, Photoshop, and Illustrator tutorials for computer magazines in the UK. His personal web site, `www.27Bobs.com`, has been featured in a number of articles and international festivals, including the Flashforward Film Festival in Amsterdam and the Electronic Language International Festival in Brazil. Todd now works as lead Flash programmer at Ego7 in New York City, in addition to his freelance writing, coding, and animation projects.

ABOUT THE TECHNICAL REVIEWER

Peter Elst is a freelance multimedia application developer and runs a small business called MindStudio, which specializes in Flash development and content management tools. As a Team Macromedia volunteer, contributor to various community resources, and speaker at several international venues, he happily spends any spare time he has on replying to e-mailed questions and posting on his personal weblog (`www.peterelst.com`).

ABOUT THE COVER IMAGE

Corné van Dooren designed the front cover image for this book. After a typically vague editorial brief along the lines of: "Make us something cool and space-age, with architecture and the Earth," Corné was inspired to extend the cover of the companion title *Flash MX Designer's ActionScript Reference* (also from friends of ED), and take it in a different direction suitable for this new Flash Extensibility technology. With a colorful background as an avid cartoonist, Corné discovered the infinite world of multimedia at the age of 17—a journey of discovery that hasn't stopped since. Corné spends much of his time with most of the well-known packages from Adobe and Macromedia, for both online and offline use. His mantra has always been "The only limit to multimedia is the imagination." You can see more of his work and contact him at `www.cornevandooren.com`, and be sure to check out his chapter in the upcoming *New Masters of Photoshop: Volume 2* from friends of ED.

ACKNOWLEDGMENTS

There are a number of people whose help or advice was invaluable in the writing of this book. First, there's Steve Rycroft, to whom we originally presented the idea of this book last summer. He's been there almost daily, guiding, prodding, and pushing the project through to the end. Peter Brouwers provided some valuable early documentation of the JavaScript API. Without Robin Debreuil, we're sure we would never have figured out the fill matrix, and much of the code describing it is directly from his description of it. Sharon Selden from Macromedia was always helpful in answering questions or finding the answers, and continues to do so over in the forums at `www.flashextensibility.com`. Finally, Peter Elst gave an incredibly thorough technical review of each page of the book, including each line of the reference section, a job we can only imagine as tedious—so special thanks to Peter!

1 INTRODUCTION TO FLASH EXTENSIBILITY

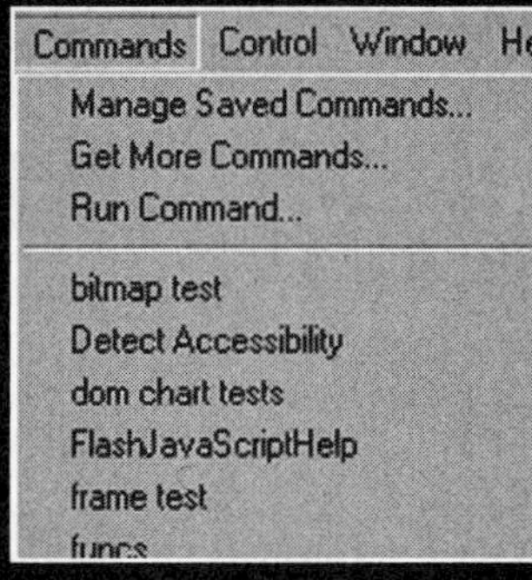

Welcome to *Extending Flash MX 2004*! This book combines a rich introduction and tutorial guide to all of the exciting new extensibility features of Macromedia Flash MX 2004, along with a comprehensive reference dictionary cataloging all of the associated extensibility technologies and language syntax. Our aim has been to make this book the best resource to Flash extensibility available—the book that you'll keep on your desk and never exhaust—complete with the most in-depth coverage possible to enhance your understanding and plenty of practical examples to inspire your creativity.

The extensibility architecture, introduced in Flash MX 2004, is one of the most powerful enhancements to the authoring environment ever seen. As such, it's probably a good idea to take a look at exactly what we mean by **extensibility**—what it can do, what it can't do—and dive in with a few examples to get your feet wet.

> *We should mention here that everything we'll cover in this book applies to both Flash MX 2004 and Flash MX Professional 2004. The main difference is that the Professional version comes with a built-in script editor with which you can create your extensibility scripts. That's certainly a nice bonus for users of this version, but users of the standard version needn't worry—these scripts are created in plain text, so you can use any text editor you like to do the same thing.*

Personally, when we first heard the term, we initially associated it, incorrectly as you'll see, with concepts and buzzwords like *accessibility* and *usability*. All well and good, but not too exciting. Since many new features are available in Flash MX 2004, it's easy to overlook extensibility as some other minor enhancement that you may or may not need someday. But when we're discussing the extensibility architecture, we're literally talking about the ability to extend the authoring environment in Flash. And this doesn't only mean that Flash MX 2004 is just extended beyond Flash MX—that much is obvious. What we're talking about is you, the Flash user, being able to extend Flash MX 2004 to make it do things that it couldn't do when you installed it. For example, you can add new drawing tools to the toolbar to create any kind of shape or drawing imaginable, including some basic real-time 3D effects. In fact, we'll show you how to do just that in **Chapter 3**! You can create commands that perform complex, time-consuming tasks instantly. These can be simple macro-type commands or full programs that create new Flash documents, add content to them, and publish them. Most of these enhancements make use of a new scripting language called **JavaScript Flash**, or **JSFL**, which can be used to manipulate the authoring environment and its various elements. We'll present on overview of JSFL shortly, and you'll be getting *very* familiar with the practical side of JSFL starting in Chapter 2.

What Is Flash Extensibility?

Let's take a look at the five main areas that fall under the heading of extensibility in Flash:

1. Commands
2. Tools
3. Timeline Effects
4. Behaviors
5. Advanced tools

Commands

If you take a look at the Flash MX 2004 authoring environment, you'll see a menu item that wasn't there in previous versions of Flash—Commands—as shown in Figure 1-1.

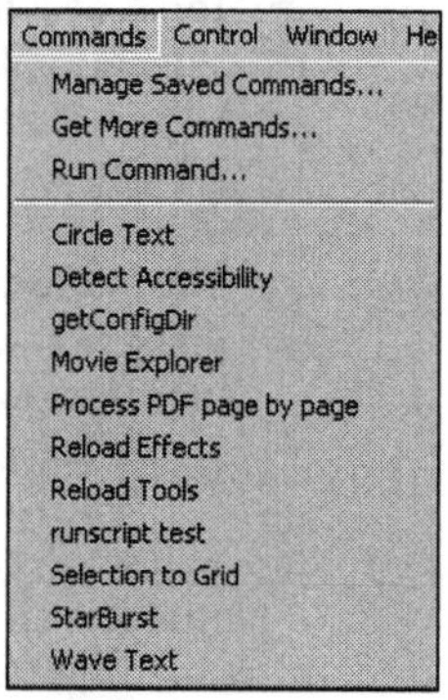

In Flash MX 2004, you can create new custom commands that can be run from this menu. In Figure 1-1, you can tell that we've already been going crazy with our own custom commands; if you haven't yet played around with this feature, your menu is likely to read No Commands Found at the moment. Not to worry though, you'll soon be brimming with ideas for new commands!

Commands Control Window He
Manage Saved Commands...
Get More Commands...
Run Command...
Circle Text
Detect Accessibility
getConfigDir
Movie Explorer
Process PDF page by page
Reload Effects
Reload Tools
runscript test
Selection to Grid
StarBurst
Wave Text

Figure 1-1.
The Commands menu

The commands functionality of Flash MX 2004 is probably the simplest level of Flash extensibility to get started with, as it doesn't really require any technical know-how about the extensibility framework at all. If you've ever recorded a macro in other popular programs, this can be just as simple—you perform the actions you want and then save them as a command. Anytime you need to perform those actions again, simply select that command from the Commands menu, and those actions will be replayed.

But don't take that to mean your commands need to be simple. You can record almost any number of actions into a command, and you can then go in and edit the resulting file to customize it even further. As you become more confident, you can even create your own commands from scratch, as simply as writing a script. Since these commands are merely text files, you can easily share these with others in your work group, or if you create a particularly useful one, distribute it to whoever might find it handy. We're sure you'll soon be able to download any number of commands from various open source repositories.

> *A key resource, and perhaps the first one online, is the companion website to this book,* `www.flashextensibility.com`*. There you'll find all the commands discussed in this book, as well as all of the other files created here. In addition, visitors will be able to upload their own commands and share ideas and techniques. This site will soon consist of a library of hundreds of useful extensibility tools for you to use or study as examples.*

Tools

No doubt you're pretty familiar with the trusty toolbar in Flash, shown in Figure 1-2. You've got your selection tools, your drawing tools, eyedropper, eraser, etc., all there, right where you need them. Right where they've always been, like they're carved in stone. Well say goodbye to that concept. In Flash MX 2004, you can not only rearrange the existing tools however you like, but also add any number of new tools, created in the same way you would code a custom command.

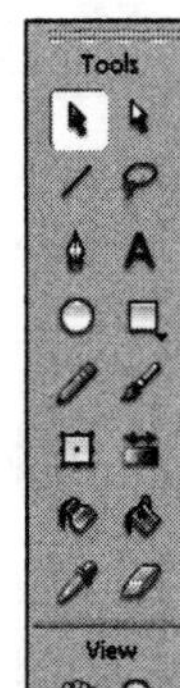

Figure 1-2.
The Flash toolbar

Tools are quite a bit more complex than commands, though. Although a command is generally a linear script that performs a series of actions and then ends, tools become activated when selected and deactivated when another tool is selected. While active, they are basically little programs running in the authoring environment, responding to various actions in a fully event-driven framework.

The most common use for tools is in creating custom drawing shapes. Up to Flash MX, we had a Line, Oval, Rectangle, and freehand drawing tools to draw with. Now with Flash MX 2004 extensibility, any shape or form that can be mathematically or programmatically defined can be inserted right into the toolbar.

Macromedia has provided one new tool in this version of Flash, the PolyStar tool, which was created with the new extensibility architecture. You can find it on your toolbar right under the Rectangle tool. Just click and hold over the rectangle icon and the PolyStar tool will slide out. We can imagine that before long, libraries of stars, arrows, callouts, smiley faces, and lightning bolts will be circulating the Web, begging to be plugged into your toolbar. In fact, you'll beat them to the punch when we demonstrate how to create a couple of custom-built tools in Chapter 3.

Timeline Effects

Face it: The first thing you likely did when you started using Flash was create a **tween**. Following some book or tutorial, you put a shape on frame one, added some frames, created a tween, made another keyframe, and changed the shape somehow. You probably also remember, at some later point, digging into the advanced tutorials, trying to create some really cool effect, struggling along trying to follow precisely what the author was saying, and most likely making far too many mistakes before you either got it right or gave up. Wouldn't it be nice if instead the author could have just recorded the actions you needed to take, and you could just supply your symbol and say, "Yeah, do *that* to *this!*"

That's essentially what **Timeline Effects** are: prescripted tweens. You supply the symbol and let the effect do its magic on it. These can even include user interfaces based on Shockwave Flash (SWF), where you can tweak various parameters and preview the effect. For a quick example of this, draw something onstage, a simple ellipse say, and right-click it (CMD-click for Mac). From the context menu, choose Timeline Effects ➤ Effects ➤ Blur (you can also get to this option via the Insert menu), and a panel opens up with the effect interface created in Flash as you see in Figure 1-3—in fact, this is a SWF itself.

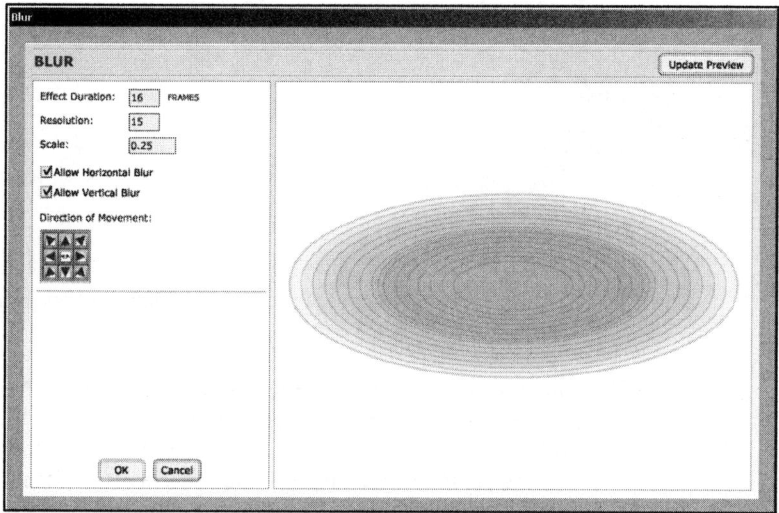

Figure 1-3. User interface for the Blur Timeline Effect

Set up some parameters and click OK and test your movie. Admittedly not a hugely exciting effect, but it shows off Flash's ability to create reasonably complex tweens at the click of a button.

Once again, you're going to see a ton of these circulating around. From a creative standpoint, we should advise you to use them with caution: A visitor to your site seeing the same canned Timeline Effect they've seen on ten other websites isn't going to be very impressed. With that in mind though, Timeline Effects can be a huge timesaver, particularly if you know how to create effects of your own, which is exactly what is covered in detail in Chapter 4. And don't forget to visit our website, `www.flashextensibility.com`, to check out some of the cool effects available for download.

Behaviors

Behaviors are like a distant cousin to Timeline Effects. Rather than a pre-scripted tween, here we're talking about a pre-scripted script. The simpler behaviors are largely going to be for the designer who wants an object to have a certain behavior that can only be scripted, but doesn't want to go through the trouble of learning ActionScript.

For another quick demo, create a movie clip on the stage and select it. Open the Behaviors panel (Windows ➤ Development Panels ➤ Behaviors or *SHIFT+F3*) and click the plus symbol. A context-sensitive list of potential behaviors occurs. Choose Start Dragging Movieclip as shown in Figure 1-4.

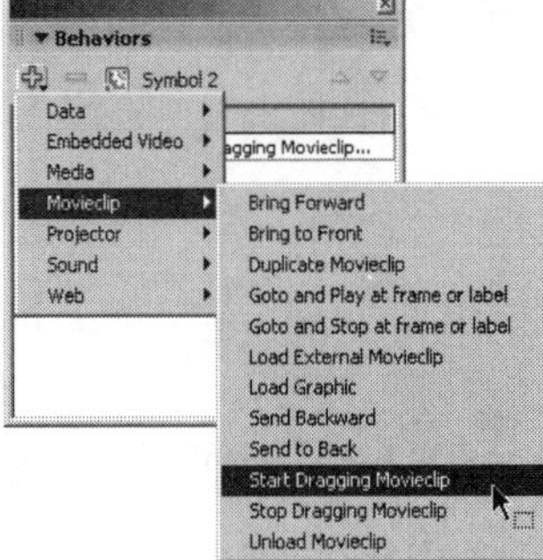

Figure 1-4.
The Behaviors panel and associated options

You can also choose an event that will trigger the behavior, so set it as On Press. Test your movie (CTRL/CMD+ENTER) and click the movie clip. It should start dragging (following the mouse). Of course, you'll probably also want to add a Stop Dragging Movieclip command for On Release. All of this dragging and responding to mouse events is obviously done behind the scenes with ActionScript, but you didn't have to write (or know) a single line of code.

Multiple behaviors can be applied to the same object, based on the same or different events, so some complex behaviors can be created through such "layering."

In this book we'll be demonstrating how to create behaviors, and we don't insist anywhere that your behaviors be as simple as *Start Dragging*. Virtually any code you can write into an event handler in ActionScript can be turned into a custom behavior. It goes without saying that there will be plenty of these behaviors available at `www.flashextensibility.com`.

Advanced Tools

Finally, if all the features you've seen so far don't get some wild ideas going in your head about what you can do, we've come to the section of items we'll lump together generally as **advanced tools**. These mainly consist of a little command called MMExecute and another tool that is used at the command line.

MMExecute is actually a new ActionScript built-in function. It takes a single argument, which is a string. The string itself is actually a program in the same language as the commands, tools, and Timeline Effects are written in, JSFL. For example, the following is a very simple program written in JSFL that simply adds a circle to the current document:

```
var the_doc = fl.getDocumentDOM();
the_doc.addNewOval({top:100, bottom:100, left:200, right:200});
```

You can encode that into a string and store it in a variable like so:

```
theJSFL = "var the_doc =
➥fl.getDocumentDOM();the_doc.addNewOval({top:100, bottom:100,
➥left:200, right:200});"
```

Then, you could use that string inside MMExecute to run that JSFL program:

```
MMExecute(theJSFL);
```

Don't worry if you don't follow this code yet—all will be revealed later in this book. Essentially, this means that you can not only extend Flash through a menu, toolbar, and the special timeline and behaviors functions, but also automatically run one of these extensibility scripts from a SWF *running in the authoring environment*. That last phrase is important; the extensibility tools only have power from within the authoring environment. Thus, `MMExecute` must be contained in a SWF running in the authoring environment, such as a live preview or custom UI SWF, for it to have any effect at all. The JSFL code that is run affects the document that is open in the authoring environment. It does nothing at all to the SWF that contains the MMExecute command.

This makes a whole bunch of things possible in the field of component creation. Flash MX 2004 components contain live previews, which are SWFs that can contain `MMExecute` statements. In this way, once a component is added to a document, it can take certain actions on that document such as adding or modifying content.

Lastly is the fact that these scripts can now be run from the command line, or even by double-clicking the icon for a script. This will automatically open up Flash and perform any actions you want, including creating documents, exporting SWF, and so on. This opens up almost the entire Flash authoring application programming interface (API) to be run from a command line, via an extensibility script. While this allows for batch processing or even creation of Flash movies, you can also envision a program operating outside of Flash, feeding scripts to the command-line tool. This could mean a whole new Flash UI! Another concept is using Flash on a web server, where a web page calls a PHP or ASP script, creating a script for Flash, and then runs that script, creating a brand new SWF on the server, which is then fed back to the calling web page.

What Extensibility Isn't

As touched upon previously, the extensibility tools only have power within the Flash authoring environment itself. The final SWF movie that you publish and put on a website or CD or whatever isn't going to be able to do anything that it couldn't do before you extended Flash. These tools are all strictly for you, the Flash author, to make your job easier or to add more power to your creative abilities.

For example, certain extensibility commands enable you to create new movie clips and insert graphic content into them. These would be called from a command, tool, or Timeline Effect, or perhaps from a SWF running as a custom UI; but in any case, they would be called from within the authoring environment. In a final exported SWF, the only way to create a movie clip is the ActionScript function `createEmptyMovieClip`, which remains unchanged since Flash MX. To add new graphics to it, you might use the ActionScript drawing API, as in Flash MX.

Also available are extensibility commands to change the stage size or color or even change the frame rate of a movie. This is only in the course of authoring a movie. There is still no way to directly perform these actions from within a published SWF (though you still have plenty of ways to fake it, of course!).

This mostly gets confusing when running the MMExecute function. When you have some ActionScript in a movie with a line like `setFPS(30)`, it's easy to get excited about how you can now control the frame rate of a movie. We just want to save you the disappointment later when you realize it doesn't work exactly like that.

To reiterate, the new extensibility features are enhancements to the authoring environment of the Flash IDE. They are there to speed up the workflow for you, the Flash designer or developer, or to make it possible to simply do things you just couldn't do before. Once your movie is exported to a SWF or published on a web page, the end audience isn't going to have access to any of these features. The main benefit that they will see is higher quality work and more of it, produced faster by you and your design team!

The Underlying Technologies

In addition to extensibility architecture, you might have heard the terms **JavaScript API** and **JSFL**. This has caused confusion among some, giving the impression that this somehow enables some communication between a Flash movie and JavaScript within a browser. Remember, extensibility has nothing to do with the final SWF in the browser. We even had one person tell us that Macromedia has done away with ActionScript and replaced it with JavaScript! So, let's look over the technologies that we'll be using throughout the book, and how JavaScript relates to it all.

JSFL—JavaScript Flash

The simple fact is that these extensibility scripts, which we've so vaguely been referring to up to now, are written in JavaScript. Why JavaScript, you ask, when all the rest of Flash is based on ActionScript? Well, that's a question for the engineers who designed it all, and they probably had very good reasons. The good news, though, is that both JavaScript and ActionScript are based on the same standard, ECMA. So, if you have more than a raw beginner's experience in ActionScript, you should feel quite at home with JSFL.

As mentioned, a JSFL file is a simple text file containing a script. You can create a JSFL file with any text editor, or you can use the built-in editor in Flash MX Professional 2004. If you *are* using the Professional version, you'll have the advantage of syntax highlighting, code hinting and completion in the editor. This is a very useful feature, especially when you're still learning JSFL. However, many fine external code editors are available out there that can be configured to do the same thing. A popular one among Flash developers is SciteFlash, available free for download at `www.bomberstudios.com/sciteflash/`. This already has code completion and highlighting for ActionScript, and it will only be a matter of time before configuration files are created for JSFL as well. In fact, SciteFlash has several useful features not available in the built-in editor, such as code folding, through which you can collapse a function or code block into a single line. With all due respect to the good folks at Macromedia, it wouldn't surprise us if many Flash Pro users continue to use this fine external editor.

Although the syntax of the script you create for your extensibility tools will be that of JavaScript, a large number of new objects, properties, and methods relate directly to Flash. It's these objects and methods that are collectively known as the JavaScript API. In hand coding your new extensions, you'll be dealing with these new methods and properties for the largest share of functionality of your script. Toward the end of this book you'll find a comprehensive reference dictionary to all of these objects, methods, and properties.

The DOM

The Document Object Model (DOM) is the model of choice for all the objects in a Flash document. If you've ever programmed in JavaScript, this will be a familiar concept to you. The DOM for a web page is a way of representing everything on the page as an object that can be manipulated in a JavaScript program. Thus, you have predefined objects for the document itself, for each element in it, and even for such things as the browser and the screen. Each of these objects has properties and perhaps methods that can be applied to change the appearance or behavior of that particular element, or to manipulate and present data within it. For example, in a browser, the document object refers to the HTML document being displayed in the browser. This object has various methods and properties. An example of one of its methods is write. Anything given to this method as a parameter will be written into the document. You can test this directly by typing the following into the address bar of your browser:

```
javascript:document.write("Hello browser")
```

Press *Enter* and the message will be written to the browser window. An example of a document property is bgColor, with which you can read or set the background color of the current document. Enter this into your browser to see it at work:

```
javascript:document.bgColor=0xff44bb;document.write("Hello browser!")
```

Similarly, JSFL has a Document Object Model that represents virtually every aspect of a Flash movie in the authoring environment, a portion of which you can see in Figure 1-5. Actually, the DOM encompasses the full authoring environment itself, any documents in it, and several of the panels you see and use.

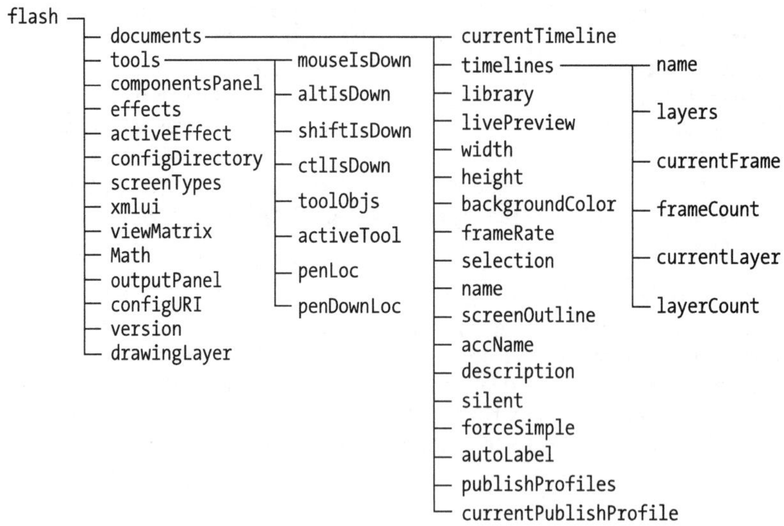

Figure 1-5. Tree diagram showing just a few sections of the Flash DOM

We'll get into this in a lot more detail later, but to give you a rough idea of it, the base-level object in the DOM is the flash object, which can also be accessed as `fl`. One of the key properties of `fl` is documents, which is an array containing all the documents currently opened in Flash (see Figure 1-6). Thus, you can access the first document in the authoring environment with the expression `fl.documents[0]`. Likewise, you can access the currently active document at any time with `fl.getDocumentDOM()`.

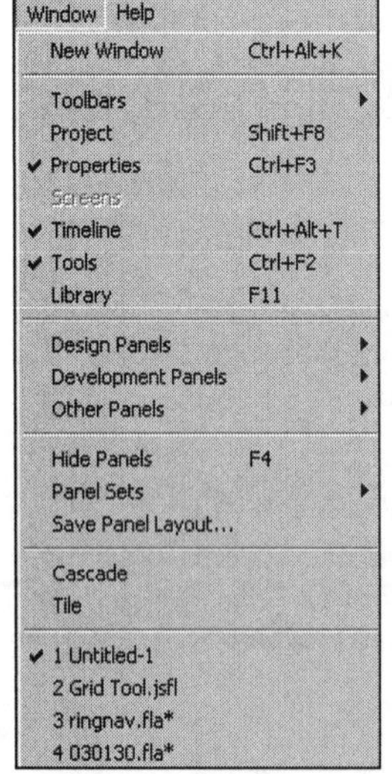

Figure 1-6.
Here you can see multiple documents open in Flash. Each document is an element in the `fl.documents` array.

A document object most importantly contains a `timeline` object, which is accessed through the document method `getTimeLine()`. Once you have a reference to the timeline, you can get access to the various layers of the timeline through a property called, obviously enough, `layers`. Again, this is an array, with each element representing a layer in the timeline.

You're probably getting a clearer idea of this now, and may have even guessed that frames is a property of each layer—it's an array containing all the frames in that layer.

Finally, you have the `elements` property of each frame. This is an array containing each object in that frame, whether it's a button, movie clip, graphic, or simple shape, as shown in Figure 1-7.

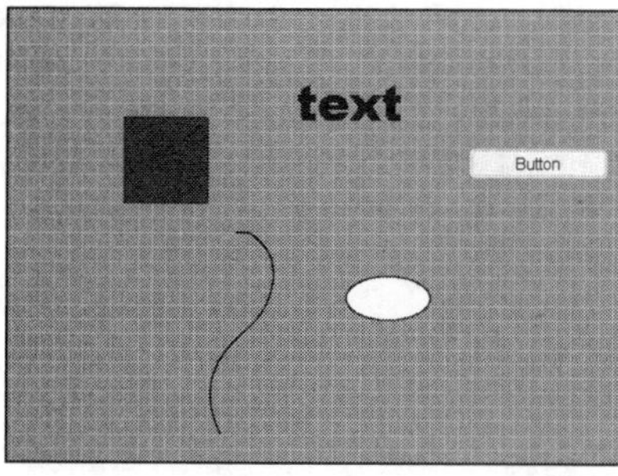

Figure 1-7.
Each document has a timeline, which can have several layers. Each layer can have many frames, and each frame can contain multiple elements.

So, to access the first element in frame one of the active movie, you would enter something like this:

```
the_elem =
➥fl.getDocumentDOM().getTimeline().layers[0].frames[0].elements[0];
```

From here, you could access the element's properties, or set them like so:

```
w = the_elem.width;
the_elem.height = 100;
```

Simple, right? Well, sort of . . . this book will help you get the hang of it soon enough!

Of course, each of these objects has many other properties and methods. And many of the properties are themselves objects, with their own properties and methods. We'll be examining quite a few of these as needed as we progress through the book.

XML to UI

In addition to JavaScript, a fair amount of XML is utilized in the Flash extensibility architecture, particularly with behaviors, which are themselves created in XML.

The XML to UI interface is a specific set of XML tags recognized by Flash, for use in creating dialog boxes. This can come in handy when you need some input or feedback from the user in order to customize the actions you're about to perform.

In simple terms, you would just write the XML tags for each individual dialog box item, such as buttons, input fields, check boxes, and so on. Flash reads in the XML, and based on that creates the dialog box for you. Users enter their data, click OK, and the resulting data is sent back to your script for use in customizing whatever it is you're creating. In Figure 1-8 you can see a picture of a dialog box created using XML to UI. This is for a command we'll show you how to create in the next chapter called Selection to Grid. From this sneak preview of the next chapter, you can see just a few of the possible controls you can add to the interfaces for your commands, tools, effects, and behaviors:

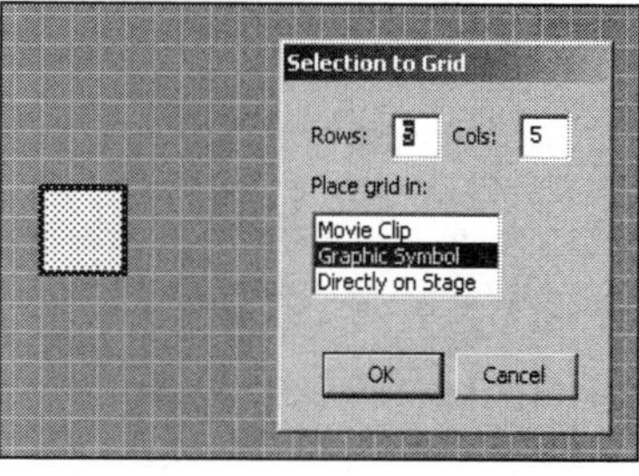

Figure 1-8.
An example of a dialog box for a command created using XML to UI

Throughout the first few chapters of the book, we'll cover just enough XML to UI to get you by for the simple projects we'll be walking you through. Further on we devote an entire chapter, Chapter 5, to the subject, which even covers the advanced topic of putting a SWF in one of these XML to UI dialog boxes. This enables you to create all sorts of custom controls in Flash, and use them in a dialog box in the authoring environment. These controls can include oddly shaped or animated buttons, rotating knobs, sliders, or just about any other type of control you could create in Flash.

Creating Your First Command

All right, enough theory—let's see Flash extensibility in action! We're going take you through the steps for creating a simple new command to add to the Commands menu, using the History panel.

1. If you haven't already done so, start up Flash MX 2004 (or Flash MX Professional 2004, if that's what you're using). Create a new Flash document and open up the History panel (Window ➤ Other Panels ➤ History or *ALT+F10*). If this is a brand new file, the panel should be empty. If any items appear in it, click the Options Menu button in the top-right corner and select Clear History. Answer Yes to the warning that appears, and your History panel should now be as pristine as the one in Figure 1-9.

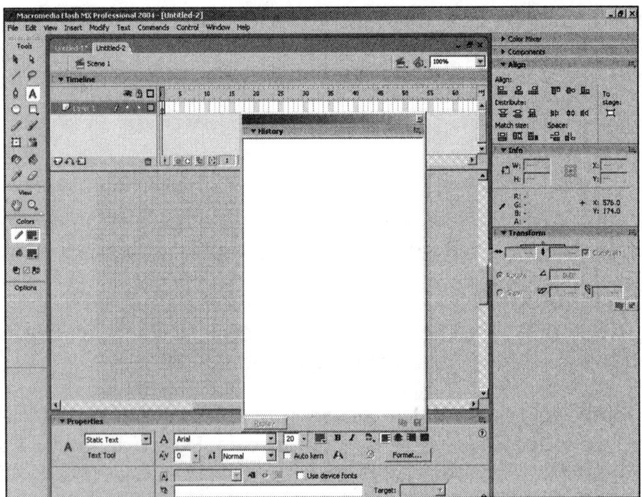

Figure 1-9. A nice clean History panel

2. Now click the Oval tool (O) in the toolbar and drag out a shape of your choosing. You should end up with a new item in the panel. Depending on your settings, the item may just say Oval or it may give you a bunch of numbers describing the oval you just created. Also, if you mouse over the history item itself, you'll get some additional information—this pretty precisely describes the action you just performed (see Figure 1-10).

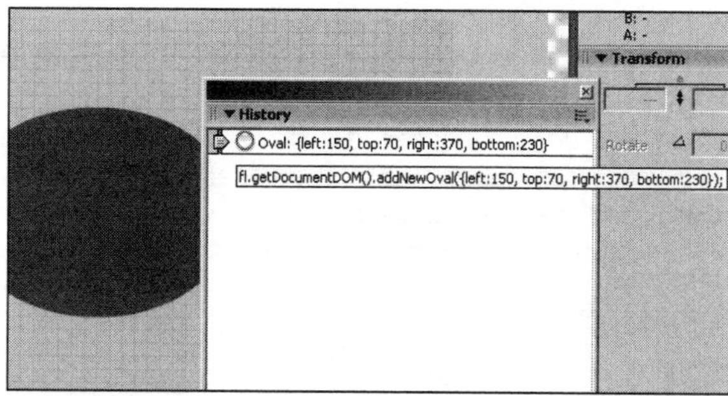

Figure 1-10. An item in the History panel

1

3. Now you'll turn this into a command. Click the item in the History panel to select it. Now, either right-click (*CMD*-click on a Mac) the item, or click the panel menu button. Then choose the menu item Save As Command. This gives you the dialog box, shown in Figure 1-11, requesting that you provide a name for the command, so choose something self-explanatory, like My Oval, and hit OK.

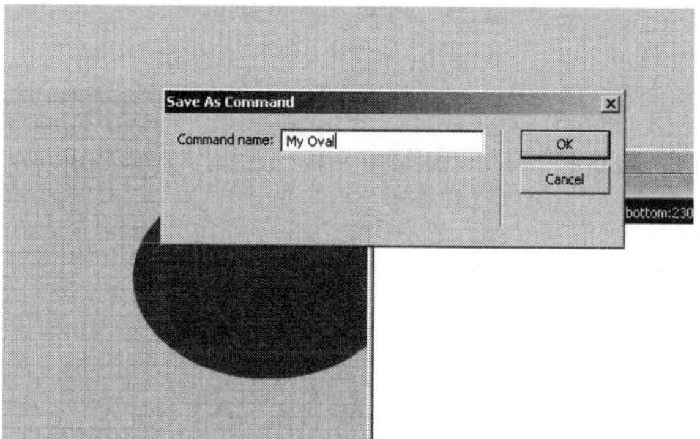

Figure 1-11. Name your command.

4. Next, delete the shape you just drew from the stage. If you're very observant, you might notice that the History panel continues to record whatever specific actions you took to do so (see Figure 1-12).

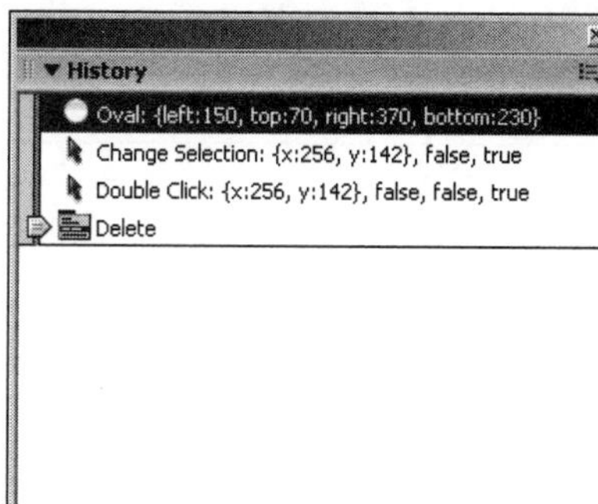

Figure 1-12. The History panel continues to record as you delete the shape.

5. Now go to the Commands menu and you should see your brand new command, My Oval, there in all its glory. Select it and see what happens—you shouldn't be too surprised!

6. Chances are, you don't really need to create that particular shape all that often, so there isn't much sense in having it sticking around cluttering up the Commands menu. From that menu, select Manage Saved Commands as shown in Figure 1-13, and you'll see a list of commands there. Select My Oval and delete it. It's gone!

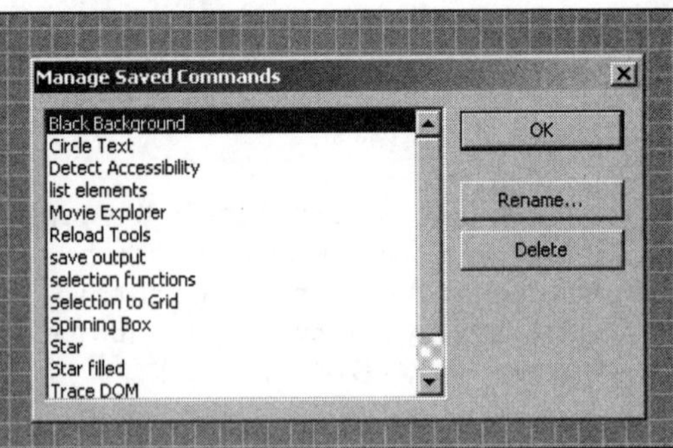

Figure 1-13.
The Manage Saved Commands dialog box

You can probably see how addictive using commands can be, because they're so easy to create and manage. That's pretty much the rock-bottom simplest level of the extensibility architecture in Flash MX 2004. In Chapter 2, you'll have a chance to look into commands in much greater detail, and you'll get into your first JSFL scripting. From there, we'll cover the rest of the areas mentioned previously and get you started building a whole library of powerful, timesaving extensibility tools.

More Than Just a Book . . .

This package is really more than just a single book—it consists of four complementary elements:

1. Tutorial-based chapters
2. Accompanying reference section
3. Downloadable sample files
4. Support website and forums

Tutorials

The chapters in the first half of this book present an introduction to the Flash extensibility architecture and a series of detailed tutorials relating to each element. These tutorial chapters show you how to use the various new technologies to literally extend and customize your Flash user interface. All the chapters come with a set of illustrative example files and source code (FLAs, SWFs, JSFLs, etc.).

Reference

The comprehensive reference section takes the form of a detailed syntax dictionary to the Flash JavaScript API. This comprises the last part of the book, and contains entries for *every* object, method, and property in these Flash languages. These printed entries encapsulate the *essential* reference material that you reach for all the time when you're coding with the extensibility technologies: syntax, a detailed description of the element, information on when you might use it, usage examples, and so on.

Sample Files and Supporting Website

Readers of this book are encouraged to visit its supporting website, `www.flashextensibility.com` (see Figure 1-14), where you can download the source code for all of the examples featured in this book. There's also a searchable electronic version of the reference dictionary available for those who choose to register, and lots more interesting extensibility-related content.

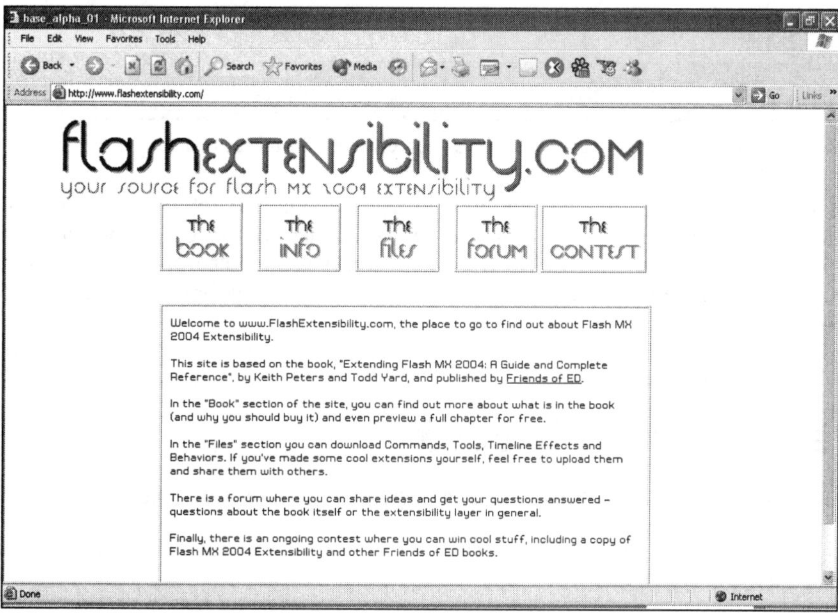

Figure 1-14. www.flashextensibility.com

friends of ED Forums

You can visit our support forums at `www.friendsofed.com/forums` (see Figure 1-15) for help, inspiration, or just to chat with like-minded Flash designers and developers:

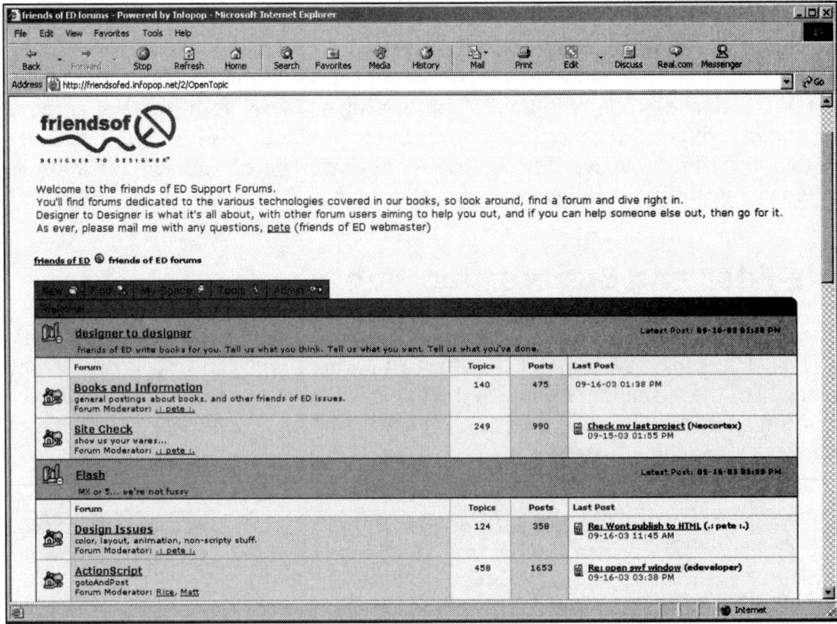

Figure 1-15. friends of ED Designer Forums—a lively place for advice and gossip

And if you run into any trouble in this book—maybe you have a problem with a certain file or tutorial, or you're just plain confused about a particular topic—leave a message on the forum, and we'll get you sorted in no time. Even if you don't have problems, e-mail `feedback@friendsofed.com` to let us know what you think of this book—we'd love to hear from you!

Styles Used in This Book

We use some simple layout conventions to make things clearer throughout the book:

- We'll use **this style** to introduce **new terms**, and to stress **important things** in the text.
- We use `this style` for code that appears in text.

```
Blocks of code
Will appear in this style,
And we'll also use
This style to highlight new code,
Or code that deserves your attention
```

When we want to draw your attention to something really important, we'll put it in a bubble like this.

- Filenames will appear in this style: `myFlashFile.swf`.
- Where we're indicating that you need to input text, you'll see this style: "type `monkeyBoy` into the Var field."
- URLs will be shown in this style: `www.friendsofed.com`
- Menu path descriptions will appear like this: File ➤ Open ➤ Monkey ➤ Banana.
- Keyboard stroke sequences will be displayed in this style: *F4* and *CTRL+ALT+DEL*. Also, wherever possible and relevant, we'll suggest the Mac equivalents of all paths and keyboard shortcuts. For example, "Now press *CTRL/CMD+ENTER* to test your Flash movie."

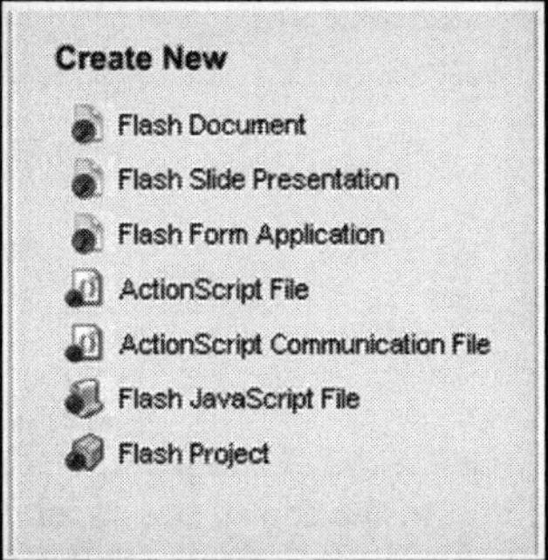

Create New

- Flash Document
- Flash Slide Presentation
- Flash Form Application
- ActionScript File
- ActionScript Communication File
- Flash JavaScript File
- Flash Project

Manage Saved Commands

bitmap test
Detect Accessibility
dom chart tests
FlashJavaScriptHelp
frame test
funcs
getConfigDir
gradient fill
key down test
lib test
Movie Explorer
My Oval
Process PDF page by page

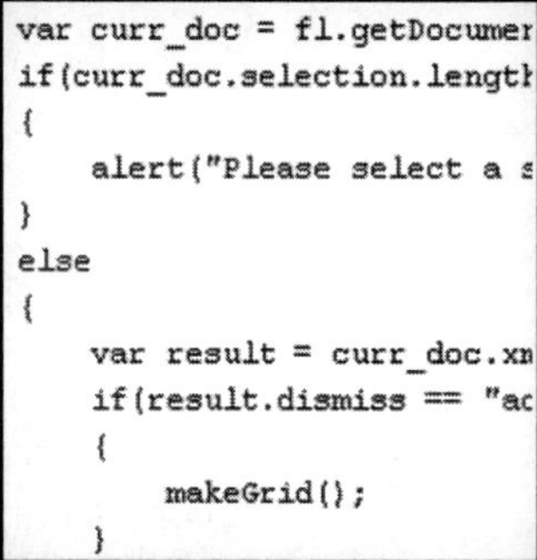

```
var curr_doc = fl.getDocumer
if(curr_doc.selection.length
{
    alert("Please select a s
}
else
{
    var result = curr_doc.xm
    if(result.dismiss == "ac
    {
        makeGrid();
    }
```

In the previous chapter, you saw a quick demonstration of how you can add a custom command to the Commands menu using the History panel. If you skipped over that chapter, you might want to just take a look at that last example and run through it. It shouldn't take more than a couple of minutes and serves as the perfect setting for this chapter.

Back to this chapter on custom commands, we'll start off with a more in-depth look at the History panel and how you can best use it to make customized commands. After this, we'll up the pace a little and show you how to code your commands with JavaScript Flash (JSFL).

The History Panel

As the History panel is the easiest jumping-off point for creating commands, we might as well dig into it in a bit more detail so you can see just how much you can do with it. It's a pretty cool tool in its own right, without even getting into saving commands. If you've used Adobe Photoshop much, you'll quickly see the similarity to the History panel in that program. Unfortunately, Flash's version isn't quite as robust just yet and doesn't include such actions as snapshots and deleting individual history items, but it's still quite handy.

Go ahead and start Flash MX 2004, create a new Flash document, and open up the History panel (*Ctrl/Cmd+F10*)—it should be blank at first. Now select from the various tools and draw some completely random objects on the stage; select them, move them around, rotate them, change colors, and so on. For each action you take, you should see a corresponding entry added to the History panel as demonstrated in Figure 2-1.

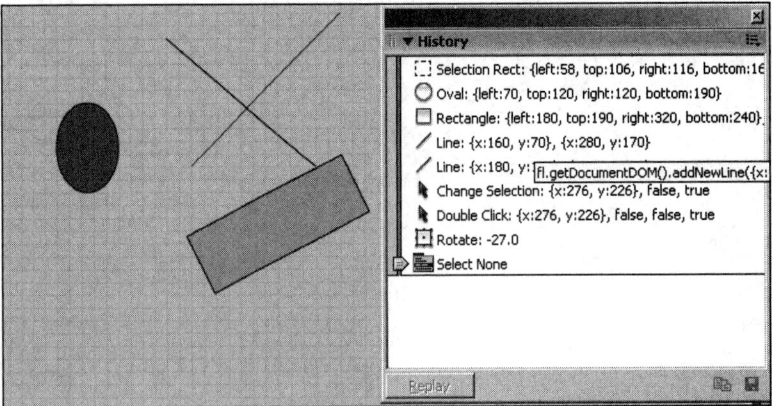

Figure 2-1. The History panel in action

You should also notice a little drag button on the left edge of the panel that points to the last action taken. Grab hold of it and drag it right up to the top of the panel. As you do so, all the content you created should disappear and the history items will be grayed out as shown in Figure 2-2. Drag it back down again slowly and you'll see the exact steps you just took re-created.

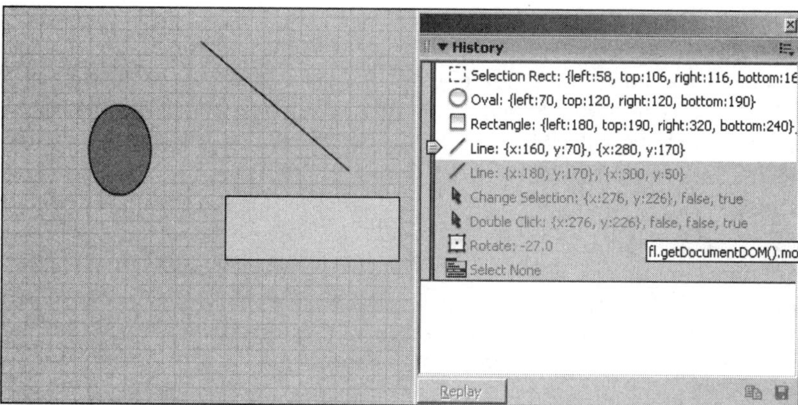

Figure 2-2. Back to the future

This is great if you're drawing something intricate and it starts going wrong. You can easily backtrack to an earlier point and then slide forward to the last point the drawing was still good. Of course, you could do that in earlier versions with undo/redo, but being able to slide back and forth like that, as if you had a sort of vertical timeline, is invaluable. Unfortunately, there is no way to delete a single history item or rearrange the existing items—but maybe in the next version!

One thing you might be wondering about as you look at the various items is that some of them may be marked with a little red X, as shown in Figure 2-3. This doesn't mean you did something wrong. There are a number of tools that will cause this—mostly the tools that operate in a **freehand** manner: the Lasso, Pen, Pencil, and Brush tools. The other tools, such as the Rectangle and Oval tools, can generally be described quite simply with a few values, i.e., position and size, or maybe angle and color. A square might go from 0, 0 to 100, 100. But a freehand path may end up with thousands of individual coordinates describing its exact shape. While it isn't impossible to write code that would have recorded all these points, the long and the short of it is that Macromedia didn't do it that way. Thus, these freehand-type tools and a few others will not work with the more advanced actions we are about to look into.

The first place you'll notice this is in replaying commands.

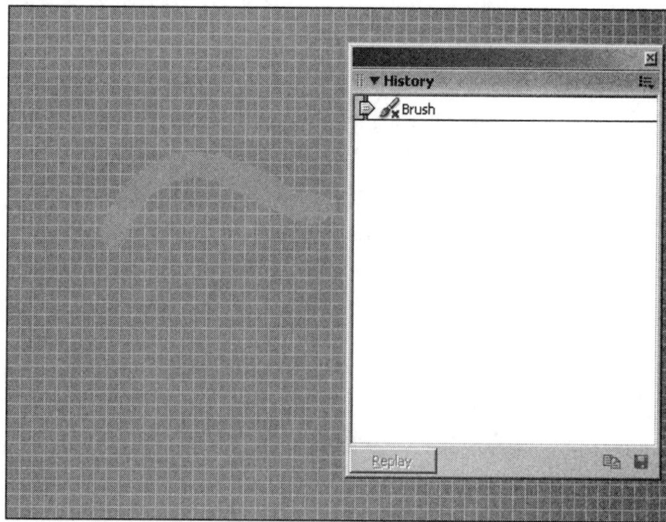

Figure 2-3. An unsupported History panel command shows a red X.

In addition to scrolling back and forth, you can selectively replay a single command out of the History panel items. Go ahead and try that right now—just select any existing command, without the red X, in the History panel, right-click it or use the panel menu in the top-right corner, and select Replay Steps. You might not notice anything happening onstage. This could be because you're simply redrawing an existing object. Try deleting everything offstage first, and then rerunning the command.

Note that if you try to do this with a command marked with a red X, the Replay Steps menu item will be inactive.

If you were quite observant there, you noticed that the menu item is Replay Steps—note the pluralization. Yes, you can actually select more than one step to replay at a time. This works in just about any way you can select multiple items out of a standard list: You can click the first item and drag down over the rest; or you can click the first, and then *Shift*-click the last to select all of the items in between. You can even select nonconsecutive items by pressing the *Ctrl/Cmd* key as you click each one. Play around with this for a while to get a feel for it. You should now begin to get the idea of how you can build a complex series of actions using the History panel.

This is another point where you can run into some trouble with your red X items. Luckily, you at least get a warning. If, in your multiple selection, you've included some red X items, you'll still be able to replay the overall sequence. However, a dialog box will pop up as shown in Figure 2-4.

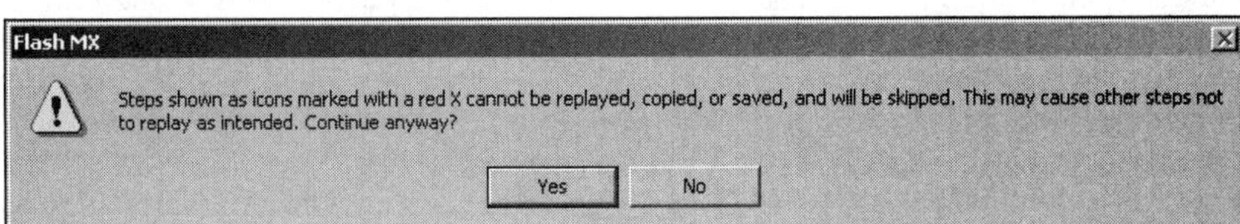

Figure 2-4. Error message for unsupported history items

Now, it's pretty obvious that these steps aren't saved and can't be replayed. We've just gone over that. But it's worth taking a look at how this may affect other steps, and how it may cause them not to replay as directed.

Take the following actions in an empty file. You can clear the History panel to make things less cluttered first. You do this by clicking the panel menu button in the top-right corner or right-clicking any step, and choosing Clear History from the menu.

1. Create a filled rectangle covering most of the stage.
2. Using the Pencil tool, make a closed free-form shape in the middle of the rectangle. Make sure it's a closed shape, i.e., the end of the line you draw should touch the beginning of it.
3. Switching to the Selection (arrow) tool, select the area of fill inside the free-form shape.
4. Hit Delete to clear out this fill.

You should now have something that looks similar to Figure 2-5: a rectangle with a squiggly shape cut out of it.

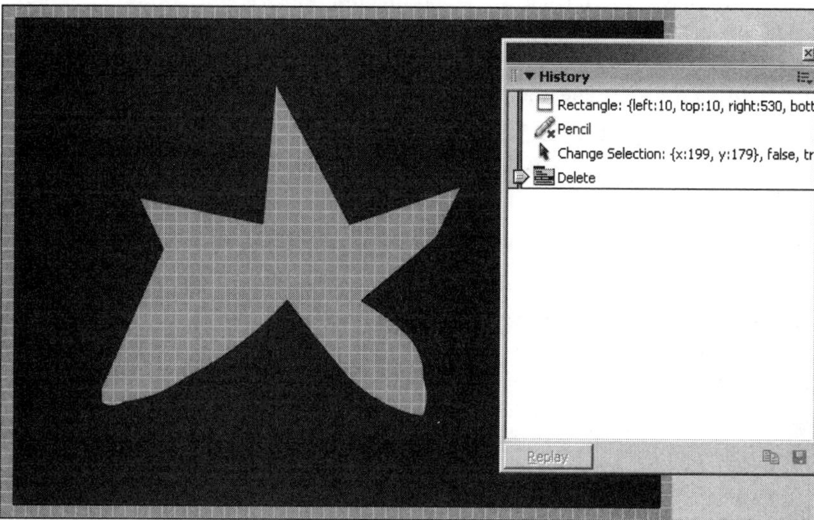

Figure 2-5. A free-form shape drawn and deleted from a rectangle

Your History panel will have four steps listed, like those seen in Figure 2-5. If your panel merely shows the tool name and not the parameters, click the panel menu button and you'll be able to choose how much detail you want shown in the History panel. Choosing View ➤ Arguments in Panel gives you a display like the one in the example.

Simple enough so far. Now, delete everything from the stage so you're starting fresh. Then highlight all four of those items and select Replay Steps. You'll get a warning as shown earlier, due to the use of the Pencil tool. Click Yes to continue.

What you wind up with is quite different from what you might expect. You should now just have an empty, nonfilled rectangle on the stage. It makes sense if you think about it. In fact, if you go through steps 1 to 4 that we described previously, and redo them manually, skipping step 2, you'll wind up with the exact same thing. Since the free-form shape was not drawn this time around, step 3, selecting the fill, selected the entire fill of the rectangle, and step 4 deleted it all. The moral of the story is, be very wary of the red X when using history items.

Commands Through the History Panel

Since you're now thoroughly indoctrinated in the ways of the History panel, its powers, and pitfalls, let's start using it to make some commands.

One of the first commands I, Keith, made from the History panel was called `Black Background`. On my site, I made individual SWF files that load into a level in the main interface. Since a SWF loaded into a level will have a transparent background, I often found myself creating a big rectangle covering the stage of the loaded SWF, to serve as a colored background. I realized I could create a command to do this automatically.

Let's re-create what I first did, and see the problem I ran into.

1. Starting with a blank stage and clear History panel, choose the rectangle tool.
2. Choose a black outline and a black fill color.
3. Draw a rectangle that covers the entire stage. It'll help if you have a 10-pixel grid and snap-to-grid turned on by selecting options from View ➤ Grid and View ➤ Snapping.

This should generate a history item like the one in Figure 2-6.

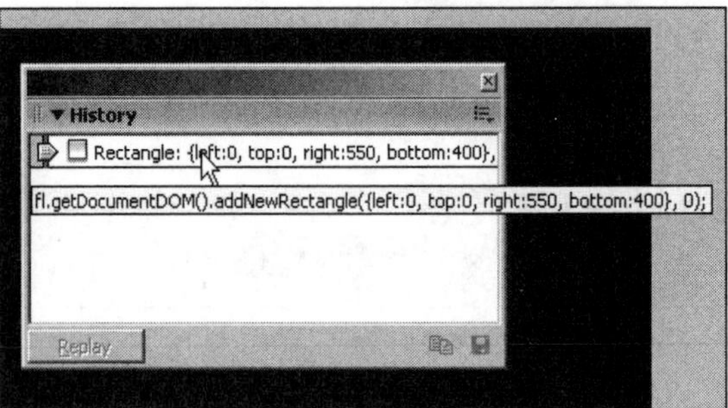

Figure 2-6.
The History panel in action

If you're wondering what that final zero is, it's the setting for the corner radius of a rounded rectangle. Since we didn't specify a rounding value, it defaults to zero, creating square corners.

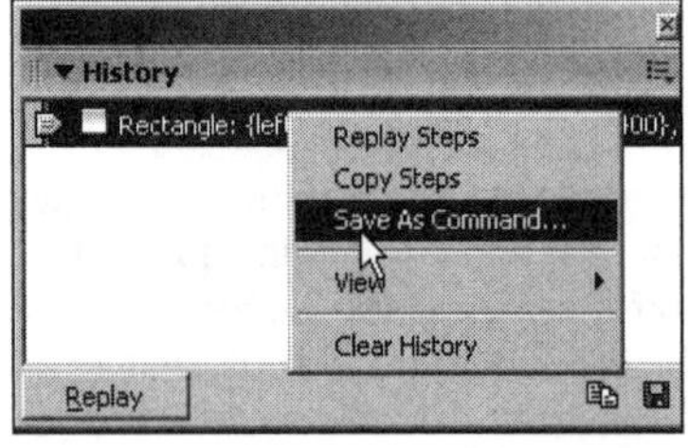

Figure 2-7.
Saving a command

Select this item, right-click (or CMD-click), and save it as a command named "Black Background" (see Figure 2-7).

Delete the shape onstage and run the command from the Command menu. Works great, eh? But eventually I found a big bug in it. Because I had recently created a red fill, the next time I went to use the command, the fill color selector was still on red. I ran the `Black Background` command, and to my shock it created a *red* background.

It turns out that any drawing tools in commands will take the currently active colors from the toolbar or the Properties and Color panels. Go ahead and try it. Using the toolbar color controls or the Color Mixer panel, select a different color for the fill and rerun the command. In addition to the fill, Flash will grab the currently active settings for stroke color, width, and style.

At first, this may seem like a bug in Flash, but if you think about it, it's the same way any tool works. If you select the Oval tool, it'll draw an oval with the currently selected colors. The same is true of shapes drawn using commands or custom-built tools. Also, if you look at the History panel, the Rectangle tool history item makes no mention of color or stroke at all. It only defines the size and position of the rectangle. The important thing to notice is that step 2 of the preceding example, choosing a fill and stroke, did not create any entry in the History panel.

Of course, I wasn't about to give up there. I wanted a *black* background, darn it!

Specifying Fill and Stroke Colors

Here's what you need to do. First, draw your rectangle in some *other* color than black, say red. Now, double-click it to select the entire rectangle. You'll see some history items record your actions. With the entire rectangle selected, change the fill and stroke colors to black using the color selection tool of your choice. Doing so generates a series of history items like the ones in Figure 2-8.

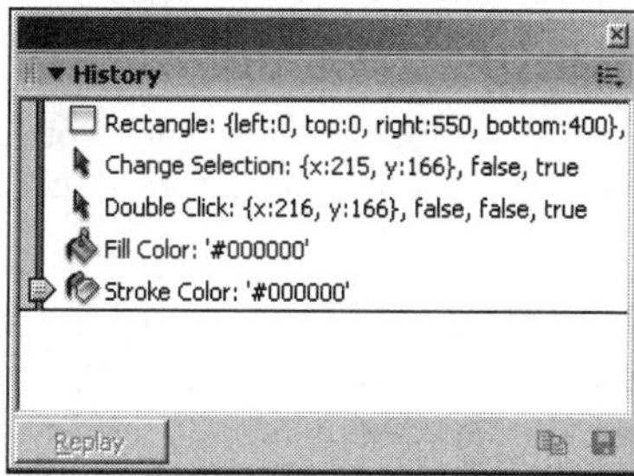

Figure 2-8.
Setting fills and strokes

Now you've recorded the act of changing the color, and learned an important point. A history item is only generated for changes in fill color if there is a fill currently selected. In other words, Flash only records the changing of color of an existing fill. If nothing is selected, you can change the color all you want and the history feature will ignore you. The same is true for stroke color and size.

Later, when you start learning JSFL, you should notice a command that sets the stroke and fill attributes for *future* drawing actions. But there is no easy way to do this from the History panel. Note also that if you set an attribute to the value it already is, such as setting a black fill to black, no history item is generated. Only *changes* are recorded. So you may have to change it to something else and change it back again to get the action to show up in the History panel.

You can now, of course, use what you have learned about selecting multiple history items to turn the preceding history series into a *real* `Black Background` command! So select all the items—the rectangle, selection, double-click, and whatever fill/stroke changes you made, and save them as a command. Flash will warn you that a command with that name already exists, but in this case it's obviously fine to save over the old one. Now this command will work as it should!

By now, you're probably quite anxious to jump into some JSFL coding and create something more interesting than black rectangles—so let's turn to JSFL commands for the rest of this chapter.

JSFL Commands

Rather than start from scratch, let's take a look at a JSFL file that was already written. Actually, we'll show you the JSFL you just created yourself in making the Black Background file.

First of all, you need to know where to find JSFL command files on your hard drive. Well, they reside in the Commands folder in the Flash MX 2004 configuration files. But where is that? It varies on different platforms and operating systems. On Windows 2000 and XP, for instance, it's here (note that you might have to select Show hidden files and folders in your folder view options):

```
C:\Documents and Settings\<user name>\Local Settings\Application
Data\Macromedia\Flash MX 2004\en\Configuration\Commands
```

When you find your configuration folder, you might want to note exactly where it is, or even create a shortcut to it. In addition to the Commands folder, you'll notice several other folders where extensibility-related files are stored: Behaviors, Effects, and Tools, for example.

Now that you're oriented, you need to know how to open these files. If you're using Flash MX Professional 2004, it comes equipped with a built-in JSFL editor. You can simply go to File ➤ Open and navigate to your Commands folder. But don't fret, JSFL files are simply text files, and can be edited with any editor that handles plain text, even Notepad! We've already mentioned a popular editor amongst Flash users, SciteFlash, available at www.bomberstudios.com/sciteflash, but you can use whatever you're comfortable with.

Either way, get down into your Commands folder and look around. What do you know? There's a file there named Black Background.jsfl! Open it up and have a look. Remember, as you read (and soon write) JSFL files, this is JavaScript, not ActionScript. They are very similar, both being based on ECMA, but you'll find some subtle differences here and there that may have you convinced that you've found some typos. We'll try to point these out as we run into them.

Here's what the code in our Black Background JSFL file looks like. Yours may vary slightly but should be essentially the same:

```
//
// Black Background
//
// This command was recorded by Macromedia Flash MX 2004.
//

// Rectangle: {left:0, top:0, right:550, bottom:400}, 0
fl.getDocumentDOM().addNewRectangle({left:0, top:0, right:550,
➥bottom:400}, 0);

// Change Selection: {x:251.1, y:225.6}, false, true
fl.getDocumentDOM().mouseClick({x: 251.1, y:225.6}, false, true);
```

```
// Double Click: {x: 251.1, y:225.6}, false, false, true
fl.getDocumentDOM().mouseDblClk({x: 251.1, y:225.6}, false, false,
➥true);

// Fill Color: '#000000'
fl.getDocumentDOM().setFillColor('#000000');

// Stroke Color: '#000000'
fl.getDocumentDOM().setStrokeColor('#000000');

// Stroke Size: 1
fl.getDocumentDOM().setStrokeSize(1);

// Stroke Style: solid
fl.getDocumentDOM().setStrokeStyle('solid');
```


OK, let's get to work dissecting this creature and see what you can learn from it. As you see, it consists of pairs of comments and code. The comment is essentially the same as the text from the History panel. Under that is pure JSFL code. We'll take a closer look at the first line.

```
fl.getDocumentDOM().addNewRectangle({left:0, top:0, right:550,
➥bottom:400}, 0);
```

In the introduction, we briefly talked about the DOM—Document Object Model. Here you have the first look at it in practice. The first two letters there, `fl`, are shorthand for Flash, and refer to the Flash MX 2004 program itself: the authoring environment. This is the top-level object, which makes sense because everything else is a "member" of Flash.

Actually, you can refer to this object as either flash or fl. Either will work in coding your JSFL files. Throughout this book, we'll use `fl`—it's shorter!

When you open Flash, you generally either start a new document or load one or more previously created documents (FLA files). Flash may have several documents open at any one time. Each one of these documents is an object in the DOM. They are stored in an array called, obviously enough, `documents`. This array is a property, or member of the `fl` object. Thus, if you had only one document open, you could access it with

```
fl.documents[0]
```

As you open additional documents, they will become

```
fl.documents[1]
fl.documents[2]
fl.documents[3]
// and so on...
```

In ActionScript, JavaScript, and most other languages, arrays are zero-indexed, which means that the first element is element 0; thus the first document open will be numbered zero.

In most cases though, when you apply a command, behavior, tool, etc. you'll merely be applying it to the *active* document. When you're writing the command, you won't know much about the circumstances under which it'll be executed. You won't know how many documents are open in Flash, or which one is which. Usually, you just want to apply the command to the currently active document. Well, you get that with the function getDocumentDOM(), which is a method of the fl object. Thus you can always access the current document with the line

```
fl.getDocumentDOM()
```

In fact, if you want, you can store this in a variable so you don't have to continually type it all out:

```
var myDoc_doc = fl.getDocumentDOM();
```

Note that this example shows the suffix _doc being used to name the document object. This will allow for code hinting and completion in the script editor, as well as helping you to remember what type of object each variable stands for. Throughout the book, we'll be using these suffixes for various objects where appropriate.

Finally we get to the last part of the command, addNewRectangle. This is a method of the document object. As you might guess, other drawing methods such as addNewLine and addNewOval are available. A full listing of all the methods and properties of all the objects in the DOM is available in the Flash extensibility reference section at the end of the book.

addNewRectangle takes two arguments. The first is an object, as signified by the curly brackets. In JavaScript, as well as in Flash, you can create a generic object by using the statement

```
myObject = new Object();
```

and then filling in its properties like this:

```
myObject.name = "Steve";
myObject.job = "Editor";
```

Or, you can use a shortcut by listing your properties inside curly brackets as follows:

```
myObject = {name:"Steve", job:"Editor"};
```

In this case, you don't even assign the object created to a variable, you just feed it straight into the function. This object is of type rect. ActionScript doesn't have a built-in rect type, but remember, this is actually JavaScript. For the purposes of this example, there is nothing very special about a rectangle object. It's an object the same as you'd use in ActionScript, but it should always contain these four properties: left, right, top, bottom. The numbers for this rect object are automatically generated when you click the mouse to create the rectangle.

The second argument is that zero we mentioned earlier for the round corner value. If you want a rectangle with rounded corners, enter a number for the radius here. A value of ten will create a rectangle with round corners that have a 10-pixel radius—all pretty straightforward.

There you have it—your first JSFL statement; pretty simple actually! Take a look at the next two lines:

```
fl.getDocumentDOM().mouseClick({x:215.1, y:225.6}, false, true);
fl.getDocumentDOM().mouseDblClk({x:215.1, y:225.6}, false, false,
➥true);
```


Here you see a mouse click and then a double click. Why both? Well, that's essentially what Flash saw. First you clicked the mouse and it registered that click. When you clicked again within a certain time frame, Flash realized you intended a double click. It didn't go back and replace the click, it just added the double click to the list.

As you see, these two methods are pretty similar. `mouseClick` takes three arguments. The first is a "point" type object. Again, this is just a normal object which contains an x and y value. This is the location of the mouse click.

The next argument is a Boolean value for whether or not the *SHIFT* key was being held down when the mouse was clicked. The final Boolean argument specifies whether *SHIFT*-select is active or not. Setting these both to true allows you to make multiple selections as if you were pressing the *SHIFT* key and selecting several shapes on the screen.

The `mouseDblClk` command simply adds one argument, which specifies whether the *ALT* key is being held down. This is the second argument, after the coordinate point.

You may be looking at these lines of code as simple recordings of *what happened*. While that isn't untrue in the case of a history-generated command, you should begin to look at them as instructions for Flash to carry out. This will come more naturally when you start to write commands from scratch, in which case you aren't recording anything, just composing a script for Flash to follow.

In this case, you're actually telling Flash to *simulate* a mouse click and a double click. Whatever a real mouse click or double click would do at that point is what will occur in the Flash authoring environment. Here, it'll cause the entire rectangle, including the fill, to be selected.

If you want, you can delete the whole line containing the single mouse click. `mouseDblClick` will do just fine by itself. This brings up a good point—that of using the History panel to kind of sketch out a command, and then going into the code itself to tweak and optimize it. It's also a great way to start learning about the JavaScript API, or JS API (in addition to reading this book, obviously!) because you can see the various methods in action and relate them to what they actually do.

The next line is pretty obvious:

```
fl.getDocumentDOM().setFillColor('#000000');
```

It simply sets the fill color for the current document. The automatically generated code uses the format `#rrggbb` for hexadecimal color numbers. But when you're writing your own code, you'll find that it's pretty flexible. You can use a string format like that, or a hex number such as `0xffffff`, or even a decimal number like `12631`.

Next, you set the stroke properties:

```
fl.getDocumentDOM().setStrokeColor('#000000');
fl.getDocumentDOM().setStrokeSize(1);
fl.getDocumentDOM().setStrokeStyle("solid");
```

Not much discussion needed there; you should be getting the hang of it by now. As usual, check the Flash extensibility reference section at the end of the book for all the possible stroke styles.

You can even fix this up a bit more by storing the document object in a variable like we just talked about, and rounding off the decimals on the double click:

```
var myDoc_doc = fl.getDocumentDOM();
myDoc_doc.addNewRectangle({left:0, top:0, right:550, bottom:400}, 0);
myDoc_doc.mouseDblClk({x:215, y:225}, false, false, true);
myDoc_doc.setFillColor('#000000');
myDoc_doc.setStrokeColor('#000000');
myDoc_doc.setStrokeSize(1);
myDoc_doc.setStrokeStyle("solid");
```

And this is exactly how we would write this command by hand. This is a great way to get started with commands—create a base file using the History panel and then fix it up by hand.

Coding It By Hand

All right, enough of the History panel. Let's jump in and create something from scratch. Although it takes a bit of time to learn the language, doing it this way is far more flexible and powerful than trying to piece together history steps.

So far you've looked at some pretty simple drawing commands and colors. For this next example, you'll actually be working with the Library creating and editing symbols, specifically, movie clips.

First, you need to create a JSFL file. If you're working with Flash MX Professional 2004, going to File ➤ New will give you a list of possible files to create. Choose Flash JavaScript File and the script editor will open. If you aren't using the Pro version, simply open up your favorite editor and start a new file.

You might as well save it right now as `Starburst.jsfl` in the `Commands` folder (if you want to have a sneak peek at what you're about to create, this file is available for download from `www.flashextensibility.com`, along with all the other examples featured in this book). Once you do that, it should show up in your Commands menu, ready to run. Now give it something to do.

First of all, you'll get a reference to the current document and to the Library of that document:

```
var star_doc = fl.getDocumentDOM();
var star_lib = star_doc.library;
```

We've covered that first line in the previous example. In the second line, note that `library` is a property of the `document` object, because any document has its own Library, which you can see by opening the Library panel (*F11*). This contains all the symbols used in the document. The library property is actually an object itself, with many powerful methods and useful properties. Note the `_lib` suffix.

One of the most important properties of the `library` object is the array `items`. Naturally, this contains a reference to each item in the Library, hence the line


```
fl.getDocumentDOM().library.items[0]
```

would be a reference to the first item in the Library of the current document.

You can also create a new item in the Library with the method `addNewItem(type, name)`. `type` would be a string set to describe what type of item you want to add. You can add movie clips, buttons, graphics, bitmaps, even videos to the Library. The strings for these types would be `movie clip`, `button`, `graphic`, `bitmap`, and `video`. You can also add a folder to the Library by adding an item of type `folder`. Obviously, the `name` parameter is the identifier you'll give the new Library item.

Go ahead and add a new movie clip named `star` to the Library now:

```
var star_doc = fl.getDocumentDOM();
var star_lib = star_doc.library;
star_lib.addNewItem("movie clip", "star");
```

If you want to see this in action, save the file, open a new Flash file, and run the `Star` command. Check the Library and you'll see a movie clip named `star` sitting there. Of course, it's just an empty movie clip at this point, so let's continue.

Next, you want to edit this symbol. In the authoring environment, you would simply right-click the item in the Library and choose Edit, or even simpler just double-click it. Either action would take you into edit mode for that particular symbol. In JSFL, you have the method `editItem` to do the same thing. `editItem` is a method of the `library` object, and takes the name of the item you want to edit as a parameter. You can add that right to the file:

```
star_lib.editItem("star");
```

Feel free to save and test the file again. If you use the same Flash file you used before, you'll get an error message saying the name star is already taken, and asking you to choose a different name.

There are a few ways to handle this. The simplest, though not necessarily the safest for all projects, is to simply check if star exists in the Library, and if so, delete it. The following code incorporates this solution:

```
var star_doc = fl.getDocumentDOM();
var star_lib = star_doc.library;
if(star_lib.itemExists("star"))
{
```

```
  star_lib.deleteItem("star");
}
star_lib.addNewItem("movie clip", "star");
star_lib.editItem("star");
```

This should be pretty clear: if the item star exists, delete the item star. Try it and see that the error message has gone.

Again, this may not be the safest solution. You never know when this command will be run. You might already have a totally different movie clip in the Library named star that took you several hours to painstakingly create. Running this command will wipe out all your hard work. Also, you may want to use this command multiple times to create multiple stars. No reason to limit it to a single star. A better idea would be to keep generating new names until you find one that is safe. Let's try that:

```
var star_doc = fl.getDocumentDOM();
var star_lib = star_doc.library;
var starname = "star";
var tryCount = 1;
while (star_lib.itemExists(starname)){
  starname = "star" + tryCount;
  tryCount++;
}
star_lib.addNewItem("movie clip", starname);
star_lib.editItem(starname);
```

Note that although it serves you well for a specific test like this, in many cases it's not ideal to use a while *loop without an appropriate escape mechanism. For instance, you might want to declare a* maxCount *variable to time out the loop after the defined number of iterations.*

Here, you take a variable called starname and set it equal to the string star. If a symbol named star already exists in the Library, you tag on the number 1 to star and try star1. If there's already a star1, increment the number and try star2. This continues until you find a free slot in the Library, at which point you add the item and start to edit it. Try running this command several times to see that it continues to create sequentially numbered clips in the Library.

Anyway, now that you successfully have a movie clip in the Library and are ready to edit it, let's put some content in it.

You'll just add a few random lines emerging from the center:

```
for(var i=0; i<20; i++)
{
  star_doc.addNewLine({x:0, y:0}, {x:Math.random()*100-50,
➥y:Math.random()*100-50});
}
```

Here you see another drawing command, addNewLine. Unlike the ActionScript line drawing function, lineTo, which only needs one x, y point to draw a line to, this command needs both the beginning and end points. Each are point objects containing x and y properties. In this case, the beginning point is 0, 0, and the end point is random.

If you're a veteran of ActionScript, you'll be happy to see the Math.random method there. The Math object in ActionScript is a pretty standard object, implemented quite similarly in many languages. Thus you can use most of the same Math methods in JSFL that you have become used to in ActionScript. Here, Math.random returns a number between 0 and 1. Multiplying that times 100, you get a number from 0 to 100. If you subtract 50 from *that*, you get something between –50 and +50.

Now that you're done editing the star, you should remember to exit edit mode. That's pretty simple:

```
star_doc.exitEditMode();
```

If you run the command, you'll see that the newly created movie clip now has some content. You could drag an instance of it to the stage, or you can do that automatically, too:

```
star_lib.addItemToDocument({x:275, y:200}, starname);
```

The first argument is a point object saying where you want the item placed, and the second is the name of the item to add. Remember that you already stored this name in the variable starname. To add a bit of a professional touch, you can deselect the object, leaving it sitting pristinely onstage as if it had appeared out of nowhere:

```
star_doc.selectNone();
```

And in Figure 2-9 you can see the results of the command being applied several times.

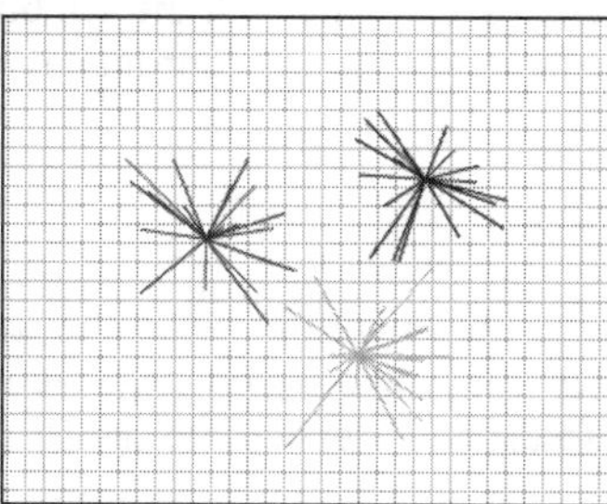

Figure 2-9.
Several starbursts onstage

There you have it. In case you got lost along the way, here's the relevant code in full (see also Starburst.jsfl):

```
var star_doc = fl.getDocumentDOM();
var star_lib = star_doc.library;
var starname = "star";
var tryCount = 1;
while(star_lib.itemExists(starname))
{
```

```
    starname = "star" + tryCount;
    tryCount++;
  }
  star_lib.addNewItem("movie clip", starname);
  star_lib.editItem(starname);
  for(var i=0; i<20; i++)
  {
    star_doc.addNewLine({x:0, y:0}, {x:Math.random()*100-50,
  ➥y:Math.random()*100-50});
  }
  star_doc.exitEditMode();
  star_lib.addItemToDocument({x:275, y:200}, starname);
  star_doc.selectNone();
```

Congratulations! You've made your first command from scratch. Note that it'll draw the starburst in whatever color is currently selected for strokes. See if you can change it to always use a specific color. Hint: Try using the `selectAll` and `setStrokeColor` methods.

Trimmed down, this serves as a pretty good template for creating any kind of item in the Library:

```
var name_doc = fl.getDocumentDOM();
var name_lib = myDoc.library;
name_lib.addNewItem(type, name);
name_lib.editItem(name);
// draw into the symbol here
name_doc.exitEditMode();
name_lib.addItemToDocument({x:___, y:___}, name);
name_doc.selectNone();
```

Just replace name with the name of your choice, and type with the symbol type you want to create, draw something where indicated, and add the x, y coordinates.

Timelines, Layers, and Frames

So far we've shown you how to get access to documents, draw on the stage, create symbols, and put them onstage. But once you've put something on stage, you need some way to have access to it. To do that, you need to dig a bit deeper into the DOM.

Working backwards, you can see that any element—shape, movie clip, text box, etc.—onstage actually resides within a particular frame or series of frames. Frames exist within a particular layer, and a number of layers make up a timeline. Also, a Flash movie (or "document" to be technically accurate) can have several scenes. Each scene is a timeline. These are all structured as a series of arrays. For instance, the first item in frame one, layer one, scene one of the first open document in Flash is as follows:

```
fl.documents[0].timelines[0].layers[0].frames[0].elements[0]
```

It might be a bit complex to always keep track of where you are in this tree, but you have a few shortcuts available to help you out. As you've already seen, `fl.getDocumentDOM()`

returns the currently active document. Similarly, you can get the currently active timeline of a particular document by writing

```
var curr_doc = fl.getDocumentDOM();
var curr_tl = curr_doc.getTimeline();
```

This gives you a very useful object to work with—it's whatever timeline you happen to be currently editing in the authoring environment. This applies not only to scenes; remember that every movie clip has its own timeline, so if you had a movie clip open for editing, like you just had in the starburst example, you could get access to its timeline in that way, without having to drill down through the layers and frames of where that movie clip is located.

Once you have the current timeline object, you can use a couple of its properties to locate the current layer and frame that is being edited:

```
var curr_doc = fl.getDocumentDOM();
var curr_tl = curr_doc.getTimeline();
var layerNum = curr_tl.currentLayer;
var frameNum = curr_tl.currentFrame;
```

These work a little differently. They are actually *properties,* not methods, and simply give you the number of the current frame or layer, not a reference to it. You can use those numbers as array indexes:

```
var curr_frame = curr_tl.layers[layerNum].frames[frameNum];
```

You can use this code to create a useful little function called `getCurrentFrame`:

```
function getCurrentFrame()
{
  var curr_doc = fl.getDocumentDOM();
  var curr_tl = curr_doc.getTimeline();
  var layerNum = curr_tl.currentLayer;
  var frameNum = curr_tl.currentFrame;
  var curr_frame = curr_tl.layers[layerNum].frames[frameNum];
  return curr_frame;
}
```

You can put that in any script and then get a reference to the frame currently being edited by just saying

```
curr_frame = getCurrentFrame();
```

Very useful indeed, we hope you'll agree!

Now that you have the current frame, you can access anything in that frame by using the elements array: `curr_frame.elements`.

Every item on the stage is an element and is stored in a slot in the `elements` array of that particular frame. For example, if you had a text box, a movie clip, a graphic symbol, a button, a component, and a shape onstage, there would be six elements, stored in `elements[0]` through `elements[5]`.

One thing to beware of is that all shapes in a frame are stored in a single element. By *shape* we mean a simple shape drawn on the stage using a drawing tool from the toolbar, or a method such as `addNewRectangle`. If you were to draw two rectangles on stage, or a hundred, they would still only make up one element. If you want to be able to access each shape as a separate element, you have to select the shape and group it, or convert it to a symbol. Each group or symbol counts as one element.

Accessing the Output Panel

When writing ActionScript, it's a fairly common practice to use the `trace` command to debug scripts. When something isn't working right, you just say `trace(myValue)` and it shows up in the Output panel. Then you discover something like `myValue` is undefined rather than what you thought it should be. This helps you track down where things are going wrong.

In the JS API, you have full access to the Output panel. It's a member of the `fl` object. To trace a value, just say

```
fl.outputPanel.trace(myValue);
```

In fact, those bright folks at Macromedia correctly guessed that this would be such a useful feature, they even provided a simpler shortcut to the `trace` function. You can call it directly from the `fl` object as follows:

```
fl.trace(myValue);
```

In fact, if like us, you're used to just writing trace like in ActionScript, you can create your own shortcut to it in the beginning of any file:

```
var trace = fl.trace;
```

Now you can call `trace(myValue)` just like in ActionScript.

Unlike in ActionScript, though, the Output panel isn't cleared each time you run a command. After a few times testing a particular command with traces in it, the panel can get pretty full, and you may get confused over which values are from which run. To solve that, you can manually clear the panel before tracing to it:

```
fl.outputPanel.clear();
```

It's sometimes handy to put that line at the top of a command file during the testing phase, in order to keep things clean and readable.

Finally, if your trace data is really important, you can save it to a text file like so:

```
fl.outputPanel.save (URI, bAppend);
```

The bAppend argument is a Boolean (true/false) value saying whether or not you want to overwrite the existing text in the file, or add the current output text to whatever is already in the file. By setting this as `false`, you could set up a log file that would contain an entry for each time the command was run. Remember, though, that this only works in the authoring environment. Once you publish your SWF, Flash still has all the same restrictions about writing to the hard drive.

URI stands for Universal Resource Identifier. It's essentially a URL, but it's a bit broader term. You can think of it as the file path and name. It generally starts with `file:///` and is then followed by the path and filename of the file you want to save. Here's an example for a file on a Windows system:


```
file:///c:/saved_text/output.txt
```

Here's another useful little property of the `fl` object: `fl.configURI`. It'll give you the URI of your configuration directory. So, say you want to save the output content into your Commands directory, you could use the following command:

```
fl.outputPanel.save(fl.configURI + "/Commands/output.txt", true);
```

The convenience of doing it this way is that you can then share this command with anyone using any system, and although the configuration directory will vary, this will always put it in the right spot. Remember that the configuration directory is different in different operating systems, so if Mac users tried to run a command pointing to something in `c:/` they wouldn't get far at all! Using `fl.configURI` gets around all of this.

Using some of these various methods and properties we just showed you, you can create some cool little utility commands. The following one loops through the entire DOM of a movie and traces its structure:

```
fl.outputPanel.clear();
var the_doc = fl.getDocumentDOM();
fl.trace("Document: "+ the_doc.name);
for(var t = 0; t<the_doc.timelines.length; t++)
{
  fl.trace("  +-Scene " + (t+1));
  var the_tl = the_doc.timelines[t];
  for(var l=0; l<the_tl.layers.length; l++)
  {
    fl.trace("  +-Layer " + (l+1));
    the_layer = the_tl.layers[l];
    for(var f=0; f<the_layer.frames.length; f++)
    {
      fl.trace("    +-Frame " + (f+1));
      the_frame = the_layer.frames[f];
      for(var e=0; e<the_frame.elements.length; e++)
      {
        the_elem = the_frame.elements[e];
        fl.trace("      +-Element " + e);
        fl.trace("          Type: " + the_elem.elementType);
        if(the_elem.elementType == "instance")
        {
          fl.trace("          (" + the_elem.instanceType + ")");
          if(the_elem.instanceType == "symbol")
```

```
                    {
                      fl.trace("           (" + the_elem.symbolType + ")");
                    }
                  }
                  if(the_elem.elementType == "text")
                  {
                    fl.trace("           (" + the_elem.textType + ")");
                  }
                  fl.trace("           Name: " + the_elem.name);
                }
              }
            }
          }
```

Here's a quick run-through of what it does:

1. First you clear the Output panel, get a reference to the current document, and trace its name. This will be its filename.
2. Then you loop through each member of its `timeline` array, and trace that. Remember, each scene in a movie is a timeline. Here, you trace (`t + 1`), since arrays start at zero, but scenes start at one.
3. With each timeline, you loop through all the layers. And with each layer, you loop through all the frames.
4. That gets you to the `elements` array. Looping through that, you get a reference to each element. Note that we've highlighted in bold this section of the code to point out a few interesting properties. Each element has an `elementType` property. This could be `shape`, `instance`, or `text`. So first, you trace that out.
5. If it is an instance element, that means it's an instance of either a graphic, movie clip, or button symbol. If so, the element will have an additional property, `instanceType`, which can have the value `symbol`, `bitmap`, `embedded video`, `linked video`, or `compiled clip`. If an instance element is a symbol, the element will also have a `symbolType` property, which can be `movie clip`, `graphic`, or `button`.
6. On the other hand, if the element is a text field, it'll either be static, dynamic, or input. This is stored in the `textType` property.
7. If the element is either instance or text, it may have a name. If so, it's in the `name` property. This file traces all of these properties out as appropriate. Note this doesn't cover the properties of the elements shown, or even all of the element types, merely some of the more interesting ones. Feel free to dig through the Flash extensibility reference section at the end of the book and update the file to show as much as you want about the structure of the movie.

At any rate, try this command. Save it in your `Commands` directory with a name like Movie Explorer, pull up an existing FLA file, or create a new one with various types of elements on various frames and layers. Run the command and get a listing of everything there.

As an interesting and useful exercise, you could try making this into a recursive function that would trace out the DOM of a movie, and when it encountered a movie clip instance it would trace the DOM of that clip. If you're interested, there is a file called `traceDOM.jsfl` on the book's website, `www.flashextensibility.com`, that does just that.

Another point to realize is that many of these properties are writable, not just readable, so they can be changed. A real-world example is a recent project we did—a large Flash movie with several hundred frames, each containing up to a hundred individual static text boxes, along with a lot of graphics. Each text box had to be changed to a dynamic text box. Doing this by hand would have literally taken days. We couldn't do a select all operation because there were many other types of elements. Each text box had to be selected individually and converted, and none could be missed.

In the end, we were able to write a JSFL script that looped through each frame, checked each element to see if it was a text box, and set each one it found to be dynamic. It took just a matter of minutes to convert the entire FLA (and the boss was very happy!).

Before moving on, you might want to take a look at some of the other properties and methods of frames, layers, and timelines. Just looking through them can give you an idea of the amount of power you now have over a movie. You can add and remove frames, keyframes, and layers; reorder layers and frames; create tweens; and almost anything else you could do in the authoring environment. We'll get into all that in more detail in Chapter 4.

Selections

Once you get a reference to a particular element, you can find out all about it by reading its properties, and depending on what type of element it is, you can change some of those properties. But you're still pretty limited in what you can actually *do* to that particular element. To really be able to manipulate a particular object, you need to *select* it. Doing so gives you a much wider variety of possible actions you can take with it. This of course mirrors the authoring environment, where you would first select an item, and then do something to it.

Once an object is selected, you can move it, rotate it, color it, delete it, turn it into a symbol, edit it, copy/cut/paste it, etc.

When an item is selected, it's added to an array that is a member of the document object. This array is named `selection`. Thus, if you had one element selected in a document named `my_doc`, you could access it with `my_doc.selection[0]`. Additional objects in a multiple selection would be in `selection[1]`, `selection[2]`, etc. Once you have a reference to an element like that, you can do such things as find its name (for an instance of a symbol, etc.), or its position or size, and you can manipulate these values and more.

So, how do you get items into this selection array? One of the simplest ways is `document.selectAll()`. This takes all items onstage in the currently active frame and selects them, putting them in the `selection` array. This is great if you want to select everything and group it or convert it to a symbol.

If you want to limit your selection though, you can use the `setSelectionRect` method, which is also a member of the document object. This takes two arguments. The first is a rect object describing the area of stage that you want to select. This is analogous to using the Selection tool to drag a rectangle over some objects on the stage. It'll select anything that falls completely within that rectangle, leaving out anything that is outside or only partly inside. The second argument is a Boolean value saying whether you want to replace the current selection (true) or add to it (false). The latter would be like holding the *SHIFT* key down to select multiple items.

One of the limitations of this method is that if you want to select a particular object, you have to know its location, or be able to calculate its location. Another is that you may end up selecting more than one object if there is another smaller object lying within that rectangle.

Another technique for selection is one we've already discussed—the `mouseClick` or `mouseDblClick` methods. Again, though, you have to know the exact location of what you want to select. And if something happens to be on top of what you're trying to select, you might wind up selecting that instead.

The moral of the story is that these tools are good in a brand new movie or at least a timeline of a new movie clip, where you have complete control over everything that is put there, and thus know exactly where everything is. In many cases though, you want to affect an object that is already onstage. You won't know its exact location or shape beforehand. Of course, you can find it by its location in the DOM, but how do you get it into the selection array?

The obvious method would be to get a reference to a particular element and just plug that into a slot in the selection array, like so:

```
my_doc.selection[0] = my_elem;
```

Or, perhaps use a standard array method such as push, which adds an item to an array:

```
my_doc.selection.push (my_elem);
```

Oddly enough, these usual methods have no effect at all! The correct way to select an element is a little more complicated.

First, you need to create a new array, then put the element into *that* array. Then, you assign that array to the variable `selection`. Here's an example code snippet showing that:

```
var selArray = new Array();
selArray[0] = my_elem;
my_doc.selection = selArray;
```

Here, `selArray` is created and `my_elem` is put into it. Then you set `selection` equal to `selArray`. Now, when Flash looks into `selection` to see what items should be selected, it'll see `my_elem`. There is a bit of strange behavior here though. Normally, you would expect `selArray` to replace the existing array, `selection`. But in practice, it actually adds the contents of `selArray` to the existing selection. Any currently selected items will remain selected and any new items in `selArray` will also be selected. Thus, if you want to *replace* the existing selection, you should make a call to `document.selectNone()` before proceeding as described.

Using this, you can make two more useful utility functions, getCurrentElements and selectElement. As ever, they are pretty straightforward:

```
function getCurrentElements()
{
  var curr_frame = getCurrentFrame();
  return curr_frame.elements;
}

function selectElement(elem, bReplace)
{
  if(bReplace)
  {
    fl.getDocumentDOM().selectNone();
  }
  var selArray = new Array;
  selArray[0] = elem;
  fl.getDocumentDOM().selection = selArray;
}
```

The getCurrentElements function gets a reference to the current frame by calling the getCurrentFrame function you created earlier in this chapter (make sure you include it in the file). The selectElement function takes an element reference as the first argument, and a Boolean argument, bReplace, which determines whether the current selection will be replaced or not.

If bReplace is true, you first call selectNone on the current document.

Then you create an array, put the element in it, and assign that to the selection array. That's all. The chosen element is now selected.

Here's an example of the use of these functions:

```
var my_doc = fl.getDocumentDOM();
var elems = getCurrentElements();
for(var i=0; i<elems.length; i++)
{
  selectElement(elems[i], true);
  my_doc.scaleSelection(.5, .5);
  my_doc.rotateSelection(45);
}
```

This uses getCurrentElements to put a reference to the elements array into the variable elems. Looping though the array, it selects each element and scales and rotates it. Make sure you include all the functions in your file. You can take a look at the scaleSelection and rotateSelection functions in the Flash extensibility reference section in the back of the book for more info on them.

Obviously, you can do a whole lot more than a simple scale and rotation like that, but this should give you a taste of how to start using this stuff. As you proceed through the chapter and the rest of the book, you'll see many more useful examples.

User Input with XML to UI

Up to now, you've pretty much been stuck with whatever code you wrote in the example scripts. If you want to change some parameter or aspect of some command, you need to open it up, rewrite it, save it again, and then run the command. Not too flexible, is it?

Well, here comes XML to UI to the rescue! That doesn't roll off the tongue quite as well as we'd hoped, but it's still pretty cool stuff. In this chapter, we'll just take brief look at XML to UI . . . just enough so you are able to do a little customizing of your commands. Actually, it's a pretty powerful tool, and we devote a whole chapter to it later in the book (Chapter 5). For now, you'll just get your toes wet with some of the basics.

First, let's look at what XML to UI, sometimes called XMLUI or XML2UI, stands for. XML is Extensible Markup Language, which simply put is a way of describing information as text inside of tags much like HTML. UI is user interface, which is some way for the *user* to *interface* or interact with the program. It usually consists of buttons, check boxes, menus, text boxes, etc., allowing the user to make various choices and set parameters.

So, XML to UI allows you to lay out a dialog box with these various controls, very similar to laying out an HTML page. Your command script then contains a line that calls up this dialog box, retrieves the values from it, and uses them later in the script.

To get your toes even more wet with XML to UI tags, you'll create a quick command that will call up a dialog box so you can see what you've created.

Create a new JSFL file starting with these two lines:

```
var the_doc = fl.getDocumentDOM();
the_doc.xmlPanel(fl.configURI + "/Commands/test.xml");
```

Save it as "Test XML to UI" in the `Commands` directory. The `xmlPanel` function is what calls up the dialog box. Note that it uses the `configURI` property to get the directory, and then goes into the `Commands` directory and grabs a file named `test.xml`.

Now, using your favorite text editor, create a new file and save it in your `Commands` directory under the name `test.xml`. In this file, insert the following:

```
<dialog buttons="accept, cancel" title="Test XML to UI">
</dialog>
```

The top-level tag is always `<dialog>`. That means the first line of an XML to UI file should always be `<dialog>` (plus internal attributes) and the last line is always the closing tag, `</dialog>`.

The `<dialog>` tag has two attributes. These are values contained in quotes. They are `buttons` and `title`. The buttons attribute can contain any of the values `accept`, `cancel`, or `help`. Just separate them with commas and contain them all within one set of quotes. Examples:

```
buttons= "accept, cancel, help"
buttons= "accept"
buttons= "accept, help
```

The title attribute is simply the text that will be displayed in the title bar of the dialog box. You can also include an id attribute, but it isn't necessary for the purposes of this example. Go ahead and save this XML file and then run the Test XML to UI command from the Commands menu. You should get a dialog box like the one in Figure 2-10.

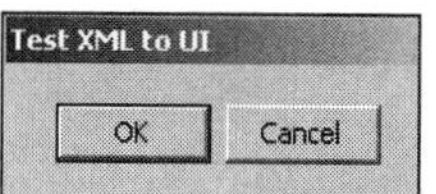

Figure 2-10. An XML to UI dialog box

2

Now, let's add some controls. Add the following to test.xml:

```
<dialog buttons="accept, cancel" title="Test XML to UI">
  <hbox>
    <label value=" Amount"/>
    <textbox id="amt" value="100">
  </hbox>
</dialog>
```

The first tag inside <dialog> is <hbox>. This is a layout tag. Anything inside of it will be laid out horizontally, one after the other.

Inside this you have two control tags. First is <label>, and this simply puts a text label in the dialog box at the specified spot. The value attribute is the text that will be displayed. Note that you close the tag with /> rather than just >. If a tag has no child tags, you can use this shortcut to close the tag. This is equivalent to saying

```
<label value="Amount">
</label>
```

Next, you have a textbox control. You give this an id attribute, which you'll later use to retrieve its value in JSFL. And you give it a default value, which will show up when the dialog box is created. There are other possible attributes here, but you'll keep it simple for now.

Save and test this and you'll get something like the dialog box in Figure 2-11.

If you want, you can change the <hbox> tag to a <vbox> tag, which will lay things out vertically, and give you something like the dialog box in Figure 2-12.

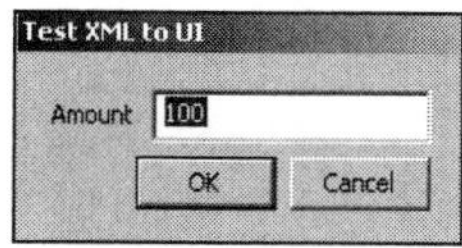

Figure 2-11. XML to UI dialog box with a textbox control

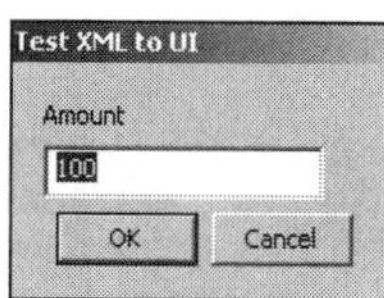

Figure 2-12. XML to UI dialog box with a vertical layout

You can also nest <hbox> and <vbox> tags to come up with a more complicated layout like this:

```
<dialog buttons="accept, cancel" title="Test XML to UI">
  <vbox>
    <hbox>
      <label value="Amount 1"/>
      <textbox id="amt1" value="100"/>
```

```
        </hbox>
        <hbox>
          <label value="Amount 2"/>
          <textbox id="amt2" value="200"/>
        </hbox>
        <hbox>
          <label value="Amount 3"/>
          <textbox id="amt3" value="300"/>
        </hbox>
        <hbox>
          <label value="Amount 4"/>
          <textbox id="amt4" value="400"/>
        </hbox>
      </vbox>
    </dialog>
```

Here you have a series of <hbox> tags laying their controls out left to right, and each of these is laid out top to bottom in the dialog box (see Figure 2-13).

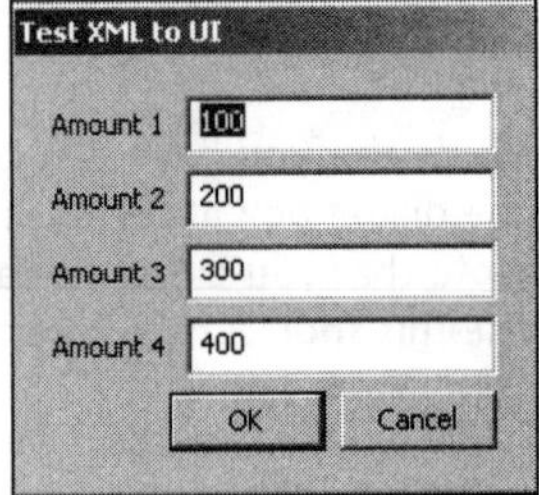

Figure 2-13.
XML to UI dialog box with nested <vbox> and <hbox> elements

There are plenty more controls you can use in your dialog boxes, and more ways to control layout. Some of these will be used as you progress through the book, and they are all fully explained in Chapter 5. You may also find useful a tool called Dialog Designer, available for download on this book's website. The Dialog Designer was created by Todd Yard, and it allows you to choose what elements you want, what attributes, and how to lay them out, and then generates the XML for you.

Next, let's look at how to retrieve the values that are set in the dialog box. You'll use the last version of `test.xml` with the four values listed. Go back into your `Test XML to UI` `JSFL` file and change it to look like this:

```
var the_doc = fl.getDocumentDOM();
var result = the_doc.xmlPanel(fl.configURI + "/Commands/test.xml");
fl.outputPanel.clear();
fl.trace("Amount 1: " + result.amt1);
fl.trace("Amount 2: " + result.amt2);
fl.trace("Amount 3: " + result.amt3);
fl.trace("Amount 4: " + result.amt4);
```

When the `xmlPanel` function is finished, i.e., the user clicks either the OK or Cancel button in the dialog box, the `xmlPanel` function returns an object. Here, you store that object in the variable `result`.

In the dialog box, you set an id attribute for each of the text boxes. These ids now become properties of the returned object, and their values will be whatever was put into the text box. Thus, whatever was in the first text box will be available to JSFL as

```
result.amt1
```


and so forth. This script merely traces those variables out to the Output panel. But, there is one problem here. Run the command again, but this time hit Cancel instead of OK. XML to UI still returns all the original values, and JSFL still traces them all out.

You can handle that. There is another property of the returned object called dismiss. This has two possible values, accept or cancel, which obviously correspond to the button that the user pressed. The following revised script checks the value of dismiss before doing anything, and then acts accordingly:

```
var the_doc = fl.getDocumentDOM();
var result = the_doc.xmlPanel(fl.configURI + "/Commands/test.xml");
fl.outputPanel.clear();
if(result.dismiss == "accept")
{
  fl.trace("Amount 1: " + result.amt1);
  fl.trace("Amount 2: " + result.amt2);
  fl.trace("Amount 3: " + result.amt3);
  fl.trace("Amount 4: " + result.amt4);
}
else
{
  alert("Command cancelled");
}
```

Generally speaking, when users hit the Cancel button, it means that they don't want to run that command at this time. Thus, you should always check the value of dismiss and put your whole command in an if block that only executes if dismiss is equal to accept.

Here you make use of the native JavaScript command alert (note that not all native JavaScript commands are available to you in JSFL). This simply pops up an alert box with the specified text if the user chooses Cancel. You don't really need to do anything in the else section, but we think it's a nice touch to acknowledge that the user cancelled the command, letting that person know that you didn't alter the file in any way.

Putting It All Together: Some Useful Commands

Well, we've covered quite a bit so far. By now you should have a basic understanding of commands, the DOM, basic JSFL syntax, and how to get data from the user.

You can go several directions from here. You can create relatively simple commands that do a small, specific function, such as changing the alpha or color of all the elements onstage, based on a value retrieved from an XML to UI dialog box. And we highly suggest that you play around with doing things just like that. It's a great way to learn the language.

However, for the rest of this chapter, we're going to up the pace a bit, and demonstrate building several real-world, useful commands. We'll walk through each step of them and explain any new concepts that arise. While these commands are pretty cool in their own right, they should also give you a glimpse of what is possible with JSFL and hopefully inspire you to do even more.

Selection to Grid

Your first complete command will take whatever shape, symbol, or other element is currently selected, duplicate it a bunch of times, and arrange it in a grid. The size of the grid will be user-configurable.

The strategy will be to grab the current selection, cut it to the clipboard, and then copy it numerous times, moving each new copy into place on the grid. The user will also be able to choose whether the resulting grid will be placed in a graphic symbol, a movie clip, or directly onstage.

Sounds like a lot to do, but actually, there's not a whole lot here that we haven't covered. So, let's jump in.

You'll start by making the XML to UI file, since that's probably simplest approach. You need a choice for number of columns, number of rows, and whether the grid should be put in a movie clip, graphic, or onstage. You'll get to look at a new XML to UI control too—the `listbox`.

Here's the XML (see also `selToGrid.xml`):

```
<dialog buttons="accept, cancel" title="Selection to Grid">
  <vbox>
    <hbox>
      <label value="Rows: "/>
      <textbox id="rows" value="5" size="3"/>
      <label value="Cols: "/>
      <textbox id="cols" value="5" size="3"/>
    </hbox>
    <vbox>
      <label value="Place grid in: "/>
      <listbox id="container" rows="3">
        <listitem label="Movie Clip" value="movie clip"/>
        <listitem label="Graphic Symbol" value="graphic"/>
        <listitem label="Directly on Stage" value="stage"/>
      </listbox>
    </vbox>
  </vbox>
</dialog>
```

Most of this should be pretty familiar by now, and the new listbox control is shown in bold. Basically, it has an id like other controls, and the rows attribute determines how many items will be visible in the listbox. If rows is less than the total number of list items, you'll be able to scroll up or down to see the hidden items (see Figure 2-14).

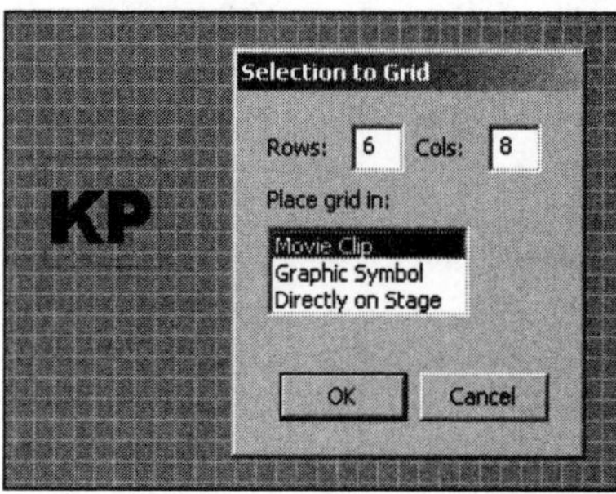

Figure 2-14.
The Selection to Grid dialog box, with a selected element

Within the <listbox> tag you have a number of listitem elements. Each one has a label, which is the text that will be shown in the dialog box (Movie Clip, Graphic Symbol, Directly on Stage), and a value (movie clip, graphic, stage), which is what will be passed back to your JSFL file via the listbox id attribute. You can save this in your Commands folder as selToGrid.xml.

Here is a shell of your Selection to Grid JSFL command script (see Selection to Grid.jsfl). This just calls the dialog box and traces the results. It's sometimes a good idea to get this part working before you do any heavy coding.

```
var curr_doc = fl.getDocumentDOM();
var result = curr_doc.xmlPanel(fl.configURI +
➥"/Commands/selToGrid.xml");
if(result.dismiss == "accept")
{
  fl.trace("rows: " + result.rows);
  fl.trace("cols: " + result.cols);
  fl.trace("container: " + result.container);
}
else
{
  alert("Command cancelled.");
}
```

If you run this as a command now, you should successfully call up the dialog box and be able to set values. When you hit OK, Flash should trace out whatever you chose, or if you hit Cancel, you should get an alert box. Once you have that working, you can remove all those traces and start working on the real code. You're going to put the code that does all the real work into its own function called makeGrid, so you can just call that function here.

Also, the command depends on something being selected so that it can duplicate it and arrange it. If nothing is selected, there's not much sense in even calling up a dialog box. You can just tell the user to select something and retry, and end off there. The following code will stand pretty much as you see it. Everything else will be put into the makeGrid function. Note that the utility functions you created earlier, getCurrentFrame, getCurrentElements, and selectElement, are also included, as you'll make good use of them:

```
var curr_doc = fl.getDocumentDOM();
if(curr_doc.selection.length == 0)
{
  alert("Please select a stage element and retry command.");
}
else
{
  var result = curr_doc.xmlPanel(fl.configURI +
➥"/Commands/selToGrid.xml");
  if(result.dismiss == "accept")
  {
    makeGrid();
  }
  else
  {
    alert("Command cancelled.");
  }
}
function getCurrentFrame()
{
  var curr_doc = fl.getDocumentDOM();
  var curr_tl = curr_doc.getTimeline();
  var layerNum = curr_tl.currentLayer;
  var frameNum = curr_tl.currentFrame;
  var curr_frame = curr_tl.layers[layerNum].frames[frameNum];
  return curr_frame;
}

function getCurrentElements()
{
  var curr_frame = getCurrentFrame();
  return curr_frame.elements;
}
function selectElement(elem, bReplace)
{
  if(bReplace)
  {
    fl.getDocumentDOM().selectNone();
  }
  var selArray = new Array;
  selArray[0] = elem;
  fl.getDocumentDOM().selection = selArray;
}
```

Now you start to create your makeGrid function. This is only the beginning, and will require a bit of explanation.

```
function makeGrid()
{
  if(result.container != "stage")
  {
    var gridname = "grid";
    var tryCount = 1;
    while(curr_doc.library.itemExists(gridname))
    {
      gridname = "grid" + tryCount;
      tryCount++;
    }
    curr_doc.convertToSymbol(result.container, gridname, "center");
    curr_doc.align("vertical center", true);
    curr_doc.align("horizontal center", true);
    curr_doc.enterEditMode();
    curr_doc.editingSymbol = true;
    curr_doc.selectAll();
  }
}
```

First you check the value of result.container. This will contain the choice the user made from the XML to UI list box. If this isn't "stage", then the user chose to put the grid in a movie clip or graphic. This section of the code handles that.

Using the naming loop you developed for the starburst file, you choose a name for the grid symbol. Once you have an acceptable name, you convert the selection to a symbol with the line

```
curr_doc.convertToSymbol(result.container, gridname, "center”);
```

Note that the container variable now contains either movie clip or graphic. These strings just happen to be the valid arguments to this method to tell it what kind of symbol to make. OK, they don't just happen to be that way. We had you set it up like that on purpose to save you from having to write more code! The next argument is the name of the symbol, which you just determined. Finally, you see the registration point, which you'll keep centered.

When you convert a selection to a symbol, that newly created symbol becomes the new selection. The next two lines merely center this new symbol on the stage—vertically and horizontally.

Finally, you enter edit mode on this selected symbol and do a selectAll to make sure all its content is now in the selection array. You also set a variable in there, editingSymbol, to be true. This just serves as a reminder to exit edit mode when you are done, as you'll see in a moment.

At this point, you'll be in one of two places: either inside a symbol, with its content (the original selection) selected, or pretty much right where you started from—onstage with the original selection still selected.

What you do from here is mostly the same in any case:

1. Cut the current selection to the clipboard.
2. Copy it back on the stage.
3. Move it into position on the grid.
4. Repeat steps 2 and 3 until the grid is filled.

Before you do anything, you need to know how much space you'll be moving things each time. If you divide the document size by how many rows and columns, you'll have your spacing. These are the next two lines in the function:

```
var xDist = curr_doc.width/result.cols;
var yDist = curr_doc.height/result.rows;
```

Then, you simply cut the selection into the clipboard.

```
curr_doc.clipCut();
```

The next chunk of code just loops through the columns and rows, pastes what you just cut to the clipboard, and calculates how much to move it:

```
for(var i = 0; i<result.cols; i++)
{
  for(var j = 0; j<result.rows; j++)
  {
    curr_doc.clipPaste(false);
    var moveX = xDist*i - curr_doc.width/2 + xDist/2;
    var moveY = yDist*j - curr_doc.height/2 + yDist/2;
    curr_doc.moveSelectionBy({x:moveX, y:moveY});
  }
}
```

The variables `moveX` and `moveY` are how much each new shape will move. When you paste an element onstage or into a symbol, you have the choice of pasting it in place by saying `clipPaste(true)`. If you specify `false` inside the function call, it'll paste to the center of the current stage. Knowing that, you move it on the x axis the value of `xDist` times the current column. But since you started in the center, you move back half a screen . . . and then forward half a space to even things out. Then you do the same thing on the y axis. Not the most elegant code (or the most elegant explanation), but it works. Feel free to improve upon it!

Once you figure the distance to move, you do the moving with the `moveSelectionBy` function. This takes a point object as its only argument. Note the important `By` element to the command—this doesn't absolutely position the current selection, but moves it relative to where it already is.

You wrap up by exiting edit mode if necessary and deselecting everything. For the record, here's what the complete function looks like now:

```
function makeGrid()
{
  if(result.container != "stage")
  {
    var gridname = "grid";
    var tryCount = 1;
    while(curr_doc.library.itemExists(gridname))
    {
      gridname = "grid" + tryCount;
      tryCount++;
    }
    curr_doc.convertToSymbol(result.container, gridname, "center");
    curr_doc.align("vertical center", true);
    curr_doc.align("horizontal center", true);
    curr_doc.enterEditMode();
    curr_doc.editingSymbol = true;
    curr_doc.selectAll();
  }
  var xDist = curr_doc.width/result.cols;
  var yDist = curr_doc.height/result.rows;
  curr_doc.clipCut();
  for(var i = 0; i<result.cols; i++)
  {
    for(var j = 0; j<result.rows; j++)
    {
      curr_doc.clipPaste(false);
      var moveX = xDist*i - curr_doc.width/2 + xDist/2;
      var moveY = yDist*j - curr_doc.height/2 + yDist/2;
      curr_doc.moveSelectionBy({x:moveX, y:moveY});
    }
  }
  if(curr_doc.editingSymbol)
  {
    curr_doc.exitEditMode();
  }
  curr_doc.selectNone();
}
```

And there you have it. The complete file is also downloadable from `www.flashextensibility.com` as `Selection to Grid.jsfl`. You can select any object onstage, choose the command, set the parameters, and it'll create a grid of the selected object as shown in Figure 2-15. Note that the object can be *any* item onstage—a shape, a line, a graphic symbol, movie clip, button, component, text box, or even a combination of these items. Whatever is selected will be duplicated. Pretty nifty, eh? We're sure you can use what you've learned so far to make it even more useful. Perhaps add a parameter for rotating or scaling each item as it's pasted. Over to you!

Figure 2-15. Result of Selection to Grid command

Text Effects

For your next trick, you're going to make a text effect. You'll concentrate on one, but with what you learn, you can turn it into just about any type of effect you want. This effect will be to arrange text in a circle. The concept is that the user will select a text field—it could be static, dynamic, or input text—and then `applies` the command. Whatever text is in that field will be arranged in a circle.

Now for your basic strategy. You first ensure the text is the only item selected, so you know where to find it—in the `selection` array. You convert it to a symbol, then break it apart. Now you have a bunch of text fields inside the symbol—each one containing one letter. You use a bit of fancy math to move them around a circle and rotate them and voila—circle text!

Once again, you'll start with your XML to UI file. You'll need two parameters—`radius` and `arc`. The `radius` parameter controls how big the circle is, while `arc` determines how much the text will go around the circle. If the user chooses `360`, the last letter will wind up right next to the first letter. `180` will wind up looking like text arranged on a rainbow. The XML is pretty simple for this one (see `Circle Text.xml`):

```
<dialog buttons="accept, cancel" title="Circle Text">
  <vbox>
    <hbox>
      <label value="Radius: "/>
      <textbox id="radius" value="100" size="5"/>
    </hbox>
    <hbox>
```

```
        <label value="Arc:     "/>
        <textbox id="arc" value="270" size="5"/>
      </hbox>
    </vbox>
  </dialog>
```

You just have two rows, each with a label and a text box, and one for each parameter.

Next, create a new file in your Commands directory and name it, predictably, Circle Text.jsfl (or, more easily, use the file from this chapter's example files). You might as well get it out of the way, and copy all of your utility functions in there: getCurrentFrame, getCurrentElements, and selectElement—you'll need them here, too. If you find yourself using the same functions over and over, you can put them in an external JSFL file, and then call those functions with the function fl.runScript. This is documented in the Flash extensibility reference section, and there are some examples of it in Chapter 8. For now though, you'll just include them in this file.

You'll continue by making sure you have the right kind of selection. You only want a single item to be selected, and that item must be a text field. If more or less than one item is in the selection array, or if that item isn't text, you send an alert:

```
curr_doc = fl.getDocumentDOM();
if((curr_doc.selection.length != 1) ||
(curr_doc.selection[0].elementType != "text"))
{
  alert("Please select a single text field and retry command.");
}
else
{

}
```

As a note, each bit of code we give you here should stand on its own, so feel free to test it as you go along. It may not do much at first, but it shouldn't generate any errors.

If you meet both of those selection requirements, you wind up in the else section, and you can get down to business. First, you display the XML panel, and make sure you get accept as a result.

```
curr_doc = fl.getDocumentDOM();
if((curr_doc.selection.length != 1) ||
(curr_doc.selection[0].elementType != "text"))
{
  alert("Please select a single text field and retry command.");
}
else
{
  var result = curr_doc.xmlPanel(fl.configURI + "/Commands/Circle
➥Text.xml");
  if(result.dismiss == "accept")
```

```
    {
      makeCircle();
    }
    else
    {
      alert("Command cancelled.");
    }
  }
```

Now, assuming you're still OK, Flash will call the `makeCircle` function, which will be the meat of what you're doing here. You'll start out once again by finding a suitable name for your circle. In this case, you'll just convert the text to a movie clip and start editing it.

```
function makeCircle()
{
  var circleName = "circle";
  var tryCount = 1;
  while(curr_doc.library.itemExists(circleName))
  {
    circleName = "circle" + tryCount;
    tryCount++;
  }
  curr_doc.convertToSymbol("movie clip", circleName, "center");
  curr_doc.enterEditMode();
  curr_doc.breakApart();
}
```

There shouldn't be any discussion required so far. You've seen this all before.

In the last line, you break apart the text field into individual letters. This couldn't be easier. You just use the `breakApart` function.

Now things get trickier. You'll need to know each character's exact position along the line of text. Not just that it's the third or fourth character, but *how many pixels* from the start of the text, and *what percentage* along the whole line it falls. You'll need to know its linear position in order to correctly determine its position around the circle.

So, first off you need to get the position of the first character and the last character. These will be in the current elements array that you can get with your `getCurrentElements` function.

```
var elems = getCurrentElements();
```

The first character will be `elems[elems.length-1]`, and the last will be `elems[0]`. It happens that when Flash breaks up a text field, the resulting elements go in the array right to left, so the first character is the last element. Also, remember that an array's last element is always numbered one less than its length. For example, a ten-element array will have a length of 10. Its elements will be numbered 0 through 9.

As far as an element's positions, the best you can do is read its properties, `top`, `left`, `width`, and `height`, which are pretty self-explanatory.

The starting position of the string will thus be elems[elems.length-1].left. The end of the string will be elems[0].left. Once you have the start and end positions, you can get the length with simple subtraction. Hopefully, Figure 2-16 will help to make this a bit clearer.

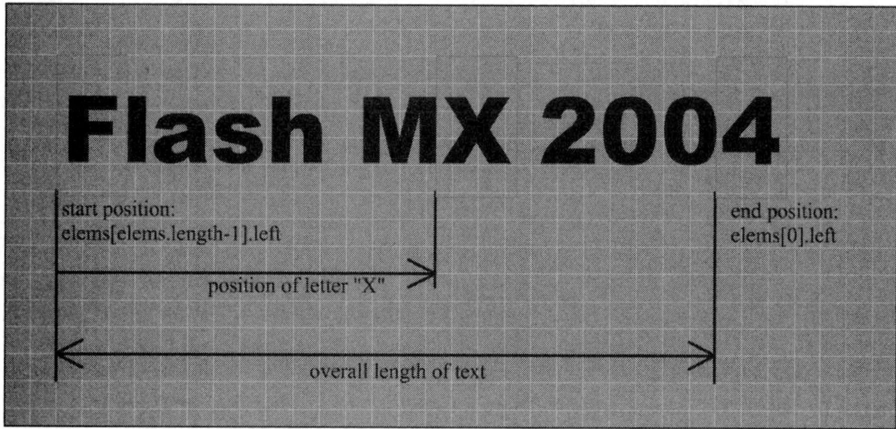

Figure 2-16. Figuring the relative position of a particular letter

Here's how your function is shaping up so far:

```
function makeCircle()
{
  var circleName = "circle";
  var tryCount = 1;
  while(curr_doc.library.itemExists(circleName))
  {
    circleName = "circle" + tryCount;
    tryCount++;
  }
  curr_doc.convertToSymbol("movie clip", circleName, "center");
  curr_doc.enterEditMode();
  curr_doc.breakApart();
  var elems = getCurrentElements();
  var startX = elems[elems.length-1].left;
  var endX = elems[0].left;
  var textWidth = endX - startX;
  var totalArc = result.arc*Math.PI/180;
}
```

We slipped in one last line again. This converts the value of arc, chosen by the user, into radians. As with most programming languages, JSFL uses radians rather than degrees for all angles. So you need to convert with the formula *radians = degrees * PI / 180*.

Now you need to loop through the elements and find each one's position as a percent of the entire length. Multiplying that percent times `totalArc`, you find where along the arc it'll fall:

```
...
  var textWidth = endX - startX;
  var totalArc = result.arc*Math.PI/180;
  for(var i=0; i<elems.length; i++)
  {
    curr_elem = elems[i];
    var xpos = curr_elem.left - startX;
    var percent = xpos/textWidth;
    var angle = percent * totalArc;
  }
}
```

Next, you select the element and center it. Then use some basic trigonometry to position it around the center, based on the angle. We'll avoid including yet another Flash trig tutorial here, but you don't need to fully understand the math for the command to work anyway. As a quick explanation, if you have an angle and a radius (distance from a center point), you can find the resulting point by the following formulas:

```
x = cos(angle) * radius
y = sin(angle) * radius
```

Here's how it looks in JSFL:

```
...
  for(var i=0; i<elems.length; i++)
  {
    curr_elem = elems[i];
    var xpos = curr_elem.left - startX;
    var percent = xpos/textWidth;
    var angle = percent * totalArc;
    selectElement(curr_elem, true);
    curr_doc.align("horizontal center", true);
    curr_doc.align("vertical center", true);
    var xDist = Math.cos(angle) * result.radius;
    var yDist = Math.sin(angle) * result.radius;
    curr_doc.moveSelectionBy({x:xDist, y:yDist});
  }
}
```

You can try that out and play around with it. You can see that you're getting there! The text actually forms a circle! Or part of one, if that's what you wanted (see Figure 2-17). You need to fix up a couple things though.

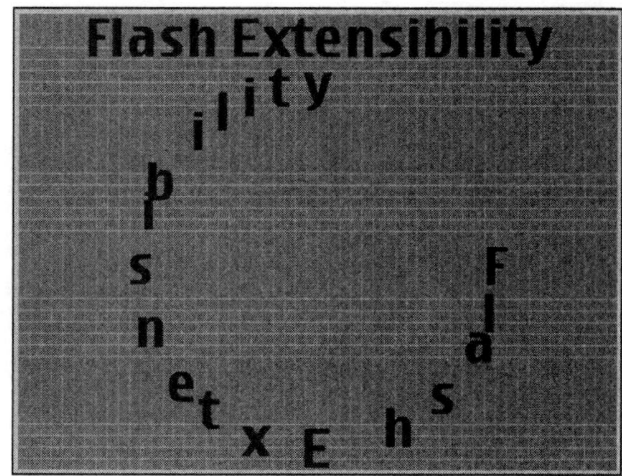

Figure 2-17. Text before and after applying the command. You should make the text start on the left, and rotate each character.

First of all, the text starts on the right-hand side and goes around clockwise. We think it'd look better starting on the left. To do that, you just need to add 180 degrees to the angle. 180 degrees happens to be 3.14159 . . . or PI radians. You can just add that to the angle before you compute your distances, with a simple line like

```
angle += Math.PI;
```

As an exercise, try adding in a `startingAngle` parameter to the XML to UI file, and using this to determine where the text circle will start.

The other issue is that you should rotate the text so it's aligned with the circumference of the circle. Strangely enough, the rotation function does in fact use degrees, just like ActionScript. Don't ask us why they use two different systems. Just get used to it! The long and the short of it is now you have to convert the variable, angle, back to degrees. You just reverse the formula:

```
var rotation = angle * 180/Math.PI;
```

Actually, if you left it at that, the letters would be lined up with their backs to the circle. To make it look like they are sitting on the circle as shown in Figure 2-18, you need to rotate them just a bit more:

```
var rotation = angle * 180/Math.PI + 90;
```

That ought to do it. Here's the final function. Note that we wrapped up by exiting edit mode and deselecting everything:

```
function makeCircle()
{
  var circleName = "circle";
  var tryCount = 1;
```

```
    while(curr_doc.library.itemExists(circleName))
    {
      circleName = "circle" + tryCount;
      tryCount++;
    }
    curr_doc.convertToSymbol("movie clip", circleName, "center");
    curr_doc.enterEditMode();
    curr_doc.breakApart();
    var elems = getCurrentElements();
    var startX = elems[elems.length-1].left;
    var endX = elems[0].left;
    var textWidth = endX - startX;
    var totalArc = result.arc*Math.PI/180;
    for(var i=0; i<elems.length; i++)
    {
      curr_elem = elems[i];
      var xpos = curr_elem.left - startX;
      var percent = xpos/textWidth;
      var angle = percent * totalArc;
      selectElement(curr_elem, true);
      curr_doc.align("horizontal center", true);
      curr_doc.align("vertical center", true);
      angle += Math.PI;
      var xDist = Math.cos(angle) * result.radius;
      var yDist = Math.sin(angle) * result.radius;
      curr_doc.moveSelectionBy({x:xDist, y:yDist});
      var rotation = angle * 180/Math.PI + 90;
      curr_doc.rotateSelection(rotation);
    }
    curr_doc.exitEditMode();
    curr_doc.selectNone();
}
```

Figure 2-18. The corrected results of the Circle Text command

You might notice some irregularities still in the spacing of the letters. This is due to the fact that you calculated the position of each letter based on its `left` property. To be more accurate, you could calculate its center point. This would be its left position plus one half of its width, for example:

```
elems[0].left + elems[0].width/2;
```


We'll leave this to you as a project to pursue. We think the file as shown is complicated enough!

Once again, this command is pretty useful, and at the same time is almost a template for any text effect you can think of creating. You can use 90 percent of it as-is for other effects. The routine is the same: Put the text in a movie clip, break it apart, find each letter's position, loop through, and apply some formula to each letter based on its position. Have fun with it.

Adding ActionScript

Up to now, everything you've created has been fairly static. Essentially you've just been creating things and pushing them around and letting them sit there. If users then want to add some ActionScript to animate the results, that's up to them.

But, using JSFL you can apply some prewritten ActionScript just as easily as anything else you've done. It can get pretty surreal writing ActionScript within JavaScript, but for simple scripts it's not that bad.

Note that if you have a preexisting movie clip or button and you want to create a tool to add some prewritten ActionScript to it, and nothing else, then you're probably looking at something that would be much suited to behaviors, covered in detail in Chapter 6.

Creating ActionScript within a command would mostly be when you first want to create some content from scratch, or manipulate some existing content in some way, and *also* want to put some script in it. For example, a command could create a shape, and then have it spin around. Let's do just that so you get the idea.

This next file is more of a lesson than something that will be really useful in and of itself. You'll create a spinning rectangle. You'll keep it as simple as possible, just to point out how you would add the ActionScript.

First, create a `Spinning Box.jsfl` file in your Commands directory. In it you'll create a new symbol in the Library, edit it, draw a square in it, and put it onstage. We've covered all the steps needed to do this, so here's the code without further ado:

```
var curr_doc = fl.getDocumentDOM();
var curr_lib = curr_doc.library;
var boxname = "box";
var tryCount = 1;
while(curr_lib.itemExists(boxname))
{
  boxname = "box" + tryCount;
```

```
    tryCount++;
  }
  curr_lib.addNewItem("movie clip", boxname);
  curr_lib.editItem(boxname);
  curr_doc.addNewRectangle({left:-50, right:50, top:-50, bottom:50}, 0);
  curr_doc.exitEditMode();
  curr_lib.addItemToDocument({x:275, y:200}, boxname);
```

Now you have a movie clip with a square in it sitting onstage. If in the authoring environment you wanted to add some ActionScript to spin this around, you would have three main options:

1. Name the movie clip, and put some code on the timeline where the box is. This code would assign an `onEnterFrame` handler function to the clip, use `setInterval`, or otherwise create a repeating block of code that would rotate the clip.
2. You could assign some code directly on the movie clip itself, Flash 5 style, using `onClipEvent(enterFrame)`.
3. You could put some code inside the clip, on the clip's own timeline. If you took this option, you would also need to add one extra frame, as timelines with only one frame don't loop.

You can actually do all of these straight from JSFL. So you will! It turns out that frames, as well as movie clip `instance` element objects, have a property called `actionscript`. This property holds a string, and this string contains an ActionScript statement, a series of statements, a function, or, potentially, a lengthy program.

The `actionscript` property works both ways. You can read it and get access to existing ActionScript on a frame or movie clip or button. For example, if a frame contained some ActionScript, and you had a reference to that frame (`curr_frame`), you could find the script in the variable `curr_frame.actionscript`.

You can also create a string containing some ActionScript statements and assign it to the `actionscript` property of a frame of a movie clip. Flash will put that script in that spot, and when you run the movie, that script will be executed.

Going back to your list of options, try out the first method. First, copy in the function `getCurrentFrame` to the file. You'll use that to get a reference to the current frame, and then assign some script to the `actionscript` property of that frame:

```
curr_frame = getCurrentFrame();
curr_frame.actionScript =  "box_mc.onEnterFrame = function() {\n";
curr_frame.actionScript += "     this._rotation+=3;\n";
curr_frame.actionScript += "};";
```

Note that the first two lines end with \n. This is the newline character, and works the same as if you'd pressed *ENTER* to start a new line. See how the three lines are split up and tacked on to each other with the += operator. This isn't particularly necessary, but it makes things a bit easier to read.

Now you just need to name the movie clip in order to have the function apply to it. Since you just added the clip to the document, it'll be the only thing selected. It'll be in curr_doc.selection[0]. You just need to set the name property:

```
curr_doc.selection[0].name = "box_mc";
```

And here is the whole file, minus the getCurrentFrame function:


```
var curr_doc = fl.getDocumentDOM();
var curr_lib = curr_doc.library;
var boxname = "box";
var tryCount = 1;
while(curr_lib.itemExists(boxname))
{
  boxname = "box" + tryCount;
  tryCount++;
}
curr_lib.addNewItem("movie clip", boxname);
curr_lib.editItem(boxname);
curr_doc.addNewRectangle({left:-50, right:50, top:-50, bottom:50}, 0);
curr_doc.exitEditMode();
curr_lib.addItemToDocument({x:275, y:200}, boxname);
curr_frame = getCurrentFrame();
curr_frame.actionScript = "box_mc.onEnterFrame = function() {\n";
curr_frame.actionScript += "     this._rotation+=3;\n";
curr_frame.actionScript += "}";
curr_doc.selection[0].name = "box_mc";
```

Now, if you run the command, you'll see two differences. One is that the square movie clip created now has a name if you look in the Properties panel. You'll also see a little a in the current frame. Click it and open the Actions panel to see the JSFL-generated code. If all is well, you should be able to test this FLA and have a spinning cube.

Now, let's look at version two, using onClipEvent code. This is probably even easier. Again, you have a reference to the new clip in the selection array. You just need to write your ActionScript string right into its actionScript property. Easy enough:

```
var curr_doc = fl.getDocumentDOM();
var curr_lib = curr_doc.library;
var boxname = "box";
var tryCount = 1;
while(curr_lib.itemExists(boxname))
{
  boxname = "box" + tryCount;
  tryCount++;
}
curr_lib.addNewItem("movie clip", boxname);
curr_lib.editItem(boxname);
curr_doc.addNewRectangle({left:-50, right:50, top:-50, bottom:50}, 0);
curr_doc.exitEditMode();
```

```
curr_lib.addItemToDocument({x:275, y:200}, boxname);
curr_doc.selection[0].actionScript = "onClipEvent(enterFrame){\n";
curr_doc.selection[0].actionScript += "     this._rotation+=3;\n";
curr_doc.selection[0].actionScript += "}";
```

Now, on to the third method, code on the movie clip's timeline. You'll do that before you exit edit mode. First you'll get a reference to the current frame (hint: include the `getCurrentFrame` function), and you'll add the code right to that frame's `actionScript` property.

```
var curr_frame = getCurrentFrame();
curr_frame.actionScript = "_rotation+=3;";
```

Then, as mentioned, you'll need to add another frame to allow for looping. To do this, you need a reference to the current timeline. From that, you call the `insertFrames` function to add one frame. Here's the whole thing.

```
var curr_doc = fl.getDocumentDOM();
var curr_lib = curr_doc.library;
var boxname = "box";
var tryCount = 1;
while(curr_lib.itemExists(boxname))
{
  boxname = "box" + tryCount;
  tryCount++;
}
curr_lib.addNewItem("movie clip", boxname);
curr_lib.editItem(boxname);
curr_doc.addNewRectangle({left:-50, right:50, top:-50, bottom:50}, 0);
var curr_frame = getCurrentFrame();
curr_frame.actionScript = "_rotation+=3;";
var curr_tl = curr_doc.getTimeline();
curr_tl.insertFrames(1);
curr_doc.exitEditMode();
curr_lib.addItemToDocument({x:275, y:200}, boxname);
```

A word of caution when adding ActionScript to a document with JSFL: Be very careful about adding code to preexisting objects or frames. You never know exactly under what circumstances the command will be run. In the first example, you wrote your code directly into the current frame. When the command is run sometime in the future, it's just possible that there could be a whole load of code on that frame. Well, your command just wiped it out. You could make some Flash developer very angry if you do stuff like that.

If you're putting code onto or into an object you just created, you can be pretty certain of what is in there. If you're adding code to something already existing, you're better off appending it with the += operator. It's a good idea to add some comments too, to show where this code is coming from. You could revise the first example as follows:

```
curr_frame.actionScript += "\n\n";
curr_frame.actionScript += "// ==================================\n";
```

```
curr_frame.actionScript += "// Code added by Spinning Box Command\n";
curr_frame.actionScript += "box_mc.onEnterFrame = function() {\n";
curr_frame.actionScript += "     this._rotation+=3;\n";
curr_frame.actionScript += "}\n";
curr_frame.actionScript += "// ==================================\n";
```

This tacks on everything to the end of any existing code on the frame, adds a couple of spaces, and boxes it off with comments that tell why the code is there and where it came from.

2

One last warning, along similar lines, is that even if you successfully append your ActionScript to some existing ActionScript, you could wind up creating all kinds of conflicts. If could end up overwriting variable names, functions, or event handlers. Try to use unique variable names, even if they end up being longer, such as `spinningBoxSpeed` rather than just speed, and be very careful about applying any code to anything you didn't create within the command, such as saying `_root.onEnterFrame = ...`

Now that you know all three methods, which one should you use? Since Flash MX, it has been the accepted best practice to put all ActionScript on frames, and keep anything out of onClipEvent statements on instances. This centralizes all the code and saves you or others from hunting through the movie to find the snippet of code causing some stray action to occur. However, as you'll soon see, the new Flash MX 2004 behaviors rely on `onClipEvent` statements for their functionality. This is most likely to avoid code conflicts on the timeline as described previously, and to a certain degree to purposely hide the code, the reasoning being that hard-core coders—those who would worry about best coding practices—would probably code such behaviors by hand, or use classes or other structures, rather than relying on behaviors. With those comments, we now leave it up to your informed decision on where to place your code!

Summary

Well, we've covered a huge amount of ground in this chapter. By now, you should have a good idea of how to run commands, how to create your own from scratch, and where to put them. You probably are getting a good grip on the Document Object Model for a Flash document, and have a pretty good feeling for what properties and methods exist and how to use them. You've even learned how to customize your commands to grab user data from dialog boxes created in XML to UI. In short, you're well on your way to controlling the Flash API via JSFL.

In the next chapter, we're going to pump up your knowledge even further, by demonstrating how to create custom tools and add them to the toolbar. In addition, we'll be exploring even more of the DOM and its various methods and properties.

3 CUSTOM TOOLS

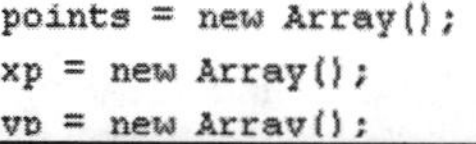

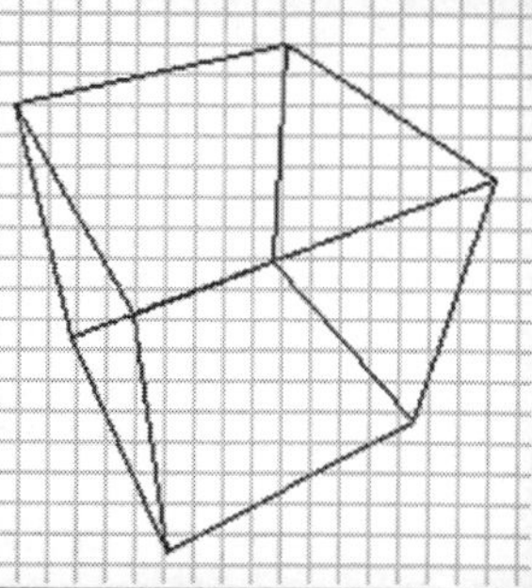

Personally, we find customized tools to be one of the most exciting portions of the JavaScript API. They have a rich architecture that is fun to work with from a programming viewpoint, and the results can be quite useful to both developers and designers. Let's take a look at what they are and how they work. As you go through this chapter, we urge you to be patient. Creating the simplest tool requires a lot of steps, and this is all brand new ground, above and beyond what we covered on custom commands. There are quite a few concepts to study before you can even start coding a tool, and if you jump ahead too far, you'll soon be lost.

In all versions of Flash so far, the toolbar has been sitting, fairly innocuously, over on one side of the screen, happily minding its own business. There have been a few changes over the years, but all in all, it's been pretty much the same old toolbar. You're no doubt pretty familiar with what's on it by now, and up until to now, what you got with Flash was what you were stuck with.

Well, with Flash MX 2004, Macromedia has removed the padlock and let you in to explore and play around. The first thing that might offer a clue to this newfound freedom is in the Edit menu, which has a new item, Customize Tools Panel. Go ahead and check it out; you'll get a panel something like the one in Figure 3-1.

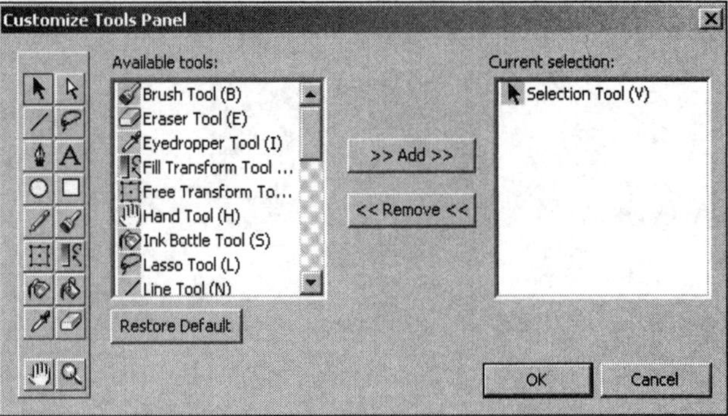

Figure 3-1. The Customize Tools Panel

With that, you can add, remove, or rearrange tools on your toolbar to your heart's content, including brand new tools that never existed before—tools that don't exist because *you* haven't written them yet. But you'll remedy that soon. We'll get more into the Customize Tools Panel a little later. That was just a sneak peak to whet your appetite!

Tools are written in JSFL, just as commands are, and can also use the XML to UI dialog boxes. But tools are miles ahead of commands, both in complexity and in power. To get an outside concept of what tools can do, check out the PolyStar tool on the toolbar.

Ah, but first you have to find it. Taking the hint from many other programs with toolbars, Flash now has drop-down tools. If you look at the Rectangle tool, you'll see a small arrow in the lower-right corner. That's a hint that it contains a drop-down toolbar. If you simply click the button for this tool, you'll get the Rectangle tool. But click and hold for a second, and you'll see the PolyStar tool drop down.

Unfortunately, you can't actually add rows or columns to the toolbar, you just have two columns to work with. There are 16 buttons labeled Tools, then 2 labeled View. Below that you have the Colors and Options areas. You can customize any of the buttons in the Tool or View sections. Recognizing that developers will probably be building and sharing many custom tools, Macromedia implemented the drop-down tools in order to let you cram as much as possible in the limited real estate of the toolbar.

If you choose PolyStar and start drawing on the stage, you'll see a pentagon shape appear where you clicked. It will grow, shrink, and rotate as you move the mouse. When you release the button, that pentagon shape will be permanently drawn onstage in whatever colors are selected. But you might also notice something else if you happen to have the Properties panel open when you select the PolyStar tool. It's subtle, but there is an additional button in there, labeled Options (see Figure 3-2).

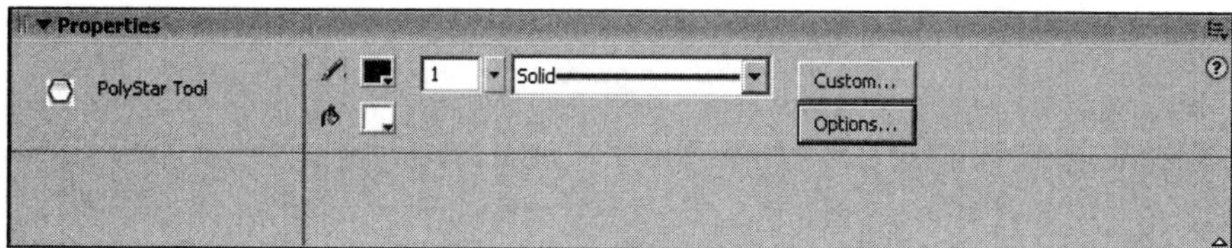

Figure 3-2. The Properties panel. Note the Options button.

Click that button, and you get a dialog box like the one in Figure 3-3.

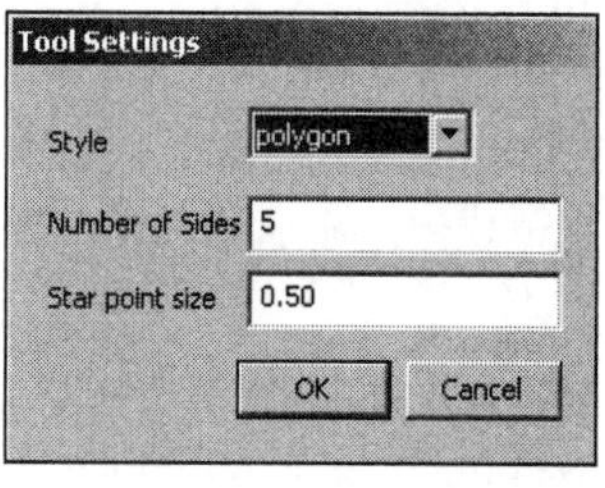

Figure 3-3. The PolyStar tool settings

You can now choose between a polygon and a star (now you know where they got the name PolyStar!), how many sides, and the star's point size. You might immediately guess that this dialog box was made in XML to UI. Not quite! Although you can of course create additional dialog boxes using XML to UI (see Chapter 5 for more details), you're given one "free" dialog box that gets linked to the Options button in the Properties panel. You just specify the parameters you want, their types, and their values. You still have to write it in an XML file, but it's a bit different to the way you use XML to UI. We'll give you a look at how to write that XML shortly.

Now that you've seen a custom tool in action, you're probably ready to jump in and make one of your own. Don't worry, you'll be doing just that soon enough. But first you need to learn a little about the structure of custom tool files. As we said, they are quite a bit more complex than a command. So this initial examination will be worth it in the long run.

Event-Based Code

If you look over the command files you created in Chapter 2, you'll see that they're pretty much linear code. You run the file and Flash starts with the first line, executes it, and moves to the next. Of course, when Flash encounters a function, it will jump to the point where the function is defined and run through that code, then back to where it left off.

When it hits the last executable line, that's it, show's over, command is done. If you want it to do more, you have to run it again.

Furthermore, short of an XML to UI dialog box, there is no interaction with the user. If you set some parameters and click OK, the command does its thing and presents you the results. There is no preview of what you're going to get. You simply have to click OK and hope for the best. Imagine trying to make something like a star shape with commands and dialog boxes alone. You'd have to guess at the size, location, number of points, point size, and rotation, then see how it looks. No good? Undo and try some slightly different parameters. Try again. Closer? Try again. Compare that to the ease of using the PolyStar tool.

Don't get us wrong, commands are pretty smart—but soon you'll see just how much more flexible tools are. This is largely due to their event-based structure. So let's discuss that for a moment.

If you've done much with Flash MX ActionScript, you probably have a pretty good idea of what events are and how an event-based program works. In ActionScript you would define various functions as handlers for various events. For example, you would have a function that runs each time the mouse button is clicked. This would be set as the `onMouseDown` handler. Or most commonly, you write an `onEnterFrame` handler function, which responds each time Flash enters a new frame.

Unlike a linear program that starts right in on the first statement and works its way through, a fully event-based program doesn't really do *anything* when you first run it. It just kind of sits there, waiting for some event to occur—a mouse click or movement, a key press, some content finishing loading, or whatever.

And that's basically how tool scripts work. You may define some variables at the beginning of the script, but everything else is all enclosed within functions. When Flash starts up, it executes all the JSFL files in the tool directory, even if they aren't on the toolbar! At this point, a specific function is executed to configure the tool. Then, each tool lies dormant, waiting to be activated. Of course, if a tool isn't on the toolbar, there is no way to activate it, but it sits there waiting anyway.

Once it is activated, it executes another function. And then it waits for something else to happen, such as a mouse action.

The key concept to remember is that tools shouldn't have any code in them that isn't contained in functions. Several of these functions are specifically named, and conform to specific events that occur. When a particular event occurs, Flash will look in your script for a function with the correct name, and run that function. For example, if you define a `mouseDown` function, it will automatically be called whenever the user presses the mouse button.

Standard Tool Functions

Let's run through the functions that you'll most likely define in your tools. For each one, we'll look at its name, when it executes, and what you should probably do inside of it.

First you have the administrative type functions, which handle setting things up and breaking things down:

- `configureTool`
- `activate`
- `deactivate`
- `notifySettingsChanged`
- `setCursor`

Then the functions for handling keyboard input:

- `keyUp`
- `keyDown`

And finally the mouse-handling functions:

- `mouseUp`
- `mouseDown`
- `mouseMove`
- `mouseDblClk`

We'll focus on each of these functions in the following sections.

configureTool

This fires when Flash is starting up. As part of all the actions it takes to set up the authoring environment, it executes each JSFL file it finds in the `tools` folder. This is the reason you don't want any code outside of functions, because that code will be executed as soon as Flash loads, regardless of whether the tool is even used on the toolbar. As it executes each tool file, it also looks for a `configureTool` function and runs it. Here you would put any code to initialize variables, etc.—anything that the tool needs to be set up and ready to run. There are a few statements that *need* to be in here, and these will set the tools icon, name, and so on.

activate

This function runs when you choose the tool on the toolbar. This is where you do any last minute setup for the tool. Where you do the setup—`configureTool` or `activate`—is up to you. You might want to do the bulk of the work in `configureTool` so that the tool is mostly ready to run when you select it. In `activate`, you'll probably minimally grab a reference to the `activeTool` property here, with the line `var curr_toolObj = fl.tools.activeTool`, and then get any properties off the Tool Settings dialog box after clicking the Options button in the Properties panel, if you chose to include one. You'll see more of this later.

deactivate

As you probably guessed, this fires when you deselect the tool, usually by selecting another one. Often, you don't need to do anything here, but if you have any cleanup to do, this would be the place to do it.

notifySettingsChanged

As mentioned earlier, you have the option of having a Tool Settings dialog box. If you created one, and the user uses it to change some setting, this function will fire as soon as that user clicks OK. In this function you need to manually grab these new settings and incorporate them into your code.

setCursor

Two functions have this name. One is `fl.tools.setCursor(cursorNumber)`, which allows you to manually change the appearance of the cursor. *This* `setCursor`, though, is different. It is an event-handling function. From time to time, Flash or the operating system may need to change the cursor to indicate various things, such as changing to an hourglass when the CPU is busy, or changing to standard icons when you move the mouse back over the desktop or other application. When they decide to hand control of the cursor back over to your script, Flash calls the `setCursor` function, if you've included it. Here, you can do whatever you want. Generally speaking this consists of setting the cursor you want your tool to have. Again, more on this later.

keyUp

This is pretty obvious. It fires when a key that has been pressed is released. While tools usually rely on the mouse, it is possible to build in some keyboard interaction.

keyDown

Yes, this fires when any key on the keyboard is pressed down.

mouseUp

Again, pretty self-explanatory. When the mouse button is pressed, and then you release it, this function is run, if you've defined it.

mouseDown

Fires when you press the mouse button. The common way to write these is to have Flash enter temporary drawing mode when the mouse is pressed. A temporary drawing is drawn to a special object called the drawing layer. You can see this in the PolyStar as well as other tools. When you draw with the tool, a kind of faint outline of the shape is visible. Then, when the mouse button is released (`mouseUp`), the actual shape is drawn to the stage, using whatever stroke and fill settings are active.

mouseMove

You guessed it, this fires when you move the mouse. Usually, this is where your temporary drawing will occur. When the mouse is moved, some shape is drawn, larger or smaller, or rotated differently. When it is moved again, the earlier shape is gone and a newer version, based on current mouse position, is redrawn.

mouseDblClk

Another very obvious one, this function fires when the mouse is double-clicked. As you saw in the previous chapter, a double click will actually generate two events: first, a `mouseDown` occurs for the first click, and then if the second click is close enough to the first, a `mouseDblClk` event will fire.

OK, those are all the basic event-handling functions. You could create a pretty basic template for a tool by simply putting all of these functions into a new JSFL file in the following format:

```
function configureTool(){
}
```

Of course, you don't need to handle *all* of these functions. If you aren't going to be handling keyboard input or double clicks, you can either leave those functions empty, or leave them out of the file altogether.

Setting Up a New Tool

We know, we know, you're probably dying to dive in and start creating a new tool by now. But remember, this is more complicated than just writing a command. You have quite a bit of work to do before you can even have a tool show up in the toolbar.

First of all, if you haven't already done so, take a look in the `Tools` directory in your Flash configuration directory. As you saw in Chapter 2, this is found within the `Configuration` directory (`C:\Documents and Settings\<user name>\Local Settings\Application Data\Macromedia\Flash MX 2004\en\Configuration\`) on Windows systems. You'll see a few files there already for the PolyStar tool. There's `PolyStar.jsfl`, `PolyStar.png`, and `PolyStar.xml`.

The JSFL file obviously contains the script itself. However, if you try to open it, you won't see much. It has been encrypted with a special tool available only to Macromedia and select developers. The tools you make will be open for anyone to look at though.

The PNG is a graphics file—PNG stands for Portable Network Graphics. This is the icon image that shows up in the toolbar. In addition to your JSFL file, you'll need to supply a PNG icon for your tool. When you're just starting out creating a new tool, it's fine to use the `PolyStar.png`, or any other existing tool icon PNG in the directory. Flash doesn't complain about using the same one more than once. But by the time you wrap up your tool, you'll want to create a nice icon for it. The easiest way to do that is to open up the `PolyStar.png` in Fireworks, Photoshop, or whatever graphics editor you prefer, change it and save it with a new filename. If you're starting from scratch, just make a 16 × 15 pixel, 24-bit (8 bits per channel) graphic saved as a PNG file.

The XML file is the file for the Options dialog box and is completely optional. Your first few files won't use it, but you'll check into it later on.

You should also see a file called `toolConfig.xml` and one called `toolDefaultConfig.xml`. Feel free to look at these and get an idea of how they are made up. The `toolConfig.xml` file is what Flash uses to load the toolbar up when it starts. This tells it where to place each tool. And `toolDefaultConfig.xml` is used to reset the tools when `toolConfig.xml` is missing or you choose to return to the default configuration after you've heavily customized the toolbar. You don't need to edit these files manually. They are created automatically when you use the Customize Tools panel. You use the panel to set up the configuration, and when you click OK, it saves to the XML file automatically.

So now you're almost ready to start making a tool. But first, you're going to make one more command! What? Go backwards? Trust us. This command is a simple workflow enhancement and will take about 30 seconds to make; it'll save you hours in the long run!

Create a JSFL file in your `Commands` directory called `Reload Tools.jsfl`. It just needs one line of code:

```
fl.reloadTools();
```

Why do you need this? As we covered earlier, when Flash loads up, it goes through the Tools folder and loads the JSFL file for each custom tool it finds there and executes its `configureTool` function. After that, it never touches the JSFL file on the hard disk again.

So, if you're in the process of writing a tool, you save the JSFL file and use the Customize Tools panel to add it to the toolbar. Then you test it out. If you're like us, it doesn't do much of anything on the first try, with the possible exception of generating some interesting error messages. So you go back in and find the bugs and save the file again. But Flash has already loaded the tool and has no idea that you've changed it. It will keep on using the code it loaded into memory.

You have three options:

1. Shut down Flash and restart it.
2. Go into the Customize Tools panel, remove the tool from the menu, close it, open it again, and add it back in. This should load the new code into memory.
3. Run your newly created Reload Tools command. This just tells Flash to redo the process of loading up the toolbar. You'll probably see the toolbar flicker a bit. This is your clue that it has reloaded successfully.

Creating a Tool

Finally! We've covered all the necessary prerequisites for you to be able to actually start coding a tool. Let's go through it step by step. Your first tool won't do much of anything, but at least you'll be able to see it in the toolbar and get a feel for the process of creating a tool and familiarize yourself with some of the different events and when they fire.

1. First off, create a simple icon of whatever design takes your fancy. Again, this should be a 16-by-15 PNG file. You can skip this step if you want, and just use the `PolyStar.png` file. Save it as `TestTool.png` in your Tools directory.
2. Next, create a new JSFL file in your `Tools` directory. Name it `TestTool.jsfl`. Using the function names mentioned previously, set up a basic tool file including each function. Inside each one, put a `fl.trace` statement tracing the name of the function. This should look something like the following:

```
function configureTool(){
  fl.trace("configureTool");
}
```

```
function activate(){
  fl.trace("activate");
}

function deactivate(){
  fl.trace("deactivate");
}

function keyDown(){
  fl.trace("keyDown");
}

function keyUp(){
  fl.trace("keyUp");
}

function mouseDblClk(){
  fl.trace("mouseDblClk");
}

function mouseDown(){
  fl.trace("mouseDown");
}

function mouseMove(){
  fl.trace("mouseMove");
}

function mouseUp(){
  fl.trace("mouseUp");
}

function notifySettingsChanged(){
  fl.trace("notifySettingsChanged");
}

function setCursor(){
  fl.trace("setCursor");
}
```

3. You still need to do a bit more to actually get this tool running, or even be visible on the toolbar, but if you now run your Reload Tools command, you should see a trace of `configureTool`. As you can see, Flash has found the JSFL file, found its `configureTool` function, and executed it. But in order to have the tool accessible, you need to add a few things to this function. In fact, if you look in the Customize Tools panel, you won't even see the tool there available to add. When Flash reloaded the tools, it did not find enough info in the `configureTool` function to be able to add it there.

4. So, add the following lines to the configureTool function:

```
function configureTool(){
  fl.trace("configureTool");
  var curr_toolObj = fl.tools.activeTool;
  curr_toolObj.setIcon("TestTool.png");
  curr_toolObj.setMenuString("Test Tool");
  curr_toolObj.setToolName("Test Tool");
  curr_toolObj.setToolTip("Test Tool");
}
```

   Let's take a look at this new code. First, you grab a reference to the "active tool." In the fl object, there is another object called tools. The tools object contains an array called toolObjs, which contains a reference to each tool. The tools object also contains a property called activeTool, which contains a reference to whatever tool is active. When a tool is chosen on the toolbar, it is the activeTool. Also, while a tool is loaded and configured when Flash is starting up or reloading the tools, it becomes the activeTool during that period.

   Anyway, you store a reference to the activeTool in a variable called curr_toolObj. A toolObj is an object with several methods and properties. Here you see the important ones for configuring a tool:

   - You set the icon. Remember, if you didn't create a custom icon for this tool, use the PolyStar.png filename here.
   - Then you set the menu string. This is the name you'll see in the drop-down tools list.
   - Then you set the tool name, which is what will show up in the Properties panel when the tool is active.
   - Finally you set the tool tip, which is the name that pops up when you mouse over a particular tool icon.

   All these names are generally set to the same thing, though that isn't required.

5. Save this, and once again open your Customize Tools panel. Now you'll see your Test tool with its icon, ready to add. Click a spot on the toolbar where you want to add the tool. You can stick it in with the Rectangle and PolyStar tools, or tack it onto any other tool. You could even remove an infrequently used tool from its slot and put your custom tool right on the top level if you want. Once you have a spot picked out for it, click its name in the Available Tools list, then click the Add button. Click OK and check out your new, customized toolbar, complete with your new tool!

You should already receive a message for configureTool in the Output panel. That's a good sign. Now, select your tool and you should get an activate message. As you move the mouse around, you should get a flurry of mouseMove and setCursor messages. Try out the mouse up and down actions too. Finally, select another tool and you should see a deactivate message, and that should be the end of it until you select the tool again.

When you're done with this particular learning experience, you'll want to go into the Customize Tools panel and remove it from the toolbar. In addition, you'll probably want to remove the JSFL file from your Tools directory, lest you get an annoying trace message every time you reload your tools (you'll be doing that quite a lot as you progress through this chapter).

Grid Tool

Interesting as that was, you'll now create a tool that actually does something! Once again you're going to go with the grid theme, creating a tool that will draw a grid. The first major idea you'll be learning about is the drawing layer. This is a special object in the Flash DOM that allows you to preview what you'll be drawing without actually drawing any content to the document itself.

There's still a lot of material to cover just to make a simple tool like this. In fact, most of the rest of this chapter will be spent just going through the different requirements and options using this same file.

1. First you'll need an icon. You can make your own, naming it `grid.png`, or just download the one that has already been created and is available on this book's website, along with all the other example files.
2. Next, you'll need to start a JSFL file named `grid.jsfl`. To start with, you'll need to include the following event-handler functions:
   - `configureTool`
   - `activate`
   - `mouseDown`
   - `mouseUp`
   - `mouseMove`

   You can set these up as empty functions for the moment, and you'll fill them up with code as you go. You can start setting up the `configureTool` function right off the bat. Most of this we've already covered:

```
function configureTool(){
  var curr_toolObj = fl.tools.activeTool;
  curr_toolObj.setIcon("grid.png");
  curr_toolObj.setMenuString("Grid Tool");
  curr_toolObj.setToolName("Grid Tool");
  curr_toolObj.setToolTip("Grid Tool");
}
```

   After saving this file, your tool will be set up enough to add to the toolbar. So go ahead and open up the Customize Tools panel and add it wherever you want it. If your Grid tool isn't in the list of available tools, make sure it is saved in the Tools directory, along with the icon file, and check the syntax of the code in the file. If there is any major error that prevents `configureTool` from running, Flash will not be able to get enough information about the tool to list it. Once you successfully add the tool and have it show up in the toolbar, you can move on.

3. Next, you'll set up the activateTool function. You really only need one line here to grab a reference to the current tool. This reference will then be available for as long as the tool is active:

```
function activate(){
  curr_toolObj = fl.tools.activeTool;
}
```

Now, in any other function, you can refer to the activeTool with curr_toolObj without having to set a reference. Remember, you can add other variables or statements here as needed for your particular tool. This is all you need for now though.

4. Next, you'll add some code to mouseDown and mouseUp. If you think about the other drawing tools in Flash, nothing too much happens until you click the mouse to start drawing. At that point, you enter a kind of interactive drawing mode, which exists until you release the mouse button. At that point, you exit the interactive mode, your drawing is placed on the stage, and Flash waits for you to do something else.

   All of the actual drawing will take place in the mouseMove function. All you need to do here is enter or exit that drawing mode. You do that with the commands fl.drawingLayer.beginDraw() and fl.drawingLayer.endDraw(). This tells the drawing layer (the fl.drawingLayer object) to get ready to receive some drawing commands. Always remember to call beginDraw before doing any drawing, and endDraw when you're done.

   Also, a drawing tool usually draws something at the physical location where the mouse was first clicked. So it will be good to make note of this point for future reference. Here are the two functions:

```
function mouseDown(){
  startPoint = fl.tools.penDownLoc;
  fl.drawingLayer.beginDraw();
}

function mouseUp(){
  fl.drawingLayer.endDraw();
}
```

   Here you store the starting point in the variable startPoint. Notice how you get that point. The tools object contains a property called penDownLoc. This is a point object with x and y properties. It holds the location of the last place where the mouse was clicked. You don't really need to grab this point right at this time, since it will still be available in penDownLoc later, but it makes the subsequent drawing code a little clearer.

5. All right, you're ready to start some interactive drawing! This will all happen in the mouseMove function. As mentioned, this temporary drawing occurs in an object called the drawing layer. It has methods drawing lines and other shapes, but remember, the shapes you draw on the drawing layer are temporary. They don't get saved to the drawing. They are just a kind of preview. In effect, you need two whole chunks of code to draw the same shape—one in mouseMove, using the drawing layer methods, and another that will occur when the user releases the mouse. This code will use the document drawing methods and draw to the stage. Since the

drawing commands for the two modes aren't exactly the same, there is no way of writing just one function that handles both of them. You have to do the double work. (Actually, there is one shortcut to this process, which you'll learn about when we get into the path object.)

Before you start drawing, you have to issue one more setup command—fl.drawingLayer.beginFrame(). This has nothing to do with the frame object or frames in Flash at all. But, since you're doing a sort of animation—drawing a slightly different shape over and over again—it does have to do with frames in a more general sense in any animation. The mouse moves, you begin a frame, you draw something to it, and then you end the frame. Then the mouse moves a little more and you need to update what was drawn, so you begin a new frame, clearing the screen and redrawing a shape.

So, much like beginDraw and endDraw bracket the entire drawing phase, beginFrame and endFrame should bracket each individual instance of drawing your shape.

Here's the beginnings of it:

```
function mouseMove(){
  if(fl.tools.mouseIsDown){
    fl.drawingLayer.beginFrame();
    fl.drawingLayer.moveTo(startPoint.x, startPoint.y);
    fl.drawingLayer.lineTo(fl.tools.penLoc.x, startPoint.y);
    fl.drawingLayer.lineTo(fl.tools.penLoc.x, fl.tools.penLoc.y);
    fl.drawingLayer.lineTo(startPoint.x, fl.tools.penLoc.y);
    fl.drawingLayer.lineTo(startPoint.x, startPoint.y);
    fl.drawingLayer.endFrame();
  }
}
```

Note that first, you check whether the mouse is down. There's no need to do anything if the mouse isn't pressed. You can find this out by checking the tools property fl.tools.mouseIsDown. If it is down, you begin the frame and start drawing.

But hey, wait just a second! Not only are you back to moveTo- and lineTo-style commands, but you're supplying them with individual x and y properties rather than a single point object! Just when you started getting used to the JSFL style, addNewLine(startPoint, endPoint), now it looks like you're back in ActionScript. Not very consistent is it? We're not sure exactly why they switched just for this one object. All we can say is be flexible and roll with it, because that's how it is.

Anyway, that's pretty basic drawing. It draws a rectangle from the point you first clicked (startPoint), to the current mouse position, which can be found with fl.tools.penLoc.

Test this out and you should be able to draw a rectangle on the screen. Don't forget to reload your tools with the Reload Tools command. If done exactly per the code here, it should be a nice, smooth drawing operation. If you're getting a lot of flickering or artifacts, you've probably messed up the placement of your begin or end drawing or frame commands. If you find your tool suddenly disappears off the toolbar, you have some major error in the code that isn't allowing configureTool to run. If that's the case, you won't even get an error message, it will just disappear.

Other runtime errors may show up in the Output panel as you run the command, so look for them as you develop and test your own extensions.

6. This is the outline for your grid. Next, you need to fill in the individual grid lines. First you'll need to determine how many lines to draw vertically and horizontally. Later, you can let the user change this with the Options button, but for now you'll just hard code it to five rows and columns. If this were going to stay hard coded, you could do it in the configureTool function and be done with it. But since it's going to wind up being dynamic, you'll put it where it's eventually going to go, in the activateTool function.

```
function activate(){
  curr_toolObj = fl.tools.activeTool;
  rows = 5;
  cols = 5;
}
```

Simple enough!

7. Now you jump back to your mouseMove function and change the drawing code. Remember, though, that it all needs to fall between the pair of beginFrame and endFrame methods:

```
function mouseMove(){
  if(fl.tools.mouseIsDown){
    fl.drawingLayer.beginFrame();
    var gridHeight = fl.tools.penLoc.y - startPoint.y;
    for(var r = 0; r<=rows; r++){
      var offset = gridHeight/rows*r;
      fl.drawingLayer.moveTo(startPoint.x, startPoint.y + offset);
      fl.drawingLayer.lineTo(fl.tools.penLoc.x, startPoint.y + offset);
    }
    var gridWidth = fl.tools.penLoc.x - startPoint.x;
    for(var c = 0; c<=cols; c++){
      offset = gridWidth/cols*c;
      fl.drawingLayer.moveTo(startPoint.x + offset, startPoint.y);
      fl.drawingLayer.lineTo(startPoint.x + offset, fl.tools.penLoc.y);
    }
    fl.drawingLayer.endFrame();
  }
}
```

What you're doing this time is first finding the height of the grid by subtracting the beginning point from the end point. Then you loop through and draw a series of horizontal lines from the start point to the current mouse position. You determine the y position of the lines by dividing the height by the number of rows, then multiplying by the current row being drawn. You then loop through and draw the vertical lines. Figure 3-4 may help to explain this.

Save the file, again as grid.jsfl, in the Tools directory, reload your tool, and test it out. Try playing around with the settings for rows and columns and make sure everything is working so far.

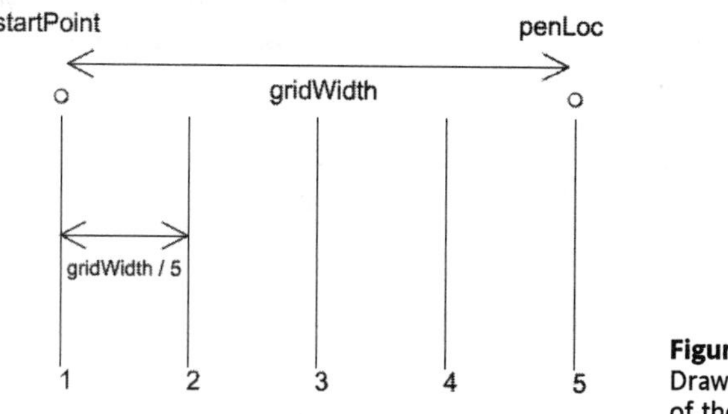

Figure 3-4.
Drawing the vertical lines of the grid

3

8. Next, you need to write some code to permanently draw the grid into the document. This occurs after users draw their grid to the size and shape they want and then release the mouse button. Thus, this code should go in the `mouseUp` function. Essentially this code does exactly the same thing as the drawing layer code, it just uses the `document` object `addNewLine` method instead. Here is the new `mouseUp` function:

```
function mouseUp(){
  fl.drawingLayer.endDraw();
  var endPoint = fl.tools.penLoc;
  var curr_doc = fl.getDocumentDOM();
  var gridHeight = endPoint.y - startPoint.y;
  for(var r = 0; r<=rows; r++){
    var offset = gridHeight/rows*r;
    var lineStart = {x:startPoint.x, y:startPoint.y + offset};
    var lineEnd = {x:endPoint.x, y:startPoint.y + offset};
    curr_doc.addNewLine(lineStart, lineEnd);
  }
  var gridWidth = endPoint.x - startPoint.x;
  for(var c = 0; c<=cols; c++){
    offset = gridWidth/cols*c;
    var lineStart = {x:startPoint.x + offset, y:startPoint.y};
    var lineEnd = {x:startPoint.x + offset, y:endPoint.y};
    curr_doc.addNewLine(lineStart, lineEnd);
  }
}
```

After ending drawing mode, you grab the current mouse position. That way the value you're using doesn't change slightly during the execution of this function, which could throw off what you're drawing. Then you get a reference to the current document. This must be old hat to you by now!

The rest of the function should look pretty similar. Much of it is exactly the same. You get the width and height and offset, and draw the lines. The only difference is that you create `lineStart` and `lineEnd` point objects to store the points in, and then pass the points to the `addNewLine` function. This just results in cleaner code than trying to pass lengthy statements to the function directly.

OK, what you've now got here is a pretty handy tool that will draw any grid you want . . . as long as it's a 5-by-5 grid like the one in Figure 3-5. Now let's dig into that Options button and make it a little more flexible.

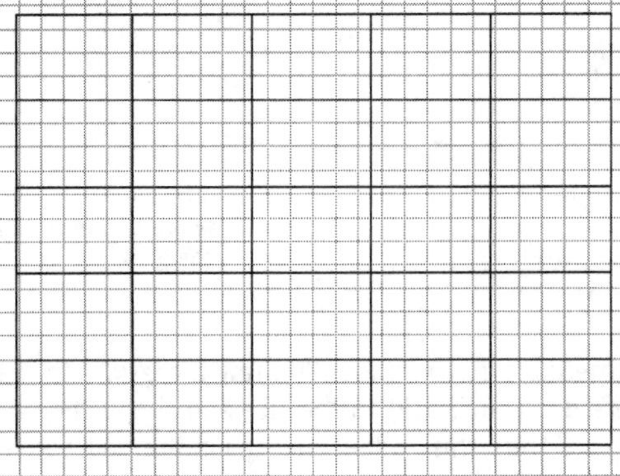

Figure 3-5.
A 5-by-5 grid drawn with the Grid tool

Adding Options

You've already had a taste of XML to UI in making commands (Chapter 2), so this next section should come pretty easy to you. In fact, the XML used to create the Tool Settings (Options) panel is even simpler than XML to UI. Let's take a look at the `PolyStar.xml` file as an example:

```
<properties>
  <property name="Style" variable="style" list="polygon,star"
➥defaultValue="0" type="Strings" />
  <property name="Number of Sides" variable="nsides" min="3" max="32"
➥defaultValue="5" type="Number" />
  <property name="Star point size" variable="pointParam" min="0"
➥max="1" defaultValue=".5" type="Double" />
</properties>
```

The XML's root tag is `<properties>`, and contains a number of `<property>` tags. Each `<property>` tag has several attributes. name is basically the label that will be shown in the Options dialog box, and `variable` is the actual variable name that will be passed to the tool. You'll see exactly how it is passed in a moment. From there you jump down to type. This is the data type of the variable and can be set to any one of the following:

- `Number`: Creates a text box accepting integers
- `Double`: Creates a text box accepting floating-point numbers
- `Boolean`: Creates a check box for setting any true/false values
- `String`: Creates a text box that will accept a string
- `Strings`: Creates a drop-down list box for choosing one of several strings
- `Color`: Creates a color chip that will pop open a color chooser

Depending on which data type you specify, other attributes can be set. The `Number` and `Double` types allow you to set minimum and maximum allowable values with the `min` and `max` attributes. You can also specify a `defaultValue` attribute, which is the value that will initially appear in the dialog box.

The `Boolean` type also has a `defaultValue` attribute that can be set to `true` or `false`, and the `String` type has the `defaultValue` attribute as well. The `Strings` type has an attribute called `list`; this is a comma-separated list of strings. The entire list is enclosed in a single set of quotes like so: `list="dogs,cats,birds"`. Each comma-separated value will be one item in the list box. The `defaultValue` attribute accepts an integer corresponding to which list item you want to show up first in the dialog box. The list is zero indexed, so in the preceding example, `defaultValue="0"` will result in dogs being the default string. Finally, the `Color` type can take a default value.

These variable type definitions are summarized in the following table:

Table 3-1. Variable Types for the Tool Settings Panel

Variable Type	Interface Element Created	Attributes
Number	Text field	1. min 2. max 3. defaultValue (integer)
Double	Text field	1. min 2. max 3. defaultValue (floating-point number)
Boolean	Check box	1. defaultValue (true/false)
String	Text field	1. defaultValue (string)
Strings	Drop-down list	1. list (comma separated strings) 2. defaultValue (index number)
Color	Color chooser	1. defaultValue (color value)

If you don't want to hand code all this XML, or can't remember all the options, you can also use the Dialog Designer available on this book's accompanying website (`www.flashextensibility.com`).

Well, that's all you need to know to get started, so let's go forth and create XML.

1. For your Grid tool, you just need two integer values: one for rows and one for columns. You'll set the minimum at 1 and maximum at 20 for each one.

```
<properties>
  <property name="Rows" variable="rows" min="1" max="20"
➥defaultValue="5" type="Number"/>
```

```
  <property name="Columns" variable="cols" min="1" max="20"
➥defaultValue="5" type="Number"/>
</properties>
```

Just save that in your Tools directory as grid.xml.

2. Then you need to tell the script that it should use this XML file as its options file. This goes in the configureTool function:

```
function configureTool(){
  var curr_toolObj = fl.tools.activeTool;
  curr_toolObj.setIcon("grid.png");
  curr_toolObj.setMenuString("Grid Tool");
  curr_toolObj.setToolName("Grid Tool");
  curr_toolObj.setToolTip("Grid Tool");
  curr_toolObj.setOptionsFile("grid.xml");
}
```

3. Now you need to have your script grab these values. This will be done as soon as the tool is selected, so you'll put it in the activate function. This is why we originally chose to have you hard code the values for rows and columns in this function. Now you can simply change the code in that location. The properties you defined in the XML will become properties of the activeTool. You already got a reference to that object, so you can easily read these two properties and assign them to your variables. Here's the updated activate function:

```
function activate(){
  curr_toolObj = fl.tools.activeTool;
  rows = curr_toolObj.rows;
  cols = curr_toolObj.cols;
}
```

You can save and reload and test this. If all works well, you shouldn't really notice a difference. When the tool is activated, it grabs the default values for rows and columns and uses them. You should notice though that the Options button is now available in the Properties panel. If you click it, you should get a dialog box allowing you to change the values (see Figure 3-6).

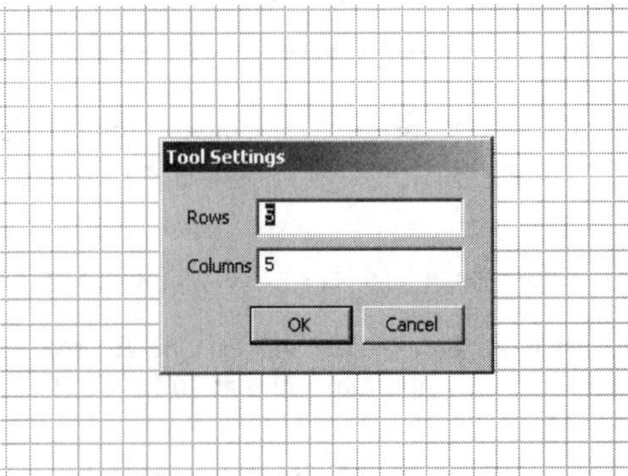

Figure 3-6.
Tool Settings dialog box for the Grid tool

4. By now you've probably noticed, however, that changing these values has no effect. That's because you only check the values in the activate function. Actually, if you set some values, then change to another tool and change back to the grid, activate will run again, grabbing the new values. But you want to grab those values as soon as they change. As briefly mentioned earlier, when the user clicks OK in the Options dialog box, the notifySettingsChanged function will be called, if it has been defined. So you need to define it!

   You've already got a reference to the active tool, so all you need to do here is grab the updated properties off it.

```
function notifySettingsChanged(){
  rows = curr_toolObj.rows;
  cols = curr_toolObj.cols;
}
```

   Do the old save, reload, test routine and play around with it. You should be able to change the settings and have them instantly respond.

You've come a long way, and you have a pretty useful tool here. You may think you're just about finished, but if you were to make a tool like this and set it free in the world, you would receive a flood of complaints! Believe it or not, there is a still a fair amount of work to do on this thing. So, let's forge on to make a really professional job of it.

Custom Cursors

If you try using one of the other built-in drawing tools, notice the cursor as you select it and then move around the screen. As soon as you choose the tool and move it onstage, it changes to a crosshair (plus sign). This is a kind of visual cue that you're in drawing mode. Then, if you roll over the toolbar, timeline, or some panel, the cursor changes back to an arrow. Now try the same with the Grid tool. You'll notice that it never changes from the original arrow. It's a minor point, but it goes a long way to making the tool look and feel professional.

Fortunately, all that switching functionality is built into Flash. When Flash decides that the cursor needs to be a particular shape, such as an arrow, it will grab the control and change it. When it deems that it's safe to hand control of the cursor back to your tool, it will call the setCursor event handler, if it is defined. Though you can do anything you want in that function, generally all you want to do is change the cursor to a particular shape, in this case the crosshair. You can do this with the function fl.tools.setCursor. This takes one argument, an integer from 0 to 7. Here's what those numbers mean:

- 0: Plus cursor (crosshair)
- 1: Black arrow
- 2: White arrow
- 3: Four-way arrow
- 4: Two-way horizontal arrow
- 5: Two-way vertical arrow
- 6: X cursor
- 7: Hand cursor

So, you just need to make a function like this:

```
function setCursor(){
  fl.tools.setCursor(0);
}
```

It doesn't get much easier than that. Test it out. Isn't that much nicer?

Note that you could also do more advanced cursor handling, using conditionals. Maybe if the cursor is within a certain area you would want to have it look one way, or if it is in another area, have it look another way, as the following pseudo-code shows:

```
if(condition1){
  fl.tools.setCursor(1);
} else if(condition2){
  fl.tools.setCursor(2);
}
```

Snap to Grid

You may or may not use a grid and the snap-to-grid feature, but many Flash users do (check the menus View ➤ Grid ➤ Show Grid and View ➤ Snapping ➤ Snap to Grid). These options allow you to set a grid on which objects and drawing tools will jump to the nearest point. It may not be useful for free-form drawing or cartooning, but for creating interface elements or other items that must be a specific size or line up at specific locations, it is quite useful. There's a good chance that someone drawing a grid will want it to snap to a particular size or location, so let's code in that functionality.

The good news is that there is a function in JSFL that allows you to do so rather easily: `fl.tools.snapPoint`. This function takes a point object as an argument and returns a point object. What this does internally is first check if Snap to Grid is set in the authoring environment. If so, it finds the point on the grid that is closest to the point supplied as an argument, and returns this point. If Snap to Grid isn't set, it simply returns the original point. Thus, as a programmer, you never have to worry about whether or not the user wants to snap. You simply convert your points using this function and the user's settings will determine what happens.

You need to apply this function in three places. The first is when the user first clicks the mouse to begin drawing—in the `mouseDown` function. You already store this point in a variable called `startPoint` with the line

```
startPoint = fl.tools.penDownLoc;
```

You simply change this to the following:

```
startPoint = fl.tools.snapPoint(fl.tools.penDownLoc);
```

Now, the starting point will always snap to the grid (if the user so wishes).

The second place you need to change it is during the drawing process itself—actually in the drawing layer preview code in `mouseMove`. It isn't crucial to snap to the grid at this point, but you may as well have your preview be an exact copy of the final drawing, so you'll snap to the grid.

Let's take another look at the function as it stands:

```
function mouseMove(){
  if(fl.tools.mouseIsDown){
    fl.drawingLayer.beginFrame();
    var gridHeight = fl.tools.penLoc.y - startPoint.y;
    for(var r = 0; r<=rows; r++){
      var offset = gridHeight/rows*r;
      fl.drawingLayer.moveTo(startPoint.x, startPoint.y + offset);
      fl.drawingLayer.lineTo(fl.tools.penLoc.x, startPoint.y + offset);
    }
    var gridWidth = fl.tools.penLoc.x - startPoint.x;
    for(var c = 0; c<=cols; c++){
      offset = gridWidth/cols*c;
      fl.drawingLayer.moveTo(startPoint.x + offset, startPoint.y);
      fl.drawingLayer.lineTo(startPoint.x + offset, fl.tools.penLoc.y);
    }
    fl.drawingLayer.endFrame();
  }
}
```

The parts in bold are where the current mouse location is referred to. These will be the "unsnapped points." Rather than converting them four times, you can create a new variable called penPoint that will be the snapped version of penLoc. Then you use penPoint to do your drawing layer drawing. Here's the corrected version:

```
function mouseMove(){
  if(fl.tools.mouseIsDown){
    fl.drawingLayer.beginFrame();
    var penPoint = fl.tools.snapPoint(fl.tools.penLoc);
    var gridHeight = penPoint.y - startPoint.y;
    for(var r = 0; r<=rows; r++){
      var offset = gridHeight/rows*r;
      fl.drawingLayer.moveTo(startPoint.x, startPoint.y + offset);
      fl.drawingLayer.lineTo(penPoint.x, startPoint.y + offset);
    }
    var gridWidth = penPoint.x - startPoint.x;
    for(var c = 0; c<=cols; c++){
      offset = gridWidth/cols*c;
      fl.drawingLayer.moveTo(startPoint.x + offset, startPoint.y);
      fl.drawingLayer.lineTo(startPoint.x + offset, penPoint.y);
    }
    fl.drawingLayer.endFrame();
  }
}
```

Finally, when the user releases the mouse (mouseUp) and you start to draw the final lines in the document, you want to snap there as well. Again, you've already got a variable, endPoint. You just need to snap it to the grid. So, in the mouseUp function, the line

```
var endPoint = fl.tools.penLoc;
```

becomes

```
var endPoint = fl.tools.snapPoint(fl.tools.penLoc);
```

And that pretty much does it for snapping to the grid. Try that out and see that it does indeed cause items to snap to the grid. You'll need to enable Snap to Grid in the View ➤ Snapping menu, and it helps if you select Show Grid in the View ➤ Grid menu. All you have to remember is to pass any points to fl.tools.snapPoint, and use the returned point instead. You can even assign a point back to itself such as myPoint = fl.tools.snapPoint(myPoint). Most of the time, though, you'll be snapping points obtained through fl.tools.penLoc or fl.tools.penDownLoc, and assigning them to brand new variables.

Bit by bit, your tool is becoming very professional. Let's see what else you can do to it.

Constraining a Shape

Another feature of almost any drawing tool is to be able to hold down the *Shift* key and constrain the drawing to a particular shape. For example, if you hold *Shift* while drawing a line, you'll get a perfectly horizontal line, vertical line, or 45-degree-angle line. Constraining the Rectangle tool allows you to draw a perfect square, and with the Oval tool you get a perfect circle. Why should you be left out of all this neat constraining action?

Similar to snapPoint, fl.tools has a method called constrainPoint. This takes two point objects as arguments, and returns a single point. The best way to describe it is that it takes the position of the second point and snaps it to the nearest point, which is either vertically or horizontally aligned with the first point, or 45 degrees from it. It's probably best to see it in action, and it can best be seen with the Line tool. If you draw a line with this tool, with the *Shift* key held down, you can think of the first point as where you first clicked. The second point is where the mouse currently is located. The return point is where the end of the line falls. Notice that if you get close enough to horizontal or vertical, the line will snap to that. If you're closer to where the end point will be at 45 degrees, it will snap to that.

Also similarly to snapPoint, which returns a snapped point only if Snap to Grid is on, constrainPoint only returns a constrained point if the *Shift* key is held down. Otherwise, it just returns the value of the second point.

So, how do you use it? The only points you need to use constrainPoint occur when you're drawing. These will be mouseMove and mouseUp.

Looking at the first few lines of mouseMove, recall that you've just snapped the current pen location and stored it in the variable, penPoint. That's the guy you want to constrain. And you want penPoint to line up with startPoint, so that's the first argument. Just add this line after defining penPoint:

```
function mouseMove(){
  if(fl.tools.mouseIsDown){
    fl.drawingLayer.beginFrame();
    var penPoint = fl.tools.snapPoint(fl.tools.penLoc);
    penPoint = fl.tools.constrainPoint(startPoint, penPoint);
    //...continued
```

Now, if *Shift* is being held down while drawing, penPoint will either be lined up with startPoint vertically, horizontally, or at 45 degrees.

Then you do the same thing with endPoint in mouseUp:

```
function mouseUp(){
  fl.drawingLayer.endDraw();
  var endPoint = fl.tools.snapPoint(fl.tools.penLoc);
  endPoint = fl.tools.constrainPoint(startPoint, endPoint);
  //...continued
```

This makes sure the final drawing is the same as the preview drawing. You can go ahead and try that out. Now, you can hold down *Shift* and get a square grid if that's what you want. But it's still not quite right. If you get too close to vertical or horizontal, it snaps to that and just draws a line. No need to use a Grid tool to draw a line. Anyway, the Rectangle and Oval tools don't constrain this way. They always form a square or circle. So let's be consistent.

Rather than trying to fix the existing constrainPoint function, just go ahead and make your own function called constrain45. All it does is compare the two points and adjust the second point accordingly. We won't go into an in-depth explanation of it, but it should be pretty easy to follow if you want to figure it out. Or, you could just plug it into your function and trust us that it works.

```
function constrain45(p1, p2){
  if (fl.tools.shiftIsDown)
  {
    var dx = Math.abs(p2.x - p1.x);
    var dy = Math.abs(p2.y - p1.y);
    var offset = Math.max(dx, dy);
    if(p2.y < p1.y)
    {
      p2.y = p1.y - offset;
    }
    else
    {
      p2.y = p1.y + offset;
    }
    if(p2.x > p1.x)
    {
      p2.x = p1.x + offset;
    }
    else
```

```
        {
          p2.x = p1.x - offset;
        }
      }
    }
```

One thing to note about this function is that it directly changes the coordinates of the second point, rather than returning a new point like constrainPoint. So when you use it, there's no need to catch the return value.

So, your mouseUp and mouseMove functions become this:

```
function mouseMove(){
  if(fl.tools.mouseIsDown){
    fl.drawingLayer.beginFrame();
    var penPoint = fl.tools.snapPoint(fl.tools.penLoc);
    constrain45(startPoint, penPoint);
    //...continued

function mouseUp(){
  fl.drawingLayer.endDraw();
  var endPoint = fl.tools.snapPoint(fl.tools.penLoc);
  constrain45(startPoint, endPoint);
  //...continued
```

Again, we're just giving the first few lines. Now, your grid is constrained to a square only if *Shift* is held down.

Enter the Matrix

OK, you're almost finished! There is just one more thing you need to do before you set this tool free. It actually contains a major bug that we haven't addressed so far. You may have even run into this bug if you've played around with this tool enough. If not, follow these steps and see just how bad it is:

1. Create a large shape onstage—a big rectangle will do.
2. Select it and convert it into a movie clip.
3. Now double-click to edit it in place.
4. Inside this shape, choose your Grid tool and draw a grid.

Hey, what's happening here? The grid isn't matching up with the mouse. It gets worse. Go back to the original clip, scale it a bit on different axes, and rotate it some. Now go back inside and try another grid.

You see the bug now (shown in Figure 3-7)? Pretty bad isn't it? Can you even see the grid you're drawing? It's there. You might have to scale down a little or scroll around as it could be offstage. What a mess! How did your grid go so awfully wrong after so much work?

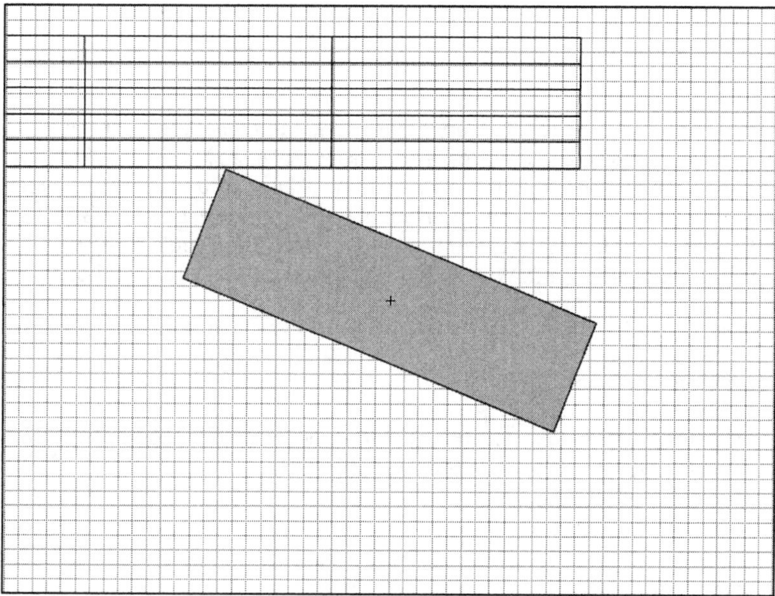

Figure 3-7. A grid gone horribly wrong inside a transformed movie clip

Actually, your grid didn't do anything wrong. It's just in kind of a time-space warp. It seems that the pen locations that you get from `fl.tools.penLoc` and `fl.tools.penDownLoc` are always in relation to coordinates of the movie clip you're drawing inside. But the `drawingLayer` drawing functions, as well as the document functions `addNewLine`, and so on, all work with the global, root-level stage coordinates. Unless the clip's registration point happens to line up with 0, 0 on the stage, you're already starting out poorly. Once you rotate or scale it, you're compounding the problem, as the internal coordinates aren't even going to be close to the stage coordinates.

So what do you do to fix it? The answer is in the matrix. No, we're not going all sci-fi on you. The answer is in a document property called the `viewMatrix`. The `viewMatrix` property holds all the information on how the current view has been translated (moved off center), rotated, and scaled.

By itself, the `viewMatrix` does nothing. It simply holds the relevant information. It's up to you to use that to transform `penLoc` or `penDownLoc` into the correct point to draw to.

Simple, right? Well not really, unless you happen to know something about matrix math. There really isn't space in this chapter to get into a long discussion about such a subject, not to mention that if we were going to teach it to you, we'd have to learn it ourselves. Instead, we're just going to hand you a function that will take care of this for you, and show you how to use it. You just have to include this function in any tool file and call it when needed. Here it is:

```
function transformPoint(aPoint, matrix) {
  var x = aPoint.x * matrix.a + aPoint.y * matrix.c + matrix.tx;
  var y = aPoint.x * matrix b + aPoint.y * matrix.d + matrix.ty;
```

```
    aPoint.x = x;
    aPoint.y = y;
}
```

You need to apply this function to every point you get using penLoc or penDownLoc. Once again, this means three locations—mouseDown, mouseMove, and mouseUp. You have to do some minor rearranging, but nothing too painful. You'll just grab the point from penLoc or penDownLoc and store it in a variable. Then you'll transform the variable. This little function will handle all the rotation, scaling, and translation issues. Then you'll continue on as usual by snapping and constraining it. Wow, this little point is getting a real workout!

Here are the revised functions, just showing the first few lines for the longer ones:

```
function mouseDown(){
  startPoint = fl.tools.penDownLoc;
  transformPoint(startPoint, fl.getDocumentDOM().viewMatrix);
  startPoint = fl.tools.snapPoint(startPoint);
  fl.drawingLayer.beginDraw();
}

function mouseUp(){
  fl.drawingLayer.endDraw();
  var endPoint = fl.tools.penLoc;
  transformPoint(endPoint, fl.getDocumentDOM().viewMatrix);
  endPoint = fl.tools.snapPoint(endPoint);
  constrain45(startPoint, endPoint);
  //...continued

function mouseMove(){
  if(fl.tools.mouseIsDown){
    fl.drawingLayer.beginFrame();
    var penPoint = fl.tools.penLoc;
    transformPoint(penPoint, fl.getDocumentDOM().viewMatrix);
    penPoint = fl.tools.snapPoint(penPoint);
    constrain45(startPoint, penPoint);
    //...continued
```

Go ahead and test it out under the conditions described earlier. The grid should stay straight and in place no matter how you've transformed the outer movie clip.

For completeness, here's the final code for your Grid tool (see also grid.jsfl):

```
function configureTool(){
  var curr_toolObj = fl.tools.activeTool;
  curr_toolObj.setIcon("grid.png");
  curr_toolObj.setMenuString("Grid Tool");
  curr_toolObj.setToolName("Grid Tool");
  curr_toolObj.setToolTip("Grid Tool");
  curr_toolObj.setOptionsFile("grid.xml");
}
```

```
function activate(){
  curr_toolObj = fl.tools.activeTool;
  rows = curr_toolObj.rows;
  cols = curr_toolObj.cols;
}
function notifySettingsChanged(){
  rows = curr_toolObj.rows;
  cols = curr_toolObj.cols;
}
function mouseDown(){
  startPoint = fl.tools.penDownLoc;
  transformPoint(startPoint, fl.getDocumentDOM().viewMatrix);
  startPoint = fl.tools.snapPoint(startPoint);
  fl.drawingLayer.beginDraw();
}
function setCursor(){
  fl.tools.setCursor(0);
}
function mouseUp(){
  fl.drawingLayer.endDraw();
  var endPoint = fl.tools.penLoc;
  transformPoint(endPoint, fl.getDocumentDOM().viewMatrix);
  endPoint = fl.tools.snapPoint(endPoint);
  constrain45(startPoint, endPoint);
  var curr_doc = fl.getDocumentDOM();
  var gridHeight = endPoint.y - startPoint.y;
  for(var r = 0; r<=rows; r++){
    var offset = gridHeight/rows*r;
    var lineStart = {x:startPoint.x, y:startPoint.y + offset};
    var lineEnd = {x:endPoint.x, y:startPoint.y + offset};
    curr_doc.addNewLine(lineStart, lineEnd);
  }
  var gridWidth = endPoint.x - startPoint.x;
  for(var c = 0; c<=cols; c++){
    offset = gridWidth/cols*c;
    var lineStart = {x:startPoint.x + offset, y:startPoint.y};
    var lineEnd = {x:startPoint.x + offset, y:endPoint.y};
    curr_doc.addNewLine(lineStart, lineEnd);
  }
}
function mouseMove(){
  if(fl.tools.mouseIsDown){
    fl.drawingLayer.beginFrame();
    var penPoint = fl.tools.penLoc;
    transformPoint(penPoint, fl.getDocumentDOM().viewMatrix);
    penPoint = fl.tools.snapPoint(penPoint);
    constrain45(startPoint, penPoint);
    var gridHeight = penPoint.y - startPoint.y;
    for(var r = 0; r<=rows; r++){
```

```
          var offset = gridHeight/rows*r;
          fl.drawingLayer.moveTo(startPoint.x, startPoint.y + offset);
          fl.drawingLayer.lineTo(penPoint.x, startPoint.y + offset);
        }
        var gridWidth = penPoint.x - startPoint.x;
        for(var c = 0; c<=cols; c++){
          offset = gridWidth/cols*c;
          fl.drawingLayer.moveTo(startPoint.x + offset, startPoint.y);
          fl.drawingLayer.lineTo(startPoint.x + offset, penPoint.y);
        }
        fl.drawingLayer.endFrame();
      }
    }
    function transformPoint(aPoint, matrix){
      var x = aPoint.x * matrix.a + aPoint.y * matrix.c + matrix.tx;
      var y = aPoint.x * matrix.b + aPoint.y * matrix.d + matrix.ty;
      aPoint.x = x;
      aPoint.y = y;
    }
    function constrain45(p1, p2)
    {
      if (fl.tools.shiftIsDown)
      {
        var dx = Math.abs(p2.x - p1.x);
        var dy = Math.abs(p2.y - p1.y);
        var offset = Math.max(dx, dy);
        if(p2.y < p1.y)
        {
          p2.y = p1.y - offset;
        }
        else
        {
          p2.y = p1.y + offset;
        }
        if(p2.x > p1.x)
        {
          p2.x = p1.x + offset;
        }
        else
        {
          p2.x = p1.x - offset;
        }
      }
    }
```

And, with that, we think we can safely say that you have a professional and robust custom-built Grid tool! We warned you that it was more complex than a command, and hopefully now you see why. With experience, you'll soon become very familiar with the construction process.

That's about all you need to do with that command, but there are more objects and functions available for you to use in making commands. We'll walk you through making a couple more tools that once again will be useful, and we'll also explore some of the other possibilities.

Arrow Tool

This tool will allow the user to instantly draw an arrow on the stage. You'll allow the user to adjust the length and the width of the arrow shaft via the tool's Options panel.

The Grid tool covered just about all the major bases of the process for creating a tool, and can almost be used as a tool template. In fact, you can start this tool by simply saving the `GridTool.jsfl` file as `Arrow.jsfl`. You'll just go through and change what you need to, which is surprisingly little. (Of course, you can also refer to the file `arrow.jsfl` to see the final version of your tool, which is available to download from `www.flashextensibility.com`.)

First of all, let's hit the `configureTool` function. You just need to change the names in the various settings from `Grid` to `Arrow`:

```
function configureTool(){
  var curr_toolObj = fl.tools.activeTool;
  curr_toolObj.setIcon("arrow.png");
  curr_toolObj.setMenuString("Arrow Tool");
  curr_toolObj.setToolName("Arrow Tool");
  curr_toolObj.setToolTip("Arrow Tool");
  curr_toolObj.setOptionsFile("arrow.xml");
}
```

You'll also need to create another icon file, or download `arrow.png`.

Next, you'll create the XML file:

```
<properties>
  <property name="Shaft Width (percent):" variable="shaftWidth" min="0"
➥max="1" defaultValue=".6" type="Double" />
  <property name="Shaft Length (percent):" variable="shaftLength"
➥min="0" max="1" defaultValue=".6" type="Double" />
</properties>
```

As you can see, `shaftWidth` and `shaftLength` are floating-point variables that can be from 0 to 1. A shaft length of 0.5 would mean that the shaft extends to half the length of the arrow, and the rest of it is the point. Similarly, a shaft width of 0.5 would produce a shaft that is half as wide as the width of the point.

All you have to do to get these properties is grab them in the `activate` and `notifySettingsChanged` functions:

```
function activate(){
  curr_toolObj = fl.tools.activeTool;
```

```
    shaftWidth = curr_toolObj.shaftWidth;
    shaftLength = curr_toolObj.shaftLength;
  }
  function notifySettingsChanged(){
    shaftWidth = curr_toolObj.shaftWidth;
    shaftLength = curr_toolObj.shaftLength;
  }
```

The functions mouseDown, setCursor, transformPoint, and constrain45 don't need to change a bit. All you really need to change at this point is the code that draws the shape itself. If you look at Figure 3-8, you'll see that we've numbered the points 1 to 7 for reference:

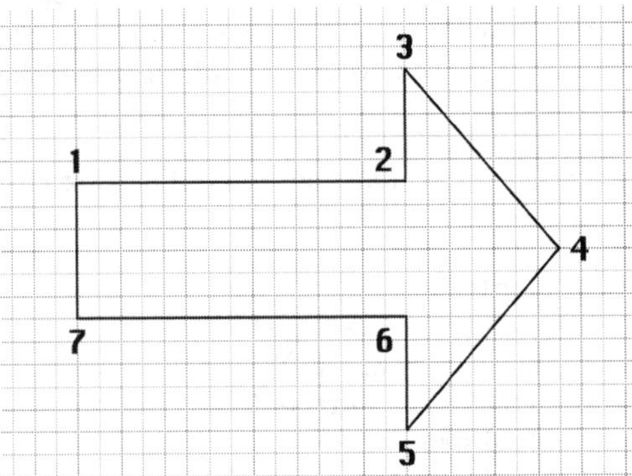

Figure 3-8. The seven points of an arrow shape

In the mouseMove function, you're simply going to move to point 1, then execute a bunch of lineTo commands to points 2, 3, 4, 5, 6, 7, and then back to 1:

```
function mouseMove(){
  if(fl.tools.mouseIsDown){
    fl.drawingLayer.beginFrame();
    var penPoint = fl.tools.penLoc;
    transformPoint(penPoint, fl.getDocumentDOM().viewMatrix);
    penPoint = fl.tools.snapPoint(penPoint);
    constrain45(startPoint, penPoint);
    var w = penPoint.x - startPoint.x;
    var h = penPoint.y - startPoint.y;
    fl.drawingLayer.moveTo(startPoint.x, startPoint.y - h *
➥shaftWidth);
    fl.drawingLayer.lineTo(startPoint.x + w * shaftLength, startPoint.
➥y - h * shaftWidth);
    fl.drawingLayer.lineTo(startPoint.x + w * shaftLength, startPoint.
➥y - h);
    fl.drawingLayer.lineTo(penPoint.x, startPoint.y);
    fl.drawingLayer.lineTo(startPoint.x + w * shaftLength, penPoint.y);
```

```
    fl.drawingLayer.lineTo(startPoint.x + w * shaftLength, startPoint.
➥y + h * shaftWidth);
    fl.drawingLayer.lineTo(startPoint.x, startPoint.y + h *
➥shaftWidth);
    fl.drawingLayer.lineTo(startPoint.x, startPoint.y - h *
➥shaftWidth);
    fl.drawingLayer.endFrame();
  }
}
```


We won't go into detail about how we figured each point. If you're intrigued, you might want to look at each line and graph it out on a piece of paper to double-check.

Finally, you do essentially the same thing in mouseUp to add the final lines to the document:

```
function mouseUp(){
  fl.drawingLayer.endDraw();
  var endPoint = fl.tools.penLoc;
  transformPoint(endPoint, fl.getDocumentDOM().viewMatrix);
  endPoint = fl.tools.snapPoint(endPoint);
  constrain45(startPoint, endPoint);
  var curr_doc = fl.getDocumentDOM();
  var w = endPoint.x - startPoint.x;
  var h = endPoint.y - startPoint.y;
  var p1 = {x:startPoint.x, y:startPoint.y - h * shaftWidth};
  var p2 = {x:startPoint.x + w * shaftLength, y:startPoint.y - h *
➥shaftWidth};
  var p3 = {x:startPoint.x + w * shaftLength, y:startPoint.y - h};
  var p4 = {x:endPoint.x, y:startPoint.y};
  var p5 = {x:startPoint.x + w * shaftLength, y:endPoint.y};
  var p6 = {x:startPoint.x + w * shaftLength, y:startPoint.y + h *
➥shaftWidth};
  var p7 = {x:startPoint.x, y:startPoint.y + h * shaftWidth};
  curr_doc.addNewLine(p1, p2);
  curr_doc.addNewLine(p2, p3);
  curr_doc.addNewLine(p3, p4);
  curr_doc.addNewLine(p4, p5);
  curr_doc.addNewLine(p5, p6);
  curr_doc.addNewLine(p6, p7);
  curr_doc.addNewLine(p7, p1);
}
```

In this case, since you need to use point objects, you go through and create the seven points first, and then just draw the lines between them.

Now, although this code works—it successfully draws an arrow as specified on the screen (you can play with the options for shaft length and width and get an idea how those work)—it isn't pretty. Indeed, you can improve upon it quite a bit. One of the major drawbacks to creating a shape with lines like this is that there is no simple way to fill it.

You've only created the outline of an arrow, and it's up to the user to fill it. For the grid, this isn't bad, as it's just a grid of lines. But you would expect a shape like this to have a fill.

Also, as you get into more and more complicated shapes, it would be ridiculous to have to write all the code to re-create the shape twice—once for the drawing layer and once for the document. For a simple shape like this with just seven lines, it's already getting pretty messy.

The Path

Here comes a new object to your rescue: path is simply an object that holds a bunch of points and/or curves. For this tool, you'll concentrate on using points. Here are the simple steps to using it:

1. Make a new path with the drawing layer function newPath. This returns a reference to the newly created path.
2. Add some points to it with the path object function addPoint(x, y).
3. If you want a closed path, you can add a line from the last point to the first one with the path function close.
4. Finally, draw the path to the drawing layer with the drawing layer function drawPath. This takes as an argument the name of the path you're drawing.

Implementing a path, your mouseMove function thus becomes as follows:

```
function mouseMove(){
  if(fl.tools.mouseIsDown){
    fl.drawingLayer.beginFrame();
    var penPoint = fl.tools.penLoc;
    transformPoint(penPoint, fl.getDocumentDOM().viewMatrix);
    penPoint = fl.tools.snapPoint(penPoint);
    constrain45(startPoint, penPoint);
    var w = penPoint.x - startPoint.x;
    var h = penPoint.y - startPoint.y;
    var points = new Array();
    points[0] = {x:startPoint.x, y:startPoint.y - h * shaftWidth};
    points[1] = {x:startPoint.x + w * shaftLength, y:startPoint.y - h *
➥shaftWidth};
    points[2] = {x:startPoint.x + w * shaftLength, y:startPoint.y - h};
    points[3] = {x:penPoint.x, y:startPoint.y};
    points[4] = {x:startPoint.x + w * shaftLength, y:penPoint.y};
    points[5] = {x:startPoint.x + w * shaftLength, y:startPoint.y + h *
➥shaftWidth};
    points[6] = {x:startPoint.x, y:startPoint.y + h * shaftWidth};
    arrow_path = fl.drawingLayer.newPath();
    for (var i = 0; i < points.length; i++) {
      arrow_path.addPoint(points[i].x, points[i].y);
    }
    arrow_path.close();
    fl.drawingLayer.drawPath(arrow_path);
```

```
        fl.drawingLayer.endFrame();
    }
}
```

You see you first create seven points in an array called points. Then you create a path called arrow_path and add your seven points to it. Then you close it and draw it—simple enough. But the real advantage to paths is about to be revealed. Notice that when you declare arrow_path in the line, like this:

```
arrow_path = fl.drawingLayer.newPath();
```


you don't use the keyword var. Doing so would make the variable a local variable, only available from within the mouseMove function. When the function is over, it would be destroyed. You want it to stick around, because you have one more job for it.

Remember the last version's mouseUp function? There was something like 25 lines of code just to draw seven lines on the stage. Well, here's your new version using paths:

```
function mouseUp(){
  fl.drawingLayer.endDraw();
  arrow_path.makeShape();
}
```

No more double work! You simply call the makeShape method of the path object, and it is drawn to stage (see Figure 3-9).

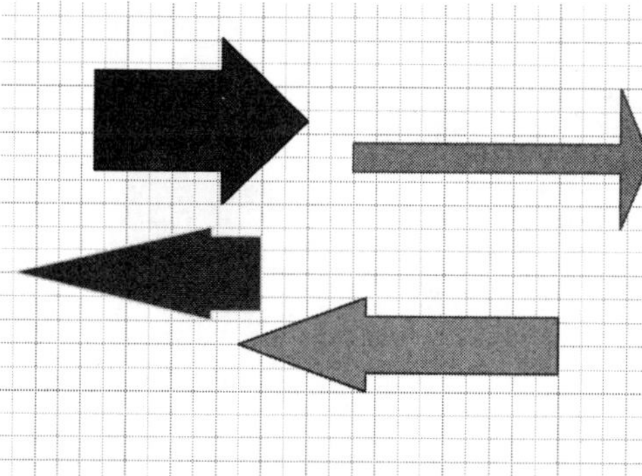

Figure 3-9.
Some of the arrows you can draw with the Arrow tool

There is a little more you should know about this command. It actually has two arguments, both Boolean. The first will suppress the fill of the shape if true, and the second will suppress the stroke. So, if you just wanted an outline arrow, you could say

```
arrow_path.makeShape(true, false);
```

And likewise, if you wanted just an arrow shape with no outline, you could say

```
arrow_path.makeShape(false, true);
```

Of course, setting them both to true would result in nothing being drawn. Also, if you want to draw both the outline and the stroke, just omit both arguments—they will default to false.

Now, this would all be great, except Macromedia decided to throw you a little curveball. Remember when you learned about the transformation matrix stuff? (Come on, it was only a few pages back!) You learned that inside a transformed movie clip, penLoc and penDownLoc report coordinates local to that clip, and the various drawing tools use global stage coordinates, so you needed to make a conversion. Well, it turns out that path operations work with the local, transformed coordinates. While the preceding code works fine for drawing on the main stage, inside a movie clip, it might go very much awry. Try it. See, back to where you started!

The simple solution would seem to be to just not transform the points penPoint and startPoint. If you want to try that, go ahead. You'll see that it is a bit better, but still not perfect.

The solution is to transform the original points you're drawing from and to (startPoint and penPoint), and then set all the in-between points, as you're doing. Then, you need to kind of "untransform" them. In other words, take them from global stage coordinates, and convert them back to local movie clip coordinates.

So we wrote two new functions, transform and invert, which handle these actions. The transform function is a little different from the transformPoint function you've been using, which is why we gave it a different name. These functions are pretty short, but would take several pages to explain. Fortunately, you don't need to understand them, just use them! Here they are:

```
function transform( pt,  mat )
{
  var x = pt.x*mat.a + pt.y*mat.c;
  var y = pt.x*mat.b + pt.y*mat.d;
  pt.x = x;
  pt.y = y;
}

function invert( pt, mat )
{
  var det = mat.a*mat.d-mat.b*mat.c;
  var x = pt.x * mat.d/det + pt.y * -mat.c/det;
  var y = pt.x * -mat.b/det + pt.y * mat.a/det;
  pt.x = x;
  pt.y = y;
}
```

You'll use the transform function in place of transformPoints in both mouseDown and mouseMove to transform startPoint and penPoint. Then, you'll invert each point before you add it to the path. Here are the two final mouse functions showing the changes:

```
function mouseDown() {
  startPoint = fl.tools.penDownLoc;
  transform(startPoint, fl.getDocumentDOM().viewMatrix);
  startPoint = fl.tools.snapPoint(startPoint);
  fl.drawingLayer.beginDraw();
}
function mouseMove(){
  if(fl.tools.mouseIsDown){
    fl.drawingLayer.beginFrame();
    var penPoint = fl.tools.penLoc;
    transform(penPoint, fl.getDocumentDOM().viewMatrix);
    penPoint = fl.tools.snapPoint(penPoint);
    constrain45(startPoint, penPoint);
    var w = penPoint.x - startPoint.x;
    var h = penPoint.y - startPoint.y;
    var points = new Array();
    points[0] = {x:startPoint.x, y:startPoint.y - h * shaftWidth};
    points[1] = {x:startPoint.x + w * shaftLength, y:startPoint.y - h *
➥shaftWidth};
    points[2] = {x:startPoint.x + w * shaftLength, y:startPoint.y - h};
    points[3] = {x:penPoint.x, y:startPoint.y};
    points[4] = {x:startPoint.x + w * shaftLength, y:penPoint.y};
    points[5] = {x:startPoint.x + w * shaftLength, y:startPoint.y + h *
➥shaftWidth};
    points[6] = {x:startPoint.x, y:startPoint.y + h * shaftWidth};
    arrow_path = fl.drawingLayer.newPath();
    for (var i = 0; i < points.length; i++) {
      invert(points[i], fl.getDocumentDOM().viewMatrix);
      arrow_path.addPoint(points[i].x, points[i].y);
    }
    arrow_path.close();
    fl.drawingLayer.drawPath(arrow_path);
    fl.drawingLayer.endFrame();
  }
}
```

And once again, you're back on the straight and narrow!

Setting the Properties Panel

In all the tools you've created so far, you've let the Properties panel just kind of do its own thing. Let's learn how to rope it in and control it.

To demonstrate just what you can do with it, you'll create a brand new tool. This will create a *callout*, which is essentially a line with some text attached to it. Callouts are useful to annotate diagrams or pictures with intricate parts with pointers and labels. A line comes off a particular item and connects to a text box off on the side explaining what the item is. In this case, you'll implement a simple click-drag functionality to create the pointer, and then add text after some user input.

Since you'll be creating some shapes and some text, you'll need access to the properties for both. If you observe the Properties panel as you work in Flash, you'll notice it has three main modes:

1. **Shape** mode: This is what you see when you select any of the drawing tools. You have options for stroke color, size, style, and fill color (see Figure 3-10).

Figure 3-10. Properties panel in shape mode

2. **Text** mode: Whenever you select the text tool or are editing a text box, you see the large array of options for creating or modifying text (see Figure 3-11).

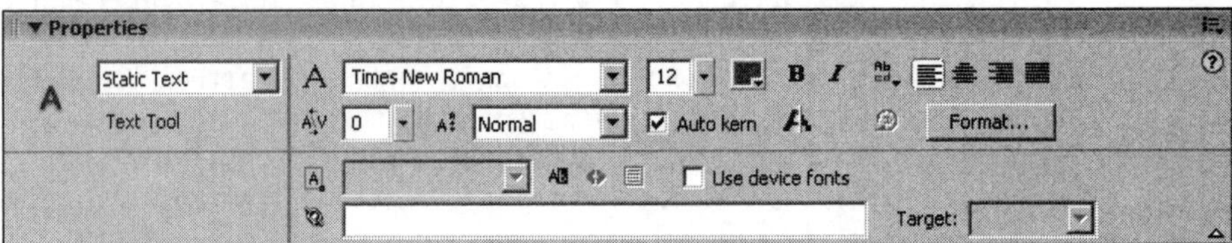

Figure 3-11. Properties panel in text mode

3. **Movie** mode: This is what appears at pretty much any other time. It actually has several different styles depending on what is currently selected—symbol, frame, stage—but basically shows the various options available for that selection (see Figure 3-12).

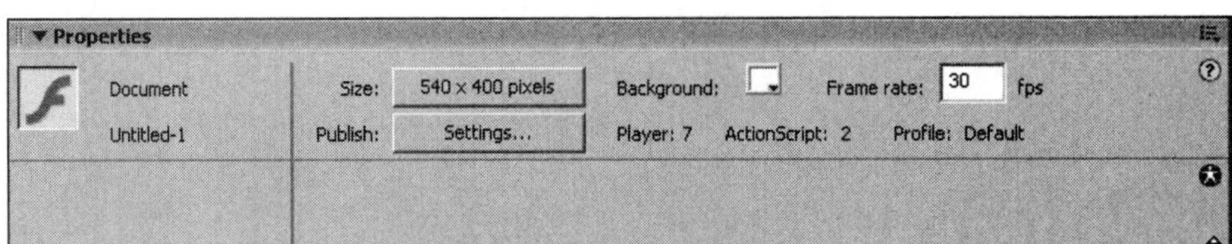

Figure 3-12. Properties panel in movie mode

You can manually set which mode the Properties panel will go into via the `toolObj` function, `setPI` (PI for Property Inspector, as this panel is also known). This function takes a string containing one of the following: `shape`, `text`, or `movie`. The Properties panel will go into that mode and stay there until something else happens to change it, such as selecting an object or another tool. If you don't set the Properties panel, it will default to shape.

In the Callout tool, you'll first set the Properties panel to shape mode in the activate function. This will allow you to draw the line for the callout. Once the line is drawn, you switch it to text mode so users can choose their text style.

You'll use a few other advanced features in this file as well, such as a JavaScript alert to notify users they should set their font preferences, and an XML to UI dialog box to get the text to add to the callout.

You'll also make your first use of dynamic functions. Up to now, all of your event-handling functions (mouseDown, mouseUp, etc.) were permanently assigned. Since you have different modes in this file, you need different behaviors at different times. You can do this by swapping functions in and out for the event handlers.

First let's configure the tool and activate it (don't forget to create an icon too):


```
function configureTool(){
  var curr_toolObj = fl.tools.activeTool;
  curr_toolObj.setIcon("callout.png");
  curr_toolObj.setMenuString("Callout Tool");
  curr_toolObj.setToolName("Callout Tool");
  curr_toolObj.setToolTip("Callout Tool");
}
function activate(){
  curr_toolObj = fl.tools.activeTool;
  curr_toolObj.setPI("shape");
  mouseDown = mouseDownFunc;
  mouseUp = mouseUpFunc;
  mouseMove = mouseMoveFunc;
}
```

The configureTool function should be nothing surprising. You're not using an option file here, so that gets left out. Note how you set the Properties panel to shape mode in the second line of the activate function, and then set the three mouse event-handler functions to other function names. You'll create those next:

```
function mouseDownFunc(){
  startPoint = fl.tools.penDownLoc;
  transform(startPoint, fl.getDocumentDOM().viewMatrix);
  startPoint = fl.tools.snapPoint(startPoint);
  fl.drawingLayer.beginDraw();
}
```

Again, the mouseDownFunc should be nothing new. It's exactly what you used earlier for mouseDown. The advantage to assigning it this way is that you can change it later to something else, and then change it back. Note that since you'll be using paths again, you'll use the new transform function rather than transformPoint.

```
function mouseMoveFunc(){
  if(fl.tools.mouseIsDown){
    fl.drawingLayer.beginFrame();
    penPoint = fl.tools.penLoc;
    transform(penPoint, fl.getDocumentDOM().viewMatrix);
    penPoint = fl.tools.snapPoint(penPoint);
    penPoint = fl.tools.constrainPoint(startPoint, penPoint);
```

```
            if(penPoint.x > startPoint.x){
              offset = -20;
            }
            else
            {
              offset = 20;
            }
            points = new Array();
            points[0] = {x:startPoint.x, y:startPoint.y};
            points[1] = {x:penPoint.x + offset, y:penPoint.y};
            points[2] = {x:penPoint.x, y:penPoint.y};
            points[3] = {x:penPoint.x, y:penPoint.y - 20};
            points[4] = {x:penPoint.x, y:penPoint.y + 20};
            call_path = fl.drawingLayer.newPath();
            for(var i=0;i<points.length;i++){
              invert(points[i], fl.getDocumentDOM().viewMatrix);
              call_path.addPoint(points[i].x, points[i].y);
            }
            fl.drawingLayer.drawPath(call_path);
            fl.drawingLayer.endFrame();
          }
        }
```

The mouseMoveFunc function is also pretty basic. It just creates a few points calculated by the mouse position, inverts them, and adds them to a path. Same thing you did for the arrow, but a different shape.

```
function mouseUpFunc(){
  fl.drawingLayer.endDraw();
  call_path.makeShape();
  curr_toolObj.setPI("text");
  mouseUp = nullFunc;
  mouseMove = nullFunc;
  mouseDown = addTextBox;
  alert("Set font properties and click on the stage.");
}
function nullFunc(){
}
```

The mouseUpFunc function contains some important new features. The first couple of lines just end drawing mode and make a shape using the path you just made. Next, you change the Properties panel to text mode. Then you start messing with the mouse event handlers. At this point, you don't want anything to happen on mouseUp or mouseMove, so you assign those to an empty function called nullFunc, which you include here.

Then you set mouseDown to a function called addTextBox, which you'll see shortly. Finally, you alert users to set the font properties and tell them to click the stage when they're done (see Figure 3-13).

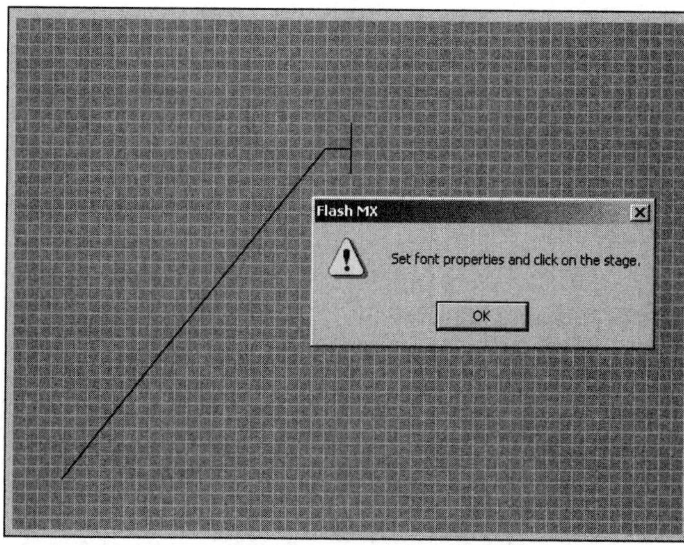

Figure 3-13. The alert box informing users what to do next

3

When users clear the alert, change the font settings, and then click the stage, this will activate your addTextBox function, which is right here:

```
function addTextBox(){
  curr_doc = fl.getDocumentDOM();
  testResult = curr_doc.xmlPanel(fl.configURI+"/Tools/callout.xml");
  if(testResult.dismiss == "accept"){
    curr_lib = curr_doc.library;
    var textName = "Callout Text";
    var tryCount = 0;
    while(curr_lib.itemExists(textName)){
      tryCount++;
      textName = "Callout Text" + tryCount;
    }
    curr_lib.addNewItem("movie clip", textName);
    curr_lib.editItem(textName);
    curr_doc.addNewText({top:0, left:0, right:10, bottom:10});
    var selArray = new Array();
    selArray[0] =
➥curr_doc.getTimeline().layers[0].frames[0].elements[0];
    curr_doc.selection = selArray;
    curr_text = curr_doc.selection[0];
    curr_text.autoExpand = true;
    curr_text.setTextString(testResult.text);
    curr_doc.exitEditMode();
    curr_lib.addItemToDocument({x:0, y:0}, textName);
    curr_doc.moveSelectionBy(penPoint);
    if(penPoint.x > startPoint.x){
```

```
      curr_doc.moveSelectionBy({x:curr_doc.selection[0].width/2+10,
➥y:0});
    }
    else {
      curr_doc.moveSelectionBy({x:-curr_doc.selection[0].width/2-10,
➥y:0});
    }
    curr_doc.selectNone();
  }
  else {
    alert("Callout Text cancelled.");
  }
}
```

This is a biggie, so we'll describe it a little at a time. First you call an XML to UI dialog box and make sure the user clicked OK.

```
curr_doc = fl.getDocumentDOM();
testResult = curr_doc.xmlPanel(fl.configURI+"/Tools/callOut.xml");
if(testResult.dismiss == "accept"){
```

And here is the XML for the dialog box shown in Figure 3-14 (see `callout.xml`):

```
<dialog buttons="accept, cancel" title="Callout Tool Options">
  <hbox>
    <label value="Callout Text"/>
    <textbox id="text"/>
  </hbox>
</dialog>
```

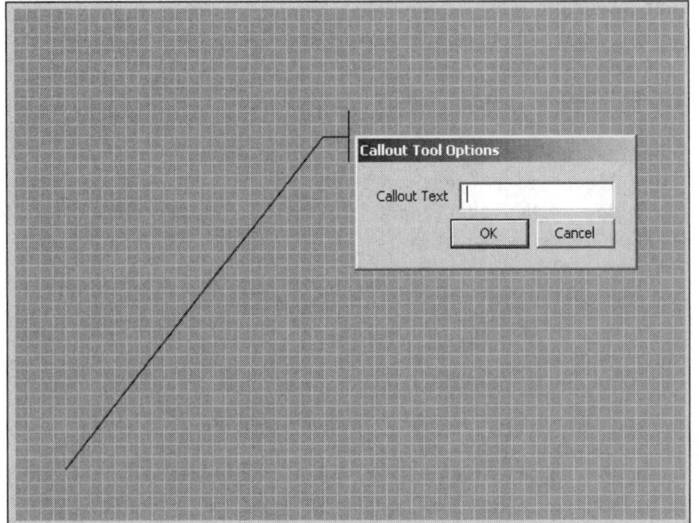

Figure 3-14. The XML to UI dialog box requesting the callout text

So the XML file just defines one property called text. Easy enough. Next, if the user did click OK, you create a new movie clip in the Library, finding a unique name first, and then start editing that movie clip.

```
curr_lib = curr_doc.library;
var textName = "Callout Text";
var tryCount = 0;
while(curr_lib.itemExists(textName)){
  tryCount++;
  textName = "Callout Text"; + tryCount;
}
curr_lib.addNewItem("movie clip”, textName);
curr_lib.editItem(textName);
```


Once you're inside this new clip and editing it, you add a new text box and put it into the selection array.

```
curr_doc.addNewText({top:0, left:0, right:10, bottom:10});
var selArray = new Array();
selArray[0] =
➥curr_doc.getTimeline().layers[0].frames[0].elements[0];
curr_doc.selection = selArray;
curr_text = curr_doc.selection[0];
```

The size of the text box doesn't really matter, since you'll let it expand to allow for whatever text is put in it. Also, note that because this is a brand new movie clip, you know there is no other content. Thus you can get a reference to the text box by selecting the current timeline, layer zero, frame zero, element zero. You now have a variable, `curr_text`, that refers to this text box. You change some settings, add some text (the text returned from the XML to UI dialog box), exit edit mode, and add the item to the stage at 0, 0.

```
curr_text.autoExpand = true;
curr_text.setTextString(testResult.text);
curr_doc.exitEditMode();
curr_lib.addItemToDocument({x:0, y:0}, textName);
```

At this point, the newly added movie clip will be the only thing selected, and it will be at 0, 0. You need to move it to the end of the callout line. The object `penPoint` refers to the end of the line you just drew. You can move the movie clip to that point using `curr_doc.moveSelectionBy(penPoint)`, as follows:

```
curr_doc.moveSelectionBy(penPoint);
```

Then, depending if the callout line is going left or right, you slide it over half its width one way or another (plus another 10 pixels as an offset). You then use `selectNone()` for a truly professional finish.

```
if(penPoint.x > startPoint.x){
  curr_doc.moveSelectionBy({x:curr_doc.selection[0].width/2+10,
➥y:0});
}
else {
```

```
            curr_doc.moveSelectionBy({x:-curr_doc.selection[0].width/2-10,
➥y:0});
          }
          curr_doc.selectNone();
        }
```

Finally, you wrap up by alerting users that the action was cancelled if they chose Cancel in the dialog box.

```
        else {
          alert("Callout Text cancelled.");
        }
      }
```

The rest of the functions that follow are nothing new at all, but we'll include them here for completeness:

```
      function setCursor(){
        fl.tools.setCursor(0);
      }
      function transformPoint(aPoint, matrix){
        var x = aPoint.x * matrix.a + aPoint.y * matrix.c + matrix.tx;
        var y = aPoint.x * matrix.b + aPoint.y * matrix.d + matrix.ty;
        aPoint.x = x;
        aPoint.y = y;
      }
      function constrain45(p1, p2)
      {
        if (fl.tools.shiftIsDown)
        {
          var dx = Math.abs(p2.x - p1.x);
          var dy = Math.abs(p2.y - p1.y);
          var offset = Math.max(dx, dy);
          if(p2.y < p1.y)
          {
            p2.y = p1.y - offset;
          }
          else
          {
            p2.y = p1.y + offset;
          }
          if(p2.x > p1.x)
          {
            p2.x = p1.x + offset;
          }
          else
          {
            p2.x = p1.x - offset;
          }
        }
      }
```

Test your new Callout tool to see it in action (see Figure 3-15).

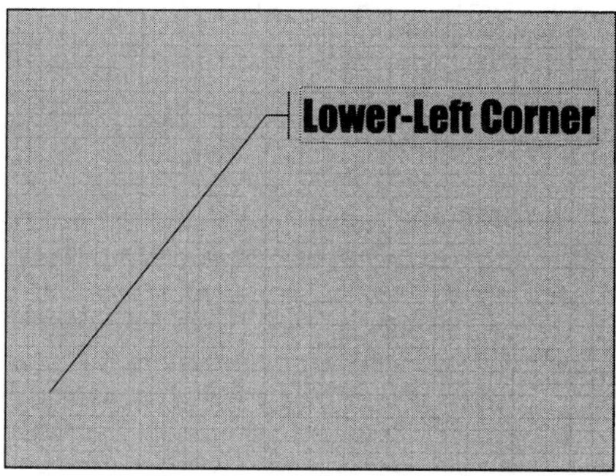

Figure 3-15.
The completed callout

We've covered most of what you need to know to build tools. Let's finish off with one final impressive example for inspiration.

3D Cube Tool

We don't really have the space to get into a big explanation of all the math involved in this next example tool, but we wanted to include it here as a brief look at just how neat these tools can be. This one creates a cube that you can rotate around in 3D space. Although the 3D perspective math is a bit complex, there are no real JSFL concepts here that we haven't thoroughly covered. We'll give you the functions one at a time and give a brief explanation of what is happening in each one. You can also refer to cube3d.jsfl to play around with the completed code.

```
function configureTool(){
  theTool = fl.tools.activeTool;
  theTool.setToolName("Cube3D");
  theTool.setIcon("Cube3D.png");
  theTool.setMenuString("Cube 3D Tool");
  theTool.setToolTip("Cube 3D Tool");
  theTool.setOptionsFile( "Cube3D.xml" );

  points = new Array();
  xp = new Array();
  yp = new Array();
  xp = new Array();
  xp = [-1, 1, 1, -1, -1, 1, 1, -1];
  yp = [-1, -1, 1, 1, -1, -1, 1, 1];
  zp = [-1, -1, -1, -1, 1, 1, 1, 1];
}
```

In configureTool you do your normal setup actions, and then create a few arrays. The points array holds the 3D points for each corner of the cube. xp, yp, and zp hold the relative positions of each point on each axis. The Cube3D.xml file is shown here:

```
<properties>
  <property name="X Size"  variable="xSize" min="5" max="300"
➥defaultValue="100"  type="Number" />
  <property name="Y Size"  variable="ySize" min="5" max="300"
➥defaultValue="100"  type="Number" />
  <property name="Z Size"  variable="zSize" min="5" max="300"
➥defaultValue="100"  type="Number" />
  <property name="Perspective"  variable="pers" min="100" max="500"
➥defaultValue="200"  type="Number" />
</properties>
```

Next:

```
function setPoints(){
  for(var i=0;i<8;i++){
    points[i] = new Object;
    points[i].x = xp[i]*xSize/2;
    points[i].y = yp[i]*ySize/2;
    points[i].z = zp[i]*zSize/2;
  }
}
```

The setPoints function just takes the relative coordinates in xp, yp, and zp, and multiplying them times the sizes retrieved from the Options dialog box, creates a 3D point for each corner, storing it in the points array.

```
function activate(){
  curr_toolObj = fl.tools.activeTool;
  xSize = curr_toolObj.xSize;
  ySize = curr_toolObj.ySize;
  zSize = curr_toolObj.zSize;
  pers = curr_toolObj.pers;
  if(xSize>pers){
    xSize = curr_toolObj.xSize=pers;
  }
  if(ySize>pers){
    ySize = curr_toolObj.ySize=pers;
  }
  if(zSize>pers){
    zSize = curr_toolObj.zSize=pers;
  }
  setPoints();
}
function notifySettingsChanged(){
  curr_toolObj = fl.tools.activeTool;
  xSize = curr_toolObj.xSize;
```

```
        ySize = curr_toolObj.ySize;
        zSize = curr_toolObj.zSize;
        pers = curr_toolObj.pers;
        if(xSize>pers){
          xSize = curr_toolObj.xSize=pers;
        }
        if(ySize>pers){
          ySize = curr_toolObj.ySize=pers;
        }
        if(zSize>pers){
          zSize = curr_toolObj.zSize=pers;
        }
      }
```


The activate and notifySettingsChanged functions are the same. In fact, if you wanted to you could create a function called getSettings and dynamically assign this to both of these handlers. All this does is grab the properties out of the Options dialog box and adjust some of them if necessary.

```
function mouseDown(){
  fl.drawingLayer.beginDraw();
}
function setCursor(){
  fl.tools.setCursor(0);
}
```

Nothing very complicated here. In this file, snapping and constraining doesn't really make sense, so you don't need to use them. Since you didn't do anything to it, you can just grab fl.tools.penDownLoc later when needed.

```
function mouseMove(){
  if(fl.tools.mouseIsDown){
    // get the view matrix
    var viewMat = fl.getDocumentDOM().viewMatrix;
    // get the distance moved on x and y
    var dx = fl.tools.penLoc.x - fl.tools.penDownLoc.x;
    var dy = fl.tools.penLoc.y - fl.tools.penDownLoc.y;
    // using these distances as angles to rotate the cube,
    // get the sine and cosine of the angles
    var cosx = Math.cos(dy*.01);
    var sinx = Math.sin(dy*.01);
    var cosy = Math.cos(dx*.01);
    var siny = Math.sin(dx*.01);
    // loop through each point
    for(var i = 0; i<8; i++){
      // some fancy math to rotate the points in 3D
      var x1 = points[i].x*cosy - points[i].z * siny;
      var z1 = points[i].z*cosy + points[i].x * siny;
      var y1 = points[i].y*cosx - z1*sinx;
      var z2 = z1*cosx + points[i].y * sinx;
```

```
      // apply perspective
      var scale = pers/(pers+z2);
      points[i].xp = x1 * scale + fl.tools.penDownLoc.x;
      points[i].yp = y1 * scale + fl.tools.penDownLoc.y;
      // apply the transformation matrix
      transformPoint(points[i], viewMat);
    }
    // draw all the lines that make the cube
    fl.drawingLayer.beginFrame();
    fl.drawingLayer.moveTo(points[0].xp, points[0].yp);
    fl.drawingLayer.lineTo(points[1].xp, points[1].yp);
    fl.drawingLayer.lineTo(points[2].xp, points[2].yp);
    fl.drawingLayer.lineTo(points[3].xp, points[3].yp);
    fl.drawingLayer.lineTo(points[0].xp, points[0].yp);
    fl.drawingLayer.lineTo(points[4].xp, points[4].yp);
    fl.drawingLayer.lineTo(points[5].xp, points[5].yp);
    fl.drawingLayer.lineTo(points[6].xp, points[6].yp);
    fl.drawingLayer.lineTo(points[7].xp, points[7].yp);
    fl.drawingLayer.lineTo(points[4].xp, points[4].yp);
    fl.drawingLayer.moveTo(points[1].xp, points[1].yp);
    fl.drawingLayer.lineTo(points[5].xp, points[5].yp);
    fl.drawingLayer.moveTo(points[2].xp, points[2].yp);
    fl.drawingLayer.lineTo(points[6].xp, points[6].yp);
    fl.drawingLayer.moveTo(points[3].xp, points[3].yp);
    fl.drawingLayer.lineTo(points[7].xp, points[7].yp);
    fl.drawingLayer.endFrame();
  }
}
```

Wow! Don't get scared. First you grab a reference to the viewMatrix, since you'll be using it a bunch of times. Then you figure out how much the mouse has moved by subtracting penDownLoc from penLoc. You use that in a bunch of fancy trigonometry to rotate the 3D points in the points array in relation to how much the mouse has moved.

Then you do some 3D perspective to locate the 2D screen positions of the 3D points and apply the transform matrix to those points. For a full discussion of all the trigonometry and perspective code used here, look into *Macromedia Flash MX Studio*, also available from friends of ED.

Finally, you draw a bunch of lines to make the cube.

```
function mouseUp(){
  fl.drawingLayer.endDraw();
  fl.getDocumentDOM().addNewLine({x:points[0].xp, y:points[0].yp},
➥{x:points[1].xp, y:points[1].yp});
  fl.getDocumentDOM().addNewLine({x:points[1].xp, y:points[1].yp},
➥{x:points[2].xp, y:points[2].yp});
  fl.getDocumentDOM().addNewLine({x:points[2].xp, y:points[2].yp},
➥{x:points[3].xp, y:points[3].yp});
```

```
  fl.getDocumentDOM().addNewLine({x:points[3].xp, y:points[3].yp},
➥{x:points[0].xp, y:points[0].yp});
  fl.getDocumentDOM().addNewLine({x:points[4].xp, y:points[4].yp},
➥{x:points[5].xp, y:points[5].yp});
  fl.getDocumentDOM().addNewLine({x:points[5].xp, y:points[5].yp},
➥{x:points[6].xp, y:points[6].yp});
  fl.getDocumentDOM().addNewLine({x:points[6].xp, y:points[6].yp},
➥{x:points[7].xp, y:points[7].yp});
  fl.getDocumentDOM().addNewLine({x:points[7].xp, y:points[7].yp},
➥{x:points[4].xp, y:points[4].yp});
  fl.getDocumentDOM().addNewLine({x:points[0].xp, y:points[0].yp},
➥{x:points[4].xp, y:points[4].yp});
  fl.getDocumentDOM().addNewLine({x:points[1].xp, y:points[1].yp},
➥{x:points[5].xp, y:points[5].yp});
  fl.getDocumentDOM().addNewLine({x:points[2].xp, y:points[2].yp},
➥{x:points[6].xp, y:points[6].yp});
  fl.getDocumentDOM().addNewLine({x:points[3].xp, y:points[3].yp},
➥{x:points[7].xp, y:points[7].yp});
}
function transformPoint(pt, mat){
  var x = pt.xp*mat.a + pt.yp * mat.c + mat.tx;
  var y = pt.xp*mat.b + pt.yp * mat.d + mat.ty;
  pt.xp = x;
  pt.yp = y;
  return;
}
```

In the mouseUp function, you essentially duplicate the mouseMove drawing code, using the document drawing methods instead. If you want to try to convert this into a path, go right ahead. The problem is that it isn't a simple path that goes from one point, through some others, and ends somewhere. You'd either have to make several paths to form one cube, or do some backtracking. That may be more efficient, but this way seemed a bit more obvious to us, even if more wordy.

And in Figure 3-16, you can see some of the 3D cubes you can draw using this new tool.

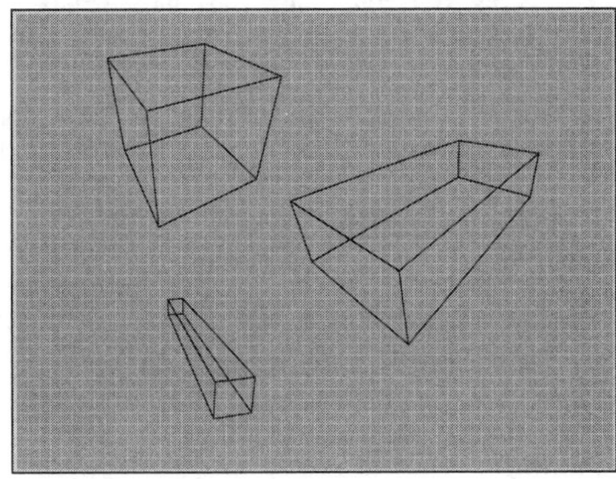

Figure 3-16.
Some cubes made with the 3D Cube tool

Packaging Extensions

At this point, it would be a good idea to look into how you can package your extensions (commands, tools, effects, behaviors) for distribution. Whether you plan to sell them, give them away, or just keep them around for your own use, packaging them correctly goes a long way toward having them be truly professional. You could simply zip up the JSFL, PNG, XML, and any other files in an archive and let others figure out where to install it. For a tool, this would include having users figure out how to get it onto the toolbar. You might end up doing a lengthy instruction and installation manual and still have users get it wrong.

Fortunately, Macromedia has given you a way to package up extensions for distribution and installation. All end users have to do is double-click a file and everything gets installed in the right place. It's required that users have the Macromedia Extension Manager installed on their system. But even that is a breeze to download and install. In fact, this is the same tool that you'll use to package your extensions, so why don't you go ahead and download and install the latest version right now, if you don't already have it. You can find it at www.macromedia.com/exchange/em_download/.

The latest version as of this writing is version 1.6, and you'll need at least that version to be able to package Flash MX 2004 extensions. Downloading and installing the Extension Manager couldn't be easier. Just download and run the file, and it will run a standard installation program. Now you're ready to package your extensions.

Flash MX users who became knowledgeable with creating and distributing components will already know that a packaged extension is known as a Macromedia Extension Package (MXP) file, and that the Extension Manager is used to create MXPs. First, though, you have to describe to the Extension Manager exactly what files will be packaged in the MXP, where they will go, what they are for, and some general information about what the extension does and who made it. This is all done in XML, and the resulting XML file is called a Macromedia Extension Installation (MXI) file.

Following is a sample MXI file for the 3D Cube tool that you've just seen:

```
<macromedia-extension name="3D Cube Tool" version="1.0.0" type="flash
➥tool" requires-restart="true">
  <description><![CDATA[A drawing tool for your tool bar. Creates a 3D
➥cube that you can rotate in real time. User adjustable size and
➥perspective.]]></description>
  <ui-access><![CDATA[You will find this tool on your tool bar]]>
➥</ui-access>
  <products>
    <product name="Flash" version="7" primary="true" />
  </products>
  <author name="Keith Peters" />
  <files>
    <file source="cube3d.jsfl" destination="$Flash\Tools" />
    <file source="cube3d.xml" destination="$Flash\Tools" />
    <file source='cube3d.png" destination="$Flash\Tools" />
  </files>
```

```
  <configuration-changes>
    <toolpanel-changes>
      <toolpanel-item-insert name="Cube3D" depth="0" position="7" />
    </toolpanel-changes>
  </configuration-changes>
</macromedia-extension>
```

This is pretty much all you'll need for any extension. In fact, extensions other than tools will be even shorter. Let's walk through each tag:

```
<macromedia-extension name="3D Cube Tool" version="1.0.0" type="flash
➥tool" requires-restart="true">
```


This is the root-level tag. It contains, as attributes, the name of the extension, the version, what type of extension it is (tool, command, behavior, effect), and whether or not Flash should be restarted after installation. You should set this to `true`, as the Extension Manager installs extensions into a special folder called `First Run`. When Flash starts up, it copies anything in the `First Run` folder to the appropriate configuration directory. Until this happens, the extension will not be in the right place and will not be available.

```
<description><![CDATA[A drawing tool for your tool bar. Creates a 3D
➥cube that you can rotate in real time. User adjustable size and
➥perspective.]]></description>
```

The `description` tag is just that, a description of what the extension is. This is enclosed in a CDATA tag exactly as shown. Other than that it is pretty free form. This data will be displayed to users by the Extension Manager when your extension is being installed.

```
<ui-access><![CDATA[You will find this tool on your tool bar]]>
➥</ui-access>
```

The `<ui-access>` tag is pretty similar, and just tells users how to access your tool. You can tell them where it is on the toolbar, or which menu, or how to locate Timeline Effects or behaviors. Again, this is shown by the Extension Manager during the installation.

```
<products>
  <product name="Flash" version="7" primary="true" />
</products>
```

Next is a products section, which will contain all the products that the extension is valid for. For the most part, this will probably just contain one `<product>` tag giving the name of the product, Flash, and its version (MX 2004 is version 7). The `primary` attribute is for extensions that could be used on more than one product to say which is the primary product. Since Flash is the only product here, it is of course the primary one!

```
<author name="Keith Peters" />
```

The `<author>` tag is self-explanatory. Take credit for all your hard work!

```
<files>
  <file source="cube3d.jsfl" destination="$Flash\Tools" />
```

```
    <file source="cube3d.xml" destination="$Flash\Tools" />
    <file source="cube3d.png" destination="$Flash\Tools" />
  </files>
```

Then you have the listing of files, in the <files> tag. Each file gets its own <file> tag. List the source file that you want packaged, and the destination of where you want it to go. For the source, the path can be relative to where the MXI file will be. The preceding syntax assumes that the three files are in the same directory as the MXI file. The destination uses the term $Flash to refer to the configuration directory where the files will be installed. To put them in a subdirectory, such as Tools, simply tack that on.

```
  <configuration-changes>
    <toolpanel-changes>
      <toolpanel-item-insert name="Cube3D" depth="0" position="7" />
    </toolpanel-changes>
  </configuration-changes>
```

The <configuration-changes> tag only applies to tools. Commands, effects, and behaviors all automatically insert themselves in the proper menus as soon as they are added and reloaded. Tools either have to be manually placed on the toolbar, or can be automatically installed with the preceding XML. Inside <configuration-changes>, you have a <toolpanel-changes> tag. Inside that you have a <toolpanel-item-insert> tag. You give it the name of the tool, which is the name as specified in the configureTool function under setToolName. Depth refers to the level of the drop-down menu where the tool icon will appear. The position is which slot on the toolbar you want the tool to be added to. You count them starting from zero and going across and then down. So here, position seven is under the rectangle tool.

That does it for your MXI file. Save it with a file extension .mxi, and you're ready to create an MXP file.

Start up the Extension Manager. It will show you a list of installed extensions, if you have any installed of course—if this is your first time with the Extension Manager, then it's likely to be empty. Now go to the File menu and choose Package Extension. A file dialog box will open asking you to choose which extension to package. Navigate to wherever your MXI file is located, and you'll see the available MXI files to package.

Choose your MXI file and click OK. You'll then be asked where and under what name to save the final MXP file. If all goes well, you'll be told that the extension has been successfully created. If you get any errors, it usually means an error in your XML, or a file that is referenced couldn't be located.

The final result is an MXP file that, when double-clicked, will install the extension to the correct location and tell the user to restart Flash, if it is already running. Remember that MXP files aren't self-executable programs; you'll have to inform your customers or colleagues that they will need to install the Extension Manager, shown in Figure 3-17, in order to install your extension.

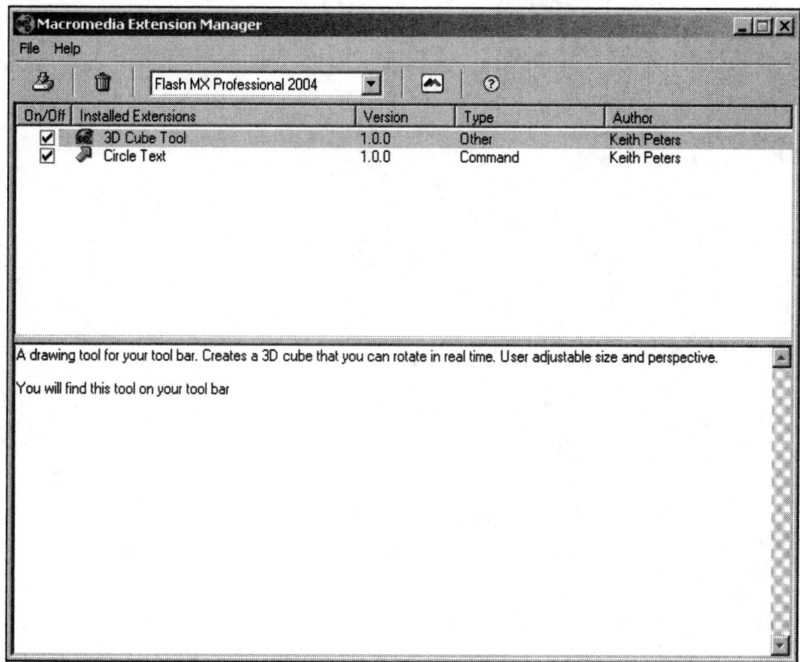

Figure 3-17. The Extension Manager

There you have it, a nice packaged extension. Be sure to see the additional documentation at Macromedia's website for additional features such as adding documentation, but the preceding instructions are enough for you to create a simple, workable packaged extension.

Summary

Well, you've made some huge leaps forward in this chapter; over your study of how you create custom-built tools, you've actually learned the bulk of the basic JavaScript API. And to cap it all, you've seen how to package your tools into neat little files that enable easy distribution. By now, we're sure you've started experimenting with your own custom tools.

In the next chapter, we'll push it up another notch or two and show you the specialized techniques of creating Timeline Effects.

4 TIMELINE EFFECTS

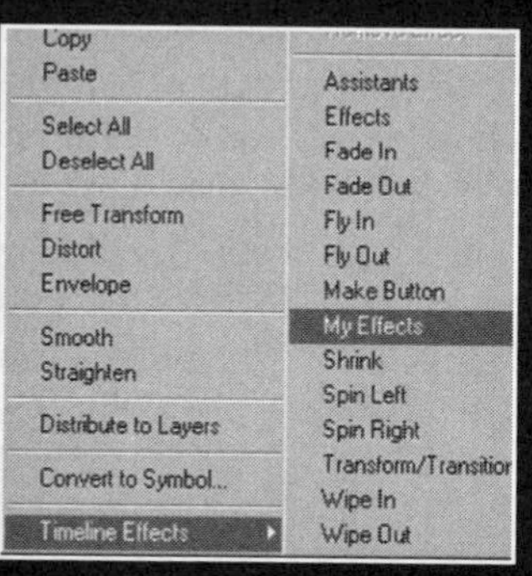

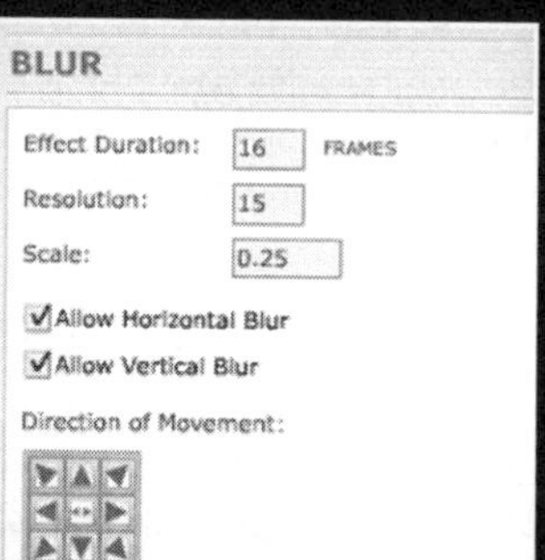


```
function configureEffect() {
}
function executeEffect() {
//   fl.trace("hello");
    curr_eff = fl.activeEffect
    rows = curr_eff.rows;
    cols = curr_eff.cols;
    curr_doc = fl.getDocumentI
    curr_tl = curr_doc.getTime
    curr_tl.insertFrames(rows*
    curr_doc.enterEditMode();
    curr_tl = curr_doc.getTime
```

Up to this point in the book, we've been discussing commands and tools, so we haven't done much with frames, layers, and timelines in Flash. Short of using them to find a specific element, we've hardly touched on them at all. This wasn't an oversight; we've simply been saving the bulk of this discussion for the extensibility tool specifically designed to work with those objects—Timeline Effects.

As discussed briefly in Chapter 1, Timeline Effects are basically scripted tweens. You apply an effect to an object, and it adds frames and maybe new layers, creates keyframes and tweens, and applies just about any type of motion or tween you could create by hand. In fact, since Timeline Effects are written in JSFL, you can go a lot further than that, and do just about anything you could do in a command. In practice, the reverse is true as well—most of the JSFL script for modifying frames and layers in an effect could just as easily be written into a command.

Timeline Effects vs. Commands

So, how do Timeline Effects differ from commands? They differ in the following four ways:

1. First, you can specify what type of object you'll allow your effect to be applied to. To apply a Timeline Effect, you first select which item you'll apply it to, and then choose the effect. If you make a neat text effect, you can make sure that it's only applied to a text field. We showed you how to do this manually in Chapter 2, but in the case of effects, it's automatic.
2. Secondly, when you apply an effect, the resulting tween is automatically put into a symbol. If you apply the effect to a movie clip, the resulting symbol will be a movie clip. If you start with a graphic symbol, you'll wind up with a symbol. If you apply the effect to any other element, the element will be embedded inside a newly created graphic symbol. But either way, this is a special symbol. Its contents are locked up from any prying eyes. Double-clicking it will have no effect. There are some back doors to get inside of it, which we'll check into, but using these will counteract some of the special features of Timeline Effects, particularly the enabling of the undo and edit effect functions.
3. The associated special symbol has the effect embedded inside of it, and you can remove this effect or edit it as easily as selecting one of those options from a menu, something you could never do with a manually created tween.
4. Effects also make use of XML files for the various properties of how they will be applied. This XML is essentially the same as what you used for tool option files, with a few additions. Actually, the effect itself is defined in the XML, and contains a link to the JSFL file that is used to apply the effect. In this way, you could actually create several different effects from one JSFL file, using separate XML files to call the same JSFL file with different options.

Now it's time to see all this in action. First we'll give you an in-depth look at existing effects that are built into Flash MX 2004 to get an idea of how they work so you can make your own work in the same way.

Blur Effect

The Blur effect ships with Flash MX 2004 and is a simple example of an effect. We'll use it to examine how effects work.

Although we took a very brief introductory look at this effect in Chapter 1, it's worth familiarizing yourself with how Timeline Effects work again. First, you'll need something onstage to apply the effect to. Using the drawing tool of your choice (or even a custom tool you've made yourself, hopefully inspired by the previous chapter!), draw something onstage. Preferably, make something you can see easily so you can see exactly what happens to it once you apply the effect—you'll opt for the ubiquitous filled circle for this demonstration.

Now, with the shape fully selected, choose the Timeline Effects menu. This can be found in two places: the main menu, under `Insert`, or in the context-sensitive menu found by right-clicking (CMD-click for those on a Mac) on the shape itself, as shown in Figure 4-1.

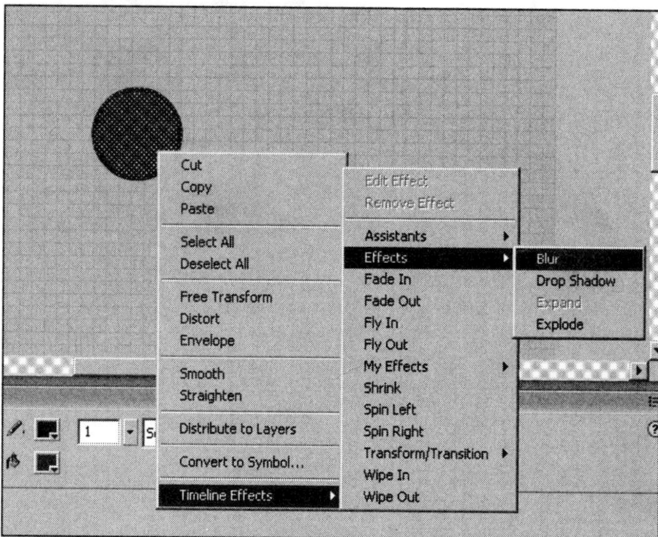

Figure 4-1. The Timeline Effects menu (with several extra effects installed in this case)

When you choose this menu, you should see a list of all the effects installed on your machine. Note that the menu has several submenus, minimally Assistants, Effects (where you'll find Blur), and Transform/Transition. Explore each submenu and see what is there. Before you jump in and choose one, note that some of them are inactive—this is what we were referring to earlier about limiting effects to a particular type of element. Any effect that isn't intended to be applied to shape elements will be inactive here. If you were to select a movie clip instead, you might see that those effects are now active, and perhaps some others become inactive.

The Blur effect can be applied to a shape though, so it should be active. Go ahead and choose it. The first thing you'll notice is the dialog box that pops up (see Figure 4-2). As you probably guessed, this is a SWF embedded into an XML to UI dialog box. You should also take note of the fact that there is now a blue outline around your shape, and a registration point in it. It has already been converted into a graphic symbol. When you get into creating your own effects later in this chapter, you'll see that you can also choose to convert the selection to a movie clip. If any other elements appear on the same layer, you should also notice that your selection has been moved to its own layer, called something like `Blur 1`, depending on how many layers you already have.

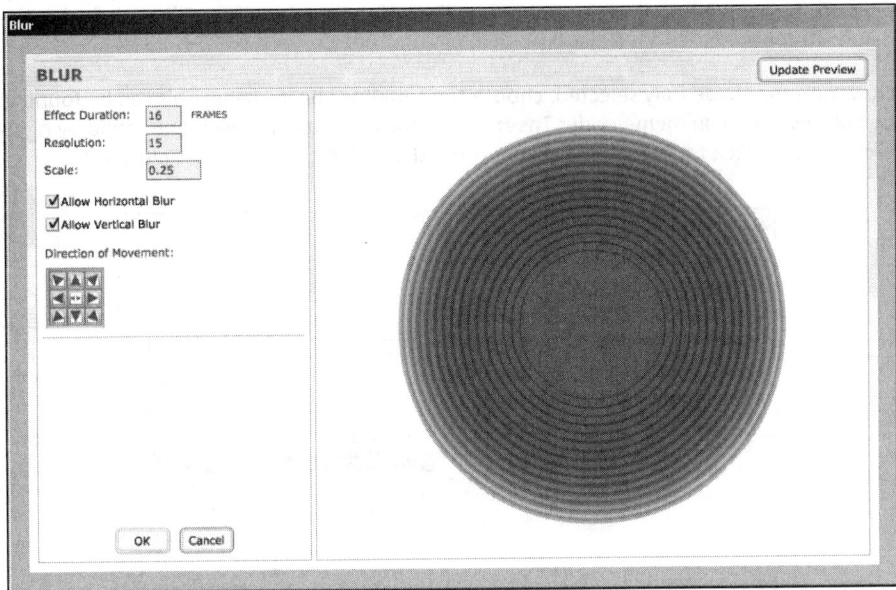

Figure 4-2. SWF-based UI dialog box of the Blur Timeline Effect

Choose any options you want in the dialog box—they should be pretty self-explanatory, but take note of the Effect Duration parameter. You can use the Update Preview button to check out your effect in action to make sure that you're happy with it, so click `OK` when you've had a chance to play around with the parameters. The first things you should notice back on the main timeline is that it has been extended with a bunch of new frames. The number of frames added is of course equal to the number you chose for Effect Duration in the dialog box. If you select the symbol now, you'll see that it's indeed a graphic symbol, and probably claims to be an instance of a graphic symbol named something like `Blur 1` (see Figure 4-3).

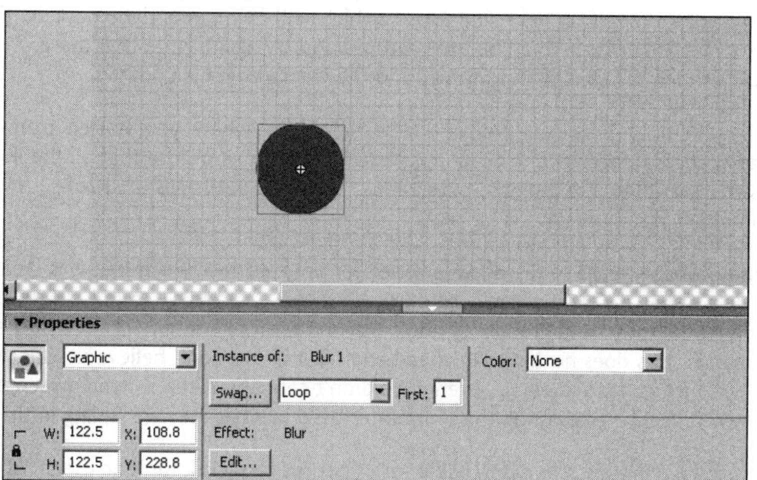

Figure 4-3. A new graphic symbol, an instance of Blur 1

Next, go ahead and test your movie and see the tween that it created. It should be doing pretty much what you saw in the preview SWF. When you're done admiring your work, right-click once again on the symbol and choose Timeline Effects again. Notice now that the only options available are Edit Effect and Remove Effect as shown in Figure 4-4. Point taken—you can't apply multiple effects to the same object.

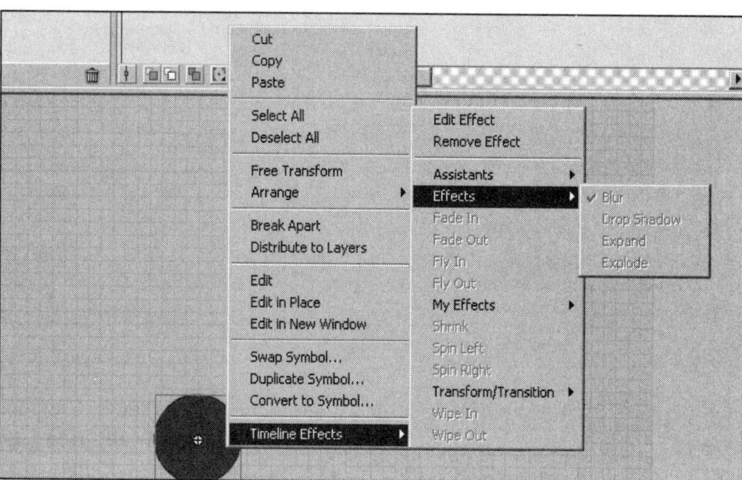

Figure 4-4. Edit Effect and Remove Effect are the only available options on a symbol with an effect applied.

You can also see this in the main menu; if you go to Insert ➤ Timeline Effects, all the options will be inactive, but Modify ➤ Timeline Effects gives you the options to edit or remove.

So, using either menu, choose Edit Effect, which will bring you right back to the Blur options dialog box menu. Change some settings and try again. Note that there is no need to undo first. Simply change the settings and the whole effect is updated.

Finally, try Remove Effect and voila—you're right back where you started from, with a selected shape onstage, as if it never happened! You may also note that all the individual actions that went into creating the effect aren't recorded in the History panel, just the fact that the effect was applied.

Now you probably want to dig down and see for yourself the tween that was created. Go ahead and apply the effect again so that you have a graphic symbol sitting onstage. Normally, to look inside a graphic symbol you would simply double-click it. But, as mentioned earlier, this does nothing. Go ahead and try it if you don't believe us! But inquiring minds like ours want to know . . . even if we didn't care about the internal tween, the fact that we can't see it makes us all the more interested in what they are hiding in there.

So the next logical step is to right-click it (or of course CMD-click for Mac users). Ah, you're in luck! You now have the option to Edit, Edit in Place, or Edit in New Window. Choose what you will and you'll get the warning message in Figure 4-5.

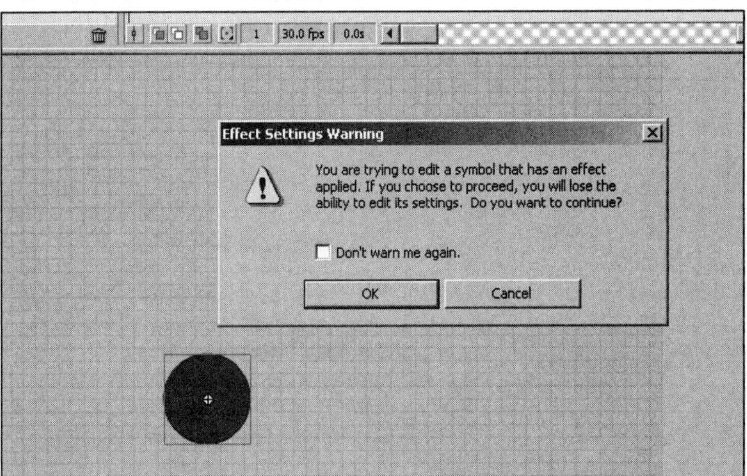

Figure 4-5. Warning! Warning!

So they were hiding something in there after all, and now you can see it. Click OK to jump in. And what do you have? A bunch of layers, each containing a tween (see Figure 4-6). Obviously this command has created a number of layers, added some frames to each one, and created a tween in each one. Each tween is slightly different, according to the parameters set when applying the effect.

You'll often want to go into symbols like this as you're developing effects, to see what was created, and how it conforms to (or differs from) what you intended the effect to do.

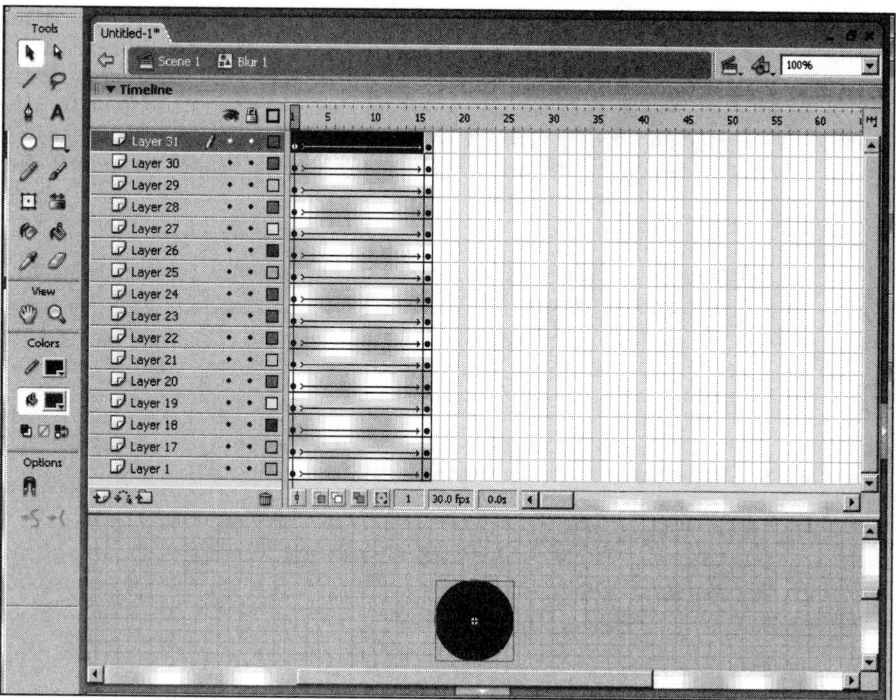

Figure 4-6. Inside an effect

Exit edit mode at this point, using the navigation bar above the timeline, and go back to where your original shape was. Once again, right-click the symbol created by the effect and choose Timeline Effects. Notice that, as warned, the options to edit and remove are now gone and now any effects that can be applied to graphic symbols are now active. Furthermore, you can now double-click the symbol to get back inside of it. Kind of like looking behind the curtain to see the Wizard of Oz—you saw what's behind there, but you also destroyed all the magic. It's now nothing more than a symbol with a tween inside.

You now know just about all you need about *applying* Timeline Effects, so you're ready to start creating your own effects.

Creating Timeline Effects

Timeline Effects are a two-part file package. You have the XML file that defines the name of the effect, what it can be applied to, and its properties, and you have the JSFL file that does all the work. We'll discuss the XML file to begin with as this is the first thing you need for an effect to even be available. You'll start out by making a very simple effect—one that simply slides an object across the stage.

Before you begin, you should create a Reload Effects command (alternatively, you can use the file Reload Effects.jsfl that is available with this chapter's downloadable source files). This works the same way as the Reload Tools command you created in the last chapter. It simply causes Flash to reload the JSFL and XML files for the current Timeline Effects. You'll need to do this each time you change or update the JSFL or XML of an effect you're working on. The command is a simple one-line JSFL file in your Commands folder:

```
fl.reloadEffects();
```

Name it Reload Effects and you're all set. Just remember to run the command each time you change something in your effect.

Slide Effect

OK, as promised, let's start by creating the XML. The root tag for this file is <group>. This means that the XML should begin with <group> and end with </group>. All other tags should come in between these two.

The group tag has one attribute, name. If you recall the submenus that came off the Timeline Effects menu, each submenu is a group. You can add an effect to an existing group, say, Effects, by stating:

```
<group name="Effects">
```

Or, you could create a whole new submenu by putting something else in here, such as the following:

```
<group name="My Effects">
```

Let's go with the latter. Create a new XML file named slide.xml in the Effects folder of your local Flash Configuration directory (see Chapter 2). Create your opening and closing group tag:

```
<group name="My Effects">

</group>
```

To start with, you'll create three child tags that will configure the effect. The first tag inside <group> is <effect>, which also contains a name attribute. This is the name of the effect itself, what will show up in the submenu. Let's call it Slide:

```
<effect name="Slide">
```

Next up is <source>, which points to the JSFL file that does all the work of manipulating the frames and content. This goes in the file attribute:

```
<source file="slide.jsfl">
```

Obviously, slide.jsfl doesn't exist yet, but it will soon enough.

Next you have the <allow> tag. This is where you specify what objects the effect can be applied to. The attribute is types. This is a comma-separated list of types of objects, for example, button, movie clip, graphic, text, bitmap, shape. You can just build your list depending on which types you want to include. For example, if you only wanted an effect to be applied to movie clips and graphics, you would use

```
<allow types="movie clip, graphic">
```

Now, if someone looks at the list of effects while a shape, text, or anything other than a movie clip or graphic is selected, your effect will be inactive and can't be applied to that object.

If you create a text effect that should really only be applied to text, it would be

```
<allow types="text">
```

4

As a shortcut, if you don't care what it's applied to, you can just specify all:

```
<allow types="all">
```

Now your effect is open to any object, so you'll stick with that. Here's how your XML is shaping up so far:

```
<group name="My Effects">
  <effect name="Slide">
  <source file="slide.jsfl">
  <allow types="all">
</group>
```

Now all you need to add is the properties. This is done inside a <properties> tag, with individual <property> tags for each property. This is precisely the same way you created an options file for tools in Chapter 3. The only difference is that <properties> is now a child tag of <group> rather than being the root tag of the file.

For this file, you need three properties—the distances to slide on the x and y axes and the duration, in frames, of the effect. You'll call those xDist, and yDist, and duration. You'll make them integers of type Number and set the default value to zero for the distances and 20 for the duration. You won't limit the user to any maximum or minimum value on the distances, but you should have a minimum duration of 1:

```
<group name="My Effects">
  <effect name="Slide">
  <source file="slide.jsfl">
  <allow types="all">
  <properties>
    <property name="X Distance" variable="xDist" defaultValue="0"
➥type="Number"/>
    <property name="Y Distance"  variable="yDist" defaultValue="0"
➥type="Number"/>
    <property name="Effect Duration" variable="duration"
➥defaultValue="20" min="1" max="16000" type="Number"/>
```

```
    </properties>
  </group>
```

You can save that as slide.xml in your Effects directory (which you probably already know is in your local Flash Configuration directory).

An interesting point about XML files for Timeline Effects is that in addition to a properties tag, you can include a <dialog> tag written in XML to UI. This allows you to take advantage of the more interesting controls available in XML to UI, including embedding a SWF file in the dialog box. This is useful for showing a preview of the effect. For the most part, we'll stick with the <properties> tag in the example files in this chapter, but for completeness we'll show you one example that utilizes a SWF-based UI like this at the end of the chapter.

OK, now you're ready for some more JSFL! Similar to tools, effects have an event-driven architecture. Nothing should go into the JSFL file except event-handling functions and any additional functions you want to include. Fortunately, an effect file is much simpler than a tool. There are only three events you need to set up handlers for:

1. configureEffect
2. executeEffect
3. removeEffect

The general meaning of these should be pretty clear. The first one sets up any variables, etc., that should be ready before the effect is executed. The next is all the code that performs the effect itself, and the last sets everything back the way it was—wipes the fingerprints off the doorknob and makes it look like nobody was ever there.

Generally, configureEffect doesn't need to do anything at all, though we'll be using it once later in the chapter. We'll include it here just so nobody thinks it's forgotten. The vast majority of the work will obviously be done in executeEffect and any additional functions you write to assist it. So let's dive right into that.

```
function executeEffect(){
  var curr_eff = fl.activeEffect;
  var curr_doc = fl.getDocumentDOM();
  var curr_tl = curr_doc.getTimeline();
  var theFrame = curr_tl.currentFrame;
  curr_tl.insertFrames(curr_eff.duration-1);
}
```

The statements listed here are ones that you probably want to put at the beginning of any effect you make. Let's take a look at them in detail. First you get a reference to the current effect. This is stored in fl.activeEffect. Then you grab references to the active document and timeline.

Next you take note of the current frame. A little refresher: The currentFrame property of the timeline object will give you an integer, not a reference to a frame object. That's all you need here. You're simply saving it so you can return to it when you're done.

Finally, you insert some frames. Remember the duration variable you defined in the XML file? It's now a property of `fl.activeEffect` (which you just assigned to `curr_eff`). In order for the effect to play itself out for the number of frames the user specified, you need to make sure that the object is onstage for that many frames. Imagine if the next frame was a keyframe in which the object didn't exist. You wouldn't see much of an effect, would you? By inserting that many frames into the current timeline, at the point where the object currently is, you can ensure that the object will stick around long enough for at least one cycle of the effect.

You can go ahead and try this out. Save the file as `slide.jsfl` in your `Effects` directory and reload your effects. Draw a simple shape on the stage, select it, and call up the `Timeline Effects` menu by right-clicking. Navigate to the `Slide` effect and choose it. You should see a dialog box like the one in Figure 4-7 pop up.

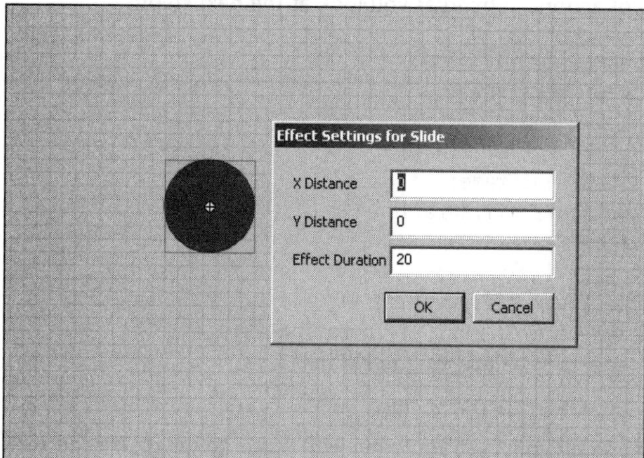

Figure 4-7.
Effect settings for the Slide effect

Also notice that the shape is now embedded in a graphic symbol, even though you didn't issue any type of convert to symbol command in your JSFL file. In fact, the JSFL file hasn't even run yet. This is an automatic feature of `Timeline Effects`.

Choose OK without changing any values and notice what happens. You have now added 19 frames to the timeline. If there was only 1 frame to begin with, you now have 20. If you double-click the new symbol, you'll see that it's locked, and if you check the Timeline Effects menu, you'll see that all the effects are inactive.

Try removing the effect. It removes the symbol and restores your shape to simple shape status. But you're still stuck with an extra 19 frames. Remember that. You'll have to clear those up manually in the `removeEffect` function.

Now try something else: Clear the stage and remove the extra frames. Repeat the first steps previously described, creating a shape and applying the effect with a default 20-frame duration. Now choose Edit Effect from the Timeline Effects menu. Change the duration to 10 frames and click OK. Instead of reducing the frames to 10, Flash has added on extra frames to the existing ones.

The reason for this is that when you choose Edit Effect and change the parameters, Flash executes the removeEffect function, and then executes the executeEffect function with the new parameters. Internally, it isn't so much an editing of the effect, but an undoing and redoing of it. You can prove this to yourself by putting a trace action inside the removeEffect function and then editing the effect. You'll see that the trace is called after changing the parameters.

But all of that is just a note on why you need to supply a function to remove the effect. Getting back on track, you'll next create a tween inside of this new symbol.

Remember that JSFL simply replicates in code the actions you would manually take yourself in the authoring environment. Think of the actions you would take to make a tween. Normally you would add some frames, make the last frame a keyframe, create a motion tween on the frames in between, and somehow change the object in the keyframe you just created. Keep that sequence of actions in mind as you look at the next steps:

```
function executeEffect(){
  var curr_eff = fl.activeEffect;
  var curr_doc = fl.getDocumentDOM();
  var curr_tl = curr_doc.getTimeline();
  theFrame = curr_tl.currentFrame;
  curr_tl.insertFrames(curr_eff.duration-1);
  curr_doc.enterEditMode();
  curr_tl = curr_doc.getTimeline();
  curr_tl.insertFrames(curr_eff.duration-1);
  curr_tl.createMotionTween(0, curr_eff.duration-1);
  curr_tl.convertToKeyframes(curr_eff.duration-1);
}
```

As usual we'll run through it line by line. First you enter edit mode to get inside the symbol. Then you reset curr_tl to point to the timeline you arrive at inside the symbol. Again, you insert frames. Then you create a motion tween with the function createMotionTween (this isn't exactly rocket science!). This takes a start and end frame as parameters. Remember that while frames in the authoring environment start at one, in JSFL they are stored in an array starting at zero. Thus you use 0 and curr_eff.duration-1 as the first and last frames. Finally, you convert that last frame to a keyframe.

At this point, you have a tween, but the keyframes on both ends contain the same thing. You need to change something in the second keyframe. In this case, you need to take the object there and move it on the x and y axes to produce your desired Slide Timeline Effect. You get the values to move it from curr_eff.xDist and curr_eff.yDist.

Now, a number of ways are available for you to accomplish this. There is no wrong way as long as it does exactly what you want it to and has no negative side effects. Here's the strategy we came up with: Go to that keyframe, select all, and then use curr_doc.moveSelectionBy to move them on the two axes. So here's the code you use:

```
function executeEffect(){
  var curr_eff = fl.activeEffect;
  var curr_doc = fl.getDocumentDOM();
```

```
    var curr_tl = curr_doc.getTimeline();
    theFrame = curr_tl.currentFrame;
    curr_tl.insertFrames(curr_eff.duration-1);
    curr_doc.enterEditMode();
    curr_tl = curr_doc.getTimeline();
    curr_tl.insertFrames(curr_eff.duration-1);
    curr_tl.createMotionTween(0, curr_eff.duration-1);
    curr_tl.convertToKeyframes(curr_eff.duration-1);
    curr_tl.currentFrame = curr_eff.duration-1;
    curr_doc.selectAll();
    curr_doc.moveSelectionBy({x:curr_eff.xDist, y:curr_eff.yDist});
    curr_doc.exitEditMode();
    curr_tl = curr_doc.getTimeline();
    curr_tl.currentFrame = theFrame;
}
```


To recap, Figure 4-8 describes pictorially what you're achieving with all of this code.

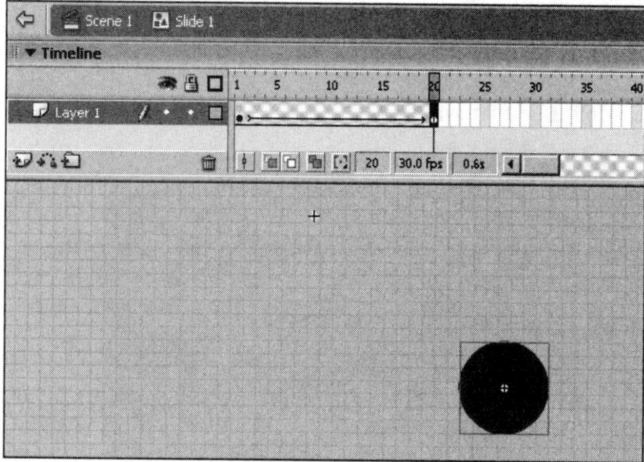

Figure 4-8. After adding frames to the main timeline and to the symbol's timeline, a motion tween is created from frame one to twenty, the last frame is converted to a keyframe, and the object is moved.

You can see in the code that you end up exiting edit mode and returning to the frame where you started. You can save this file now, reload your effects, and try it out. Again, select an object onstage and apply the effect. Choose some real values for the x and y distance this time. Test the resulting file and see that the tween does what it's supposed to.

You should also use the context menu (right-click or *CMD*-click) to edit the symbol and check inside. See for yourself that it's just a simple tween that was created. Make sure it's the right length and moves in the right direction.

While you're in there, take note of the fact that your simple shape is embedded in yet another graphic symbol. No magic this time. This is exactly what would happen in the authoring environment. Only symbols can be tweened. If you try to apply a motion tween to a shape or other element, it will always be converted to a graphic element before tweening. This extends to multiple elements of any type. If, for instance, you selected a graphic, shape, movie clip, and text box and then created a motion tween or applied this effect, all four elements would be wrapped in a single graphic symbol, and that symbol would be the one that was tweened.

Removing an Effect

There is no really straightforward way to undo an effect. It all depends on what effect you made and how you did it. It's up to you to make sure all your modifications are undone when the user selects this option. Generally, this consists of working through your code and changing back anything that you moved, resizing or reorienting anything you moved or changed, and deleting anything you added. Of course, the last point is key. There is no need to reset positions of objects in frames that you then delete. The last step, converting the symbol back to whatever it was to begin with, is done automatically by Flash.

Thus, if you think of the removing process when you're creating the `executeEffect` function, you can actually make things easier on yourself. Notice that in your effect, you start off with a copy of your original element inside a graphic symbol on layer one, frame one, and nothing else. That's exactly where you want to end up. Again, Flash will handle the last step of removing the symbol.

So what did you do inside that symbol?

- You added some frames.
- You created a tween.
- Although you didn't do it manually, creating a tween embedded the element in another graphic symbol.
- You created a keyframe and moved the element.

So, what you need to do to remove the effect is

- Delete the frames you added.
- Set the property of the remaining frame so it isn't a tween.
- Break apart the remaining symbol so it's back to whatever it was originally.

You don't need to worry about the added keyframe or changed location, since you just deleted those frames anyway.

Let's look at how to do these steps:

```
function removeEffect(){
  var curr_doc = fl.getDocumentDOM();
  curr_doc.enterEditMode();
  var curr_tl = curr_doc.getTimeline();
  var numFrames = curr_tl.layers[0].frameCount;
  curr_tl.removeFrames(1, numFrames);
  curr_tl.setFrameProperty("tweenType", "none", 0);
  curr_tl.currentFrame = 0;
```

```
        curr_doc.selectAll();
        curr_doc.breakApart();
        curr_doc.exitEditMode();
    }
```

First you just get references to the current document. Then you enter edit mode to go inside the symbol created by the effect and get the current timeline inside that symbol.

Next you need to remove the extra frames. But how many to remove? You can't rely on the `duration` property, as the user may have reused the effect on another symbol in the meantime and changed the value. Instead, you can find out how many frames are in the current layer (which you know is layer zero because it's the only one). You then remove all the frames from one to the end. You're now back to the original frame (zero) you started with.

Then you remove the tween. This is done by setting the `frame` property:

```
curr_tl.setFrameProperty("tweenType", "none", 0);
```

This function takes three arguments: the property to set, what you want to set it to, and what frame to apply it to. For a full list of available frame properties, see the listing for the `frame` object in the Flash extensibility reference section at the back of the book. If you wanted to set properties of multiple frames, you could add a fourth parameter of another ending frame. Flash would set that property for all frames in between those two frames. Here you're setting the tweenType property of frame zero to none.

In order to break apart the tween symbol, you need to select it. You can do that by going to frame zero and selecting all, then breaking it apart. Finally you exit edit mode and you're back to the original timeline. Flash will handle breaking apart the final symbol, so you have your original element sitting onstage.

But if you left it like this, you'd still have a bunch of extra frames sitting around on the timeline. Remember, that's the first thing you did in applying the effect. This isn't as simple as removing the frames inside the symbol. In there, you knew there was only one layer, and only so many frames, because you created them. You knew that your original element was in frame zero.

Out here in the real world you have no idea what the current conditions are. The symbol might be on frame one, or one hundred one, or one thousand two hundred seventy-four. And you can't just keep track of where it was when it was created. The user could have inserted or deleted frames prior to the symbol, thus changing its position. Furthermore, you won't know how many frames the effect covers. Again, the active effect parameters can't be relied on, as they may have changed. Puts you in a bit of a predicament, doesn't it?

Fortunately, there is a way to find out where the symbol is and how many frames it's taking up. If you select a symbol that has an effect applied to it, and look at the timeline, you'll see that the whole sequence of frames containing that symbol are now selected (see Figure 4-9). Knowing that this is the case, you just have to find out which frames are selected. You do just that with the next two lines of the function:

```
curr_tl = curr_doc.getTimeline();
var selFrames = curr_tl.getSelectedFrames();
```

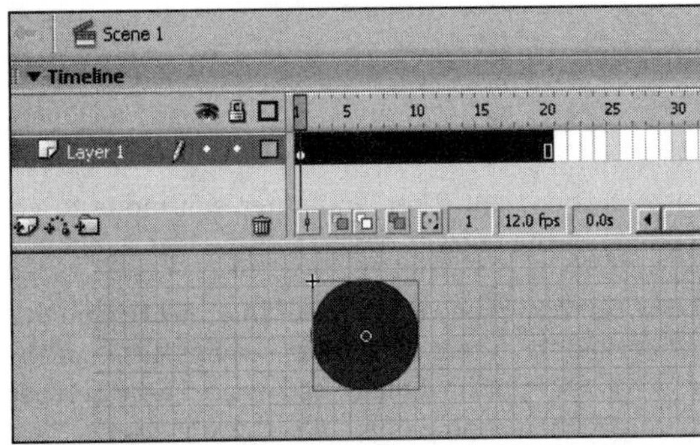

Figure 4-9.
Selecting a symbol selects the entire range of frames it exists in.

The `timeline` object function `getSelectedFrames` returns an array containing information about which frames are currently selected. But it isn't quite what you might expect—an array with each element containing a frame. Actually, it just contains three frames no matter how many frames are selected. Note that we said the array contains *information about* the frames. Here is exactly what information it will contain:

- `selFrames[0]`: Contains the number of the layer where the selected frames are.
- `selFrames[1]`: Contains the number of the first selected frame in the sequence.
- `selFrames[2]`: Contains the number of the frame *after* the last selected frame in the sequence. In other words, the next *unselected* frame.

Thus, if you have an array with the values [`1, 5, 11`], it would mean that frames five through ten in layer two (remember layer one is element `0`, two is element `1`, etc.) are selected.

Returning the frame *after* the last selected frame may seem a little strange. You might expect that Flash would return the last frame that is actually selected. Luckily, the other functions that deal with ranges work the same way, so you don't have to worry about it too much. For example, the next line will use the `removeFrames` function. The two values it takes are the first frame to remove and the frame *after* the last frame to remove. So you can just feed back in the value you got with `getSelectedFrames`.

Remember you don't want to remove all the frames. You should keep the first frame in place, and just remove the rest of the sequence. Thus, you get the next line:

```
curr_tl.removeFrames(selFrames[1]+1, selFrames[2]);
```

Finally, you can end in a professional manner by resetting the selection to the one frame where the symbol is left. Here's the whole function:

```
function removeEffect(){
  var curr_doc = fl.getDocumentDOM();
  curr_doc.enterEditMode();
  var curr_tl = curr_doc.getTimeline();
  var numFrames = curr_tl.layers[0].frameCount;
  curr_tl.removeFrames(1, numFrames);
  curr_tl.setFrameProperty("tweenType", "none", 0);
  curr_tl.currentFrame = 0;
```

```
    curr_doc.selectAll();
    curr_doc.breakApart();
    curr_doc.exitEditMode();
    curr_tl = curr_doc.getTimeline();
    var selFrames = curr_tl.getSelectedFrames();
    curr_tl.removeFrames(selFrames[1]+1, selFrames[2]);
    curr_tl.setSelectedFrames(selFrames[1], selFrames[1]);
}
```

And there you have it, a fully functional Timeline Effect! Not a very exciting one, you understand. But it works like it should, which is the most important thing. Now you can use what you learned and just create more complex effects.

Move in Circle Effect

For your next effect, you're going to try something a little different. You're actually going to skip the whole tween scene and make a frame-by-frame animation. It would probably be possible to make this same effect using a tween, but it will be good practice here, and there are some effects that you could only do with a frame-by-frame approach.

You'll also be exploring a new concept in JSFL, that of storing **persistent data** in the document. Up to now, most variables would be lost or reinitialized on the subsequent running of a particular command, tool, or effect. Nothing at all would survive closing a document and reopening it. But you can in fact create persistent data. This is data that can be stored in a document, element, or Library item. You set the data and it's stored in the FLA document such that the next time you open the document in the authoring environment, it's still there.

The idea for this simple effect is to move a selected object around in a circle. Of course, you'll be needing some data from the user as well—specifically, the size of the circle, whether the object should move in a clockwise or counterclockwise direction, whether the object should align itself to the circular path, and you can't forget your old friend, the duration of the effect.

The first thing you'll do is create the effect XML file, `moveInCircle.xml`, which will gather all the preceding information for you. Here it is:

```
<group name="My Effects">
  <effect name="Move in Circle">
  <source file="moveInCircle.jsfl">
  <allow types="all">
</group>
<properties>
  <property name="Radius" variable="radius" defaultValue="100" min="1"
➥max="1000" type="Number"/>
  <property name="Direction"  variable="direction"
➥list="Clockwise,Counterclockwise" defaultValue="0" type="Strings"/>
  <property name="Align to Path" variable="alignPath" type="Boolean"/>
```

```
  <property name="Effect Duration" variable="duration"
➥defaultValue="20" min="1" max="16000" type="Number"/>
</properties>
```

Figure 4-10 shows the dialog box created by this XML.

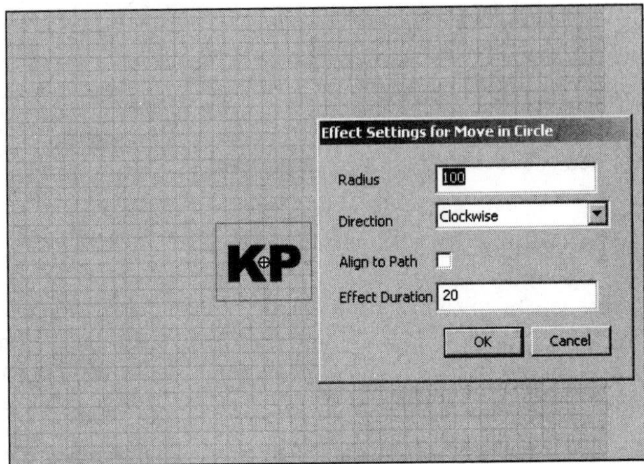

Figure 4-10. The effect settings set up by the XML file

Nothing too groundbreaking here; you just set up the effect with its group, name, source file, and allow types, then specify the properties. You don't need to do any configuration, so you'll leave that empty:

```
function configureEffect(){
}
```

Then you begin the executeEffect function with pretty much the same code you used in the last effect:

```
function executeEffect(){
  var curr_eff = fl.activeEffect;
  var curr_doc = fl.getDocumentDOM();
  var curr_tl = curr_doc.getTimeline();
  var theFrame = curr_tl.currentFrame;
  curr_tl.insertFrames(curr_eff.duration-1);
  curr_doc.enterEditMode();
  curr_tl = curr_doc.getTimeline();
  curr_tl.insertFrames(curr_eff.duration-1);
}
```

This gets the necessary references, adds frames to the current timeline, enters edit mode on the symbol, and adds the same number of frames there.

Here is where you start the different approach though. Rather than creating a tween, you're going to convert the entire sequence to keyframes. You can do that with one line, just specifying the start and end frames to convert:

```
curr_tl.convertToKeyframes(0, curr_eff.duration);
```

Once again here, the end frame is the frame *after* the last frame you want to convert. Now you can start to see the logic of why Macromedia made it that way. Say the duration chosen was 20. You want to convert frames 0 to 19. You can easily use the duration number in the function, since the duration corresponds to the first unaffected frame.

The next bunch of code loops through each frame and moves the content into a new position. This uses a bit of basic trigonometry to calculate the points around a circle. First it takes a full circle that is `PI*2` radians (see Chapter 2 for a discussion of degrees and radians), and divides it by the number of frames. Then it multiplies that value times the number of the current frame. This gives you the angle that the current element should be placed at. In Flash, angles go around clockwise as they increase. If the user chose counterclockwise, you invert it, making it a negative angle:


```
function executeEffect(){
  var curr_eff = fl.activeEffect;
  var curr_doc = fl.getDocumentDOM();
  var curr_tl = curr_doc.getTimeline();
  var theFrame = curr_tl.currentFrame;
  curr_tl.insertFrames(curr_eff.duration - 1);
  curr_doc.enterEditMode();
  curr_tl = curr_doc.getTimeline();
  curr_tl.insertFrames(curr_eff.duration - 1);
  curr_tl.convertToKeyframes(0, curr_eff.duration);
  for(var i = 0; i < curr_eff.duration; i++){
    var angle = Math.PI * 2 / curr_eff.duration * i;
    if(curr_eff.direction == "Counterclockwise"){
      angle = -angle;
    }
  }
}
```

You then use the cosine and sine of that angle, along with the chosen radius to determine how much to move the element. And you move to that frame, select all, and move the selection by the distance just determined:

```
function executeEffect(){
  var curr_eff = fl.activeEffect;
  var curr_doc = fl.getDocumentDOM();
  var curr_tl = curr_doc.getTimeline();
  var theFrame = curr_tl.currentFrame;
  curr_tl.insertFrames(curr_eff.duration - 1);
  curr_doc.enterEditMode();
  curr_tl = curr_doc.getTimeline();
  curr_tl.insertFrames(curr_eff.duration - 1);
```

```
    curr_tl.convertToKeyframes(0, curr_eff.duration);
    for(var i = 0; i < curr_eff.duration; i++){
      var angle = Math.PI * 2 / curr_eff.duration * i;
      if(curr_eff.direction == "Counterclockwise"){
        angle = -angle;
      }
      var xDist = Math.cos(angle)*curr_eff.radius;
      var yDist = Math.sin(angle)*curr_eff.radius;
      curr_tl.currentFrame = i;
      curr_doc.selectAll();
      curr_doc.moveSelectionBy( {x:xDist, y:yDist} );
    }
  }
```

Finally, you check if the user chose to align to path. If so, you want to rotate the elements by the chosen angle. As discussed in Chapter 2, the rotation function jumps back to degrees, so you'll need to make a conversion. Also, similar to what you did in that chapter, you'll then add 90 degrees to make the selection lie flat on the circle, not perpendicular to it. You then simply wrap up by jumping out of edit mode and making sure the current frame is where you started.

```
function executeEffect(){
  var curr_eff = fl.activeEffect;
  var curr_doc = fl.getDocumentDOM();
  var curr_tl = curr_doc.getTimeline();
  var theFrame = curr_tl.currentFrame;
  curr_tl.insertFrames(curr_eff.duration - 1);
  curr_doc.enterEditMode();
  curr_tl = curr_doc.getTimeline();
  curr_tl.insertFrames(curr_eff.duration - 1);
  curr_tl.convertToKeyframes(0, curr_eff.duration);
  for(var i = 0; i < curr_eff.duration; i++){
    var angle = Math.PI * 2 / curr_eff.duration * i;
    if(curr_eff.direction == "Counterclockwise"){
      angle = -angle;
    }
    var xDist = Math.cos(angle)*curr_eff.radius;
    var yDist = Math.sin(angle)*curr_eff.radius;
    curr_tl.currentFrame = i;
    curr_doc.selectAll();
    curr_doc.moveSelectionBy( {x:xDist, y:yDist} );
    if(curr_eff.alignPath){
      curr_doc.rotateSelection(angle*180/Math.PI+90);
    }
  }
  curr_doc.exitEditMode();
  curr_tl = curr_doc.getTimeline();
  curr_tl.currentFrame = theFrame;
}
```

And in Figure 4-11 you can see the effect created by the code so far.

Figure 4-11.
The Move in Circle effect in action

As a little hint, if you're applying any effect that does any scaling or rotation of dynamic or input text fields, you'll need to embed the font in the field. If you don't, the text will disappear while it's being changed. You could even build a function into the effect to check whether a text field is being used and, if so, automatically embed the font.

Well that's about it for the effect itself. Now you need to think about undoing it. This will be a little different from the last time, obviously, since you did some slightly different actions. You can start out pretty much the same though, by removing all the extra frames you created:

```
function removeEffect(){
  var curr_doc = fl.getDocumentDOM();
  curr_doc.enterEditMode();
  var curr_tl = curr_doc.getTimeline();
  var numFrames = curr_tl.layers[0].frameCount;
  curr_tl.removeFrames(1, numFrames);
}
```

Next, you move to frame zero and select all. Last time you created a tween that automatically put any elements into a graphic symbol. Since you didn't do that this time, anything here should be in its original state.

Also, last time you didn't do anything to the elements in frame zero. This time around, you did move it, and possibly rotated it. First you'll handle resetting the movement. When the effect symbol was created, any content in it would have been centered on the symbol's internal registration point, so you just need to recenter it.

Remember, though, that the user may have selected more than one item. If you just center everything there, each individual item will be centered rather than having the whole group centered. You'll handle that by grouping the selection first, centering the group, and then ungrouping it. This will ensure that each element retains its original position.

Then you'll wrap up the same way you did before, exiting edit mode and removing the extra frames on the timeline.

```
function removeEffect(){
  var curr_doc = fl.getDocumentDOM();
  curr_doc.enterEditMode();
  var curr_tl = curr_doc.getTimeline();
  var numFrames = curr_tl.layers[0].frameCount;
  curr_tl.removeFrames(1, numFrames);
  curr_tl.currentFrame = 0;
  curr_doc.selectAll();
  curr_doc.group();
  curr_doc.align("horizontal center", true);
  curr_doc.align("vertical center", true);
  curr_doc.unGroup();
  curr_doc.exitEditMode();
  curr_tl = curr_doc.getTimeline();
  var selFrames = curr_tl.getSelectedFrames();
  curr_tl.removeFrames(selFrames[1]+1, selFrames[2]);
  curr_tl.setSelectedFrames(selFrames[1], selFrames[1]);
}
```

Now you come to the point of removing any rotation that might be left on the remaining object. It turns out that if `align to path` was chosen, the remaining element will always be rotated 90 degrees. All you have to do is rotate it back -90, as shown here:

```
function removeEffect(){
  var curr_doc = fl.getDocumentDOM();
  curr_doc.enterEditMode();
  var curr_tl = curr_doc.getTimeline();
  var numFrames = curr_tl.layers[0].frameCount;
  curr_tl.removeFrames(1, numFrames);
  curr_tl.currentFrame = 0;
  curr_doc.selectAll();
  curr_doc.group();
  curr_doc.align("horizontal center", true);
  curr_doc.align("vertical center", true);
  curr_doc.rotateSelection(-90);
  curr_doc.unGroup();
  curr_doc.exitEditMode();
  curr_tl = curr_doc.getTimeline();
  var selFrames = curr_tl.getSelectedFrames();
  curr_tl.removeFrames(selFrames[1]+1, selFrames[2]);
  curr_tl.setSelectedFrames(selFrames[1], selFrames[1]);
}
```

But wait . . . if you just do that, it will rotate the remaining object *every time*. If the user didn't choose `align to path`, then you definitely *don't* want to rotate the object back. But there is no easy way to determine whether or not the element was rotated. You can't just check the active effect's `alignPath` property. Remember, that user may be removing the effect a long time after it was created. The effect could have been applied to several other elements in the meantime, and the user may have even closed the document or entire program and restarted it. So that property is useless and can't be relied upon to refer to the current element. You could add some ActionScript to the object to indicate that it was rotated, but as mentioned in Chapter 2, automatically adding ActionScript to existing elements carries the potential danger of interfering with existing ActionScript.

Here's where persistent data comes in handy. You can set some data in the element to tell you whether or not it was rotated. This data will exist in the element as long as the element exists. It will be saved along with the FLA file. So, you can open up the document sometime later, and when you go to remove the effect, it checks to see if it was originally rotated or not, and acts accordingly.

First you need to jump back to your `executeEffect` function and add the data. You'll use the function

```
element.setPersistentData(name, type, value)
```

where `name` is a string containing the name of the data you want to set (you can think of it as a variable), and `type` is also a string and can consist of `integer`, `integerArray`, `double`, `doubleArray`, `string`, or `byteArray`. And finally, `value` is simply the value you want the data to contain. As you can see, you could potentially store a wealth of information in an `element`, `item`, or `document`.

You'll only set this data if `align to path` was chosen. Normally you would probably set a Boolean value to `true` or `false`, but you'll have to "fake it" with another type. Here you use a string:

```
function executeEffect(){
  var curr_eff = fl.activeEffect;
  var curr_doc = fl.getDocumentDOM();
  var curr_tl = curr_doc.getTimeline();
  var theFrame = curr_tl.currentFrame;
  curr_tl.insertFrames(curr_eff.duration - 1);
  curr_doc.enterEditMode();
  curr_tl = curr_doc.getTimeline();
  curr_tl.insertFrames(curr_eff.duration - 1);
  curr_tl.convertToKeyframes(0, curr_eff.duration);
  for(var i = 0; i < curr_eff.duration; i++){
    var angle = Math.PI * 2 / curr_eff.duration * i;
    if(curr_eff.direction == "Counterclockwise"){
      angle = -angle;
    }
    var xDist = Math.cos(angle)*curr_eff.radius;
    var yDist = Math.sin(angle)*curr_eff.radius;
    curr_tl.currentFrame = i;
    curr_doc.selectAll();
    curr_doc.moveSelectionBy( {x:xDist, y:yDist} );
    if(curr_eff.alignPath){
      curr_doc.rotateSelection(angle*180/Math.PI+90);
```

```
      }
    }
    curr_doc.exitEditMode();
    if(curr_eff.alignPath){
      var curr_elem = curr_doc.selection[0];
      curr_elem.setPersistentData("aligned", "string", "true");
    }
    curr_tl = curr_doc.getTimeline();
    curr_tl.currentFrame = theFrame;
  }
```

Note that you apply this action right after you exit edit mode, where the symbol will be the only thing selected. You get a reference to that element from the selection array, and then set its data.

Now, in removeEffect, you again get a reference to the element. Again, it should be the only thing selected, so you can grab it out of the selection array. Then you see if it has a persistent data element named aligned. If so, you check if the value of this data is true. Actually this check is a bit redundant, as the data is only set if the element is rotated, and will either be equal to true or not exist at all. We included it so you could see both functions, and know how to not only check if data exists, but also get its value.

In any case, if the persistent data variable, aligned, equals true, you set a local variable, aligned, to true. This just makes the data easier to access later on inside the symbol.

```
  function removeEffect(){
    var curr_doc = fl.getDocumentDOM();
    var curr_elem = curr_doc.selection[0];
    if(curr_elem.hasPersistentData("aligned")){
      if(curr_elem.getPersistentData("aligned") == "true"){
        var aligned = true;
      }
    }
    curr_doc.enterEditMode();
    var curr_tl = curr_doc.getTimeline();
    var numFrames = curr_tl.layers[0].frameCount;
    curr_tl.removeFrames(1, numFrames);
    curr_tl.currentFrame = 0;
    curr_doc.selectAll();
    curr_doc.group();
    curr_doc.align("horizontal center", true);
    curr_doc.align("vertical center", true);
    if(aligned){
      curr_doc.rotateSelection(-90);
    }
    curr_doc.unGroup();
    curr_doc.exitEditMode();
    curr_tl = curr_doc.getTimeline();
    var selFrames = curr_tl.getSelectedFrames();
    curr_tl.removeFrames(selFrames[1]+1, selFrames[2]);
```

```
    curr_tl.setSelectedFrames(selFrames[1], selFrames[1]);
  }
```

Inside the symbol, you check the value of the local variable, `aligned`, and if it's `true`, you do the rotation.

Test this out, try different types of elements, multiple elements, and different parameters. Make sure the effect works and make sure that removing it really does set things back the way they were.

Easing the Pain of Development

One of the great things about being authors is that after you, the reader, spend a couple of frustrating hours trying to figure something out, you come and read something here that seems nice and clear and simple and we look like geniuses. What you don't see is the day and a half we spent tearing our hair out trying to figure it out, and the other half a day trying to make it sound simple!

Before moving on to creating another effect, we'll take a brief time-out to introduce a few more tips and techniques to help you do what you want to get done. Drawing on the stage was easy enough. Manipulating frames got a little more complex. As you begin to add layers, things get quite a bit more complicated.

One trick we figured out early on is to start our effects as commands. Commands require no setup other than creating the file itself. Don't worry about parameters, and so on, just hard code some values to start with. Commands can also generally be undone with a simple undo, and you don't have to break into a locked symbol to see what is happening inside. When you have the basic functionality you want, create the effect XML file and move everything inside the `executeEffect` function. You'll probably have to adjust a few things to get it working in the new context, but overall, you'll save time.

Another very helpful feature comes to you straight from standard JavaScript—catching exceptions. An exception is a fancy word for an error. As you've seen, certain errors can cause some extensibility tools to disappear or not run at all. Some will cause an error to be traced to the Output window. But others sneak by without a word and merely mess up your program. Catching exceptions can help you find more errors, find out more about them, and stop them before they go too far.

The principle is to put your questionable code inside a `try` block. This is merely the word "try" followed by curly braces. And this is followed by a `catch` block—the word "catch" with a pair of parentheses surrounding a variable of your choice—then another set of curly braces.

Flash will attempt to run the code within the try block. If it encounters any errors, it will cancel the operation and run the `catch` block. The error it caught will be sent via the variable after `catch`. This is what it looks like:

```
try {
  // statements to execute here
} catch(error) {
```

```
    // statements to handle the error
  }
```

Handling the error in this case will usually just consist of telling you what the error is. You can include a trace or alert like so:

```
try {
  curr_dod.enterEditMode();
} catch(error) {
  alert(error);
}
```

Here, we intentionally misspelled curr_doc. Assuming this variable doesn't exist, it will throw an exception. The catch block calls up an alert box with the text of the exception, which will be something like: `ReferenceError: curr_dod is not defined.`

You can also add a `finally` block after the `catch` block. Anything here will execute after the `try` and `catch` blocks, regardless of whether or not an error is caught. It looks like this:

```
try {
  // statements
} catch(error) {
  // handle error
} finally {
  // always do this
}
```

Exception catching can be used at development time only, or you could build it into your final effect. Of course, you should work out all the bugs such as undefined variables being referenced, but new users will always find a way to break your code by doing something you never expected; so if you want to be safe, you can enclose your entire effect, or at least the trickier parts, in a `try` block. In the `catch` block, you can use an alert to tell the user something went wrong, and then call `removeEffect` and hopefully undo any damage. After you gain a little more experience predicting and catching errors, you can learn about the various exceptions that can be thrown and test for them in the catch block, and maybe even save the function.

We'll leave all that to you. To keep the code simple for learning purposes here, we'll leave it out. Also, remember that this is a standard part of the JavaScript language, and you can find out a lot more about it in any good book on JavaScript.

Checkerboard Transition Effect

For the next effect, you'll take your first small steps toward creating and manipulating timeline layers. You'll create a new layer above the existing content, turn it into a mask layer and put some animation into it. And then of course, you'll have to figure out how to undo it all.

The effect is a standard transition. First there is one image onstage, or perhaps nothing. Then, another image slowly builds up through randomly placed squares in a checkerboard pattern. The image that is revealed is what users originally selected when they applied the effect. The checkerboard is a mask with randomly placed rectangles drawn into it.

First your XML file. You'll need two parameters to represent rows and columns. Of course, you want to limit it somewhat—for example, 25 rows and columns equates to 625 rectangles, each of which will get its own frame. At 30 frames per second, that's over 20 seconds of animation, so that's a good maximum to work with.

```
<group name="My Effects">
  <effect name="Checkerboard">
  <source file="checkerboard.jsfl">
  <allow types="all">
</group>
<properties>
  <property name="Rows" variable="rows" defaultValue="5" min="1"
➥max="25" type="Number"/>
  <property name="Columns" variable="cols" defaultValue="5" min="1"
➥max="25" type="Number"/>
</properties>
```


This file, `checkerboard.xml`, produces the Effect Settings dialog box shown in Figure 4-12.

Figure 4-12. The Effect Settings dialog box for the Checkerboard effect, being applied to a bitmap

Now onto the associated JSFL. The first chunk should be starting to look familiar by now, you just need to incorporate your rows and cols variables:

```
function configureEffect(){
}
function executeEffect() {
  curr_eff = fl.activeEffect;
  rows = curr_eff.rows;
  cols = curr_eff.cols;
  curr_doc = fl.getDocumentDOM();
  curr_tl = curr_doc.getTimeline();
  curr_tl.insertFrames(rows*cols);
  curr_doc.enterEditMode();
  curr_tl = curr_doc.getTimeline();
  curr_tl.insertFrames(rows*cols);
}
```

You have your shell of a configureEffect function and then jump into executeEffect. Here you grab your parameters, insert some frames into the timeline—enough for each rectangle, or rows times columns—and then enter edit mode and do the same thing inside the new symbol.

In the next few lines, you basically find out the size of the selected elements:

```
function executeEffect() {
  curr_eff = fl.activeEffect;
  rows = curr_eff.rows;
  cols = curr_eff.cols;
  curr_doc = fl.getDocumentDOM();
  curr_tl = curr_doc.getTimeline();
  curr_tl.insertFrames(rows*cols);
  curr_doc.enterEditMode();
  curr_tl = curr_doc.getTimeline();
  curr_tl.insertFrames(rows*cols);
  contentLayNum = curr_tl.currentLayer;
  curr_tl.layers[contentLayNum].name = "content";
  curr_doc.selectAll();
  curr_doc.group();
  curr_elem = curr_doc.selection[0];
  xpos = curr_elem.left;
  ypos = curr_elem.top;
  w = curr_elem.width;
  h = curr_elem.height;
}
```

First you find out the number of the current layer. Remember that the timeline object contains a property, layers, which is an array containing each layer. Actually, you know this should be layer zero, but you'll do it this way to be in good form. You then set the name of this layer to content. This will help you find it later, when its layer number changes.

Next you group any and all elements that were selected. This puts them all into a single element that you can find in the first slot of the `selection` array. Knowing that, you grab its position and size and store those in variables.

Carrying on from there, you create an array of rectangles, which, forming a grid, will completely cover the selected objects.

```
    // continues from previous code...

    xSize = w/cols;
    ySize = h/rows;
    boxArray = new Array();
    for (x=0; x<cols; x++) {
      for (y=0; y<rows; y++) {
        t = ypos + y * ySize;
        b = ypos + y * ySize + ySize;
        l = xpos + x * xSize;
        r = xpos + x * xSize + xSize;
        box = {top:t, bottom:b, left:l, right:r};
        boxArray.push(box);
      }
    }
  }
```

Dividing the selection width by the number of columns, and its height by rows, you get the size of each rectangle. You make an array, `boxArray`, and looping through each of the columns and rows, you create a rectangle object and push it into the array.

Now this array holds a very orderly arrangement of rectangles, not the random placement you want. The next code shakes it up a bit:

```
    // continues from previous code...
    randArray = new Array();
    while (boxArray.length>0) {
      index = Math.floor(Math.random()*boxArray.length);
      box = boxArray[index];
      boxArray.splice(index, 1);
      randArray.push(box);
    }
  }
```

Now, you create a new array called `randArray`. You choose a random element from the `boxArray` and copy it into `randArray`. Then you remove that element from `boxArray` using the `splice` function. This takes an argument of which element to start removing at, and how many to remove. In this case, you just take out one at a time.

4

At some point, you'll have deleted all the elements from boxArray. When that happens, boxArray.length will be zero, and the while loop will end. randArray will then be filled with all the same rectangles that were in boxArray, but in a random order.

Next you draw one of these boxes in each frame of a mask, on top of the content.

```
    // continues from previous code...
    newLayNum = curr_tl.addNewLayer("mask", "mask", true);
    curr_tl.setSelectedLayers(newLayNum, true);
    for (i=0; i<randArray.length; i++) {
      curr_tl.currentFrame = i;
      curr_doc.addNewRectangle(randArray[i], 0, false, true);
      curr_tl.convertToKeyframes(i+1);
    }
  }
```

The first new line there adds the new layer. The addNewLayer function takes three parameters: the name of the new layer, its type, and whether or not it should be added above the current layer. You can omit these and accept the default name and normal layer type, and have it added below the current layer. But you want to specify all three here—you'll name the layer "mask" so you can find it later. Its type is also mask. Other possible types are normal, guide, and folder. Lastly, you specify true, making it appear above the current layer, which is of course necessary for a mask layer.

You then select this layer by specifying its number in setSelectedLayers. The true here specifies that this selection replaces any former selection.

Next you loop through randArray. Each time, you move to the next frame and draw a rectangle there. Then you convert the *next* frame to a keyframe. Doing it this way ensures that each frame will contain all the previously drawn rectangles, plus the newly drawn one (see Figure 4-13).

Only a few things left to wrap it up:

```
    // continues from previous code...
    contentLayNum = curr_tl.findLayerIndex("content");
    curr_tl.layers[contentLayNum].parentLayer =
  ➥curr_tl.layers[newLayNum];
    curr_doc.exitEditMode();
  }
```

Here, you need to tell the content layer that it should be masked by the mask layer. As it stands, it's simply another layer underneath the mask layer. In order for a mask layer to mask something, it must not only lie above it, but also be set as the parentLayer of the layer it's masking.

Now, originally you knew that the content layer was layer zero, because it was the only layer. But now, when you created the mask layer *above* it, it was pushed down. You could (correctly) guess that it's now layer one, but in a more complex effect, there might be all kinds of insertions and deletions of layers, and you couldn't assume that.

Figure 4-13. Inside the Checkerboard effect. Here you can see the mask layer, masking the content layer, with individual keyframes that each add one block.

Remember, though, that you named it "content". Here, you find out what number the content layer is by using the `findLayerIndex` function. Then you can gain access to that layer by using the `layers` array. Also, when you created the mask layer, you saved its number in a variable called `newLayNum`. You use that to find it in the layers array. The next line just sets the mask layer as the `parentLayer` of the `contentLayer`. Now it will correctly function as a mask. All that's left is to jump out of edit mode and your effect is almost complete . . .

. . . except for the `removeEffect` function, of course! Luckily this isn't too hard. We've already covered many of the actions you need to do:

```
function removeEffect(){
  curr_doc = fl.getDocumentDOM();
  curr_doc.enterEditMode();
  curr_tl = curr_doc.getTimeline();
  curr_tl.layers[1].parentLayer = null;
  curr_tl.deleteLayer(0);
  curr_tl.currentLayer = 0;
  numFrames = curr_tl.layers[0].frameCount;
  curr_tl.removeFrames(1, numFrames);
  curr_tl.currentFrame = 0;
  curr_doc.selectAll();
  curr_doc.unGroup();
```

```
        curr_doc.exitEditMode();
        curr_tl = curr_doc.getTimeline();
        var selFrames = curr_tl.getSelectedFrames();
        curr_tl.removeFrames(selFrames[1]+1, selFrames[2]);
        curr_tl.setSelectedFrames(selFrames[1], selFrames[1]);
    }
```

Line 5 is the first one that you should note. Having made our point about how to find a layer index, we have you use a shortcut here, knowing that the content is layer number one in this simple file. If you add things to this file to make it more complex, you may want to go back to finding its index via its name. Anyway, you set that layer's `parentLayer` to `null`, since you're about to get rid of its parent.

The next line does just that: It deletes layer zero, which is again a shortcut, owing to the simple layer structure of a basic effect like this. The next couple of lines remove the extra frames—you've seen that already. Then you go to frame zero, select everything, and ungroup it (remember that you grouped it in order to get its overall position and size). Finally, you exit edit mode and remove the extra frames on the main timeline using the same method as discussed earlier.

Remember, you can download the associated files for this example—`checkerboard.jsfl` and `checkerboard.xml`—from the book's website, `www.flashextensibility.com`. Figure 4-14 shows a snapshot of the effect in action.

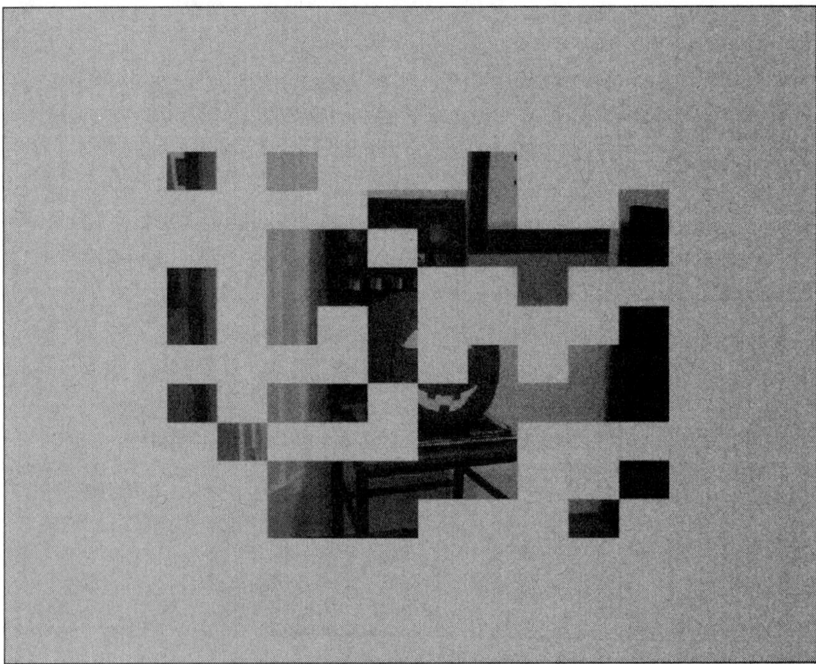

Figure 4-14. The Checkerboard effect in action

Custom Effect UI and Preview

As promised, we'll now show you how to make an effect with a custom SWF-based user interface and preview. This is a pretty advanced technique, so for the sake of clarity, we'll use a very simple effect. Once you have the basics down, you can apply this to any effect at all.

Before you start, let's plan out the sequence of what needs to happen to have a custom UI with an effect preview.

1. First you execute the effect with default values, *without* calling up any dialog box.
2. You then take the symbol that has been created by applying the effect, and export it as a SWF file on the user's hard drive. This is the preview.
3. At that point, you call up an XML to UI dialog box, containing a SWF.
4. The SWF uses `loadMovie` to load in the previously created preview SWF.
5. The SWF also has some controls to change the properties, and a button to reset the preview. When the user resets the preview, the properties will be updated in the JSFL file.
6. Then the effect will be removed and re-created with the new properties, and a new preview SWF will be saved to disk. The XML to UI dialog box will be called again, and will load the new preview.
7. If the user clicks `OK` in the dialog box at any time, you just need to exit, as the effect is already created. If the user clicks `Cancel`, you remove the effect.

Don't panic just yet—we'll walk you through each step slowly and methodically. First create the effect itself as if it were going to use a regular interface, then you'll upgrade it from there.

You'll call this effect Grow. It simply scales the movie clip up or down to a certain percentage, specified by the user, over a number of frames, also specified by the user. The first two parameters you'll need are `scale` and `duration`. The third is a Boolean value that will be used to indicate if the preview is being reset (`true`), or accepted or canceled (`false`). Here's the initial XML file:

```
<group name="My Effects">
  <effect name="Grow">
  <source file="grow.jsfl">
  <allow types="all">
  <properties>
    <property name="Scale" variable="scale" defaultValue="200" min="0"
➥max="1000" type="Number"/>
    <property name="Duration" variable="duration" defaultValue="20"
➥min="2" max="500" type="Number"/>
    <property name="reset" variable="reset" defaultValue="false"
➥type="Boolean"/>
  </properties>
</group>
```

Save that as grow.xml. And now the JSFL file itself:

```
function configureEffect(){
}
function executeEffect(){
  var curr_eff = fl.activeEffect;
  var curr_doc = fl.getDocumentDOM();
  var curr_tl = curr_doc.getTimeline();
  theFrame = curr_tl.currentFrame;
  curr_tl.insertFrames(curr_eff.duration-1);
  curr_doc.enterEditMode();
  curr_tl = curr_doc.getTimeline();
  curr_tl.insertFrames(curr_eff.duration-1);
  curr_tl.createMotionTween(0, curr_eff.duration-1);
  curr_tl.convertToKeyframes(curr_eff.duration-1);
  curr_tl.currentFrame = curr_eff.duration-1;
  curr_doc.selectAll();
  curr_doc.scaleSelection(curr_eff.scale/100, curr_eff.scale/100,
➥"center");
  curr_doc.exitEditMode();
  curr_tl = curr_doc.getTimeline();
  curr_tl.currentFrame = theFrame;
}
function removeEffect(){
  var curr_doc = fl.getDocumentDOM();
  curr_doc.enterEditMode();
  var curr_tl = curr_doc.getTimeline();
  var numFrames = curr_tl.layers[0].frameCount;
  curr_tl.removeFrames(1, numFrames);
  curr_tl.setFrameProperty('tweenType', 'none', 0);
  curr_tl.currentFrame = 0;
  curr_doc.selectAll();
  curr_doc.breakApart();
  curr_doc.exitEditMode();
  curr_tl = curr_doc.getTimeline();
  var selFrames = curr_tl.getSelectedFrames();
  curr_tl.removeFrames(selFrames[1]+1, selFrames[2]);
  curr_tl.setSelectedFrames(selFrames[1], selFrames[1]);
}
```

Save this file as grow.jsfl in your Effects folder. By now, there shouldn't be a need to go over this line by line. It's almost exactly the same as the Slide effect.

The only major difference is the line in bold. The scaleSelection method takes three arguments: how much to scale in the x and y directions, and which direction to scale in. Notice that you divide your scale value by 100. Unlike the scaling functions in ActionScript, this one doesn't take percentages to scale, but simply multiplies the width and height by the value you give it for scale. Thus 1 is the same as 100 percent, 2 would be 200 percent, and so on. To scale down, use decimals: 0.5 would be 50 percent, and so on. Here you use center as direction, which will scale it up or down equally in all directions. See the document object entries in the Flash extensibility reference section at the back of the book for other possible values to use as the scaleSelection parameters.

OK, that's the effect. You should be able to reload your effects and have this work as expected. Now you start hacking it up so that you can use your custom SWF-based UI.

The first thing you're going to do is to remove all the code from the executeEffect and removeEffect functions and put them in separate external functions, because you need to perform all these actions over and over as you apply the effect repeatedly to generate a preview. But executeEffect and removeEffect do additional things behind the scenes, such as converting to symbols and breaking up symbols. You only want to do that when you initially create the effect, and when you remove it. So you'll create some new functions that do all the same things, but externally.


```
function executeEffect(){
  doEffect();
}
function removeEffect(){
  undoEffect();
}
function doEffect(){
  var curr_eff = fl.activeEffect;
  var curr_doc = fl.getDocumentDOM();
  var curr_tl = curr_doc.getTimeline();
  theFrame = curr_tl.currentFrame;
  curr_tl.insertFrames(curr_eff.duration-1);
  curr_doc.enterEditMode();
  curr_tl = curr_doc.getTimeline();
  curr_tl.insertFrames(curr_eff.duration-1);
  curr_tl.createMotionTween(0, curr_eff.duration-1);
  curr_tl.convertToKeyframes(curr_eff.duration-1);
  curr_tl.currentFrame = curr_eff.duration-1;
  curr_doc.selectAll();
  curr_doc.scaleSelection(curr_eff.scale/100, curr_eff.scale/100,
➥"center");
  curr_doc.exitEditMode();
  curr_tl = curr_doc.getTimeline();
  curr_tl.currentFrame = theFrame;
}
function undoEffect(){
  var curr_doc = fl.getDocumentDOM();
  curr_doc.enterEditMode();
  var curr_tl = curr_doc.getTimeline();
  var numFrames = curr_tl.layers[0].frameCount;
  curr_tl.removeFrames(1, numFrames);
  curr_tl.setFrameProperty('tweenType', 'none', 0);
  curr_tl.currentFrame = 0;
  curr_doc.selectAll();
  curr_doc.breakApart();
  curr_doc.exitEditMode();
```

```
  curr_tl = curr_doc.getTimeline();
  var selFrames = curr_tl.getSelectedFrames();
  curr_tl.removeFrames(selFrames[1]+1, selFrames[2]);
  curr_tl.setSelectedFrames(selFrames[1], selFrames[1]);
}
```

None of the code has been changed, just moved around a bit. See that executeEffect calls doEffect, and removeEffect calls undoEffect as their only actions.

1. Now let's take care of step 1 outlined earlier, applying the effect with default values (that is, with no dialog box). Here's the first point that you need to use the configureEffect function. In this, you tell the effect to not use the XML to UI dialog box.

   ```
   function configureEffect(){
     curr_eff = fl.activeEffect;
     curr_eff.useXMLToUI = false;
   }
   ```

   Then you need to set up some default values for the duration and scale. You can do that in executeEffect, since it only needs to happen once.

   ```
   function executeEffect(){
     duration = 20;
     scale = 200;
     doEffect();
   }
   ```

   You can go ahead and try that out if you want and see that the effect is instantly applied with those values. Don't forget to reload your effects to get the configureEffect function to reconfigure things.

2. The next step relates to exporting the symbol as a SWF file. This is done via the exportSWF function, naturally enough. You just need to give it a URI describing where to save the SWF. But this function is a method of a Library item, not an instance on the stage. So, first you need to find out which Library item this symbol is based on. You can do that with these two lines:

   ```
   curr_elem = curr_doc.selection[0];
   curr_item = curr_elem.libraryItem;
   ```

   Then you need to change that item from a graphic symbol to a movie clip, so it will retain its animation when it's exported to SWF and loaded in later. The next two lines convert it to a clip and export it:

   ```
   curr_item.symbolType = "movie clip";
   curr_item.exportSWF(fl.configURI + "/Effects/growPreview.swf");
   ```

   Note the location that you save the SWF, in the Effects folder. This code will all go in right after you exit edit mode, and the newly created symbol is sitting onstage, selected:

   ```
   function doEffect(){
     var curr_eff = fl.activeEffect;
   ```

```
  var curr_doc = fl.getDocumentDOM();
  var curr_tl = curr_doc.getTimeline();
  theFrame = curr_tl.currentFrame;
  curr_tl.insertFrames(curr_eff.duration-1);
  curr_doc.enterEditMode();
  curr_tl = curr_doc.getTimeline();
  curr_tl.insertFrames(curr_eff.duration-1);
  curr_tl.createMotionTween(0, curr_eff.duration-1);
  curr_tl.convertToKeyframes(curr_eff.duration-1);
  curr_tl.currentFrame = curr_eff.duration-1;
  curr_doc.selectAll();
  curr_doc.scaleSelection(curr_eff.scale/100, curr_eff.scale/100,
➥"center");
  curr_doc.exitEditMode();
  curr_elem = curr_doc.selection[0];
  curr_item = curr_elem.libraryItem;
  curr_item.symbolType = "movie clip";
  curr_item.exportSWF(fl.configURI + "/Effects/growPreview.swf");
  curr_tl = curr_doc.getTimeline();
  curr_tl.currentFrame = theFrame;
}
```

4

If you run the file at this point, you won't notice any difference, but if you dig around your `Effects` folder, you should find a file named `growPreview.swf`. Go ahead and check it out and make sure that it reflects the effect you just created.

3. Now you're almost ready to call up your XML to UI dialog box with enclosed SWF. But before you do that, you need to save your properties (duration and scale) in a way that the SWF UI can access them. We found that the most reliable way to do so is to add it as persistent data in the document. This way, not only is it accessible by the SWF UI, but it will remain with the document as it's closed and reopened.

   Once you've saved the data, you can call up the XML to UI file. This goes right at the end of the function.

```
function doEffect(){
  var curr_eff = fl.activeEffect;
  var curr_doc = fl.getDocumentDOM();
  var curr_tl = curr_doc.getTimeline();
  theFrame = curr_tl.currentFrame;
  curr_tl.insertFrames(curr_eff.duration-1);
  curr_doc.enterEditMode();
  curr_tl = curr_doc.getTimeline();
  curr_tl.insertFrames(curr_eff.duration-1);
  curr_tl.createMotionTween(0, curr_eff.duration-1);
  curr_tl.convertToKeyframes(curr_eff.duration-1);
  curr_tl.currentFrame = curr_eff.duration-1;
  curr_doc.selectAll();
  curr_doc.scaleSelection(curr_eff.scale/100, curr_eff.scale/100,
➥"center");
  curr_doc.exitEditMode();
```

```
  curr_elem = curr_doc.selection[0];
  curr_item = curr_elem.libraryItem;
  curr_item.symbolType = "movie clip";
  curr_item.exportSWF(fl.configURI + "/Effects/growPreview.swf");
  curr_tl = curr_doc.getTimeline();
  curr_tl.currentFrame = theFrame;
  curr_doc.addDataToDocument("duration", "string", duration);
  curr_doc.addDataToDocument("scale", "string", scale);
  var result = curr_doc.xmlPanel(fl.configURI + "/Effects/grow.xml");
}
```

Now if you try it out at this point, you'll get an error, because the xmlPanel function is looking in the XML for a <dialog> tag and not finding it. So add a <dialog> tag in there that will load the SWF:

```
<group name="My Effects">
  <effect name="Grow2">
  <source file="grow2.jsfl">
  <allow types="all">
  <properties>
    <property name="Scale" variable="scale" defaultValue="200" min="0"
➥max="1000" type="Number"/>
    <property name="Duration" variable="duration" defaultValue="20"
➥min="2" max="500" type="Number"/>
    <property name="reset" variable="reset" defaultValue="false"
➥type="Boolean"/>
  </properties>
  <dialog id="grow_ui_dialog" buttons="accept, cancel">
    <flash id="grow_ui" src="growUI.swf" width="300" height="200">
      <property id="scale" />
      <property id="duration" />
      <property id="reset" />
    </flash>
  </dialog>
</group>
```

Here you see you can add the XML to UI <dialog> tag right in with the Effect setup XML. The dialog node has one child node, flash. This contains attributes for its ID, source file, width, and height. The ID can be any unique string you want, and the rest are pretty self-explanatory.

Inside the flash node you include three property tags—these are the properties that you want the SWF file to be able to have access to.

4. Next you need to create the Flash interface itself. You can download this file from the book's website—it's called growUI.swf (along with its corresponding FLA). But it's essentially a pretty simple file. It contains only two input text fields, a button, and some code, as shown in Figure 4-15.

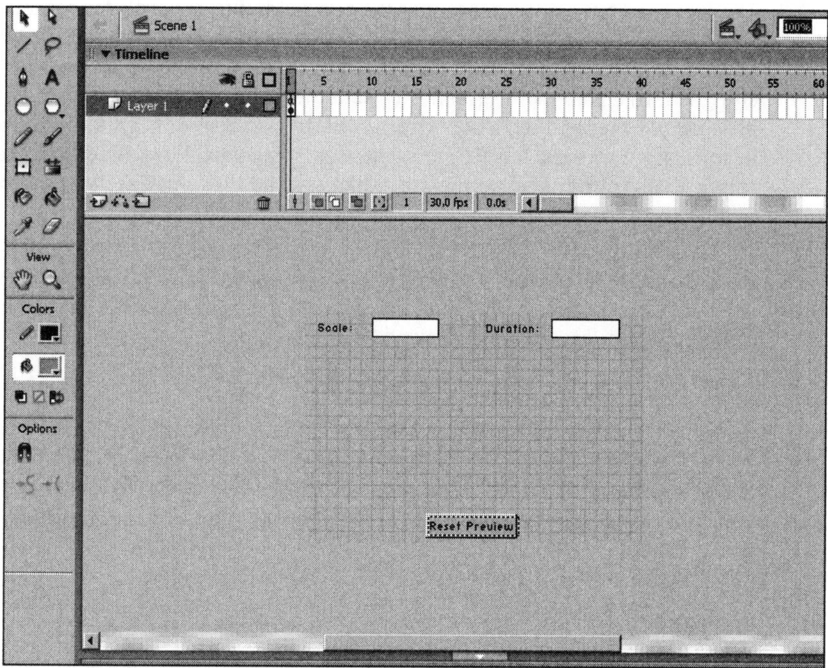

Figure 4-15. The SWF UI for the Grow effect

The text fields are named duration_txt and scale_txt, while the button is reset_btn. Here is the ActionScript on frame one of the main timeline:

```
scale_txt.text =
➥MMExecute("fl.getDocumentDOM().getDataFromDocument(\"scale\");");
duration_txt.text =
➥MMExecute("fl.getDocumentDOM().getDataFromDocument(\"duration\");");
createEmptyMovieClip("holder", 0);
holder._x = 200;
holder._y = 100;
holder.loadMovie("growPreview.swf");
reset_btn.onRelease = function() {
  XMLUI.set("scale", scale_txt.text);
  XMLUI.set("duration", duration_txt.text);
  XMLUI.set("reset", "true");
  XMLUI.accept();
};
```

4

The first two lines set the content of the text fields. But now you see something you haven't run into before, MMExecute. This is covered in full detail in Chapter 7, but you get a sneak peek at it here. MMExecute takes a string as an argument. That string is a JSFL statement or series of statements. This is very similar to when you assigned a string to the ActionScript property of a frame or symbol in Chapter 2. In this case, however, the JSFL statement is immediately executed. If there is any return value from that statement, it's then returned from MMExecute. For example, in line 1, you have

```
scale_txt.text =
➥MMExecute("fl.getDocumentDOM().getDataFromDocument(\"scale\");");
```

This string translates to the following JSFL statement:

```
fl.getDocumentDOM().getDataFromDocument("scale");
```

Remember that you added data to the document in the configureEffect function, under the name scale. This statement will return the value of that data to the MMExecute function, which then assigns it to the text property of the scale_txt text field. Phew! That's quite an operation for one line of code. Figure 4-16 illustrates it more clearly.

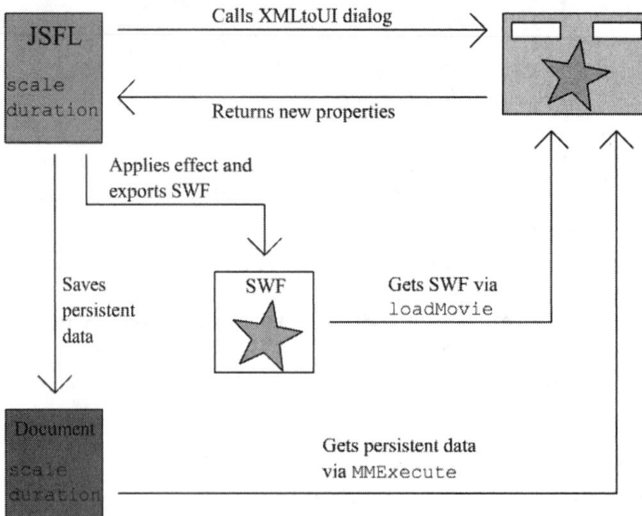

Figure 4-16. Creating a preview SWF file

You then do the same thing for the duration text field. Then you create an empty movie clip and load the previously created preview SWF file into it. You know it's already created, because you took care of that before you called up the dialog box. And you know it's in the Effects folder. If you keep this SWF file in the Effects folder as well, you can just call it up directly.

5. Finally you set the actions for the button. This is what will happen if the user clicks Reset Preview:

```
XMLUI.set("scale", scale_txt.text);
XMLUI.set("duration", duration_txt.text);
XMLUI.set("reset", "true");
XMLUI.accept();
```

The XMLUI object is a new addition to ActionScript. It's a way for a Flash movie to communicate with the XML to UI dialog box that contains it. Here you use it to set a couple of properties: It sets the duration and scale values to whatever is currently in the two text fields. These presumably changed since the file first loaded, which is why the user is resetting the preview. You also set reset to true (you'll see why shortly).

Then you call XMLUI.accept(). This is the same as if the user clicked the OK button. It closes the dialog box and gives control back to the JSFL file, which will continue with the next line after the xmlPanel call.

6. OK, still tracking with everything so far? Feel free to go over it a few times to make sure you follow the sequence of actions up to now. We know it gets pretty complex; after all, you're dealing with interaction between four different files: JSFL, XML, preview SWF, and UI SWF.

Returning to the JSFL file, you now have three possibilities: The user has either clicked OK, Cancel, or Reset Preview. You'll examine reset first.

You've saved the return value of the xmlPanel call in a variable called result. If the user clicked Reset, then this variable should now contain three properties: duration, scale, and reset (in addition to the dismiss property it gets automatically). First, you'll check if the reset property is true and, if so, you'll update the duration and scale properties in the JSFL file itself. Then you'll undo the effect and apply it again with the new values. Now you see why you moved the execute and remove code to new functions.

```
function doEffect(){
  var curr_eff = fl.activeEffect;
  var curr_doc = fl.getDocumentDOM();
  var curr_tl = curr_doc.getTimeline();
  theFrame = curr_tl.currentFrame;
  curr_tl.insertFrames(curr_eff.duration-1);
  curr_doc.enterEditMode();
  curr_tl = curr_doc.getTimeline();
  curr_tl.insertFrames(curr_eff.duration-1);
  curr_tl.createMotionTween(0, curr_eff.duration-1);
  curr_tl.convertToKeyframes(curr_eff.duration-1);
  curr_tl.currentFrame = curr_eff.duration-1;
  curr_doc.selectAll();
  curr_doc.scaleSelection(curr_eff.scale/100, curr_eff.scale/100,
➥"center");
  curr_doc.exitEditMode();
  curr_elem = curr_doc.selection[0];
  curr_item = curr_elem.libraryItem;
```

```
    curr_item.symbolType = "movie clip";
    curr_item.exportSWF(fl.configURI + "/Effects/growPreview.swf");
    curr_tl = curr_doc.getTimeline();
    curr_tl.currentFrame = theFrame;
    curr_doc.addDataToDocument("duration", "string", duration);
    curr_doc.addDataToDocument("scale", "string", scale);
    var result = curr_doc.xmlPanel(fl.configURI + "/Effects/grow.xml");
    if(result.reset){
      duration = result.duration;
      scale = result.scale;
      undoEffect();
      doEffect();
    }
  }
```

When the script calls the doEffect again, it will re-create the effect with the new properties. It will then automatically save a new preview SWF and once again call up the XML to UI dialog box. The SWF UI will load and display the preview. Even though the dialog box is closing and reopening again, unless you have a very complex effect, it should not look like more than a flicker to the user.

7. This cycle of reapplying the effect, exporting a preview, and calling up the dialog box will continue as long as the user keeps hitting reset. If that user hits anything else, the program will simply end off the function and be done. Since the effect has already been created and previewed, there is nothing more to do.

The only thing left to handle is if the user clicks Cancel. In this case, you'll want to remove the effect. You can do this directly with the removeEffect function. However, since you've kind of shortcut the usual process, you'll need to break apart the final symbol manually, so here is the relevant code addition for the doEffect function:

```
function doEffect(){
  var curr_doc = fl.getDocumentDOM();
  var curr_tl = curr_doc.getTimeline();
  theFrame = curr_tl.currentFrame;
  curr_tl.insertFrames(duration-1);
  curr_doc.enterEditMode();
  curr_tl = curr_doc.getTimeline();
  curr_tl.insertFrames(duration-1);
  curr_tl.createMotionTween(0, duration-1);
  curr_tl.convertToKeyframes(duration-1);
  curr_tl.currentFrame = duration-1;
  curr_doc.selectAll();
  curr_doc.scaleSelection(scale/100, scale/100, "center");
  curr_doc.exitEditMode();
  curr_elem = curr_doc.selection[0];
```

```
  curr_item = curr_elem.libraryItem;
  curr_item.symbolType = "movie clip";
  curr_item.exportSWF(fl.configURI + "/Effects/growPreview.swf");
  curr_tl = curr_doc.getTimeline();
  curr_tl.currentFrame = theFrame;
  curr_doc.addDataToDocument("duration", "string", duration);
  curr_doc.addDataToDocument("scale", "string", scale);
  var result = curr_doc.xmlPanel(fl.configURI + "/Effects/grow.xml");
  if(result.reset){
    duration = result.duration;
    scale = result.scale;
    undoEffect();
    doEffect();
  } else if(result.dismiss == "cancel"){
    removeEffect();
    curr_doc.breakApart();
  }
}
```

4

There is one last detail to take care of to make this more professional. As it stands, if the user closes the file and reloads it and goes to edit the effect, the default values will be applied, rather than the last saved values. These values are stored in the file, so it's no problem to load them up. You just need to check for them and load them if they exist, and otherwise use the default values. This happens in executeEffect:

```
function executeEffect(){
  var curr_doc = fl.getDocumentDOM();
  if(curr_doc.documentHasData("duration")){
    duration = curr_doc.getDataFromDocument("duration");
  } else {
    duration = 20;
  }
  if(curr_doc.documentHasData("scale")){
    scale = curr_doc.getDataFromDocument("scale");
  } else {
    scale = 200;
  }
  doEffect();
}
```

This could be made even more professional by storing the data in the symbol itself, so that if the effect were applied to multiple objects in the same document, each would have its own values (see Figure 4-17). But we think we've given you enough to chew on for now!

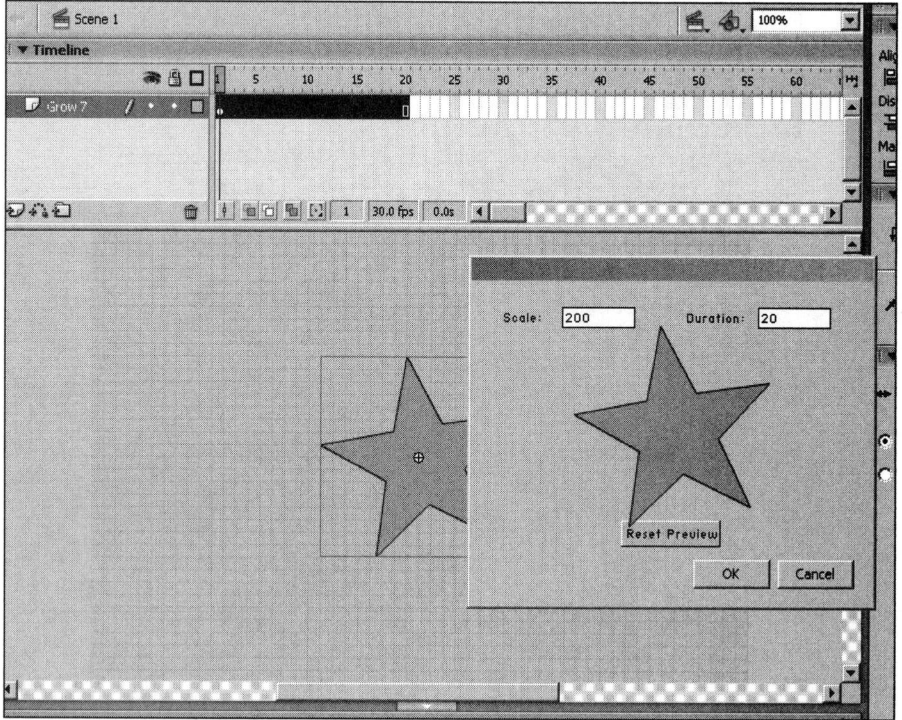

Figure 4-17. The Grow effect in action

Summary

Well, once again, we've covered a lot of territory in this chapter on implementing robust `Timeline Effects`. You should now have all the tools and techniques in your hands to create some pretty stunning effects that can be applied with a few mouse clicks. But more important than specific techniques is the fact that you're gaining an increasingly solid understanding of the DOM and the various objects and methods you can use with JSFL and how each one works. This knowledge will enable you to create many more productive tools with the Flash MX 2004 extensibility architecture. You're slowly but surely becoming a *Master of Extensibility*.

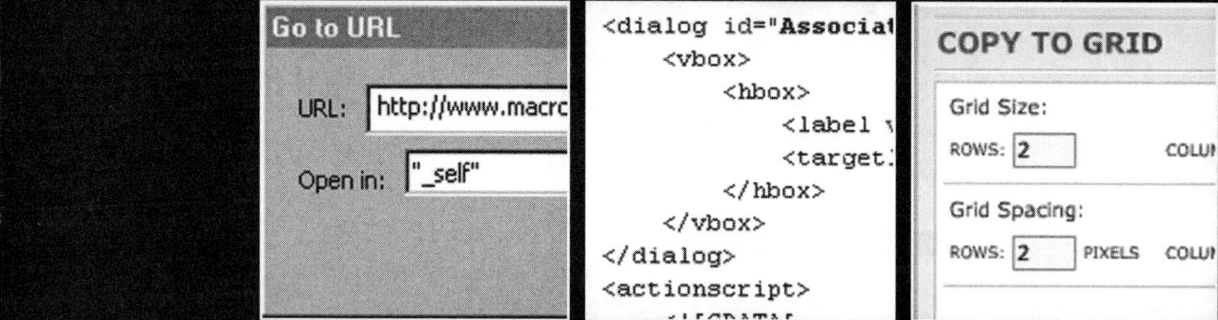
Go to URL
URL:
http://www.macro
Open in:
"_self"
<dialog id="Associat
<vbox>
<hbox>
<label
<target
</hbox>
</vbox>
</dialog>
<actionscript>
COPY TO GRID
Grid Size:
ROWS: 2
Grid Spacing:
ROWS: 2
PIXELS

What the heck is up with all of the acronyms in the title of this chapter? Is it yet another government agency created to bury us in bureaucracy? Perhaps a track from a new hip hop album? In fact, XML to UI, or Extensible Markup Language to User Interface, provides a method in Macromedia Flash MX 2004 for developers to easily create dialog boxes for their behaviors and effects. By utilizing XML to UI, you can give users a way to enter and change parameters for your behavior and effect scripts without being required to create common interface containers or any other such "widgets."

Although we've already shown you XML to UI while presenting commands, tools, and Timeline Effects in the previous chapters, it's an important and useful concept and therefore deserves a chapter to itself for reference. So, in this chapter, after a brief overview of XML, we'll present reference tables describing all of the available XML to UI tags. The real meat of this chapter comes in the latter half, where we demonstrate how to use all of the XML to UI tags in practice by looking at several examples on creating custom dialog boxes for your extensibility tools.

XML to UI in Action

Let's take a look at how XML to UI dialog boxes can work hand in hand with a behavior by using one of the behaviors that is provided with Flash. Note that we'll cover behaviors in detail in the next chapter.

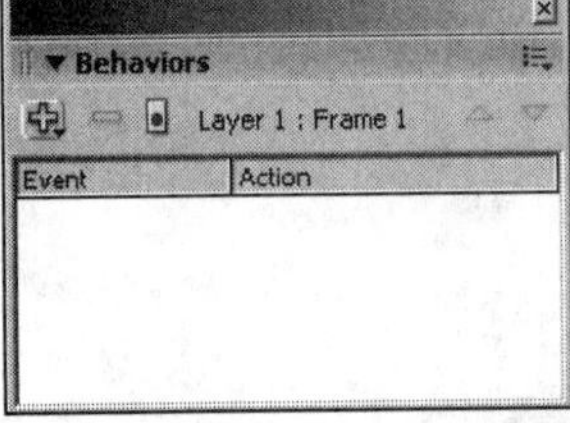

Figure 5-1. The Behaviors panel

Create a new Flash document and open your Behaviors panel, shown in Figure 5-1, by pressing *SHIFT+F3* (again, we'll explore this panel in more depth in Chapter 6).

Click the plus sign at the top left of the panel to access all the behaviors available to your main timeline, and then select Movieclip ➤ Load Graphic. Figure 5-2 shows the dialog box that appears.

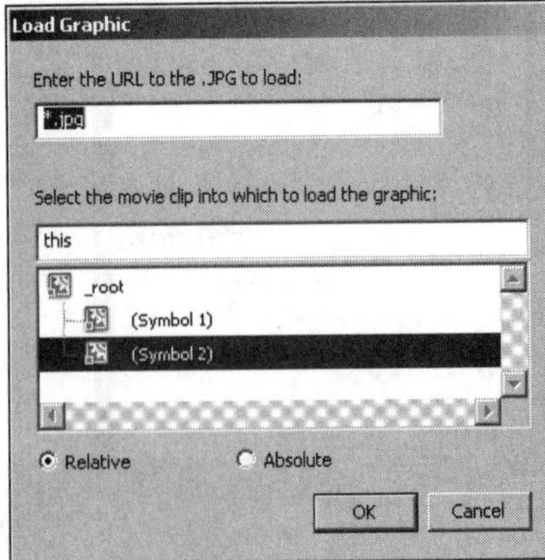

Figure 5-2. The dialog box that appears when the Load Graphic behavior is selected

If you've already added any symbols to the stage, they'll appear below the *_root* element. You might be surprised to know that the XML that follows is all that is required of the developer to create such a dialog box. In fact, opening any behavior that results in a UI dialog box is controlled by similar XML.

```
<!- Copyright 2003 Macromedia, Inc. All Rights Reserved.->
<?xml version="1.0"?>

<flash_behavior version="1.0">

<dialog id="Load Graphic-dialog" title="Load Graphic" buttons="accept,
cancel">
  <grid>
    <columns>
      <column>
        <rows>
          <row align="center">
            <vbox>
              <label value="Enter the URL to the .JPG to load:"/>
              <textbox literal="true" width="40" id="graphic"
➥required="true"/>
            </vbox>
          </row>
        </rows>
        <rows>
          <row align="center">
            <vbox>
              <label value=""/>
              <label value="Select the movie clip into which to load
➥the graphic:"/>
              <targetlist id="target" class="movieclip"/>
            </vbox>
          </row>
        </rows>
      </column>
    </columns>
  </grid>
</dialog>

</flash_behavior>
```

The XML used to create behaviors and effects that ship with Flash MX 2004 can be found in your Flash `Configuration` folder. For example, the commented version of the preceding file is located at `C:\Documents and Settings\Administrator\Local Settings\Application Data\Macromedia\Flash MX 2004\en\Configuration\Behaviors\Graphic_load_graphic.xml` (on a Windows system). The actual file contains a little bit more XML used to create the full behavior, but the dialog box is created with only the preceding lines, and will be the focus of this chapter. (Don't worry, we cover behaviors in detail in the next chapter.)

The Beauty of XML

Before we can show you how to use XML to UI, you need to know exactly what XML is. XML, as noted earlier, stands for Extensible Markup Language and is simply a way to mark and describe structured data or information by tagging it, much like you tag the header or body in an HTML document. XML is ideal for passing data from one application to another since it isn't actually tied to a specific application. Instead, it allows you to define your own structure and tags for data that can then be read by any application set up to read such a structure, like Macromedia Flash is able to do. Let's look quickly at a simple example.

Let's say you want to create a structure for a day planner. You know that the planner will need to show information for years, months, days, and times. Here's an unstructured way of writing information for 1:00 p.m. and 5:00 p.m. on December 3, 2004:

```
December 3, 2004 @ 1:00 p.m. : lunch with Keith at Spago
December 3, 2004 @ 5:00 p.m. : meet with Steve at office
```

Easy to read? Sure. Can you get Flash (or another application) to read that and use it for a day planner? That could prove difficult since an application doesn't know what each element in the preceding lines represents. How can it tell apart the 3 from the 2004? Those are just numbers that could represent anything. To solve this problem, let's use some tags to structure the data in a form that's not only easily readable, but also defines what each element represents:

```
<year value="2004">
  <month value="12">
    <day value="3">
      <appointment>
        <time>1:00 p.m.</time>
        <place>Spago</time>
        <activity>lunch with Keith</activity>
      </appointment>
      <appointment>
        <time>5:00 p.m.</time>
        <place>office</time>
        <activity>meet with Steve</activity>
      </appointment>
    </day>
  </month>
</year>
```

OK, now you have a nice little hierarchy of information that's not only human-readable, but also structured in a way in which an application might be able to utilize it. Each element of information is separated into a different tag, and you can easily discern which elements are contained within other elements. Thus, you can put multiple appointments within a single day, and many days within a single month, and so on.

So now that you've seen generally how XML works, we'll break it down and define each individual element, starting with, well, the **elements**.

Elements

XML is composed primarily of *elements* (also referred to as *nodes*), which are the individual tags in the structure. In the preceding example, the first element you see is the `<year>` node. Likewise, year is the node name for the element. Whatever you choose for the node name (and you can name them whatever you please), it must be in lowercase. Also, each element must be enclosed in the standard <> symbols, and must contain an open and close tag. So for every `<year>`, you'll also have a `</year>`, for every `<month>`, a `</month>`, and so on. If an element has no children (other elements or character data contained within), then it may be closed within the same tag: `<year />`. Note that since element names are case sensitive (or rather, lowercase sensitive), the open and close tags must both be in all lowercase.

Attributes

Looking back at your day planner XML, you'll see that some elements have additional information within their opening tags. These name/value pairs, like `value="2004"` for the `<year>` node, are called **attributes**. You may have as many attributes as you wish within any single node (some people *only* use attributes to hold their XML data), and you may use whatever names you wish for the attributes, as long as the attribute names are lowercase. The only thing you need to be certain of is that each attribute is given a value contained within quotation marks, and this value can't contain certain characters like &, <, or >, which will need to be "escaped."

Character Data

Any data that lies outside of the <> symbols in a tag is referred to as **character data**. This character data is a child of the element in which it's located. In the day planner example, the lines "lunch with Keith" and "meet with Steve" are character data, each a child of a separate `<activity>` element. Often the character data, if used at all, is contained within the innermost elements of the XML hierarchy, though it can be included with any node within the structure.

In addition, character data may be enclosed in a special `<![CDATA[]]>` tag. This tag instructs the XML parser to ignore any characters usually reserved for markup. In this way, you can include certain characters that need to be passed to the application without interpretation. You'll use this extensively with behaviors when you need to pass ActionScript commands to Flash.

Comments

As with HTML, ActionScript, or any other type of script or code, XML allows for **commenting** by the developer. This doesn't affect the structure itself, but is merely a helpful way for developers to compose their scripts. Each comment is opened by <!-- and closed with -->. A comment may be single or multiline as well.

Root

Every XML document contains a single **root node** that holds all other elements. In the day planner example, you might define the root as <planner> and contain all of the years within this element. In the behavior XML to UI example that you saw earlier, the root node is defined as <flash_behavior>. Notice that all other elements are contained within this <flash_behavior> node.

Declaration

The first thing that must appear in an XML document is the **declaration**, which tells whichever application that is reading the XML some important information. Look to the behavior example once more. The first line you see is

```
<?xml version="1.0"?>
```

The declaration is enclosed in <?xml ?> tags, and in this case contains a single attribute defining the version number. Additional attributes can be included, such as encoding or standalone. These aren't required for your use in XML to UI, so we won't discuss them here. Just remember that this line is the first one you need when creating an XML file.

XML to UI tags

OK, so if XML doesn't contain any predefined tags (that's the beauty of XML, right?), we bet you're wondering how you create those lovely dialog boxes. The answer? XUL! Wait a minute! Is this yet another acronym for you to digest? Yep, but it's an important one for your XML to UI knowledge. **XUL** (pronounced *zool*) stands for XML User Interface Language, and is a set of tags developed to define feature-rich cross-platform applications with XML. In other words, some really nice folk have already created the means for you to create dialog boxes through XML. If you want to find out more on XUL, head to www.mozilla.org/projects/xul/. The XML to UI tags you'll be using are actually a subset of XUL, which means that although you don't have as many options available for your dialog boxes as you would if you used the entirety of XUL, at least you have fewer tags to learn!

So what tags are available for your use? We'll look at each element individually in the examples that follow later in this chapter, but first we present a couple of tables for you to refer to during your learning and development. The content of these tables is divided between the **layout** and **control** tags of XML to UI.

Layout Tags

Tag	Description	Attributes	Child Nodes
<dialog>	The element to hold the entirety of the box (i.e., all other elements)	1. id: Identification for dialog box 2. title: Label for title bar dialog 3. buttons: Default buttons in dialog box: accept, cancel, or both	<hbox> <vbox> <grid>
<hbox>, **<vbox>**	Horizontal and vertical boxes in which to lay out widgets	None	<hbox> <vbox> <spacer> <separator> Any control element
<grid>	Tabular layout definition for widgets	None	<columns> <rows>
<columns>	Vertical element within the grid element	None	<column>
<rows>	Horizontal element within the grid element	None	<row>
<column>	Individual column within the grid	None	<spacer> Any control element
<row>	Individual row within the grid	None	<spacer> Any control element
<spacer>	Empty buffer space	None	None
<separator>	Vertical or horizontal bar to separate elements	None	None

Control Tags

Tag	Description	Attributes	Child Nodes
`<button>`	Button for users to press	1. id: Identification for button 2. label: Label for button 3. tabindex: Position in tab ordering 4. accesskey: Keyboard key which, when pressed, will call button's function 5. oncommand: JavaScript function to be called when button is pressed	None
`<checkbox>`	On/off toggle	1. id: Identification for check box 2. label: Label for check box 3. tabindex: Position in tab ordering 4. checked: Whether the check box is checked by default (true or false) 5. accesskey: Keyboard key which, when pressed, will toggle the check box	None
`<colorchip>`	Array of color swatches	1. id: Identification for color chip 2. color: Initial color displayed in color chip	None
`<flash>`	Flash movie embedded in a dialog box	1. id: Identification for Flash movie 2. width: Width for display of SWF height: Height for display of SWF 3. src: File path to SWF	`<property>`
`<label>`	Static text to mark widget	1. control: Associated control element for label 2. value: Text displayed in label	None
`<listbox>`	List of items to choose from	1. id: Identification for list box 2. tabindex: Position in tab ordering 3. rows: Number of rows displayed in list	`<listitem>`
`<listitem>`	Individual item in the list box	1. label: Text displayed in item 2. value: Value for item to be used in scripts 3. selected: Item selected by default when dialog box is opened (true or false)	None
`<menulist>`	Drop-down list	1. id: Identification for drop-down list 2. tabindex: Position in tab ordering	`<menupop>`
`<menupop>`	Pop-up list for the menu list	None	`<menuitem>`

Table continues on the following page

Tag	Description	Attributes	Child Nodes
<menuitem>	Individual item in the menu list	1. label: Text displayed in item 2. value: Value for item to be used in scripts 3. selected: Item selected by default when dialog box is opened (true or false)	None
<popupslider>	Slider bar to adjust values within a range	1. id: Identification for slider 2. tabindex: Position in tab ordering 3. minvalue: The minimum value allowed in slider 4. maxvalue: The maximum value allowed in slider	None
<property>	Dialog box property defined within <flash> element	1. id: Name of property being defined	None
<radiogroup>	Group of radio buttons, in which only one option may be selected	1. id: Identification for group of radio buttons 2. tabindex: Position in tab ordering	<radio>
<radio>	Individual radio option	1. label: Label for radio option 2. accesskey: Keyboard key which, when pressed, will select the radio option 3. selected: Option selected by default when dialog box is opened (true or false)	None
<targetlist>	Tree hierarchy of objects in document	1. id: Identification for target list 2. height: Height of element 3. width: Width of element 4. class: Type of objects that the list will display 5. required: Whether a value (such as a reference to a movie clip in the document) is necessary in order for the dialog box to be accepted and closed	None

Table continues on the following page

5

Tag	Description	Attributes	Child Nodes
<textbox>	Input field in which users may type a value	1. `id`: Identification for text box 2. `maxlength`: Maximum number of text characters allowed in text box 3. `tabindex`: Position in tab ordering 4. `value`: Initial text in field when dialog box is opened 5. `multiline`: Whether the text box allows for multiple lines of text (`true` or `false`) 6. `size`: Maximum length (width) of text box in characters 7. `literal`: Whether the text value, when returned, should be wrapped in quotes	None

These are all the tags you'll need to familiarize yourself with. Now let's get cracking on defining some dialog boxes so you can see how it all fits together!

Creating a Dialog Box

XML to UI dialog boxes can be utilized in a number of areas to get feedback from the user. For instance, most behaviors will have a dialog box for users to enter parameters—go ahead and drop some of the preset behaviors onto the stage or a movie clip to see these in action. Timeline Effects such as those found under Insert ➤ Timeline Effects can also take advantage of these dialog boxes (see Chapter 4), even if they consist mostly of the Flash movie embedded inside. In fact, you can create a dialog box using XML to UI any time you use the JavaScript API, whether it be in a JSFL file, or within a Flash movie that calls JavaScript commands using `MMExecute` (discussed further in Chapter 7). Don't worry about *all* of the many uses of XML to UI right now or how to incorporate them. As you work through this book, you'll begin to see how to take advantage of XML to UI for your effects and behaviors, and you'll incorporate dialog boxes using XML to UI in later chapters. Indeed, if you've been going through this book's chapters in sequential order, you'll no doubt already have a good idea of some of the possibilities. For the moment, let's concentrate on what you can do *within* the dialog box and how to use the XML tags to create the dialog boxes you need.

> *Note that XMl to UI dialog boxes are* modal, *which means that while they are open, nothing else in the interface can be accessed. The dialog box will need to be closed—either accepted or canceled out of—before the interface once again becomes available.*

In order to make testing and executing new dialog boxes easy, you're going to create a test file that you can modify and from which you can see results without having to relaunch Flash. You'll accomplish this using a SWF file you can open within the authoring environment.

SWF in a Window

1. Launch Flash and create a new Flash document using the menu command File ➤ New ➤ Flash Document. Save the new movie as `testXMLtoUI.fla`. (Alternatively, you can always download this file from `www.flashextensibility.com` and edit the ActionScript as described in step 5.) Save it anywhere for the time being, though you'll need to drop it into a specific folder in a moment.
2. Go to Modify ➤ Document and make the movie's dimensions 150-by-100 pixels. Change the background color to #666666.
3. Create a new layer in your movie. You should now have two layers in all. Name the top layer "script" and the bottom layer "button".
4. Open up your Components panel (CTRL+F7), expand the `UI Components` section, and find the Button component. Drag and drop an instance onto your stage and center it, giving the instance the name launch_bn in the Properties panel. Next, with the button selected, use the Parameters tab of the Properties panel to set the button's label to launch as shown in Figure 5-3.

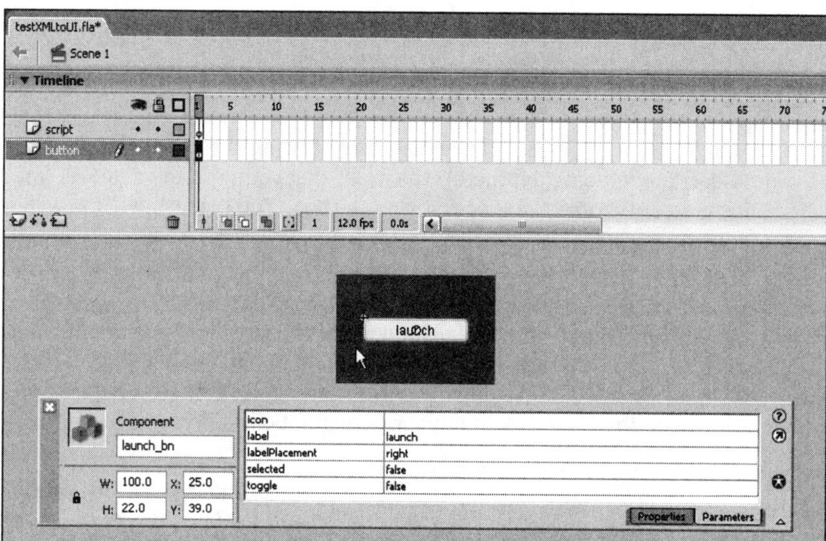

Figure 5-3. The timeline, stage, and button parameters for the interface

5. Select frame one of the movie and open your Actions panel (*F9*). Type the following:

```
function click() {
  var js = "fl.trace(fl.configURI);";
  MMExecute(js);
}
launch_bn.addEventListener("click", this);
```

So much that's new! What you have here is a function named `click` that places a string into a variable called `js`, then runs a command called `MMExecute`, sending it the `js` variable. We're going to have a whole chapter dealing with MMExecute later in this book (Chapter 7), but it's actually fairly easy to understand in this simple case. You see, `MMExecute` allows you to call any JavaScript API command from any SWF UI within the Flash authoring environment. Now that's a rather simple explanation for a fantastically powerful command. What this means is that you can create SWFs that, when opened in Flash (like in a component UI or an effect window), can alter almost any part of the Flash document. Now that's power!

`MMExecute` accepts a string argument, which is how you've formatted the JavaScript that you place in the `js` variable. Note that this command will not work within the testing environment, but only within SWFs that are opened from within the Flash authoring environment. In other words, don't expect anything to happen right now when you test your movie! However, let's break down the JavaScript so you may see what *will* happen eventually.

1. `fl`: A reference to the Flash application
2. `trace`: Displays strings to the Output panel
3. `configURI`: The path to the local `Configuration` folder of the Flash application

This first line of JavaScript then is simply tracing the path to the `Configuration` folder. You're doing this merely to ensure that you drop this test SWF you're creating into the correct folder for your testing. You'll see how this will help in a moment.

Your string is set to call the `trace` method in Flash. This will send a string to the same Output panel that opens and displays `trace` commands when you're testing movies within the authoring environment. What are you asking to be traced? The `fl.configURI` will return the path to the Configuration folder. By sending this string to your `MMExecute` command, you should get a nice message in your Output window of the correct path to your Configuration folder!

The final line in your code adds your main timeline as a listener for click events fired off by your launch_bn. When the button is clicked, the `click` function you've defined on your main timeline will be called and the Output window should display your trace.

6. Test or publish your movie in order to create a SWF file. This means you should have both a FLA file and a SWF file named testXMLtoUI. Then close the document and exit Flash (close the application entirely). This is necessary in order for you to reopen Flash and have your movie recognized as a WindowSWF to be opened in the authoring environment.

Now, you need to find the WindowSWF folder to drop this movie into. On your hard drive, you can either do a search for WindowSWF, or browse in your Local Settings for the relevant application data files. Readers who've read the earlier chapters of this book will already be familiar with dropping files into their local settings configuration folders. In this case, for a Windows system, you're looking in this location: C:\Documents and Settings\<user name>\Local Settings\Application Data\Macromedia\Flash MX 2004\en\Configuration\WindowSWF. Once the test files are in the WindowSWF folder, you can open the SWF from within Flash and your MMExecute will trace the proper location for your files (remember the trace call you wrote earlier?).

> *Note for Mac users: The* WindowSWF *folder isn't automatically created during the installation as it is on a PC. If you haven't installed an extension requiring the folder or created the folder yourself up to this point, you'll need to create a new folder named* WindowSWF *within the* Configuration *folder. Once it's created, drop* testXMLtoUI.fla *and* testXMLtoUI.swf *into this folder.*

7. Drop both testXMLtoUI.fla and testXMLtoUI.swf into your local WindowSWF folder that you found in the previous step, and then relaunch Flash.
8. Once Flash has reopened, open a new Flash Document and go to Window ➤ Other Panels and you should see testXMLtoUI underneath the separator bar (see Figure 5-4). Pretty easy adding a window into Flash, isn't it?

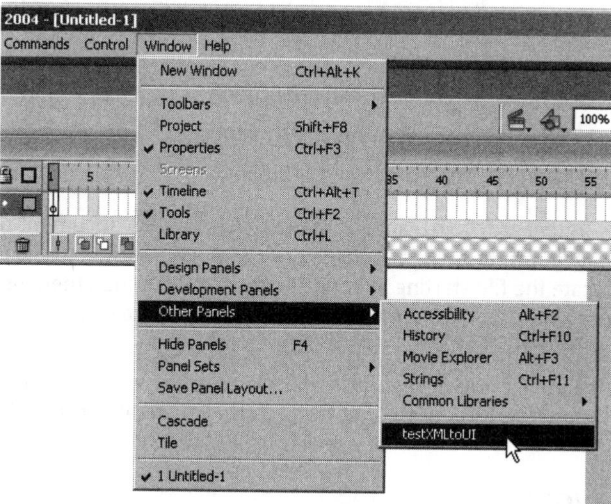

Figure 5-4. Accessing your new window

If you now open that window, you should see your movie with the button in the center of the stage. Press the button and your Output window should open with a nice path for you, as shown in Figure 5-5. There you are—a neat way to prove it was the correct path to your Configuration folder!

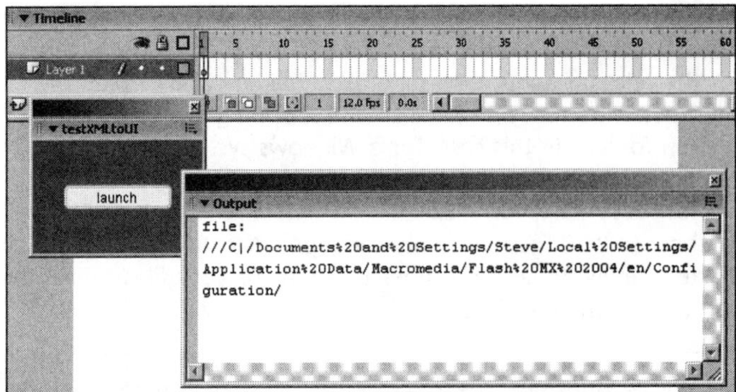

Figure 5-5. The path to the Configuration folder as traced from the WindowSWF movie

9. Now that you have your FLA and SWF files in the correct folder, you can get rid of your trace and replace it with a line that will help test your XML to UI dialog boxes. Change the click function to read as follows:

```
function click() {
  var js = "fl.getDocumentDOM().xmlPanel(fl.configURI+
➥\"WindowSWF/testXMLtoUI.xml\");"
  MMExecute(js);
}
```

   The JavaScript that you now send to your MMExecute function breaks down as follows:

   1. fl: A reference to the Flash application
   2. getDocumentDOM(): Returns the current document in the application
   3. xmlPanel(): Opens an XML to UI panel

   The argument for xmlPanel is the path to the XML document defining the XML to UI panel, formatted as a string. Notice that you're using fl.configURI to tell Flash to locate the file starting at your Configuration folder, then inside your WindowSWF folder where this test movie is located. This is where you'll save your XML file in the next exercise.

10. Compile your movie, then save and close. You now have a WindowSWF movie that will launch an XML to UI dialog box (once you create an XML file, of course!).

Dialog Layout

That previous exercise was required in order for you to be able to quickly and easily test different configurations of XML to UI dialog boxes. Because you now have a SWF that will open up in a window and read in an XML file fresh each time, you can change the XML defining your dialog box and launch the new dialog box with a simple click of a button. First, of course, you need to write some XML!

<dialog>

1. Open your favorite text editor and type in the following XML:

```
<?xml version="1.0" ?>
<dialog id="test-dialog-box" title="Test Dialog Box" >
</dialog>
```

   You don't actually need the XML declaration in order for a dialog box to work, but it doesn't hurt to include it since it's better form. Notice that you have a single element currently defined with the node name dialog. This will always be the root node of your dialog box XML. The node currently has two attributes, id and title. The id attribute doesn't serve much purpose for your dialog boxes and more than anything is included because it's good form to have an ID for your elements. It will become more important later when you write behaviors. The title attribute, however, will define the text in the title bar for your dialog box. Remember that you must close every tag you open, and so </dialog> will always end your dialog box definitions.

2. Save this file as testXMLtoUI.xml into the same Configuration/WindowSWF folder as your testXMLtoUI.fla file (as described in the previous exercise). Then open your test movie through Window ➤ Other Panel ➤ testXMLtoUI (you'll need to have at least one document opened, even a blank one, in order to access Window ➤ Other Panels). Once your test SWF file opens, click the launch button. A dialog box should open up (see Figure 5-6)! Not that it's a very pretty dialog box, or indeed at all useful . . .

   Figure 5-6. The world's smallest dialog box

   In fact, since there are no elements inside the dialog box, what you have is the smallest window the application will allow. The title can't be read and there doesn't appear to be a way to close it! Not to worry. Hit *Esc* on your keyboard to close the window and you'll try again (*Esc* can *always* be used to close an XML to UI dialog box).

3. In your testXMLtoUI.xml file, add another attribute to the <dialog> element:

```
<dialog id="test-dialog-box" title="Test Dialog Box"
➥buttons="accept,cancel">
```

   The <dialog> element takes one more attribute, buttons, that can equal either or both of the options accept and cancel; the former sends the dialog box's values back to wherever the dialog box was called (and will actually have a label of OK), while the latter exits the dialog box without sending its values back.

4. Save the XML file and click the launch button in your test movie again (you don't ever need to close this test movie window—this was the reason for all of the steps in the last section). You should see a new dialog box like the one in Figure 5-7 open and proudly displaying two horizontally laid out buttons. Nice!

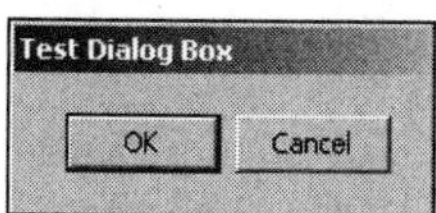

Figure 5-7. The standard system buttons for a dialog box

> *The* buttons *attribute actually accepts one other type of button:* help. *Although this is standard in XUL, it doesn't appear to have any current use in XML to UI, since you can't set any particular function to be called with the system buttons. Both* cancel *and* accept *have default functionality included.* help*, however, does not.*

Now that you have a simple dialog box, let's fill it with user interface elements (which, of course, is the entire reason for XML to UI!). There are three elements that you can use as child nodes of the `<dialog>` element: `<hbox>`, `<vbox>`, and `<grid>`. All three of these child nodes help to define the layout of the dialog box. In order to demonstrate how each works, we'll show you a control element, `<button>`, and some of the many ways you can lay it out inside the dialog box.

<hbox>

5. Add the following bold lines to your XML:

```
<dialog id="test-dialog-box" title="Test Dialog Box"
➥buttons="accept,cancel">
  <hbox>
    <button id="button1" label="one" />
    <button id="button2" label="two" />
    <button id="button3" label="three" />
  </hbox>
</dialog>
```

The <hbox> element defines a horizontal layout of elements and doesn't have any attributes to worry about. The elements within the <hbox> element will simply be laid out side by side. You can see that your `<button>` control elements currently have two attributes apiece (though we'll discuss more attributes later): `id`, which is the identifier for the element, and `label`, which defines the text for the button.

6. Save the XML file and click once more the `launch` button within your `WindowSWF` test file in Flash. Notice how the three buttons are laid out in the dialog box as shown in Figure 5-8.

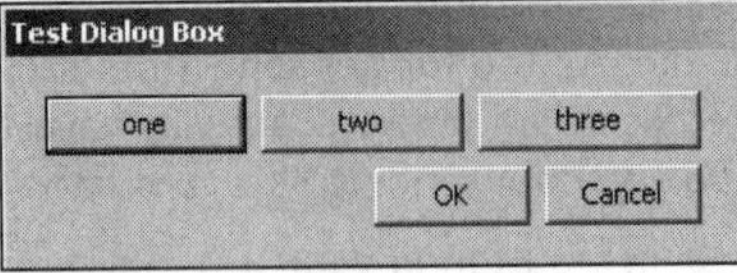

Figure 5-8. A dialog box demonstrating the <hbox> element with three buttons laid out horizontally

<vbox>

7. Now change the <hbox> element to <vbox> (remember to change both the start and end tags!). Save the XML and launch a new dialog box to see the new layout. As you can see, the <vbox> tags help to define a vertical layout of elements inside the dialog box. Notice that the `three` button is slightly wider than the `one` and `two` buttons. This is because the buttons size themselves based on their labels. Currently, there is no way for you to define the width or height of a button.

8. You can nest <hbox> and <vbox> tags within each other as well. Try this in your XML:

```
<dialog id="test-dialog-box" title="Test Dialog Box"
➥buttons="accept,cancel">
  <hbox>
    <button id="buttonLeft" label="left" />
    <vbox>
      <button id="button1" label="one" />
      <button id="button2" label="two" />
      <button id="button3" label="three" />
    </vbox>
    <button id="buttonRight" label="right" />
  </hbox>
</dialog>
```

Here you have a horizontal layout defined by the <hbox> element. Within this, though, you have a button labeled left, then a vertical layout of three buttons defined by the <vbox> element, then another button labeled right. Save the XML and launch the new dialog box to see the results. Notice in Figure 5-9 that the buttons are aligned vertically on the left within the <vbox> (there is no way to change this alignment).

5

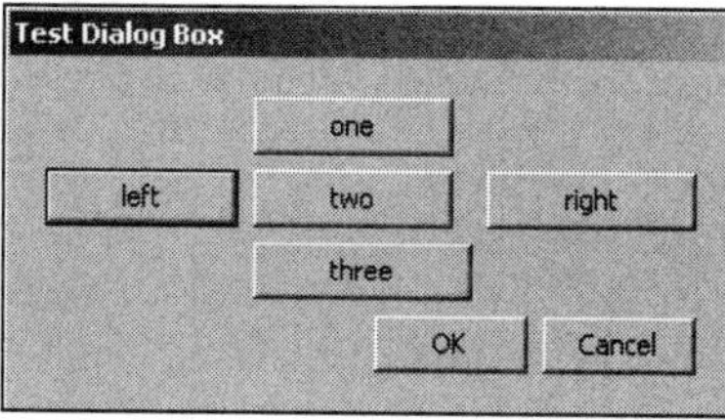

Figure 5-9.
A dialog box demonstrating the <hbox> and <vbox> elements. The center item within the horizontal layout is a vertical layout of three buttons (one, two, three).

<separator>

9. In order to visually separate controls in vertical and horizontal boxes, you can use the <separator> element, which draws a separator bar in your dialog box. Add the following nodes to your XML:

```
<dialog id="test-dialog-box" title="Test Dialog Box"
➥buttons="accept,cancel">
  <hbox>
    <button id="buttonLeft" label="left" />
    <separator />
    <vbox>
      <button id="button1" label="one" />
      <separator />
      <button id="button2" label="two" />
      <separator />
      <button id="button3" label="three" />
    </vbox>
    <separator />
```

```
    <button id="buttonRight" label="right" />
  </hbox>
</dialog>
```

You'll notice that <separator> elements inside an <hbox> element will draw vertically, while those inside a <vbox> element will draw horizontally (see Figure 5-10).

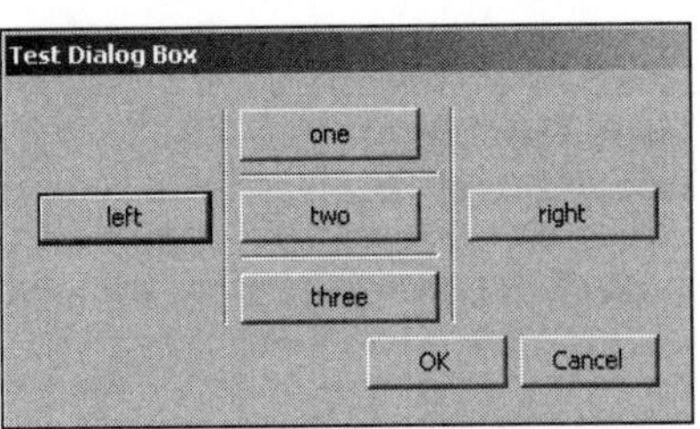

Figure 5-10.
Separator bars added to the <vbox> and <hbox> elements

<grid>, <columns>, <column>, <rows>, <row>

10. In addition to <hbox> and <vbox>, a dialog box can use the <grid> element to define a tabular layout for the dialog box. <grid> works by nesting <columns> and <rows> elements inside it to define the layout of the grid. <grid> can *only* nest these two tags within itself. <columns>, in turn, can *only* contain <column> tags and <rows> can *only* contain <row> tags.

Let's look at an example, then break it down further. Change your XML to read as follows:

```
<dialog id="test-dialog-box" title="Test Dialog Box"
➥buttons="accept,cancel">
  <grid>
    <columns>
      <column />
      <column />
      <column />
    </columns>
    <rows>
      <row>
        <button id="button1" label="one" />
        <button id="button2" label="two" />
        <button id="button3" label="three" />
      </row>
    </rows>
  </grid>
</dialog>
```

You can see here that the <dialog> element contains a single <grid> element (though you may include multiple grids), which doesn't have any attributes to define. Within the <grid> element you have a single <columns> element and a single <rows> element. Neither of these have any attributes either. Officially, these two elements are all that the <grid> element should contain (although you might find examples that contain multiple <columns> or <rows> tags, this isn't correct according to the specification of XUL).

The <columns> element can only contain one or more <column> elements, but no other kind of element. These individual <column> elements have no attributes to define and will have no children. What's the point, then? The number of <column> elements will define the number of columns in your grid. The preceding example, then, creates a grid with three columns.

The <rows> element, similar to the <columns> element, can only contain one or more <row> elements, and no other type of node. Each <row>, however, will contain any or all of the control elements for the dialog box. This would be any the visual elements like buttons, check boxes, labels, etc.

11. Save the XML and launch the dialog box once more to see the results of your XML. You have a nice horizontal layout of buttons, divided into three columns, as you can see in Figure 5-11.

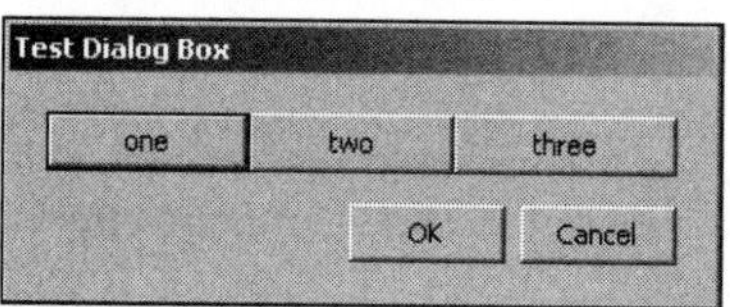

Figure 5-11.
Using a <grid> element to lay out buttons in three columns of a single row

<spacer>

12. Now alter the XML to create three rows, and then place one button on each row and in a different column:

```
<dialog id="test-dialog-box" title="Test Dialog Box"
➥buttons="accept,cancel">
  <grid>
    <columns>
      <column />
      <column />
      <column />
    </columns>
    <rows>
      <row>
        <button id="button1" label="one" />
      </row>
      <row>
        <spacer />
        <button id="button2" label="two" />
      </row>
      <row>
        <spacer />
        <spacer />
        <button id="button3" label="three" />
      </row>
    </rows>
  </grid>
</dialog>
```

You've added a new element to help control spacing in your rows, the aptly named <spacer>. In order to get the buttons in rows 2 and 3 to move into new columns, you include these spacers, which are merely transparent fills used to help position your elements in the dialog boxes. You can use <spacer> elements to help lay out controls in <hbox> and <vbox> elements as well, though within the <grid> element they only control horizontal spacing of items within each row (see Figure 5-12).

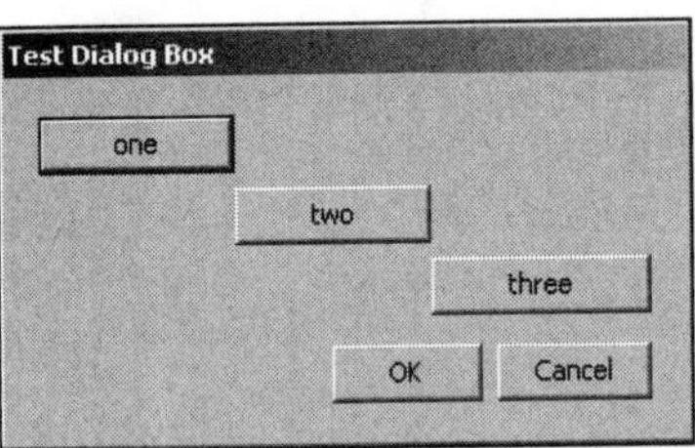

Figure 5-12.
Using a <grid> with <spacer> elements to lay out three buttons in three different columns of three different rows

Using <grid> (and thus <columns>, <rows>, <column>, and <row>), <hbox>, <vbox> and <spacer>, you have tight control over the layout of your interface controls. Guess it's time to look at those controls!

Dialog Controls

After the last exercise, you should have a fairly solid grasp on how to lay out a dialog box. What you need now are all the controls and widgets you'll place *inside* your dialog box. Since we've already touched on the <button> element, let's start there.

<button>

The <button> element for your XML to UI dialog boxes has a number of attributes, only a few of which we've addressed. In addition to the id (the button's identity) and label (the text in the button) attributes, you can include tabindex (order for tabbing), accesskey (the key on the keyboard used to call the button's function), and oncommand (the function to call when a button is pressed). Let's look at these attributes next.

1. In your testXMLtoUI.xml file, change the XML to read as follows:

```
<dialog id="test-dialog-box" title="Test Dialog Box"
buttons="accept,cancel">
  <hbox>
    <button id="button1" label="one" tabindex="3" accesskey="n"
➥oncommand="fl.trace('one');" />
    <button id="button2" label="two" tabindex="2" accesskey="w"
➥oncommand="fl.trace('two');" />
    <button id="button3" label="three" tabindex="1" accesskey= "h"
➥oncommand="fl.trace('three');" />
  </hbox>
</dialog>
```

Here you're giving each button every attribute that you have available. The tabindex is reversed from its natural left-to-right inclination so you may see it in action. In addition, you've given access keys to each button (you'll only see the underlined letter for the access keys if you press *ALT* while the dialog box is open). Now if you press *N* with the dialog box open, then the function for the one button will fire just as if you pressed the button. And what function might that be? Well, you've written a JavaScript command formatted as a string and assigned it to the `oncommand` attribute. In this case, you're tracing the name of the button to the Output panel so you may simply see how it works. What you might have guessed from this simple demonstration, though, is that you can call any of the JavaScript API commands by clicking a button in your dialog boxes. You can even call a command that will open a JSFL file and run its contents. You'll get a change to explore this functionality in more depth in the next chapter when we discuss behaviors. Unfortunately, this functionality is unique to the button—there is no way to capture or react to events from the other controls.

> *One possible workaround for the inability to capture events from controls other than the button is to include an embedded SWF file in the dialog box that runs a periodic check of the controls using* `setInterval`*. This polling of the controls' values isn't ideal, however. In instances where user feedback needs to be acted upon immediately, it's a better idea to include those controls within the embedded SWF itself (at times the entire dialog box interface might be an embedded SWF).*

5

2. Save the XML and launch a new dialog box to see the buttons in action (see Figure 5-13). Try using the access keys you assigned to fire off the buttons' functions, then you'll move on to your next control element, the check box.

Figure 5-13.
The button control can call JSFL commands, such as fl.trace();

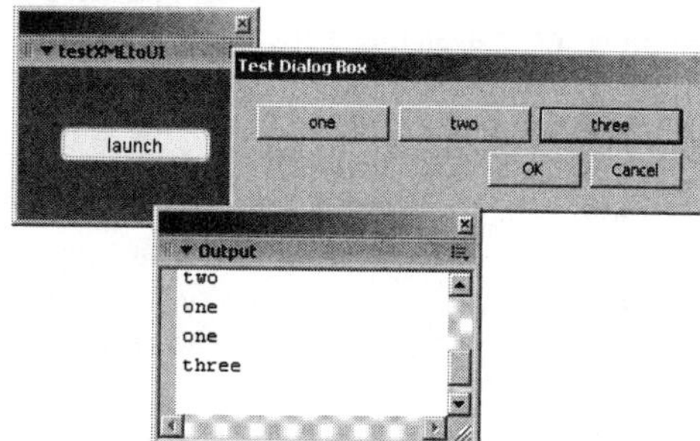

<checkbox>

3. Once more, alter your XML to read as follows:

```
<dialog id="test-dialog-box" title="Test Dialog Box" buttons="accept">
  <hbox>
    <checkbox id="checkbox1" label="click me" tabindex="1"
➥accesskey="c" checked="true" />
  </hbox>
</dialog>
```

As you can see, the check box is set up in a very similar way to the button. The only difference, in fact, is that although the check box doesn't have an oncommand attribute, it has a new checked attribute, which can hold either true or false to determine if the check box is checked by default when the dialog box is opened. Launch a new dialog box like the one shown in Figure 5-14 to see the check box working.

Figure 5-14.
A demonstration of the <checkbox> element

<radiogroup>, <radio>

4. A close relation to the check box is the radio button. A radio button doesn't stand alone, however, but is included within a radio group, which is a collection of radio buttons. Within the group, only one of the radio options may be checked. Look at the following:

```
<dialog id="test-dialog-box" title="Test Dialog Box" buttons="accept">
  <vbox>
    <radiogroup id="gender" tabindex="1" >
      <radio label="male" selected="true" accesskey="m" />
      <radio label="female" accesskey="f" />
    </radiogroup>
  </vbox>
</dialog>
```

Within this XML you define a single radio group with the ID gender (tabindex is the only other available attribute). This group has two radio button options, male and female (see Figure 5-15). The way that radio buttons work, only one of the two options may be checked at a time, with the default radio option determined by the selected attribute, which can be true or false, though to include the attribute in radio options that are false is unnecessary, as is demonstrated in the preceding example. The only other attribute for a radio option is the accesskey, which works exactly as it does in the check box and button controls.

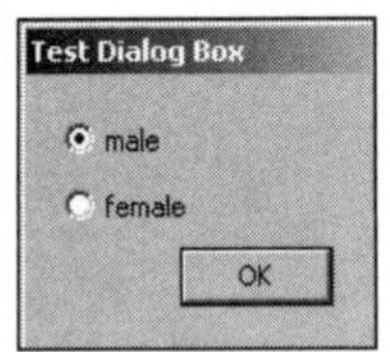

Figure 5-15.
A demonstration of using radio buttons in a vertical layout

<label>, <textbox>

5. Another common and extremely useful control you can incorporate is the text field, which we show you next, coupled with the label control (as well as your old friend the button):

```
<dialog id="test-dialog-box" title="Test Dialog Box" >
  <vbox>
    <hbox>
      <label control="name_tb" value="name" />
```

```
      <textbox id="name_tb" maxlength="10" multiline="false" value=""
➥tabindex="1" size="12" literal="false" />
    </hbox>
    <button id="trace_bn" label="trace" tabindex="2" accesskey="t"
➥oncommand="fl.trace(fl.xmlui.get('name_tb')); fl.xmlui.accept();" />
  </vbox>
</dialog>
```

We tried to throw in some fun things in this dialog box to spice it up a bit. First, notice that you're defining your dialog box without either of the standard buttons (accept and cancel). This is so you may explore how to close a dialog box through code.

Next, you have your <vbox> element defining a vertical layout of controls. Within that, you have an <hbox> element defining a horizontal layout. This means that you'll have some horizontally laid out controls at the top of the overall vertical structure.

The <hbox> element contains two child nodes, both of which are new. The <label> element is a static text field used to, well, label controls. It has two properties: value is simply the text for the label, and control is the ID of the control that the label is associated with. In XUL, clicking a label that has control defined will set focus for that particular control (for instance, clicking the label for the text box will set focus for the text box). This functionality doesn't appear to be set up in XML to UI, however, so the control attribute has no function save for clarity.

Next, you add a new element to your arsenal, <textbox>. The id and tabindex attributes are old friends, but you also have a number of new attributes to look at. maxlength sets the maximum number of characters that can be typed into the text field. multiline, when set to true, allows for multiple lines of text, and, when set to false (which it is by default), allows for a single line of text. Note that there is no way to control the height of a single or multiline text field. You *can* control the width, though, which is done using the size attribute. The number represents the number of characters that can be displayed across (not to be confused with the number of characters that may be entered into the text box). In the preceding example, you set the size to be 2 more characters than the maxlength, which provides a nice buffer to the right of the text. The last two attributes available are value, into which you can place the initial value of the text box (the text that will appear in the text box when the dialog box opens), and literal. literal, when set to true, wraps the text in quotes before processing. A false setting (by default) doesn't place quotes around the text. Whether you need quotes or not depends on what you'll be doing with the text once you leave the dialog box. For instance, if the value you need returned will actually be a string, including the quotes is helpful, since you won't have to add them in your code. For a value that will actually be a reference to, say, a function on the main timeline, you wouldn't want the quotes included. What's good to note, though, is that when literal is set to true, quotation marks that the user enters into the field are escaped with a backslash (\).

After you close your <hbox> tag, you add one final control to your dialog box, a button. Take a look at the oncommand attribute and the function you've assigned to it. Here's the function broken down into individual elements:

1. fl: Reference to the application.
2. trace: Sends a string to the Output panel.
3. xmlui: Reference to the current XML to UI dialog box.
4. xmlui.get('name_tb'): Returns the value of the property specified in the argument from the current XML to UI dialog box. In this case, you send the ID for your text box as a string in order to have the text box's text returned.
5. xmlui.accept(): The same as clicking the default accept button, this method closes the dialog box and sends the dialog box's values back to the script that called it.

   So in your oncommand attribute, you're sending two lines of JSFL, separated by a semicolon. The first line gets the text from your text box in the dialog box and sends it in a trace statement to the Output panel. The second line closes the dialog box.
6. Save the XML and launch a new dialog box in Flash. Type something into the text box as shown in Figure 5-16, then hit the trace button (or *Alt+T*) to see the text displayed in the Output panel. Now you're getting somewhere!

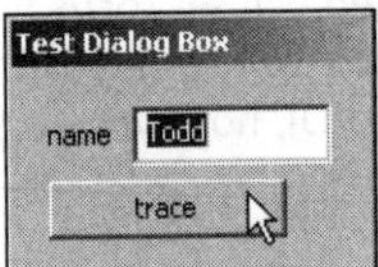

Figure 5-16. <label> and <textfield> elements demonstrated

<colorchip>, <popupslider>

7. There are a few final control elements left to explore, two of which are single elements without children. The <popupslider> element allows you to include range sliders in your dialog boxes. The <colorchip> element gives you a nice, standard color picker to work with, much like the ones you find within Flash. Change your XML to the following:

```
<dialog id="test-dialog-box" title="Test Dialog Box" >
  <vbox>
    <hbox>
      <label control="color_cc" value="background color:" />
      <colorchip id="color_cc" color="#FFFFFF" />
      <label control="fps_ps" value="framerate:" />
      <popupslider id="fps_ps" minvalue="0" maxvalue="100" />
    </hbox>
    <hbox>
      <spacer />
      <spacer />
      <button id="cancel_bn" label="cancel" accesskey="a"
➥oncommand="fl.xmlui.cancel();" />
      <button id="accept_bn" label="accept" accesskey="c"
➥oncommand="fl.getDocumentDOM().backgroundColor=fl.xmlui.get(
➥'color_cc');fl.getDocumentDOM().frameRate=parseFloat(
➥fl.xmlui.get('fps_ps'));fl.xmlui.accept();" />
```

```
    </hbox>
  </vbox>
</dialog>
```

This is getting juicy now, isn't it? Before we go over the preceding XML, save it and launch a new dialog box in Flash. Use the colorchip to set a new color for the current movie's background. Use the slider to set a framerate (see Figure 5-17).

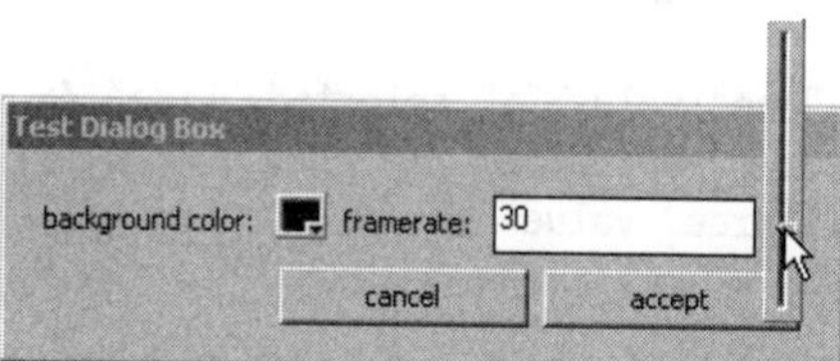

Figure 5-17. Using the <label>, <colorchip>, <popupslider>, and <buttons> elements within box elements to control the layout

When you've selected values, hit the accept button to see the effect. The dialog box closes and your stage color and framerate should change (you might have to click the stage before it takes effect).

As for the XML, within the familiar <dialog>, <hbox>, and <vbox> elements, you have <label> elements attached to your two new controls, <colorchip> and <popupslider>. <colorchip> has only two attributes to worry about, id and color, which, if you hadn't guessed, is the initial color of the colorchip. <popupslider> has id as well, plus minvalue and maxvalue, which define the minimum and maximum allowed values for the slider. Some limitations of the slider are the inability to specify a starting value or increment value and that the increments must be integers, but it's still a pretty powerful widget you can create with a single tag!

In the next <hbox> element, you add two buttons to your dialog box. You may be wondering why you don't use the standard cancel and accept buttons for this exercise. In a normal circumstance you might certainly use the default buttons. In this case, however, you have no way to assign functions to the default accept button through your XML (the default cancel button would work, but it wouldn't be aligned with your control button). This is why you use a <button> element with an oncommand attribute. The string of JavaScript that you assign to oncommand breaks down into the following lines:

```
fl.getDocumentDOM().backgroundColor = fl.xmlui.get('color_cc');
fl.getDocumentDOM().frameRate = parseFloat(fl.xmlui.get('fps_ps'));
fl.xmlui.accept();
```

The first line assigns the value from your <colorchip> to the current Flash document's background color. The second line sets the current document's framerate using the value of your <popupslider>. Notice that you have to use the JavaScript parseFloat to turn the slider value into a floating point number for the frame rate. The final line, which you met in the last step, closes the dialog box. We'll note here that you also have the option of fl.xmlui.cancel(), which closes the dialog box without returning any of its values to the calling script. For this test, however, the results would be the same, simply closing the dialog box. Hopefully, you're beginning to see the possibilities afforded to you with these dialog boxes, but you're not through yet!

<menulist>, <menupop>, <menuitem>, <listbox>, <listitem>

8. You'll now see the two list elements you have available to you in your dialog boxes, <menulist> and <listbox>, in this next step. Try the following XML:

```
<dialog id="test-dialog-box" title="Test Dialog Box" buttons="accept" >
  <vbox>
    <hbox>
      <menulist id="options_ml" tabindex="1" >
        <menupop>
          <menuitem label="one" value="1" selected="true" />
          <menuitem label="two" value="2" />
          <menuitem label="three" value="3" />
        </menupop>
      </menulist>
      <button id="set1_bn" label="SET" tabindex="2" accesskey="a"
➥oncommand="fl.xmlui.set('list_lb', fl.xmlui.get('options_ml'));" />
    </hbox>
    <hbox>
      <listbox id="list_lb" tabindex="3" rows="4" >
        <listitem label="one" value="1" />
        <listitem label="two" value="2" />
        <listitem label="three" value="3" selected="true" />
      </listbox>
      <button id="set2_bn" label="SET" tabindex="2" accesskey="a"
➥oncommand="fl.xmlui.set('options_ml', fl.xmlui.get('list_lb'));" />
    </hbox>
  </vbox>
</dialog>
```

9. Save the XML and launch the new dialog box to see what you've created as shown in Figure 5-18.

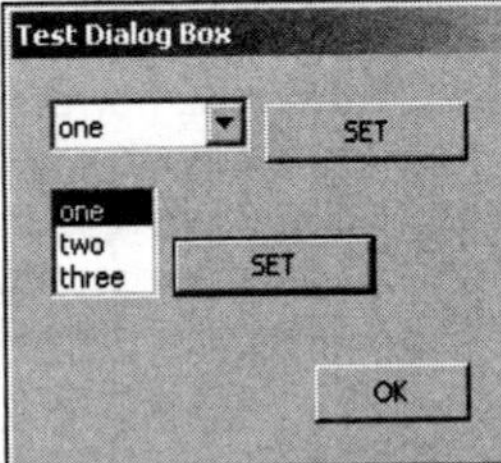

Figure 5-18.
The two available list controls, <menulist> and <listbox>

The first new element is the <menulist> element, which creates a text field with a button inside it. This element has the familiar id and tabindex attributes. The value for the id attribute is what you'll use to get or set which of the list's items are selected. <menulist> has only one child to contend with, <menupop>, which doesn't have any attributes. <menupop> defines the pop-up list that will open if you click the <menulist> button. The effect of the <menupop> element inside the <menulist> element is a drop-down list similar to Flash's ComboBox component. These two tags define the drop-down functionality, but of course you need items inside the list to be displayed. You use <menuitem> for this purpose. Each <menuitem> has a label and a value attribute (label is displayed, value is what is passed to any function requesting it). If a value isn't defined, then the label acts as the value.

In addition, you can add an attribute, `selected`, that takes a `true` or `false` value. This, of course, is the menu item selected when the dialog box opens.

The next list element is `<listbox>`, and this works similarly to the List component in Flash. This control allows for more than one menu item to be displayed at once (though there is no ability to allow for multiple selection of menu items). The `<listbox>` element has the old standards `id` and `tabindex`, but also features a `rows` attribute that determines the number of rows displayed in the control. Within `<listbox>` you have individual `<listitem>` elements. These have the same attributes available as your `<menuitem>` elements: `label`, `value`, and `selected`. In the same way as with `<menuitem>`, leaving the `value` attribute out simply means the `label` will be used for that purpose.

We've added some new button code to the preceding example as well to demonstrate how you may set values within the XML to UI dialog box. Both buttons work in a similar way, setting the opposite menu to the value displayed in the button's corresponding menu, so we'll just explain one of the `JavaScript` strings:

```
fl.xmlui.set('list_lb', fl.xmlui.get('options_ml'));
```

5

You have already seen how the `xmlui.get()` method returns the value of a control in your dialog box. You can then guess how `xmlui.set()` will set a control in much the same way. You pass it two parameters. The first is the name of the control you wish to set (formatted as a string), and the second is the value. In this case, you get the value from another one of the controls! The effect is that whenever a button next to one of your menus is pressed, the other menu has its value set to match.

<targetlist>

The `<targetlist>` element isn't a standard XUL element, but is unique to your Flash XML to UI. When you include this element in your dialog box, what is drawn is a scrollpane containing an expandable tree that displays the hierarchy of objects in your document. This is extremely useful when you need the user to select a movie clip, button, or text field (all selectable from the target list) from the current document in order to perform some action upon it.

For its attributes, you have `id`, `width`, and `height`, in addition to `class`, which specifies the type of objects you wish to appear in the list. Not specifying a class will simply include all selectable objects in your document, including movie clips, text fields, buttons, and videos. However, you can specify certain types of objects you wish to appear in the list (currently, movie clips will *always* appear in the list no matter what else is specified—this appears to be a bug that perhaps will be rectified upon later versions). For instance, if you only wish for buttons to appear, you would specify `class="button"`. The target list would then show a list of buttons and movie clips. If you wanted to have video included, you would use `class="video"`. For text fields, you would use the rather unintuitive `class="text"` (not "`textfield`").

Although all movie clips appear in the target list by default, you can also specify packages like "`mx.controls.CheckBox`" if you wished for the check box component to appear in the list and *not* instances of other classes. This confusing functionality deserves a closer look. As an example, if you had a movie with a check box, a combo box, and a basic movie clip symbol named "clip" that was unassociated with a class and you left the `class` attribute blank in the target list, all three would appear in the dialog box, since they are all movie clips. If you instead specified "mx.controls.CheckBox" for the class attribute, then the check box and the "clip" instance would appear, but not the combo box. No, it doesn't make too much sense and perhaps will also be corrected at a later date.

The final attribute, required, lets the dialog box know that it can't be accepted without an object being specified in the target list. If users fail to select an object and hit the accept button, they'll receive a friendly pop-up warning that they need to select an object. Let's add a target list to a dialog box so you may see how it looks.

10. You know the routine! Change your XML to the following (you'll make it short and sweet this time):

```
<dialog id="test-dialog-box" title="Test Dialog Box"
➥buttons="accept,cancel" >
  <vbox>
    <targetlist id="target_tl" height="300" width="400"
➥required="true"/>
  </vbox>
</dialog>
```

11. Save the XML and launch a new dialog box to see what you've added. The target list consists of three parts, really: a text field to hold the name of an object once you select it, the scrollpane containing the tree, and two radio buttons with Relative and Absolute options (see Figure 5-19). The radio buttons allow users to specify if the path to the object should be relative or absolute. For this example, it doesn't make too much sense, but when you begin to use dialog boxes when applying behaviors to symbol instances, the option can be pretty useful.

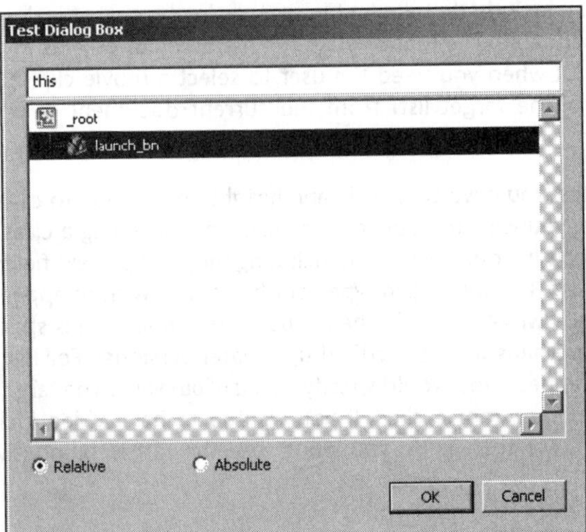

Figure 5-19. The <targetlist> element used to select objects within the Flash document

As for the tree itself, it shows you every object currently in your movie and is an impressive tool in its own right. Open a dialog box with a target list in it, and you immediately have access to the structure of your entire movie, no matter how nested the clips. One neat option you have as you explore the list is to name instances that don't as yet have instance names (unfortunately, though, you can't rename instances).

> *One thing to note about the target list control is that it isn't a standard XUL control (its functionality being unique to Flash), and one quirky consequence of this is that you can't get or set its value from within the XML to UI dialog box, as you can with other controls. Therefore, using* `fl.xmlui.get()` *for a target list will return an* `undefined` *value if you try to access it.*

> *Another issue with the target list is a certain instability with the control, especially when switching between relative and absolute paths. At times we've found this functionality to be a bit buggy, returning incorrect paths or not switching properly between a relative and absolute state. At other times, reentering a dialog box with a* `target list` *can cause erroneous results. It's a great control when working properly, but its instability should be something to consider when developing XML to UI dialog boxes.*

5

There is essentially only one element left to look at in our exploration of XML to UI, but it's possibly the most powerful. Since you're developing in Flash, and these dialog boxes will be opened and used in Flash, it only makes sense that you can include Flash in your dialog boxes!

<flash>, <property>

1. The first thing you need to do is create another Flash movie for your test. Open up `testXMLtoUI.fla` in your `Configuration/WindowSWF` folder if you don't have it open. Use File ➤ Save As to save it as the new document `trace.fla`.
2. Select the launch_bn instance on the stage and use the Properties panel to change the label for the button to trace.
3. Select the first frame (where you placed your ActionScript initially) and open up the Actions panel. Make the following changes (in bold):

```
function click() {
  var js = "fl.xmlui.set('display_tb', 'Hello from Flash!');"
  MMExecute(js);
}
launch_bn.addEventListener("click", this);
MMExecute("fl.xmlui.set('secretword', 'duck');");
```

You've changed the JavaScript that you'll call on the button click. Since you've already looked at the fl.xmlui.set() method, you should be able to tell that you're setting the value of a control with the ID display_tb with the string Hello from Flash! This will occur when the button on the stage is clicked.

In addition to that MMExecute, you have another MMExecute that will fire when the movie launches and the frame code is run. The JavaScript you send in this call is a fl.xmlui.set() command as well. This time you give secretword the value duck.

> *We've used JSFL in the preceding example, but you can also use the ActionScript command* XMLUI.set() *for the same purpose. These commands work exactly the same.*

4. Save and compile your movie into the same folder as the testXMLtoUI.swf file (Configuration/WindowSWF). Your Flash movie is done. All you have left is to construct your dialog box.
5. You'll take one final trip into your XML. Change testXMLtoUI.xml to read as follows:

```
<dialog id="test-dialog-box" title="Test Dialog Box" buttons="accept" >
  <vbox>
    <textbox id="display_tb" size="24" />
    <flash id="trace_fl" width="150" height="100" src="trace.swf">
      <property id="secretword" />
    </flash>
    <button id="trace_bn" label="trace Flash"
➥oncommand="fl.xmlui.set('display_tb', 'the secret word is ' +
➥fl.xmlui.get('secretword'));"/>
  </vbox>
</dialog>
```

You can see that you've added a text box to your dialog box with the ID display_tb. This is the control that you'll set from your button in the Flash movie. The new element you've included is <flash>. This element has an id like most of your other elements, but also a height and width attribute specifying the height and width of the SWF you'll be using (this doesn't have to correspond, but is rather silly if it doesn't), as well as a src attribute that points to the SWF you wish to include in the dialog box.

The <flash> element can also have child nodes to define properties in the XML to UI dialog box. The Flash movie embedded in the dialog box can set any value within the dialog box (which then can be utilized in the script that may have called the dialog box), but that value must be defined in the XML to begin with. If the value is one of the control elements (like display_tb earlier), then that value has already been defined in the XML. If the value isn't one of the controls, however, you can include it in your XML by using the <flash> element's <property> child node. This node only has a single attribute, id, which sets the name of the property. Once that property is defined in the XML through the <property> element, then Flash has the ability to set and get its value (unfortunately, you can't set a default value for the property, though).

So how does this work in the preceding example? Well, if you look back at your ActionScript in `trace.fla`, you'll see that when the movie is launched you set the value of `secretword` to duck. The button that you've included in your XML to UI dialog box looks to this property and, when clicked, places the value for `secretword` into the `display_tb` text box (see Figure 5-20). In addition to that, the button inside Flash sends a friendly greeting to the same text box when you click it.

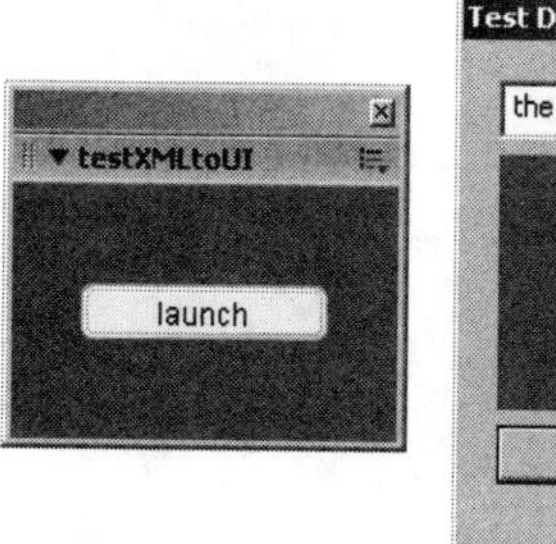

Figure 5-20.
Using an embedded SWF movie as a control and having it communicate with the dialog box

If you haven't already done so, save the XML and launch the new dialog box in Flash. Click both buttons to see the results. That's a very simple example of how an embedded Flash movie in a dialog box can both get and set values in its parent dialog box.

Dialog Designer

Now that you've gone through and learned the ins and outs of XML to UI, and are confident you can code it from scratch, blindfolded, and with your fingers trapped in Chinese handcuffs, we'd like to introduce a tool that will make creation of dialog boxes a snap. If you open the file `DialogDesigner.swf` from this chapter's source files, you'll find a simple interface that allows you to quickly construct the XML required to make whatever box you need.

To work with the Dialog Designer, drop the SWF into the same `Configuration/WindowSWF` folder as your test files from this chapter. You'll need to close and relaunch Flash to have the option for the Dialog Designer appear in your Window ➤ Other Panels submenu. When you open the interface you'll actually be in "behavior mode," which simply places some extra nodes on the tree for a behavior (you'll get a chance to revisit and explore the Dialog Designer later when we introduce behaviors). To simply make a dialog box, select `dialog mode` in the combo box at the top and you're left with a `<dialog>` element as the root node (see Figure 5-21).

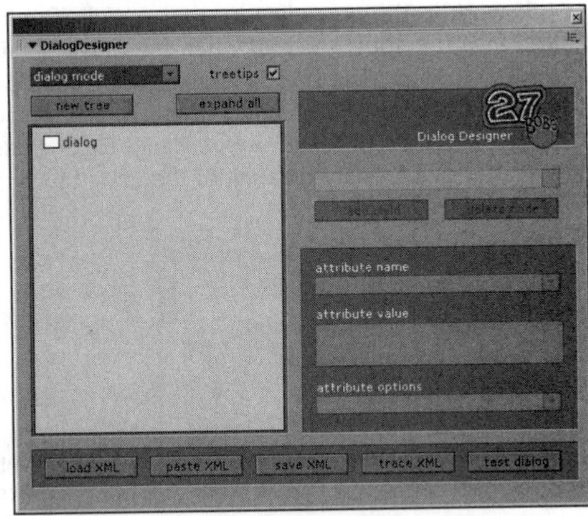

Figure 5-21. The Dialog Designer WindowSWF movie aids in the creation of XML to UI dialog boxes.

On the left of the interface is the tree representing the XML structure, while the right of the interface gives you options of what can be added to each node as you select it (see Figure 5-22). Using this tool, you can create dialog boxes from scratch, load in XML from existing dialog boxes, save your XML to one of the useful `Configuration` subfolders, and trace the XML to either the Dialog Designer interface or your Output panel. You can drag and drop nodes in the tree to other valid locations, and trust that the tree will deny invalid drops, invalid nodes, and useless attributes. Finally, using a bit of JSFL and `MMExecute` (more on that later in the book), the interface allows you to test your dialog boxes as you make them, so you can tweak to your heart's content until you get just the right look and functionality.

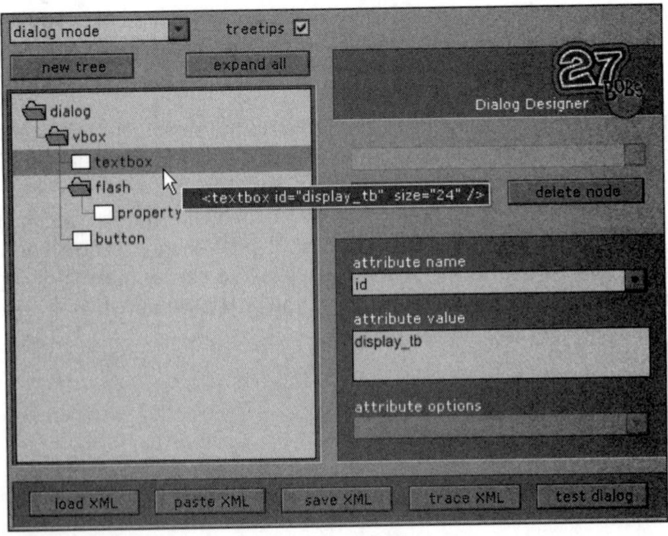

Figure 5-22. Nodes can be added and edited within the tree structure.

Have fun with the interface, and now that you know all of the XML to UI options, experiment with different dialog boxes to see how everything works together. We'll work within the interface when we discuss behaviors, but feel free to use the Dialog Designer throughout the book if an effect or command could benefit from a dialog box.

Summary

Let's face it, there's a fantastic range of things that the new Flash extensibility architecture allows you to do. You've never had this kind of access to the Flash authoring environment before, so it's time to play around and customize your environment. So why would you want to spend needless time re-creating standard UI tools and controls? Using XML to UI, you can quickly introduce the necessary controls that allow users to input information. Then you can take that information and do extraordinary things!

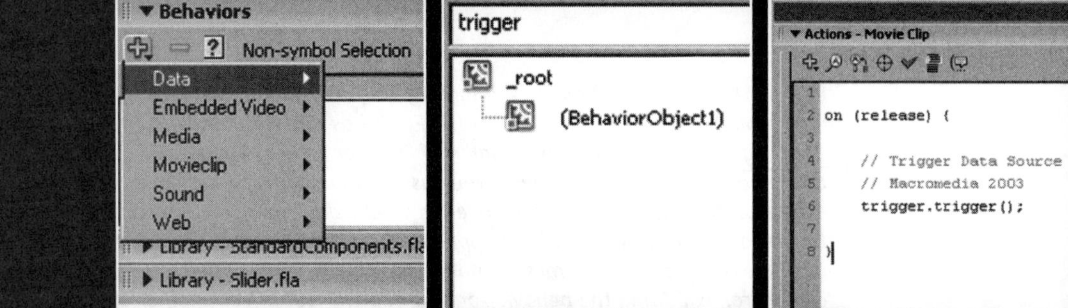

Behaviors
Non-symbol Selection
Data
Embedded Video
Media
Movieclip
Sound
Web
Library - StandardComponents.fla
Library - Slider.fla
trigger
_root
(BehaviorObject1)
Actions - Movie Clip
on (release) {
// Trigger Data Source
// Macromedia 2003
trigger.trigger();
}

One major change with the latest release of Flash that might come as a shock to certain designers is the loss of the normal mode in the Actions panel. To those who long ago moved to expert mode, this might not seem a major alteration, but to those users who never felt comfortable typing in their code, this change could prove intimidating. So will these users, so used to a simplified method of entering their code, be left behind as Flash moves forward? Not with the addition of behaviors! That's not to say that behaviors are necessarily for beginners only—they can actually provide you with a pretty nice workflow enhancement, as you'll see in the final example of this chapter. But first, let's start at the very beginning . . .

Exploring Behaviors

The term *behavior* implies a way of acting: the manner in which something functions. The idea of behaviors in Flash is that you can take a basic movie clip (for example) and make it act a certain way by applying a particular behavior. Multiple clips with the same behavior would obviously act in a similar manner.

For those who might be wondering, this isn't the same thing as a component. A component is a clip that acts a certain way, sure, but a component is a singular symbol in your Library, and multiple instances on stage are all derived from the same building block. With behaviors, you can take different symbols' instances and make them all act the same way. They are all unique as far as their makeup—they just behave alike. In addition, you can apply multiple behaviors to a single clip, including additional functionality as you need it.

Well, that's all very nice and abstract, but what *exactly* are behaviors? **Behaviors** allow developers to apply code to frames, buttons, or movie clips without having to type in, or even open up, the Actions panel. Need the movie to go to a frame? Use a behavior! Want to play a video or sound? A behavior can do that for you as well. In fact, there is very little that can't be achieved by using a behavior. They don't necessarily offer all of the functionality of the normal mode in the old ActionScript editor, which stepped users through even the simplest of commands, but behaviors can provide more complete code to accomplish common tasks, as well as the means to include code for uncommon tasks and unfamiliar syntax.

Users of Macromedia Director will already be familiar with the idea of behaviors, though the implementation within Flash has one notable difference from the drag-and-drop script functionality of Director. In Director, each behavior is defined as a single cast member in the Cast Library and instances are applied to sprites on the stage. Editing the code for a behavior in Director means editing the behavior for all sprites it was applied to. In Flash, however, behaviors actually add code to either frames or movie clips and are individually tied to each clip or frame. Editing the behavior on one clip will not affect another clip with the same behavior applied, and will in fact "break" the code's connection to the behavior and the Behavior panel.

Now, if you're reading this book, it's a pretty good bet that you're comfortable with ActionScript and won't require behaviors for simple tasks. In fact, we're sure that you'll be one of the developers writing behaviors for others! But in order to see how behaviors work, and in order to see what may be possible, let's step through a simple example.

1. Create a new Flash Document. With nothing selected, open the Behaviors panel (*SHIFT+F3*) and click the plus in the upper left. Select Web ➤ Go to Web Page as shown in Figure 6-1.

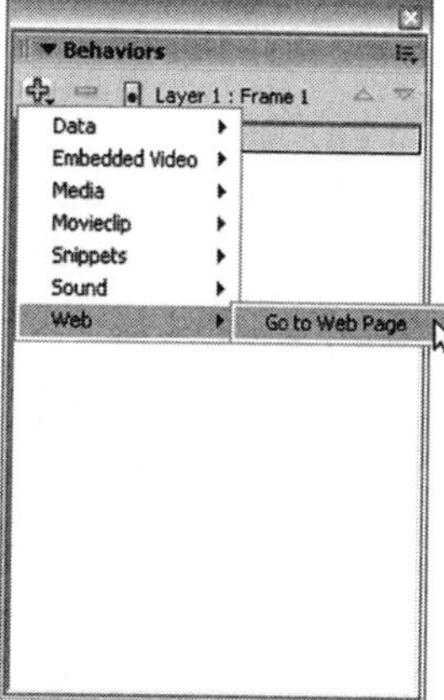

Figure 6-1.
Behaviors panel with the Go to Web Page behavior selected

2. An XML to UI dialog box opens up and prompts you to enter a URL and specify a target. Notice that the dialog box is modal and doesn't allow you to select anything else within the application. Keep the default settings in the dialog box and click OK (see Figure 6-2).

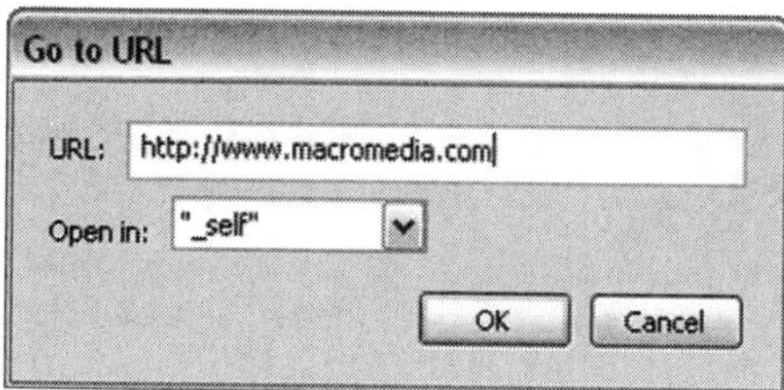

Figure 6-2.
The dialog box for the Go to Web Page behavior

A few things will now happen:

- First, and most obvious, the dialog box will close.
- Second, you might notice a small a appear in frame one of the default layer, signifying that code has been added to that frame.
- Finally, if you look to the Behaviors panel, you'll see a new line has been added to show you what behavior is applied. Under Action will appear Go to Web Page and the Event will be listed as None.

3. Open up your Actions panel and you'll find the following code has been added:

```
//Goto Webpage Behavior
getURL("http://www.macromedia.com","_self");
//End Behavior
```

Now that was easy! With just a few clicks and no need to enter the Actions panel, you have some very useful code added to your document. Perhaps you don't wish to redirect to Macromedia's site, however. How do you change this code without using the Actions panel? Let's take a look.

4. Select the first frame and then double-click the Go to Web Page field in the Behaviors panel. The dialog box reopens! Type `http://www.flashextensibility.com` into the URL field and hit OK. If your Actions panel is still open, you'll see that the code has been updated with the new site.

   But wait a moment. Perhaps you would rather the site opened a new window instead of loading in the current window. Let's edit the script directly to make this change.

5. In the Actions panel, replace the text `_self` with the text `_blank`. Now once again double-click the Go to Web Page field in the Behaviors panel. You'll see the dialog box reopen with _blank now in the drop-down menu. Cool! Editing the script automatically updated the value in the dialog box when you reopened it.

   This obviously was an example of adding code to a frame, but you can just as easily add the same code to a movie clip or button, which perhaps would be more useful in this situation.

6. Now create a simple graphic (we just drew a box) and convert it into a movie clip by hitting *F8* (the name of the symbol is unimportant). With the instance selected, click the plus in the Behaviors panel.

   You should notice that there are more options available to you now in the drop-down list. This is because you can specify in a behavior definition what class of object can receive that behavior. There are more behaviors shipped with Flash that have been set up for movie clips.

7. Select the same behavior for your movie clip, Web ➤ Go to Web Page. Once again, accept the defaults in the dialog box. Open your Actions panel if it isn't still open.

   The code results are similar to the frame code, but are now contained within an `on(release){}`. As in previous versions of Flash, code can't be applied to a movie clip unless it's within an `on(){}` or an `onClipEvent(){}` block. If you test your movie, clicking the clip will cause your browser to open and go to Macromedia's site. This button-type functionality is applied by default since behaviors, more than anything else, seem tailored to react to simple user input with common actions—going to a Web page, becoming draggable, or playing a sound perhaps.

   If you now take a look at the Behaviors panel (your movie clip will still need to be selected), you'll find that the Event field now contains the words On Release, as shown in Figure 6-3. This is the default action for a behavior applied to a clip, but you can change that if you want.

Figure 6-3.
The Behaviors panel with the Go to Web Page applied to a movie clip offers a number of events to fire the behavior.

8. Click On Release and you'll see a drop-down list of the other button events. Select On Press, and watch your code update to match!

Behind the Scenes

So what goes into creating this simple behavior? XML, pure and simple! With just a few lines of XML in a file stored in your `Behaviors` folder, you can create any kind of behavior that you can conceive. For example, open up the file `Web_Goto_Webpage.xml` in your `Behaviors` folder (ours is located at `C:\Documents and Settings\Administrator\Local Settings\Application Data\Macromedia\Flash MX 2004\en\Configuration\`). Better yet, take a look at it here:

```
<?xml version="1.0"?>
<!- Copyright 2003 Macromedia, Inc. All Rights Reserved.->
<flash_behavior version="1.0">
  <behavior_definition dialogID="GotoWebPage-dialog" category="Web"
➥name ="Go to Web Page" >
    <properties>
      <property id="URL" default="http://www.macromedia.com"/>
      <property id="targetWindow" default='"_self"'/>
    </properties>
    <dialog id="GotoWebPage-dialog" title="Go to URL" buttons="accept,
➥cancel">
      <vbox>
        <hbox>
          <label value="URL:" control="URL"/>
          <textbox literal="true" required="true" width="40" id="URL"/>
        </hbox>
        <hbox>
          <label value="Open in:" control="targetWindow"/>
          <menulist literal="true" id="targetWindow">
            <menupopup>
              <menuitem label='"_self"'/>
              <menuitem label='"_parent"'/>
              <menuitem label='"_blank"'/>
              <menuitem label='"_top"'/>
            </menupopup>
          </menulist>
        </hbox>
      </vbox>
    </dialog>
<actionscript>
<![CDATA[
  //Goto Webpage Behavior
  getURL($URL$,$targetWindow$);
  //End Behavior
]]>
</actionscript>
  </behavior_definition>
</flash_behavior>
```

6

If you went through Chapter 5, most of this XML should look familiar to you (and if you didn't, it's probably worth your time taking a look at it before you proceed). In fact, if you remove the <dialog> element for clarity, you're left with only a couple of tags.

```
<flash_behavior version="1.0">
  <behavior_definition dialogID="GotoWebPage-dialog" category="Web"
➥name ="Go to Web Page" >
    <properties>
      <property id="URL" default="http://www.macromedia.com"/>
      <property id="targetWindow" default='"_self"'/>
    </properties>
    <dialog  ... />
<actionscript>
<![CDATA[
  //Goto Webpage Behavior
  getURL($URL$,$targetWindow$);
  //End Behavior
]]>
</actionscript>
  </behavior_definition>
</flash_behavior>
```

Not too daunting, is it? In fact, if you use the Dialog Designer presented last chapter, you'll have 80 percent of your behaviors written for you—you'll only have to fill in the ActionScript!

Just as with the XML to UI, let's start off by defining the tags you'll use for your behaviors. It's a much shorter list this time:

Tag	Description	Attributes	Child Nodes
<flash_behavior>	The root tag containing the behavior and version number	version: Current build of behavior	<behavior_definition>
<behavior_definition>	Contains all the information defining the behavior	1. category: The menu that the behavior will appear under in the <actionscript> Behaviors panel 2. class: The type of object the behavior may be applied to 3. defaultEvent: The event that will fire the behavior unless otherwise specified 4. dialogID: The ID of the dialog box associated with this behavior	<properties> <dialog>

Table continues on the following page

Tag	Description	Attributes	Child Nodes
`<behavior_ definition>` *(continued)*		5. `events`: The events that will appear in the Behaviors panel under event for this behavior 6. `name`: The title of the behavior as it will appear in the Behaviors panel	
`<properties>`	Contains the list of properties that will be passed back to Flash for use with the behavior	None	`<property>`
`<property>`	The name of a variable whose value will be sent back to Flash	1. `default`: The value this property will have when the behavior is applied (if not changed with a dialog box) 2. `id`: The name of the variable holding the value	None
`<dialog>`	Contains the information to build an XML to UI dialog box	See Chapter 5	See Chapter 5
`<actionscript>`	Contains the code that will be added to the instance or frame in the authoring environment	None	None

We'll go through each of these tags and their attributes as we take you through the next few examples. The best way to learn about behaviors, as with most things, is by doing. So let's get started!

Snippet Behaviors

Behaviors don't necessarily need to have a dialog box, so the first behavior we'll discuss will be of this simple nature. Not requiring a dialog box means that the behavior has no need for user input. These behaviors will most probably be of the "snippet" variety—behaviors that simply add common code to your movies without requiring you to retype it every time. You'll code this first behavior from scratch, but subsequent examples will utilize the Dialog Designer to speed up the process (that way you can explore and create more!).

Root Preloader

1. Create a new Flash Document. Select the first frame, open the Actions panel, and type in the following:

```
this.onEnterFrame = function() {
  var loaded = this.getBytesLoaded();
  var total = this.getBytesTotal();
  var percent = loaded/total;
  this.loaded_tf.text = Math.round(loaded/1024) + "kb";
  this.total_tf.text = Math.round(total/1024) "kb";
  this.percent_tf.text = Math.round(percent*100) + "%";
  if (percent == 1) {
    delete this.onEnterFrame;
    play();
  }
};
stop();
```

   We've found that it's always a good idea to start behaviors within Flash itself. Even though this code will eventually go into an XML file, the Actions panel will give you feedback and error messages while you work and develop the behavior. Once code has been "approved" in Flash, you can move it into an XML editor (like Dreamweaver or EditPlus—even Notepad will do the trick!) where you'll create your XML. After you try a few more complex behaviors, you'll better appreciate working initially in Flash.

   The preceding code shouldn't be anything too strange. In fact, it's likely you've used similar code in your own movies. This script is a simple preloader that will assess the load of your main timeline (although the `MovieClipLoader` is a new and very useful object in Flash MX 2004, it doesn't work for the main timeline as it loads). We've referenced three text fields in the code, `loaded_tf`, `total_tf`, and `percent_tf`. This obviously assumes the presence of these three fields, but won't break if the fields aren't there. Again, this is a quick snippet that will take you only a few seconds to drop into your movie. If you then need to delete a line or two or change a reference, you've still saved quite a few seconds!

2. Once you've tested the code and don't receive any errors, go ahead and open up your favorite text editor. Macromedia's Dreamweaver is a great environment for editing XML, but more often than not we find ourselves in good ol' Notepad when working with fairly simple XML.

3. Save a new file as `PreloadMovie.xml` into your `Configuration/Behaviors` folder. In the file, type the following declaration and tags:

```
<?xml version="1.0"?>
<flash_behavior version="1.0" >
</flash_behavior>
```

   Here you open and close your root node, which will always have the node name `flash_behavior`. The only attribute for this node is version, which you've set as 1.0.

4. Within the <flash_behavior> node, add the following:

```
<flash_behavior version="1.0" >
  <behavior_definition category="Snippets" name="Preload Movie">
  </behavior_definition>
</flash_behavior>
```

<behavior_definition> is the only child node of <flash_behavior>. This element has a number of attributes, only a few of which do you need for your snippet. category is the attribute that defines which menu the behavior will appear under in the Behaviors panel. The menus that are already defined are Data, Embedded Video, Media, Movieclip, Sound, and Web, with Projector and Screen appearing under special circumstances. However, this doesn't mean that you're limited to these menus. By defining Snippets as shown previously, you'll create a new menu to hold your snippets as you make them.

The name attribute should be fairly self-explanatory. This is how your behavior will appear in your Snippets menu. You don't need any of the other <behavior_definition> attributes yet for your behavior, but you'll explore them in later exercises.

5. One final tag to add:

```
<?xml version="1.0"?>
<flash_behavior version="1.0" >
  <behavior_definition category="Snippets" name="Preload Movie">
    <actionscript><![CDATA[]]></actionscript>
  </behavior_definition>
</flash_behavior>
```

Would you believe that's it for tags? This last one looks a little odd, though, so let's look at it more closely. The <actionscript> element is a child of the <behavior_definition> element. It doesn't contain any attributes, but its character data (whatever comes between its start and end tags) contains the ActionScript that will be placed back in the Flash authoring environment. It's important that this ActionScript is sent back exactly as you need it, so you'll place it inside the <![CDATA[]]> section so that it isn't interpreted by the XML parser. You'll just paste the code that you wrote up in step 1 between the [ ] symbols. Before you do that, you'll "prepare" by altering your XML to look like this:

```
<?xml version="1.0"?>
<flash_behavior version="1.0" >
  <behavior_definition category="Snippets" name="Preload Movie">
<actionscript>
<![CDATA[

]]></actionscript>
  </behavior_definition>
</flash_behavior>
```

6

We typed it the other way first so you could better see the hierarchy, but this is the form that will work best for your behaviors. You see, any whitespace in your XML will translate into whitespace in your ActionScript, so you place your <actionscript> tag flush left without indentation, since that's how you'll want your code to appear in your Actions panel.

6. Now head back to Flash and copy your preloader code from step 1 onto your clipboard. Return to your XML and paste it within the CDATA section so it looks like the following:

```
<?xml version="1.0"?>
<flash_behavior version="1.0" >
  <behavior_definition category="Snippets" name="Preload Movie">
<actionscript>
<![CDATA[
this.onEnterFrame = function() {
  var loaded = this.getBytesLoaded();
  var total = this.getBytesTotal();
  var percent = loaded/total;
  this.loaded_tf.text = Math.round(loaded/1024) + "kb";
  this.total_tf.text = Math.round(total/1024) + "kb";
  this.percent_tf.text = Math.round(percent*100) + "%";
  if (percent == 1) {
    delete this.onEnterFrame;
    play();
  }
};
stop();
]]></actionscript>
  </behavior_definition>
</flash_behavior>
```

Save your XML and return to Flash (`PreloadMovie.xml` is also available for download from `www.flashextensibility.com`). If you open the menu in the upper right of the Behaviors panel, you'll see an option to reload the behaviors. You'll need to do this anytime you make a change to the XML (or create a new behavior XML file) in order for Flash to recognize the change. Flash automatically does this when you launch the application, so changes you make while Flash is closed will be recognized the next time you open the application.

Now that the behaviors have been reloaded, clicking the plus sign in the Behaviors panel should reveal a new Snippets menu, which contains your Preload Movie behavior. Go ahead and apply it to something—select a frame in the main timeline of a new Flash document, for example, and you'll see your preload code added to that frame (with nothing selected on the stage, the behavior will automatically be applied to the current layer and current frame). As you can see, it would be pretty straightforward to create an entire library of snippet behaviors!

Button Action Behaviors

The snippet behaviors will come in handy for frequently used code, but behaviors were intended more for instances of interacting with the user. In fact, when applied to clips by default, behaviors enclose their code within an `on(){}` block for common button actions. In this next exercise, you'll take advantage of this functionality as well as the ability to assign multiple behaviors as you create a few basic, but useful, physics behaviors.

Once again, you'll initially build your behaviors in Flash for testing purposes. Once you're happy with the code and are sure everything is working properly, you'll write your XML. Although this section might appear pretty lengthy, it's actually composed of three smaller behaviors that are all fairly straightforward. Let's take a look . . .

Drag and Throw Physics in Flash

1. Create a new Flash document and draw a small circle on the stage. Convert the circle into a movie clip and name the instance `dragClip`. (You can also follow this example by using the example file `dragPhysics.fla`.) With the instance selected, open up the Actions panel, shown in Figure 6-4.

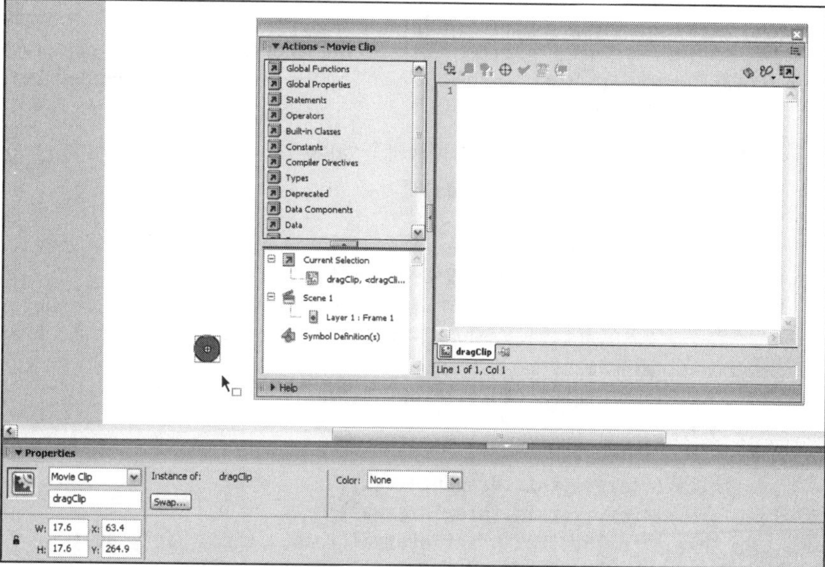

Figure 6-4. The Actions panel with the `dragClip` instance selected

2. Add the following code to the editor:

```
on (press) {
  this.dragClip = function() {
    this._x = this._parent._xmouse - this.offsetX;
    this._y = this._parent._ymouse - this.offsetY;
    updateAfterEvent();
  };
  clearInterval(this.dragInterval);
  this.dragInterval = setInterval(this, "dragClip", 40);
  this.offsetX = this._xmouse;
  this.offsetY = this._ymouse;
}
```

Here you have a function defined within the on(press) handler. Of course, ideally you wouldn't want to define this function every time the clip is pressed, but this is how it must be configured if it's contained within a single behavior (we'll show you a workaround in later exercises featuring a custom event). This function will update the position of the clip each time it's called. Below the function definition you set a new interval call (after first clearing any previous interval call) to occur every 40 milliseconds. You also record the offset position of the mouse, which will keep the clip from snapping to the mouse position when dragged.

The reason you're using this method to drag instead of the simpler startDrag() is because you'll need to record the movements of the clip as it's being dragged. This will allow you to have the clip "thrown" by the user when it's released. Let's look to that handler next.

3. Add the following code to your script window:

```
on (release, releaseOutside) {
  $weight$ = .9;
  this.throwClip = function() {
    this._x += (this.moveX*=$weight$);
    this._y += (this.moveY*=$weight$);
    if (Math.abs(this.moveX - this._x) < 1 && Math.abs(this.moveY -
➥this._y) < 1) {
      clearInterval(this.throwInterval);
    }
  }
  clearInterval(this.dragInterval);
  clearInterval(this.throwInterval);
  this.throwInterval = setInterval(this, "throwClip", 40);
}
```

At the top of your handler you define a new variable named $weight$. Why the strange notation? Actually, this is the form you'll need to give any variables in the XML behavior that receive their values from the XML itself (as returned from a dialog box, for instance), so we include it here so swapping out later is a cinch. You'll look at it more closely when you construct the XML. For now, just understand that $weight$ will represent how quickly a clip will come to rest after being thrown.

Next within the handler, you define a new function called throwClip. throwClip, like dragClip in the onPress handler, will update the clip position based on its weight and two new variables, moveX and moveY. These variables will be used solely in your ActionScript and aren't set by the XML itself, so you don't use the special dollar sign notation. You'll set these variables in the next step. The if statement that follows just checks to see if the clip should come to rest.

After throwClip is defined, you clear the dragInterval call and create a new interval call every 40 milliseconds (again, after clearing a previous interval that might be running). Basically, when the clip is released, it will continue moving as long as either of its moveX and moveY variables are above 1. Now you have to define those variables!

4. Update the onPress code to read as follows (changes in bold):

```
on (press) {
  this.dragClip = function() {
    this._x = this._parent._xmouse - this.offsetX;
    this._y = this._parent._ymouse - this.offsetY;
    this.moveX = this._x - this.prevX;
    this.moveY = this._y - this.prevY;
    this.prevX = this._x;
    this.prevY = this._y;
    updateAfterEvent();
  };
  clearInterval(this.throwInterval);
  clearInterval(this.dragInterval);
  this.dragInterval = setInterval(this, "dragClip", 40);
  this.offsetX = this._xmouse;
  this.offsetY = this._ymouse;
  this.prevX = this._x;
  this.prevY = this._y;
}
```

In the dragClip function, you set your moveX and moveY variables that you saw in the last step. These variables hold how far the clip has moved since the previous function call. You do this by subtracting the previous position from the current position. The previous position is stored in prevX and prevY, which you then set to be equal to the clip's current position. These variables are saved in the scope of your clip, and so are available the next time you enter the dragClip function.

After the function, you clear a throwInterval if it's still running and set your initial prevX and prevY variables before you start your dragInterval (the first dragInterval call won't actually occur immediately, but after 40 milliseconds have passed). Now when you drag and release the clip, it will continue moving based on how fast it was moving when released. Test the movie and see.

With dragging and throwing implemented, let's add one final piece to your code—collision detection. You'll specify another clip on the stage that will act as the boundary for your dragged clip.

5. Draw a large rectangle that covers most of the stage. Convert it into a movie clip and name the instance `boundary`. Make sure that the `boundary` instance is below the `dragClip` instance, as shown in Figure 6-5, by either placing `boundary` on a layer below `dragClip`, or by sending it to the bottom of the stack (*Ctrl* and down arrow key).

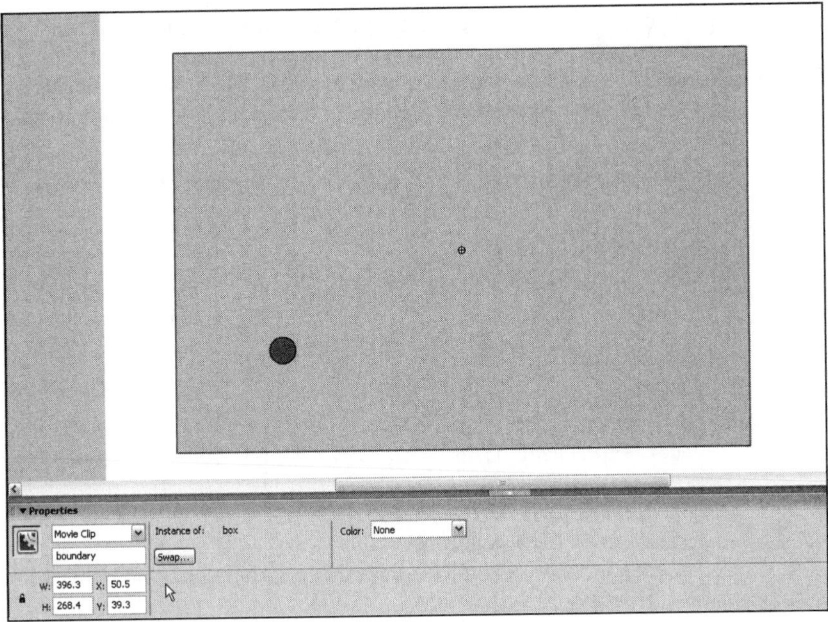

Figure 6-5. A `boundary` instance placed under the `dragClip` instance

6. Select `dragClip` once more and add the following code. All code should be on `dragClip`—`boundary` will *not* contain any code.

```
onClipEvent (load) {
  $boundingClip$ = this._parent.boundary;
  this.bounds = $boundingClip$.getBounds(this._parent);
  this.checkBounds = function() {
    // if hitting right boundary
    if (this._x + this._width/2 > this.bounds.xMax) {
      this._x = this.bounds.xMax - this._width/2;
      if (this.thrown) this.moveX *= -1;
    // if hitting left boundary
    } else if (this._x - this._width/2 < this.bounds.xMin) {
      this._x = this.bounds.xMin + this._width/2;
      if (this.thrown) this.moveX *= -1;
    }
    // if hitting bottom boundary
    if (this._y + this._height/2 > this.bounds.yMax) {
      this._y = this.bounds.yMax - this._height/2;
      if (this.thrown) this.moveY *= -1;
```

```
      // if hitting top boundary
      } else if (this._y - this._height/2 < this.bounds.yMin) {
        this._y = this.bounds.yMin + this._height/2;
        if (this.thrown) this.moveY *= -1;
      }
    }
  }
```

You don't actually want the collision detection occurring on a button-type event (onPress, onRelease, etc.). All you actually need to do is define a function that will check boundaries, and the best place to do that is when the clip loads. Once again, you set a new variable using the dollar sign notation that will become important when you move to XML. In this case, you set `$boundingClip$` to reference the boundary instance you created last step. You then store the bounds of the boundary clip within a new bounds variable (this doesn't need the dollar signs since you're setting its value here—it doesn't receive its value from the XML).

The checkBounds function that then follows contains two `if/else` if statements to ensure your clip stays within its boundaries. The nested `if` statements (`if (this.thrown)` . . .) check to see if the object is no longer in the user's control. If it's being dragged (not thrown), then the checkBounds function merely keeps the clip from moving outside the boundaries. If the user has released the mouse button, however, the clip's directional vector (stored in moveX and moveY) is reversed on one axis, causing a nice bounce off in the opposite direction.

Now you just need to update your onPress and onRelease handlers to work with the boundaries.

7. Add the following bold lines to the two handlers:

```
on (press) {
  this.dragClip = function() {
    this._x = this._parent._xmouse - this.offsetX;
    this._y = this._parent._ymouse - this.offsetY;
    this.moveX = this._x - this.prevX;
    this.moveY = this._y - this.prevY;
    this.prevX = this._x;
    this.prevY = this._y;
    this.checkBounds();
    updateAfterEvent();
  };
  clearInterval(this.throwInterval);
  clearInterval(this.dragInterval);
  this.dragInterval = setInterval(this, "dragClip", 40);
  this.offsetX = this._xmouse;
  this.offsetY = this._ymouse;
  this.prevX = this._x;
  this.prevY = this._y;
  delete this.thrown;
}
on (release, releaseOutside) {
  $weight$ = .9;
```

```
this.throwClip = function() {
  this._x += (this.moveX*=$weight$);
  this._y += (this.moveY*=$weight$);
  this.checkBounds();
  if (Math.abs(this.moveX) < 1 && Math.abs(this.moveY) < 1) {
    delete this.thrown;
    clearInterval(this.throwInterval);
  }
  updateAfterEvent();
}
clearInterval(this.dragInterval);
clearInterval(this.throwInterval);
this.throwInterval = setInterval(this, "throwClip", 40);
this.thrown = 1;
}
```

Now you have both interval functions call checkBounds each time the respective function is run. You also create a new variable thrown when the clip is released, which is removed when the clip comes to a stop or is pressed again. This will allow for the clip to bounce when it hits a boundary after being released. Test your movie now to see it all working nicely together. You have the code where you need it. It's time you make some XML to define your behavior.

Designing the Drag Dialog Box

8. If you haven't yet dropped the `DialogDesigner.swf` file into your `WindowSWF` folder, do so now and relaunch Flash. The `WindowSWF` folder will be located in your `Configuration` folder, along with the `Behaviors` folder you looked into at the start of the chapter. If you are on a Mac and have not yet created a WindowSWF folder, you will need to do so within your `Configuration` folder.

9. Open the Dialog Designer from Window ➤ Other Panels ➤ DialogDesigner. By default, you'll be in behavior mode (the combo box menu defines the mode), which means the necessary tags have already been set up for you (see Figure 6-6).

10. Select the `<behavior_definition>` node and the category attribute should appear in the attribute name field at right. Enter `Drag Physics` as the category, as shown in Figure 6-7, which will be a new menu in the Behaviors panel containing your collection of behaviors.

11. For the next `<behavior_definition>` attribute, select class from the attribute name combo box and enter `movieclip` in the attribute value. This attribute controls what clips the behavior will appear for in the Behaviors panel. For instance, setting no class value will mean that the attribute will be available for any frame, button, or movie clip. If you specify `button`, it will only be available and appear for buttons. You can be very specific about the class, perhaps specifying `mx.controls.CheckBox` if you only wanted a behavior applied to instances of the check box component. You can also specify multiple classes in the attribute, such as "`buttons, mx.controls.CheckBox`". For your Drag Clip behavior, you specify `MovieClip` as the class of choice.

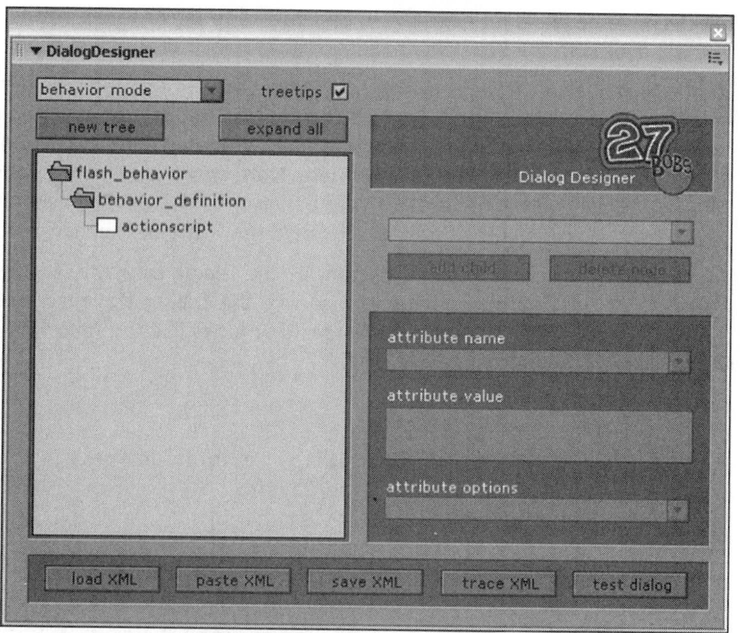

Figure 6-6. The Dialog Designer set up to construct behavior XML

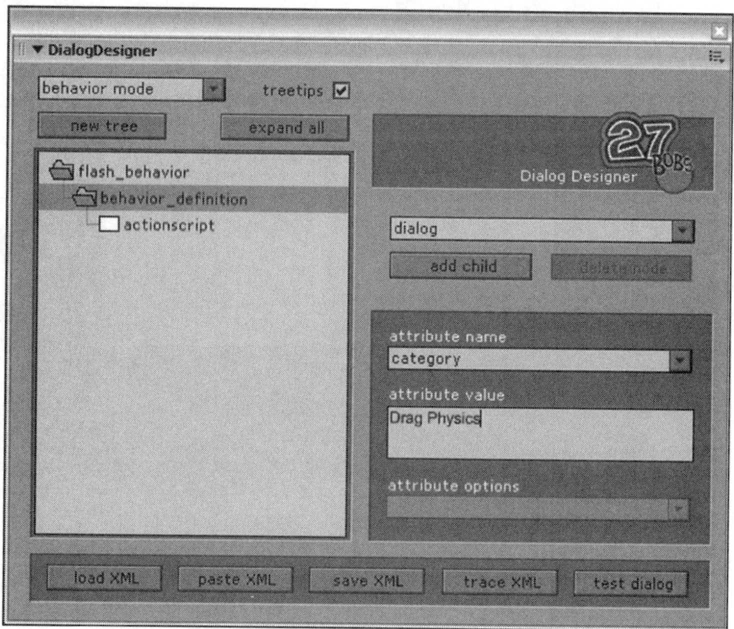

Figure 6-7. Adding the behavior information to the Dialog Designer

6

12. Select the name attribute next and enter `Drag Clip` for its value. This is the name as it will appear in the Behaviors panel.

13. For the final `<behavior_definition>` attribute, select events and set its value to `On Press`. If you didn't specify an event, then all of the button events would appear in the Behaviors panel for this behavior. However, you only want this action to occur when a clip is pressed, so you specify it here. Now, *only* this event will appear in the Behaviors panel and will be used for your behavior by default. The `events` attribute can accept a list of events as well, which you'll see in the next behavior you create.

14. Hit the trace XML button at the bottom of the Dialog Designer, add whitespace when prompted and trace to here, meaning the Dialog Designer interface. As shown in Figure 6-8, you should have XML that looks like the following (or if you wish to type in the behavior, here it is):

```
<?xml version="1.0"?>
<flash_behavior version="1.0" >
  <behavior_definition name="Drag Clip"  events="On Press"
➥class="movieclip"  category="Drag Physics" >
    <actionscript><![CDATA[]]></actionscript>
  </behavior_definition>
</flash_behavior>
```

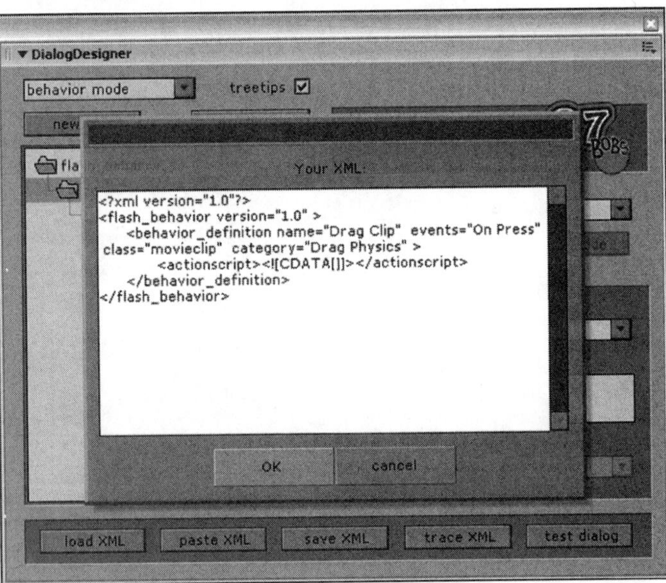

Figure 6-8. The XML produced for the Drag Clip behavior

Now, you can copy and paste this into a new text file and save it as XML, or have the Dialog Designer do it for you. We'll take the latter method, thank you!

15. Close the trace window and click the save XML button at the bottom of the Dialog Designer interface. Save the file as DragClip (you don't need the .xml file extension) and select the Behaviors folder when prompted. That's it! You've now set up your behavior and are ready to paste in your ActionScript.

16. In your text editor of choice, open the DragClip.xml file, which you should now find in your Configuration/Behaviors folder. You need to include your dragging ActionScript from your Flash movie in the CDATA section of the <actionscript> node, so copy the code within the on(press){} block from your Actions panel in Flash. The results should look like the following:

```
<?xml version="1.0"?>
<flash_behavior version="1.0" >
  <behavior_definition name="Drag Clip"  events="On Press"
class="movieclip"  category="Drag Physics" >
<actionscript>
<![CDATA[
  this.dragClip = function() {
    this._x = this._parent._xmouse - this.offsetX;
    this._y = this._parent._ymouse - this.offsetY;
    this.moveX = this._x - this.prevX;
    this.moveY = this._y - this.prevY;
    this.prevX = this._x;
    this.prevY = this._y;
    this.checkBounds();
    updateAfterEvent();
  };
  clearInterval(this.throwInterval);
  clearInterval(this.dragInterval);
  this.dragInterval = setInterval(this, "dragClip", 40);
  this.offsetX = this._xmouse;
  this.offsetY = this._ymouse;
  this.prevX = this._x;
  this.prevY = this._y;
  delete this.thrown;
]]>
</actionscript>
  </behavior_definition>
</flash_behavior>
```

Note that you don't include the actual on(press){} lines since the behavior will automatically add them for you, which it does by default. Now resave your XML file and close it. That's it! One interactive behavior complete. Let's now quickly move through the other two pieces in your Drag Physics behavior group.

6

Throwing Behaviors Around

17. Head back to Flash and the Dialog Designer and click the new tree button. Enter the following attribute values for the <behavior_definition> node:

Attribute	Value
category	`Drag Physics`
class	`movieclip`
defaultEvent	`On Release`
dialogID	`throw-dialog-id`
events	`On Release, On Release Outside`
name	`Throw Clip`

The `category`, `class`, `name`, and `events` attributes you'll recall from the Drag Clip behavior (although notice you supply two possible events in the events list this time). `defaultEvent` is necessary when you want to specify which of the events out of those possible will be selected for the behavior by default. Finally, `dialogID` is the ID of the dialog box that will be associated with this behavior and its properties. This will make more sense in a moment when you create your dialog box.

18. With the `<behavior_definition>` node still selected, select `properties` under the node combo box on the upper right. This combo box shows which child nodes are available for the selected node. Click the add child button to add the `<properties>` node to your XML.

19. Select `<properties>` in the tree at left and you'll see that it doesn't have any attributes available. Instead, you can add `<property>` nodes as child nodes of `<properties>`. These child nodes will set which properties are associated with this behavior and will be sent back to Flash. Add a `<property>` node to the selected `<properties>` node, then select the new node.

20. `<property>` has two attributes you can set (and no child nodes available). The first in the attribute name combo box is id, which will hold the name of your property. Remember in your `on(release){}` ActionScript where you set the variable `$weight$`? Look way back at step 3 to refresh your memory. This variable, whose value you want the user to be able to set in a dialog box, will be defined by a property in the XML. Enter `weight` as the ID *without the dollar signs* (see Figure 6-9). The dollar signs will only be used in your CDATA to specify the variables that will be replaced by property values.

    The second attribute for `<property>` is `default`, and can hold an initial value for your property. This will be the value set when the behavior is first applied (or when the dialog box opens as you apply it), but isn't required. Set the default to 2.

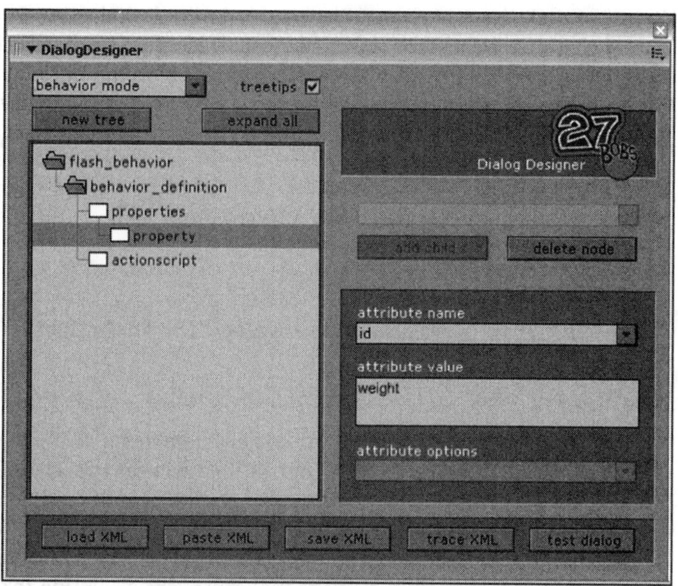

Figure 6-9. Adding properties and values to the XML

Trace your XML and it should look like the following so far:

```
<?xml version="1.0"?>
<flash_behavior version="1.0" >
  <behavior_definition dialogID="throw-dialog-id"  name="Throw Clip"
➥defaultEvent="On Release"  events="On Release,On Release Outside"
➥class="movieclip"  category="Drag Physics" >
    <properties>
      <property default="2"  id="weight" />
    </properties>
    <actionscript><![CDATA[]]></actionscript>
  </behavior_definition>
</flash_behavior>
```

21. Now you need to add a dialog box so the user can enter a weight value. Add a `<dialog>` node to the `<behavior_definition>` node and give it the following attribute values:

Attribute	Value
buttons	`accept, cancel`
id	`throw-dialog-id`
title	`Throw Clip`

6

We covered all these attributes thoroughly in the last chapter. The only thing to note is that the dialog box id attribute corresponds to the dialogID as set in <behavior_definition>. This is necessary to let the behavior know that the values that come from the dialog box will set the properties for the behavior.

22. Add an <hbox> node, then a label and popupslider to the dialog box so that your XML will resemble the following:

```
<dialog title="Throw Clip"  id="throw-dialog-id"
➥buttons="accept,cancel" >
  <hbox>
    <label value="weight" />
    <popupslider maxvalue="9"  minvalue="1"  id="weight" />
  </hbox>
</dialog>
```

The most important thing to note in the new elements is that you've set the id of your popupslider to weight. This control then will set the value for your weight property. Are you beginning to see how everything fits together? The property names are set in each <property> child of the <properties> element in the <behavior_definition>. That <behavior_definition> has a dialogID that is associated with a <dialog> child element that shares the id. Inside this dialog box is a control with an id value associated with a property name, as shown in Figure 6-10. When the user changes the value of a control (in this case, by moving the slider), they are actually setting the property value, which will be included in the ActionScript sent back to Flash, indicated by dollar signs in your code! Go ahead and test the dialog box by hitting the test dialog button at the lower right. Looking good!

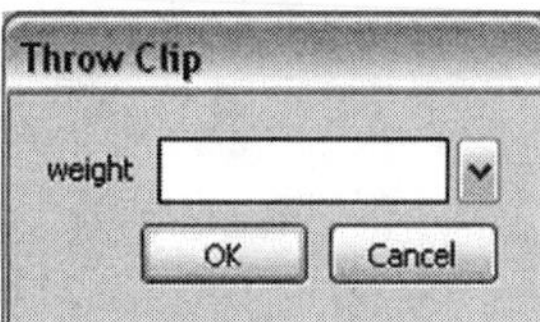

Figure 6-10. The dialog box generated for the Throw Clip behavior

23. Save this behavior as ThrowClip.xml into your Behaviors folder. Open it up in your text editor and paste in the on(release){} code from your Flash movie (remembering to *not* include the actual on(release){} lines). The XML should now look like the following:

```
<?xml version="1.0"?>
<flash_behavior version="1.0" >
  <behavior_definition dialogID="throw-dialog-id"  name="Throw Clip"
➥defaultEvent="On Release"  events="On Release,On Release Outside"
➥class="movieclip"  category="Drag Physics" >
    <properties>
      <property default="2"  id="weight" />
    </properties>
    <dialog title="Throw Clip"  id="throw-dialog-id"
➥buttons="accept,cancel" >
      <hbox>
        <label value="weight" />
        <popupslider maxvalue="9"  minvalue="1"  id="weight" />
      </hbox>
    </dialog>
<actionscript>
```

```
<![CDATA[
  $weight$ = .9;
  this.throwClip = function() {
    this._x += (this.moveX*=$weight$);
    this._y += (this.moveY*=$weight$);
    this.checkBounds();
    if (Math.abs(this.moveX) < 1 && Math.abs(this.moveY) < 1) {
      delete this.thrown;
      clearInterval(this.throwInterval);
    }
    updateAfterEvent();
  }
  clearInterval(this.dragInterval);
  clearInterval(this.throwInterval);
  this.throwInterval = setInterval(this, "throwClip", 40);
  this.thrown = 1;
]]>
</actionscript>
  </behavior_definition>
</flash_behavior>
```


Almost there! Since `weight` will be set in your dialog box, you need to delete where you set it in your code (that was there just so you could test it). The final step is to slightly alter your `$weight$` lines.

24. Make the following changes to the preceding ActionScript:

```
<actionscript>
<![CDATA[
  this.throwClip = function() {
    this._x += (this.moveX*=(1-.$weight$));
    this._y += (this.moveY*=(1-.$weight$));
    this.checkBounds();
```

First of all you delete the explicit variable definition (`$weight$ = .9`). Remember, the dollar sign notation tells Flash to replace the variable between the dollar signs with the value of the property in the XML (usually set by the XML to UI dialog box). In this case, `$weight$` will become a value between 1 and 9, which are the minimum and maximum values of your control slider. Since you want to multiply your `moveX` and `moveY` variables by a number between .1 and .9, you add a decimal point before `$weight$`, and it will subtract this value from 1.

If this manner of adding a decimal seems confusing (at least, it confused us at first), just consider that the `$weight$` variable will be replaced by a number *before* it's sent back to Flash and processed. So if the user sets the slider to 5, the actual ActionScript lines when they appear in Flash will read as follows:

```
this._x += (this.moveX*=(1-.5));
this._y += (this.moveY*=(1-.5));
```

That's pretty cool—automatically you have a decimal!

Later on, you'll do the same thing with strings. Consider this: a combo box with an ID of greeting contains the items hello, hi, and what's up?. You want to put the selected value into a text field back in Flash. You might expect the following line in the CDATA section to work for you:

```
this.textfield_tf.text = $greeting$;
```

However, supposing what's up? was selected, this will become the following back in Flash:

```
this.textfield_tf.text = what's up?;
```

Obviously, this will produce a parsing error. Instead, your ActionScript in the CDATA tag should contain the necessary quotes to make the property value a string:

```
this.textfield_tf.text = "$greeting$";
```

If you haven't yet saved your XML file with the changes, be sure to do so before moving to your final behavior in this group.

Keeping Things in Check

25. Using either the Dialog Designer or typing by hand, create a new XML file named BoundaryCheck.xml with the following lines:

```
<?xml version="1.0"?>
<flash_behavior version="1.0" >
  <behavior_definition dialogID="boundary-dialog-id"  events="custom"
➥name="Boundary Check"  class="movieclip"  category="Drag Physics" >
    <properties>
      <property id="boundingClip" />
    </properties>
    <dialog title="Boundary Check"  id="boundary-dialog-id"
➥buttons="accept,cancel" >
      <hbox>
        <label value="bounding clip:" />
        <targetlist required="true"  id="boundingClip"
➥class="movieclip" />
      </hbox>
    </dialog>
    <actionscript><![CDATA[]]></actionscript>
  </behavior_definition>
</flash_behavior>
```

There is nothing new in this XML except the line we've made bold for emphasis. Although we discussed the events attribute before, we didn't mention that one of the best options you can give it is custom. By default, when a behavior is applied to a clip, it's placed within the standard button event handlers. This isn't always what you want, however. By specifying custom as the event, you override that default functionality and the code will not be included within the on() events. Now, since you need to include code within *some* kind of block when placed on a clip (or else you'll get an error), the best option is to include all of your code inside an onClipEvent(load), which is actually how you'll construct the rest of your components in this chapter (and, indeed, that's how we've constructed the majority of our own components).

26. Add the onClipEvent(load) code block from your Flash movie (see step 6 earlier in this chapter), without the initial $boundingClip$ definition, so that your <actionscript> node looks like the following:

```
<actionscript>
<![CDATA[
onClipEvent (load) {
  this.bounds = $boundingClip$.getBounds(this._parent);
  this.checkBounds = function() {
    // if hitting right boundary
    if (this._x + this._width/2 > this.bounds.xMax) {
      this._x = this.bounds.xMax - this._width/2;
      if (this.thrown) this.moveX *= -1;
    // if hitting left boundary
    } else if (this._x - this._width/2 < this.bounds.xMin) {
      this._x = this.bounds.xMin + this._width/2;
      if (this.thrown) this.moveX *= -1;
    }
    // if hitting bottom boundary
    if (this._y + this._height/2 > this.bounds.yMax) {
      this._y = this.bounds.yMax - this._height/2;
      if (this.thrown) this.moveY *= -1;
    // if hitting top boundary
    } else if (this._y - this._height/2 < this.bounds.yMin) {
      this._y = this.bounds.yMin + this._height/2;
      if (this.thrown) this.moveY *= -1;
    }
  }
}
]]>
</actionscript>
```

Once again, you don't need to set your $boundingClip$ variable since it will be set in your dialog box, so you remove that line. Also notice that this time you *do* include your onClipEvent(){} block tags. Remember, if you choose custom as the event, Flash will not wrap your code inside a block, so you'll need to do this yourself.

27. Make sure all three XML files are saved, and then in Flash reload your behaviors using the Reload option in the Behaviors panel menu. Now on the stage, make a box movie clip for your boundary and a small circle for your draggable clip, then apply your three new behaviors, which you'll find in the Behaviors panel under Drag Physics. Test the movie to see the result of your new physics behaviors stacked on one clip! It should look something like Figure 6-11. (You can also see this in action in dragPhysics.swf.)

6

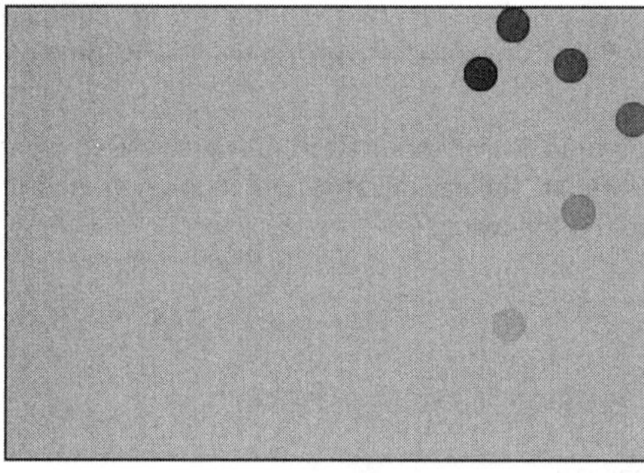

Figure 6-11.
The finished Drag Clip, Throw Clip, and Boundary Check behaviors working together

One addition that you'll find is necessary is to add a second Throw Clip behavior with the `Event` *set as* `On Release Outside`. *If you do this and then open up your Actions panel, you'll see the exact same code for both the* `on(release)` *and* `on(releaseOutside)` *blocks. In a later exercise, you'll look at a way of avoiding this redundancy in your code.*

Dynamic Properties with SWF Dialog Boxes

An issue we've run into when developing behaviors is the inability to dynamically set additional properties/variables for a behavior using the standard XML to UI controls. Every property you wish to be passed to Flash must be named in the `<properties>` node. This means that if you wanted the user to enter a list of items that could number anywhere between one and a hundred, you would have to define property names for one hundred properties even if the user needed only one. There is one way to get over this hurdle, however, and the answer lies in embedded SWF controls.

You'll recall from Chapter 5 that one control you can include in your dialog boxes is a SWF file. What this allows is the ability to have much more extensive control over how the user can enter variables in the dialog box. In this next exercise, you'll explore the possibilities by creating a SWF interface that provides a means for the user to enter a list of values.

A Flash Component Interface

A new feature made possible in Flash MX 2004 is the ability to add custom commands to the user's right-click menu. One of the first behaviors we developed was a simple means for a developer to define custom right-click menu items for a movie clip. Let's step through the process:

1. Create a new Flash document and save it as `addOptions.fla` into your `Configuration/Behaviors` folder. This will be the SWF control in a dialog box, so it's important that the file is in the same folder as your behavior (this isn't absolutely necessary, but will make things a lot easier!). Make the movie's dimensions 300 by 170.

2. Drag a TextInput field from the `UI Components` folder in your Components panel onto the upper left of the stage. Give it an instance name of `newOption_ti`. Put a Button component (again from `UI Components`) next to it with the instance name `addOption_bn` and the label "add option". We also added a label above the TextInput instance with the text "add option" (see Figure 6-12).

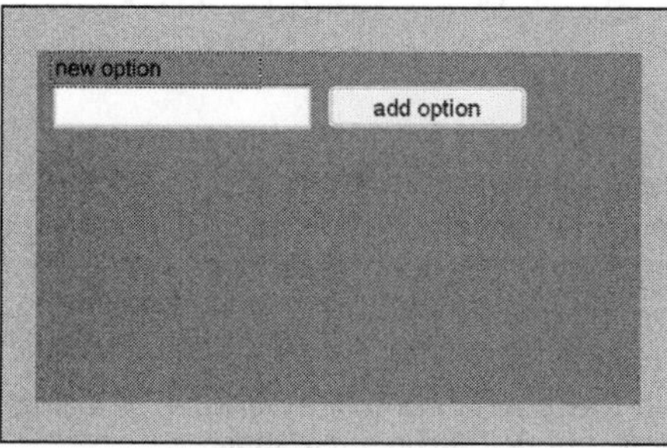

Figure 6-12.
Laying out the interface elements for the Add Right-Click Options behavior

3. Next drag a List from `UI Components` onto the stage and give it an instance name `options_lb`. To its right, drop another two TextInput fields, naming them `optionName_ti` and `handlerName_ti`. Give them the labels "option name" and "option handler".

6

4. Finally, drag another Button component onto the stage and place it at the bottom of the interface, giving it the instance name `removeOption_bn` and the label "remove option" as shown in Figure 6-13.

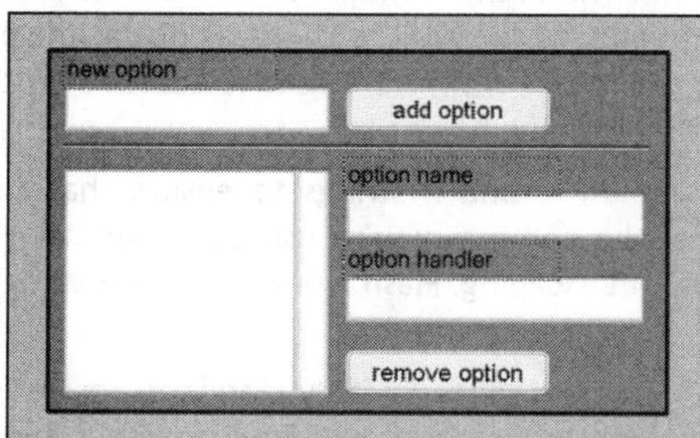

Figure 6-13.
The finished interface for the Add Right-Click Options behavior, including List, TextInput, and Button components

Just for kicks, we added some lines and a border to the interface. Feel free to enhance it any way you wish before moving on to the code.

5. Create a new layer named code and with its first frame selected, open your Actions panel. Type the following:

```
_global.style.setStyle("fontSize", 11);
options = [];
// sets options and handlers variable in XML-to-UI dialog box
function setOptions() {
  var o = "";
  var h = "";
  for (var i = 0; i < options.length; i++) {
```

```
    o += options[i].name + ",";
    h += options[i].handler + ",";
  }
  o = o.slice(0, -1);
  h = h.slice(0, -1);
  var js = "fl.xmlui.set('options','" + escape(o) + "');";
  js += "fl.xmlui.set('handlers','" + escape(h) + "');";
  MMExecute(js);
};
```

The first line in the preceding example merely changes the text size in your components. The second line initializes an array you'll use to store your right-click options within this movie. The juicy bit, though, is the setOptions() function below that. What this function will do is run through your options array, which will be full of option names and handler names, and place all the values into two string variables, o and h. It will send these variables to the XML to UI dialog box, in this way compressing many options into two distinct variables.

You start the function off by initializing your o and h variables, which will hold strings for your **options** and **handlers**. You then run through your options array. In each index you'll store an object containing a name and handler property. You'll add the value for each of these properties to your o and h strings, separating them all by commas. Once this is complete, you use slice to take off the last comma of the string, since it's the final option and doesn't need a comma because no other options follow. In the final two lines, you use MMExecute to send back two JavaScript commands. The first command sets the property options to the o value, while the second places the h value within the handlers property. Thus you've taken an array of values and sent them back to the XML to UI dialog box as the property options and handlers. (You could just as easily have used XMLUI.set for the same purpose of communicating with the dialog box.)

By the way, you have to escape the o and h strings to ensure that characters entered by the user (as well as the commas you're using in your string) are all allowed in your dialog box. Without escaping, Flash would throw up an ugly dialog box reprimanding you!

The rest of the code for your Flash interface is fairly standard, so we won't go through it line by line. The only thing you might not be familiar with is the new way to work with components and their events. We'll discuss this briefly after you take a look at the rest of the code:

```
// adds option to list
addOption_ln = {};
addOption_ln.click = function() {
  if (newOption_ti.text != "") {
    options_lb.addItem(newOption_ti.text, "");
    options.push({name:newOption_ti.text, handler:""});
    newOption_ti.text = "";
    setOptions();
  }
};
addOption_bn.addEventListener("click", addOption_ln);
```

```
// removes option from list
removeOption_ln = {};
removeOption_ln.click = function() {
  options.splice(options_lb.getSelectedIndex(), 1);
  options_lb.removeItemAt(options_lb.getSelectedIndex());
  setOptions();
};
removeOption_bn.addEventListener("click", removeOption_ln);

// changes option name
optionName_ti.onKillFocus = optionName_ti.onChanged = function() {
  options[options_lb.getSelectedIndex()].name = this.text;
  options_lb.replaceItemAt(options_lb.getSelectedIndex(), this.text,
➥handlerName_ti.text);
  setOptions();
};

// changes handler name
handlerName_ti.onKillFocus = handlerName_ti.onChanged = function() {
  options[options_lb.getSelectedIndex()].handler = this.text;
  options_lb.replaceItemAt(options_lb.getSelectedIndex(),
➥optionName_ti.text, this.text);
  setOptions();
};

// sets fields based on item selected
option_ln = {};
option_ln.change = function() {
  optionName_ti.text = options_lb.getSelectedItem().label;
  handlerName_ti.text = options_lb.getSelectedItem().data;
};
options_lb.addEventListener("change", option_ln);
```

Instead of specifying changeHandlers or clickHandlers for components as you did in Flash MX, you now have a much more robust method of dealing with component events. The process makes a lot of sense once you get used to it and involves adding listeners to hear events broadcast by the components. For example, when a button is pressed, it sends a click event out to any object registered to hear the event. Each listener object must then have a function defined named click that will run when that event is fired.

In the preceding code, you create listeners for every component. Each component then adds the appropriate listener to hear the proper events, which correspond to functions defined in the listener objects. So when addOption_bn is clicked, the click function in the addOption_ln object is run.

What exactly does this interface do then? It allows the user to enter a menu option label and add it to a list (option_lb). When an item in the list is selected, the user can change its name as well as enter a name for the option's handler, which will be the function called when the option is clicked in the right-click menu.

6

The `removeOption_bn` obviously will remove the selected option from the list. Notice how nearly all of the functions call your `setOptions()` function, so that the properties in the dialog box will be constantly updated.

6. Test the movie to make sure all of the code is working properly, adding and removing options, and then close out of the addOptions movie (see Figure 6-14).

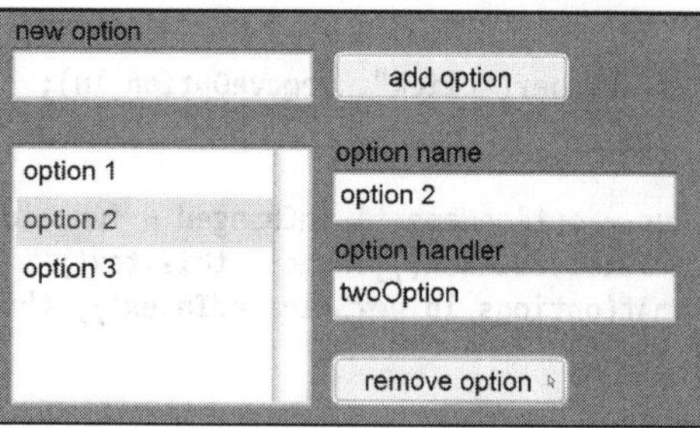

Figure 6-14.
The Add Right-Click Options interface working

You're now ready to create your behavior, but first let's look at the ActionScript you'll need to add right-click menu options since this is a new feature you might not have explored.

Custom Right-Click Menu

7. Create a new Flash document and within it create a new movie clip of any shape and name its instance `clip`. Now select frame one of the main timeline, open the Actions panel, and type in the following code:

```
function mainHandler() {
  trace("menu opened");
}
function oneHandler() {
  trace("option one clicked");
}
function twoHandler() {
  trace("option two clicked");
}

cM = new ContextMenu(mainHandler);

one = new ContextMenuItem("option one", oneHandler);
two = new ContextMenuItem("option two", twoHandler);

cM.customItems.push(one);
cM.customItems.push(two);

clip.menu = cM;
```

First, you define three functions. The first will be the function called whenever the right-click menu is opened, before any options are selected. The next two functions will be called when a particular option is pressed. You then create a new

ContextMenu instance, which is a new object in Flash MX 2004, passing the mainHandler function in the constructor. The next two lines create your two options using the ContextMenuItem constructor. Here you pass the option's name as it will appear in the menu, as well as the function that will be called upon selecting the option.

Once you have your options, you can place them within the ContextMenu instance's customItems array. The final line sets the clip's menu to equal your new custom menu. Now, when you right-click the clip, the first two options will be your custom options. Test it and see. You should get something like the result in Figure 6-15.

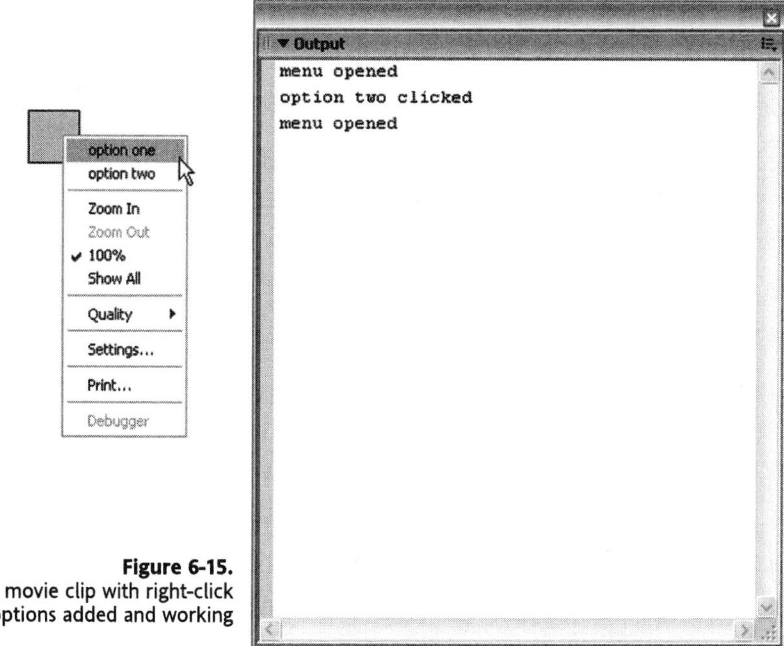

Figure 6-15. A movie clip with right-click options added and working

For your behavior, though, you won't know exactly how many options the user will want for the menu, so you'll have to use a loop to count. The properties you'll have the user define in the dialog box are menuHandler (the name of the function called when the menu is opened), options (the string containing all of the option names, separated by commas), handlers (the string containing all of the handler names, separated by commas), and target (the path to the clip the menu should be applied to). Here is some dummy code for clarification (you don't need to put this anywhere):

```
$target$ = this;
$menuHandler$ = mainHandler;
$options$ = "option one, option two";
$handlers$ = "oneHandler,twoHandler";

var cM = new ContextMenu($menuHandler$);
var o = $options$.split(",");
```

```
var h = $handlers$.split(",");
for (var i = 0; i < o.length; i++) {
  var item = new ContextMenuItem(o[i], this._parent[h[i]]);
  cM.customItems.push(item);
}
$target$.menu = cM;
```

Do you see how it will work? options and handlers will be split into arrays. The length of these arrays can be used to add the appropriate number of ContextMenuItems to the ContextMenu. All you need to do now is build the behavior around this.

8. Either using the Dialog Designer or typing by hand, save a new file named RightClick.xml with the following XML:

```
<?xml version="1.0"?>
<flash_behavior version="1.0" >
  <behavior_definition events="custom" dialogID="Right_Click-dialog"
➥category="Movieclip"  class="movieclip"  name="Add Right Click
➥Options" >
    <properties>
      <property id="menuHandler" />
      <property id="target"  default="this" />
      <property id="options" />
      <property id="handlers" />
    </properties>
    <dialog id="Right_Click-dialog"  title="Add Right Click Options"
➥buttons="accept, cancel" >
      <grid>
        <columns>
          <column/>
        </columns>
        <rows>
          <row>
            <label value="menu handler:" />
          </row>
          <row>
            <textbox id="enuHandler" />
          </row>
          <row>
            <label value="apply to:" />
          </row>
          <row>
            <targetlist required="true"  class="movieclip, button"
➥id="target" />
          </row>
          <row>
            <flash src="addOptions.swf"  height="170"  width="300"
➥id="flashMovie" >
              <property id="options" />
              <property id="handlers" />
```

```
                </flash>
              </row>
            </rows>
          </grid>
        </dialog>
        <actionscript>
<![CDATA[
onClipEvent(load) {
  // be sure to define functions on parent timeline

  var m = new ContextMenu(this._parent.$menuHandler$);
  var o = unescape("$options$").split(",");
  var h = unescape("$handlers$").split(",");
  for (var i = 0; i < o.length; i++) {
    var item = new ContextMenuItem(o[i], this._parent[h[i]]);
    m.customItems.push(item);
  }
  $target$.menu = m;
}
]]>
    </actionscript>
  </behavior_definition>
</flash_behavior>
```

Most of this should be quite familiar to you by now, so we just highlighted the lines you should pay attention to. First, of course, is the fact that you're again setting the events to custom in order to bypass the default button events. You also need to be sure to set a dialogID that will correspond to the id attribute of your dialog box. Next, you define all four of the properties you want passed to Flash. The only one you give a default value to is target.

Down in your dialog box, you've included a <flash> element with a src attribute that points to your SWF file (if you didn't drop the SWF into your Behaviors folder, this is where you would specify your own path). The id attribute is included here, but unnecessary. Special interest should be paid to the <flash> child nodes, though. Here you define the two properties that the SWF will set in the dialog box. Since a SWF file can only set properties that have been defined *in the dialog box* (not just in the <property> nodes in the behavior definition), these need to be included with the <flash> element.

Finally, notice down in your ActionScript contained within the CDATA section that you must "unescape" your options and handlers variables since you escaped them within the SWF file. Also, to make them strings, you need to place quotes around the variables. This might seem unintuitive since both options and handlers *contain* string values, but remember that these variables will be evaluated before they are sent back to Flash. This means that if options had the value of option%20one%2Coption%20two and you left out the quotes, then the ActionScript would become

```
var o = unescape(option%20one%2Coption%20two).split(",");
```

6

Therefore, you need to include the quotes for the line to read as follows:

```
var o = unescape("option%20one%2Coption%20two").split(",");
```

9. Go ahead and save the XML file (test the dialog box first if you like), then in Flash reload the behaviors using the reload command in the Behaviors panel menu (remember you need to do this each time you create or edit one of the behavior XML files). Make a new movie clip in a movie and apply your new behavior. The dialog box shown in Figure 6-16 should open for you to enter your options. In order for the menu options to appear in the published movie, you'll also need to define the functions on the clip's parent timeline. (Flash is smart that way and won't show the menu options if the corresponding functions don't exist.)

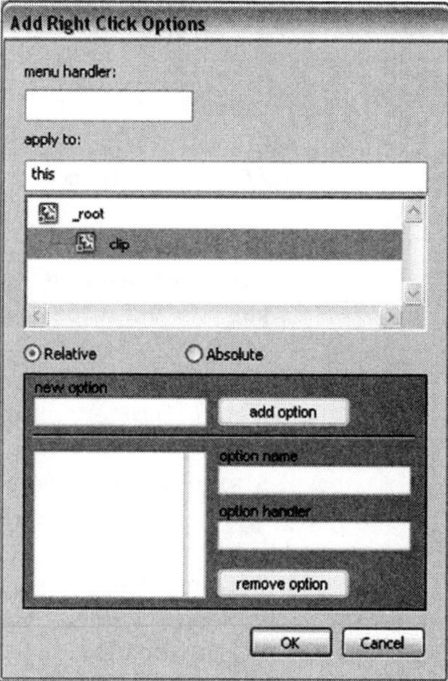

Figure 6-16. The dialog box for the Add Right-Click Options behavior

Behavior Clips

Two of the biggest issues we've found with behaviors concern how behaviors place code directly on instances. First, with the release of Flash MX and its new dynamic event model, you learned to centralize your code and leave behind the ways of Flash 5, which often saw code spread out onto every clip and nested clip in your movies. Now with behaviors, it seems as if Macromedia is encouraging you to return to your less productive and more frustrating ways. Second, if you have multiple clips with the same behavior, the code is placed on all clips. You're left with redundant code and the inability to edit the code in one central location in order for it to affect all clips.

It's obvious that behaviors aren't intended for the advanced Flash user, and are geared more toward the beginner, or the developer less interested in learning the ways of ActionScript. Does this mean that advanced users should ignore behaviors, or if developing behaviors for others you should ignore the best coding practices? We say to thee, "No!"

The final exercise in this chapter will explore developing a behavior that creates a centralized instance in the Library, much like a component. Clips that have the behavior applied to them will simply attach the behavior from the Library. In this way you prevent redundancy of code and provide a way to edit the behavior for all instances it's applied to.

Following the Leader

The behavior you'll make is a "follower" behavior. Clips with this action applied to them will follow the mouse around the screen, either when the mouse is down, or to the last clicked position, or continuously (see Figure 6-17).

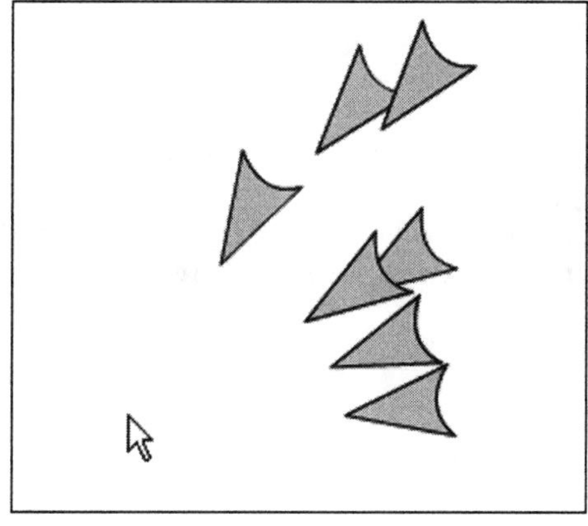

Figure 6-17.
A set of movie clips with behaviors to follow and turn toward the mouse

1. Using either the Dialog Designer or by typing it by hand, create a new file named `MouseFollower.xml` with the following XML:

```
<?xml version="1.0"?>
<flash_behavior version="1.0" >
  <behavior_definition dialogID="follower-dialog"  name="Mouse
➥Follower"  events="custom"  class="movieclip"  category="Movieclip" >
    <properties>
      <property default="2"  id="xRate" />
      <property default="2"  id="yRate" />
      <property id="followOption" />
      <property default="false"  id="hideMouse" />
    </properties>
    <dialog title="Mouse Follower"  id="follower-dialog" >
      <vbox>
        <hbox>
          <label control="xRate"  value="rate on x-axis:" />
          <popupslider id="xRate"  minvalue="1"  maxvalue="10" />
        </hbox>
        <hbox>
          <label value="rate on y-axis:"  control="yRate" />
          <popupslider maxvalue="10"  minvalue="1"  id="yRate" />
        </hbox>
        <vbox>
          <label control="followOption"  value="follow option:" />
          <menulist id="followOption" >
            <menupop>
```

```
                <menuitem value="onDown"  label="move only while mouse is
➥down" />
                <menuitem value="onClick"  label="move when mouse is
➥clicked" />
                <menuitem value="onMove"  label="move continuously" />
              </menupop>
            </menulist>
            <checkbox label="hide mouse"  id="hideMouse"  accesskey="h" />
          </vbox>
          <hbox>
            <button label="cancel" oncommand="fl.xmlui.cancel();"
➥id="cancel_bn" accesskey="c" />
            <button label="accept" oncommand="fl.runScript(fl.configURI +
➥'/Behaviors/MouseFollower.jsfl');fl.xmlui.accept();" id="accept_bn"
➥accesskey="a" />
          </hbox>
        </vbox>
      </dialog>
  </behavior_definition>
</flash_behavior>
```

We won't address the behavior XML since you've seen it all before in previous examples and in Chapter 5. The important lines are in bold. You don't set any default buttons in the <dialog> node, but instead create two of your own accept and cancel buttons within the dialog box. The cancel button merely calls the cancel method and closes the box, but the accept button does something much more interesting. It runs a JSFL script found in the Behaviors folder before calling the standard accept method of the dialog box, which closes the box and sends its values back to Flash. Because of what you do with the JSFL file, though, you can't apply your ActionScript in the manner you have in previous examples. Notice that the <actionscript> node has been left out of this behavior entirely. Obviously the meat of your behavior must then lie in that JSFL file—so let's write that code now.

2. Create a new Flash JavaScript file named MouseFollower.jsfl and save it into your Behaviors folder. Add the following lines of code:

```
var doc = fl.getDocumentDOM();
var sel = doc.selection[0];
var fO = fl.xmlui.get("followOption");
var hM = fl.xmlui.get("hideMouse");
var xR = fl.xmlui.get("xRate");
var yR = fl.xmlui.get("yRate");
```

After storing the reference to the current document, you find the current selection and place it in the sel variable. Then you grab all four of the property values from the dialog box. You'll need these to add to your selected clip.

3. Add these lines of code next:

```
var script =  "onClipEvent(load) {\n";
script +=     "  this.attachMovie(\"MouseFollower\", \"myFollower\",
➥this.getNextHighestDepth(), {followOption:\"" + fO + "\", xRate:(11-"
➥+ xR + "), yRate:(11-" + yR + ")});\n";
script +=     "  if (" + hM + ") Mouse.hide();\n";
script +=     "}";
sel.actionScript = script;
```

The first four of these lines construct a long string and store it in the script variable. This string (which is four lines of ActionScript) is then added to the current selection. Basically, this means that when you click the accept button in the dialog box, the following lines of code will be added to the selected clip (supposing the values for the four behavior properties):

```
onClipEvent(load) {;
  this.attachMovie("MouseFollower", "myFollower",
➥this.getNextHighestDepth(), {followOption:"onClick",
➥xRate:(11-2), yRate:(11-2)});
  if (true) Mouse.hide();
};
```

6

Obviously then your clip will attach another clip from the Library with the export identifier of MouseFollower. In the initClip, you pass to the attached clip three of the properties from the dialog box. The fourth property, hideMouse, doesn't really need to be passed, and you use its value (which will be either true or false) directly in the final line of ActionScript code.

The majority of your code must then lie within the MouseFollower clip in the Library. Let's look to see how you attach that.

4. Add the following code to your editor:

```
var lib = doc.library;
if (!lib.itemExists("Behavior Clips/MouseFollower")) {
  lib.addNewItem("movieclip", "Behavior Clips/MouseFollower");
  lib.selectItem("Behavior Clips/MouseFollower");
  var i = lib.getSelectedItems()[0];
  i.linkageExportForAS = true;
  i.linkageExportInFirstFrame = true;
  i.linkageIdentifier = "MouseFollower";
  lib.editItem("Behavior Clips/MouseFollower");
  var tl = doc.getTimeline();
  tl.currentLayer = 0;
  tl.setSelectedFrames([0,0,0]);
```

After you store a reference to the document's Library, the if statement checks to see if the clip has already been added to that Library. If it has, the remaining code will not be run—one behavior clip of this type is enough. If it hasn't, though, you need to create it. You do this using addNewItem (the Behavior Clips folder will automatically be created for you if it isn't already there). You then select the item and store a reference to that item in the i variable. You set the item's export values (notice MouseFollower) and enter edit mode for the item. The final three lines are needed to select the first frame of your new MouseFollower clip.

5. The next bit of code holds all of the ActionScript that your MouseFollower will hold, first stored in the script variable. Notice that all of the paths reference the parent timeline since this clip will be attached to the clips it will need to control.

```
script =   "// called to reset movie clip's position\n";
script +=   "this.followMouse = function() {\n";
script +=   "  this._parent._x -= (this._parent._x -
➥_root._xmouse)/this.xRate;\n";
script +=   "  this._parent._y -= (this._parent._y -
➥_root._ymouse)/this.yRate;\n";
script +=   "  updateAfterEvent();\n";
script +=   "};\n";
script +=   "// sends movie clip to last place mouse was clicked\n";
script +=   "this.gotoClick = function() {\n";
script +=   "  this._parent._x -= (this._parent._x -
➥this.endX)/this.xRate;\n";
script +=   "  this._parent._y -= (this._parent._y -
➥this.endY)/this.yRate;\n";
script +=   "  if (Math.abs(this._parent._x - this.endX) < 1 &&
➥Math.abs(this._parent._y - this.endY) < 1) {\n";
script +=   "    this._parent._x = this.endX;\n";
script +=   "    this._parent._y = this.endY;\n";
script +=   "    clearInterval(this.moveInterval);\n";
script +=   "  }\n";
script +=   "  updateAfterEvent();\n";
script +=   "}\n";
script +=   "// begins to follow mouse when mouse is clicked\n";
script +=   "this.startMouseFollow = function() {\n";
script +=   "  if (this.followOption == \"onDown\") {\n";
script +=   "    clearInterval(this.moveInterval);\n";
script +=   "    this.moveInterval = setInterval(this,
➥\"followMouse\", 40);\n";
script +=   "    this.onMouseUp = function() {
➥clearInterval(this.moveInterval) };\n";
script +=   "  } else {\n";
script +=   "    this.endX = _root._xmouse;\n";
script +=   "    this.endY = _root._ymouse;\n";
script +=   "    clearInterval(this.moveInterval);\n";
```

```
  script +=   "    this.moveInterval = setInterval(this, \"gotoClick\",
➥40);\n";
  script +=   "  }\n";
  script +=   "}\n";
  script +=   "switch (this.followOption) {\n";
  script +=   "  // move to clicked position only\n";
  script +=   "  case \"onClick\":\n";
  script +=   "    this.onMouseDown = this.startMouseFollow;\n";
  script +=   "    break;\n";
  script +=   "  // move continuously\n";
  script +=   "  case \"onMove\":\n";
  script +=   "    this._parent._x = _root._xmouse;\n";
  script +=   "    this._parent._y = _root._ymouse;\n";
  script +=   "    clearInterval(this.moveInterval);\n";
  script +=   "    this.moveInterval = setInterval(this,
➥\"followMouse\", 40);\n";
  script +=   "    break;\n";
  script +=   "  // move to mouse only when mouse is down\n";
  script +=   "  case \"onDown\":\n";
  script +=   "    this.onMouseDown = this.startMouseFollow;\n';
  script +=   "    break;\n";
  script +=   "}\n";
```

You can put this all on one long line of code, but it's a little easier to read in this form (well, at least a *little*). We won't go through the code since it's all basic ActionScript and contains helpful comments. Just understand that it controls the behavior of its parent clip based on the three variables passed to it: followOption, xRate, and yrate.

6. The ActionScript was the long part, so now you can finish it up with just a couple lines of code:

```
  tl.setFrameProperty("actionScript", script);
  doc.exitEditMode();
}
```

tl holds a reference to the MouseFollower's timeline. You set the actionscript property of that timeline (and its selected frames) to equal your long script variable. You then exit edit mode and return to the main timeline.

7. Save the JSFL file, and then return to Flash and reload the behaviors in the Behaviors panel. Create a new movie and a new movie clip symbol. With a symbol instance selected, apply your new Mouse Follower behavior. The JSFL and the XML file work together to add a new MouseFollower symbol to the Library and apply the necessary attaching code to your clip (see Figure 6-18). If you create new movie clip instances and apply the same behavior, you'll see that only a few extra lines of code are added to each clip, with the majority of the code resting inside a single symbol in your Library!

6

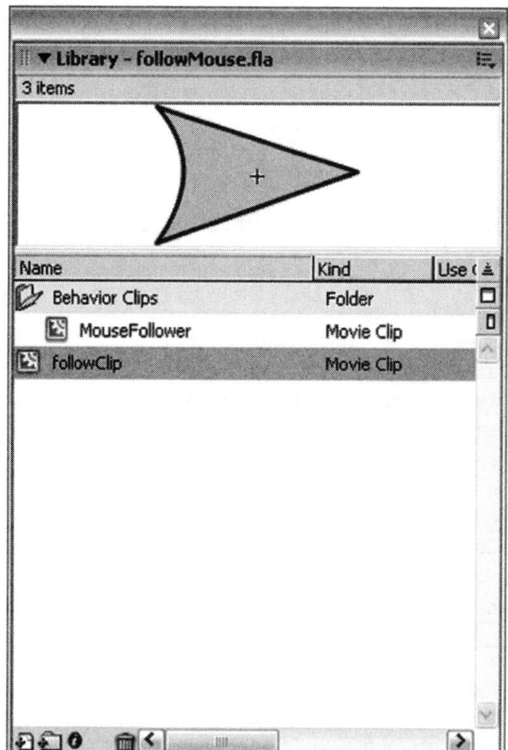

Figure 6-18.
The MouseFollower behavior clip added to the library, storing all behavior code in a central location

> *The* `MouseFollower.jsfl` *file included with this chapter's download files (and available from* `www.flashextensibility.com`*) contains some additional lines that first check whether an* `onClipEvent(load)` *block exists on the selected clip before adding the mouse follower code. Because of this, multiple behaviors can be applied to a single clip. In the file* `followMouse.fla`*, included with the download files as well, a FaceMouse behavior has been combined with a MouseFollower behavior for each clip, with different parameters for each clip.*

With behavior clips set up in this way, code is kept centralized in the Library with a minimal amount placed on the actually clips. Designers and developers with an aversion to code will have it kept tucked safely away, and applying multiple instances won't bloat up the file of their movie with superfluous code.

Summary

There are plenty more examples of behaviors for you to explore before you set off developing your own custom behaviors. In addition to the behaviors that ship with Flash and those available at Macromedia Exchange, this chapter's downloadable files contain several additional behaviors not covered within the text of this chapter. Our web site, `www.flashextensibility.com`, features behaviors created by other developers as well—be sure to check them out.

Behaviors offer a new way of developing in Flash MX 2004 that not only is more user friendly for those uncomfortable within the Actions panel, but also provides a means for rapid development of complex, multiple actions, even for the advanced developer. A multitude of additional functionality can be combined and applied to clips throughout your movie, keeping common code separate and easily accessible. The inclusion of these behaviors, like much of the new extensibility features, requires a new way of thinking for ideal application, but the possibilities these behaviors provide are numerous and exciting.

7 WINDOWSWF AND MMEXECUTE

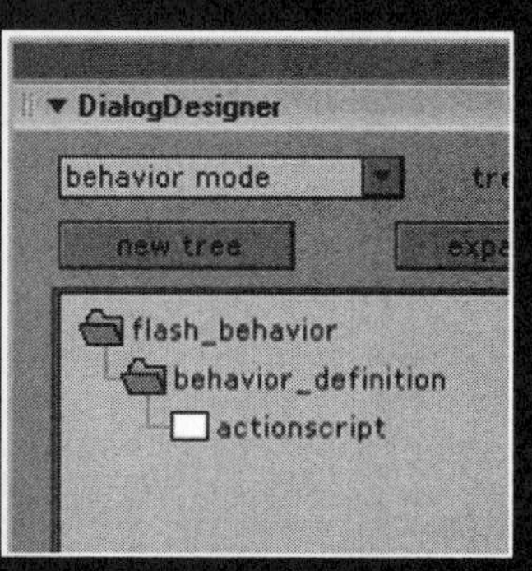


```
var js =    "function
js +=       "   var s
js +=           "   v
js +=           "   f
js +=           "
js +=           "   }
js +=           "   f
js +=           ")";
MMExecute(js);
```

We love this feature. There, we've said it, and we're not ashamed. And by the end of this chapter, we believe you'll share our feelings for WindowSWF movies. What exactly are they? Really, this feature isn't anything new with Flash—you've had the ability to create custom user interfaces that you could open in the Flash authoring environment for the last couple of versions. What *is* new, however, is the ability to use these movies to make changes and interact with the application via the JavaScript API. This unlocks so many possibilities for new tools and enhancements that it's truly staggering.

In this chapter, we'll step through the creation of two new useful tools that can aid you when developing. The first is simply a text field in a window that you can use to directly enter your JSFL commands and have them executed (see Figure 7-1).

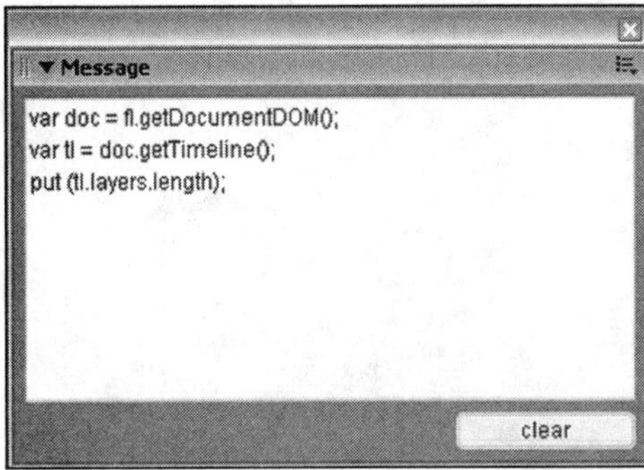

Figure 7-1.
The Message WindowSWF panel allows you to type in JSFL code and have it executed immediately in the authoring environment.

The second, and much more complex, is a search-and-replace tool similar in functionality to the new Find and Replace tool in MX 2004 (Edit ➤ Find and Replace). This application, shown in Figure 7-2, will run through all text in your document (scripts on frames and instances as well as text in text fields) and find phrases that you can alter or replace.

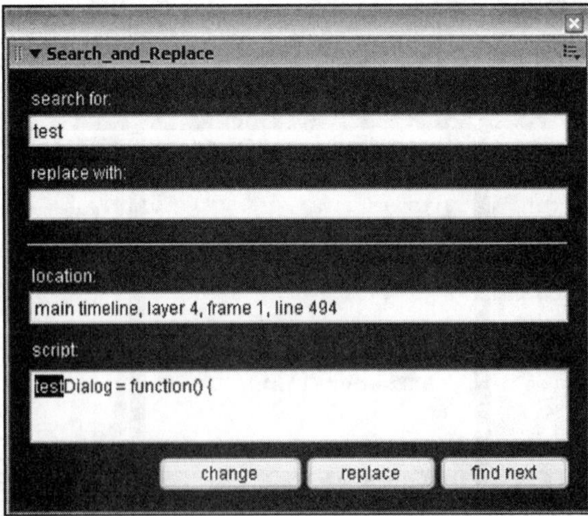

Figure 7-2.
The Search and Replace WindowSWF panel allows you to search for and replace text or code instances in your document.

These tools will hopefully serve to introduce you to what can be accomplished with WindowSWF movies and get you started with developing your own cool interface enhancements.

What's New with WindowSWF?

One of the great things about working through this chapter is that there is very little that you aren't already familiar with, from either working through the previous chapters in this book or from your current ActionScript knowledge. Is there any new ActionScript involved? One command that we've already discussed. Is there any JavaScript API related only to WindowSWF that hasn't been covered elsewhere in this book? Not a thing.

You might be wondering what's so great about WindowSWF movies if they require nothing new to implement them. You've already seen how to use Flash movies as interfaces within XML to UI dialog boxes. Those dialog boxes are modal, which means that while they are open, the user can no longer interact with the authoring environment. With WindowSWF Flash movies, however, you can use all of your ActionScript and JavaScript API knowledge to create nonmodal windows to run your scripts. The user can have the windows open yet still interact with and work in the authoring environment (which has implications on the way you must code these movies, as the state of the authoring environment can change while the window is open). This opens so many doors that we could spend an entire book just on the possibilities. As it is, we devote a hefty chapter to the topic that will not only get your feet wet, but also should leave you bubbling over with ideas on additional tools you could develop.

WindowSWF windows can be opened from the Window ➤ Other Panels menu. SWF movies that appear in this menu have simply been placed in the WindowSWF folder in either the `First Run` folder for your Flash installation (`C:\Program Files\Macromedia\Flash MX 2004\en\First Run` on Windows systems) or the local `Configuration` folder. As noted earlier in this book, the path to `Configuration` will be different for different users and operating systems; for our Windows installation (and we accepted the default path) the folder can be found at `C:\Documents and Settings\Administrator\Local Settings\Application Data\Macromedia\Flash MX 2004\en\Configuration\WindowSWF`. If you're unsure, the best way to find it is run a search for `WindowSWF`. If you are using a Mac, remember that you may have to create this folder yourself in the `Configuration` directory.

We demonstrated the WindowSWF feature in Chapters 5 and 6, most notably when opening the Dialog Designer. The Dialog Designer, shown in Figure 7-3, is good example of how a WindowSWF movie can be used to enhance the authoring environment, make tasks easier, and increase productivity.

Most of the functionality is provided by good ol' ActionScript (in fact, the interface was originally built in Flash MX for another purpose), with the Flash extensibility architecture stepping in to allow the user to save files and test dialog boxes. These added features were made possible by one simple command, `MMExecute()`.

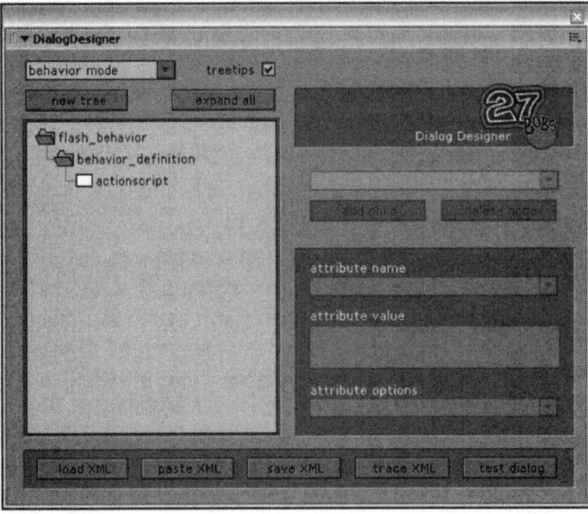

Figure 7-3.
The Dialog Designer WindowSWF panel introduced in Chapter 5 allows you to create XML to UI dialog boxes easily.

MMExecute

As we mentioned a couple of paragraphs before, you have only one command that is new for this chapter, and yet it's one that we've utilized in many previous examples in this book. MMExecute() is an incredibly versatile command that runs JavaScript API commands from within Flash movies that are opened in the authoring environment (it has no effect in a browser or standalone player). Any JSFL code you've learned so far can be passed as the single argument formatted as a string that is then executed. For instance, if you wanted to have a message passed to the Output panel, you might use

```
MMExecute("fl.trace('message');");
```

Notice that the actual JSFL command, fl.trace('message');, is exactly how you would include the line in a separate JSFL file. The only difference is that you must first place the command in quotes to send in MMExecute(). This means that additional quotation marks inside the quotes either need to be escaped (\" or \'), or of a different type, as was demonstrated previously with single quotes included within the double quotes. To write the same line with escaped quotes, you would use

```
MMExecute("fl.trace(\"message\");");
```

MMExecute() will return whatever value might be executed by the JSFL. You can use this functionality to utilize variables and values returned by a JSFL command in your Flash movie interface. As an example, imagine in a SWF interface you have a text field on the stage named myField_tf. If you wished to display the name of the current document in the text field whenever this movie loaded, you might use the following command:

```
myField_tf.text = MMExecute("fl.getDocumentDOM().name;");
```

The JSFL runs and returns the name of the current document, which is then returned by MMExecute(). This value is then placed in the appropriate text field.

It's also good to note that multiple commands can be sent to MMExecute() in a single call, as long as the commands are included in the single string argument. If you wished to grab the current document's name and send it to the Output panel, you could use

```
MMExecute("var n = fl.getDocumentDOM().name;fl.trace(n);");
```

The document name is placed in the variable n and then traced to the Output panel. Even with two lines, this code can get to be pretty confusing to look at. Thankfully, you have a couple of additional options when you wish to execute multiple lines of JSFL. First, you can simply call MMExecute() once for each line, as in the following:

```
MMExecute("var n = fl.getDocumentDOM().name;");
MMExecute("fl.trace(n);");
```

Here, n is remembered from one call to the next, so splitting it to multiple lines in this case keeps the same result while making it more legible. You could also place both lines into a string variable and send the variable in a single call of MMExecute():

```
var js = "var n = fl.getDocumentDOM().name;";
js +=    "fl.trace(n);";
MMExecute(js);
```

This becomes necessary when you wish to have multiple line conditionals or loops, or perhaps create a function. As an example of this, consider this script, which creates and names three new layers:

```
var js = "var doc = fl.getDocumentDOM();";
js +=    "var t = doc.getTimeline();";
js +=    "var lNames = ['one', 'two', 'three'];";
js +=    "for (var i = 0; i < lNames.length; i++) {";
js +=    "  var l = t.addNewLayer(lNames[i]);";
js +=    "}";
MMExecute(js);
```

Could you imagine reading that if it was all contained on one line? Building your scripts in this way allows you to construct complex actions that can be run with a single call to MMExecute().

7

Case Study 1: Message Window

Users of Macromedia Director might be familiar with that application's Message window. It contains a handy little input field that not only acts like the Output panel in Flash, tracing messages sent by the movie, but also allows developers to type in commands that can then alter or affect the authoring environment. The first exercise you'll go through is creating a window that will mimic this latter functionality in Flash. Basically, you'll create an input field in a window that a developer can type JSFL commands into and have them be immediately executed, without having to go to an external JSFL file or relaunch Flash to test. This window will allow a user to not only test and debug JSFL commands instantly (perhaps to then include them in a separate JSFL script), but also enable the quick deployment of additional JavaScript API features for the application or movie.

Creating the Interface

The first step is to create a simple interface for users to enter their JSFL commands. This will consist of a single text field and a button to clear the field. Both will be components taken from the Components panel, since these will provide all the functionality you need, and you don't have to code them!

1. Create a new Flash document and save it as `Message.fla` into your `Configuration/WindowSWF` folder (if you save it into the `First Run` folder instead, you'll have to relaunch Flash each time you change the SWF file, which of course would be undesirable). You stepped through a lengthy process of finding this folder back in Chapter 5, but a quick search of your hard drive should allow you to find the folder without much fuss. Make the movie 350 by 200 pixels with a dark background color of your choice.
2. Once you've saved the file into the proper folder, publish or test the movie to create a SWF. This is the movie that will appear in the Window ➤ Other Panels menu. To see the movie appear in the menu, close your Flash application and relaunch. This is only necessary the first time you create the file (again, as long as you saved the FLA in the `Configuration/WindowSWF` folder). Unlike the XML that Flash reads to create commands and behaviors, the SWF used to produce the movies in a window are read only when the window is launched from the menu. This means that you can make changes to your FLA, publish a new SWF, and then immediately open the new SWF from the Window ➤ Other Panels menu as shown in Figure 7-4.

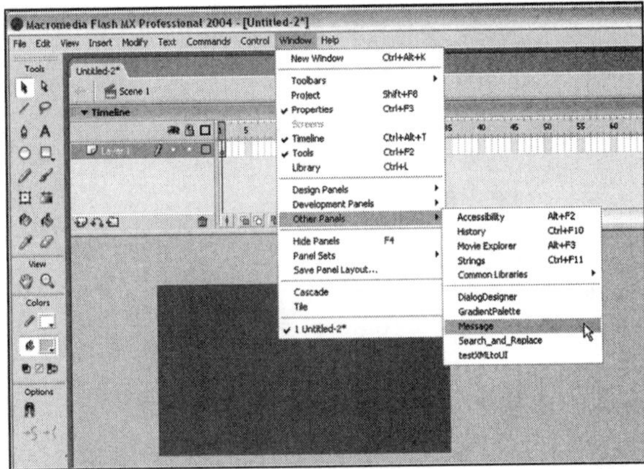

Figure 7-4. The Message WindowSWF file can be accessed from the Window ➤ Other Panels menu.

3. Once you've relaunched Flash and ensured the movie has appeared in the Window menu, create two new layers in your `Message.fla` file. Name the three layers now on the timeline interface, functions, and code.
4. On the interface layer, drag a TextArea and a Button component from the Components panel onto your stage. Resize the TextArea until it covers the majority of the stage and place the Button to the lower right. Name the TextArea instance `input_ta` and the Button `clear_bn`. As shown in Figure 7-5, set the Button component's label as `clear`.

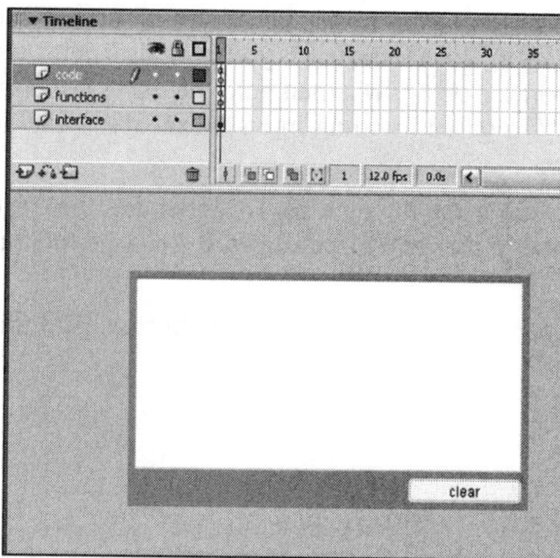

Figure 7-5.
The simple interface for the Message panel

Interface Code

After such few simple steps for laying out your interface, you must be thinking that all of the hard work will lie in the code, correct? Actually, this movie will require so little code it'll perhaps surprise you. You're going to add some amazing functionality to the Flash interface with less than 40 lines!

5. On the code layer, select the first and only frame and open up your ActionScript editor. Type the following:

```
function change(c) {
  var s = c.target.text;
  var c = Selection.getBeginIndex() - 1;
  var pos = s.substr(c, 1);
  if (pos == "\r") {
    var sub = s.substr(0, c);
    lastPos = sub.lastIndexOf("\r") + 1;
    js = s.substr(lastPos, c-lastPos);
    MMExecute(js);
  }
}
input_ta.addEventListener("change", this);
```

Here you create a function to handle the change event fired off by the TextArea component. The c passed as an argument will be a reference to the component itself, so in the function's first line you store the TextArea's text in the variable s. You then find the cursor's position in the field by using the `Selection` object. Once you know the position of the cursor, you use the `substr()` method to check the character right before the cursor position. If this character is a return (`\r` counts as one character), you know the user has just hit the *Enter* key. When this occurs, you'll execute a JSFL command based on the user's last typed line.

Inside the `if` conditional, you place all the text in the TextArea up until the last return into the `sub` variable. Using `lastIndexOf()`, you can also determine the position of the previous return in the text. js will then hold the user's last entire line from one return to the next. You pass this string in an `MMExecute()` call and are done with your change handler.

After the function, you add your main timeline as a listener for the TextArea's change event. Now when the text in the TextArea changes, the change function that you just wrote will be called.

6. You have the TextArea working, so it's time to work on the button. Add this code to your ActionScript:

```
function click(c) {
  input_ta.text = "";
}
clear_bn.addEventListener("click", this);
```

Simple—when the button is clicked, the TextArea will be cleared. Test your movie to compile a new SWF.

To see your Message window in action, open it up from the menu Window ➤ Other Panels ➤ Message. The movie should open up in its own window. Go ahead and type the following into the TextArea:

```
fl.trace("hello");
```

It works! Be a little more adventurous and try the following:

```
fl.getDocumentDOM().library.addNewItem("movieclip", "myFolder/myClip");
```

A new folder with a movie clip inside will be added to your document as shown in Figure 7-6.

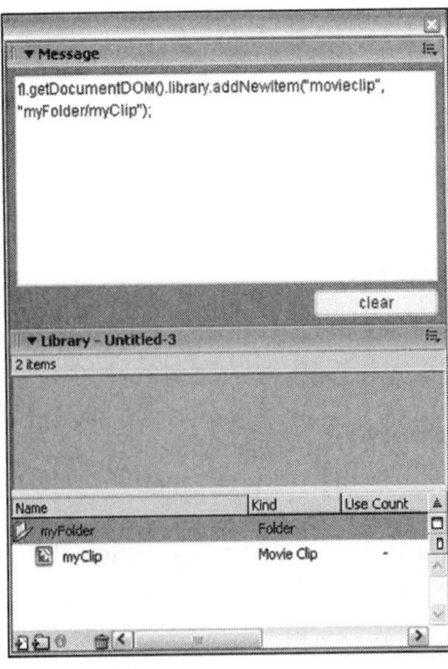

Figure 7-6.
Entering a single JSFL line creates a new folder and nested symbol in your library.

Custom Functions

One thing you can do to enhance your Message window is provide some custom commands for the user to make things even easier than they currently are. First, let's create a `put` command (taken from Director's Lingo) to mimic the `trace` action in Flash. Sure, `fl.trace()` doesn't take terribly long to type, but `put()` does relieve at least a couple of strokes!

7. On the functions layer, select the first frame and enter the following into your ActionScript window:

```
MMExecute("function put(p) { fl.trace(p) }");
```

> *If you wish to test this command, remember to first republish and then reopen the movie as a window.*

In one line you create a function for your Message window. Now users will be able to use `put()` anytime they wish to have something traced to the Output panel. What's good to note about this is that by calling `MMExecute()` when the movie is opened (as you do here), the function is declared and ready to be used, even though it's in a previous `MMExecute()` call. Let's add two more functions to explore this more and supply additional functionality.

7

8. Enter the following after the previous `MMExecute()` call:

```
MMExecute("function getSelected() { return
➥fl.getDocumentDOM().selection[0] }");
```

The function `getSelected()` will return the current selection (at least the first in the array) in the current document. This will be useful when you wish to alter the properties of a certain item on the stage.

9. Let's add one more function, `run`, which will extend the Message window's functionality even further. This function will call a script stored in an external JSFL file. In this way, you can write more complex scripts outside of the `Message.fla` file and include them as you need to.

Add these lines after the `getSelected()` declaration:

```
var js =   "function run() { ";
js +=     "  var s = arguments[0];";
js +=      "  var a = [];";
js +=      "  for (var i = 1; i < arguments.length; i++) {";
js +=      "    a.push(arguments[i]);";
js +=      "  }";
js +=      "
fl.runScript(fl.configURI+\"WindowSWF/MessageScripts.jsfl\", s,
➥a.join(\"^\"));";
js +=      "}";
MMExecute(js);
```

Here you construct your JSFL over several lines and store it in the js variable. The first thing you do inside the function is grab the first index in the arguments array, which is the array that stores all of the arguments sent to the function (each function has access to its own arguments array). The index will hold the name of the function you wish to call in an external script. Every other argument will be variables to be passed to the function. Since different functions will have a different number of variables, you'll put these arguments all together into one string with each argument separated by a ^. You accomplish this by placing each index of arguments into a new array, a (unfortunately you can't call the slice()method on the arguments array as you would expect, so you simply create a new array). Once you have your new array filled with arguments, you call the runScript() method to read from a new JSFL file named MessageScripts.jsfl and pass first the name of the function you wish to be run and the arguments to be passed to the function, which you format into a string by calling the array's join() method. Finally, you call MMExecute() and send your string of JavaScript.

Of course, to get this to work you need to do two things. First, you must republish your SWF and open it again in a window. Second, you must create a new JSFL file—let's do that now.

10. Create a new Flash JavaScript file named MessageScripts.jsfl and save it into the same WindowSWF folder as Message.fla. You'll just put in two functions so you may see how to utilize this external file. Type the following into the script window:

```
function getDocData() {
  var a = arguments[0].split("^");
  fl.trace(fl.getDocumentDOM().getDataFromDocument(a[0]));
}
function setDocData() {
  var a = arguments[0].split("^");
  fl.getDocumentDOM().addDataToDocument(a[0], a[1], a[2]);
}
```

getDocData() and setDocData() get or set the persistent data stored with the current document. You can see that the first thing you do in either function is split the array that is sent to the function into separate arguments stored in the variables. getDocData() then traces the persistent data variable that is sent to the function, while setDocData() sets a variable using a variable name (a[0]), type (a[1]), and value (a[2]).

11. To see how all of your functions work, save the JSFL file and open the Message window once more. Type the following:

```
run("setDocData", "creator", "string", "Todd Yard");
run("getDocData", "creator");
put(getSelected());
```

Hopefully you can now see how easy it is to add functions to be called in the Message window. You're still missing one final piece, however, which is the ability to enter multiple lines of script without MMExecute() being called after each line. This will become necessary if you wish to use a for loop or an if conditional, or even declare a new function.

12. Return to Message.fla and the code layer. You'll add a "fake function" to your code to handle multiline scripts. Alter the change-handler code to look like the following:

```
function change(c) {
  var s = c.target.text;
  var c = Selection.getBeginIndex() - 1;
  var pos = s.substr(c, 1);
  if (pos == "\r") {
    var sub = s.substr(0, c);
    lastPos = sub.lastIndexOf("\r") + 1;
    js = s.substr(lastPos, c-lastPos);
    if (js == "startScript:") {
      script = "";
    } else if (js == "endScript") {
      MMExecute(script);
      delete script;
    } else if (script != undefined) {
      script += js;
    } else {
      MMExecute(js);
    }
  }
}
```

You've added an if conditional before you call MMExecute(). This first checks to see if the line typed was startScript:. This is a flag for your Message window to simply record all following commands without running MMExecute(). It will store these commands in the variable script, which it initializes as an empty string. The next check in the conditional is to see whether the endScript keyword has been used. This tells the movie to run all of the script stored in the script variable, which it then deletes. If neither of those conditions are met, you check to see whether script currently exists. If it does, you know you're in the middle of a multiline script and so simply add the last line to your script variable. If none of these three options are true, you run the line of code through MMExecute().

To test this, republish your movie and open the Message window from the menu once more. Type the following into the TextArea:

```
startScript:
for (var i = 0; i < 5; i++) {
  fl.trace(i);
}
endScript
```

Nice! You've now added a new tool to the Flash authoring environment that will aid you greatly when writing your JSFL. Now for something a little more complex . . .

Case Study 2: Search and Replace

We'll be honest, you're going to tread through some pretty complex code in this next section. Our initial thought for this chapter was to create a number of small, useful tools, but as we developed the Search and Replace window, we realized that tackling this larger project would not only give you a strong foundation in constructing WindowSWF movies, but also, because of the nature of the Search and Replace application, help solidify the hierarchy of objects in Flash's DOM.

But why develop such a tool when you have an efficient Find and Replace tool already available in Flash? More than anything else, building such an application will teach you how to step through the document hierarchy and affect elements at different levels. It will teach you the power and flexibility that WindowSWF movies may have, and how to work with external scripts and communicate between the window and these scripts. Finally, you may find a way to improve on the functionality presented in the current Find and Replace tool. Since you can't build onto what Macromedia has provided in their tool, re-creating the tool and improving upon that is your best (and possibly only) option.

We believe that if you work through this chapter you'll walk away with a thorough understanding of what is capable with WindowSWF movies and how to use them to affect any object within a document. That's no small task, so let's get cracking!

The Search and Replace tool, shown in Figure 7-7, will allow for a developer to search through an entire Flash document for any phrase located in a script in a frame, in a script on an instance, or in the text of a text field and replace the phrase with another, or overwrite the line containing the phrase completely. The search will be conducted by running through each movie clip symbol in the Library, and then the main timeline. Within each symbol and on the root, you'll delve down from timeline to layer to frame to element to line of script or text.

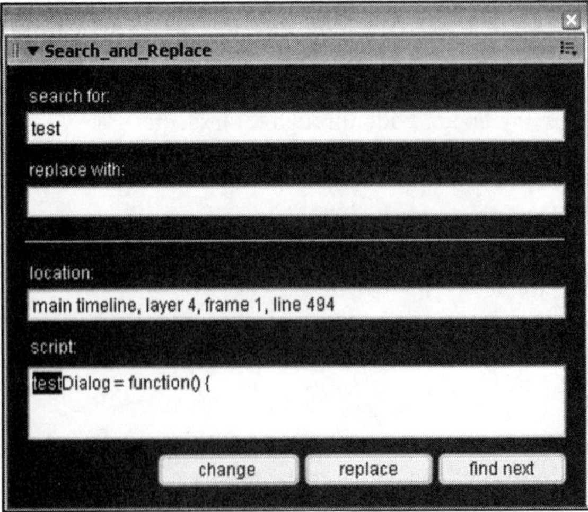

Figure 7-7.
The Search and Replace panel returning an instance of a search phrase

A flowchart of the search will better illuminate how the code will flow. You would read the chart in Figure 7-8 as "Start the search. Are there Library items that haven't been checked? If yes, are there more layers within the current Library item to check? If yes, are there more frames within the current layer of the current Library item to check?" and so on.

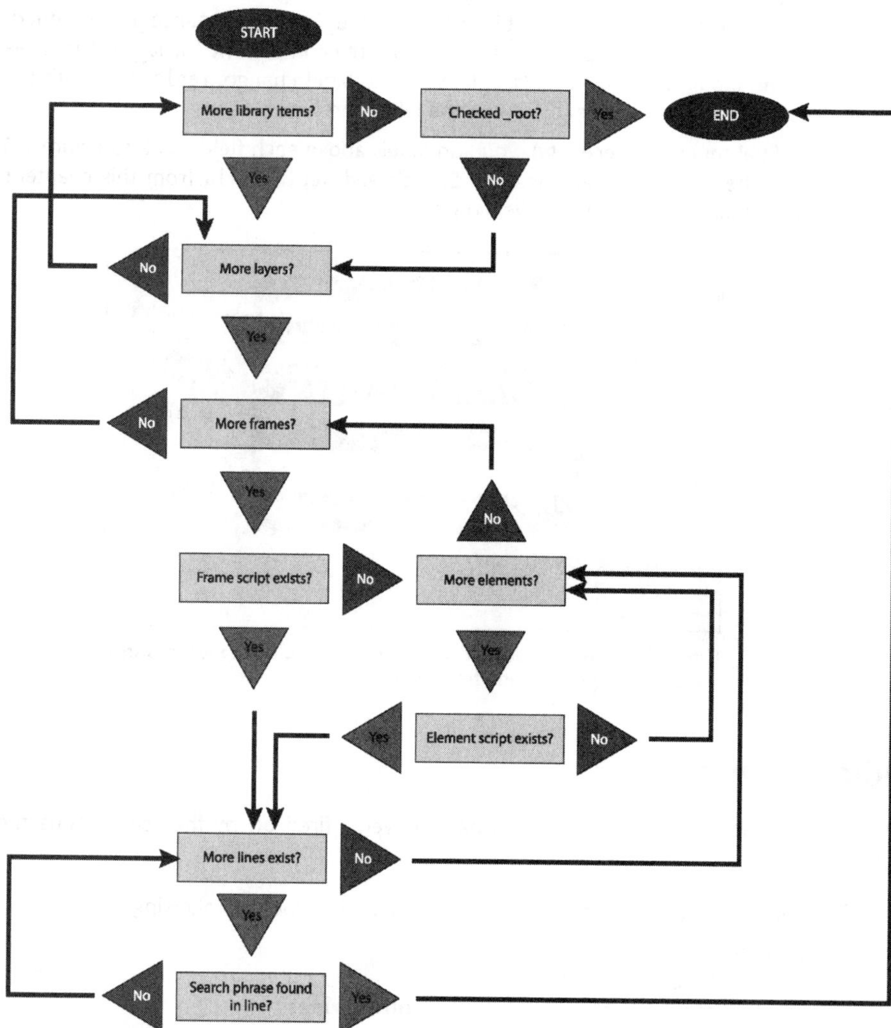

Figure 7-8. A flowchart for the application's logic

User Interface

Your first step is to construct the interface for the user to type in search-and-replace phrases. Since constructing Flash movies shouldn't be anything new to you, we'll go quickly through these initial steps so you can get to the interesting code.

1. Create a new Flash document named Search_and_Replace.fla and save it into your WindowSWF folder. Make the movie 400 by 300 pixels with a dark background color. Create two layers, one named interface and the other code.
2. Drag three TextInput components, one TextArea component, and three Button components from the Components panel onto the stage. Label the three TextInput instances search_ti, replace_ti, and instance_ti. Set instance_ti as noneditable in the Properties panel. Name the TextArea component found_ta. The three buttons should be named change_bn with the label change, replace_bn with the label replace, and findNext_bn with the label find next.

   As a final touch (or necessity), you add labels above each field. Look to Figure 7-9 to see the finished layout, or open Search_and_Replace.fla from this chapter's downloadable files to see our version.

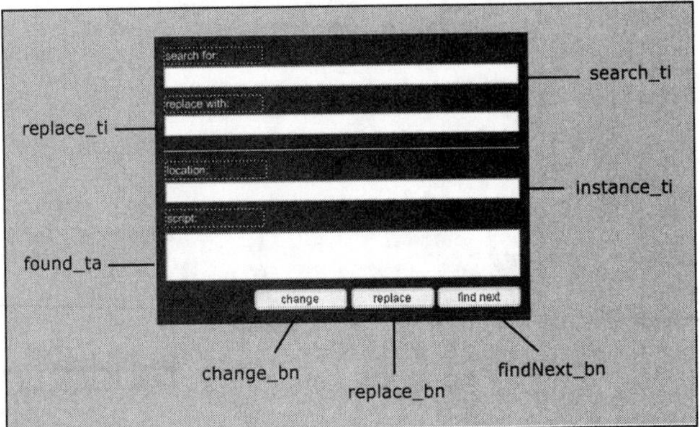

Figure 7-9. The interface for the Search and Replace panel consists of standard components and text fields.

Finding a Phrase

Next, you'll add code to your movie to handle events fired off by the user clicking the buttons.

3. Select the code layer and open the Actions panel. Type the following:

```
findNext_ln = {};
findNext_ln.click = function() {
  if (search_ti.getText() == "") return false;
  searchText = search_ti.getText();
MMExecute("fl.runScript(fl.configURI+\"WindowSWF/
➥Search_and_Replace.jsfl\", \"find\", \"" + searchText + "\");");
}
findNext_bn.addEventListener("click", findNext_ln);

change_ln = {};
change_ln.click = function() {
  if (search_ti.getText() == "") return false;
```

```
    // more code to come
    findNext_ln.click();
  }
  change_bn.addEventListener("click", change_ln);

  replace_ln = {};
  replace_ln.click = function() {
    if (search_ti.getText() == "") return false;
    // more code to come
    findNext_ln.click();
  }
  replace_bn.addEventListener("click", replace_ln);
```

Here you do a very similar thing for all three buttons, so we've included their scripts together for you. Each button will have its own listener for its respective click. You can see that the first thing you do is create a new object, `findNext_ln`, that will serve as a listener for the `findNext_bn`'s `click` event. You then write a `click` function for the listener. Inside this function (and this is true for all three listeners' functions) you check to see if the search field is empty. If it is, you exit the function. If you continue in the `findNext` function, you place the text into a new variable, `searchText`, and send this variable as an argument for the function `find` in the JSFL file `Search_and_Replace.jsfl` located in the same `WindowSWF` folder. You'll construct most of your search-and-replace functionality in this external JSFL file. After the function is complete, you add the `findNext_ln` object as an event listener for `findNext_bn`'s click event.

7

For the remaining two buttons you do the exact same thing, creating a new object for each, giving these objects `click` functions, and then adding the objects as listeners for the respective buttons. Inside these `click` functions, you do the same check to see if the search field is empty, run some additional code to be written shortly, and then call the `findNext_ln` `click` function. If you think of standard search-and-replace functionality, once you click to either replace or change an occurrence of a search phrase, the application should automatically then go and search for the next occurrence. This is what you take care of by calling the `findNext_ln`'s click function.

You'll take care of all the replace functionality later. For now, you'll concentrate on finding phrases within a document. As it stands, you've enabled the ability to enter a phrase and initiate a search by clicking a button. Create your JSFL file that will then take this phrase and search for it.

4. Create a new Flash JavaScript file and save it as `Search_and_Replace.jsfl` into your `WindowSWF` folder. Type the following into the script window:

```
function find(t) {
  init();
  initializeVars();
  searchText = t;
  phraseFound = 0;
  return findNext();
}
```

```
function init() {
  doc = fl.getDocumentDOM();
  lib = doc.library;
}
```

The find function is what you call from your Flash movie. It will hold the search phrase, which you place into the searchText variable. phraseFound is a flag you'll use to determine if you've successfully found the phrase. You also call three additional functions. The first, init(), which we also added in this step's code, simply sets some variables you'll access throughout your script, namely the current document and its Library. The next function is initializeVars(), which you keep separate from init() for an important reason that will come to light later in the script. The final function, findNext(), is what you'll use for each search of a phrase. You'll tackle this in a moment, but first, let's take care of initializeVars().

5. Add the following function to your script window:

```
function initializeVars() {
  checkedMain = 0;
  itemNum = 0;
  symbolName = "";
  layerNum = 0;
  frameNum = 0;
  elementNum = -1;
  elementName = "";
  lineNum = 0;
  charNum = 0;
}
```

As you run through the document while searching for a phrase, you'll need to keep track of where you are in all of the respective arrays. You should know what each variable represents by its name (layerNum, frameNum, elementNum, etc.). lineNum and charNum will represent points within the text itself. checkedMain is a flag you'll use to determine if the occurrence of the phrase is on the main timeline or within a symbol in the Library.

6. You've now come to the findNext function, which is the heart of your search script:

```
function findNext() {
  while (itemNum < lib.items.length) {
    var it = lib.items[itemNum];
    if (it.itemType == "movie clip" && lib.editItem(it.name)) {
      break;
    } else {
      itemNum++;
    }
  }
}
```

itemNum holds the current item in the Library that is being searched, and was initialized at 0 in your initializeVars function. Here, you use a while loop to check to see if the current item (found in the Library's items array) is editable and whether it's of the itemType movieclip. One of the great advantages of using editItem() in the conditional is that not only will it return true if the item is editable, but it will also enter into edit mode for the item, placing you in a nice position to search through the item's text.

If the item meets your criteria, you break out of the loop and prepare for the next step. If not, you increment the itemNum and check the next item in the Library until you've run through them all.

7. Add to findNext() with the following changes:

```
function findNext() {
  while (itemNum < lib.items.length) {
    var it = lib.items[itemNum];
    if (it.itemType == "movie clip" && lib.editItem(it.name)) {
      break;
    } else {
      itemNum++;
    }
  }
  if (itemNum < lib.items.length) {
    symbolName = lib.items[itemNum].name;
  } else {
    doc.exitEditMode();
    if (!checkedMain) initializeVars();
    checkedMain = 1;
    itemNum = 160000;
  }
return checkTimeline();
}
```

After you've either found a searchable item or run out of items to search, you hit a new conditional that checks to see if the item is within the Library's items count. If so, you place the item's name into symbolName. If you've run out of items in the Library to search, it's time to check the main timeline. You call exitEditMode() to get back to the main timeline if you're not already there, reinitialize your variables if you haven't been this way before, then set checkedMain to flag the fact that you're now running a search on the main timeline. Finally, no matter which option (Library item or main timeline), you call checkTimeline() to continue the search at a new level.

8. Each of the next several functions will be similar, but deal with a new level in the DOM. Here you write the function to check a timeline, whether it be a movie clip or the main timeline. If you understand the process of this function, you'll have a head start on each of the functions that follow.

```
function checkTimeline() {
  if (phraseFound) return false;
  curTimeline = doc.getTimeline();
  if (layerNum < curTimeline.layers.length) {
    return checkLayer(curTimeline);
  } else {
```

```
      if (checkedMain) {
        formatReturn("search complete");
        return phraseFound = 1;
      } else {
        itemNum++;
        layerNum = 0;
        return findNext();
      }
    }
  }
```

The first thing you check is whether a phrase has been found. You'll be using a bit of recursion in these scripts, so it becomes necessary to have this flag to inform functions when they should stop running. You'll see this line in many of the following functions, and it serves the same purpose. If the phrase has not been found, you set your curTimeline variable with the current timeline, whether it's that of a symbol or the root timeline. Your next step is to see whether you have layers left to check. layerNum holds the number of the current layer to be searched. If this number is less than the number of layers for this timeline, then you need to search this layer. You do that by calling checkLayer().

However, if you've exceeded the number of layers for this timeline, then the search through this timeline is complete. If the current timeline is the main timeline, which is the last thing you check, then the entire search is complete and you call a new function, formatReturn(), which will take care of sending all of the variables back to your Flash movie. You'll take care of that function after you've delved down all the way into DOM.

The final else statement runs if you've finished searching through the current timeline and the current timeline is an item in the Library. If this is the case, you increment the itemNum variable, reset the layerNum variable to 0 for the next timeline, and call the findNext function to find the next item that can be searched (this is where your recursion begins).

9. Here is the next level in the search, which goes through a timeline's layer structure:

```
function checkLayer() {
  if (phraseFound) return false;
  curLayer = curTimeline.layers[layerNum];
  if (frameNum < curLayer.frames.length) {
    return checkFrame();
  } else {
    layerNum++;
    frameNum = 0;
    return checkTimeline();
  }
}
```

As you can see, it's almost exactly like checkTimeline(), except it doesn't need to know whether the current timeline is a symbol or the _root. Here you check to see if frameNum is within the number of frames for the current layer (accessed in the layer's frames array). If it is, you check this frame by calling checkFrame(). If not, you increment layerNum, reset frameNum to 0 for the next layer, and call checkTimeline().

10. We bet we won't even have to explain this one. Enter this code in the script window:

```
function checkFrame() {
  if (phraseFound) return false;
  curFrame = curLayer.frames[frameNum];
  if (elementNum < curFrame.elements.length &&
➥curFrame.startFrame == frameNum) {
    return checkElement();
  } else {
    frameNum++;
    elementNum = -1;
    return checkLayer();
  }
}
```

Are you beginning to see how this all fits together? You check to see if elementNum is within the number of elements (found in this frame's elements array). Also, you do a check to see whether this frame is a keyframe by looking at its startFrame property. If this property value equals the number of the current frame, you know it's a keyframe and should be searched. If not, or if the elementNum is greater than the number of elements in the current frame, you increment frameNum, reset elementNum to -1 (more on that in the next function), and call checkLayer(). Otherwise, you proceed by calling checkElement().

11. Almost down to the bottom of the stack! Here you check the current element:

```
function checkElement() {
  if (phraseFound) return false;
  ascript = "";
  var type = "as";
  if (elementNum < 0) {
    elementName = "";
    ascript = curFrame.actionScript;
  } else {
    var el = curFrame.elements[elementNum];
    if (el != undefined) {
      elementName = ", instance '" + el.name + "'";
      if (el.elementType == "text") {
        type = "text";
        ascript = el.textRuns[0].characters;
      } else {
        ascript = el.actionScript;
      }
    }
  }
  if (ascript != undefined && ascript != "") {
    return checkScript(type);
  } else {
```

7

```
      elementNum++;
      lineNum = 0;
      return checkFrame();
    }
  }
```

Here is something a little bit different. At the top of the function you initialize a new string variable, ascript. You also set a local variable type to as, which stands for ActionScript. Since you're searching through both script and text, it becomes important to know which type the current element holds.

The if statement that follows checks to see whether elementNum is less than zero. You might recall that you initialized the elementNum variable to -1 for each frame. You do this so that the first thing you check in a frame is its frame code before searching through its elements array, which starts at 0. If elementNum is -1, you store the frame's code in ascript. If not, you find the current element for the frame. If that element exists, you store its name (which will be its instance name) within the elementName variable. Next you check to see if the element is a text field by looking at its elementType property. If it is, you reset the type variable to "text" and store the text field's text, found in the characters property of the first index of the text field's textRuns array. If the element isn't a text field, though, you store the instance's ActionScript (if it has any) in the ascript variable.

Once you've run through that conditional, you check to see if there is anything to check in the ascript variable. If there is, you call checkScript(), sending the script's type (as or text) as an argument. If there is no text to be searched, you increment elementNum, reset lineNum to 0, and check the next frame.

12. Finally you've reached the bottom level for your search—the text. You can now look to see if the search phrase is present.

```
function checkScript(type) {
  if (phraseFound) return false;
  var s = ascript;
  if (type == "text") s = changeReturns(s);
  s = s.split("\n");
  while (lineNum < s.length) {
    var ln = s[lineNum];
    var i = ln.indexOf(searchText, charNum);
    if (i > -1) {
      charNum = i + searchText.length;
      formatReturn(s[lineNum]);
      return phraseFound = 1;
    } else {
      charNum = 0;
      lineNum++;
    }
  }
  lineNum = 0;
  elementNum++;
  return checkFrame();
}
```

After placing a script into a temporary variable, you check to see if you're dealing with the type text. If so, you call a new function, changeReturns(), which will replace all of the text field's \r line breaks with \n to match the script window. We found when we developed this that text fields onstage register line breaks as \r, while the scripts in the ActionScript editor register as \n. To make them both the same in order to have this script work for both types, we included a changeReturns function to manage this. You'll write that in a moment.

The next line splits your s string into an array based on the line breaks (which will now be consistent between text fields and the script window). You then run through the each index of the array using lineNum, which represents a single line of text or code. You store each line as you check it in the ln variable and use indexOf() to see whether your search phrase appears within the line. charNum is used to start the search midline. This is necessary to ensure that multiple occurrences of the search phrase on a single line can be caught. Basically, if the search phrase is found on the line, the current character index (the next character after the occurrence of the search phrase) is stored in charNum so that the next time this function is called it continues searching on that same line.

Once charNum is stored, you call formatReturn() once again to get things ready to send back to your Flash movie, sending the line where the search phrase occurred back as an argument. If the search phrase doesn't exist in the current line, though, you set charNum back to 0, increment lineNum, and the while loop carries on until all of the script has been checked or the phrase has been found. Once all of the script has been searched, you increment elementNum, reset lineNum to 0, and check the frame for the next element to search.

You're almost at the point where you can check your movie. First you need to write the two functions you've called in your scripts but have yet to include, formatReturn() and changeReturns().

13. Add the following two new functions to your script window:

```
function changeReturns(s) {
  var i = 0;
  while (s.indexOf('\r', i) > -1) {
    var i = s.indexOf('\r', i);
    s = s.substr(0, i) + "\n" + s.substr(i+1);
    i+=2;
  }
  return s;
}

function formatReturn(m) {
  fl.trace(m);
}
```

As we said earlier, changeReturns() simply swaps out all \r occurrences with \n. formatReturn(), which you'll beef up in a moment, currently sends the line containing the search phrase to the Output window.

If you haven't yet published your Search_and_Replace.swf and closed and relaunched Flash, do so now so you may check the progress of the tool. Open a movie that contains plenty of text and code and run a search for a phrase using the new WindowSWF movie. Your Output window should return whether a phrase is found or if the search is complete.

There is the possibility in a larger movie that you'll get an alert box stating that the script has stopped due to too much recursion. You'll see how to deal with this eventuality in a later step.

Continuing the Search

The problem with the tool currently is that it only returns the first phrase found and stops. Clicking the find next button restarts the search instead of continuing on from the last position. You can take care of this issue in the find function, which is the first function called in your script.

14. Change the find function to look like the following:

```
function find(t, initialize) {
  init();
  searchText = t;
  if (initialize) {
    initializeVars();
  } else {
    getVars();
  }
  phraseFound = 0;
  return findNext();
}
```

You'll send an additional variable from Flash to let the function know if this is a new search or a continuation of a previous search. If it's new, you reinitialize the variables. If not, you call a new function that will get the previous search's variables. You'll look at that function in a moment. But first you need to figure out a way to save the previous search.

Here is a trick we have found to pass variables back and forth easily between a script and a Flash interface. If all you're sending is a single variable, then you can simply return it in a function. However, if you're dealing with many variables and lots of recursion as you are in this case, that isn't really a viable answer. Here is a solution: What you'll do is create a temporary item in the Library that you can pass variables through by giving the item persistent data that both the JSFL script and the Flash interface can set and read. When you're done passing values, you'll delete the symbol to keep things tidy.

15. Add a new function and amend the init function as follows:

```
function init() {
  doc = fl.getDocumentDOM();
  lib = doc.library;
  if (!lib.itemExists("$Search and Replace$")) {
    lib.addNewItem("movieclip", "$Search and Replace$");
  }
}

function getVars() {
  var i = lib.items[lib.findItemIndex("$Search and Replace$")[0]];
  checkedMain = i.getData("checkedMain");
  itemNum = i.getData("item");
  symbolName = "";
  layerNum = i.getData("layer");
  frameNum = i.getData("frame");
  elementNum = i.getData("element");
  elementName = "";
  lineNum = i.getData("line");
  charNum = i.getData("character");
}
```


The init function now checks to see if there is an item in the Library with the name $Search and Replace$. If there isn't, it creates one. getVars() is the function you called in the find function when you wanted to continue your search. All it does is check for the persistent data stored in the new Library item using the getData() method. Now all you need to do on this side is send the variables back to the Flash interface in the same way you get them. You'll do that in the formatReturn function.

16. Change your formatReturn function to read as follows (it's all new!):

```
function formatReturn(m) {
  var i = lib.items[lib.findItemIndex("$Search and Replace$")[0]];
  i.addData("checkedMain", "integer", checkedMain);
  i.addData("item", "integer", itemNum);
  i.addData("layer", "integer", layerNum);
  i.addData("frame", "integer", frameNum);
  i.addData("element", "integer", elementNum);
  i.addData("line", "integer", lineNum);
  i.addData("character", "integer", charNum);
  i.addData("message", "string", m);
  i.addData("symbolName", "string", symbolName);
  i.addData("elementName", "string", elementName);
}
```

Pretty much the same thing as getVars(), right? Here obviously you're setting the variables instead of getting them. You also send back one additional variable, message, which holds the line where your search phrase was found, or search is complete.

17. Now you need to change your FLA so that it deals with these changes. In your Search_and_Replace.fla, change the findNext_ln's click function to read as follows:

```
findNext_ln.click = function() {
  if (search_ti.getText() == "") return false;
  var init = 1;
  if (search_ti.getText() == searchText) {
    init = 0;
    createLibraryLink();
  }
  searchText = search_ti.getText();
  MMExecute("fl.runScript(fl.configURI+\"WindowSWF/Search_and_Replace.
➥jsfl\", \"find\", \"" + searchText + "\"," + init + ");");
  var js =   "var doc = fl.getDocumentDOM();";
  js +=    "var lib = doc.library;";
  js +=     "var sar =
➥lib.items[lib.findItemIndex(\"$Search and Replace$\")[0]];";
  MMExecute(js);
  item = Number(MMExecute("sar.getData(\"item\");"));
  var symbolName = MMExecute("sar.getData(\"symbolName\");");
  layer = Number(MMExecute("sar.getData(\"layer\");"));
  frame = Number(MMExecute("sar.getData(\"frame\");"));
  element = Number(MMExecute("sar.getData(\"element\");"));
  var elementName = MMExecute("sar.getData(\"elementName\");");
  line = Number(MMExecute("sar.getData(\"line\");"));
  character = Number(MMExecute("sar.getData(\"character\");"));
  checkedMain = Number(MMExecute("sar.getData(\"checkedMain\");"));
  var m = MMExecute("sar.getData(\"message\");");
  MMExecute("lib.deleteItem(\"$Search and Replace$\");");
}
```

Trust us, it's not as bad as it looks. You've dealt with most of this code already "on the other side." When you first get into the function, you check to see if the search text has changes since the last time the find next button was clicked. This is what will determine whether you start a new search or continue a previous one. createLibraryLink() is a function you'll use to create the new item in your Library. First, though, note how you send the additional flag init in your runScript() call. This tells the find function in the JSFL file whether to reinitialize the variables or not.

After the runScript call, you have several lines of JavaScript that place a reference to your Library item link in the variable sar (short for "search and replace"). Using this reference, you set the value of variables within the Flash movie to correspond with the link's values. Remember that MMExecute() returns the value of the last JavaScript command, so you can use this to place the values into variables in your interface. Once you've safely received these variables, you delete the item from the Library.

18. You're almost done with the find functionality! You just need to create the initial link in the Library to send the variables values *back* to the JSFL script when you continue a search. This is taken care of in the createLibraryLink function, so add this code to your Search_and_Replace.fla:

```
function createLibraryLink() {
  var js = "var doc = fl.getDocumentDOM();";
  js +=    "var lib = doc.library;";
  js +=    "lib.addNewItem(\"movieclip\", \"$Search and Replace$\");";
  js +=    "sar = lib.items[lib.findItemIndex(\"$Search and
➥Replace$\")[0]];";
  js +=    "sar.addData(\"checkedMain\", \"integer\", " +
➥checkedMain + ");";
  js +=    "sar.addData(\"item\", \"integer\", " + item + ");";
  js +=    "sar.addData(\"layer\", \"integer\", " + layer + ");";
  js +=    "sar.addData(\"frame\", \"integer\", " + frame + ");";
  js +=    "sar.addData(\"element\", \"integer\", " + element + ");";
  js +=    "sar.addData(\"line\", \"integer\", " + line + ");";
  js +=    "sar.addData(\"character\", \"integer\", " +
➥character + ");";
  MMExecute(js);
}
```

You've seen similar code in three other instances, so we're confident you can see what's going on here. Now that you have a link established between your interface and the external JSFL script, you can take the information returned by the script and use it to populate the text fields in your interface.

19. These next lines take the information received from the external script and format it to place it in the text fields. It's all taken care of in the click function of finNext_ln. New lines are in bold:

```
findNext_ln.click = function() {
  if (search_ti.getText() == "") return false;
  var init = 1;
  if (search_ti.getText() == searchText && !resetSearch) {
    init = 0;
    createLibraryLink();
  }
  delete resetSearch;
  searchText = search_ti.getText();
  MMExecute("fl.runScript(fl.configURI+\"WindowSWF/Search_and_Replace.
➥jsfl\", \"find\", \"" + searchText + "\"," + init + ");");
  var js = "var doc = fl.getDocumentDOM();";
  js +=    "var lib = doc.library;";
  js +=    "var sar = lib.items[lib.findItemIndex(\"$Search and
➥Replace$\")[0]];";
  MMExecute(js);
  item = Number(MMExecute("sar.getData(\"item\");"));
  var symbolName = MMExecute("sar.getData(\"symbolName\");");
```

7

```
  layer = Number(MMExecute("sar.getData(\"layer\");"));
  frame = Number(MMExecute("sar.getData(\"frame\");"));
  element = Number(MMExecute("sar.getData(\"element\");"));
  var elementName = MMExecute("sar.getData(\"elementName\");");
  line = Number(MMExecute("sar.getData(\"line\");"));
  character = Number(MMExecute("sar.getData(\"character\");"));
  checkedMain = Number(MMExecute("sar.getData(\"checkedMain\");"));
  var m = MMExecute("sar.getData(\"message\");");
  found_ta.setText(removeReturns(m));
  Selection.setFocus(found_ta);
  Selection.setSelection(character-searchText.length, character);
  if (m == "search complete") {
    instance_ti.setText("");
    Selection.setFocus(search_ti);
    replace_bn.enabled = change_bn.enabled = 0;
    resetSearch = 1;
  } else {
    replace_bn.enabled = change_bn.enabled = 1;
    if (checkedMain) {
      var i = "main timeline, layer " + (layer+1) + ", frame " +
➥(frame+1) + elementName + ", line " + (line+1);
    } else {
      var i = "symbol '" + symbolName + "', layer " + (layer+1) + ",
➥frame " + (frame+1) + elementName + ", line " + (line+1);
    }
    instance_ti.setText(i);
  }
  MMExecute("lib.deleteItem(\"$Search and Replace$\");");
}
```

The variable m contains the message sent back from your script. You place this in found_ta (after reformatting the returns, in a similar way to the changeReturns function you wrote earlier). You set the focus to this field and then highlight the occurrence of the search phrase based on the value of character.

If the message returned is search complete, you turn off the necessary buttons, clear the instance_ti text field, and set resetSearch to 1. If you look at the top of the function, you use this flag to determine whether to reset your variables to be able to search through the movie a second time. If the search isn't complete and you received back an occurrence of the search phrase, you place the information for that occurrence in the instance_ti field based on the variables received back.

20. The final step to get your find functionality working (and 80 percent of the functionality of your movie) is the addition of your removeReturns function you called in the preceding script. Add this to your script:

```
function removeReturns(t) {
  var i = 0;
  while (t.indexOf('\n', i) > -1) {
    var i = t.indexOf('\n', i);
```

```
      t = t.substr(0, i);
      i+=1;
    }
    var i = 0;
    while (t.indexOf('\r', i) > -1) {
      var i = t.indexOf('\r', i);
      t = t.substr(0, i);
      i+=1;
    }
    return t;
}
```

Here you simply go through the text sent and strip it of any returns and line breaks.

Go ahead and republish your SWF, save your JSFL, and open the Search and Replace window in a movie to test it (you won't need to restart Flash if you've saved the FLA file in the Configuration/WindowSWF folder). Everything is working splendidly now, with phrases being found throughout a document and all relevant information being returned as well. Now all you need is the ability to replace items!

Replacing Phrases

7

You have two methods of replacing text in your tool. The first, clicking the replace button will replace the highlighted phrase in found_ta with whatever the user has specified in the replace_ti field. The second method will involve the user typing something new in the found_ta field and clicking the change button, which will replace the line returned with the line the user types.

For the first method, you'll have to save the current selection when the replace button is pressed, since that will then have focus and any selection in the text field will be lost.

21. Add the following lines to your Search_and_Replace.fla:

```
this.onMouseDown = function() {
  savedSelection = {focus:eval(Selection.getFocus()),
➥startSel:Selection.getBeginIndex(), endSel:Selection.getEndIndex()};
};
```

Here you've created a new object to hold where the current focus is and what the selection is. You'll access this information in the click handler of your replace_ln listener.

22. Alter the replace_ln and change_ln click handlers to read as follows:

```
change_ln = {};
change_ln.click = function() {
  if (search_ti.getText() == "") return false;
  var t = found_ta.getText();
  replaceLine(t);
  findNext_ln.click();
}
change_bn.addEventListener("click", change_ln);
```

```
replace_ln = {};
replace_ln.click = function() {
  if (search_ti.getText() == "") return false;
  if (savedSelection.focus != found_ta.label) return false;
  var t = found_ta.getText();
  var begin = t.substr(0, savedSelection.startSel);
  var end = t.substr(savedSelection.endSel);
  var s = begin + replace_ti.getText() + end;
  replaceLine(s);
  findNext_ln.click();
}
replace_bn.addEventListener("click", replace_ln);
```

For the change button, you merely need to grab the text from the found_ta field and send it to a new function, replaceLine(). For the replace button, you first check to make sure that found_ta just had focus when the button was clicked. You then use the saved selection to find the portion of the text that needs to be replaced. You cut out this portion and replace it with the text from your replace_ti field. This new string you send to replaceLine().

Obviously then it's replaceLine() where you need to go to see the next step.

23. Add this new function to the Actions panel:

```
function replaceLine(t) {
  var i = 0;
  while (t.indexOf('"', i) > -1) {
    var i = t.indexOf('"', i);
    t = t.substr(0, i) + "\\" + t.substr(i);
    i+=2;
  }
  removeReturns(t);
  createLibraryLink();
  MMExecute("fl.runScript(fl.configURI+\"WindowSWF/Search_and_Replace.
➥jsfl\",\"replaceLine\",\""+t+"\");");
  character -= searchText.length;
  MMExecute("lib.deleteItem(\"$Search and Replace$\");");
}
```

When you enter this function, the first thing you do is escape any quotes inside the string. This is very important as you pass variables to external scripts. You then remove any returns within the string—remember that your tool replaces single lines. Next, you create your Library link, which will be passed the values of the current search and therefore the location where the replace is to occur, and call your external script, this time specifying the replaceLine function and sending your string. Because your replace string might be fewer characters than your search string, you subtract from character so that when you continue the search you don't accidentally skip over another occurrence of the search phrase. Finally, just as before, you delete your link item once you're done with it.

That's it for your Flash movie! Now you move back to your JSFL to finish up by writing, as you may have guessed, the `replaceLine` function.

24. Return to the JSFL file `Search_and_Replace.jsfl` and add the following function to your ever-expanding code:

```
function replaceLine(t) {
  init();
  getVars();
  if (checkedMain) {
    doc.exitEditMode();
  }
  var tl = doc.getTimeline();
  var ly = tl.layers[layerNum];
  if (ly == undefined) return false;
  var fr = tl.layers[layerNum].frames[frameNum];
  if (elementNum < 0) {
    var el = fr;
    var script = el.actionScript;
    var type = "as";
  } else {
    var el = fr.elements[elementNum];
    if (el.elementType == "text") {
      var script = el.textRuns[0].characters;
      var type = "text";
    } else {
      var script = el.actionScript;
      var type = "as";
    }
  }
}
```

Here is the first half of the function that will take care of finding and replacing the appropriate line in the document. After running `init()` and `getVars()` to get the variable values from the Library link, you exit back to the main timeline if that is where the replace will occur. You then store the correct timeline and layer and check to see if the layer returns `undefined`, exiting if this is the case. After storing the necessary frame, you check to see if you're dealing with frame code (`elementNum < 0`) or an element. If it's a frame, you store a reference to the frame in the variable `el`, the ActionScript in `script`, and set the `type` as `as`. If instead you're dealing with an element, you store a reference to the element in `el` and check to see whether you're dealing with a text field or not, setting `script` and `type` appropriately.

25. Now that you have the proper elements stored, you can replace the text with the following lines:

```
  } else {
    var el = fr.elements[elementNum];
    if (el.elementType == "text") {
      var script = el.textRuns[0].characters;
      var type = "text";
```

```
      } else {
        var script = el.actionScript;
        var type = "as";
      }
    }
    if (type == "text") script = changeReturns(script);
    var s = script.split("\n");
    s[lineNum] = t;
    var str = "";
    for (var i = 0; i < s.length; i++) {
      str += (s[i] + ((type == "text") ? "\r" : "\n"));
    }
    if (type == "text") {
      el.textRuns[0].characters = str.substr(0, str.length-1);
    } else {
      el.actionScript = str.substr(0, str.length-1);
    }
  }
```

Once more you check to see if you're dealing with a text field and swap out the returns for line breaks if this is the case. Then you split the `script` variable and replace the appropriate line with the text sent to the function. Next you run through the array and put it back together as a single string (notice you add returns to the text field and line breaks to the ActionScript editor). Finally, you place your new string into the appropriate property of your element.

That's it! Save, republish, and test your movie in a window. You now can replace text in your documents!

Recursion, Recursion, Recursion!

Perhaps we spoke too soon when we said, "That's it!" If you tested the search-and-replace functionality with a fairly hefty document, you might have received a long message stating that the script was stopped due to recursion. Flash doesn't really like to keep loops and functions running for long periods of time, which can of course occur when you're running through every line in a document! To take care of this issue, you need to add a few lines to the file to stop the search before a recursion message pops up.

26. First, you need to initialize a new variable when you start each search. You do this in the `find` function in your JSFL file:

```
function find(t, initialize) {
  init();
  searchText = t;
  if (initialize) {
    initializeVars();
  } else {
    getVars();
  }
```

```
    count = 0;
    phraseFound = 0;
    return findNext();
}
```

This will hold the current number of times you've called your findNext function.

27. Add the following new code to findNext():

```
function findNext() {
  if (count++ > 50) {
    phraseFound = 1;
    formatReturn("recursion limit reached; please press 'find next'
➥to continue search");
    return;
  }
  if (phraseFound) {
    formatReturn(phrase);
    return;
  }
  while (itemNum < lib.items.length) {
    var it = lib.items[itemNum];
    if (it.itemType == "movie clip" && lib.editItem(it.name)) {
      break;
    } else {
      itemNum++;
    }
  }
  if (itemNum < lib.items.length) {
    symbolName = lib.items[itemNum].name;
  } else {
    doc.exitEditMode();
    if (!checkedMain) initializeVars();
    checkedMain = 1;
    itemNum = 160000;
  }
  return checkTimeline();
}
```

If you call this function more than 50 times, you'll exit this script and send back a recursion message to your Flash interface. We've added another conditional as well to ensure you exit this function once the phrase has been found. This is just another added level of security to make sure things aren't called more than necessary.

And that's really it for your JSFL file (honest!). Save it and head back to the FLA where you'll complete your code.

28. In the click handler for findNext_ln, add the bold lines to your code to handle the recursion message being returned:

```
if (m == "search complete" || m == "recursion limit reached; please
➥press 'find next' to continue search") {
  instance_ti.setText("");
  Selection.setFocus(search_ti);
  replace_bn.enabled = change_bn.enabled = 0;
  resetSearch = (m == "search complete");
} else {
```

Ladies and gentlemen, you're now finished! You've created a fully functional search-and-replace tool for your Flash environment, along the way exploring the DOM extensively and learning how to navigate through and manipulate it effectively. If you got lost anywhere along the way, just download the relevant example files from www.flashextensibility.com and study them.

Summary

We've said it before and we'll say it again: We love this new feature! It's difficult to summarize what can be accomplished as the possibilities are many and varied. In this chapter you've created a tool to test JSFL and run simple commands as well as a tool that can run through an entire document and edit it. In previous chapters you've utilized the Dialog Designer to edit, save, and test XML within Flash.

How about a tool that allows you to automatically increment and save backup documents (Guy Watson from www.flashguru.co.uk already has a great tool that automatically saves your files as you work on them), or perhaps restructures your document based on specific criteria? You might want to create a 3D construction tool that draws the shapes onto the stage or one that places text onto user-defined paths (in fact, these ideas were both component interfaces we previously developed that we're currently adapting for WindowSWF movies–stay tuned to www.flashextensibility.com for more details).

Each of these examples have very little in common except for the fact that you can create such interfaces in Flash, and now you can get them to interact and manipulate the authoring environment via the JavaScript API. There are endless possibilities for what can be achieved with this feature, and we're hoping you'll help us prove this by creating as many exciting and useful WindowSWF movies as possible!

8 FLASH FROM THE COMMAND LINE

If you've gone through all the material thus far in the book, you'll have learned numerous new ways of adding content to, or modifying content in, a Flash document. You can automate actions with commands, create custom tools and encapsulated timeline effects, and create behaviors that can add complex scripting to a movie clip with the click of a button. In this chapter, you may learn a few more tricks about JSFL, but for the most part we're going to show you how to step right outside the program and control it from a distance.

Believe it or not, although this chapter contains some of the most powerful information in this book, most of the examples don't require the direct use of Flash at all! Of course, the exception to this would be if you're working with Flash MX 2004 Professional and prefer that as your code editor for JSFL.

Most of the examples in this chapter are specific for Windows-based systems but should work on any version of Windows. While the general concepts for Flash that we discuss here should apply to Mac-based systems as well, the specifics on how to execute programs from the command line (or the Mac "terminal") will obviously be different. You can find additional information on how to perform these same functions on a Mac system on the book's companion website, `www.flashextensibility.com`.

Why the Command Line?

First of all, it's probably a good idea to discuss exactly what we're talking about when discussing executing Flash from the command line, and why this would be desirable. After all, you have this really powerful interface within the Flash authoring environment. Why would you want to revert to typing commands in at a DOS prompt?

One simple answer is automation. Say you had a bunch of Flash files that you needed to process somehow. Maybe you needed to go through them and add some data, or convert all the text fields to be dynamic, or maybe you simply had a whole bunch of FLA files that you needed to publish to a tight deadline.

You could start up Flash, open up each file, do what you needed to do with it, and then save it, close it, and open the next one. Or, you could write a JSFL script that would perform the same function on every file in a list. It could actually take care of the whole process, including starting Flash, opening each file, processing it, saving and/or publishing it, and when it was done, it would shut down Flash again. It might take a bit of time to write the script the first time, but if this was something you needed to do on a regular basis, you'd just need to change the filenames each time and rerun the script. You'd never even have to open Flash by yourself.

We'll be using just such an example as we go through this chapter and build up both the complexity of the script and the ease of its use.

Another concept would be building a new front-end for Flash. If you know any other programming languages, such as C++ or Visual Basic, you can build a custom interface that accepts user data and perhaps performs some kind of processing on the data. This program could then output a JSFL file and have Flash execute the script contained in it. The JSFL file would most likely include commands to open or create a document and do something to it, then save or publish, and close down Flash. Users would only ever deal with the custom interface. Of course, it would require that they have Flash installed on their computers in order to do the final execution of the script. These things don't replace Flash, but add new functionality to it.

We'll also evolve our example into something very similar, but rather than using a high-level language like those just mentioned, we'll use a simple DOS batch file that you can create with any text editor and a few batch commands.

How to Execute a JSFL File

There are three basic ways to execute a JSFL file in Windows (that is, outside of the Flash IDE):

1. Running Flash from the command line with the JSFL file as a parameter
2. Calling the JSFL file directly from the command line
3. Executing a file from its icon

We'll look at each of these methods in detail in the next three sections, and then we'll move on to some practical examples.

8

Calling Flash from the Command Line

The first method is via the command line, using the path to the Flash executable. First, you need to get a command line or, as it's sometimes called, a command prompt, which is where you can enter text-based commands to run programs or perform actions on the system. You can find the command prompt on the Windows Start menu under Start ➤ All Programs ➤ Accessories, or you can go to Start ➤ Run, and enter cmd as shown in Figure 8-1.

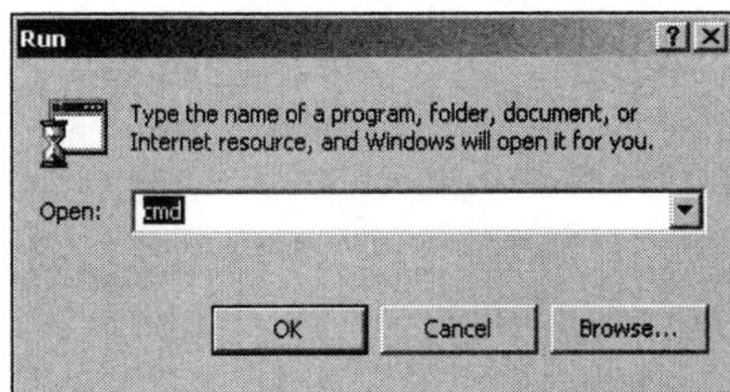

Figure 8-1.
Starting a command prompt with the Run dialog box

Either way, you should wind up with a window with a black background and white lettering and the characters C:\> followed by a blinking cursor, as you see in Figure 8-2.

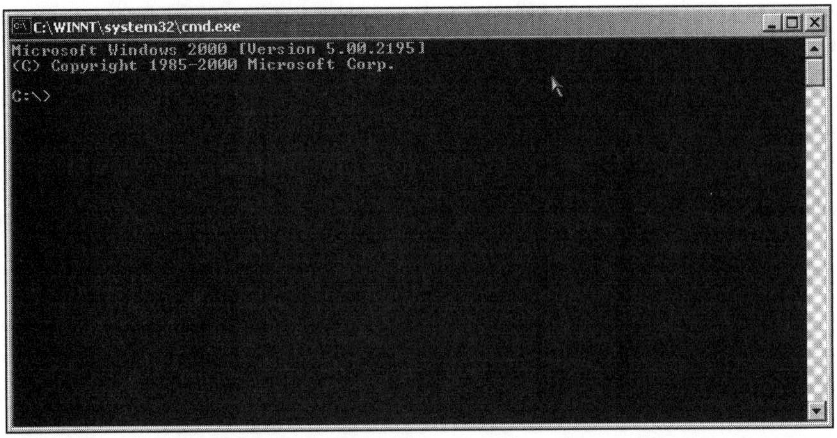

Figure 8-2. The Windows command prompt

Here you can type various system commands or launch any program by typing its path and name. For example, you can launch Flash by typing

```
"C:/Program Files/Macromedia/Flash MX 2004/Flash.exe"
```

Note that the entire line is enclosed in quotes. This is due to the spaces in `Program Files` and `Flash MX 2004`. Without the quotes, the system would see each space as the end of one command and the start of something else. Enclosing it in quotes tells the system that it's all one command. Flash should now run just as if you had chosen it on the Start menu or double-clicked its icon on the desktop. (Of course, this assumes that Flash is installed in the default location. If you've installed Flash on a different drive or in a different directory, you'll have to type in the path where the executable is actually located.)

Furthermore, you can pass a filename to Flash right on the command line by typing the filename (and path if necessary) right after `Flash.exe`, as shown in Figure 8-3. Assuming you had a file named `myScript.jsfl` in a directory called `jsfl_files`, you could send it to Flash as follows:

```
"C:/Program Files/Macromedia/Flash MX 2004/Flash.exe"
➥C:/jsfl_files/myScript.jsfl
```

Note the space after the command and the start of the file path. Also note that because this path doesn't include any spaces, it doesn't need any quotes.

> *What happens when you open a JSFL file like this is very important to understand. Remember that in Flash MX 2004 Professional, you can edit JSFL files right in the authoring environment. But in this case, Flash doesn't open the JSFL file for editing. Instead, it opens it up and executes it, much as if it were a command selected from the* Commands *menu. In fact, it's this behavior that enables you to do some pretty cool stuff—so read on!*

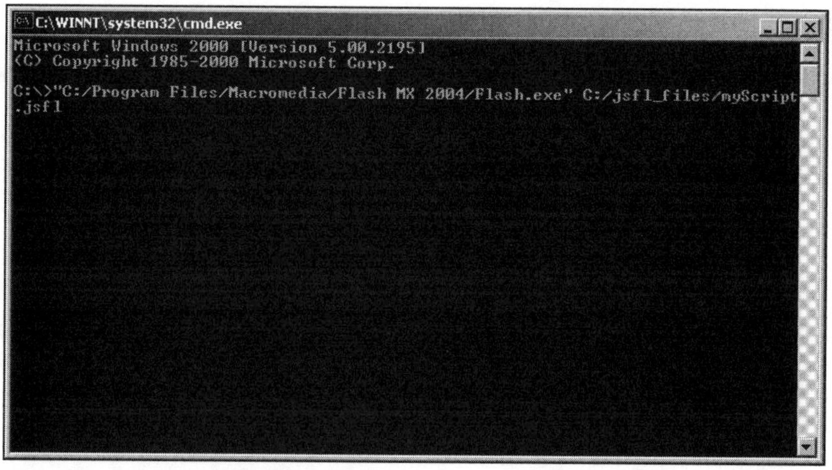

```
C:\WINNT\system32\cmd.exe
Microsoft Windows 2000 [Version 5.00.2195]
(C) Copyright 1985-2000 Microsoft Corp.

C:\>"C:/Program Files/Macromedia/Flash MX 2004/Flash.exe" C:/jsfl_files/myScript
.jsfl
```

Figure 8-3. Typing in a command with an argument

So go ahead and create a new directory called `jsfl_files` right in the root directory (C:\). Actually, it doesn't really matter where this directory is located; we just found that having it close to the root directory makes it more easily accessible from the command line, where you have to type in paths or navigate to directories by typing.

As a side note, you might notice that we separate our directories with forward slashes, whereas the paths that DOS prints out use back slashes. DOS and Windows prefer the back slashes, but will accept your typing in forward slashes. Since most other operating systems, as well as URLs and URIs, use forward slashes, we've gotten in the habit of using them too.

8

In this directory, create a new JSFL file named `newdoc.jsfl`. You'll notice that we avoid any spaces in our directory or filenames, which saves us from typing in quotes later. In this file, insert one line:

```
fl.createDocument();
```

Remember that when you first start up Flash, the default behavior is for the start page to appear. If you want a new document to work with, you have to create one. This command takes an optional parameter of the type of document to create, which can be `timeline`, `presentation`, or `application`—these refer to a regular Flash movie, a Flash slide presentation, and a Flash form application, respectively. Omitting the parameter will give you the default, which is `timeline`.

You can now test this out on the command line by typing the following in the command prompt window:

```
"C:/Program Files/Macromedia/Flash MX 2004/Flash.exe"
➥C:/jsfl_files/newdoc.jsfl
```

On pressing *ENTER*, Flash should start up if it isn't already running, and a new document will be created. Congratulations! You just created a new Flash document without touching Flash!

Calling the JSFL File Directly

This second method is even easier. Conveniently, the extension `.jsfl` is associated with Flash by default. In other words, Windows has been told that when it encounters a file ending with that extension, it should execute the file using Flash. Therefore, all you have to do is type in the filename itself at the command prompt. The system will automatically start Flash and pass the filename to it as a parameter. Try it by typing the following at the command prompt:

```
C:/jsfl_files/newdoc.jsfl
```

The result should be the same as if you had typed out the path to the Flash executable along with the file—Flash will start up and create a new document. If you don't want to type the whole path every time, you can navigate to the `jsfl_files` directory by using the `cd` (change directory) command:

```
cd jsfl_files
```

After typing this at the command prompt, the prompt should change to the following:

```
C:\jsfl_files>
```

Then, you can simply type the name of your file, without the path, to execute it:

```
newdoc.jsfl
```

With no path, the system will look for a file of that name in the current directory, and finding it, will execute it.

Executing a File from Its Icon

The last way of executing a JSFL file is even easier! Close down the command prompt window by clicking the close button or typing *EXIT*. Open up Windows Explorer and navigate to the `jsfl_files` directory. Depending on your settings, you should see either a list of files in the directory (which should only include the `newdoc.jsfl` file at this point), with a small icon next to each, or a larger icon sitting there in the window.

We're sure we don't have to tell you how to run a file from an icon. Go ahead and double-click it, or however else you would normally start any application or open any document. Once again, Flash will start up and execute the JSFL file.

Adding Content via the Command Line

Now that you've got Flash to open and create a document, let's have it put something into this document. With all that you've learned so far, and your own creativity, we don't think we have to belabor the point on creating content with JSFL. Here we've made a script that draws a whole bunch of multicolored, randomly sized circles to the stage:

```
// make a document
fl.createDocument();
curr_doc = fl.getDocumentDOM();
curr_doc.width = 400;
curr_doc.height = 300;

// create a fill
curr_fill = new Object();
curr_fill.style = "solid";

for(i=0; i<100; i++){
  // set fill to a random color
  curr_fill.color = Math.floor(Math.random()*0xffffff);
  curr_doc.setCustomFill(curr_fill);
  // get a random location and size
  l = Math.random() * 350;
  t = Math.random() * 250;
  circleSize = Math.random()*50;
  r = l + circleSize;
  b = t + circleSize;
  // draw the circle
  curr_doc.addNewOval({top:t, bottom:b, left:l, right:r});
}
```

This script creates a new document and an object, curr_fill, to hold parameters for the type of color fill you want. You set the fill style to solid. Next you loop through 100 times and do the following:

1. Select a random color for the fill.
2. Set the custom fill to the color you just chose by applying setCustomFill using the curr_fill object.
3. Choose a random size and position for the circle.
4. Finally, you draw the circle.

Save this file to the jsfl_files directory under the name randomCircles.jsfl. Then execute it using one of the three methods we just discussed. Flash should start up, create a document, and draw 100 circles in it like the ones in Figure 8-4.

Run it again and another document will open with a new random arrangement of circles. OK, now you've created Flash *content* without touching Flash! Let's continue at this pace . . .

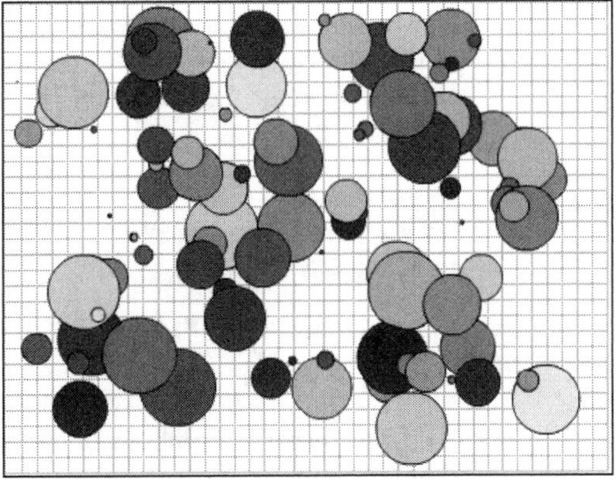

Figure 8-4. One hundred circles

Saving and Publishing

Normally when you create a Flash movie, you test it and eventually publish it and probably save it to your hard drive in case you want to do something more to it later. Since the goal is to automate this whole process, let's look at each of those functions.

Before you publish, you need to save the document. This will give it a name and location, which will also become the name and location of the published HTML and SWF files. You can use a couple of methods to save a document. The document object has a save method, but this is only good if the document has already been saved at least once and therefore already has a name and location. Otherwise, you'll get the Save As dialog box asking you where and under what name to save the document. There is no way to name the document and specify where to save it with this method.

Luckily, there is another method, on the fl object, called saveDocument. The first argument of this method is the document you want to save. The second argument is the URI specifying the path and name you want to save it as. If you omit this second argument, this method will function exactly like the document save method. But if you specify the URI, the document will be saved to that name and location, even if it hasn't been saved before. You can add this line to the end of the randomCircles.jsfl file:

```
fl.saveDocument(curr_doc, "file:///c:/jsfl_files/CircleMovie.fla");
```

Finally, now that you've saved the document, publishing it is a piece of cake. Just tack on this line to the end of the file:

```
curr_doc.publish();
```

This will publish the document, creating an HTML file and a SWF. As is, this will publish the movie using the default publish settings. If you want to publish in a different format, say a projector or QuickTime movie, rather than just HTML and SWF, or change any of the other publish settings, you can modify the settings programmatically using the publishProfile object, which is a property of the document object. publishProfile's properties and methods are listed in the Flash extensibility reference section of the book, so feel free to experiment with them.

Now double-click (or otherwise run) the randomCircles.jsfl file once again. When it has finished doing its magic, check out your jsfl_files directory. There should be a few files in there, namely CircleMovie.fla, CircleMovie.swf, and CircleMovie.html. You can check out the HTML and SWF files and see that they do indeed show your 100 random circles.

Now you've created a SWF and HTML file, ready to put on the Web, all without even touching Flash itself.

Closing Flash

Well, we keep talking about doing all this work without ever touching Flash. It seems a shame to just leave it sitting there on the desktop when you're done, waiting for you to manually close it down. Fortunately, you can take care of that with a couple more lines.

```
curr_doc.close(false);
fl.quit(true);
```

These both function pretty much the same. The document close method closes the specified document. The one argument determines whether or not Flash should prompt the user to save any changes. If set to `true`, and the document either has never been saved or has changed since the last save, the user will be prompted to save it before closing. If `false`, Flash will immediately close the document regardless of its status.

The `quit` method of the fl object closes all documents and shuts down the whole program. Again, if the argument is `true`, it will prompt the user for each unsaved document, and if `false`, it will immediately close all documents and shut down.

In this case, you definitely want to close the document you just opened. You know exactly what happened to it. You created it, added some content, and saved and published it. There shouldn't be any changes to it since the last save, so it's safe to shut it down. However, it's entirely possible that when the script is executed, Flash could already be open with some other documents. You would have some pretty irate users on your hands if you shut down Flash on them and destroyed the files they had just spent the last couple hours working on, but forgot to save. Therefore, you let Flash prompt the user to save if there are any unsaved documents open when you're done.

Another option here that you could try is to check the length of the `documents` array after you close the document you opened. If the length is zero, then there are no other documents open and it's safe to shut down. If it's more than zero, then the user has something else open and you shouldn't even bother trying to shut down. As you can see, there are usually several ways of doing any action, and it's up to you, the developer, to think it through and decide on the method you want to use.

8

Here's the entire file for reference:

```
// make a document
fl.createDocument();
curr_doc = fl.getDocumentDOM();
curr_doc.width = 400;
curr_doc.height = 300;

// create a fill
curr_fill = new Object();
curr_fill.style = "solid";

for(i=0; i<100; i++){
  curr_fill.color = Math.floor(Math.random()*0xffffff);
  curr_doc.setCustomFill(curr_fill);
  l = Math.random() * 350;
  t = Math.random() * 250;
  circleSize = Math.random()*50;
  r = l + circleSize;
  b = t + circleSize;
  curr_doc.addNewOval({top:t, bottom:b, left:l, right:r});
```

```
}
fl.saveDocument(curr_doc, "file:///c:/jsfl_files/CircleMovie.fla");
curr_doc.publish();
curr_doc.close(false);
fl.quit(true);
```

Processing Existing Files

Circles are very nice, but let's make something a little more useful. You'll start creating the script we talked about earlier, one that will take a list of FLA files and open and publish them. First you need an FLA file to publish. Create a new Flash movie document, put whatever you want in it, and save it as `testMovie.fla` in the `jsfl_files` directory.

Then create a new JSFL file in the `jsfl_files` directory named `flashPublish.jsfl`. Put the following code in this file:

```
filename = "file:///C:/jsfl_files/testMovie.fla";
fl.openDocument(filename);
curr_doc = fl.getDocumentDOM();
curr_doc.publish();
curr_doc.close(false);
fl.quit(true);
```

Here you simply store the path to the FLA file in a variable called `filename`, and then you open the document, publish it, close it, and finally close Flash as long as no other documents are unsaved.

Now you can double-click or otherwise execute `flashPublish.jsfl` and it will publish your test movie. Not bad, but it needs some improvement. If you have a list of files you want to publish, you'd need to open the file for editing, change the name, save it, and run it. Repeat for each file. That's hardly a timesaver. So you need to fix up the file to handle multiple movies.

All you need to do is create an array that contains the name of each file and loop through the array, publishing each file. Let's say you have a series of five movies, named `testMovie1` through `testMovie5`. The code would look like this:

```
filenames = ["file:///C:/jsfl_files/testMovie1.fla",
             "file:///C:/jsfl_files/testMovie2.fla",
             "file:///C:/jsfl_files/testMovie3.fla",
             "file:///C:/jsfl_files/testMovie4.fla",
             "file:///C:/jsfl_files/testMovie5.fla"];
for(i = 0; i < filenames.length; i++){
  fl.openDocument(filenames[i]);
  curr_doc = fl.getDocumentDOM();
  curr_doc.publish();
  curr_doc.close(false);
}
fl.quit(true);
```

Now that's a little better. You can now open the file and enter one file or a hundred. All you need to do is list the files in the array, save, and execute the file. Flash will open up and publish each file on the list. It still needs some work though . . .

Handling External Files from JSFL

The main thing we dislike about the preceding script is that the data and the code are too connected. There is something wrong about having to go in and edit a program to change the data that it processes. It's always best to separate the two. Ideally, you would have some kind of data-loading function in JSFL with which to do this. Something like `loadVariables` or `loadVars` in Flash ActionScript. The best you have available is something called `runScript`. This is designed to run an external JSFL script or function therein, but you can use it to create a sort of external data source. First let's look at exactly how it works.

The `runScript` method is a property of the `fl` object, and takes one or more parameters as you can see here:

```
fl.runScript(URI, function, arg1, arg2, arg3, etc.);
```

The first argument is the URI of another JSFL script. If this is the only argument you use, that other script will be run in its entirety. Of course, if any functions are defined in that script, they won't be run unless they are explicitly called in that script.

The second argument is the name of a function within that external script. If you include a function name here, Flash will first execute the external script as a whole, and then run the particular function that you named. These are important to remember. If you had an external JSFL script named `funcs.jsfl` that contained the following:

```
fl.trace("outside");
function myfunc(){
  fl.trace("inside");
}
```

and you called this from another script in the same directory, using just the file URI as shown here:

```
fl.runScript("file:///funcs.jsfl");
```

it would only trace `outside`. (Note that if the file you're referencing is in the same directory, you can skip the drive letter and path and just reference the filename.) The internal function, `myfunc`, wouldn't be run. If you called it using the function name like so:

```
fl.runScript("file:///funcs.jsfl", "myfunc");
```

it would first run the entire file, tracing `outside`, and then it would run the function, tracing `inside`.

Thus, if you're setting up a kind of library of external functions to run, you probably want to make sure that no code appears outside of the function definitions themselves. If some does, it will get run every time you call any function in the file.

8

OK, the last optional thing you can feed the runScript function is one or more function arguments. Any values included after the function name are sent to the function as arguments. So, code like this:

```
fl.runScript("file:///funcs.jsfl", "myfunc", 1, 2, "hello");
```

is the same as if you had called the function like this:

```
myfunc(1, 2, "hello");
```

If any values are returned from the function, they will then be returned from runScript. An example of using this would be the utility functions you used in Chapters 2 and 3. You could put them all in an external JSFL file called utilityFuncs.jsfl. Since these could be used by tools, commands, and other scripts, it would probably be best to place this file directly in the Configuration directory. Then, any time you wanted to get the current frame, in any JSFL file, you could say:

```
curr_frame = fl.runScript(fl.configURI + "/utilityFuncs.jsfl",
➥"getCurrentFrame");
```

OK, it doesn't exactly roll off the keyboard, but it's better than retyping the entire function! Now you see why we chose to include the functions right in our scripts, and call them with this simple line:

```
curr_frame = getCurrentFrame();
```

All right then—now that you know all about runScript, let's see how to use it to separate your code and data. Return to the flashPublish.jsfl file you just made, cut out the first line that lists the files, and replace it with the following:

```
fl.runScript("file:///fileList.dat");
for(i = 0; i < filenames.length; i++){
  fl.openDocument(filenames[i]);
  curr_doc = fl.getDocumentDOM();
  curr_doc.publish();
  curr_doc.close(false);
}
fl.quit(true);
```

Now create a new file in the same directory, name it fileList.dat, and paste that file list into it as follows:

```
filenames = ["file:///C:/jsfl_files/testMovie1.fla",
             "file:///C:/jsfl_files/testMovie2.fla",
             "file:///C:/jsfl_files/testMovie3.fla",
             "file:///C:/jsfl_files/testMovie4.fla",
             "file:///C:/jsfl_files/testMovie5.fla"];
```

An interesting point here is that you name the data file with a .dat extension. It's still a valid JSFL file, but changing the extension lets you know that this contains data only, not code that is meant to be executed on its own. It doesn't change any functionality, just acts as a visual reminder as to the purpose of the file.

Now, when you run `flashPublish.jsfl`, the first thing it does is execute `fileList.dat`, which creates the array of filenames; it then continues through and processes them as before. As for editing the list, it's much cleaner to open up a data file containing only a list of files to edit, rather than editing the entire script.

Abstracting It Even Further with Batch Files

The preceding setup is pretty good, but even with the separated file list data, it isn't really anything to write home about. You still have to open up a text editor, open the data file, edit the filenames, save it, close the text editor, and run the JSFL file. This is clearly better than loading and processing each file manually, but you can do better!

The main problem is that JSFL isn't dynamic. You can't pass any parameters to a JSFL file when you execute it like this:

```
flashPublish.jsfl myMovie.fla
```

and have it publish the file you give it. Everything has to be prescripted and saved before execution. We knew we could reap huge benefits if this limitation could be overcome. Since the JSFL itself isn't dynamic, the solution was to dynamically create JSFL files! In other words, you take some live data and use it to generate a brand new JSFL file based on that data, and then execute that file. After looking into various complex ways of doing this, we realized there was an ancient technology sitting on our computers that was perfect for this chore—DOS batch files!

8

If you happen to be too young to recall the pre-Windows era, we'll explain: A batch file is a simple script used to automatically execute various system commands from the command prompt. Less than a dozen batch commands are available, but they can write some pretty powerful scripts. In addition to the batch-specific commands, you can use any DOS command in a batch file, such as `dir` for a directory listing, `del` to delete a file, and so on.

You save these scripts to a simple text file with a `.bat` extension, and when it's executed—either by typing in its name or double-clicking its icon—the commands execute from top to bottom.

Note, however, that batch files aren't the only way or even necessarily the best way to accomplish these tasks. If you're familiar with and have access to a C++ compiler or another programming language that can write files and execute programs, that would work just as well, and probably give you even more options. We went with batch files because they're free and very easy to learn while still giving you a fair share of power and flexibility.

Echoing Data

Perhaps one of the most useful commands for the purposes of this example is the echo command. This allows you to send any text to the console, or redirect it to a file. This is how you'll create a new JSFL file. Let's try it out.

1. Using any text editor, create a new text file and save it as `test.bat` in your `jsfl_files` directory.
2. Type in the following:

   ```
   echo Hello World
   ```

   and save the file. Notice how loose this scripting language is—no quotes needed, no end-of-line semicolon or other character. Anything that follows the echo command (which is case-insensitive by the way, as are all DOS commands) will be sent to the console.
3. Open up a command prompt (console window) as described earlier in the chapter.
4. Change the directory to the jsfl_files directory:

   ```
   cd jsfl_files
   ```

5. Type in `test.bat` or simply `test`. You should see the text `Hello World` echoed on your screen.
6. Now try sending it to a file. This is done using the redirection operator, >, followed by the name of the file you want to put the text in. Change the code in the `test.bat` file to the following:

   ```
   echo Hello World > output.txt
   ```

   and rerun the file as in step 5. There should now be a new file in the directory named `output.txt`. Examine it and you'll find that it's a simple text file containing the words `Hello World`.

Getting Arguments

Another powerful aspect of batch files is that they are able to accept arguments. If you called the `test.bat` file with an argument like this one:

```
test 100
```

the value 100 would be available inside the batch file in the variable `%1`. Try that by changing `test.bat` to the following:

```
echo You entered %1
```

then run the file, giving it an argument. It should echo back, telling you what you entered.

Additional arguments can be contained in variables `%2` through `%9` (later, you'll use a little trick to access arguments beyond the ninth). Try changing the batch file to this:

```
echo You entered %1 %2 %3 %4 %5 %6 %7 %8 %9
```

and you can now enter up to nine arguments and have them trace back.

Creating a JSFL File

Let's look at how you can use what you've learned so far to create a new JSFL file based on an argument fed to the batch file.

1. Create a new batch file named `flashPublish.bat` in the `jsfl_files` directory.

2. In this example, the argument fed into the batch file will be a filename, stored in the variable `%1`. If you remember your original `flashPublish.jsfl`, which handled only one file, it started out by defining the filename with the following line:

   ```
   filename = "file:///C:/jsfl_files/testMovie.fla";
   ```

   You can re-create that dynamically by echoing it to a new, temporary JSFL file you'll call `tempPublish.jsfl`:

   ```
   echo filename = "file:///%1"; > tempPublish.jsfl
   ```

   Notice that you need to add the quotes and `file:///` in order to have the filename appear as a valid URI.

3. Now run this batch file from the command prompt with a filename as an argument like this:

   ```
   flashPublish myMovie.fla
   ```

4. Look in the `jsfl_files` directory and you should now see a `tempPublish.jsfl` file. Inside, it should indeed have one line:

   ```
   filename = "file:///myMovie.fla";
   ```

   Voila! Dynamic JSFL. Of course, the argument as given previously assumes that there is a file called `myMovie.fla` in the directory from which the command is called. If it's somewhere else, you would need to type the full path in addition to the filename in the argument. One problem you now face though is that each time you echo data to a file using >, it erases any previous data in the file. If you're going to be adding a full script, you need a way to add to the file rather than replacing it. You can do that with the >> operator. So your first line will use > to create a fresh file, and each line thereafter will use >> to add additional lines of code.

5. Now you just need to create the rest of the file:

   ```
   echo filename = "file:///%1"; > tempPublish.jsfl
   echo fl.openDocument(filename); >> tempPublish.jsfl
   echo curr_doc = fl.getDocumentDOM(); >> tempPublish.jsfl
   echo curr_doc.publish(); >> tempPublish.jsfl
   echo curr_doc.close(false); >> tempPublish.jsfl
   echo fl.quit(true); >> tempPublish.jsfl
   ```

   The rest of the lines are straight out of the original file, with the echo command added to the front and the file redirection added to the end. Run the batch file again with a filename as an argument. Then open up the `tempPublish.jsfl` file. This should be identical to the original `flashPublish.jsfl` file, but will contain the filename you specified. You can even execute this JSFL file and have it open and publish your file.

Pretty good, but you're still in a two-stage process: Run the batch file, and then run the JSFL file. For a truly professional workflow, you can do even better!

8

Executing Files from a Batch File

It would be nice if, after building the custom JSFL file, you could automatically execute it from the batch file. Well, as a matter of fact you can, with the Windows `start` command. The syntax of this command in its simplest form is

```
start program argument1 argument2 [additional arguments]
```

For the purposes of this example, program is the entire path to the Flash executable file, and the argument (there will be only one in this case) is the JSFL file that you've just created. Remember to use quotes to enclose any file paths that contain spaces. Here's how it's shaping up:

```
echo filename = "file:///%1"; > tempPublish.jsfl
echo fl.openDocument(filename); >> tempPublish.jsfl
echo curr_doc = fl.getDocumentDOM(); >> tempPublish.jsfl
echo curr_doc.publish(); >> tempPublish.jsfl
echo curr_doc.close(false); >> tempPublish.jsfl
echo fl.quit(true); >> tempPublish.jsfl
start "C:/Program Files/Macromedia/Flash MX 2004/Flash.exe"
➥tempPublish.jsfl
```

Works well so far. But there's one annoying point—each line is echoed to the console as it executes. You get this sudden scrolling of a half a page of information, which isn't going to make much sense to the average user. There are two ways to suppress the echoing. One is to put an @ symbol at the beginning of each line you don't want to echo to the screen, as demonstrated here:

```
@echo filename = "file:///" + %1; > tempPublish.jsfl
```

But, there's an even better method that allows you to shut it off altogether. You can just use the statement echo `off` at the beginning of the file. No further statements will be echoed. But you'll have to prefix this with @ to prevent it from echoing itself. So you can now add this as the first line of the file:

```
@echo off
```

Handling Multiple Arguments

As it stands, the batch file only handles a single argument. Let's fix it up so it handles as many as you feed it.

The brute force method would be to repeat all the code for %1, %2, %3, etc. Obviously that would be horrible coding practice, so you can just ignore that option. You need a loop to execute once for each argument given. But there's another problem. Earlier we mentioned that the first nine arguments to the batch file are contained in variables %1 through %9. What if the user enters more than nine? How do you access the rest?

The answers to both issues are in the batch file command shift. What shift does is discard the value in %1, and shift over all the other variables one slot down. %2 now becomes %1,

%3 becomes %2, and so on. And the tenth, unnamed variable is now found in %9. So, you just need to continue your loop until %1 is empty. At that point you know that you've used up all the arguments. (Actually, if you want to get technical about it, there is another variable, %0, which initially holds the first thing typed at the command prompt, the name of the batch file itself. The shift command discards this value and shifts %1 into %0.)

So, how do you loop? Batch files don't have any commands like while, do/while, or for (there is a for/in loop, but it doesn't really work for the purposes of this example). What you do have is if, goto, and labels. You can test for a certain condition, and if true go to one label, and if false go to another. Labels are created by typing a colon followed by the label name. Here's some pseudo-code to show the basic arrangement:

```
:start
(do something in here)
if someCondition goto end
goto start
:end
```

Here you have two labels, start and end. After executing some code, you check a condition, and if true, go to the end label. If the condition doesn't test true, the batch file will continue with the next line, which tells it to go back to start. In your Flash publishing batch file, you'll be testing to see if the variable %1 has any value. If it has no value (an empty string, or "") then you go to end, otherwise you loop back to start. Here's the final file:

```
@echo off
echo // >tempPublish.jsfl
:start
echo filename = "file:///%1"; > tempPublish.jsfl
echo fl.openDocument(filename); >> tempPublish.jsfl
echo curr_doc = fl.getDocumentDOM(); >> tempPublish.jsfl
echo curr_doc.publish(); >> tempPublish.jsfl
echo curr_doc.close(false); >> tempPublish.jsfl
shift
if "%1" == "" goto end
goto start
:end
echo fl.quit(true); >> tempPublish.jsfl
start "C:/Program Files/Macromedia/Flash MX 2004/Flash.exe"
➥tempPublish.jsfl
```

8

To clarify, here's a quick rundown of what you're doing: You create the tempPublish.jsfl file with an empty comment (//). This wipes out any previous content in it. You handle the first argument, writing out all the code to publish that file. Then you shift the arguments and check if there is another filename in %1. If so, you go back to start and write out the code to publish the next file. When it finally returns an empty string, you go to the end, write out the final code for the file, and then execute it. Go ahead and test the batch file, handing it multiple files to compile (ensuring that these FLAs exist):

```
flashPublish myMovie1.fla myMovie2.fla myMovie3.fla myMovie4.fla
```

There you have it—creating multiple SWF files with a single line! If you looked at the code generated inside the JSFL file, it does pretty much resemble the brute force method of running through each file with a ton of code duplication. But since it's only a temporary file designed to be run only once and is never actually seen by human eyes, you should be able to live with that.

Summary

Hopefully by now, you're starting to see some of the powerful things you can do in executing Flash from the command line with JSFL. Again, these batch files have a lot of limitations, and as you work with this file, we're sure you'll run across them. But given that, you've created a pretty powerful command-line Flash compiler that will work in most circumstances and can save you hours of work!

If you have some knowledge in any other languages, you could take this simple file a lot further. Imagine being able to drag FLA files onto this program's icon and have them automatically published, or even have a file selector where you could choose a number of FLA files, and click a button, and bang! They're all published. Our original idea was to create a server-side PHP script that would use Flash to generate SWFs on the fly, much like the older application, Macromedia Generator. This not only proved tougher than we thought, but in retrospect, we can only imagine the effects of dozens of users logging on to the script to create SWFs. Still, it's a concept that we're sure someone out there will be interested in pursuing!

In the meantime, hopefully this chapter has given you a start in the right direction and some inspiration. We can't wait to see what kind of cool applications start to appear in the next year or so!

JSFL REFERENCE

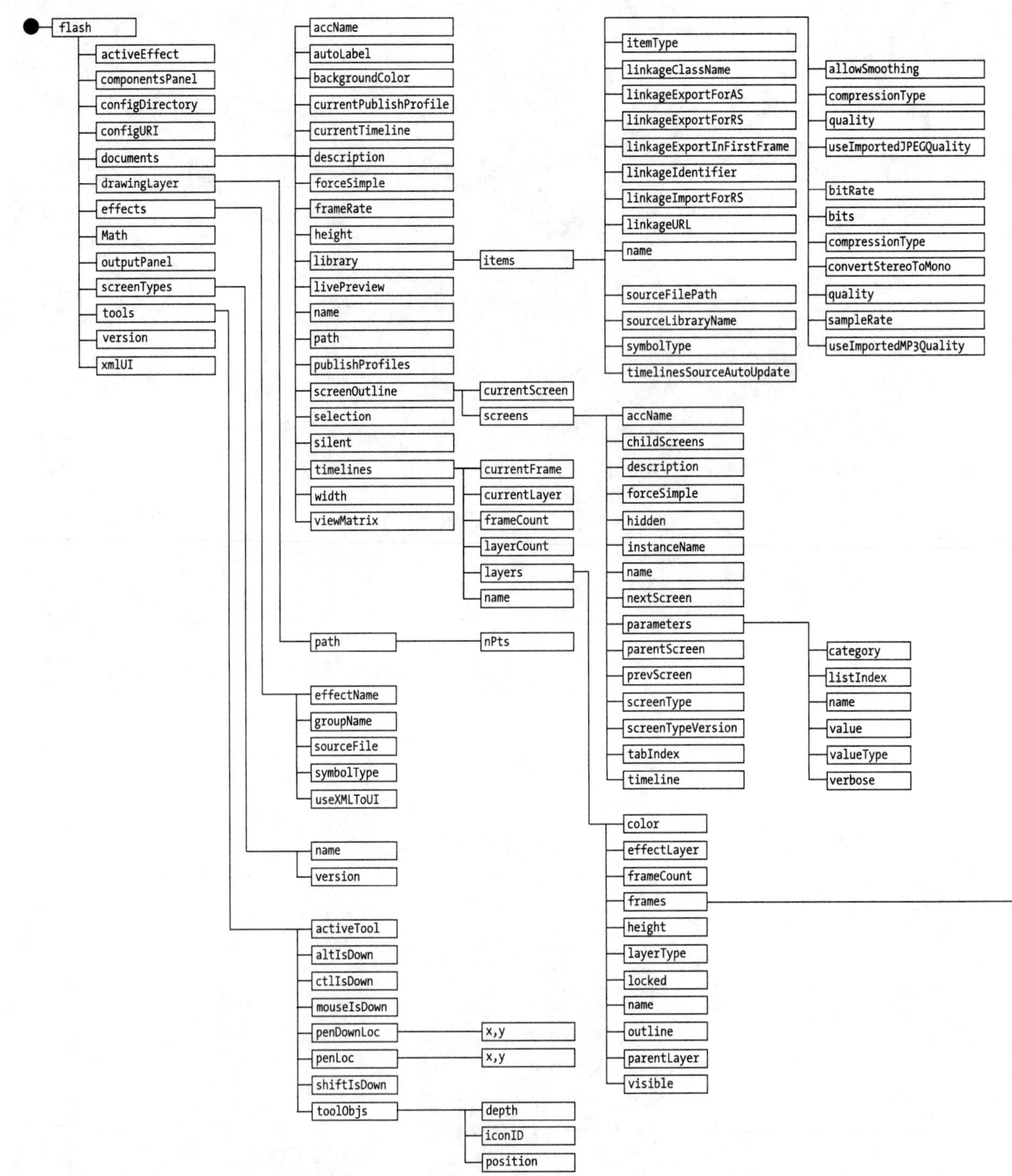

Figure 9-1. JSFL DOM Overview

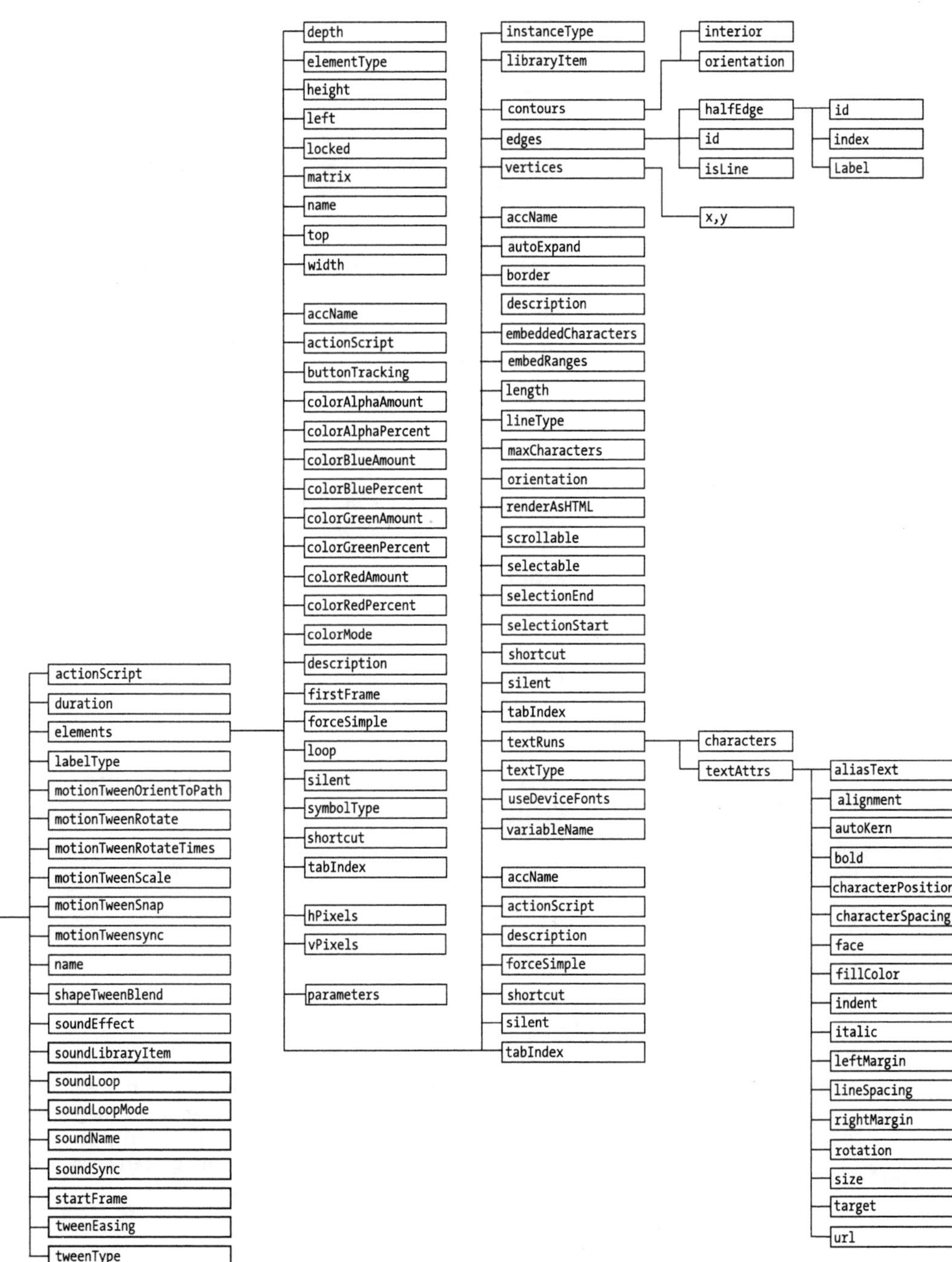
actionScript
duration
elements
labelType
motionTweenOrientToPath
motionTweenRotate
motionTweenRotateTimes
motionTweenScale
motionTweenSnap
motionTweensync
name
shapeTweenBlend
soundEffect
soundLibraryItem
soundLoop
soundLoopMode
soundName
soundSync
startFrame
tweenEasing
tweenType
depth
elementType
height
left
locked
matrix
name
top
width
accName
actionScript
buttonTracking
colorAlphaAmount
colorAlphaPercent
colorBlueAmount
colorBluePercent
colorGreenAmount
colorGreenPercent
colorRedAmount
colorRedPercent
colorMode
description
firstFrame
forceSimple
loop
silent
symbolType
shortcut
tabIndex
hPixels
vPixels
parameters
instanceType
libraryItem
contours
edges
vertices
accName
autoExpand
border
description
embeddedCharacters
embedRanges
length
lineType
maxCharacters
orientation
renderAsHTML
scrollable
selectable
selectionEnd
selectionStart
shortcut
silent
tabIndex
textRuns
textType
useDeviceFonts
variableName
accName
actionScript
description
forceSimple
shortcut
silent
tabIndex
interior
orientation
halfEdge
id
isLine
x,y
id
index
Label
characters
textAttrs
aliasText
alignment
autoKern
bold
characterPosition
characterSpacing
face
fillColor
indent
italic
leftMargin
lineSpacing
rightMargin
rotation
size
target
url

BitmapInstance

Subclass of Instance. Represents a bitmap on the stage.

Methods:

- getBits
- setBits

Properties:

- hPixels
- vPixels

Methods of the bitmapInstance Object

getBits

`bitmapInstance.getBits()`

Gets bits from bitmap

Description
Gets information from the bitmap instance for manipulation. The object returned by the method has width and height properties (in pixels), depth (the bit depth of image), and two arrays, bits and cTab. bits is a byte array of color information and cTab holds values for the bitmap's color table (if it has one) with each index in the form of #rrggbb. This method was intended for developers to use to make bitmap effects, by extracting the color information and sending it to a program or extension outside of Flash, and then using setBits to alter the bitmap with the manipulated values sent back to Flash. Within Flash itself, the byte array, and therefore the basic color information, isn't meaningful.

Argument(s)
None

Returns
Object holding bitmap's color information—*object*

Example
```
var c = fl.getDocumentDOM().selection[0].
➥ getBits();
fl.trace(c.bits.length);
fl.trace(c.depth);
```

setBits

`bitmapInstance.setBits( bitmap )`

Sets bits of bitmap

Description
Intended to be used along with bitmapInstance .getBits() to create bitmap effects. setBits() sets the bitmap's color information to equal the manipulated values sent in the bitmap argument.

Argument(s)
bitmap—*object*—An object with the following properties:

width (*integer*)

height (*integer*)

depth (*integer*)

bits (*byte array*)

cTab (*array of colors in the form "#rrggbb", only necessary for images with bit depth of 8 or less*)

Returns
Nothing

Example
```
fl.getDocumentDOM ().selection[0].
➥ setBits(colorObj);
```

Properties of the bitmapInstance Object

hPixels

`bitmapInstance.hPixels`

Width of bitmap in pixels

Description
Holds the pixel width of the bitmap, disregarding any transformations upon it onstage. Therefore if a bitmap that was imported with a width of 200 pixels is placed on the stage and scaled horizontally by half, the instance's hPixel property will still hold a value of 200 pixels. This property may be retrieved, but not set.

Value(s)
integer—Width in pixels

Example

```
var bInstance = fl.getDocumentDOM().
➥ getTimeline().layers[0].frames[0].
➥ elements[0];
fl.trace(bInstance.hPixels);
```

vPixels

`bitmapInstance.vPixels`

Height of bitmap in pixels

Description

Holds the pixel height of the bitmap, disregarding any transformations upon it onstage. Therefore if a bitmap that was imported with a height of 200 pixels is placed on the stage and scaled vertically by half, the instance's `vPixel` property will still hold a value of 200 pixels. This property may be retrieved, but not set.

Value(s)

integer—Height in pixels

Example

```
var bInstance = fl.getDocumentDOM().
➥ getTimeline().layers[0].frames[0].
➥ elements[0];
fl.trace(bInstance.vPixels);
```

BitmapItem

Subclass of `Item`. Represents a bitmap symbol in the Library.

Properties:

- `allowSmoothing`
- `compressionType`
- `quality`
- `useImportedJPEGQuality`

Properties of the bitmapItem Object

allowSmoothing

`bitmapItem.allowSmoothing`

If `true`, smooths edges of bitmap with antialiasing

Description

This property, when set to `true`, antialiases the edges of a bitmap in the published movie.

Value(s)

Boolean—`true`, `false`

Example

```
fl.getDocumentDOM().library.items[0].
➥ allowSmoothing = true;
```

compressionType

`bitmapItem.compressionType`

Specifies compression type for export

Description

Determines how the bitmap is compressed upon export of the movie. Valid values are `"photo"` and `"lossless"`. If `"photo"`, the compression quality is set at a value between 0 and 100 if the `useImportedJPEGQuality` is set to `false`. If `useImportedJPEGQuality` is set to `true`, the default document quality is used (determined in the Publish Profile).

Value(s)

string—`"photo"` or `"lossless"`

Example

```
fl.getDocumentDOM().library.items[0].
➥ compressionType = "photo";
```

quality

`bitmapItem.quality`

Quality for JPEG compression

Description

Determines the compression quality of bitmap if `compressionType` is `"photo"` and `useImportedJPEGQuality` is `false`. You can still get and set the quality setting when `useImportedJPEGQuality` is `true`, but the value is never used.

Value(s)

integer—An integer between 0 and 100, inclusive; this will hold -1 if `useImportedJPEGQuality` is set to `true` and `quality` has never been set.

Example

```
fl.getDocumentDOM().library.items[0].
➥ quality = 60;
```

useImportedJPEGQuality

`bitmapItem.useImportedJPEGQuality`

If true, uses default document JPEG compression quality for export

Description
Determines whether a bitmap with a compressionType of "photo" uses the default document compression value (true) or a quality value specific to the bitmap (false).

Value(s)
Boolean—true, false

Example
```
fl.getDocumentDOM().library.items[0].
➥ useImportedJPEGQuality = false;
fl.getDocumentDOM().library.items[0].
➥ quality = 50;
```

CompiledClipInstance

Subclass of SymbolInstance. Represents a compiled clip instance on the stage.

Properties:

- accName
- actionScript
- description
- forceSimple
- shortcut
- silent
- tabIndex

Properties of the compiledClipInstance Object

accName

`compiledClipInstance.accName`

Name of object, used by screen reader

Description
The accName property holds the name of the symbol instance that appears in the Accessibility panel and will be exposed to screen reader technology. This property may be both retrieved and set.

Value(s)
string—The name of the instance for the screen reader

Example
```
var my_elem = fl.getDocumentDOM().
➥ getTimeline().layers[0].frames[0].
➥ elements[0];
my_elem.silent = false;
my_elem.description = "go to last page";
my_elem.accName = "back";
```

actionScript

`compiledClipInstance.actionScript`

String representing ActionScript on an instance

Description
This property holds all of the ActionScript that is placed on a symbol instance (the ActionScript inside the instance must be accessed from the timeline, layer, and frame on which it appears) and may be both set and retrieved. Since you may perform any string operations on the ActionScript, it is possible to not only replace all of an instance's code, but also insert within or add to existing code. Remember that code placed on an instance (not within a frame) must appear within an on() or onClipEvent() block in order for the movie to not produce an error.

Value(s)
string—Code on an instance

Example
```
// inserts code within an existing block if it
// exists, else creates a new block
var my_elem = fl.getDocumentDOM().
➥ selection[0];
var aScript = my_elem.actionScript;
if (aScript.length > 0) {
  var close = aScript.lastIndexOf("}");
  aScript = aScript.substr(0, close) +
➥ "\n\ttrace(\"here\");\n}";
} else {
  aScript =  "onClipEvent(load) {\n";
  aScript += "  trace(\"here\");\n";
  aScript += "}";
}
my_elem.actionScript = aScript;
```

description

`compiledClipInstance.description`

Description of object, used by screen reader

Description

The `description` property holds the textual information about the symbol instance that appears in the Accessibility panel and will be exposed to screen reader technology. This property may be both retrieved and set.

Value(s)

string—Description of an instance for the screen reader

Example

```
var my_elem = fl.getDocumentDOM().
➥ getTimeline().layers[0].frames[0].
➥ elements[0];
my_elem.silent = false;
my_elem.description = "go to last page";
my_elem.accName = "back";
```

forceSimple

`compiledClipInstance.forceSimple`

If `true`, children of object aren't accessible to screen reader.

Description

This property specifies whether a compiled clip instance's child objects will be made accessible to a screen reader and corresponds (inversely) with the Make child objects accessible check box in the Accessibility panel. When `true`, the child objects *won't* be accessible. When `false`, the child objects *will* be accessible. This property may be both set and retrieved.

Value(s)

Boolean—`true`, `false`

Example

```
var my_elem = fl.getDocumentDOM().
➥ selection[0];
my_elem.silent = false;
my_elem.forceSimple = true;
```

shortcut

`compiledClipInstance.shortcut`

Object's shortcut key

Description

The shortcut key used for accessibility and exposed by a screen reader. This property corresponds with the shortcut field in the Accessibility panel. It may be retrieved or set. To have the shortcut key actually work with an object, however, you still need to use ActionScript to detect a keyDown event for that key and provide whatever functionality is required.

Value(s)

string—The key or key combination used to access the object

Example

```
var my_elem = fl.getDocumentDOM().
➥ getTimeline().layers[0].frames[0].
➥ elements[0];
my_elem.silent = false;
my_elem.shortcut = "Control+B";
my_elem.accName = "back";
```

silent

`compiledClipInstance.silent`

If `true`, object isn't read by screen reader

Description

This property controls whether an object is visible and accessible to a screen reader, and may be both set and retrieved. Setting this property to `true` will make it invisible and corresponds with deselecting the Make Object Accessible check box in the Accessibility panel.

Value(s)

Boolean—`true`, `false`

Example

```
var my_elem = fl.getDocumentDOM().
➥ getTimeline().layers[0].frames[0].
➥ elements[0];
my_elem.silent = false;
my_elem.shortcut = "Control+B";
my_elem.accName = "back";
```

tabIndex

`compiledClipInstance.tabIndex`

`tabIndex` value of object

Description
This property corresponds with the same value found in ActionScript. tabIndex is used to control tab ordering on a page and determines order for a screen reader. This property may be both set and retrieved.

Value(s)
integer—The index in tab order

Example
```
fl.getDocumentDOM().selection[0].
➥ tabIndex = 5;
```

ComponentInstance

Subclass of SymbolInstance. Represents a component instance on the stage.

Properties:

- parameters

Properties of the componentInstance Object

parameters

componentInstance.parameters

Component's parameters

Description
An object array of parameter objects for the component. This array can be accessed either using an index (parameters[0]) or with the name of the parameter (parameters["icon"] or parameters.icon). Although individual parameters may have their values set, the array itself is static and can't be manipulated, meaning that you can't add to or delete items in the array.

Value(s)
object—The collection of parameter objects for the component

Example
```
fl.getDocumentDOM().selection[0].
➥ parameters["label"].value = "play";
fl.trace(fl.getDocumentDOM().selection[0].
➥ parameters[1].value);
```

ComponentsPanel

An object representing the Components panel in the Flash authoring environment

Methods:

- addItemToDocument

Methods of the componentsPanel Object

addItemToDocument

componentsPanel.addItemToDocument
➥ (*position*, *categoryName*, *componentName*)

Adds component to document

Description
Adds the specified component to the current document

Argument(s)
position—*point object*—The x, y position onstage to place the component

categoryName—*string*—The category in the components panel where the component is located

componentName—*string*—The name of the component

Returns
Nothing

Example
```
fl.componentsPanel.addItemToDocument
➥ ({x:100, y:200}, "UI Components",
➥ "CheckBox");
```

Contour

A closed path of half edges on a shape

Methods:

- getHalfEdge

Properties:

- interior
- orientation

Methods of the contour Object

getHalfEdge

contour.getHalfEdge()

Returns halfEdge object

Description

Returns a halfEdge object on the contour (see the entry for HalfEdge). Multiple calls to this method will return different half edges.

Argument(s)

None

Returns

halfEdge—*A halfEdge object on the contour*

Example

```
var my_doc = fl.getDocumentDOM();
var my_tl = my_doc.getTimeline();
var my_layer = my_tl.layers[0];
var my_frame = my_layer.frames[0];
var my_elem = my_frame.elements[0];
var my_contour = my_elem.contours[0];
var my_halfEdge = my_contour.getHalfEdge();
fl.trace(my_halfEdge);
```

Properties of the contour Object

interior

contour.interior

If true, contour encloses an area

Description

Property is true if contour encloses an area, false otherwise. A shape that consists of a closed path will have two contours. The first index in the contours array will hold a reference to the exterior contour, while the second index will hold a reference to the interior.

Value(s)

Boolean—true, false

Example

```
var my_doc = fl.getDocumentDOM();
var my_tl = my_doc.getTimeline();
var my_layer = my_tl.layers[0];
var my_frame = my_layer.frames[0];
var my_elem = my_frame.elements[0];
fl.trace(my_elem.contours[0].interior);
fl.trace(my_elem.contours[1].interior);
```

orientation

contour.orientation

Integer indicating orientation of contour

Description

An integer value specifying the orientation of the vertices of the contour: -1 for counterclockwise, 1 for clockwise, and 0 for a contour with no enclosed area.

Value(s)

integer—1, 0, 1

Example

```
var my_doc = fl.getDocumentDOM();
var my_tl = my_doc.getTimeline();
var my_layer = my_tl.layers[0];
var my_frame = my_layer.frames[0];
var my_elem = my_frame.elements[0];
fl.trace(my_elem.contours[0].orientation);
```

Document

An object representing the stage of any open document

Methods:

- addDataToDocument
- addDataToSelection
- addItem
- addNewLine
- addNewOval
- addNewPublishProfile
- addNewRectangle
- addNewScene
- addNewText
- align
- allowScreens
- arrange
- breakApart

- canEditSymbol
- canRevert
- canTestMovie
- canTestScene
- clipCopy
- clipCut
- clipPaste
- close
- convertLinesToFills
- convertToSymbol
- deletePublishProfile
- deleteScene
- deleteSelection
- distribute
- distributeToLayers
- documentHasData
- duplicatePublishProfile
- duplicateScene
- duplicateSelection
- editScene
- enterEditMode
- exitEditMode
- exportPublishProfile
- exportSWF
- getAlignToDocument
- getCustomFill
- getCustomStroke
- getDataFromDocument
- getElementProperty
- getElementTextAttr
- getSelectionRect
- getTextString
- getTimeline
- getTransformationPoint
- group
- importPublishProfile
- importSWF
- match
- mouseClick
- mouseDblClk
- moveSelectedBezierPointsBy
- moveSelectionBy
- optimizeCurves
- publish
- removeDataFromDocument
- removeDataFromSelection
- renamePublishProfile
- renameScene
- reorderScene
- resetTransformation
- revert
- rotateSelection
- save
- saveAndCompact
- scaleSelection
- selectAll
- selectNone
- setAlignToDocument
- setCustomFill
- setCustomStroke
- setElementProperty
- setElementTextAttr
- setFillColor
- setInstanceAlpha
- setInstanceBrightness
- setInstanceTint
- setSelectionBounds
- setSelectionRect
- setStroke
- setStrokeColor
- setStrokeSize
- setStrokeStyle
- setTextRectangle
- setTextSelection
- setTextString
- setTransformationPoint
- skewSelection
- smoothSelection

- space
- straightenSelection
- swapElement
- testMovie
- testScene
- traceBitmap
- transformSelection
- unGroup
- unlockAllElements
- xmlPanel

Properties:

- accName
- autoLabel
- backgroundColor
- currentPublishProfile
- currentTimeline
- description
- forceSimple
- frameRate
- height
- library
- livePreview
- name
- path
- publishProfiles
- screenOutline
- selection
- silent
- timelines
- viewMatrix
- width

Methods of the document Object

Note: Many of the document methods operate on whatever elements are currently selected in the document at the time the command is run. For instance, `document.addDataToSelection()` sets persistent data in the currently selected objects. But note that although the elements are receiving the action, the method belongs to the document object, not the elements.

addDataToDocument

```
document.addDataToDocument
➥ ( name, type, data )
```

Stores persistent data in document

Description

Saves the specified data in a Flash document. The data will be saved in the FLA and be available when it is closed and reopened.

Argument(s)

name—*string*—The name of the variable in which you will store the data.

type—*string*—A string containing the type of data you want to save. Valid values are "integer", "integerArray", "double", "doubleArray", "string", and "byteArray".

data—*Type depends on specified type of data*—The data that will be saved.

Returns

Nothing

Example

```
my_doc = fl.getDocumentDOM();
my_doc.addDataToDocument("myName",
➥ "string", "Keith");
myNumbers = [1, 2, 3];
my_doc.addDataToDocument
➥ ("myNums", "integerArray", myNumbers);
```

addDataToSelection

```
document.addDataToSelection( name, type,
➥ data )
```

Stores data with selected objects

Description

Saves the specified data in the selected element in a Flash document. The data will be saved in the FLA and be available when it is closed and reopened.

Argument(s)

name—*string*—The name of the variable in which you will store the data.

type—*string*—A string containing the type of data you want to save. Valid values are "integer", "integerArray", "double", "doubleArray", "string", and "byteArray".

data—*Type depends on specified type of data*—The data that will be saved.

Returns
Nothing

Example
```
my_doc = fl.getDocumentDOM();
my_doc.addDataToSelection("myName",
➥ "string", "Keith");
myNumbers = [1, 2, 3];
my_doc.addDataToSelection("myNums",
➥ "integerArray", myNumbers);
```

addItem

document.addItem(*position*, *item*)

Adds item from Library to stage

Description
Creates an instance of a Library item on the stage of the specified document.

Argument(s)
position—*point*—The x, y point at which the newly created instance will be placed.

item—*object*—A reference to the Library item you wish to add. See the entry for library.item.

Returns
Value stating whether the operation was successful or not—*Boolean*

Example
```
my_doc = fl.getDocumentDOM();
my_doc.addItem({x:100, y:100},
➥ my_lib.items[0]);
```

addNewLine

document.addNewLine(*startPoint*,
➥ *endPoint*)

Draws line onstage

Description
Draws a new line on the stage of the specified document. As with all drawing methods, it will use the current settings for the stroke color, width, and style.

Argument(s)
startPoint—*point*—The x, y point at which to begin drawing the line

endPoint—*point*—The x, y point specifying the end of the line

Returns
Nothing

Example
```
my_doc = fl.getDocumentDOM();
my_doc.addNewLine({x:0, y:0},
➥ {x:100, y:100});
```

addNewOval

document.addNewOval(*boundingRectangle*
➥ [, *bSuppressFill*] [, *bSuppressStroke*])

Draws oval onstage

Description
Draws an oval shape on the stage of the specified document. Will use the current settings for fill and stroke, unless the second and third arguments are set as true.

Argument(s)
boundingRectangle—*rect*—An object containing properties top, bottom, left, and right

bSuppressFill—*Boolean*—Specifies if the oval will be drawn with or without a fill (optional, default is false)

bSuppressStroke—*Boolean*—Specifies if the oval will be drawn with or without a stroke (optional, default is false)

Returns
Nothing

Example
```
// draw oval with fill and stroke:
my_doc = fl.getDocumentDOM();
my_doc.addNewOval({top:100, left:100,
➥ bottom:200, right:200});
// draw oval with stroke only:
my_doc = fl.getDocumentDOM();
my_doc.addNewOval({top:100, left:100,
```

```
➥ bottom:200, right:200}, true, false);
// draw oval with fill only:
my_doc = fl.getDocumentDOM();
my_doc.addNewOval({top:100, left:100,
➥ bottom:200, right:200}, false, true);
```

addNewPublishProfile

document.addNewPublishProfile
➥ ([*profileName*])

Adds new Publish Profile

Description
Creates a new Publish Profile for the current document. It will become the current Publish Profile.

Argument(s)
profileName—*string*—The name of the new profile. If omitted, default name will be used.

Returns
Index of new profile, –1 if not successful—*integer*

Example
```
my_doc = fl.getDocumentDOM();
my_doc.addNewPublishProfile("betaVersion");
```

addNewRectangle

document.addNewRectangle(*boundingRectangle*,
➥ *roundness* [, *bSupressFill*]
➥ [, *bSuppressStroke*])

Draws new rectangle onstage

Description
Draws a rectangle shape on the stage of the specified document. Will use the current settings for fill and stroke, unless the third and fourth arguments are set as true.

Argument(s)
boundingRectangle—*rect*—An object containing properties top, bottom, left, and right.

roundness—*integer*—The radius of the rectangle corners. A value of zero will produce square corners.

bSuppressFill—*Boolean*—Specifies if the rectangle will be drawn with or without a fill (optional, default is false).

bSuppressStroke—*Boolean*—Specifies if the rectangle will be drawn with or without a stroke (optional, default is false).

Returns
Nothing

Example
```
// draw rectangle with fill and stroke:
my_doc = fl.getDocumentDOM();
my_doc.addNewRectangle({top:100, left:100,
➥ bottom:200, right:200}, 0);
// draw rectangle with stroke only:
my_doc = fl.getDocumentDOM();
my_doc.addNewRectangle({top:100, left:100,
➥ bottom:200, right:200}, 0, true, false);
// draw rectangle with fill only:
my_doc = fl.getDocumentDOM();
my_doc.addNewRectangle({top:100, left:100,
➥ bottom:200, right:200}, 0, false, true);
// draw rectangle with 10 pixel
// round corners:
my_doc = fl.getDocumentDOM();
my_doc.addNewRectangle({top:100, left:100,
➥ bottom:200, right:200}, 10);
```

addNewScene

document.addNewScene([*name*])

Adds new scene

Description
Creates a new scene (timeline object). The new scene will be inserted after the current scene and will become the new current scene.

Argument(s)
name—*string*—The name of the new scene

Returns
true if successful, otherwise false—*Boolean*

Example
```
my_doc = fl.getDocumentDOM();
my_doc.addNewScene("Fred");
```

addNewText

document.addNewText(*boundingRectangle*)

Inserts new empty text field

Description

Creates a new text field in the specified document, in the size and location specified by the bounding rectangle. Type of text field, font, color, etc., will be determined by the current settings in the text property inspector. The text field will be selected and ready for input.

Argument(s)

boundingRectangle—*rect*—An object with the following properties: top, left, bottom, right

Returns

Nothing

Example

```
// create a 100 by 20 pixel text field at
// 10, 10 on the stage:
my_doc = fl.getDocumentDOM();
my_doc.addNewText({top:10, left:10,
➥ bottom:30, right:110});
```

align

```
document.align( alignmode
➥ [, bUseDocumentBounds] )
```

Aligns selection

Description

Aligns any selected elements as specified

Argument(s)

alignmode—*string*—Determines how the document will be aligned. Valid values are "left", "right", "top", "bottom", "vertical center", and "horizontal center".

bUseDocumentBounds—*Boolean*—If true, the elements will be aligned to the bounds of the document. If false, elements will be aligned to the bounding box surrounding the selection.

Returns

Nothing

Example

```
// have selected elements align to a
// common left edge:
my_doc = fl.getDocumentDOM();
my_doc.align("left", false);
// align selected elements to
// left edge of stage:
my_doc = fl.getDocumentDOM();
my_doc.align("left", true);
```

allowScreens

```
document.allowScreens()
```

Checks if screen outline is available

Description

Returns true or false specifying whether or not screens are allowed in this document

Argument(s)

None

Returns

true if allowed, false if not—*Boolean*

Example

```
my_doc = fl.getDocumentDOM();
trace(my_doc.allowScreens());
```

arrange

```
document.arrange( arrangeMode )
```

Arranges selection

Description

Duplicates the Bring to Front, Bring Forward, Send Backward, and Send to Back menu items by moving the selected element on the z axis. As in the authoring environment, this only works on nonshape elements.

Argument(s)

arrangeMode—*string*—Where to send the element. Valid values are "back", "backward", "forward", and "front".

Returns

Nothing

Example

```
// send the selected element behind
// all other elements
my_doc = fl.getDocumentDOM();
my_doc.arrange("back");
```

breakApart

```
document.breakApart()
```

Breaks apart current selection

Description

Duplicates the Break Apart menu item in the authoring environment. Breaks apart the currently selected element, if applicable. Generally, if applied to a symbol, the symbol will be broken apart to its individual members. If applied to a text field, it will be broken into its individual letters. If applied to a text field containing an individual letter, this method will break the letter into a vector shape.

Argument(s)

None

Returns

Nothing

Example

```
my_doc = fl.getDocumentDOM();
my_doc.breakApart();
```

canEditSymbol

`document.canEditSymbol()`

If `true`, `editSymbol()` method can be used.

Description

Indicates whether or not there is a symbol to be edited. If no symbol is selected, this should return `false`.

Argument(s)

None

Returns

`true` if symbol can be edited, otherwise `false`—*Boolean*

Example

```
my_doc = fl.getDocumentDOM();
if(my_doc.canEditSymbol()){
  fl.trace("can edit symbol");
}else{
  fl.trace("cannot edit symbol");
}
```

canRevert

`document.canRevert()`

Indicates if document can be reverted

Description

Indicates whether or not the `revert` method can be used

Argument(s)

None

Returns

`true` if reversion is possible, otherwise `false`—*Boolean*

Example

```
my_doc = fl.getDocumentDOM();
if(my_doc.canRevert()){
  fl.trace("can revert");
}else{
  fl.trace("cannot revert");
}
```

canTestMovie

`document.canTestMovie()`

Indicates if movie can be tested

Description

Indicates whether or not the movie can be tested

Argument(s)

None

Returns

`true` if movie can be tested, otherwise `false`—*Boolean*

Example

```
my_doc = fl.getDocumentDOM();
if(my_doc.canTestMovie()){
  fl.trace("can test");
}else{
  fl.trace("cannot test");
}
```

canTestScene

`document.canTestScene()`

Indicates if current scene can be tested

Description

Indicates whether or not the scene can be tested

Argument(s)

None

Returns

`true` if scene can be tested, otherwise `false`—*Boolean*

Example

```
my_doc = fl.getDocumentDOM();
if(my_doc.canTestScene()){
  fl.trace("can test");
}else{
  fl.trace("cannot test");
}
```

clipCopy

`document.clipCopy()`

Copies selection to clipboard

Description

Copies any elements that are currently selected into the clipboard. These can later be pasted to the same or a different location using `document.clipPaste()`.

Argument(s)

None

Returns

Nothing

Example

```
my_doc = fl.getDocumentDOM();
my_doc.clipCopy();
```

clipCut

`document.clipCut()`

Cuts selection to clipboard

Description

Cuts any elements that are currently selected into the clipboard. These can later be pasted to the same or a different location using `document.clipPaste()`.

Argument(s)

None

Returns

Nothing

Example

```
my_doc = fl.getDocumentDOM();
my_doc.clipCut();
```

clipPaste

`document.clipPaste( [`*`bInPlace`*`] )`

Pastes clipboard into document

Description

Pastes any elements that have previously been cut or copied back into the specified document

Argument(s)

`bInPlace`—*Boolean*—If `true`, elements will be pasted to the location they were originally cut or copied from. If `false`, generally pastes into the center of the screen. Defaults to `false` if not specified.

Returns

Nothing

Example

```
my_doc = fl.getDocumentDOM();
my_doc.clipPaste(true);
```

close

`document.close( [`*`bPromptToSaveChanges`*`] )`

Closes current document

Description

Closes the current document

Argument(s)

`bPromptToSaveChanges`—*Boolean*—If `true`, and the document has not been saved, or has been changed since the last save, users will get an alert prompting them to save the changes. If `false`, the document will immediately be closed and any unsaved changes will be lost.

Returns

Nothing

Example

```
my_doc = fl.getDocumentDOM();
my_doc.close(true);
```

convertLinesToFills

`document.convertLinesToFills()`

Converts lines to fills on selected objects

Description
Duplicates the Convert Lines to Fills menu item in the authoring environment. The strokes of any selected shape elements will be converted to fills, retaining their shape and color.

Argument(s)
None

Returns
Nothing

Example
```
my_doc = fl.getDocumentDOM();
my_doc.convertLinesToFills();
```

convertToSymbol

```
document.convertToSymbol( type, name,
➥ registrationPoint )
```

Converts selected items to new symbol

Description
Converts any selected elements to a graphic symbol, movie clip, or button

Argument(s)
`type`—*string*—The type of symbol to create. Can be `"movie clip"`, `"button"`, or `"graphic"`.

`name`—*string*—The name you want to give the symbol. If set to a blank string (`""`), Flash will assign a default name.

`registrationPoint`—*string*—Where in the symbol to place the registration point. Valid values are `"top left"`, `"top center"`, `"top right"`, `"center left"`, `"center"`, `"center right"`, `"bottom left"`, `"bottom center"`, and `"bottom right"`.

Returns
Reference to the new symbol—*object*

Example
```
my_doc = fl.getDocumentDOM();
my_mc = my_doc.convertToSymbol
➥ ("movie clip", "myClip", "center");
```

deletePublishProfile

```
document.deletePublishProfile()
```

Deletes current Publish Profile

Description
Deletes the current Publish Profile. If only one profile exists, this method doesn't delete it, and returns the index to that profile.

Argument(s)
None

Returns
Index to new current profile—*integer*

Example
```
my_doc = fl.getDocumentDOM();
my_doc.deletePublishProfile();
```

deleteScene

```
document.deleteScene()
```

Deletes current scene

Description
Deletes the current scene (timeline). When a scene is deleted, the next scene in the timeline array becomes the current scene. If there is only one scene in the movie, and thus only one element in the `document.timelines` array, it won't be deleted and the method will return `false`.

Argument(s)
None

Returns
`true` if more than one scene and scene was deleted, otherwise `false`—*Boolean*

Example
```
my_doc = fl.getDocumentDOM();
my_doc.deleteScene();
```

deleteSelection

```
document.deleteSelection()
```

Deletes selection from stage

Description
Deletes any selected elements from the specified document

Argument(s)
None

Returns
Nothing

Example
```
my_doc = fl.getDocumentDOM();
my_doc.deleteSelection();
```

distribute

```
document.distribute( distributemode
➥ [, bUseDocumentBounds] )
```

Distributes selection

Description
Distributes all selected elements on the stage, according to the selected mode and bounds

Argument(s)
distributeMode—*string*—Determines how the elements will be distributed. Valid values are "left edge", "horizontal center", "right edge", "top edge", "vertical center", and "bottom edge".

bUseDocumentBounds—*Boolean*—If true, elements will be distributed across the entire stage. If false, elements will be distributed across the bounding box of the selection

Returns
Nothing

Example
```
my_doc = fl.getDocumentDOM();
my_doc.distribute("horizontal center", true);
```

distributeToLayers

```
document.distributeToLayers()
```

Distributes current selection to layers

Description
Duplicates the Distribute to Layers menu item in the authoring environment. If multiple elements are selected, each one will be placed on a separate layer.

Argument(s)
None

Returns
Nothing

Example
```
my_doc = fl.getDocumentDOM();
my_doc.distributeToLayers();
```

documentHasData

```
document.documentHasData( name )
```

If true, there is persistent data.

Description
Checks for any persistent data stored in the document under the specified name

Argument(s)
name—*string*—The name of the stored data you want to check for

Returns
true if the data exists, otherwise false—*Boolean*

Example
```
my_doc = fl.getDocumentDOM();
if( my_doc.documentHasData("myVar") ){
  fl.trace("this document has data.");
}
  fl.trace("this document doesn't
➥ have data.");
}
```

duplicatePublishProfile

```
document.duplicatePublishProfile
➥ ( [profileName] )
```

Duplicates current profile

Description
Duplicates the current Publish Profile and makes the new profile the current profile

Argument(s)
profileName—*string*—The name for the new profile. If omitted, default name will be provided.

Returns
Index to new profile—*integer*

Example

```
my_doc = fl.getDocumentDOM();
my_doc.duplicatePublishProfile
➥ ("betaVersion2");
```

duplicateScene

`document.duplicateScene()`

Duplicates current scene

Description
Duplicates the current scene and makes it the new current scene

Argument(s)
None

Returns
`true` if successful, otherwise `false`—*Boolean*

Example

```
my_doc = fl.getDocumentDOM();
my_doc.duplicateScene();
```

duplicateSelection

`document.duplicateSelection()`

Duplicates selection

Description
Duplicates any selected elements in the new document. The newly duplicated elements become the new selection.

Argument(s)
None

Returns
Nothing

Example

```
my_doc = fl.getDocumentDOM();
my_doc.duplicateSelection();
```

editScene

`document.editScene( *index* )`

Sets specified scene to be the current one

Description
Sets the current timeline to the specified scene

Argument(s)
`index`—*integer*—The number of the timeline you want to set at the current timeline

Returns
Nothing

Example

```
// edits the first scene
my_doc = fl.getDocumentDOM();
my_doc.editScene(0);
```

enterEditMode

`document.enterEditMode( [*editMode*] )`

Enters edit mode for symbol or group

Description
Enters edit mode on the currently selected symbol. `document.getTimeline()` will now return a reference to the timeline of the symbol being edited.

Argument(s)
`editMode`—*string*—Determines in what mode the symbol will be edited. Valid values are `"inPlace"` or `"newWindow"`.

Returns
Nothing

Example

```
my_doc = fl.getDocumentDOM();
my_doc.enterEditMode("inPlace");
```

exitEditMode

`document.exitEditMode()`

Exits edit mode

Description
Goes out of edit mode on the current symbol being edited and moves up one level to the parent object's timeline or

the main timeline. document.getTimeline() will now return a reference to the parent timeline.

Argument(s)
None

Returns
Nothing

Example
```
my_doc = fl.getDocumentDOM();
my_doc.exitEditMode();
```

exportPublishProfile

document.exportPublishProfile(*fileURI*)

Exports current Publish Profile to file

Description
Exports the current Publish Profile to an XML file

Argument(s)
fileURI—*URI string*—Valid URI to an XML file in which to store information about the current Publish Profile

Returns
Nothing

Example
```
// assumes you have a directory
// "myprofiles" in C:/
my_doc = fl.getDocumentDOM();
my_doc.exportPublishProfile
➥ ("file:///C:/myprofiles/betaVersion.xml");
```

exportSWF

document.exportSWF([*fileURI*]
➥ [, *bCurrentSettings*])

Exports document as SWF file

Description
Creates a new SWF file based on the specified document

Argument(s)
fileURI—*string*—The path and name at which the new SWF will be exported. Must be a valid URI string. Usually this will start with "file:///" followed by a file path and name. You can use fl.configURI as a shortcut URI to the Configuration directory.

bCurrentSettings—*Boolean*—If true, SWF will be created using the current publish settings. If false, the SWF Export Settings dialog box will be displayed.

Returns
true if export is successful—*Boolean*

Example
```
my_doc = fl.getDocumentDOM();
my_doc.exportSWF
➥ ("file:///C:/myMovie.swf", true);
```

getAlignToDocument

document.getAlignToDocument()

Returns value of Align to Stage setting

Description
Gets the current mode for aligning, distributing, matching, or spacing elements. These operations can either be done in relation to the entire stage or the current selection.

Argument(s)
None

Returns
true if alignment, etc., will be in relation to stage, otherwise false—*Boolean*

Example
```
my_doc = fl.getDocumentDOM();
fl.trace(my_doc.getAlignToDocument());
```

getCustomFill

document.getCustomFill([*locationOfFill*])

Returns fill object of selection or toolbar

Description
Returns an object that contains data about the current custom fill as shown in the toolbar, current selection, or specified element. See the entry for Fill for more information about its properties.

Argument(s)
locationOfFill—*string*—Valid values are "toolbar" and "selection". If "toolbar" is specified, the method returns the currently selected fill properties set in the toolbar. If "selection", it will return the fill properties of the selected shape.

Returns

fill object—*object*

Example

```
my_doc = fl.getDocumentDOM();
my_fill = my_doc.getCustomFill
➥ ("selection");
fl.trace(my_fill.color);
```

getCustomStroke

document.getCustomStroke
➥ ([*locationOfStroke*])

Returns stroke object or toolbar setting

Description

Returns an object that contains data about the current custom stroke as shown in the toolbar, current selection, or specified element. See the entry for Stroke for more information about its properties.

Argument(s)

locationOfStroke—*string*—Optional path to element to get stroke information from

Returns

stroke object—*object*

Example

```
my_doc = fl.getDocumentDOM();
my_stroke = my_doc.getCustomStroke();
fl.trace(my_stroke.color);
```

getDataFromDocument

document.getDataFromDocument(*name*)

Returns value of named data

Description

Returns the value of the persistent data stored in the specified document under the specified name

Argument(s)

name—*string*—The name under which the data was saved

Returns

Persistent data—*Type of data depends on the data that was saved.*

Example

```
my_doc = fl.getDocumentDOM();
authorName = my_doc.getDataFromDocument
➥ ("myname");
```

getElementProperty

document.getElementProperty
➥ (*propertyName*)

Returns specified Element property

Description

Returns the value of the specified property for the currently selected element

Argument(s)

propertyName—*string*—The name of the property you want to retrieve

Returns

Element property value—*Type depends on particular property chosen.*

Example

```
my_doc = fl.getDocumentDOM();
leftEdge = my_doc.getElementProperty
➥ ("left");
```

getElementTextAttr

document.getElementTextAttr(*attrName*
➥ [, *startIndex*] [, *endIndex*])

Returns specified TextAttrs property

Description

If the selected element(s) is a text element, returns the specified property of the textAttr object for the text, or portion of text, between startIndex and endIndex. If the results would be different for multiple selected elements, or for multiple characters in the specified text, this method returns undefined.

Argument(s)

attrName—*integer*—The name of the attribute you want to retrieve

startIndex—*integer*—The first character you want to check

endIndex—*integer*—The character after the last character you want to check

Returns

The value of the attribute specified—*Type depends on attribute type.*

Example

```
my_doc = fl.getDocumentDOM();
my_doc.getElementTextAttr("lineSpacing",
➥ 0, 100);
```

getSelectionRect

```
document.getSelectionRect()
```

Returns bounding rectangle of selection

Description

Returns a rectangle object (contains properties top, left, bottom, right) describing the bounding box of the currently selected item or items

Argument(s)

None

Returns

Rectangle describing bounding box—*rect object*

Example

```
my_doc = fl.getDocumentDOM();
box = my_doc.getSelectionRect();
topEdge = box.top;
leftEdge = box.left;
```

getTextString

```
document.getTextString( [startIndex]
➥ [, endIndex] )
```

Returns text string of selected text

Description

If the selected element(s) is a text element, returns the text contained in that element, or portion thereof

Argument(s)

startIndex—*integer*—The first character

endIndex—*integer*—The character after the last character

Returns

The text contained in the element—*string*

Example

```
my_doc = fl.getDocumentDOM();
myName = my_doc.getTextString();
```

getTimeline

```
document.getTimeline()
```

Returns current timeline

Description

Returns a reference to the current timeline being edited. Will return a reference to the timeline inside of a symbol if the symbol is open for editing.

Argument(s)

None

Returns

Timeline—*object*

Example

```
my_doc = fl.getDocumentDOM();
// get a reference to the main timeline:
main_tl = my_doc.getTimeline();
// enter edit mode on a selected symbol:
my_doc.enterEditMode();
// now get a reference to the timeline
// of that symbol:
mc_tl = my_doc.getTimeline();
```

getTransformationPoint

```
document.getTransformationPoint()
```

Returns location of transformation point

Description

Returns the transformation point of the currently selected object

Argument(s)

None

Returns

Transformation point—*point object*

Example

```
my_doc = fl.getDocumentDOM();
myPoint = my_doc.getTransformationPoint();
fl.trace(myPoint.x);
fl.trace(myPoint.y);
```

group

`document.group()`

Converts selection to a group

Description

Converts the currently selected element or elements to a group. This is useful for separating shape objects. Multiple shape objects will count as one item in the elements array or the selection array. However, a shape element that has been grouped will always be counted as a single item in the elements or selection array.

Argument(s)

None

Returns

Nothing

Example

```
my_doc = fl.getDocumentDOM();
my_doc.selectAll();
my_doc.group();
```

importPublishProfile

`document.importPublishProfile( fileURI )`

Imports Publish Profile from file

Description

Loads an external XML file containing a Publish Profile

Argument(s)

`fileURI`—*URI string*—Valid URI to an XML file containing a Publish Profile

Returns

Index of the newly imported profile, –1 if unsuccessful—*integer*

Example

```
// assumes you have a directory named
// "myprofiles" in C:/
my_doc = fl.getDocumentDOM();
my_doc.importPublishProfile
➥ ("file:///c:/myprofiles/bigprofile.xml");
```

importSWF

`document.importSWF( fileURI )`

Imports SWF into document

Description

Pulls an external, previously compiled Flash SWF file into the current document

Argument(s)

`fileURI`—*URI string*—Must be a valid URI string. Usually this will start with `"file:///"` followed by a file path and name. You can use `fl.configURI` as a shortcut URI to the `Configuration` directory.

Returns

Nothing

Example

```
my_doc = fl.getDocumentDOM();
my_doc.importSWF
➥ ("file:///C:/mySWFs/myMovie.swf");
my_doc.importSWF(fl.configURI +
➥ "/Commands/myMovie.swf");
```

match

`document.match( bWidth, bHeight ➥ [, bUseDocumentBounds] )`

Makes size of selected objects equal

Description

Makes the selected objects the same size, or makes the selected objects the size of the stage

Argument(s)

`bWidth`—*Boolean*—If `true`, will affect the width of the selected objects.

`bHeight`—*Boolean*—If `true`, will affect the height of the selected objects.

`bUseDocumentBounds`—*Boolean*—If `true`, objects will be made the same size as the stage; otherwise all selected objects will be made the size of the largest selected object.

Returns
Nothing

Example

```
// make all selected objects the same
// size as the stage:
my_doc = fl.getDocumentDOM();
my_doc.match(true, true, true);
// make all selected objects the same
// width as the largest selected object:
my_doc = fl.getDocumentDOM();
my_doc.match(true, false, false);
```

mouseClick

document.mouseClick(*position*,
➥ *bShiftDown, bShiftSel*)

Performs mouse click

Description
Simulates a mouse double click at the specified point using the arrow tool. This will result in the same actions that would occur if you actually double-clicked the mouse in that position. A single click on a shape element will only select the fill or the stroke, depending on the exact position. Double-clicking on a fill will select the fill and the stroke.

Argument(s)
position—*point*—An object containing x and y properties, indicating the point onstage where the click will be simulated.

bShiftDown—*Boolean*—Simulates the *SHIFT* key being held down during the mouse click.

bShiftSel—*Boolean*—Sets the Shift Select option as found in the Preferences panel (Edit ➤ Preferences). If true, allows you to select (or deselect) multiple elements by *SHIFT*-clicking on each one. If false, clicking a new element will deselect all previously selected items, even if *SHIFT* is down.

Returns
Nothing

Example

```
// select multiple items onstage:
my_doc = fl.getDocumentDOM();
my_doc.mouseClick({x:100, y:100}, true,
➥ true);
my_doc.mouseClick({x:200, y:100}, true,
➥ true);
my_doc.mouseClick({x:300, y:100}, true,
➥ true);
```

mouseDblClk

document.mouseDblClk(*position, bAltDown,*
➥ *bShiftDown, bShiftSelect*)

Performs mouse double click

Description
Simulates a mouse double click at the specified point using the arrow tool. This will result in the same actions that would occur if you actually double-clicked the mouse in that position. A single click on a shape element will only select the fill or the stroke, depending on the exact position. Double-clicking a fill will select the fill and the stroke.

Argument(s)
position—*point*—An object containing x and y properties, indicating the point onstage where the double click will be simulated.

bAltDown—*Boolean*—Simulates the *ALT* key being held down during the double click.

bShiftDown—*Boolean*—Simulates the *SHIFT* key being held down during the double click.

bShiftSel—*Boolean*—Sets the Shift Select option as found in the Preferences panel (Edit ➤ Preferences). If true, allows you to select (or deselect) multiple elements by *SHIFT*-double-clicking each one. If false, double-clicking a new element will deselect all previously selected items, even if *SHIFT* is down.

Returns
Nothing

Example

```
// select multiple items onstage:
my_doc = fl.getDocumentDOM();
my_doc.mouseDblClk({x:100, y:100}, true,
➥ true, true);
my_doc. mouseDblClk({x:200, y:100}, true,
➥ true, true);
my_doc. mouseDblClk({x:300, y:100}, true,
➥ true, true);
```

moveSelectedBezierPointsBy

```
document.moveSelectedBezierPointsBy
➥ ( delta )
```

Moves selected Bezier points

Description
If the current selection contains a path with Bezier points, moves all selected Bezier points the amount specified in the argument

Argument(s)
`delta`—*point object*—Contains x and y properties indicating how much to move the points

Returns
Nothing

Example
```
my_doc = fl.getDocumentDOM();
my_doc.moveSelectedBezierPointsBy({x:10,
➥ y:10});
```

moveSelectionBy

```
document.moveSelectionBy( distanceToMove )
```

Moves selection

Description
Moves any selected elements on the x or y axis

Argument(s)
`distanceToMove`—*point object*—Contains x and y properties. Selection will move the distance of those properties.

Returns
Nothing

Example
```
// move the selection 100 pixels to the
// right and 20 pixels down:
my_doc = fl.getDocumentDOM();
my_doc.moveSelectionBy({x:100, y:20});
```

optimizeCurves

```
document.optimizeCurves( smoothing,
➥ bUseMultiplePasses )
```

Opimizes curves of selected shape

Description
Optimizes any curves in any shape elements in the current selections

Argument(s)
`smoothing`—*integer*—From 0 to 100, being no smoothing to maximum smoothing.

`bUseMultiplePasses`—*Boolean*—If `true`, smoothing will be done in multiple passes; if `false`, one pass.

Returns
Nothing

Example
```
my_doc = fl.getDocumentDOM();
my_doc.optimizeCurves( 50, true);
```

publish

```
document.publish()
```

Publishes document

Description
Publishes the current document. Generally, this will create a SWF and HTML file based on the current movie. What is actually published is dependent on the current Publish settings in the authoring environment, or the current `publishProfile` object.

Argument(s)
None

Returns
Nothing

Example
```
my_doc = fl.getDocumentDOM();
my_doc.publish();
```

removeDataFromDocument

```
document.removeDataFromDocument( name )
```

Removes persistent data from document

Description
Removes any persistent data stored in the document under the specified name

Argument(s)
name—*string*—The name under which the data was stored

Returns
Nothing

Example
```
my_doc = fl.getDocumentDOM();
my_doc.removeDataFromDocument("myData");
```

removeDataFromSelection

`document.removeDataFromSelection( name )`

Removes persistent data from selected objects

Description
Removes any persistent data stored in the currently selected objects under the specified name

Argument(s)
name—*string*—The name under which the data was stored

Returns
Nothing

Example
```
my_doc = fl.getDocumentDOM();
my_doc.removeDataFromSelection("myData");
```

renamePublishProfile

`document.renamePublishProfile`
`➥ ( [profileNewName] )`

Renames current Publish Profile

Description
Gives a new name to the current Publish Profile

Argument(s)
profileNewName—*string*—The new name given to the profile. If omitted, a default name will be used.

Returns
true if successful, otherwise false—*Boolean*

Example
```
my_doc = fl.getDocumentDOM();
my_doc.renamePublishProfile("New Profile");
```

renameScene

`document.renameScene( name )`

Renames current scene

Description
Renames the current scene to the name specified in the argument. Scenes are also known as timelines.

Argument(s)
name—*string*—The new name for the scene

Returns
true if successful, false if a scene already exists with that name—*Boolean*

Example
```
my_doc = fl.getDocumentDOM();
my_tl = my_doc.getTimeline();
my_doc.renameScene("OpeningScene");
```

reorderScene

`document.reorderScene( sceneToMove,`
`➥ sceneToPutItBefore )`

Reorders specified scene

Description
Repositions the specified scene to the new position specified. Scenes are also known as timelines and are stored in the timelines array of the document object.

Argument(s)
sceneToMove—*integer*—Zero-based index to the timelines array. The first scene would thus be scene 0.

sceneToPutItBefore—*integer*—The number of the scene you want to move the scene before.

Returns
Nothing

Example
```
// move scene 3 to position 0
// (move it before 1):
my_doc = fl.getDocumentDOM();
my_doc.reorderScene(3, 1);
```

resetTransformation

```
document.resetTransformation()
```

Resets transformation matrix

Description

If an element or elements have been scaled, rotated, or skewed, this data is stored in a transformation matrix object (see the entry for `Math.matrix`). This method sets the element back to 100 percent scale, no rotation or skew.

Argument(s)

None

Returns

Nothing

Example

```
my_doc = fl.getDocumen
tDOM();
my_doc.resetTransformation();
```

revert

```
document.revert()
```

Reverts specified document

Description

Reverts the specified document to its last saved state. Equivalent to closing the document without saving it and reopening it.

Argument(s)

None

Returns

Nothing

Example

```
my_doc = fl.getDocumentDOM();
my_doc.revert();
```

rotateSelection

```
document.rotateSelection( angle
➥ [, rotationPoint] )
```

Rotates election

Description

Rotates any selected elements to the specified angle. Rotates around the point specified.

Argument(s)

`angle`—*float*—The angle in degrees to rotate the selection(s).

`rotationPoint`—*string*—The point around which the selection(s) will be rotated. Valid values are `"top right"`, `"top left"`, `"bottom right"`, and `"bottom left"`. If not specified, the transformation point of the selection will be used.

Returns

Nothing

Example

```
my_doc = fl.getDocumentDOM();
my_doc.rotateSelection(45, "top left");
```

save

```
document.save( [bOkToSaveAs] )
```

Saves document

Description

Saves the specified document under its previously saved filename and location, or brings up a Save As dialog box. If you want to save a document for the first time, and specify its name via JSFL, use `fl.saveDocument()`.

Argument(s)

bOkToSaveAs—*Boolean*—If `true` and the document has not previously been saved, allows the Save As dialog box to appear. If `false`, and document has not been saved, does nothing and document won't be saved.

Returns

`true` if successful, `false` if not—*Boolean*

Example

```
my_doc = fl.getDocumentDOM();
my_doc.save(true);
```

saveAndCompact

```
document.saveAndCompact( [bOkToSaveAs] )
```

Saves and compacts document

Description
Saves the specified document under its previously saved filename and location, or brings up a Save As dialog box. If you want to save a document for the first time, and specify its name via JSFL, use `fl.saveDocument()`. Due to the method used to save documents in Flash, the document size will only grow as you add and remove objects to it. If an object is deleted from the file, the document size on disk won't decrease. This method rewrites the file from scratch, saving only those items still actually in existence in the document.

Argument(s)
bOkToSaveAs—*Boolean*—If `true` and the document has not previously been saved, allows the Save As dialog box to appear. If `false`, and document has not been saved, does nothing and document won't be saved.

Returns
`true` if successful, `false` if not—*Boolean*

Example
```
my_doc = fl.getDocumentDOM();
my_doc.saveAndCompact(true);
```

scaleSelection

`document.scaleSelection(` *xScale, yScale*
➥ `[,` *whichCorner*`] )`

Scales selection

Description
Scales the selected element(s) on the x and/or y axis

Argument(s)
xScale—*float*—How much to scale the element's width. A value of `1.0` is equal to 100 percent.

yScale—*float*—How much to scale the element's width. A value of `1.0` is equal to 100 percent.

whichCorner—*string*—From which direction the scaling will occur. Valid values are `"bottom left"`, `"bottom right"`, `"top right"`, `"top left"`, `"top center"`, `"right center"`, `"bottom center"`, and `"left center"`. If not specified, scaling will be done from the element's transformation point.

Returns
Nothing

Example
```
my_doc = fl.getDocumentDOM();
my_doc.scaleSelection(2.0, .5, "top left");
```

selectAll

`document.selectAll()`

Selects all items onstage

Description
Selects all elements currently available in the timeline and document being edited

Argument(s)
None

Returns
Nothing

Example
```
my_doc = fl.getDocumentDOM();
my_doc.selectAll();
```

selectNone

`document.selectNone()`

Deselects all items onstage

Description
Deselects any and all currently selected elements

Argument(s)
None

Returns
Nothing

Example
```
my_doc = fl.getDocumentDOM();
my_doc.selectNone();
```

setAlignToDocument

`document.setAlignToDocument(` *bToStage* `)`

If `true`, objects are aligned, distributed, sized, or spaced to stage

Description

Sets the current mode for aligning, distributing, matching, or spacing elements. These operations can either be done in relation to the entire stage or the current selection. Note: The align, distribute, match, and space methods all have an argument for their own align mode, and will default to `false`. Using `setAlignToDocument` seems to have no actual effect on the functionality of these methods.

Argument(s)

`bToStage`—*Boolean*—If `true`, alignment, etc., will be in relation to stage; otherwise alignment actions will act on the selection size.

Returns

Nothing

Example

```
my_doc = fl.getDocumentDOM();
my_doc.setAlignToDocument(false);
```

setCustomFill

`document.setCustomFill( fill )`

Sets current fill settings of selection or toolbar

Description

Sets the fill color and style on the toolbar, or changes the fill color and style of a currently selected shape

Argument(s)

`fill`—*fill object*—See the entry for `Fill`.

Returns

Nothing

Example

```
my_fill = new Object();
my_fill.color = 0xff0000;
my_fill.style = "solid";
my_doc = fl.getDocumentDOM();
my_doc.setCustomFill(my_fill);
```

setCustomStroke

`document.setCustomStroke( stroke )`

Sets current stroke settings of selection or toolbar

Description

Sets the stroke color and style on the toolbar, or changes the stroke color and style of a currently selected shape

Argument(s)

`stroke`—*stroke object*—See the entry for `Stroke`.

Returns

Nothing

Example

```
my_stroke = new Object();
my_stroke.color = 0xff0000;
my_stroke.style = "solid";
my_stroke.thickness = 10;
my_doc = fl.getDocumentDOM();
my_doc.setCustomStroke(my_stroke);
```

setElementProperty

```
document.setElementProperty( property,
➥ value )
```

Sets specified property of element object

Description

Sets the specified property of the selected elements(s) to the given value

Argument(s)

`property`—*string*—The property you wish to change. For a full list of properties available, see the entries for `Element` and its various subclasses.

`value`—*Dependent on property type*—The new value you are setting the property to.

Returns

Nothing

Example

```
// puts the selected element on the
// left edge of the stage
my_doc = fl.getDocumentDOM();
my_doc.setElementProperty("width", 100);
```

setElementTextAttr

```
document.setElementTextAttr( attrName,
➥ attrValue [, startIndex] [, endIndex] )
```

Sets specified property of selected text items

Description

Sets the specified text attribute of the selected text element(s) to the value given. If `startIndex` and `endIndex` are specified, the changes will only affect the range of characters defined by them. If they aren't specified, changes will affect all text in the element.

Argument(s)

`attrName`—*string*—The name of the text attribute to change. See the entry for `TextAttr` for a full list of available properties.

`attrValue`—*Dependent on attribute type*—The value to set this property.

`startIndex`—*integer*—The first character in the text element to be affected (zero-indexed).

`endIndex`—*integer*—The character *after* the last affected character.

Returns

`true` if successful, otherwise `false`—*Boolean*

Example

```
// set the whole text element to use
// the Arial font:
my_doc = fl.getDocumentDOM();
my_doc.setElementTextAttr("face", "Arial");
// set the first character to size 20:
my_doc = fl.getDocumentDOM();
my_doc.setElementTextAttr("size", 20,
➥ 0, 1);
```

setFillColor

`document.setFillColor( color )`

Changes fill color of selection

Description

Changes the fill color of a selected shape object or objects. Only affects a fill that is currently selected. Won't change the toolbar fill color.

Argument(s)

`color`—*integer, string, or null*—The color as a string (#rrggbb) or base 10 or hex integer (0 to 16777216 or 0xrrggbb). If set to null, a "no fill" will be specified for the selected objects and their fill will be deleted. You can also specify an alpha for the fill by adding on the hex values from 00 to FF after the color definition as a string. Example: "#FF00007F" creates a red fill with approximately 50 percent alpha.

Returns

Nothing

Example

```
// set selected fill to red:
my_doc = fl.getDocumentDOM();
my_doc.setFillColor(0xff0000);
```

setInstanceAlpha

`document.setInstanceAlpha( opacity )`

Sets opacity of instance

Description

Sets the transparency of any currently selected instance element. Has no effect on noninstance elements.

Argument(s)

`opacity`—*int*—A value of zero makes the instance fully transparent. 100 makes it fully opaque.

Returns

Nothing

Example

```
my_doc = fl.getDocumentDOM();
my_doc.setInstanceAlpha(50);
```

setInstanceBrightness

`document.setInstanceBrightness(brightness)`

Sets brightness of instance

Description

Sets the brightness of any currently selected instance element. Has no effect on noninstance elements.

Argument(s)

`brightness`—*int*—A value from –100 to +100 specifying how bright the object will be (fully black to fully white). A value of zero will leave the instance with its original brightness.

Returns

Nothing

Example

```
my_doc = fl.getDocumentDOM();
my_doc.setInstanceBrightness(50);
```

setInstanceTint

`document.setInstanceTint(color, strength)`

Sets tint of instance

Description
Changes the tint of any currently selected instance element. Has no effect on noninstance elements.

Argument(s)
color—*integer or string*—The color as a string (#rrggbb) or base10 or hex integer (0 to 16777216 or 0xrrggbb)

strength—*int*—A value from 0 to 100. Zero will cause the color to have no effect on the instance. 100 will cause the instance to appear as a solid swatch of the specified color. Values in between will tint the image to that degree.

Returns
Nothing

Example

```
// give the instance a strong red tint:
my_doc = fl.getDocumentDOM();
my_doc.setInstanceTint(0xff0000, 50);
```

setSelectionBounds

```
document.setSelectionBounds
➥ (boundingRectangle)
```

Moves and resizes selection

Description
Forces any selected element(s) to fit within the specified bounding rectangle. Will move and resize the entire selection. Individual elements within a multiple selection will retain their relative size in relation to the selection as a whole.

Argument(s)
boundingRectangle—*rect object*—An object with properties left, right, top, bottom, specifying the bounds of the selection after it is changed

Returns
Nothing

Example

```
// force all objects onstage to fit
// into a 50x50 box in the top-left
// corner onstage:
my_doc = fl.getDocumentDOM();
my_doc.selectAll();
my_doc.setSelectionBounds({top:0, left:0,
➥ bottom:50, right:50});
```

setSelectionRect

```
document.setSelectionRect( rect
➥ [, bReplaceCurrentSelection] )
```

Sets selection rectangle

Description
Selects any elements in the current frame that fall within the specified rectangle

Argument(s)
rect—*rect object*—An object containing the properties left, right, top, bottom, describing the area of stage you want to select.

bReplaceCurrentSelection—*Boolean*—If true (default), any previously selected items will be deselected. If false, this action will add to the current selection.

Returns
Nothing

Example

```
// select all elements lying completely
// on the left half of a 550x400 stage:
my_doc = fl.getDocumentDOM();
my_doc.setSelectionRect({top:0, left:0,
➥ bottom:400, right:275});
```

setStroke

`document.setStroke( color, size, style )`

Sets stroke properties of selected stroke

Description
Sets the properties for the stroke of a currently selected shape object

Argument(s)
color—*integer, string, or null*—The color as a string (#rrggbb) or base10 or hex integer (0 to 16777216 or

0xrrggbb). If set to null, a "no stroke" will be specified for the selected objects and their strokes will be deleted. You can also specify an alpha for the fill by adding on the hex values from 00 to FF after the color definition as a string. Example: "#FF00007F" creates a red fill with approximately 50 percent alpha.

size—*integer*—The width of the line making the stroke.

style—*string*—What kind of stroke you want the element to have. Valid values are "hairline", "solid", "dashed", "dotted", "ragged", "stipple", and "hatched".

Returns
Nothing

Example
```
my_doc = fl.getDocumentDOM();
my_doc.setStroke(0xff00ff, 10, "stipple");
```

setStrokeColor

`document.setStrokeColor( color )`

Changes stroke color of selected stroke

Description
Changes the color only of the stroke of the currently selected shape element(s).

Argument(s)
color—*integer, string, or null*—The color as a string (#rrggbb) or base10 or hex integer (0 to 16777216 or 0xrrggbb). If set to null, a "no stroke" will be specified for the selected objects and their strokes will be deleted. You can also specify an alpha for the fill by adding on the hex values from 00 to FF after the color definition as a string. Example: "#FF00007F" creates a red fill with approximately 50 percent alpha.

Returns
Nothing

Example
```
my_doc = fl.getDocumentDOM();
my_doc.setStrokeColor(0x00ff00);
```

setStrokeSize

`document.setStrokeSize( size )`

Changes stroke width of selected stroke

Description
Changes the size only of the stroke of the currently selected shape element(s)

Argument(s)
size—*integer*—The width of the line making the stroke

Returns
Nothing

Example
```
my_doc = fl.getDocumentDOM();
my_doc.setStrokeSize(3);
```

setStrokeStyle

`document.setStrokeStyle( style )`

Changes stroke style of selected stroke

Description
Changes the stroke style only of the stroke of the currently selected shape element(s).

Argument(s)
style—*string*—What kind of stroke you want the element to have. Valid values are "hairline", "solid", "dashed", "dotted", "ragged", "stipple", and "hatched".

Returns
Nothing

Example
```
my_doc = fl.getDocumentDOM();
my_doc.setStrokeStyle("ragged");
```

setTextRectangle

```
document.setTextRectangle
➥ ( boundingRectangle )
```

Changes bounding rectangle for selected text item

Description
Changes the size and position of any currently selected text element. Note that the element isn't scaled, and the text inside will reflow to fill the new shape. For horizontal static text, only the width is changed; the height will be adjusted to fit all the text. For vertical static text, the opposite is true. Has no effect on nontext elements.

Argument(s)

boundingRectangle—*rect object*—An object containing the properties top, bottom, left, right, which will specify the size and position of the changed text field

Returns

true if at least one text element was changed, otherwise false—*Boolean*

Example

```
my_doc = fl.getDocumentDOM();
my_doc.setTextRectangle({top:0, left:0,
➥ bottom: 50, right: 100});
```

setTextSelection

```
document.setTextSelection( startIndex,
➥ endIndex )
```

Sets text selection of selected text field

Description

In the selected text element(s), causes the text between the two indexes specified to be selected. The text will then be activated for editing.

Argument(s)

startIndex—*integer*—The first character to be selected

endIndex—*integer*—The next nonselected character

Returns

true if successful, otherwise false—*Boolean*

Example

```
// selects the first three characters
// in a selected text field
my_doc = fl.getDocumentDOM();
my_doc.setTextSelection(0, 3);
```

setTextString

```
document.setTextString( text [, startIndex]
➥ [, endIndex] )
```

Adds specified text string to selected text field

Description

Sets the text in any selected text element to the specified string. If the element is currently activated and being edited, and the optional index parameters aren't specified, the new text will replace any currently selected characters, or be inserted at the cursor position. If the element isn't being edited, and the index parameters aren't specified, the new text will replace all text in the element. If both index parameters are specified, the new text will replace the text specified by the indexes. If only the start index is specified, new text will be inserted at that point.

Argument(s)

text—*string*—The text to add to the element

startIndex—*type*—The first character to replace (if endIndex is specified), or the point at which to insert the text

endIndex—*type*—The first character that won't be replaced

Returns

true if at least one insertion/replacement occurred—*Boolean*

Example

```
// replace all text in the field (
// if not being edited):
my_doc = fl.getDocumentDOM();
my_doc.setTextString("new text");
// insert text at the beginning
// of the element:
my_doc = fl.getDocumentDOM();
my_doc.setTextString("text: ", 0);
// replace text between the
// 3rd and 5th characters:
my_doc = fl.getDocumentDOM();
my_doc.setTextString("new text", 2, 5);
```

setTransformationPoint

```
document.setTransformationPoint
➥ ( transformationPoint )
```

Moves transformation point of selection

Description

Moves the transformation point of the selected element using x and y of the supplied argument. This works differently for different types of elements:

- *For shape elements:* The transformation point specified will be in relation to the 0, 0 point of the stage.
- *For symbol elements:* The transformation point specified will be in relation to the symbol's current registration point.

- *For text, bitmap, and video elements*: The transformation point specified will be in relation to the top-left corner of the element.
- *For groups:* The transformation point specified will be in relation to the 0, 0 point of the stage.

Argument(s)
transformationPoint—*point object*—An object containing x and y properties, specifying the location of the new transformation point.

Returns
Nothing

Example
```
my_doc = fl.getDocumentDOM();
my_doc.setTransformationPoint({x:0, y:0});
```

skewSelection

document.skewSelection(*xSkew, ySkew*
➥ [, *whichEdge*])

Skews selection

Description
Skews the selected element(s) on the x and y axis

Argument(s)
xSkew—*float*—The amount to skew the selection on the x axis.

ySkew—*float*—The amount to skew the selection on the y axis.

whichEdge—*string*—The point around which the selection will be skewed. If omitted, Flash will use the transformation point. Valid values are "top center", "right center", "bottom center", and "left center".

Returns
Nothing

Example
```
my_doc = fl.getDocumentDOM();
my_doc.skewSelection(10, 20,
➥ "left center");
```

smoothSelection

document.smoothSelection()

Smoothes selected curve of shape

Description
Recalculates the curves in the stroke of a selected shape element to make them smoother

Argument(s)
None

Returns
Nothing

Example
```
my_doc = fl.getDocumentDOM();
my_doc.smoothSelection();
```

space

document.space(*direction*
➥ [, *bUseDocumentBounds*])

Spaces objects of selection evenly

Description
Spaces the selected elements evenly across the stage or the bounding box of all selected elements

Argument(s)
direction—*string*—Can be either "horizontal" or "vertical"

bUseDocumentBounds—*Boolean*—If true, spaces the elements out across the entire stage width. If false, spaces elements across the bounding box of the selection.

Returns
Nothing

Example
```
my_doc = fl.getDocumentDOM();
my_doc.space("horizontal", true);
```

straightenSelection

document.straightenSelection()

Straightens selected curve of shape

Description
Recalculates the curves in the stroke of a selected shape element to make them straighter

Argument(s)
None

Returns
Nothing

Example
```
my_doc = fl.getDocumentDOM();
my_doc.straightenSelection();
```

swapElement

`document.swapElement( name )`

Swaps selected symbol with specified one

Description
Swaps the selected symbol instance with the Library item specified. Has no effect If the selected element isn't a symbol item.

Argument(s)
`name`—*string*—The name and path if necessary of the Library item you want to use to replace the selected element

Returns
Nothing

Example
```
my_doc = fl.getDocumentDOM();
my_doc.swapElement("new clip");
```

testMovie

`document.testMovie()`

Tests movie

Description
Duplicates the Test Movie command in the authoring environment. Creates a SWF file based on the current document and displays it with the internal player.

Argument(s)
None

Returns
Nothing

Example
```
my_doc = fl.getDocumentDOM();
my_doc.testMovie();
```

testScene

`document.testScene()`

Tests current scene

Description
Duplicates the Test Scene command in the authoring environment. Creates a SWF file based on the current scene of the current document and displays it with the internal player.

Argument(s)
None

Returns
Nothing

Example
```
my_doc = fl.getDocumentDOM();
my_doc.testScene();
```

traceBitmap

```
document.traceBitmap( threshold,
➥ minimumArea, curveFit, cornerThreshold )
```

Traces bitmap

Description
Duplicates the Trace Bitmap action in the authoring environment. Converts the selected bitmap element into a shape element.

Argument(s)
`threshold`—*integer*—A number from 0 to 500. Controls the number of colors in the final shape.

`minimumArea`—*integer*—A number from 0 to 1000. The minimum pixel radius of a color to create a new fill for.

`curveFit`—*string*—How closely to fit curves of a fill to the colored areas in the bitmap. Valid values are `"pixels"`, `"very tight"`, `"tight"`, `"normal"`, `"smooth"`, and `"very smooth"`.

cornerThreshold—*string*—How closely to fit corners to the colored areas in the bitmap. Valid values are "many corners", "normal", and "few corners".

Returns
Nothing

Example
```
my_doc = fl.getDocumentDOM();
my_doc.traceBitmap(0, 5, "normal",
➥ "normal");
```

transformSelection

`document.transformSelection( a, b, c, d )`

Performs general transformation

Description
Transforms the selected element(s) based on the matrix values given.

Argument(s)
a—*float*—See the entry for Matrix for a description of these four properties.

b—*float*

c—*float*

d—*float*

Returns
Nothing

Example
```
my_doc = fl.getDocumentDOM();
object.method(0, 1, 0, 1);
```

unGroup

`document.unGroup()`

Ungroups selected group

Description
Ungroups any grouped elements contained in the current selection. Has no effect on nongrouped elements.

Argument(s)
None

Returns
Nothing

Example
```
my_doc = fl.getDocumentDOM();
my_doc.unGroup();
```

unlockAllElements

`document.unlockAllElements()`

Unlocks all symbols on current frame

Description
Sets the locked property of all elements in the current frame to false

Argument(s)
None

Returns
Nothing

Example
```
my_doc = fl.getDocumentDOM();
// lock an element:
my_doc.selection[0].locked = true;
// unlock all elements:
my_doc.unlockAllElements();
```

xmlPanel

`document.xmlPanel( fileURI )`

Displays specified XML to UI dialog box

Description
Displays a dialog box based on the XML file given in the argument. The dialog box is modal and will need to be closed before further actions (scripted or manual) take place in the authoring environment. Returns an object that contains a property named dismiss. If this is equal to the string "accept", then the dialog box ended by the user clicking OK. If the user cancelled, then dismiss will contain the string "cancel".

Argument(s)
fileURI—*string (URI)*—The location of the XML file to base the dialog box on. Must be a valid URI string. Usually this will start with "file:///" followed by a file path and name. You can use fl.configURI as a shortcut URI to the Configuration directory.

Returns

Result object—Object containing any properties set in the dialog box as well as the dismiss property

Example

```
my_doc = fl.getDocumentDOM();
result = my_doc.xmlPanel(fl.configURI +
➥ "/Commands/mySettings.xml");
if(result.dismiss == "accept"){
  // process further properties of
  // result, which were set as properties
  // in the dialog box:
} else {
  alert("Dialog was cancelled.");
```

Properties of the document Object

accName

`document.accName`

Name of movie, used by screen reader

Description

For accessibility purposes, this is the name of the document that will be seen and used by a screen reader. It can be different than the name used by the document for other purposes.

Value(s)

string—The name of the document for the screen reader

Example

```
my_doc = fl.getDocumentDOM();
my_doc.accName = "Main Document";
```

autoLabel

`document.autoLabel`

If `true`, turns on automatic labelling for screen reader

Description

Turns on or off automatic labelling, which uses text objects for labels, rather than making them visible as objects to the screen reader.

Value(s)

Boolean—`true` turns on auto labelling; `false` turns it off.

Example

```
my_doc = fl.getDocumentDOM();
my_doc.autoLabel = true;
```

backgroundColor

`document.backgroundColor`

A color representing the background

Description

The color that will be used as the background of the specified document.

Value(s)

integer or string—The color as a string (#rrggbb) or base10 or hex integer (0 to 16777216 or 0xrrggbb)

Example

```
my_doc = fl.getDocumentDOM();
my_doc.backgroundColor = 0x000000;
```

currentPublishProfile

`document.currentPublishProfile`

Sets and returns name of active Publish Profile

Description

The name of the current Publish Profile

Value(s)

string—The name of the profile

Example

```
my_doc = fl.getDocumentDOM();
my_doc.currentPublishProfile = "Omega";
```

currentTimeline

`document.currentTimeline`

Represents active timeline

Description

The number of the currently active timeline of the document. Timelines are stored in the `document.timelines` array. This number will represent the array element where the timeline can be referenced. To get a reference to the current timeline object, use `document.getTimeline()`. You can set the active timeline by setting this property's value;

however, if you set it to a nonexistent value, you won't get an error. Using document.editScene(scene) is a safer method of changing the active timeline, as it will generate an error message if the scene doesn't exist.

Value(s)
integer—The index of the current timeline as found in the document.timelines array.

Example
```
my_doc = fl.getDocumentDOM();
fl.trace("This is scene " +
➥ (my_doc.currentTimeline + 1));
my_doc.currentTimeline = 3;
```

description

document.description

Description of main movie, used by screen reader

Description
For accessibility purposes, a description of the document for use by a screen reader

Value(s)
string—Movie description

Example
```
my_doc = fl.getDocumentDOM();
my_doc.description =
➥ "This is my first Flash movie.";
```

forceSimple

document.forceSimple

If true, children of object aren't accessible to screen reader.

Description
For accessibility purposes, hides any child objects from the screen reader

Value(s)
Boolean—If true, child objects won't be accessible to the screen reader. If false, they will be.

Example
```
my_doc = fl.getDocumentDOM();
my_doc.forceSimple = false;
```

frameRate

document.frameRate

Document's frames per second

Description
The rate in terms of frames per second that the movie will attempt to run at

Value(s)
integer—Frames per second

Example
```
my_doc = fl.getDocumentDOM();
my_doc.frameRate = 30;
```

height

document.height

Height of document

Description
The height in pixels of the stage of the specified document

Value(s)
integer—Height

Example
```
my_doc = fl.getDocumentDOM();
my_doc.height = 300;
```

library

document.library

Represents document's Library

Description
An object representing the Library of the specified document. This is read-only and is used to access the Library only.

Value(s)
object—Library

Example
```
my_doc = fl.getDocumentDOM();
my_lib = my_doc.library
fl.trace("There are " + my_lib.items.length
➥ + " items in my library.");
```

livePreview

`document.livePreview`

If true, visually displays components at authortime

Description

Turns on or off the live preview feature in the authoring environment. For use with components containing a live preview or compiled clips.

Value(s)

Boolean—`false` turns off live preview. `true` turns it on.

Example

```
my_doc = fl.getDocumentDOM();
my_doc.livePreview = false;
```

name

`document.name`

Name of document

Description

The name of the document, which is read-only. You set the name of the document by saving it. If not saved, it will have a name such as "Untitled-1".

Value(s)

string—The name of the document

Example

```
my_doc = fl.getDocumentDOM();
fl.trace("The current document's name is "
➥ + my_doc.name);
```

path

`document.path`

File path of document

Description

The file path of the specified document. Note: This won't be a valid URI for use in any methods requiring a URI as an argument. URIs use forward slashes and need to be prefixed by `"file:///"`. On a Windows system, the path will use backward slashes. And on no system will the path have a file prefix. You can use string manipulation functions to replace the slashes and add the prefix.

Value(s)

string—The file path of the specified document

Example

```
my_doc = fl.getDocumentDOM();
fl.trace("this document is located at: "
➥ + my_doc.path);
```

publishProfiles

`document.publishProfiles`

Array containing Publish Profiles for document

Description

An array containing the names of all the Publish Profiles for the specified document

Value(s)

array—Each element holding a string that is the name of a Publish Profile

Example

```
my_doc = fl.getDocumentDOM();
fl.trace(my_doc.publishProfiles[0]);
```

screenOutline

`document.screenOutline`

Current `screenOutline` object for document

Description

If the document is a screen-based presentation or form-based application, it will contain a `screenOutline` object.

Value(s)

object—`screenOutline` object of the document

Example

```
my_doc = fl.getDocumentDOM();
so = my_doc.screenOutline;
```

selection

`document.selection`

Array of selected element objects

Description
An array containing an element for each currently selected item.

Although some standard array methods and properties are available, such as length, others such as push(element) aren't, and it is *not* possible to select items by adding them to the array like so: my_doc.selection[1] = my_elem;. This won't work. To programmatically add elements to the array, you should create a new array, add the elements to it, and assign this to the selection array as follows:

```
selArray = new Array();
selArray[0] = my_elem;
my_doc.selection = selArray;
```

This also has an unexpected behavior of simply adding the new elements to the existing array rather than replacing the current selection. If you want to deselect currently selected items before adding your element to the selection array, you must call document.selectNone() first. A shortcut for the preceding code would be

```
my_doc.selection = [my_elem];
```

Also note that multiple selected shapes are considered a single element and will occupy one slot in the selection array. To separate individual shapes, either group each one or convert it to a symbol.

Value(s)
array—An array of selected elements

Example
```
// double the height of every
// selected element
my_doc = fl.getDocumentDOM();
for(i=0; i<my_doc.selection.length; i++){
  my_doc.selection[i].height *= 2;
}
```

silent

document.silent

If true, movie isn't read by screen reader

Description
For accessibility purposes, hides the document from being read by the screen reader

Value(s)
Boolean—If true, screen reader won't read the document. If false, it will.

Example
```
my_doc = fl.getDocumentDOM();
my_doc.silent = true;
```

timelines

document.timelines

Array containing timeline objects of document

Description
An array of the timelines contained in a movie. Each timeline is a scene in the movie. Scene 1 would be document.timelines[0]. Each element in the array contains a timeline object.

Value(s)
array—An array of timeline objects that represent the scenes of a movie.

Example
```
my_doc = fl.getDocumentDOM();
scene3_tl = my_doc.timelines[3];
```

viewMatrix

fl.viewMatrix

References TransformationMatrix object

Description
A matrix object containing data on the current translation, rotation, and scaling of the current view. This is often needed when editing content inside of a symbol onstage that may have been transformed.

Value(s)
Object—See the entry for Matrix for more information.

Example
```
my_doc = fl.getDocumentDOM();
vm = my_doc.viewMatrix;
```

width

document.width

Width of document

Description
The width in pixels of the stage of the specified document

Value(s)
integer—Width

Example
```
my_doc = fl.getDocumentDOM();
my_doc.width = 300;
```

DrawingLayer

Used by tools for creating a temporary drawing while dragging the mouse

Methods:

- beginDraw
- beginFrame
- cubicCurveTo
- curveTo
- drawPath
- endDraw
- endFrame
- lineTo
- moveTo
- newPath
- setColor

Methods of the drawingLayer Object

beginDraw

drawingLayer.beginDraw([*persistentDraw*])

Puts Flash into drawing mode

Description
Puts Flash into drawing mode. All drawing actions should be preceded by beginDraw and terminated by endDraw. See the entry for drawingLayer.beginFrame for more information.

Argument(s)
persistentDraw—*Boolean*—If true, what is visible onstage will remain until the next beginDraw of beginFrame call.

Returns
Nothing

Example
```
fl.drawingLayer.beginDraw();
```

beginFrame

drawingLayer.beginFrame()

Starting point to delimit a set of lines

Description
Tools generally draw while the mouse is dragging. Each time the mouse is moved, a shape is drawn with slightly different parameters based on the mouse position. By enclosing your drawing commands with beginFrame and endFrame, the drawing layer is cleared after each successive shape is drawn. A general template for these actions is

```
mouseDown:
  beginDraw
mouseMove:
  beginFrame
    drawing actions
  endFrame
mouseUp:
  endDraw
```

The entire drawing session is bracketed with beginDraw and endDraw and each sequential drawing action is bracketed with beginFrame and endFrame.

Argument(s)
None

Returns
Nothing

Example
```
function mouseMove(){
  fl.drawingLayer.beginFrame();
  fl.drawingLayer.moveTo(0, 0);
  fl.drawingLayer.lineTo(fl.tools.penLoc.x,
➥ fl.tools.penLoc.y);
  fl.drawingLayer.endFrame();
}
```

cubicCurveTo

```
drawingLayer.cubicCurveTo( x1Ctrl, y1Ctrl,
➥ x2Ctl, y2Ctl, xEnd, yEnd)
```

Draws a cubic curve

Description
Draws a curve from the last point drawn to (or 0, 0 if no drawing has taken place yet) through two control points, to an end point

Argument(s)
x1Ctrl—*float*—The x position of the first control point

y2Ctrl—*float*—The y position of the first control point

x2Ctrl—*float*—The x position of the second control point

y2Ctrl—*float*—The y position of the second control point

xEnd—*float*—The x position of the end point

yEnd—*float*—The y position of the end point

Returns
Nothing

Example

```
fl.drawingLayer.moveTo(0, 100);
fl.drawingLayer.cubicCurveTo(0, 0, 300,
➥ 200, 300, 100);
```

curveTo

```
drawingLayer.curveTo( xCtrl, yCtrl, xEnd,
➥ yEnd )
```

Draws a quadratic curve segment

Description
Draws a curve from the last point drawn to (or 0, 0 if no drawing has taken place yet) through a control point, to an end point

Argument(s)
xCtrl—*float*—The x position of the first control point

yCtrl—*float*—The y position of the first control point

xEnd—*float*—The x position of the end point

yEnd—*float*—The y position of the end point

Returns
Nothing

Example

```
fl.drawingLayer.moveTo(0, 100);
fl.drawingLayer.curveTo(150, 0, 300, 100);
```

drawPath

```
drawingLayer.drawPath( path )
```

Draws specified path

Description
Draws a shape based on the given path object. If the path is closed, drawPath will draw a stroke and fill based on the active settings for stroke and fill. If not closed, it will draw a stroke based on current stroke settings.

Argument(s)
path—*path*—A path object created with drawingLayer.newPath()

Returns
Nothing

Example

```
my_path = fl.drawingLayer.newPath();
my_path.addPoint(0, 0);
my_path.addPoint(100, 0);
my_path.addPoint(100, 100);
my_path.addPoint(0, 100);
my_path.close();
fl.drawingLayer.drawPath(my_path);
```

endDraw

```
drawingLayer.endDraw()
```

Exits drawing mode

Description
Takes Flash out of drawing mode. All drawing actions should be preceded by beginDraw and terminated by endDraw. See the entry for drawingLayer.beginFrame for more information.

Argument(s)
None

Returns
Nothing

Example

```
fl.drawingLayer.endDraw();
```

endFrame

`drawingLayer.endFrame()`

Erases paths drawn by drawingLayer object

Description

Ends the current frame and erases any drawings done in the drawing layer within the frame

Argument(s)

None

Returns

Nothing

Example

```
function mouseMove(){
  fl.drawingLayer.beginFrame();
  fl.drawingLayer.moveTo(0, 0);
  fl.drawingLayer.lineTo(fl.tools.penLoc.x,
➥ fl.tools.penLoc.y);
  fl.drawingLayer.endFrame();
}
```

lineTo

`drawingLayer.lineTo( x, y )`

Draws line

Description

Draws a line from the last point drawn to (or 0, 0 if no drawing has occurred) to the specified x, y point

Argument(s)

x—*float*—The x position of the end point of the line

y—*float*—The y position of the end point of the line

Returns

Nothing

Example

```
function mouseMove(){
  fl.drawingLayer.beginFrame();
  fl.drawingLayer.moveTo(0, 0);
  fl.drawingLayer.lineTo(fl.tools.penLoc.x,
➥ fl.tools.penLoc.y);
  fl.drawingLayer.endFrame();
}
```

moveTo

`drawingLayer.moveTo( x, y )`

Sets current drawing position

Description

Moves the drawing tool to the specified point. The next drawing action will take this as its starting point.

Argument(s)

x—*float*—The x position of the point to move to

y—*float*—The y position of the point to move to

Returns

Nothing

Example

```
function mouseMove(){
  fl.drawingLayer.beginFrame();
  fl.drawingLayer.moveTo(0, 0);
  fl.drawingLayer.lineTo(fl.tools.penLoc.x,
➥ fl.tools.penLoc.y);
  fl.drawingLayer.endFrame();
}
```

newPath

`drawingLayer.newPath()`

Returns new path object

Description

Creates a new path object

Argument(s)

None

Returns

path—*path object*

Example

```
my_path = fl.drawingLayer.newPath();
my_path.addPoint(0, 0);
my_path.addPoint(100, 0);
my_path.addPoint(100, 100);
my_path.addPoint(0, 100);
my_path.close();
fl.drawingLayer.drawPath(my_path);
```

setColor

`drawingLayer.setColor( color )`

Sets color of subsequently drawn data

Description
Sets the color of the lines used in the drawing layer

Argument(s)
color—*integer or string*—The color as a string (#rrggbb) or base10 or hex integer (0 to 16777216 or 0xrrggbb)

Example
```
fl.drawingLayer.setColor(0xff0000);
```

Edge

Represents an edge of an object on the stage

Methods:

- getControl
- getHalfEdge
- setControl
- splitEdge

Properties:

- id
- isLine

Methods of the edge Object

getControl

`edge.getControl( index )`

Returns control point of specified edge object

Description
Returns a point object representing one of three control points of the edge based on the argument sent. 0 will retrieve the edge's first control point values, 1 will retrieve the middle control point's values, and 2 will retrieve the end control point's values. For a straight line, 1 will retrieve the midpoint of the line. The object returned, which isn't a reference to the control point itself, has an x and y property.

Argument(s)
index—*integer*—The position of the control point to retrieve: 0, 1, 2

Returns
x, y control point coordinates—*point object*

Example
```
var my_elem = fl.getDocumentDOM().
➥ getTimeline().layers[0].frames[0].
➥ elements[0];
var pt = my_elem.edges[0].getControl(0);
pt.x = pt.x + 10;
my_elem.beginEdit();
my_elem.edges[0].setControl(0, pt.x, pt.y);
my_elem.endEdit();
```

getHalfEdge

`edge.getHalfEdge( index )`

Returns halfEdge object

Description
Returns one of the two halfEdge objects that are contained in edge. Which halfEdge is determined by the index sent as an argument.

Argument(s)
index—*integer*—0 or 1 depending on the position of the HalfEdge instance you wished returned

Returns
One halfEdge in edge—*halfEdge object*

Example
```
var my_elem = fl.getDocumentDOM().
➥ getTimeline().layers[0].frames[0].
➥ elements[0];
fl.trace(my_elem.edges[0].getHalfEdge(0).id);
```

setControl

`edge.setControl( index, x, y )`

Sets control point of edge

Description

Sets the pixel position of one of the edge's control points. Which control point depends on the index sent. 0 sets the start control point, 1 sets the middle control point, and 2 sets the end control point. For a straight line with only two control points, sending an index of 1 has no effect.

Argument(s)

index—*integer*—The position of the control point to retrieve: 0, 1, 2

x—*float*—The x pixel coordinate, relative to the current coordinate system

y—*float*—The y pixel coordinate, relative to the current coordinate system

Returns

Value—*type*

Example

```
var my_elem = fl.getDocumentDOM().
➥ getTimeline().layers[0].frames[0].
➥ elements[0];
my_elem.beginEdit();
var pt = my_elem.edges[0].getControl(0);
pt.x = pt.x + 10;
my_elem.edges[0].setControl(0, p.x, p.y);
my_elem.endEdit();
```

splitEdge

`edge.splitEdge( t )`

Divides specified edge object into two

Description

Splits the edge in two at the position specified in the parameter, which is a percentage of the full length of the line. Therefore, a value of `0.5` will split the edge in the middle.

Argument(s)

t—*float*—Percentage of line where split should occur

Returns

Nothing

Example

```
var my_elem = fl.getDocumentDOM().
➥ getTimeline().layers[0].frames[0].
➥ elements[0];
my_elem.beginEdit();
my_elem.edges[0].splitEdge(.3);
my_elem.endEdit();
```

Properties of the edge Object

id

`edge.id`

Unique identifier for edge object

Description

A unique identifier for the edges, this ID can be used to keep track of certain edges as their position changes with the shape object's edges array

Value(s)

integer—The unique ID of the edge

Example

```
var my_elem = fl.getDocumentDOM().
➥ getTimeline().layers[0].frames[0].
➥ elements[0];
fl.trace(my_elem.edges[0].id);
```

isLine

`edge.isLine`

If `true`, edge is a straight line.

Description

Specifies whether the edge is a straight line (`true`) or curve (`false`). This can become important if you wish to manipulate the middle control point, which isn't possible on a straight line.

Value(s)

Boolean—`true`, `false`

Example

```
var my_elem = fl.getDocumentDOM().
➥ getTimeline().layers[0].frames[0].
➥ elements[0];
my_elem.beginEdit();
if (!my_elem.edges[0].isLine) {
var pt = my_elem.edges[0].getControl(1);
pt.x = pt.x + 10;
my_elem.edges[0].setControl(1, p.x, p.y);
}
my_elem.endEdit();
```

Effect

An instance of a Timeline Effect

Properties:

- effectName
- groupName
- sourceFile
- symbolType
- useXMLToUI

In addition to these properties (listed in detail in the following text), an effect object may have additional properties that are assigned to it from the XML dialog box that configures the effect. The properties that follow are mainly applied in the configureEffect method inside the effect implementation JSFL script.

Properties of the effect Object

effectName

effect.effectName

Name of effect, used to create menu item

Description
The name of the effect. This is what appears in the Timeline Effects menu. An effect's name is initially defined in the XML file that configures the effect, but this property can be used to retrieve the name.

Value(s)
string—The effect name

Example
```
my_eff = fl.effects[0];
fl.trace(my_eff.effectName);
```

groupName

effect.groupName

Name of effect group, used to create menu item

Description
Name of the effect group. In the Timeline Effects menu, effects can be placed in a submenu. This submenu gets its name from this property. An effect's group name is initially defined in the XML file that configures the effect, but this property can be used to retrieve the group name.

Value(s)
string—The effect group

Example
```
my_eff = fl.effects[0];
fl.trace(my_eff.groupName);
```

sourceFile

effect.sourceFile

Name of JSFL source file

Description
The JSFL source file used to script the actions that will take place in the specified effect. An effect's source file is initially defined in the XML file that configures the effect, but this property can be used to retrieve the filename.

Value(s)
string—Path to the source file

Example
```
my_eff = fl.effects[0];
fl.trace(my_eff.sourceFile);
```

symbolType

effect.symbolType

Name of symbolType to create during initial application of effect

Description
The type of symbol that is created when the effect is applied to an element. This property is automatically set to "graphic" but can be changed via JSFL with this property.

Value(s)
string—The type of symbol to create. Can be set to "movie clip" or "graphic".

Example
```
my_eff = fl.effects[0];
my_eff.symbolType = "movie clip";
```

useXMLToUI

`effect.useXMLToUI`

If `true`, displays a XML to UI dialog box

Description
Determines whether or not an XML to UI dialog box will be displayed when the effect is applied. Displaying this dialog box is the default behavior, but can be disabled via this property.

Value(s)
Boolean—`true` will cause the dialog box to be displayed; `false` will suppress it.

Example
```
my_eff = fl.effects[0];
my_eff.useXMLToUI = false;
```

Element

Represents all objects on the stage

Methods:

- `getPersistentData`
- `hasPersistentData`
- `removePersistentData`
- `setPersistentData`

Properties:

- `depth`
- `elementType`
- `height`
- `left`
- `locked`
- `matrix`
- `name`
- `top`
- `width`

Methods of the element Object

getPersistentData

`element.getPersistentData(` *name* `)`

Returns value of named data

Description
Retrieves the value of the named data from the stage element (available only for symbols and bitmaps). If data for the name specified has not been stored with the element, then 0 is returned.

Argument(s)
name—*string*—The name of data to retrieve

Returns
Value of data or 0—*Varies depending on data*

Example
```
var my_doc = fl.getDocumentDOM();
var my_tl = my_doc.getTimeline();
var my_elem = my_tl.layers[0].frames[0].
➥ elements;
fl.trace(my_elem[0].getPersistentData
➥ ("created");
```

hasPersistentData

`element.hasPersistentData(` *name* `)`

If `true`, data with specified name is attached to object

Description
Checks to see whether persistent data of the name given has been stored with the element (`true`) or not (`false`) This method is available only for symbols and bitmaps.

Argument(s)
name—*string*—The name of data to check

Returns
`true` if named data exists—*Boolean*

Example
```
var my_doc = fl.getDocumentDOM();
var my_tl = my_doc.getTimeline();
var my_elem = my_tl.layers[0].frames[0].
➥ elements;
if (!my_elem[0].
➥ hasPersistentData("version")) {
```

```
  my_elem.setPersistentData("version",
➥ double, 1.0);
}
```

removePersistentData

`element.removePersistentData( name )`

Removes persistent data attached to object

Description

Removes persistent data of given name from element and returns true. If data doesn't exists, it returns false. This method is available only for symbols and bitmaps.

Argument(s)

name—*string*—The name of the data to remove from the element

Returns

true if data existed and was removed—*Boolean*

Example

```
var my_doc = fl.getDocumentDOM();
var my_tl = my_doc.getTimeline();
var my_elem = my_tl.layers[0].frames[0].
➥ elements;
if (!my_elem[0].
➥ hasPersistentData("toBeRemoved")) {
  my_elem.removePersistentData
➥ ("toBeRemoved");
}
```

setPersistentData

`element.setPersistentData( name, type, ➥ value )`

Stores specified data with object

Description

Stores the data of the name and type specified with the element. The data will be saved with the file and retrievable after the document has been closed and reopened.

Argument(s)

name—*string*—The name of the data to store

type—*string*—The type of data: "string", "integer", "integerArray", "double", "doubleArray", and "byteArray"

value—*Varies depending on type*—The value for the data

Returns

Nothing

Example

```
var my_doc = fl.getDocumentDOM();
var my_tl = my_doc.getTimeline();
var my_elem = my_tl.layers[0].frames[0].
➥ elements;
my_elem[0].setPersistentData("creator",
➥ "string", "Todd Yard");
my_elem[0].setPersistentData("version",
➥ "double", 1.0);
```

Properties of the element Object

depth

`element.depth`

Returns drawing order of objects onstage

Description

Holds the arrange order of the elements on the stage, with 0 representing the top of the stack, and numbers increasing towards the bottom of the stack (therefore an element at a depth of 5 is below an element at a depth of 3). However, for all layers excepting the top layer of the timeline, it appears as if all elements return the same depth, which is one greater than the depth of the element at the bottom of the stack on the top layer. So if there are four elements on the top layer with depths of 0to3, elements on all other layers will have a depth of 4. This property may be retrieved, but not set.

Value(s)

integer—The depth in the visual stack

Example

```
var my_doc = fl.getDocumentDOM();
var my_tl = my_doc.getTimeline();
var my_elem = my_tl.layers[0].frames[0].
➥ elements;
fl.trace(my_elem[0].depth);
```

elementType

`element.elementType`

Type of element object

Description

Holds the type for the element. This property may be retrieved, but not set.

Value(s)

string—"instance", "text", "shape", or "shapeObj"

Example

```
var my_doc = fl.getDocumentDOM();
var my_tl = my_doc.getTimeline();
var my_elem = my_tl.layers[0].frames[0].
➥ elements;
fl.trace(my_elem[0].elementType);
```

height

element.height

Height of element

Description

Holds the pixel height of the element. This property may be set and retrieved. When set, the element is scaled from the current location of the center point.

Value(s)

float—Pixel height

Example

```
// makes the minimum height of all
// elements on layer 100 pixels
var my_doc = fl.getDocumentDOM();
var my_tl = my_doc.getTimeline();
var my_elem = my_tl.layers[0].frames[0].
➥ elements;
for (var i = 0; i < my_elem.length; i++) {
  if (my_elem[i].height < 100) {
    my_elem[i].height = 100;
  }
}
```

left

element.left

Left side of element

Description

The pixel position of the left side of the element, as determined by its bounding box. This property may be retrieved, but not set. This doesn't necessarily correspond with the element's x value in the Property panel, as that is determined by its registration point.

Value(s)

float—Pixel position of left of element

Example

```
var my_doc = fl.getDocumentDOM();
var my_tl = my_doc.getTimeline();
var my_elem = my_tl.layers[0].frames[0].
➥ elements;
fl.trace(my_elem[0].left);
```

locked

element.locked

If true, element is locked.

Description

Holds whether element onstage is locked (true) or not (false). This property may be both retrieved and set. Shape elements may not be locked.

Value(s)

Boolean—true, false

Example

```
// locks all elements in layer
var my_doc = fl.getDocumentDOM();
var my_tl = my_doc.getTimeline();
var my_elem = my_tl.layers[0].frames[0].
➥ elements;
for (var i = 0; i < my_elem.length; i++) {
  my_elem[i].locked = true;
}
```

matrix

element.matrix

References transformationMatrix object

Description

The transformationMatrix is an object of six properties: a, b, c, d, tx, and ty. These values all relate to the transform properties of the element and are all floating-point numbers. tx and ty represent the stage coordinates in pixels. a represents _xscale and d represents _yscale, both in percents (1 is 100 percent scale, 2 is 200 percent scale, etc.). b represents vertical skew and c represents horizontal skew, both in radians (a c value of .7854 would be a 45-degree horizontal skew). All transformations occur from the element's registration point.

You may not alter a transformationMatrix directly. To change the matrix for an element you must first either copy its current transform to a variable or create a new object. After setting the copy or new object's properties, you place it into the matrix property of the element. See the example that follows. Note that the element doesn't always automatically update when setting this property. Reselecting or deselecting the transformed element usually forces an update.

Value(s)

object—An object of six properties representing a transform

Example

```
// copies current transform, then
// skews element horizontally
var my_doc = fl.getDocumentDOM();
var my_tl = my_doc.getTimeline();
var my_elem = my_tl.layers[0].frames[0].
➥ elements[0];
var mx = my_elem.matrix;
mx.c = .7854;
my_elem.matrix = mx;
// creates a new transform for an element,
// placing it at (50, 50) and scaling it
// vertically to 200%
var my_doc = fl.getDocumentDOM();
var my_tl = my_doc.getTimeline();
var my_elem = my_tl.layers[0].frames[0].
➥ elements[0];
var mx = {a:1, b:0, c:0, d:2, tx:50, ty:50};
my_elem.matrix = mx;
```

name

element.name

Instance name of element

Description

The instance name given to the element in the Property panel. If no name is given (or can't be given, as with shapes), then an empty string ("") is returned.

Value(s)

string—The element's name

Example

```
var my_doc = fl.getDocumentDOM();
var my_tl = my_doc.getTimeline();
var my_elem = my_tl.layers[0].frames[0].
➥ elements;
fl.trace(my_elem[0].name);
```

top

element.top

Top side of element

Description

The pixel position of the top side of the element, as determined by its bounding box. This property may be retrieved, but not set.

Value(s)

float—The pixel position of the top of the element

Example

```
var my_doc = fl.getDocumentDOM();
var my_tl = my_doc.getTimeline();
var my_elem = my_tl.layers[0].frames[0].
➥ elements;
fl.trace(my_elem[0].top);
```

width

element.width

Width of element

Description

Holds the pixel width of the element. This property may be set and retrieved. When set, the element is scaled from the current location of the center point.

Value(s)

float—Pixel width

Example

```
// makes the minimum width of all
// elements on layer 100 pixels
var my_doc = fl.getDocumentDOM();
var my_tl = my_doc.getTimeline();
var my_elem = my_tl.layers[0].frames[0].
➥ elements;
for (var i = 0; i < my_elem.length; i++) {
  if (my_elem[i].width < 100) {
    my_elem[i].width = 100;
  }
}
```

EmbeddedVideoInstance

Subclass of `Instance`; an embedded video instance on the stage. Refer to the entry for `Instance` for properties.

Fill

Fill settings for the selection or toolbar

Properties:

- `color`
- `colorArray`
- `matrix`
- `posArray`
- `style`

The `fill` object is returned by `document.getCustomFill()` and is used in `document.setCustomFill()`.

Properties of the fill Object

color

`fill.color`

Fill color

Description

The color of the specified fill

Value(s)

integer or string—The color as a string (#rrggbb) or base10 or hex integer (0 to 16777216 or 0xrrggbb). You can also specify an alpha for the fill by adding on the hex values from 00 to FF after the color definition as a string. Example: "#FF00007F" creates a red fill with approximately 50 percent alpha.

Example

```
my_doc = fl.getDocumentDOM();
my_fill = my_doc.getCustomFill();
// Note alpha is also set after color value.
my_fill.color = "#ff00ff33";
my_doc.setCustomFill(my_fill);
```

colorArray

`fill.colorArray`

Array of colors in gradient

Description

An array of values as colors in a linear or radial gradient fill. Note: If you use gradient fills, you must specify `color`, `colorArray`, `posArray`, and a `matrix` for the `fill` object. Omitting to create all four properties can cause Flash to crash.

Value(s)

array—An array of color values in the format specified in `fill.color`

Example

```
// the following assumes the current fill
// set in the authoring environment is
// already a gradient.
my_doc = fl.getDocumentDOM();
my_fill = my_doc.getCustomFill();
my_fill.colorArray = ["#ff00ff", "#00ff00",
➥ "#ff0000"];
my_fill.posArray = [0, 128, 255];
my_doc.setCustomFill(my_fill);
```

matrix

`fill.matrix`

`matrix` object used to control gradients

Description

A matrix used to specify the rotation, position, and size of a linear or gradient fill. Note: If you use gradient fills, you must specify `color`, `colorArray`, `posArray`, and `matrix` properties for the `fill` object. Omitting to create all four properties can cause Flash to crash.

Setting a matrix is a very advanced topic. We don't have the space to go into matrix math here, but we will try to give you at least what the matrix is based on and what each property means. If you understand how to manipulate matrix values, you can probably take it from there. The following information was offered by Robin Debreuil and serves as a pretty good set of definitions:

The matrix values are based on a square that has the following size and location in twips (twentieth of a pixel):

x: -0x4000

y: -0x4000

w: 0x8000

h: 0x8000

If we convert that to decimal and pixels, they become

x: -819.2

y: -819.2

w: 1638.4

h: 1638.4

We then have the six properties of the matrix object, which basically tell it how to scale, rotate, and translate that large square, as follows:

a—How much to scale each x coordinate in the x direction (a multiplier)

b—How much to scale each x coordinate in the y direction (a multiplier)

c—How much to scale each y coordinate in the x direction (a multiplier)

d—How much to scale each y coordinate in the y direction (a multiplier)

tx—How much to offset each point in the x direction (in pixels)

ty—How much to offset each point in the y direction (in pixels)

Again, this subject could fill a book in itself. While we don't have the space to completely explain how it works, here is a function that you can use to create a valid matrix for the fill object. You just need to specify the x and y positions where the fill will begin, the width and height of the fill, and the angle of the fill in radians. The function will return a matrix that you can use as the matrix property of a fill object:

```
function makeFillMatrix(x, y, w, h, a){
  var maxSize= 32768/20;
  var scaleX = w/maxSize;
  var scaleY = h/maxSize;
  var mat = new Object();
  mat.a = Math.round
  ➥ (Math.cos(a)*scaleX*1000)/1000;
  mat.b = Math.round
  ➥ (Math.sin(a)*scaleX*1000)/1000;
  mat.c = -Math.round
  ➥ (Math.sin(a)*scaleY*1000)/1000;
  mat.d = Math.round
  ➥ (Math.cos(a)*scaleY*1000)/1000;
  mat.tx = x + w/2;
  mat.ty = y + h/2;
  return mat;
}
```

Example

```
my_doc = fl.getDocumentDOM();
my_elem = my_doc.selection[0];
my_fill = new Object();
my_fill.color = "#ffffff";
my_fill.colorArray = ["#ff00ff", "#00ff00",
➥ "#ff0000", "#0000ff"];
my_fill.posArray = [0, 69, 159, 255];
my_fill.matrix = makeFillMatrix
➥ (my_elem.left, my_elem.top, my_elem.width,
➥ my_elem.height,2);
my_fill.style = "linearGradient";
my_doc.setCustomFill(my_fill);
```

posArray

`fill.posArray`

Indicates position of corresponding color in gradient

Description

An array of integers from 0to255 as positions of the colors in a linear or radial gradient fill. Note: If you use gradient fills, you must specify `color`, `colorArray`, `posArray`, and `matrix` properties for the `fill` object. Omitting to create all four properties can cause Flash to crash.

Value(s)

array—An array of values from 0 to 255

Example

```
// the following assumes the current
// fill set in the authoring environment
// is already a gradient, thus the matrix
// property will already exist
my_fill = my_doc.getCustomFill();
my_fill.colorArray = ["#ff00ff", "#00ff00",
➥ "#ff0000"];
my_fill.posArray = [0, 128, 255];
my_doc.setCustomFill(my_fill);
```

style

`fill.style`

Fill style

Description
The style of the fill: solid, linear gradient, or radial gradient. Note: If you use gradient fills, you must specify color, colorArray, posArray, and matrix properties for the fill object. Omitting to create all four properties can cause Flash to crash.

Value(s)
string—Valid values are "solid", "linearGradient", and "radialGradient"

Example
```
my_doc = fl.getDocumentDOM():
my_fill = my_doc.getCustomFill();
my_fill.style = "solid";
```

Flash

An object representing the Flash application

Methods:

- browseForFileURL
- closeAll
- closeDocument
- createDocument
- enableImmediateUpdates
- fileExists
- findDocumentIndex
- findScreenType
- getDocumentDOM
- invokeScreenType
- openDocument
- quit
- reloadEffects
- reloadTools
- revertDocument
- runScript
- saveAll
- saveDocument
- saveDocumentAs
- setActiveWindow
- trace

Properties:

- activeEffect
- componentsPanel
- configDirectory
- configURI
- documents
- effects
- Math
- outputPanel
- screenTypes
- tools
- version
- xmlui

Methods of the flash Object

browseForFileURL

```
fl.browseForFileURL( browseType [, title]
➥ [, previewArea] )
```

Brings up Open or Save dialog box

Description
Brings up a dialog box for selecting a filename and path. Note that this function doesn't actually save or load anything. It merely allows the user to choose a path and filename visually through a dialog box, and returns that path as a valid file URI for use in your program. The dialog box is modal, meaning all processing will stop until it is closed.

Argument(s)
browseType—*string*—Can be set to "open", "save", or "select". These merely change the various labels in the dialog box, and a Save dialog box will warn you if you choose an existing file.

title—*string*—The string that will be displayed in the dialog box's title bar. If omitted or set to an empty string, a default title will be used.

previewArea—*Boolean*—Displays a preview area for previewing images in the dialog box. May not be supported on all systems.

Returns
URI path and filename—*URI string*

Example
```
fl.browseForFileURL("open", "Pick a File,
➥ any File", false);
```

closeAll

`fl.closeAll()`

Closes all open documents

Description
Closes all open documents. If a document has not been saved, or changed since its last save, users will be asked if they want to save changes. There is no way to disable this in this function.

Argument(s)
None

Returns
Nothing

Example
```
fl.closeAll();
```

closeDocument

```
fl.closeDocument( documentObject
➥ [, bPromptToSaveChanges] )
```

Closes specified document

Description
Closes the specified document

Argument(s)
documentObject—*object*—The document object representing the document you want to close.

bPromptToSaveChanges—*Boolean*—If true (default), user will be prompted to save any changes to an unsaved document or one that has changed since its last save. If false, document will be immediately closed, discarding any changes.

Returns
Nothing

Example
```
fl.closeDocument(my_doc);
```

createDocument

`fl.createDocument( [docType] )`

Creates new document

Description
Creates a new document

Argument(s)
docType—*string*—The type of document that will be created. Valid values are "timeline"—a regular Flash movie, "presentation"—a slide-based Flash presentation, or "application"—a form-based Flash application. Default is "timeline".

Returns
A reference to the new document object—*object*

Example
```
my_new_doc = fl.createDocument("timeline");
```

enableImmediateUpdates

`fl.enableImmediateUpdates()`

If true, updates to timeline display when executing an effect. Only used for debugging effect.

Description
Enables or disables display of a timeline while an effect is being executed. This would generally be used inside the executeEffect function in a Timeline Effect. As each step of the effect is executed, it will be shown on the stage. While this may be useful while developing an effect so you can see what is happening, it is usually not used in the final effect, as the display can be distracting and causes the effect to take longer to execute.

Argument(s)
None

Returns
Nothing

Example

```
function executeEffect(){
  fl.enableImmediateUpdates();
  // code to execute the effect goes here
}
```

fileExists

`fl.fileExists( fileURI )`

Returns true if specified file exists

Description

Checks for the existence of the specified file

Argument(s)

fileURI—*URI string*—A valid URI to a file

Returns

true if file exists, otherwise false—*Boolean*

Example

```
if(fl.fileExists
➥ ("file:///myFiles/myMovie.swf")){
  my_doc.importSWF
  ➥ ("file:///C:/myFiles/myMovie.swf");
} else {
  alert("File doesn't exist!");
}
```

findDocumentIndex

`fl.findDocumentIndex( name )`

Returns specified document object's index

Description

Returns the index of the documents array in which the specified document is stored. References to every open document are kept in the array, `fl.documents`. Given the name of an open document, you can get a reference to it by finding its place in the array.

Argument(s)

name—*string*—The name of the document you are looking for.

Returns

Index—*integer*

Example

```
index = fl.findDocumentIndex
➥ ("Asteroids.fla");
fl.closeDocument(fl.documents[index]);
```

findScreenType

`fl.findScreenType( name [, version] )`

Returns specified ScreenType

Description

Returns an object containing the screen type and version specified. See the entries Screen and ScreenType for more info on screens.

Argument(s)

name—*string*—The name of the screen type

version—*string*—The version of the screen type

Returns

screenType—*object*

Example

```
st = fl.findScreenType("Slide", "1.0");
```

getDocumentDOM

`fl.getDocumentDOM()`

Returns active document object

Description

Returns a reference to the active document object. This is perhaps the most used method in the JavaScript API. Although you can work on other documents via the documents array, most often you will be performing actions on the currently active document, and most often you won't know which position it occupies in the array. This method is always available to get a reference to the document without searching through the array.

Argument(s)

None

Returns

Reference to active document—*object*

Example

```
my_doc = fl.getDocumentDOM();
```

invokeScreenType

`fl.invokeScreenType( name [, version] )`

Invokes ScreenType

Description
Invokes the specified screen type and version

Argument(s)
name—*string*—The name of the screen type

version—*string*—The version of the screen type

Returns
screenType object if successful, otherwise undefined—*object*

Example
```
s = fl.invokeScreenType("Form", "1.0");
```

openDocument

`fl.openDocument( fileURI )`

Opens specified FLA file

Description
Creates a new document object by opening the FLA file specified in the file URI. Can be used in conjunction with `fl.browseForFileURL()`. The newly opened document will appear as the top document in the authoring environment and will be the current document (accessible immediately by `fl.getDocumentDOM()`).

Argument(s)
fileURI—*URI string*—A valid URI to a FLA file

Returns
Reference to the document object created—*object*

Example
```
file = fl.browseForFileURL("open");
fl.openDocument(file);
```

quit

`fl.quit( [bPromptIfNeeded] )`

Quits Flash

Description
Quits Flash, exiting the program. Useful for scripting JSFL from outside of the authoring environment, such as from the command line. Executing a JSFL file will start Flash, and this command can be used to close it when done.

Argument(s)
bPromptIfNeeded—*Boolean*—If `true`, if any open documents haven't been saved or have been changed since their last save, the user will be prompted to save changes. If `false`, Flash will immediately exit, discarding any changes to any open documents.

Returns
Value—*type*

Example
```
fl.quit(true);
```

reloadEffects

`fl.reloadEffects()`

Reloads all effects descriptors

Description
Reloads the Timeline Effect files, updating any changes that have been made to them since Flash started. When Flash starts up, it reads the XML files that describe the installed Timeline Effects. These are located in the `Effects` folder in the `Configuration` folder. While developing effects, you will need to either reload the effects or restart the program to have changes to these XML files be reflected in the Timeline Effects menu.

Argument(s)
None

Returns
Nothing

Example
```
// Create the following one-line JSFL
// file and put it in your Commands
// folder. This will allow you to
// instantly reload the effects as you
// are developing them.
fl.reloadEffects();
```

reloadTools

`fl.reloadTools()`

Rebuilds toolbar

Description

Reloads the toolbar, updating any changes that have been made to them since Flash started. When Flash starts up, it reads and executes any JSFL files in the `Tools` folder in the `Configuration` folder. In addition, it will execute the `configureTool` function in any of those files. While developing tools, you will need to either reload the tools, restart the program, or make changes in the Customize Tools panel to have changes to these files be reflected in the toolbar.

Argument(s)

None

Returns

Nothing

Example

```
// Create the following one-line JSFL
// file and put it in your Commands
// folder. This will allow you to
// instantly reload the effects as you
// are developing them.
fl.reloadTools();
```

revertDocument

`fl.revertDocument(` *`documentObject`* `)`

Reverts specified document

Description

Reverts the specified document to its last saved state. Note that in the authoring environment, choosing Revert Document from the Files menu will warn you that changes will be lost. This command gives no such warning, and instantly reverts the document.

Argument(s)

`documentObject`—*object*—The document you want to revert

Returns

`true` if successful, `false` otherwise—*Boolean*

Example

```
fl.revertDocument(my_doc);
```

runScript

`fl.runScript(` *`fileURI`* `[,` *`funcName`*`]`
`➥ [,` *`arg`*`] )`

Executes JavaScript file

Description

Executes an external JSFL file and/or function therein. Arguments can be passed to the function. First, Flash will execute the entire file linearly as if it were a command. Function declarations will be processed, but the functions won't be executed unless called by other statements within the script. Then, if a function name is given, it will execute that function, passing any arguments to it. Thus, if you are creating an external file containing functions to be called, be sure not to include any statements not inside of functions, as they will be executed along with any function you call.

Argument(s)

`fileURI`—*URI string*—The location of the JSFL file to execute. Must be a valid URI.

`funcName`—*string*—The name of a function in the specified JSFL file. This function will be executed in addition to any statements in the file that aren't contained in functions.

`arg`—*Any type*—Data that will be passed to the named function as an argument. Additional arguments may be included, separated by commas.

Returns

Value—*type*

Example

```
fl.runScript("file:///c:/myScript.jsfl",
➥ "myFunction");
```

saveAll

`fl.saveAll()`

Saves all open documents

Description

Saves all open documents in the application using their existing name and location. For documents that haven't been previously saved, a Save As dialog box will open.

Argument(s)

None

Returns
Nothing

Example
```
fl.saveAll();
```

saveDocument

`fl.saveDocument( document [, fileURI] )`

Saves specified document

Description
Saves the specified document, using its existing name, or a newly specified name. Unlike the document method save, this method will allow you to automatically save a document for the first time with a name defined in the script. Can be used in conjunction with fl.`browseForFileURL()`.

Argument(s)
`document`—*object*—The document you want to save

`fileURI`—*URI string*—A valid URI to a filename. If not specified, document will be saved under its existing name. If the document has never been saved, the Save As dialog box will appear.

Returns
Nothing

Example
```
fileName = fl.browseForFileURL("save");
fl.saveDocument(my_doc, fileName);
```

saveDocumentAs

`fl.saveDocumentAs( document )`

Displays Save As dialog box

Description
Displays the Save As dialog box to allow the user to choose a name and location to save a document. When the user chooses, the document will be saved.

Argument(s)
`document`—*object*—The document to save

Returns
Nothing

Example
```
fl.saveDocumentAs(my_doc);
```

setActiveWindow

`fl.setActiveWindow( document )`

Sets active window to be the specified document

Description
Makes the specified document the active window and currently active document. This is now what will be returned from `fl.getDocumentDOM()`.

Argument(s)
`document`—*object*—The document you want to make active. Must be a reference to another open document.

Returns
Nothing

Example
```
fl.setActiveWindow(fl.documents[0]);
my_doc = fl.getDocumentDOM();
fl.trace(my_doc.name);
fl.setActiveWindow(fl.documents[1]);
my_doc = fl.getDocumentDOM();
fl.trace(my_doc.name);
```

trace

`fl.trace( message )`

Sends a test string to Output panel

Description
Sends the specified string to the output panel

Argument(s)
`message`—*string*—Any string that you want sent to the Output panel. Can be evaluated from any expression that will return a string.

Returns
Nothing

Example
```
my_frame = fl.getDocumentDOM().
➥ timelines[0].layers[0].frames[0];
fl.trace("number of elements = " +
➥ my_frame.elements.length);
```

Properties of the flash Object

activeEffect

`fl.activeEffect`

Effect descriptor

Description

A reference to the effect currently being applied. This would most likely be used within the executeEffect() function of an effect. This holds information about the current effect. See the entry for Effect for more information.

Value(s)

object—Contains information about the effect being applied

Example

```
function executeEffect(){
  fl.trace(fl.activeEffect.effectName);
  // actions of effect
}
```

componentsPanel

`fl.componentsPanel`

Reference to Components panel

Description

A reference to the Components Panel. This would mainly be used to add components to a document using componentsPanel.addItemToDocument().

Value(s)

object—The reference to the panel

Example

```
fl.componentsPanel.addItemToDocument
➥ ({x:100, y:100}, "UI Components",
➥ "CheckBox");
```

configDirectory

`fl.configDirectory`

Contains full path name for local user's Configuration directory

Description

Holds the full path to the Flash application's Configuration directory. The path will be formatted with backslashes and may include spaces (configURI, which holds the path to the same directory, will contain forward slashes and spaces will be replaced by "%20").

Value(s)

string—The path to the Configuration directory

Example

```
fl.trace(fl.configDirectory);
```

configURI

`fl.configURI`

Returns URI to local user's Configuration directory

Description

Returns a URI string to the Configuration directory, where Tools, Commands, Behaviors, etc., are stored. This is often used as a shortcut to get into that directory where most extensibility files are stored.

Value(s)

URI string—The path to the Configuration directory

Example

```
my_doc.xmlPanel(fl.configURI +
➥ "/Commands/myPanel.xml");
```

documents

`fl.documents`

Array of document objects

Description

An array of all open documents in the authoring environment

Value(s)

array—Each element contains a reference to one document object.

Example

```
my_doc = fl.documents[0];
```

effects

`fl.effects`

Array of effect descriptors

Description
An array of effect descriptors. Each descriptor is based on an XML file. Note that a single JSFL file can be used by multiple effects using multiple XML descriptor files. Each element in the array holds information about the effect, not a reference to the effect itself. See the entry for `Effect` for more information.

Value(s)
object—Contains information about the effect

Example
```
for(i=0; i<fl.effects.length; i++){
  fl.trace(fl.effects[i].effectName);
}
```

Math

`fl.Math`

Reference to `Math` object

Description
A reference to the `Math` object. Contains various methods for manipulating matrixes and calculating points. This is different from the standard `Math` object that is directly accessible, not a property of `fl`.

Value(s)
object—The `Math` object

Example
```
// returns 100
fl.trace(fl.Math.pointDistance({x:0, y:0},
➥ {x:100, y:0}));
// returns undefined
fl.trace(Math.pointDistance({x:0, y:0},
➥ {x:100, y:0}));
// returns undefined
fl.trace(fl.Math.PI);
// returns 3.14159
fl.trace(Math.PI);
```

outputPanel

`fl.outputPanel`

Reference to Output panel object

Description
A reference to the Output panel. Mainly used for clearing the panel or saving the information traced to it. `fl.outputPanel.trace()` is the same as `fl.trace()`.

Value(s)
object—The reference to the panel

Example
```
fl.outputPanel.clear();
```

screenTypes

`fl.screenTypes`

Array of all `screenType` objects in the system

Description
An array of all the screen types in the system

Value(s)
array of all screen types—Array

Example
```
fl.trace("There are " +
➥ fl.screenTypes.length +
➥ " screen types here.");
```

tools

`fl.tools`

Object representing the tools in Flash

Description
An object representing the tools in Flash. Contains the `toolObjs` array, which is an array of all the tools available on the toolbar, plus other properties and methods for use by tools.

Value(s)
object—The reference to the `tools` object

Example
```
fl.trace(fl.tools.penLoc.x);
```

version

`fl.version`

Returns Flash authoring tool's version

Description
Returns the version of the Flash authoring tool

Value(s)
string—Represents the platform and version number of the program

Example
```
fl.trace(fl.version);
```

xmlui

`fl.xmlui`

References XML to UI dialog box

Description
A reference to the XML to UI dialog box. Intended for setting properties in the dialog box or dynamically accepting or cancelling the dialog box. However, because an XML to UI dialog box is modal, the JSFL script won't execute while it is active, thus this object is rather useless inside of a JSFL script. It is possible to use it inside control event handlers inside of an XML to UI dialog box though. An example of this appears in Chapter 7.

Value(s)
object—The reference to the dialog box

FolderItem

Subclass of `Item`; a folder in the Library. Refer to the entry for `Item` for methods and properties.

FontItem

Subclass of `Item`; a font symbol in the Library. Refer to the entry for `Item` for methods and properties.

Frame

A frame on the timeline

Properties:

- `actionScript`
- `duration`
- `elements`
- `labelType`
- `motionTweenOrientToPath`
- `motionTweenRotate`
- `motionTweenRotateTimes`
- `motionTweenScale`
- `motionTweenSnap`
- `motionTweenSync`
- `name`
- `shapeTweenBlend`
- `soundEffect`
- `soundLibraryItem`
- `soundLoop`
- `soundLoopMode`
- `soundName`
- `soundSync`
- `startFrame`
- `tweenEasing`
- `tweenType`

Properties of the frame Object

actionScript

`frame.actionScript`

String containing ActionScript on frame

Description
Contains the ActionScript code assigned to the specified frame. You can also create a string containing valid ActionScript statements and assign it to this property. That ActionScript will then be the code seen in that frame.

Value(s)

string—Any number of ActionScript statements within a string

Example

```
my_frame = fl.getDocumentDOM().
➥ timelines[0].layers[0].frames[0];
my_frame.actionScript =
➥ "my_mc._visible = false";
my_frame.actionScript += "stop();";
```

duration

`frame.duration`

Number of frames in frame span

Description

The number of frames in the sequence of frames containing the specified frame. A sequence of frames starts with a keyframe and continues until there are no more frames or another keyframe is encountered. This could contain a tween or could simply be a continuation of the keyframe. Any frame is part of a particular sequence, even if it is the only keyframe comprising that sequence. This property tells how many frames are in that sequence.

Value(s)

integer—How many frames in the particular sequence a frame falls in

Example

```
my_frame = fl.getDocumentDOM().
➥ timelines[0].layers[0].frames[0];
if(my_frame.duration == 1){
  fl.trace("I am a keyframe.");
}
```

elements

`frame.elements`

Array of element objects

Description

An array containing all the elements that exist in that frame. Note: All shape elements in the frame will be placed in a single slot in the array and are actually considered a single element. To separate individual shapes, group them or convert them to symbols. For more information on elements, see the entry for `Element`.

Value(s)

array—Contains an array element for each screen element onstage in that frame

Example

```
my_frame = fl.getDocumentDOM().
➥ timelines[0].layers[0].frames[0];
fl.trace("There are " +
➥ my_frame.elements.length +
➥ " elements in this frame.");
```

labelType

`frame.labelType`

Specifies type of frame label

Description

Specifies the type of label that is on the current frame. This can be `"none"` (no label), `"name"`, `"comment"`, or `"anchor"`. These correspond to the label types that you can set for a frame in the authoring environment. If a frame has a label, the label itself will be available in the name property of the frame. Setting the `labelType` to `"none"` will erase that name.

Value(s)

string—The type of label: `"none"`, `"name"`, `"comment"`, or `"anchor"`

Example

```
my_frame = fl.getDocumentDOM().
➥ timelines[0].layers[0].frames[0];
my_frame.labelType = "name";
my_frame.name = "stop frame";
```

motionTweenOrientToPath

`frame.motionTweenOrientToPath`

If `true`, object tweens oriented to path

Description

If the frame contains a tween in which an object is following a path, setting this property to `true` will make the object align itself in the direction of the path.

Value(s)

Boolean—`true` will cause object to align to path; `false` will not.

Example

```
my_frame = fl.getDocumentDOM().
➥ timelines[0].layers[0].frames[0];
my_frame.motionTweenOrientToPath = true;
```

motionTweenRotate

`frame.motionTweenRotate`

Specifies if object rotates during tween

Description

Specifies how or if the tweened object in the frame will rotate during the tween

Value(s)

string—Valid values are "none", "auto", "clockwise", and "counter-clockwise"

Example

```
my_frame = fl.getDocumentDOM().
➥ timelines[0].layers[0].frames[0];
my_frame.motionTweenRotate = "clockwise";
```

motionTweenRotateTimes

`frame.motionTweenRotate`

Times number of rotations

Description

Specifies how many times the tweened object in the frame will rotate over the duration of the tween

Value(s)

integer—Number of rotations

Example

```
my_frame = fl.getDocumentDOM().
➥ timelines[0].layers[0].frames[0];
my_frame.motionTweenRotateTimes = 5;
```

motionTweenScale

`frame.motionTweenScale`

If true, object scales while tweening.

Description

Determines if the object in the frame will change size during the tween

Value(s)

Boolean—true means it will scale; false means it won't.

Example

```
my_frame = fl.getDocumentDOM().
➥ timelines[0].layers[0].frames[0];
my_frame.motionTweenScale = false;
```

motionTweenSnap

`frame.motionTweenSnap`

If true, object snaps to motion guide.

Description

Determines if the object in the frame will snap to the guide during the tween.

Value(s)

Boolean—true means it will snap; false means it will not.

Example

```
my_frame = fl.getDocumentDOM().
➥ timelines[0].layers[0].frames[0];
my_frame.motionTweenSnap = false;
```

motionTweenSync

`frame.motionTweenSync`

If true, tween synchronizes symbols.

Description

Determines if the tweened frames in a symbol will synchronize to the parent timeline. Used to ensure the animation loops correctly.

Value(s)

Boolean—true will synchronize the symbols; false will not.

Example

```
my_frame = fl.getDocumentDOM().
➥ timelines[0].layers[0].frames[0];
my_frame.motionTweenSync = true;
```

name

`frame.name`

Label of frame

Description

The text contained in the label of the frame

Value(s)

string—The label name of the frame

Example

```
my_frame = fl.getDocumentDOM().
➥ timelines[0].layers[0].frames[0];
my_frame.name = "start";
```

shapeTweenBlend

`frame.shapeTweenBlend`

Specifies blend setting for a shape tween

Description

Determines the method for calculating a shape tween

Value(s)

string—Valid values are "distributive" and "angular"

Example

```
my_frame = fl.getDocumentDOM().
➥ timelines[0].layers[0].frames[0];
my_frame.shapeTweenBlend = "angular";
```

soundEffect

`frame.soundEffect`

Effects on the sound

Description

Specifies the effect to be used on any sound attached to the frame

Value(s)

string—Valid values are "none", "left channel", "right channel", "fade left to right", "fade right to left", "fade in", "fade out", and "custom".

Example

```
my_frame = fl.getDocumentDOM().
➥ timelines[0].layers[0].frames[0];
my_frame.soundEffect = "fade left to right";
```

soundLibraryItem

`frame.soundLibraryItem`

Library item used to instantiate a sound

Description

Specifies the sound item in the Library to be attached to this frame

Value(s)

object—The reference to the Library item containing a sound

Example

```
my_frame = fl.getDocumentDOM().
➥ timelines[0].layers[0].frames[0];
fl.trace(my_frame.soundLibraryItem.name);
```

soundLoop

`frame.soundLoop`

Specifies number of times a sound loops

Description

Specifies the number of times a sound attached to the frame will play

Value(s)

integer—The number of loops

Example

```
my_frame = fl.getDocumentDOM().
➥ timelines[0].layers[0].frames[0];
my_frame.soundLoop = 999;
```

soundLoopMode

`frame.soundLoopMode`

Specifies whether sound should loop or repeat indefinitely

Description

Specifies how the frame sound will repeat

Value(s)

string—"repeat" will cause the sound to repeat indefinitely. "loop" will cause it to play the number of times specified in soundLoop.

Example

```
my_frame = fl.getDocumentDOM().
➥ timelines[0].layers[0].frames[0];
my_frame.soundLoopMode = "loop";
```

soundName

`frame.soundName`

Name of sound

Description

The name of the sound attached to this frame

Value(s)

string—The sound's name

Example

```
my_frame = fl.getDocumentDOM().
➥ timelines[0].layers[0].frames[0];
fl.trace(my_frame.soundName);
```

soundSync

`frame.soundSync`

Specifies sync behavior of sound

Description

Specifies how the sound will synchronize to the frames in the movie

Value(s)

string—Valid values are `"event"`, `"stop"`, `"start"`, and `"stream"`. These correspond to settings in the authoring environment.

Example

```
my_frame = fl.getDocumentDOM().
➥ timelines[0].layers[0].frames[0];
my_frame.soundSync = "stream";
```

startFrame

`frame.startFrame`

Frame number of first frame in span

Description

The first frame in the sequence of frames containing the specified frame. A sequence of frames starts with a keyframe and continues until there are no more frames or another keyframe is encountered. This could contain a tween or could simply be a continuation of the keyframe. Any frame is part of a particular sequence, even if it is the only keyframe comprising that sequence. This property indicates the keyframe that begins that sequence.

Value(s)

integer—The frame number of the keyframe beginning a frame sequence.

Example

```
my_tl = fl.getDocumentDOM().getTimeline();
my_frame = my_tl.layers[0].frames[0];
if(my_frame.startFrame ==
➥ my_tl.currentFrame){
  fl.trace("I am a keyframe.");
}
```

tweenEasing

`frame.tweenEasing`

Amount of easing

Description

The amount of easing to be used in the tween of which this frame is a part

Value(s)

integer—Valid values are from –100 to +100.

Example

```
my_frame = fl.getDocumentDOM().
➥ timelines[0].layers[0].frames[0];
my_frame.tweenEasing = 93;
```

tweenType

`frame.tweenType`

Type of tween

Description

The type of tween to be performed on the current frame sequence. This can be used to retrieve the type of tween that exists, or to create a tween. Usually, `timeline.createMotionTween()` would be used to create a motion tween.

Value(s)

string—Valid values are `"motion"` and `"shape"`.

Example

```
my_frame = fl.getDocumentDOM().
➥ timelines[0].layers[0].frames[0];
my_frame.tweenType = "shape";
```

HalfEdge

Indicates half of an edge of a contour

Methods:

- getEdge
- getNext
- getOppositeHalfEdge
- getPrev
- getVertex

Properties:

- id

Methods of the halfEdge Object

getEdge

halfEdge.getEdge()

Returns edge object that contains halfEdge

Description
Returns a reference to the edge object that contains the halfEdge

Argument(s)
None

Returns
Edge containing halfEdge—*edge object*

Example

```
var my_halfEdge = fl.getDocumentDOM().
➥ selection[0].contours[0].getHalfEdge();
fl.trace(my_halfEdge.getEdge().id);
```

getNext

halfEdge.getNext()

Returns next halfEdge

Description
Returns the next halfEdge on the current contour

Argument(s)
None

Returns
Next halfEdge in sequence—*HalfEdge instance*

Example

```
var firstHalfEdge = fl.getDocumentDOM().
➥ selection[0].contours[0].getHalfEdge();
var nextHalfEdge = firstHalfEdge.getNext();
```

getOppositeHalfEdge

halfEdge.getOppositeHalfEdge()

Returns opposite halfEdge object

Description
Returns the halfEdge object on the neighboring contour

Argument(s)
None

Returns
Neighboring halfEdge—*HalfEdge instance*

Example

```
var firstHalfEdge = fl.getDocumentDOM().
➥ selection[0].contours[0].getHalfEdge();
var oppHalfEdge = firstHalfEdge.
➥ getOppositeHalfEdge();
```

getPrev

halfEdge.getPrev()

Returns previous halfEdge

Description
Returns the previous halfEdge on the current contour

Argument(s)
None

Returns

Previous halfEdge in sequence—*HalfEdge instance*

Example

```
var firstHalfEdge = fl.getDocumentDOM().
➥ selection[0].edges[0].getHalfEdge(1);
var prevHalfEdge = firstHalfEdge.getPrev();
```

getVertex

halfEdge.getVertex()

Returns vertex of the halfEdge

Description

Returns a point object with x and y properties representing the vertex at the head of the halfEdge

Argument(s)

None

Returns

Vertex—*point object*

Example

```
var my_halfEdge = fl.getDocumentDOM().
➥ selection[0].edges[0].getHalfEdge(1);
var my_vertex = my_halfEdge.getVertex();
fl.trace(my_vertex.x);
fl.trace(my_vertex.y);
```

Properties of the halfEdge Object

id

halfEdge.id

Unique identifier for halfEdge

Description

A unique identifier for the halfEdge object that can be useful when keeping track of halfEdges as a shape changes

Value(s)

integer—Unique identifier

Example

```
var id = fl.getDocumentDOM().selection[0].
➥ contours[0].getHalfEdge().id;
```

Instance

Subclass of Element. Represents an instance on the stage.

Properties:

- instanceType
- LibraryItem

Properties of the instance Object

instanceType

instance.instanceType

Type of instance

Description

The type of instance on the stage. Values can include "bitmap", "compiled clip", "embedded video", "linked video", and "symbol". This property may be retrieved, but not set.

Value(s)

string—"bitmap", "compiled clip", "embedded video", "linked video", or "symbol"

Example

```
var my_elem = fl.getDocumentDOM().
➥ getTimeline().layers[0].frames[0].
➥ elements[0];
if (my_elem.instanceType == "symbol") {
  fl.trace(my_elem.symbolType);
}
```

libraryItem

instance.libraryItem

Library item used to instantiate instance

Description

The Library item that the instance is derived from. This property holds a reference to the item in the Library and may be both retrieved and set. Setting a new item to this property effectively swaps one symbol for another (similar to using fl.getDocumentDOM().swapElement() except this command can work with unselected symbols and uses a reference to the item as opposed to the item's name).

Value(s)
Item object—Library item

Example
```
var my_elem = fl.getDocumentDOM().
➥ selection[0];
var my_lib = fl.getDocumentDOM().library;
var my_item = my_lib.findItemIndex
➥ ("newSymbol");
my_elem.libraryItem =
➥ my_lib.items[my_item];
```

Item

Items in the Library

Methods:

- addData
- getData
- hasData
- removeData

Properties:

- itemType
- linkageClassName
- linkageExportForAS
- linkageExportForRS
- linkageExportInFirstFrame
- linkageIdentifier
- linkageImportForRS
- linkageURL
- name

Methods of the item Object

addData

item.addData(*name*, *type*, *data*)

Adds persistent data to item

Description
Used to add user data to an item in the Library that will remain when the document is closed and reopened

Argument(s)
name—*string*—The name of the data to set

type—*string*—The type of the data being set, "string", "integer", "integerArray", "double", "doubleArray", or "byteArray"

data—*Varies depending on type*—The value for the data

Returns
Nothing

Example
```
fl.getDocumentDOM().library.items[0].
➥ addData("creator", "string", "Todd Yard");
fl.getDocumentDOM().library.items[0].
➥ addData("version", "double", 1.1);
```

getData

item.getData(*name*)

Returns value of named data

Description
Retrieves the user-defined data from the Library item. If data was never set, 0 is returned.

Argument(s)
name—*string*—The name of the data that was previously set

Returns
Value of specified data or 0 if data undefined—*Boolean*

Example
```
var version = fl.getDocumentDOM().
➥ library.items[0].getData("version");
```

hasData

item.hasData(*name*)

If true, Library item has named data

Description
Returns true or false whether the Library item has data of the name sent in the argument

Argument(s)
name—*string*—The name of the data to check

Returns
true if data has been defined on the item—*Boolean*

Example
```
var my_item = fl.getDocumentDOM().
➥ library.items[0];
if (!my_item.hasData("version") {;
my_item.addData("version", "double", 1.0);
} else {
var v = my_item.getData("version");
my_item.addData("version", "double",
➥ v + 0.1);
}
```

removeData

`item.removeData( name )`

Removes persistent data from Library item

Description
Removes the persistent data specified in the argument from the Library item

Argument(s)
name—*string*—The name of the data to remove

Returns
Nothing

Example
```
fl.getDocumentDOM().library.items[0].
➥ removeData("version");
```

Properties of the item Object

itemType

`item.itemType`

Symbol type of item

Description
The type of Library item. This property may be retrieved, but not set.

Value(s)
string—"movie clip", "button", "graphic", "component", "video", "sound", "font", "bitmap", "folder", or "undefined"

Example
```
fl.trace(fl.getDocumentDOM().library.
➥ items[0].itemType);
```

linkageClassName

`item.linkageClassName`

Specifies ActionScript 2 class to associate with symbol

Description
The name of the class the symbol is associated with. AS 2 classes are established in external files. Paths to these files are set in the Publish Profile or Edit ➤ Preferences. To set a class, either linkageExportForAS or linkageExportForRS (or both) must be set to true. linkageImportForRS must be false.

Value(s)
string—The name of the class

Example
```
fl.getDocumentDOM().library.items[0].
➥ linkageClassName = "MouseFollower";
fl.getDocumentDOM().library.items[0].
➥ linkageClassName = "Flash3D.Model";
```

linkageExportForAS

`item.linkageExportForAS`

If true, item will be exported for ActionScript.

Description
Determines whether an item is exported for use with ActionScript and is false by default. linkageImportForRS must be set to false (which it is by default) before this may be set to true. The linkageIdentifer of the item is automatically set to its name. If another item exists that already is being exported with the item's name, an error is thrown stating a unique identifier must be specified and the operation fails.

Value(s)
Boolean—true, false

Example
```
fl.getDocumentDOM().library.items[0].
➥ linkageExportForAS = true;
```

linkageExportForRS

`item.linkageExportForRS`

If `true`, item will be exported for runtime sharing.

Description
Determines whether an item is exported for runtime sharing and is `false` by default. This property can only be set to `true` if `linkageImportForRS` is first set to `false`. As with `linkageExportForAS`, if this property is set to `true`, `linkageIdentifier` is automatically set to equal the item's name. If such an identifier already exists, the operation fails and an error is thrown.

Value(s)
Boolean—`true`, `false`

Example
```
fl.getDocumentDOM().library.items[0].
➥ linkageExportForRS = true;
```

linkageExportInFirstFrame

`item.linkageExportInFirstFrame`

If `true`, item will be exported in the first frame.

Description
Determines whether an item is exported in the first frame of the movie (`true`), meaning it must load before the first frame is rendered but then may be used from the first frame on. This property may only be set if either `linkageExportForAS` or `linkageExportForRS` are set to `true`.

Value(s)
Boolean—`true`, `false` (default)

Example
```
fl.getDocumentDOM().library.items[0].
➥ linkageExportInFirstFrame = true;
```

linkageIdentifier

`item.linkageIdentifier`

Name of symbol when referenced by ActionScript or runtime sharing

Description
The unique identifier for the item as it will be referenced in the movie's ActionScript or for runtime sharing. This can only be set if `linkageExportForAS` or `linkageExportForRS` are set to `true`.

Value(s)
string—Unique identifier

Example
```
fl.getDocumentDOM().library.items[0].
➥ linkageIdentifier = "expLogo";
```

linkageImportForRS

`item.linkageImportForRS`

If `true`, item will be imported for runtime sharing.

Description
Determines whether an item is imported from an external movie (`false` by default). If set to `true`, `linkageExportForRS` and `linkageExportForAS` must both first be set to `false`. `linkageIdentifier` is automatically set to equal the item's name, though a `linkageURL` must be set.

Value(s)
Boolean—`true`, `false`

Example
```
fl.getDocumentDOM().library.items[0].
➥ linkageImportForRS = true;
fl.getDocumentDOM().library.items[0].
➥ linkageURL = "external.swf";
```

linkageURL

`item.linkageURL`

Location of shared asset SWF

Description
The location of the SWF file containing the item to be imported for runtime sharing. This property must be set if `linkageImportForRS`has been set to `true`.

Value(s)
string—The path or address of the SWF

Example
```
fl.getDocumentDOM().library.items[0].
➥ linkageImportForRS = true;
```

```
fl.getDocumentDOM().library.items[0].
➥ linkageURL =
➥ "http://mySite.com/libraries/external.swf";
```

name

`item.name`

Name of Library item

Description
The name of the Library item

Value(s)
string—Name

Example
```
fl.trace(fl.getDocumentDOM().library.
➥ items[0].name);
fl.getDocumentDOM().library.items[0].
➥ name = "changedName";
```

Layer

A layer on the timeline

Properties:

- color
- frameCount
- frames
- height
- layerType
- locked
- name
- outline
- parentLayer
- visible

Properties of the layer Object

color

`layer.color`

Color used to outline objects on layer

Description
The color used as an outline if outlines are selected for the specified layer

Value(s)
integer or string—The color as a string (#rrggbb) or base10 or hex integer (0 to 16777216 or 0xrrggbb).

Example
```
my_layer = fl.getDocumentDOM().
➥ getTimeline().layers[0];
my_layer.color = 0xff0000;
```

frameCount

`layer.frameCount`

Total number of frames in layer

Description
The total number of frames in this layer. Equivalent to `layer.frames.length`.

Value(s)
integer—The number of frames

Example
```
my_layer = fl.getDocumentDOM().
➥ getTimeline().layers[0];
for(f=0; f<my_layer.frameCount; f++){
  my_frame = my_layer.frames[f];
  // process the frame
}
```

frames

`layer.frames`

Array of frame objects

Description
An array containing one element for each frame in the layer

Value(s)
array—Each element containing a `frame` object

Example
```
my_layer = fl.getDocumentDOM().
➥ getTimeline().layers[0];
for(f=0; f<my_layer.frameCount; f++){
  my_frame = my_layer.frames[f];
```

```
    // process the frame
}
```

height

`layer.height`

Height of layer

Description
Specifies a larger height for the layer as seen in the Timeline panel

Value(s)
integer—Valid values are 100, 200, or 300, representing percentage of default layer height

Example
```
my_layer = fl.getDocumentDOM().
➥ getTimeline().layers[0];
my_layer.height = 300;
```

layerType

`layer.layerType`

Specifies layer type

Description
Specifies the type of the layer. Note that a "masked" layer must be positioned under a "mask" layer to work as expected. Use `timeline.reorderLayer()` to change the position of a layer. Multiple "masked" layers positioned under a single "mask" layer will be masked by that layer. Also, if a layer is under a "mask" layer and the "mask" layer is set as its `parentLayer`, it will become a "masked" layer. All of the above also applies to "guide" and "guided" layers.

Value(s)
string—Valid values are `"normal"`, `"guide"`, `"guided"`, `"mask"`, `"masked"`, and `"folder"`.

Example
```
my_tl = fl.getDocumentDOM().getTimeline();
my_tl.layers[0].layerType = "mask";
my_tl.layers[1].layerType = "masked";
```

locked

`layer.locked`

If `true`, layer is locked.

Description
Locks or unlocks the layer, or reports locked condition of the layer

Value(s)
Boolean—`true` indicates layer is locked; `false` indicates it is not.

Example
```
my_layer = fl.getDocumentDOM().
➥ getTimeline().layers[0];
my_layer.locked = true;
```

name

`layer.name`

Name of layer

Description
The name of the layer as it appears in the timeline panel

Value(s)
string—The name of the layer

Example
```
my_layer = fl.getDocumentDOM().
➥ getTimeline().layers[0];
my_layer.name = "Harry";
```

outline

`layer.outline`

If `true`, layer is displayed as outlines.

Description
Specifies whether layer content or only outlines of content will be seen on the stage

Value(s)
Boolean—`true` indicates only outlines will be displayed; `false` will display all content.

Example
```
my_layer = fl.getDocumentDOM().
➥ getTimeline().layers[0];
my_layer.outline = true;
```

parentLayer

`layer.parentLayer`

Defines layer's parent layer

Description
Sets or returns the parent layer of the layer. A parent layer must be of layerType "mask" or "guide" and must be located above the specified layer. See the entries `layer.layerType` and `timeline.reorderLayer()` for more information.

Value(s)
object—The reference to the layer's parent layer

Example
```
my_tl = fl.getDocumentDOM().getTimeline();
my_tl.layers[0].layerType = "mask";
my_tl.layers[1].parentLayer = my_tl.layers[0];
```

visible

`layer.visible`

If `true`, layer is visible.

Description
Specifies whether or not a layer will be visible in the authoring environment. Has no effect in a published movie.

Value(s)
Boolean—`true` if visible, `false` if not

Example
```
my_layer = fl.getDocumentDOM().
➥ getTimeline().layers[0];
my_layer.visible = false;
```

Library

Object for the Library panel

Methods:

- `addItemToDocument`
- `addNewItem`
- `deleteItem`
- `duplicateItem`
- `editItem`
- `expandFolder`
- `findItemIndex`
- `getItemProperty`
- `getItemType`
- `getSelectedItems`
- `importEmbeddedSWF`
- `itemExists`
- `moveToFolder`
- `newFolder`
- `renameItem`
- `selectAll`
- `selectItem`
- `selectNone`
- `setItemProperty`
- `updateItem`

Properties:

- `items`

Methods of the library Object

addItemToDocument

`library.addItemToDocument(` *`position`*
`➥ [,` *`namePath`*`] )`

Adds item from Library to document

Description
Adds either the specified or, if not specified, the selected Library item to the document at the given position. The center of the instance will be placed at the coordinate position, not the symbol's registration point.

Argument(s)
`position`—*point object*—An object consisting of `x` and `y` properties representing a coordinate position on the stage

`namePath`—*string*—The Library path to the item to be added, including all parent folders holding the item

Returns
Nothing

Example

```
// adds currently selected Library
// item to document
fl.getDocumentDOM().library.
➥ addItemToDocument({x:50, y:50});
// adds library item "logo" located in
// "branding" folder to document
fl.getDocumentDOM().library.
➥ addItemToDocument({x:50, y:50},
➥ "branding/logo");
```

addNewItem

`library.addNewItem( type [, namePath] )`

Creates new item

Description

Creates and selects a new item in the document's Library of the type specified in the first argument, "video", "movieclip" or "movie clip", "button", "graphic", "bitmap", or "folder". Supplying a namePath argument will create a symbol of the specified name within the specified folder (if any folder is indicated). Specifying nonexistent folders in the path will automatically cause them to be created. If no name is specified, the new symbol will be given a default name ("Symbol *N*" for buttons, graphics, and movie clips; "Embedded Video *N*" for video; "Bitmap *N*" for bitmaps; and "untitled folder *N*" for folders).

Argument(s)

type—*string*—The type of symbol to be added to the Library, "video", "movieclip" or "movie clip", "button", "graphic", "bitmap", or "folder"

namePath—*string*—The Library path, including all parent folders, where symbol should be added

Returns

true if symbol was successfully added—*Boolean*

Example

```
fl.getDocumentDOM().library.addNewItem
➥ ("movieclip");
fl.getDocumentDOM().library.addNewItem
➥ ("movie clip", "new clip");
fl.getDocumentDOM().library.addNewItem
➥ ("graphic", "myFolder/myGraphic");
fl.getDocumentDOM().library.addNewItem
➥ ("video", "topFolder/subFolder/newVideo");
fl.getDocumentDOM().library.addNewItem
➥ ("folder", "someFolder");
```

deleteItem

`library.deleteItem( [namePath] )`

Deletes item or items from Library

Description

Deletes the specified items from the document's Library, or the selected item or items if no argument is passed. Deleting a folder will delete all items and folders within it. If multiple items in the Library are selected and no argument is passed, all selected items will be deleted. Therefore to delete all items, first select them all before calling deleteItem.

Argument(s)

namePath—*string*—The Library path, including all parent folders, of the symbol that should be deleted

Returns

true if item successfully deleted—*Boolean*

Example

```
// deletes selected item or items in library
fl.getDocumentDOM().library.deleteItem();
// deletes item "logo" in folder "branding"
fl.getDocumentDOM().library.
➥ deleteItem("branding/logo");
// deletes all items in library
var my_lib = fl.getDocumentDOM().library;
my_lib.selectAll();
my_lib.deleteItem();
```

duplicateItem

`library.duplicateItem( [namePath] )`

Makes copy of currently selected item

Description

Duplicates the specified or, if not specified, the currently selected Library item, which can be a movie clip, button, or graphic (or master symbol). The new symbol takes its name from the master symbol, with "copy" appended, or "copy *N*", with *N* representing the number of copy the new symbol represents. The new symbol is placed in the same folder as the master symbol and its index in the Library's items array is one higher than the master symbol (which means every symbol following the new symbol in the items array has its index offset by one). Folders, video, fonts, and bitmaps may not be duplicated. If multiple items are selected in the Library and no namePath is given, the operation fails.

Argument(s)

namePath—*string*—The Library path, including all parent folders, to the symbol to be duplicated

Returns

true if new symbol was successfully created—*Boolean*

Example

```
// duplicates current selection in Library
fl.getDocumentDOM().library.
➥ duplicateItem();
// duplicates symbol "logo" in folder
// "branding", then changes the new
// symbol's name
var my_lib = fl.getDocumentDOM().library;
my_lib.duplicateItem("branding/logo");
var i = my_lib.findItemIndex
➥ ("branding/logo copy");
my_lib.items[i].name = "copied logo";
```

editItem

`library.editItem( [namePath] )`

Enters edit mode for specified item

Description

Enters edit symbol mode for the specified symbol. If the symbol isn't editable or doesn't exist, the main timeline is displayed for editing. Although true is returned if the symbol is editable, true is also returned if the symbol isn't editable and the main timeline isn't currently displayed (i.e., the user is in edit mode for a symbol in the Library); false is only returned when the symbol isn't editable and main timeline is currently displayed for editing.

Argument(s)

namePath—*string*—The Library path, including all parent folders, to the symbol to be edited

Returns

true if symbol is editable or if main timeline isn't currently displayed—*Boolean*

Example

```
// enters editing mode for currently
// selected symbol. If multiple symbols
// selected or selected symbol is not
// editable, operation fails.
fl.getDocumentDOM().library.editItem();
// edits "logo" symbol in "branding" folder
fl.getDocumentDOM().library.
➥ editItem("branding/logo");
```

expandFolder

```
library.expandFolder( bExpand
➥ [, bRecurseNestedParents] [, namePath] )
```

If true, expands folder; if false, collapses it.

Description

Expands or collapses the specified or, if not specified using the namePath argument, selected folder. If bExpand is set to true, then all subfolders of the specified or selected folder will also expand or collapse based on first argument. If no namePath argument is passed and the currently selected Library item isn't a folder, this operation fails.

Argument(s)

bExpand—*Boolean*—true to expand folder, false to collapse it.

bRecursiveNestedParents—*Boolean*—true for all subfolders of specified folder to expand or collapse as well, based on first argument; if false, command only affects specified folder.

namePath—*string*—Path in the Library, including all parent folders, of folder to be affected.

Returns

true if specified or selected item is a folder—*Boolean*

Example

```
// expands selected folder in library
fl.getDocumentDOM().library.
➥ expandFolder(1);
// closes selected folder and all of
// its nested folders
fl.getDocumentDOM().library.
➥ expandFolder(0, 1);
// expands selected folder, but leaves
// nested folders as they are
fl.getDocumentDOM().library.
➥ expandFolder(1, 0);
// expands the folder "myFolder"
// and all of its nested folders
fl.getDocumentDOM().library.
➥ expandFolder(1, 1, "myFolder");
// collapses the folder "mySubFolder"
// within "myFolder", leaving its nested
// folders alone
fl.getDocumentDOM().library.
➥ expandFolder(0, 0, "myFolder/mySubFolder");
```

findItemIndex

`library.findItemIndex( namePath )`

Returns array containing index of item

Description

Returns an array of indices in the Library's items array for the items specified. Since only one parameter may be sent and since Library items of the same name can't coexist within the same folder, this method inevitably returns an array of a single index.Even though an array is returned, it can be as an integer to access a reference item in the Library's items array. If no path is specified, this method fails.

Argument(s)

namePath—*string*—Path in the Library, including all parent folders, to the item in the Library

Returns

Array of item indices—*array*

Example

```
fl.getDocumentDOM().library.
➥ findItemIndex("logo");
var my_lib = fl.getDocumentDOM().library;
var i = my_lib.
➥ findItemIndex("branding/logo");
var my_item = my_lib.items[i];
my_item.name = "logo 2";
```

getItemProperty

`library.getItemProperty( property )`

Returns specified property for selected item

Description

Returns the value for the specified property of the selected Library item. The property may be any property of the item object or its relevant subclasses—BitmapItem, SoundItem, and SymbolItem—depending on the item's type. If multiple items are selected, the method returns values for the first selected item it finds in its items array.

Argument(s)

property—*string*—The name of the property to be retrieved

Returns

Property value—*Varies based on property specified*

Example

```
// checks type of selected item,
// then, if a movie clip, exports the item
// with an identifer to match its name
var my_lib = fl.getDocumentDOM().library;
var nm = my_lib.getItemProperty("name");
var t = my_lib.getItemProperty("itemType");
if (t == "movie clip") {
  var my_item =
➥ my_lib.items[my_lib.findItemIndex(nm)];
  my_item.linkageExportForAS = true;
  my_item.linkageExportInFirstFrame = true;
  my_item.linkageIdentifier = nm;
}
```

getItemType

`library.getItemType( [namePath] )`

Returns type of specified item

Description

Returns the itemType of the specified item, which can have the value of "movie clip", "graphic", "button", "folder", "font", "video", "sound", "bitmap", "component", or "undefined". If no path is specified, this method will return the type of the currently selected item in the Library. If multiple items are selected when this method is called and no argument is passed, an error is thrown.

Argument(s)

namePath—*string*—The full path, including parent folders, of item in the Library

Returns

itemType of item—*string*

Example

```
// checks item type of "logo"
// in folder "branding"
alert(fl.getDocumentDOM().library.
➥ getItemType('branding/logo'));
// checks type of selected item,
// then, if a movie clip, exports the item
// with an identifer to match its name
var my_lib = fl.getDocumentDOM().library;
var nm = my_lib.getItemProperty("name");
if (my_lib.getItemType() == "movie clip") {
  var my_item =
➥ my_lib.items[my_lib.findItemIndex(nm)];
  my_item.linkageExportForAS = true;
  my_item.linkageExportInFirstFrame = true;
  my_item.linkageIdentifier = nm;
}
```

getSelectedItems

`library.getSelectedItems()`

Returns array containing selected items

Description
Returns an array populated with all currently selected items in the Library. This array holds references to the items, so it may be used to get information or manipulate the items.

Argument(s)
None

Returns
Array of selected items—*array*

Example
```
// traces all properties of currently
// selected items
var itms = fl.getDocumentDOM().
➥ library.getSelectedItems();
for (var i in itms) {
  fl.trace("________________");
  var my_item = itms[i];
  for (var j in my_item) {
    fl.trace(j + ": " + my_item[j]);
  }
}
```

importEmbeddedSWF

`library.importEmbeddedSWF( linkageName,`
`➥ swfData [, libName] )`

Imports contained SWF to Library

Description
Imports binary SWF data into document and embeds it in the Library as a compiled clip. This method is only significant with an external library or DLL.

Argument(s)
`linkageName`—*string*—The linkage identifier of the Library item once imported.

`swfData`—*array*—An array of binary SWF data.

`libName`—*string*—The name for the Library item once imported; this argument is optional, and if the name is not given or already exists, Flash will give the item an alternative name.

Returns
Nothing

Example
```
fl.getDocumentDOM().library.
➥ importEmbeddedSWF("newItem", itemData,
➥ "newItem");
```

itemExists

`library.itemExists( namePath )`

Returns `true` if specified item exists

Description
Returns `true` or `false` indicating whether the specified item exists in the Library

Argument(s)
`namePath`—*string*—The full path, including parent folders, of the item to check

Returns
`true` if item exists—*Boolean*

Example
```
// creates a new clip if one has
// not been created
var my_lib = fl.getDocumentDOM().library;
if (!my_lib.itemExists("logo")) {
  my_lib.addNewItem("movie clip", "logo");
}
// places symbol onstage if it exists
var my_lib = fl.getDocumentDOM().library;
if (my_lib.itemExists("logo")) {
  my_lib.
  ➥ addItemToDocument({x:0, y:0}, "logo");
}
```

moveToFolder

`library.moveToFolder( folderPath`
`➥ [, itemToMove] [, replace] )`

Moves item into folder

Description
Moves the specified item in the Library. If `folderPath` is specified as an empty string, the item is moved to top level. If no item is specified, all selected items are moved. `replace` determines whether moved items are renamed if

another item exists with the same name in the new folder; `false` (default) will cause moved items to be renamed with "copy" appended. `true` will see the moved item replace (and effectively delete) the old item.

Argument(s)

`folderPath`—*string*—The full path, including all parent folders, of the folder where the item should be moved

`itemToMove`—*string*—The full path, including all parent folders, of the item to move

`replace`—*Boolean*—Whether other items with conflicting names should be replaced with moved item

Returns

`true` if move was successful—*Boolean*

Example

```
fl.getDocumentDOM().library.
➥ moveToFolder("branding", "logo");
fl.getDocumentDOM().library.
➥ moveToFolder("", "logo", 1);
fl.getDocumentDOM().library.
➥ moveToFolder("branding/completed logos",
➥ "branding/color variations/green logo");
```

newFolder

`library.newFolder( [namePath] )`

Creates new folder

Description

Creates a new folder in the Library at the specified path. If no path is specified, the folder is created with default name ("untitled folder *N*") on top level.

Argument(s)

`namePath`—*string*—The full path, including parent folders, to where new folder should be created

Returns

`true` if new folder is created—*Boolean*

Example

```
fl.getDocumentDOM().library.newFolder();
fl.getDocumentDOM().library.
➥ newFolder("myFolder/subFolder");
```

renameItem

`library.renameItem( name )`

Renames selected item

Description

Renames a single selected item in the Library. If multiple items are selected, the operation fails. Slashes (/) in new name are converted to hyphens (-).

Argument(s)

`name`—*string*—The new name to be given to the selected item

Returns

`true` if item successfully renamed—*Boolean*

Example

```
fl.getDocumentDOM().library.
➥ renameItem("newLogo");
```

selectAll

`library.selectAll( [select] )`

Selects or deselects all items

Description

Selects or deselects all items in the Library based on the argument passed. If `true` or nothing is passed (default), then all items are selected.

Argument(s)

`select`—*Boolean*—Determines whether to select or deselect Library items (no argument passed defaults to `true`)

Returns

Nothing

Example

```
// selects all
fl.getDocumentDOM().library.selectAll();
// selects none
fl.getDocumentDOM().library.selectAll(0);
```

selectItem

```
library.selectItem( namePath
➥ [, bReplaceCurrentSelection] [, bSelect])
```

Selects specified item

Description

Selects or deselects the item specified in namePath based on parameters passed. By default, a newly selected item will be added to the current selection unless bReplaceCurrentSelection is set to true (default is false). The additional parameter bSelect determines whether the specified item should be selected (true by default) or deselected (false).

Argument(s)

namePath—*string*—The full path, including parent folders, of item to be selected/deselected

bReplaceCurrentSelection—*Boolean*—Whether new selection should replace current selection (true)

bSelect—*Boolean*—Whether item should be selected (true) or deselected (false)

Returns

true if item exists and was selected/deselected—*Boolean*

Example

```
// adds logo to selection
fl.getDocumentDOM().library.
➥ selectItem("logo");
// replaces selection with logo
fl.getDocumentDOM().library.
➥ selectItem("logo", 1);
// deselects logo, but leaves rest of selection
fl.getDocumentDOM().library.
➥ selectItem("logo", 0, 0);
// deselects all in library
fl.getDocumentDOM().library.
➥ selectItem("logo", 1, 0);
```

selectNone

library.selectNone()

Deselects all items

Description

Deselects all items in the Library

Argument(s)

None

Returns

Nothing

Example

```
fl.getDocumentDOM().library.selectNone();
```

setItemProperty

library.setItemProperty(*property*, *value*)

Sets specified property for currently selected items

Description

Sets the item property for selected items in the Library. For the "name" property on a multiple selection, the operation throws an error after the first item's name is changed since conflicting names can't exist. "type" and "itemType" may not be set with this method.

Argument(s)

property—*string*—The name of the item property to set

value—*varies depending on property*—The value to be set for the property

Returns

Nothing

Example

```
fl.getDocumentDOM().library.
➥ setItemProperty("name", "myClip");
fl.getDocumentDOM().library.
➥ setItemProperty("linkageExportForAS",
➥ true);
```

updateItem

library.updateItem([*namePath*])

Updates specified item

Description

Updates the specified item in the Library or, if no item is specified, the selected item in the Library

Argument(s)

namePath—*string*—The name of the Library item

Returns

true if at least one item was updated successfully—*Boolean*

Example

```
fl.getDocumentDOM().library.selectAll();
fl.getDocumentDOM().library.updateItem();
```

Properties of the library Object

items

`library.items`

Array containing all `item` objects in Library

Description
An array holding references to all `item` objects that exist in the Library. Array may be accessed, but not altered directly.

Value(s)
array—Item references

Example
```
//. traces names of all clips in library
var my_lib = fl.getDocumentDOM().library;
var n = my_lib.items.length;
for (var i = 0; i < n; i++) {
fl.trace(my_lib.items[i].name);
}
```

LinkedVideoInstance

Subclass of `Instance`; a linked video instance on the stage. Refer to the entry for `Instance` for properties.

Math

Used to do common mathematical operations

Methods:

- `concatMatrix`
- `invertMatrix`
- `pointDistance`

Note: This `Math` object is a property of the `fl` (or `flash`) object and is accessed as `fl.Math`. It should not be confused with the standard `Math` object that is accessed directly as `Math`, and contains many more functions. The standard `Math` object is largely identical to the same object found in ActionScript, and the ActionScript reference can be used as a guide to its properties and methods."

Methods of the Math Object

concatMatrix

`Math.concatMatrix(` *`mat1, mat2`* `)`

Adds two `matrix` objects

Description
This method takes two matrices and adds them together to return a new matrix. In this way you might perform identical transformations on multiple objects with a single transform matrix. The matrix, which can either be retrieved from the matrix property of an element or from the document's `viewMatrix`, or created as you would any other object, must have the fields `a`, `b`, `c`, `d`, `tx`, and `ty` (see the entry for `Matrix` for an explanation on how these effect a stage element). The order in a concatenation is unimportant.

Argument(s)
`mat1`—*matrix object*—An object with properties `a`, `b`, `c`, `d`, `tx`, and `ty`

`mat2`—*matrix object*—An object with properties `a`, `b`, `c`, `d`, `tx`, and `ty`

Returns
New matrix—*matrix object*

Example
```
// offsets, scales, and skews all
// elements on a layer by same amount
var transform =
➥ {a:.5, b:.7854, c:0, d:1, tx:25, ty:25};
var elmnts = fl.getDocumentDOM().
➥ getTimeline().layers[0].frames[0].elements;
for (var i in elmnts) {
  var mtrx = elmnts[i].matrix;
  elmnts[i].matrix =
➥ fl.Math.concatMatrix(mtrx, transform);
}
```

invertMatrix

`Math.invertMatrix(` *`mat`* `)`

Returns inverse of specified matrix

Description
Returns the inverse of the matrix sent in the argument. The matrix, which can either be retrieved from the `matrix` property of an element or from the document's

viewMatrix, or created as you would any other object, must have the fields a, b, c, d, tx, and ty (see the entry for Matrix for an explanation on how these effect a stage element). Multiplying a matrix by its inverse will return an identity matrix (though there isn't a built-in Math method to handle multiplication of these special matrices). The inverse of a matrix might be useful when you wish to reverse or undo transformations on an element.

Argument(s)

mat—*matrix object*—An object with properties a, b, c, d, tx, and ty

Returns

New matrix—*matrix object*

Example

```
// transforms clip, dupes it, then removes
// the transformations from the duplicate
var my_doc = fl.getDocumentDOM();
var transform =
➥ {a:.5, b:.7854, c:0, d:1, tx:25, ty:25};
var invTransform =
➥ fl.Math.invertMatrix(transform);
var my_elem = my_doc.selection[0];
my_elem.matrix =
➥ fl.Math.concatMatrix(my_elem.matrix,
➥ transform);
my_doc.clipCopy();
my_doc.clipPaste(true);
my_elem = my_doc.selection[0];
my_elem.matrix =
➥ fl.Math.invertMatrix(my_elem.matrix,
➥ invTransform);
```

pointDistance

Math.pointDistance(*pt1*, *pt2*)

Computes distance between specified points

Description

Returns the pixel distance between the two point objects sent in the arguments. The two objects must both have x and y properties. Since a shape's vertices and control points contain these properties, they may be passed without error to the method.

Argument(s)

pt1—*point object*—An object containing x and y properties holding numbers

pt2—*point object*—An object containing x and y properties holding numbers

Returns

Pixel distance—*float*

Example

```
// finds distance between two
// clips' registration points
var clip1 =
➥ fl.getDocumentDOM().selection[0];
var pt1 =
➥ {x:clip1.matrix.tx, y:clip1.matrix.ty};
var clip2 =
➥ fl.getDocumentDOM().selection[1];
var pt2 =
➥ {x:clip2.matrix.tx, y:clip2.matrix.ty};
fl.trace(fl.Math.pointDistance(pt1, pt2));
// finds distance between
// two vertices on shape
var my_elem =
➥ fl.getDocumentDOM().selection[0];
var v1 = my_elem.vertices[0];
var v2 = my_elem.vertices[1];
fl.trace(fl.Math.pointDistance(v1, v2));
```

Matrix

The transformation matrix—a special object holding values describing the current transform of an element, such as scale, placement, or skew. In general mathematical terms, a matrix is a rectangular array of numbers that allows for special operations due to the unique arrangement of numbers.

Properties:

- a
- b
- c
- d
- tx
- ty

These six properties of the matrix object control the transformations of objects. An object with no transformations has a matrix property with the default values of {a:1, b:0, c:0, d:1, tx:0, ty:0}. Resetting an object's matrix to this default will remove all of its transformations.

Properties of the matrix Object

a

`matrix.a`

Scale factor to x axis

Description

A percent that controls the scale of a transform on the x axis. A value of `1` (or `1.00`) is equivalent to 100 percent scaling, and is the default value. Therefore setting this value to `2` would mean a transform with `200` percent horizontal scale, and a value of `0.5` would mean `50` percent horizontal scale.

Value(s)

float—Scale factor (1.00 == 100%)

Example

```
// scales to 200% on x axis
var mx =
➥ fl.getDocumentDOM().selection[0].matrix;
mx.a = 2;
fl.getDocumentDOM().selection[0].matrix =
➥ mx;
```

b

`matrix.b`

Skews object on vertical axis

Description

A number in radians that controls the vertical skew of a transform. To skew a transform by degrees, first convert the degrees value to radians using the formula (degree*PI/180 = radians) before applying it to the `matrix.b` property.

Value(s)

float—Radians to skew transform vertically

Example

```
// skews vertically to 45 degrees
var mx =
➥ fl.getDocumentDOM().selection[0].matrix;
mx.b = 45*Math.PI/180;
fl.getDocumentDOM().selection[0].matrix =
➥ mx;
```

c

`matrix.c`

Skews object on horizontal axis

Description

A number in radians that controls the horizontal skew of a transform. To skew a transform by degrees, first convert the degrees value to radians using the formula (degree*PI/180 = radians) before applying it to the `matrix.c` property.

Value(s)

float—Radians to skew transform vertically

Example

```
// skews horizontally by 10 more degrees
var mx =
➥ fl.getDocumentDOM().selection[0].matrix;
mx.c += 10*Math.PI/180;
fl.getDocumentDOM().selection[0].matrix =
➥ mx;
```

d

`matrix.d`

Scale factor to y axis

Description

A percentage that controls the scale of a transform on the y axis. A value of `1` (or `1.00`) is equivalent to 100 percent scaling, and is the default value. Therefore setting this value to `2` would mean a transform with 200 percent vertical scale, and a value of `0.5` would mean 50 percent vertical scale.

Value(s)

float—Scale factor (1.00 == 100%)

Example

```
// scales by 50% on y axis
var mx =
➥ fl.getDocumentDOM().selection[0].matrix;
mx.d *= .5;
fl.getDocumentDOM().selection[0].matrix =
➥ mx;
```

tx

`matrix.tx`

Location of object along x axis

Description
Corresponds to the x coordinate for a transform. Adding to this value will translate an object in a positive direction on the parent timeline's x axis.

Value(s)
float—x coordinate in pixels for transform center (will correspond with an element's registration point)

Example
```
// moves object to right by 100 pixels
var mx =
➥ fl.getDocumentDOM().selection[0].matrix;
mx.tx += 100;
fl.getDocumentDOM().selection[0].matrix =
➥ mx;
```

ty

`matrix.ty`

location of object along y axis

Description
Corresponds to the y coordinate for a transform. Adding to this value will translate an object in a positive direction on the parent timeline's y axis.

Value(s)
float—y coordinate in pixels for tranform center (will correspond with an element's registration point)

Example
```
// moves object up by 100 pixels
var mx =
➥ fl.getDocumentDOM().selection[0].matrix;
mx.ty -= 100;
fl.getDocumentDOM().selection[0].matrix =
➥ mx;
```

OutputPanel

An object representing the Output panel

Methods:

- `clear`
- `save`
- `trace`

Methods of the outputPanel Object

clear

`outputPanel.clear()`

Clears contents from Output panel

Description
Clears the Output panel

Argument(s)
None

Returns
Nothing

Example
```
fl.outputPanel.clear();
```

save

`outputPanel.save(` *`fileURI`*
➥ `[,` *`bAppendToFile`*`] )`

Saves contents of Output panel to file

Description
Saves whatever text is currently in the Output panel to a text file

Argument(s)
`fileURI`—*URI string*—A valid URI to a text file. If the file doesn't exist, it will be created.

`bAppendToFile`—*Boolean*—If `true`, text will be added to the text in the file. If `false`, previous contents will be erased.

Returns
Nothing

Example

```
fl.outputPanel.
➥ save("file:///C:/logfile.txt", true);
```

trace

`outputPanel.trace( message )`

Sends test string to Output panel

Description

Sends the specified text to the Output panel. Equivalent to `fl.trace()`.

Argument(s)

`message`—*string*—Any valid string. Can be created by any statement that returns a string.

Returns

Nothing

Example

```
angle = 1;
fl.outputPanel.trace("sine = " +
➥ Math.sin(angle));
```

Parameter

Parameters for a screen or component

Methods:

- `insertItem`
- `removeItem`

Properties:

- `category`
- `listIndex`
- `name`
- `value`
- `valueType`
- `verbose`

The `parameter` array is used for getting or setting parameters on components or screens. As there can be many different types of components and screens, and each can have a different number and type of properties (parameters), it would be impossible to specify a different set of properties for every one. Thus, the `parameters` array can contain any number and type of `parameter` objects, and each `parameter` object can contain any of several different types of data, as well as information about what type of information it contains.

Methods of the parameter Object

insertItem

`parameter.insertItem( index, name, value,`
`➥ type )`

Inserts `parameter` object into list, object, or array

Description

If the `parameter` object is of type `List`, `Object`, or `Array`, the data is actually stored in an array. This method adds a new item into that array.

Argument(s)

`index`—*integer*—The position in the array where the item will be inserted.

`name`—*string*—The name of the data. If the parameter is of type `List` or `Array`, this argument will be ignored, as the list will be numerically indexed. But it must be included at any rate.

`value`—*string*—The value of the new item

`type`—*string*—The data type of the new item inserted

Returns

Nothing

Example

```
my_component.parameters[0].insertItem(2,
➥ "position", {_x:100, _y:100}, "Object");
```

removeItem

`parameter.removeItem( index )`

Deletes parameter from list, object, or array

Description

If the `parameter` object is of type `List`, `Object`, or `Array`, the data is actually stored in an array. This method removes an item from that array.

Argument(s)
index—*integer*—The index of the array that contains the data you want to delete

Returns
Nothing

Example
```
my_component.parameters[0].removeItem(0);
```

Properties of the parameter Object

category

parameter.category

Groups items in Components panel, or organizes screens

Description
When parameters are listed in the Property Inspector or Component Inspector panel, they can be grouped into various categories. This property indicates which category the particular property will be put in.

Value(s)
string—The name of the category

Example
```
my_component.parameters[0].category =
➥ "Basic Parameters";
```

listIndex

parameter.listIndex

Value of specified item; for type list only.

Description
If the parameter object is of type List, Object, or Array, the data is actually stored in an array. This property indicates which item in the array you are inspecting or setting.

Value(s)
integer—The index to the array

Example
```
my_component.parameters[0].listIndex = 3;
```

name

parameter.name

Name of parameter

Description
The name of the parameter

Value(s)
string—The name of the parameter

Example
```
my_component.parameters[0].name =
➥ "Position";
```

value

parameter.value

Value of parameter

Description
The value of the specified parameter

Value(s)
Type depends on the type of data stored—The data type is stored in the valueType property of the parameter object.

Example
```
my_componenent.properties[0].value =
➥ {_x:100, _y:150};
```

valueType

parameter.valueType

Parameter's value type

Description
The type of data contained by the parameter's value property

Value(s)
string—Valid data types are "Array", "Object", "List", "String", "Number", "Boolean", "Font Name", and "Color".

Example
```
my_component.parameters[0].valueType =
➥ "Object";
```

verbose

`parameter.verbose`

Determines if parameter appears in Properties panel

Description
Determines if the parameter will appear in the Property Inspector

Value(s)
Boolean—`true` will display the parameter; `false` will not.

Example
```
my_component.parameters[0].verbose = true;
```

Path

Contains a defined sequence of line segments

Methods:

- addCubicCurve
- addCurve
- addPoint
- clear
- close
- makeShape
- newContour

Properties:

- nPts

Path objects are created with the `fl.drawingLayer.newPath()` method. Although they are mainly used in drawing tools, they can be used in any extensibility script.

Methods of the path Object

addCubicCurve

```
newPath.addCubicCurve( xAnchor, yAnchor,
➥ x1, y1, x2, y2, x3, y3 )
```

Appends cubic Bezier curve segment to path

Description
Adds a new cubic curve to the path, starting at the point specified by the first two arguments, through two control points specified by the next four arguments, to the point specified by the last two arguments

Argument(s)
xAnchor—*float*—The x coordinate of the anchor point

yAnchor—*float*—The y coordinate of the anchor point

x1—*float*—The x coordinate of the first control point

y1—*float*—The y coordinate of the first control point

x2—*float*—The x coordinate of the second control point

y2—*float*—The y coordinate of the second control point

x3—*float*—The x coordinate of the end point

y3—*float*—The y coordinate of the end point

Returns
Nothing

Example
```
my_path = fl.drawingLayer.newPath();
my_path.addCubicCurve(0, 100, 0, 0,
➥ 550, 200, 550, 100);
```

addCurve

```
newPath.addCurve( x0, y0, x1, y1 )
```

Appends quadratic Bezier segment to path

Description
Adds a new quadratic curve to the path, starting at last point drawn to (or 0, 0 if no drawing has been done yet), through a single control point specified by the next two arguments, to the point specified by the last two arguments

Argument(s)
x0—*float*—The x coordinate of the control point

y0—*float*—The y coordinate of the control point

x1—*float*—The x coordinate of the end point

y1—*float*—The y coordinate of the end point

Returns
Nothing

Example

```
my_path = fl.drawingLayer.newPath();
my_path.addCurve(275, 0, 550, 100);
```

addPoint

`newPath.addPoint( x, y )`

Adds point to path

Description

Adds a single point to the path. This will create a line segment from the last point drawn to (or 0, 0 if no drawing has occurred yet) to the point

Argument(s)

x—*float*—The x position of the point

y—*float*—The y position of the point

Returns

Nothing

Example

```
my_path = fl.drawingLayer.newPath();
my_path.addPoint(0, 100);
```

clear

`newPath.clear()`

Removes all points from path

Description

Removes all points and curves from the path

Argument(s)

None

Returns

Nothing

Example

```
my_path = fl.drawingLayer.newPath();
// after adding points...
my_path.clear();
```

close

`newPath.close()`

Appends point at location of first point of path

Description

Adds a final point to the path, at the location of the first point added to the path. This has the effect of closing whatever shape has been created by the points.

Argument(s)

None

Returns

Nothing

Example

```
my_path = fl.drawingLayer.newPath();
// after adding points...
my_path.close();
```

makeShape

```
newPath.makeShape( [bSupressFill]
➥ [, bSupressStroke] )
```

Creates shape

Description

Draws the shape described by the points and curves that have been added to the path. This will be a shape object as a new element in the document in the current frame.

Argument(s)

`bSupressFill`—*Boolean*—If `true`, the shape will be drawn with no fill. If `false`, the current fill will be used.

`bSupressStroke`—*Boolean*—If `true`, the shape will be drawn with no stroke. If `false`, the current stroke will be used.

Returns

Nothing

Example

```
my_path = fl.drawingLayer.newPath();
// after adding points...
my_path.makeShape();
```

newContour

`newPath.newContour()`

Starts new contour in path

Description
Starts a new contour in the path. See the entry for Contour for more details.

Argument(s)
None

Returns
Nothing

Example
```
my_path = fl.drawingLayer.newPath();
my_path.newContour();
```

Properties of the path Object

nPts

`newPath.nPts`

Returns integer representing number of points in path

Description
Reports how many points are currently defined in the specified path

Value(s)
integer—The number of points

Example
```
my_path = fl.drawingLayer.newPath();
fl.trace(my_path.nPts);
```

Screen

A screen in the screenOutline object

Properties:

- accName
- childScreens
- description
- forceSimple
- hidden
- instanceName
- name
- nextScreen
- parameters
- parentScreen
- prevScreen
- screenType
- screenTypeVersion
- silent
- tabIndex
- timeline

Properties of the screen Object

accName

`screen.accName`

Name of object, used by screen reader

Description
For accessibility purposes. This is the name of the screen as seen by the screen reader.

Value(s)
string—The name of the screen

Example
```
my_screen.accName = "Introduction";
```

childScreens

`screen.childScreens`

Array of child screens

Description
An array containing any child screens (nested screens) that belong to this screen

Value(s)
array—An array of this screen's child screens

Example

```
fl.trace("This screen has " +
➥ my_screen.childScreens.length +
➥ " children.");
```

description

`screen.description`

Description of object, used by screen reader

Description
For accessibility purposes, a description of the screen

Value(s)
string—The description of the screen

Example

```
my_screen.description =
➥ "This is the first screen.";
```

forceSimple

`screen.forceSimple`

If `true`, children of object aren't accessible to screen reader.

Description
For accessibility purposes, hides any children of this screen from the screen reader

Value(s)
Boolean—`true` hides children; `false` exposes them

Example

```
my_screen.forceSimple = true;
```

hidden

`screen.hidden`

If `true`, screen isn't visible to any other screens.

Description
Turns on or off the visibility of the specified screen

Value(s)
Boolean—`true` hides the screen; `false` reveals it.

Example

```
my_screen.hidden = true;
```

instanceName

`screen.instanceName`

Screen's instance name

Description
The screen's instance name for use in accessing the screen object with ActionScript

Value(s)
string—The instance name of the screen

Example

```
my_screen.instanceName = "mainScreen";
```

name

`screen.name`

Name of screen

Description
The name of the screen

Value(s)
string—The screen's name

Example

```
my_screen.name = "Main Screen";
```

nextScreen

`screen.nextScreen`

Next sibling in `childScreen` array

Description
References the next screen in an array of nested or child screens

Value(s)
object—The reference to the next screen in the array

Example

```
fl.trace(my_screen.nextScreen.name);
```

parameters

`screen.parameters`

Properties in screen's Property Inspector

Description
An array of parameter objects relating to the screen

Value(s)
array—Each element contains one parameter object.

Example
```
my_screen.parameters[0].name = "position";
```

parentScreen

`screen.parentScreen`

Screen that contains this screen as a childScreen

Description
A reference to the parent screen of the specified screen. If this is a top-level screen, it won't have a parent screen and this property will be null.

Value(s)
object—The reference to the parent screen

Example
```
if(my_screen.parentScreen != null){
  fl.trace("I have a parent");
}
```

prevScreen

`screen.prevScreen`

Previous sibling in childScreen array

Description
References the previous screen in an array of nested or child screens

Value(s)
object—The reference to the previous screen in the array

Example
```
fl.trace(my_screen.prevScreen.name);
```

screenType

`screen.screenType`

screenType that created screen

Description
The name of the screenType that created this screen

Value(s)
string—screenType name

Example
```
fl.trace(my_screen.screenType);
```

screenTypeVersion

`screen.screenTypeVersion`

Template version that created screen

Description
The version of the screenType used to create this screen

Value(s)
string—The version number in string format

Example
```
fl.trace(my_screen.screenTypeVersion);
```

silent

`screen.silent`

If true, object isn't read by screen reader.

Description
For accessibility purposes, indicates whether or not the screen will be read by the screen reader

Value(s)
Boolean—true will cause the screen reader to ignore the screen; false will allow it to read the screen.

Example
```
my_screen.silent = false;
```

tabIndex

`screen.tabIndex`

Tab index value of object

Description
The relative order in which the screen will be activated by tabbing. Also used by the screen reader.

Value(s)
integer—The tab index of the screen

Example
```
my_screen.tabIndex = 33;
```

timeline

`screen.timeline`

`timeline` object for screen

Description
The `timeline` object for the screen

Value(s)
object—The timeline of the screen

Example
```
my_tl = my_screen.timeline;
```

ScreenOutline

An object representing the Screen Outline pane

Methods:

- `copyScreenFromFile`
- `deleteScreen`
- `duplicateScreen`
- `getSelectedScreens`
- `insertNestedScreen`
- `insertScreen`
- `moveScreen`
- `renameScreen`
- `setCurrentScreen`
- `setScreenProperty`
- `setSelectedScreens`

Properties:

- `currentScreen`
- `screens`

Methods of the screenOutline Object

copyScreenFromFile

```
screenOutline.copyScreenFromFile( fileURI
➥ [, screenName] )
```

Inserts all screens from specified URI

Description
Copies screens from an external FLA file into the current document

Argument(s)
`fileURI`—*URI string*—Valid URI to a FLA file containing screens.

`screenName`—*string*—The name of a screen in the external file. If omitted, will copy all the screens in the file.

Returns
Nothing

Example
```
my_doc = fl.getDocumentDOM();
my_doc.screenOutline.copyScreenFromFile
➥ ("file:///c:/myscreens.fla",
➥ "Intro screen");
```

deleteScreen

```
screenOutline.deleteScreen( [screenName] )
```

Deletes screen

Description
Deletes the named screen from the outline

Argument(s)
`screenName`—*string*—The name of the screen to delete. If not specified, current screen will be deleted.

Returns
Nothing

Example
```
my_doc = fl.getDocumentDOM();
my_doc.screenOutline.
➥ deleteScreen("placeholder");
```

duplicateScreen

```
screenOutline.
➥ duplicateScreen( [screenName] )
```

Duplicates screen

Description
Makes a copy of the named or current screen, giving it a default name

Argument(s)
screenName—*string*—The name of the screen to duplicate. If not specified, will duplicate selected screens.

Returns
true if successful, otherwise false—*Boolean*

Example
```
my_doc = fl.getDocumentDOM();
my_doc.screenOutline.
➥ duplicateScreen("Chapter Intro");
```

getSelectedScreens

```
screenOutline.getSelectedScreens()
```

Returns array of selected screens

Description
Returns an array of all currently selected screens

Argument(s)
None

Returns
Array of screens—*array*

Example
```
my_doc = fl.getDocumentDOM();
selScreens =
➥ my_doc.screenOutline.getSelectedScreens();
```

insertNestedScreen

```
screenOutline.insertNestedScreen( [name]
➥ [, referenceScreen] [, screenTypeName] )
```

Inserts child screen

Description
Inserts a nested screen that will appear as a child of the current screen

Argument(s)
name—*string*—The name for the new screen (can't contain spaces). If omitted, a default name will be supplied.

referenceScreen—*string*—The name of an existing screen. The new screen will appear as a child of this screen.

screenTypeName—*string*—The screen type assigned to the new screen.

Returns
Reference to new screen—*object*

Example
```
my_doc = fl.getDocumentDOM();
my_doc.screenOutline.
➥ insertNestedScreen("SubSection1",
➥ "Section3", "BasicScreen");
```

insertScreen

```
screenOutline.insertScreen( [name]
➥ [, referenceScreen] [, screenTypeName] )
```

Adds new screen

Description
Inserts a screen that will appear as a child of the current screen

Argument(s)
name—*string*—The name for the new screen (can't contain spaces). If omitted, a default name will be supplied.

referenceScreen—*string*—The name of an existing screen. The new screen will appear after this screen.

screenTypeName—*string*—The screen type assigned to the new screen.

Returns
Reference to new screen—*object*

Example

```
my_doc = fl.getDocumentDOM();
my_doc.screenOutline.
➥ insertScreen("Section4", "Section3",
➥ "BasicScreen");
```

moveScreen

```
screenOutline.moveScreen( screenToMove,
➥ referenceScreen, position )
```

Relocates screen

Description

Moves the specified screen to a new position.

Argument(s)

screenToMove—*string*—The name of the screen you want to move

referenceScreen—*string*—The name of the string to move it near

position—*string*—Where to move it in location to the reference screen. Values can be "before", "after", "firstChild", and "lastChild".

Returns

true if successful, otherwise false—*Boolean*

Example

```
my_doc = fl.getDocumentDOM();
my_doc.screenOutline.
➥ moveScreen("Statistics", "Information",
➥ "firstChild");
```

renameScreen

```
screenOutline.renameScreen( newScreenName
➥ [, oldScreenName] [, bDisplayError] )
```

Changes screen's name

Description

Renames the specified screen

Argument(s)

newScreenName—*string*—The name you want to give the screen (which can't contain spaces).

oldScreenName—*string*—The name of the screen to change. If omitted, will change the currently selected screen.

bDisplayError—*string*—If true, will display any error generated. Default is false.

Returns

true if successful, otherwise false—*Boolean*

Example

```
my_doc = fl.getDocumentDOM();
my_doc.screenOutline.
➥ renameScreen("Profits", "MoneyMade",
➥ false);
```

setCurrentScreen

```
screenOutline.setCurrentScreen( name )
```

Sets current screen

Description

Makes the specified screen the current screen

Argument(s)

name—*string*—The name of the screen to go to

Returns

true if successful, otherwise false—*Boolean*

Example

```
my_doc = fl.getDocumentDOM();
my_doc.screenOutline.
➥ setCurrentScreen("Profits");
```

setScreenProperty

```
screenOutline.setScreenProperty(property,
➥ value )
```

Sets specified property's value

Description

Sets the specified property of the current screen

Argument(s)

property—*string*—The name of the property to set

value—*Type depends on property*—The value to set it to

Returns
Value—*type*

Example
```
my_doc = fl.getDocumentDOM();
my_doc.screenOutline.
➥ setScreenProperty("name", "Fred");
```

setSelectedScreens

screenOutline.setSelectedScreens(*selection*, ➥ *bReplaceCurrentSelection*)

Selects one or more screens

Description
Sets which screens will be selected

Argument(s)
selection—*array*—The names of the screens you want to select.

bReplaceCurrentSelection—*Boolean*—true replaces selection; false adds to it.

Returns
Nothing

Example
```
my_doc = fl.getDocumentDOM();
my_doc.screenOutline.
➥ setSelectedScreens(["Intro",
➥ "Intermission", "Closing"], true);
```

Properties of the screenOutline Object

currentScreen

screenOutline.currentScreen

Focused screen in Screen Outline pane and onstage

Description
The currently focused screen, which will be shown on the stage

Value(s)
type—Value

Example
```
fl.trace(my_doc.screenOutline.
➥ currentScreen.name);
```

screens

screenOutline.screens

Array of screens

Description
An array of screens. Note, this will contain only references to the top-level screens. These may contain additional nested screens.

Value(s)
array—An array of screens

Example
```
my_doc = fl.getDocumentDOM();
fl.trace("There are " +
➥ my_doc.screenOutline.screens.length +
➥ " top level screens here");
```

ScreenType

An object representing a single ScreenType

Methods:

- closeWizardDialog
- getJSFLContext
- invoke
- openWizardDialog

Properties:

- name
- version

Screen types refer to classes of screens that can be created. Flash MX 2004 Professional ships with two screen types: Form and Slide. Additional classes can be created. A class is defined by an XML file in the ScreenTypes directory in the Configuration directory. It is implemented by an ActionScript class .as file. It can also have JSFL files associated with it in order to perform actions on the document, and a SWF-based wizard to help set up the screen.

Methods of the screenType Object

closeWizardDialog

`screenType.closeWizardDialog()`

Closes prior wizard

Description
Closes the current SWF-based wizard for the screen type

Argument(s)
None

Returns
Nothing

Example
```
my_screenT.closeWizardDialog();
```

getJSFLContext

`screenType.getJSFLContext()`

Calls method defined within Flash JavaScript document

Description
Returns an object that references the JSFL file associated with this screen type. You can then use this object to call any functions within that JSFL file.

Argument(s)
None

Returns
Reference to JSFL script—*object*

Example
```
myJSFL = my_screenT.getJSFLContext();
// doSomething is a function you have
// defined in the JSFL file.
myJSFL.doSomething();
```

invoke

`screenType.invoke()`

Invokes screen type wizard

Description
Invokes the wizard of the specified screen type. If there is no SWF-based wizard, a new screen of the specified type will be created.

Argument(s)
None

Returns
Nothing

Example
```
my_screenT.invoke();
```

openWizardDialog

`screenType.openWizardDialog()`

Opens screen type's wizard dialog box

Description
If there is a wizard associated with the screen type, the wizard dialog box will be opened. If not, nothing will happen.

Argument(s)
None

Returns
Nothing

Example
```
my_screenT.openWizardDialog();
```

Properties of the screenType Object

name

`screenType.name`

Name of screen type

Description
The name of the screen type

Value(s)
string—The name of the screen type

Example
```
my_screenT.name = "New Screen";
```

version

`screenType.version`

Version of screen type

Description
The version of the screen type

Value(s)
string—The version number expressed as a string

Example
```
my_screenT.version = "1.2";
```

Shape

Subclass of Element. Represents a shape on the stage.

Methods:

- beginEdit
- deleteEdge
- endEdit

Properties:

- contours
- edges
- isGroup
- vertices

Methods of the shape Object

beginEdit

`shape.beginEdit()`

Defines start of edit session

Description
All editing on a shape must take place between beginEdit() and endEdit() calls.

Argument(s)
None

Returns
Nothing

Example
```
var my_doc = fl.getDocumentDOM();
var my_tl = my_doc.getTimeline();
var my_layer = my_tl.layers[0];
var my_frame = my_layer.frames[0];
var my_elem = my_frame.elements[0];
my_elem.beginEdit();
my_elem.deleteEdge(0);
my_elem.endEdit();
```

deleteEdge

`shape.deleteEdge( index )`

Deletes specified edge

Description
Deletes the edge of the specified index from the shape and removes the edge from the shape's edges array. This method must occur within the shape's beginEdit() and endEdit() calls.

Argument(s)
index—*integer*—The index in shape's edges array of the edge to delete

Returns
Nothing

Example
```
var my_doc = fl.getDocumentDOM();
var my_tl = my_doc.getTimeline();
var my_layer = my_tl.layers[0];
var my_frame = my_layer.frames[0];
var my_elem = my_frame.elements[0];
my_elem.beginEdit();
my_elem.deleteEdge(0);
my_elem.endEdit();
```

endEdit

`shape.endEdit()`

Signals end of edit session

Description
All editing on a shape must take place between beginEdit() and endEdit() calls.

Argument(s)
None

Returns
Nothing

Example
```
var my_doc = fl.getDocumentDOM();
var my_tl = my_doc.getTimeline();
var my_layer = my_tl.layers[0];
var my_frame = my_layer.frames[0];
var my_elem = my_frame.elements[0];
my_elem.beginEdit();
my_elem.deleteEdge(0);
my_elem.endEdit();
```

Properties of the shape Object

contours

`shape.contours`

Array of contour objects

Description
An array holding references to the shape's contour objects

Value(s)
array—A collection of contour objects

Example
```
var my_doc = fl.getDocumentDOM();
var my_tl = my_doc.getTimeline();
var my_layer = my_tl.layers[0];
var my_frame = my_layer.frames[0];
var my_elem = my_frame.elements[0];
fl.trace(my_elem.contours[0].orientation);
```

edges

`shape.edges`

Array of edge objects

Description
An array holding references to the shape's edge objects

Value(s)
array—A collection of edge objects

Example
```
var my_doc = fl.getDocumentDOM();
var my_tl = my_doc.getTimeline();
var my_layer = my_tl.layers[0];
var my_frame = my_layer.frames[0];
var my_elem = my_frame.elements[0];
fl.trace(my_elem.edges[0].isLine);
```

isGroup

`shape.isGroup`

Returns `true` if selected element is a group

Description
Returns whether selected element is grouped (`true`) or not (`false`)

Value(s)
Boolean—`true`, `false`

Example
```
var my_doc = fl.getDocumentDOM();
var my_tl = my_doc.getTimeline();
var my_layer = my_tl.layers[0];
var my_frame = my_layer.frames[0];
var my_elem = my_frame.elements[0];
if (my_elem.isGroup) {
  my_doc.unGroup();
}
```

vertices

`shape.vertices`

Array of vertex objects

Description
An array holding references to the shape's vertex objects

Value(s)
array—A collection of vertex objects

Example
```
var my_doc = fl.getDocumentDOM();
var my_tl = my_doc.getTimeline();
var my_layer = my_tl.layers[0];
var my_frame = my_layer.frames[0];
var my_elem = my_frame.elements[0];
fl.trace(my_elem.vertices.length);
```

SoundItem

Subclass of Item. Represents a sound in the Library.

Properties:

- bitRate
- bits
- compressionType
- convertStereoToMono
- quality
- sampleRate
- useImportedMP3Quality

Properties of the soundItem Object

bitRate

soundItem.bitRate

MP3 compression bit rate

Description

Hold the number of kilobits per second for MP3 compression type and will only be available if useImportedMP3Quality is set to false. Acceptable values are "8 kbps", "16 kbps", "20 kbps", "24 kbps", "32 kbps", "48 kbps", "56 kbps", "64 kbps", "80 kbps", "112 kbps", "128 kbps", and "160 kbps". For any compression type other than MP3, this property will hold undefined and attempting to set it will return an error.

Value(s)

string—"8 kbps", "16 kbps", "20 kbps", "24 kbps", "32 kbps", "48 kbps", "56 kbps", "64 kbps", "80 kbps", "112 kbps", "128 kbps", or "160 kbps"

Example

```
fl.getDocumentDOM().library.items[0].
➥ compressionType = "MP3";
fl.getDocumentDOM().library.items[0].
➥ bitRate = "128 kbps";
```

bits

soundItem.bits

Type of ADPCM compression

Description

This property is only available for the ADPCM compression type and controls the level of compression. Acceptable values are "2 bit", "3 bit", "4 bit", and "5 bit".

Value(s)

string—"2 bit", "3 bit", "4 bit", or "5 bit"

Example

```
fl.getDocumentDOM().library.items[0].
➥ compressionType = "ADPCM";
fl.getDocumentDOM().library.items[0].
➥ bits = "2 bit";
```

compressionType

soundItem.compressionType

Type of compression

Description

Type of compression for a sound item in the Library. This property may be both set and retrieved.

Value(s)

string—"ADPCM", "Default", "MP3", "Raw", or "Speech"

Example

```
fl.getDocumentDOM().library.items[0].
➥ compressionType = "MP3";
```

convertStereoToMono

soundItem.convertStereoToMono

If true, converts stereo sound to mono

Description

This property, when set to true, will convert a sound from stereo to mono upon compression. This is only available for MP3 and Raw compression types, and for the former only if useImportedMP3Quality is set to false. If a sound using MP3 compression has its bit rate set to less than 20 kbps, this property is automatically set to true, and attempting to set it will throw an error.

Value(s)

Boolean—`true`, `false`

Example

```
fl.getDocumentDOM().library.items[0].
➥ useImportedMP3Quality = false;
fl.getDocumentDOM().library.items[0].
➥ convertStereoToMono = false;
```

quality

`soundItem.quality`

MP3 compression quality setting

Description

Sets the quality of MP3 compression for a sound item. Acceptable values are `"Fast"`, `"Medium"`, and `"Best"`. This value holds `undefined` for all other compression types, and attempting to set it will throw an error.

Value(s)

string—`"Fast"`, `"Medium"`, or `"Best"`

Example

```
fl.getDocumentDOM().library.items[0].
➥ compressionType = "MP3";
fl.getDocumentDOM().library.items[0].
➥ quality = "Best";
```

sampleRate

`soundItem.sampleRate`

Sample rate

Description

The samples per second in kilohertz for the sound item: `"5 kHz"`, `"11 kHz"`, `"22 kHz"`, or `"44 kHz"`. This property is available only for Raw, ADPCM, and Speech compression types. Setting this property for other compression types will throw an error.

Value(s)

string—`"5 kHz"`, `"11 kHz"`, `"22 kHz"`, or `"44 kHz"`

Example

```
fl.getDocumentDOM().library.items[0].
➥ compressionType = "ADPCM";
fl.getDocumentDOM().library.items[0].
➥ sampleRate = "22 kHz";
```

useImportedMP3Quality

`soundItem.useImportedMP3Quality`

If `true`, imported MP3 quality is used.

Description

This property specifies whether the imported MP3 quality for a sound item will be used upon export. Setting this property to `false` allows you to specify bit rate and quality.

Value(s)

Boolean—`true`, `false`

Example

```
fl.getDocumentDOM().library.items[0].
➥ useImportedMP3Quality = false;
```

Stroke

Stroke settings for the selection or the toolbar

Properties:

- `breakAtCorners`
- `color`
- `curve`
- `dash1`
- `dash2`
- `density`
- `dotSize`
- `dotspace`
- `hatchThickness`
- `jiggle`
- `length`
- `pattern`
- `rotate`
- `space`
- `style`
- `thickness`
- `variation`
- `waveHeight`

The stroke object is returned by document.getCustomStroke() and is used in document.setCustomStroke().

Properties of the stroke Object

breakAtCorners

stroke.breakAtCorners

If true, enables Sharp Corners setting in Custom Stroke dialog box

Description
Sets sharp corners for the stroke object specified

Value(s)
Boolean—true will create sharp corners; false will not.

Example

```
my_stroke = fl.getDocumentDOM().
➥ getCustomStroke();
my_stroke.breakAtCorners = true;
```

color

stroke.color

Stroke color

Description
The color of the specified stroke

Value(s)
integer or string—The color as a string (#rrggbb) or base10 or hex integer (0 to 16777216 or 0xrrggbb). You can also specify an alpha for the stroke by adding on the hex values from 00 to FF after the color definition as a string. Example: "#FF00007F" creates a red fill with approximately 50 percent alpha.

Example

```
my_stroke = my_doc.getCustomStroke();
// Note alpha is set after color value
my_stroke.color = "#ff00ff33";
my_doc.setCustomStroke(my_stroke);
```

curve

stroke.curve

Specifies curved setting; hatch line only.

Description
Sets the curve setting of the hatched stroke style. This property only has meaning if the stroke's style property is set to "hatched".

Value(s)
string—Values can be "straight", "slight curve", "medium curve", and "very curved".

Example

```
my_stroke =
➥ fl.getDocumentDOM().getCustomStroke();
my_stroke.curve = "very curved";
```

dash1

stroke.dash1

Length of solid part of dash

Description
In a dashed line, represents the length of the solid part of the dash. The blank part of the dashed line is represented by dash2. This property only has meaning if the stroke's style property is set to "dashed".

Value(s)
integer—The length of dash segment

Example

```
my_stroke =
➥ fl.getDocumentDOM().getCustomStroke();
my_stroke.style = "dashed";
my_stroke.dash1 = 5;
fl.getDocumentDOM().
➥ setCustomStroke(my_stroke);
```

dash2

stroke.dash2

Length of space between dashes

Description
In a dashed line, represents the length of the blank part of the dash. The solid part of the dashed line is represented by

dash1. This property only has meaning if the stroke's style property is set to "dashed".

Value(s)

integer— The length of dash segment

Example

```
my_stroke =
➥ fl.getDocumentDOM().getCustomStroke();
my_stroke.style = "dashed";
my_stroke.dash2 = 5;
fl.getDocumentDOM().
➥ setCustomStroke(my_stroke);
```

density

`stroke.density`

Density of stippled line

Description

In a stippled line, represents density of the dots making up the stroke. This property only has meaning if the stroke's style property is set to "stipple".

Value(s)

string—Values can be "very dense", "dense", "sparse", and "very sparse".

Example

```
my_stroke =
➥ fl.getDocumentDOM().getCustomStroke();
my_stroke.style = "stipple";
my_stroke.density = "dense";
fl.getDocumentDOM().
➥ setCustomStroke(my_stroke);
```

dotSize

`stroke.dotSize`

Dot size of stippled line

Description

In a stippled line, represents size of the dots making up the stroke. This property only has meaning if the stroke's style property is set to "stipple".

Value(s)

string—Values can be "tiny", "small", "medium", and "large".

Example

```
my_stroke =
➥ fl.getDocumentDOM().getCustomStroke();
my_stroke.style = "stipple";
my_stroke.dotSize = "tiny";
fl.getDocumentDOM().
➥ setCustomStroke(my_stroke);
```

dotspace

`stroke.dotspace`

Spacing between dots of dotted line

Description

In a dotted line, represents spacing between the dots making up the stroke. This property only has meaning if the stroke's style property is set to "dotted".

Value(s)

integer—The space between the dots

Example

```
my_stroke =
➥ fl.getDocumentDOM().getCustomStroke();
my_stroke.style = "dotted";
my_stroke.dotSpace = 18;
fl.getDocumentDOM().
➥ setCustomStroke(my_stroke);
```

hatchThickness

`stroke.hatchThickness`

Thickness of hatches in hatched line

Description

Sets the thickness setting of the hatched stroke style. This property only has meaning if the stroke's style property is set to "hatched".

Value(s)

string—Values can be "hairline", "thin", "medium", and "thick".

Example

```
my_stroke =
➥ fl.getDocumentDOM().getCustomStroke();
my_stroke.style = "hatched";
my_stroke.hatchThickness = "medium";
fl.getDocumentDOM().
➥ setCustomStroke(my_stroke);
```

jiggle

`stroke.jiggle`

Jiggle style of hatched line

Description

Sets the jiggle setting of the hatched stroke style. This property only has meaning if the stroke's style property is set to "hatched".

Value(s)

string—Values can be "none", "bounce", "loose", and "wild".

Example

```
my_stroke =
➥ fl.getDocumentDOM().getCustomStroke();
my_stroke.style = "hatched";
my_stroke.jiggle = "bounce";
fl.getDocumentDOM().
➥ setCustomStroke(my_stroke);
```

length

`stroke.length`

Length of hatched line segments

Description

Sets the stroke length of the hatched stroke style. This property only has meaning if the stroke's style property is set to "hatched".

Value(s)

string—Values can be "equal", "slight", "variation", "medium variation", and "random".

Example

```
my_stroke =
➥ fl.getDocumentDOM().getCustomStroke();
my_stroke.style = "hatched";
my_stroke.length = "random";
fl.getDocumentDOM().
➥ setCustomStroke(my_stroke);
```

pattern

`stroke.pattern`

Pattern of ragged line

Description

In a ragged line, represents the pattern used on the line. This property only has meaning if the stroke's style property is set to "ragged".

Value(s)

string—Values can be "solid", "simple", "random", "dotted", "random dotted", "triple dotted", and "random triple dotted".

Example

```
my_stroke =
➥ fl.getDocumentDOM().getCustomStroke();
my_stroke.style = "ragged";
my_stroke.pattern = "simple";
fl.getDocumentDOM().
➥ setCustomStroke(my_stroke);
```

rotate

`stroke.rotate`

Rotation style of hatched line

Description

Sets the rotation style of the hatched stroke style. This property only has meaning if the stroke's style property is set to "hatched".

Value(s)

string—Values can be "none", "slight", "medium", and "free".

Example

```
my_stroke =
➥ fl.getDocumentDOM().getCustomStroke();
my_stroke.style = "hatched";
my_stroke.rotate = "slight";
fl.getDocumentDOM().
➥ setCustomStroke(my_stroke);
```

space

`stroke.space`

Length of spaces between hatches of hatched line

Description

Sets the length of spaces in the hatched stroke style. This property only has meaning if the stroke's style property is set to "hatched".

Value(s)

string—Values can be "very close", "close", "distant", and "very distant".

Example

```
my_stroke =
➥ fl.getDocumentDOM().getCustomStroke();
my_stroke.style = "hatched";
my_stroke.space = "very close";
fl.getDocumentDOM().
➥ setCustomStroke(my_stroke);
```

style

`stroke.style`

Stroke style setting

Description

Sets the style of the stroke. Options are the same as in the authoring environment. As you may have noticed, many of the other stroke properties pertain to only one style. Here is a list of the styles and the other properties that pertain to them:

Style	Additional Properties Used
Solid	No other properties
Dashed	dash1, dash2
Dotted	dotSpace
Ragged	pattern, waveHeight, wavelength
Stipple	dotSize, variation, density
Hatched	hatchThickness, space, jiggle, rotate, curve, length

Value(s)

string—See description.

Example

```
my_stroke =
➥ fl.getDocumentDOM().getCustomStroke();
my_stroke.style = "hatched";
fl.getDocumentDOM().
➥ setCustomStroke(my_stroke);
```

thickness

`stroke.thickness`

Width of stroke

Description

The width of the stroke in pixels

Value(s)

integer—Width

Example

```
my_stroke =
➥ fl.getDocumentDOM().getCustomStroke();
my_stroke.thickness = 10;
fl.getDocumentDOM().
➥ setCustomStroke(my_stroke);
```

variation

`stroke.variation`

Variation style of stippled line

Description

In a stippled line, represents variation of the dots making up the stroke. This property only has meaning if the stroke's style property is set to "stipple".

Value(s)

string—Values can be "one size", "small variation", "varied sizes", and "random sizes".

Example

```
my_stroke =
➥ fl.getDocumentDOM().getCustomStroke();
my_stroke.style = "stipple";
my_stroke.variation = "random sizes";
fl.getDocumentDOM().
➥ setCustomStroke(my_stroke);
```

waveHeight

`stroke.waveHeight`

Wave style of ragged line

Description

In a ragged line, represents the wave height of the line. This property only has meaning if the stroke's style property is set to "ragged".

Value(s)

string—Values can be "flat", "wavy", "very wavy", and "wild".

Example

```
my_stroke =
➥ fl.getDocumentDOM().getCustomStroke();
my_stroke.style = "ragged";
my_stroke.waveHeight = "very wavy";
fl.getDocumentDOM().
➥ setCustomStroke(my_stroke);
```

SymbolInstance

Subclass of Instance. Represents a symbol instance on the stage.

Properties:

- accName
- actionScript
- buttonTracking
- colorAlphaAmount
- colorAlphaPercent
- colorBlueAmount
- colorBluePercent
- colorGreenAmount
- colorGreenPercent
- colorMode
- colorRedAmount
- colorRedPercent
- description
- firstFrame
- forceSimple
- loop
- shortcut
- silent
- symbolType
- tabIndex

Properties of the symbolInstance Object

accName

symbolInstance.accName

Name of object, used by screen reader

Description

The accName property holds the name of the symbol instance that appears in the Accessibility panel and will be exposed to screen reader technology. This property may be both retrieved and set, and is available for movie clip and button instances, but not graphic instances.

Value(s)

string—The name of the instance for the screen reader

Example

```
var my_elem = fl.getDocumentDOM().
➥ getTimeline().layers[0].frames[0].
➥ elements[0];
my_elem.silent = false;
my_elem.description = "go to last page";
my_elem.accName = "back";
```

actionScript

symbolInstance.actionScript

String representing the ActionScript on instance

Description

This property holds all of the ActionScript that is placed *on* a symbol instance (the ActionScript inside the instance must be accessed from the timeline, layer, and frame on which it appears) and may be both set and retrieved. Since you may perform any string operations on the ActionScript, it's possible to not only replace all of an instance's code, but also insert within or add to existing code. Remember that code placed on an instance (not within a frame) must appear within an on() or onClipEvent() block in order for the movie to not produce an error.

Value(s)

string—Code on an instance

Example

```
// inserts code within an existing
// block if it exists, else creates
// a new block
```

```
var my_elem =
➥ fl.getDocumentDOM().selection[0];
var aScript = my_elem.actionScript;
if (aScript.length > 0) {
  var close = aScript.lastIndexOf("}");
  aScript = aScript.substr(0, close) +
➥ "\n\ttrace(\"here\");\n}";
} else {
  aScript =   "onClipEvent(load) {\n";
  aScript +=  "  trace(\"here\");\n";
  aScript +=  "}";
}
my_elem.actionScript = aScript;
```

buttonTracking

symbolInstance.buttonTracking

Sets button options

Description

This property corresponds with the Track as Button and Track as Menu Item options that appear in the Properties panel for a button instance. Acceptable values are "menu" and "button", and may either be retrieved or set. When "menu" is set, the button's onRelease event may be fired when the user merely releases the mouse over the button. An option of "button" will require you to both press and release the mouse over the button for the onRelease to be fired. This property will return undefined for movie clip or graphic symbol instances.

Value(s)

string—"button", "menu"

Example

```
fl.getDocumentDOM().selection[0].
➥ buttonTracking = "menu";
```

colorAlphaAmount

symbolInstance.colorAlphaAmount

Reduces or increases alpha values by constant amount

Description

Part of the color transformations for an instance, this property corresponds with the A) setting on the right side of the Settings window for the advanced color mode (accessed in the Properties panel while an instance is selected). Altering this value either increases or decreases the alpha values of an instance by a constant amount. The acceptable range of values is -255 to 255, and this may be both retrieved and set.

Value(s)

integer—-255 to 255

Example

```
var my_elem =
➥ fl.getDocumentDOM().selection[0];
my_elem.colorMode = "advanced";
my_elem.colorAlphaAmount = -100;
```

colorAlphaPercent

symbolInstance.colorAlphaPercent

Reduces or increases alpha values by percentage

Description

Part of the color transformations for an instance, this property corresponds with the Alpha setting on the left side of the Settings window for the advanced color mode (accessed in the Properties panel while an instance is selected). Altering this value either increases or decreases the alpha values of an instance by a percentage. The acceptable range of values is -100 to 100, and this may be both retrieved and set.

Value(s)

integer—-100 to 100

Example

```
var my_elem =
➥ fl.getDocumentDOM().selection[0];
my_elem.colorMode = "advanced";
my_elem.colorAlphaPercent = 0;
```

colorBlueAmount

symbolInstance.colorBlueAmount

Reduces or increases blue tint by specified value

Description

Part of the color transformations for an instance, this property corresponds with the B) setting on the right side of the Settings window for the advanced color mode (accessed in the Properties panel while an instance is selected). Altering this value either increases or decreases the blue tint of an instance by a constant amount. The acceptable range of values is -255 to 255, and this may be both retrieved and set.

Value(s)

integer—-255 to 255

Example

```
var my_elem =
➥ fl.getDocumentDOM().selection[0];
my_elem.colorMode = "advanced";
my_elem.colorBlueAmount = -100;
```

colorBluePercent

`symbolInstance.colorBluePercent`

Reduces or increases blue tint by specified percentage

Description

Part of the color transformations for an instance, this property corresponds with the Blue setting on the left side of the Settings window for the advanced color mode (accessed in the Properties panel while an instance is selected). Altering this value either increases or decreases the blue tint of an instance by a percentage. The acceptable range of values is -100 to 100, and this may be both retrieved and set.

Value(s)

integer—-100 to 100

Example

```
var my_elem =
fl.getDocumentDOM().selection[0];
my_elem.colorMode = "advanced";
my_elem.colorBluePercent = 0;
```

colorGreenAmount

`symbolInstance.colorGreenAmount`

Reduces or increases green tint by specified value

Description

Part of the color transformations for an instance, this property corresponds with the G) setting on the right side of the Settings window for the advanced color mode (accessed in the Properties panel while an instance is selected). Altering this value either increases or decreases the green tint of an instance by a constant amount. The acceptable range of values is -255 to 255, and this may be both retrieved and set.

Value(s)

integer—-255 to 255

Example

```
var my_elem =
fl.getDocumentDOM().selection[0];
my_elem.colorMode = "advanced";
my_elem.colorGreenAmount = -100;
```

colorGreenPercent

`symbolInstance.colorGreenPercent`

Reduces or increases green tint by specified percentage

Description

Part of the color transformations for an instance, this property corresponds with the Green setting on the left side of the Settings window for the advanced color mode (accessed in the Properties panel while an instance is selected). Altering this value either increases or decreases the green tint of an instance by a percentage. The acceptable range of values is -100 to 100, and this may be both retrieved and set.

Value(s)

integer—-100 to 100

Example

```
var my_elem =
fl.getDocumentDOM().selection[0];
my_elem.colorMode = "advanced";
my_elem.colorGreenPercent = 0;
```

colorMode

`symbolInstance.colorMode`

Color mode as identified in instance PI

Description

This property corresponds with the Color: drop-down menu found in the Properties panel when an instance is selected and controls the type of color transformations on an object. Acceptable values are `"none"`, `"brightness"`, `"tint"`, `"alpha"`, and `"advanced"`. Note that setting any of the individual color transform properties will automatically set the `colorMode` property to `"advanced"`.

Value(s)

string—`"none"`, `"brightness"`, `"tint"`, `"alpha"`, or `"advanced"`

Example

```
var my_elem =
fl.getDocumentDOM().selection[0];
my_elem.colorMode = "advanced";
my_elem.colorGreenPercent = 0;
```

colorRedAmount

`symbolInstance.colorRedAmount`

Reduces or increases red tint by specified value

Description

Part of the color transformations for an instance, this property corresponds with the R) setting on the right side of the Settings window for the advanced color mode (accessed in the Properties panel while an instance is selected). Altering this value either increases or decreases the red tint of an instance by a constant amount. The acceptable range of values is -255 to 255, and this may be both retrieved and set.

Value(s)

integer—-255 to 255

Example

```
var my_elem =
fl.getDocumentDOM().selection[0];
my_elem.colorMode = "advanced";
my_elem.colorBlueAmount = -100;
```

colorRedPercent

`symbolInstance.colorRedPercent`

Reduces or increases red tint for selected instance by specified percentage

Description

Part of the color transformations for an instance, this property corresponds with the Red setting on the left side of the Settings window for the advanced color mode (accessed in the Properties panel while an instance is selected). Altering this value either increases or decreases the red tint of an instance by a percentage. The acceptable range of values is -100 to 100, and this may be both retrieved and set.

Value(s)

integer—-100 to 100

Example

```
var my_elem =
➥ fl.getDocumentDOM().selection[0];
my_elem.colorMode = "advanced";
my_elem.colorRedPercent = 0;
```

description

`symbolInstance.description`

Description of object, used by screen reader

Description

The description property holds the textual information about the symbol instance that appears in the Accessibility panel and will be exposed to screen reader technology. This property may be both retrieved and set, and is available for movie clip and button instances, but not graphic instances.

Value(s)

string—Description of instance for screen reader

Example

```
var my_elem =
➥ fl.getDocumentDOM().getTimeline().
➥ layers[0].frames[0].elements[0];
my_elem.silent = false;
my_elem.description = "go to last page";
my_elem.accName = "back";
```

firstFrame

`symbolInstance.firstFrame`

Specifies which frame of graphic symbol to display first

Description

Specifies which frame will appear first for a graphic symbol (for a movie clip or button, this property returns undefined), and may be both set and retrieved. If the integer sent in the argument exceeds the number of frames in the instance, the instance will accept the argument but disappear from the stage (in the same way it will if the same value is set in the Properties panel). The argument will refer to an index in the symbol's frames array, and therefore a value of 0 would mean the first frame is first displayed, a value of 10 will mean the 11th frame will be first displayed, etc.

Value(s)

integer—The index in the symbol's frames array

Example

```
// sets the last frame as the
// first to be displayed
var my_elem =
➥ fl.getDocumentDOM().selection[0];
var frameCount =
➥ my_elem.libraryItem.timeline.
➥ layers[0].frames.length;
my_elem.firstFrame = frameCount-1;
```

forceSimple

`symbolInstance.forceSimple`

If `true`, children of object aren't accessible to screen reader.

Description

This property specifies whether a movie clip instance's child objects will be made accessible to a screen reader and corresponds (inversely) with the Make child objects accessible check box in the Accessibility panel. When `true`, the child objects *won't* be accessible. When `false`, the child objects *will* be accessible. This property, which is only available for movie clips, may be both set and retrieved.

Value(s)

Boolean—`true`, `false`

Example

```
var my_elem =
➥ fl.getDocumentDOM().selection[0];
my_elem.silent = false;
my_elem.forceSimple = true;
```

loop

`symbolInstance.loop`

Specifies loop setting for graphic symbol

Description

Controls how a graphic is displayed or played. Acceptable values are `"loop"` (default), `"play once"`, and `"single frame"`. This property, which applies to only graphic symbols (this value will return undefined for both movie clips and buttons), may be both retrieved and set.

Value(s)

string—`"loop"`, `"play once"`, or `"first frame"`

Example

```
var my_elem =
➥ fl.getDocumentDOM().selection[0];
my_elem.loop = "play once";
```

shortcut

`symbolInstance.shortcut`

Object's shortcut key

Description

The shortcut key used for accessibility and exposed by a screen reader. This property, which may be applied to movie clips and buttons, but not graphic symbols, corresponds with the shortcut field in the Accessibility panel. It may be retrieved or set. To have the shortcut key actually work with an object, however, you still need to use ActionScript to detect a keyDown event for that key and provide whatever functionality is required.

Value(s)

string—The key or key combination used to access the object

Example

```
var my_elem =
➥ fl.getDocumentDOM().selection[0];
my_elem.silent = false;
my_elem.shortcut = "Control+B";
my_elem.name = "back";
```

silent

`symbolInstance.silent`

If `true`, object isn't read by screen reader.

Description

This property controls whether an object is visible and accessible to a screen reader, and may be both set and retrieved. Setting this property to `true` will make it invisible and corresponds with deselecting the Make Object Accessible check box in the Accessibility panel.

Value(s)

Boolean—`true`, `false`

Example

```
var my_elem =
➥ fl.getDocumentDOM().selection[0];
my_elem.silent = false;
```

```
my_elem.shortcut = "Control+B";
my_elem.name = "back";
```

symbolType

symbolInstance.symbolType

Specifies symbol type of instance

Description

Specifies whether the symbol instance is a "button", "graphic", or "movie clip". This property may be set or retrieved, which makes it possible to switch an instance's behavior from one type to another.

Value(s)

string—"button", "graphic", or "movie clip"

Example

```
var my_elem =
➥ fl.getDocumentDOM().selection[0];
if (my_elem.symbolType == "button") {
  my_elem.silent = "false";
}
```

tabIndex

symbolInstance.tabIndex

Tab index value of object

Description

This property, which is only available for movie clip and button instances, corresponds with the same value found in ActionScript. tabIndex is used to control tab ordering on a page and determines order for a screen reader. This property may be both set and retrieved.

Value(s)

integer—The index in tab order

Example

```
// reverses tab order on a layer
// from right to left
function sorter(a, b) { return b[1]-a[1] }
var elmnts =
➥ fl.getDocumentDOM().getTimeline().
➥ layers[0].frames[0].elements;
var clips = [];
for (var i in elmnts) {
  clips.push([elmnts[i], elmnts[i].matrix.tx]);
}
clips.sort(sorter);
for (var i = 0; i < clips.length; i++) {
  clips[i][0].tabIndex = i
}
```

SymbolItem

Subclass of Item. Represents a symbol in the Library.

Methods:

- convertToCompiledClip
- exportSWC
- exportSWF

Properties:

- sourceAutoUpdate
- sourceFilePath
- sourceLibraryName
- symbolType
- timeline

Methods of the symbolItem Object

convertToCompiledClip

symbolItem.convertToCompiledClip()

Converts a symbol to compiled clip

Description

Creates a new compiled clip in the Library from the item. The compiled clip will display and publish faster than the original symbol, but will be uneditable. The original item is unharmed.

Argument(s)

None

Returns

Nothing

Example

```
fl.getDocumentDOM().library.items[0].
➥ convertToCompiledClip();
```

exportSWC

`symbolItem.exportSWC( outputURI )`

Exports symbol to SWC file

Description
Exports item to local SWC file at the specified URI. If only `file:///` is passed as the URI, then a browse dialog box will be presented to the user.

Argument(s)
`outputURI`—*string*—The local path where SWC should be saved

Returns
Nothing

Example
```
fl.getDocumentDOM().library.items[0].
➥ exportSWC("file:///c|/My Documents/
➥ CompiledClips/test.swc");
fl.getDocumentDOM().library.items[0].exportSWC("fil
e:///");
```

exportSWF

`symbolItem.exportSWF( outputURI )`

Exports symbol to SWF file

Description
Exports item to local SWF file at the specified URI. Unlike `exportSWC`, a valid path must be passed—no browse dialog box will be opened if the path is invalid. Instead an error will be thrown.

Argument(s)
`outputURI`—*string*—The local path where SWF should be saved

Returns
Nothing

Example
```
fl.getDocumentDOM().library.items[0].
➥ exportSWF("file:///c|/My Documents/movies/
➥ test.swf");
```

Properties of the symbolItem Object

sourceAutoUpdate

`symbolItem.sourceAutoUpdate`

If `true`, Shared Library symbol updates when published.

Description
If `true`, forces the symbol to automatically update from the Shared Library when the movie is published.

Value(s)
Boolean—`true`, `false`

Example
```
fl.getDocumentDOM().library.items[0].
➥ sourceAutoUpdate = true;
```

sourceFilePath

`symbolItem.sourceFilePath`

Source path for Shared Library symbol

Description
The absolute path to the FLA where the item should be imported from

Value(s)
string—The absolute path to the FLA

Example
```
fl.getDocumentDOM().library.items[0].
➥ sourceFilePath = "C:\Documents and
➥ Settings\Administrator\My Documents\
➥ libraries\exported.fla";
```

sourceLibraryName

`symbolItem.sourceLibraryName`

Name of symbol in source file

Description
The name of the symbol in the Shared Library that this item should import

Value(s)
string—The name of the Shared Library item

Example

```
fl.getDocumentDOM().library.items[0].
➥ sourceLibraryName = "newClip";
```

symbolType

symbolItem.symbolType

Specifies symbol type

Description

The symbol type of the item. May be retrieved or set.

Value(s)

string—"movie clip", "button", or "graphic"

Example

```
fl.trace(fl.getDocumentDOM().library.
➥ items[0].symbolType);
```

timeline

symbolItem.timeline

timeline object for symbol

Description

A reference to the symbol item's timeline object, which is the timeline inside the symbol

Value(s)

Timeline—The timeline of the symbol

Example

```
fl.getDocumentDOM().library.items[0].
➥ timeline.layers[0].name = "code";
```

Text

Subclass of Element. Represents a text field on the stage.

Methods:

- getTextAttr
- getTextString
- setTextAttr
- setTextString

Properties:

- accName
- autoExpand
- border
- description
- embeddedCharacters
- embedRanges
- length
- lineType
- maxCharacters
- orientation
- renderAsHTML
- scrollable
- selectable
- selectionEnd
- selectionStart
- shortcut
- silent
- tabIndex
- textRuns
- textType
- useDeviceFonts
- variableName

Methods of the text Object

getTextAttr

text.getTextAttr(*attrName* [, *startIndex*]
➥ [, *endIndex*])

Returns specified text attribute

Description

Returns the value for specified text attribute (see the entry for TextAttrs for a list of its properties that may be passed as an argument for this function). If only the attrName argument is passed, then the value for the text attribute for the entire string will be returned. If this isn't consistent for the entire string, undefined will be returned. If the attrName and startIndex arguments are passed, but not the endIndex, then the text attribute value for the single character at the index specified by startIndex will be returned. If endIndex is also passed, the text attribute value for the range from startIndex up to but not including endIndex will be returned. If this value isn't consistent for the entire range of text, then undefined is returned. A negative number passed as the startIndex has the same effect as passing a 0.

Argument(s)

attrName—*string*—The name of the textAttrs property

startIndex—*integer*—The index in the text string to check (or start index for a range to check)

endIndex—*integer*—Determines the end of the range to check (not included in range)

Returns

Value of text attribute—*Varies depending on attribute*

Example

```
var my_elem =
➥ fl.getDocumentDOM().selection[0];
var s = my_elem.getTextAttr("size");
my_elem.setTextAttr("size", s+5, 0);
```

getTextString

```
text.getTextString( [startIndex]
➥ [, endIndex] )
```

Returns text string contained in specified range

Description

Returns the text contained in the element for the specified range. If no argument is passed, the entire text string is returned. If only a startIndex is passed, the text is returned from that index to the end of the string. If both arguments are passed, the string is returned from the startIndex up to but not including the endIndex. Passing a negative number for the startIndex works the same as passing a negative number.

Argument(s)

startIndex—*integer*—The index of the first character in a range to return

endIndex—*integer*—Determines the end of the range (not included in range)

Returns

Text in range specified—*string*

Example

```
fl.trace(fl.getDocumentDOM().
➥ selection[0].getTextString());
var t = fl.getDocumentDOM().getTimeline().
➥ layers[0].frames[0].elements[0].
➥ getTextString(0, 3);
```

setTextAttr

```
text.setTextAttr( attrName, attrValue
➥ [, startIndex] [, endIndex] )
```

Sets specified text attribute

Description

Sets text attribute properties for an entire text field or for a specified range of characters. Using this method (as opposed to setting the properties directly within the textAttrs object in a TextRun) allows you to set formatting across TextRuns. This can have the effect of creating more TextRuns within this text element's textRuns array.

If a startIndex isn't passed, then the formatting for the entire text string is set. If startIndex is passed, but not endIndex, then the formatting is set for the single character at the index specified by startIndex. If both startIndex and endIndex are passed, then the formatting is set for the range starting from startIndex and leading up to, but not including, endIndex.

Argument(s)

attrName—*string*—The name of the attribute to set

attrValue—*Varies depending on attribute*—The value for the attribute

startIndex—*integer*—Starting index for range of characters to set

endIndex—*integer*—Determines end of range to set (not included in range)

Returns

Nothing

Example

```
fl.getDocumentDOM().selection[0].
➥ setTextAttr("alignment", "center");
fl.getDocumentDOM().selection[0].
➥ setTextAttr("fillColor", "#FF0000", 0);
fl.getDocumentDOM().selection[0].
➥ setTextAttr("size", 20, 0, 1);
```

setTextString

```
text.setTextString( text [, startIndex]
➥ [, endIndex] )
```

Sets text string within text object

Description

Sets text or inserts text into a text element. If only the text argument is passed, the entire string will be replaced with the text passed. If only startIndex is passed, the text argument that is sent will be inserted at that index position. If both startIndex and endIndex are passed, the text argument sent will replace the text at that range.

Argument(s)

text—*string*—Text to be inserted into text element

startIndex—*integer*—Either index at which to begin insert or, if endIndex is passed as well, beginning of range to replace

endIndex—*integer*—Determines the end of text range to be replaced (not included in range)

Returns

Nothing

Example

```
fl.getDocumentDOM().selection[0].
➥ setTextString("I'm replacing with
➥ this text");
fl.getDocumentDOM().selection[0].
➥ setTextString("I'm inserting at index
➥ 2", 2);
fl.getDocumentDOM().selection[0].
➥ setTextString("I'm replacing a range",
➥ 5, 10);
```

Properties of the text Object

accName

```
text.accName
```

Name of object, used by screen reader

Description

The accName property holds the name of the text element that appears in the Accessibility panel and will be exposed to screen reader technology. This property may be both retrieved and set, but is only available for input text fields.

Value(s)

string—The name of the input field for the screen reader

Example

```
var my_elem =
➥ fl.getDocumentDOM().getTimeline().
➥ layers[0].frames[0].elements[0];
my_elem.silent = false;
my_elem.description =
➥ "login username field";
my_elem.accName = "username";
```

autoExpand

```
text.autoExpand
```

If true, bounding width expands to display all text

Description

This property specifies whether a text field's bounding box will expand to display all text (true) or not (false). For static text fields, the width of the text field is what will expand. For dynamic and input fields, both the width and height will expand to accommodate the text. This property may be retrieved or set.

Value(s)

Boolean—true, false

Example

```
fl.trace(fl.getDocumentDOM().
➥ selection[0].autoExpand);
```

border

```
text.border
```

If true, displays a border around dynamic or input text

Description

This property, if true, displays a border around dynamic or input text element. For a static text field, this property may be retrieved (though it has no relevance), but an error is thrown if set.

Value(s)

Boolean—true, false

Example

```
fl.getDocumentDOM().
➥ selection[0].border = true;
```

description

`text.description`

Description of object, used by screen reader

Description

The `description` property holds the textual information about the text field that appears in the Accessibility panel and will be exposed to screen reader technology. This property may be both retrieved and set, and is available for input and dynamic text fields, but not static.

Value(s)

string—Description of the text element for the screen reader

Example

```
var my_elem =
➥ fl.getDocumentDOM().getTimeline().
➥ layers[0].frames[0].elements[0];
my_elem.silent = false;
my_elem.description =
➥ "login username field";
my_elem.accName = "username";
```

embeddedCharacters

`text.embeddedCharacters`

Embeds all specified characters

Description

Specifies the font outline characters to be embedded in the SWF file. The characters are passed as a single string. This property may be both retrieved and set.

Value(s)

string—Characters to embed

Example

```
fl.getDocumentDOM().selection[0].
➥ embeddedCharacters = "USERNAME:";
```

embedRanges

`text.embedRanges`

Specifies ranges of characters to embed

Description

Specifies the ranges of characters to be embedded in SWF. The numbers in this string correspond with the row in the list of ranges found in the Character dialog window accessed in the Properties panel when a text field is selected. For instance, a value of `"1|2"` passed as an argument (each integer is separated by a bar) will embed the uppercase and lowercase characters of the text field's font—these are the first two rows in the ranges list in the Character dialog box. Passing an empty string to this property will deselect all ranges. This property may be both retrieved and set.

Value(s)

string—A string of integers, each separated by a bar. For example, `"1|3|4|7";`.

Example

```
fl.getDocumentDOM().selection[0].
➥ embedRanges = "1|2|3";
```

length

`text.length`

Number of characters in text object

Description

The number of characters in the text field. This property may be retrieved, but not set.

Value(s)

integer—The number of characters

Example

```
var my_elem = fl.getDocumentDOM().selection[0];
my_elem.setTextString(" Placing this
➥ at the end", my_elem.length);
```

lineType

`text.lineType`

Type of text line

Description

This property determines how text flows within the text field. Possible values for input and dynamic text fields include `"single line"`, `"multiline"`, and `"multiline no wrap"`. Input fields may also have `"password"` set (setting this for a dynamic text field will throw an error). For a static text field, trying to set this property will throw an error. For input and dynamic text fields, this property may be both retrieved and set.

Value(s)

string—"single line", "multiline", "multiline no wrap", and "password"

Example

```
fl.getDocumentDOM().
➥ selection[0].lineType = "single line";
```

maxCharacters

`text.maxCharacters`

Specifies maximum characters

Description

For an input field, sets the maximum number of characters a user may enter into the field. Setting this property for dynamic or static text fields will throw an error. For an input field, the property may be both retrieved and set.

Value(s)

integer—Maximum number of characters

Example

```
fl.getDocumentDOM().
➥ selection[0].maxCharacters = 10;
```

orientation

`text.orientation`

Specifies orientation of text

Description

The orientation of the text in a static text field. Acceptable values are "horizontal", "vertical right to left", and "vertical left to right". This property may be both retrieved and set. For input and dynamic fields, this property will always return "horizontal", and attempting to set it will throw an error.

Value(s)

string—"horizontal", "vertical right to left", and "vertical left to right"

Example

```
fl.getDocumentDOM().
➥ selection[0].orientation =
➥ "vertical left to right";
```

renderAsHTML

`text.renderAsHTML`

If true, text renders as HTML.

Description

When this property is set to true, the text within this text field is rendered as HTML and any recognized tags within the text will be interpreted. This property may be set and retrieved, but only applies to dynamic and input text fields. Setting this property for static text fields will throw an error (retrieving it for static text will always return false).

Value(s)

Boolean—true, false

Example

```
fl.getDocumentDOM().
➥ selection[0].renderAsHTML = true;
```

scrollable

`text.scrollable`

If true, text can be scrolled.

Description

Determines whether a text field's text is scrollable or not. With scrollable text, the field won't automatically expand to accommodate text but instead remain a static size and allow for its text to be scrolled with the mouse or arrow keys.

Value(s)

Boolean—true, false

Example

```
fl.getDocumentDOM().
➥ selection[0].scrollable = true;
```

selectable

`text.selectable`

If true, text can be selected.

Description

When this property is set to true, the user may select the text in the field, and whenever the mouse is hovered over the field, the I-bar will appear. For an input text field, this property is always set to true and may not be set. For dynamic and static text fields, this property may be both retrieved and set.

Value(s)

Boolean—true, false

Example

```
fl.getDocumentDOM().
➥ selection[0].selectable = false;
```

selectionEnd

text.selectionEnd

Offset of end of text subselection

Description

The index in the text designating the end of a selection (the character at this index is *not* included in the selection). If selectionStart is equal to selectionEnd, then there is no selection of text. When setting this property, setting a value less than the selectionStart value will set the selectionStart value to equal the selectionEnd (thus causing no selection). This property may be both set and retrieved. Note: Once a selection of a text field has been made at one point, selectionEnd and selectionStart may not be equal even when there is no selection. Only when the cursor is inserted within the text field (with no range selected) will these two values once again be equal and signify no selection.

Value(s)

integer—The index of the character directly after a selection of text

Example

```
fl.getDocumentDOM().
➥ selection[0].selectionStart = 0;
fl.getDocumentDOM().
➥ selection[0].selectionEnd = 10;
```

selectionStart

text.selectionStart

Offset of beginning of text subselection

Description

The index in the text where a selection of the text begins. If selectionStart is equal to selectionEnd, then there is no selection of text. When setting this property, setting a value greater than the selectionEnd value will set the selectionEnd value to equal selectionStart (thus causing no selection). This property may be both set and retrieved. Note: Once a selection of a text field has been made at one point, selectionEnd and selectionStart may not be equal even when there is no selection. Only when the cursor is inserted within the text field (with no range selected) will these two values once again be equal and signify no selection.

Value(s)

integer—The starting index of a text selection

Example

```
fl.getDocumentDOM().
➥ selection[0].selectionStart = 0;
fl.getDocumentDOM().
➥ selection[0].selectionEnd = 10;
```

shortcut

text.shortcut

Object's shortcut key

Description

The shortcut key used for accessibility and exposed by a screen reader. This is the key designated that, when pressed, will set the focus to the text field. This property, which may only be applied to input text fields, corresponds with the shortcut field in the Accessibility panel. It may be retrieved or set. To have the shortcut key actually work with an object, however, you still need to use ActionScript to detect a keyDown event for that key and provide whatever functionality is required.

Value(s)

string—The key or key combination used to access the object

Example

```
var my_elem =
➥ fl.getDocumentDOM().selection[0];
if (my_elem.textType == "input") {
my_elem.silent = false;
my_elem.shortcut = "U";
}
```

silent

text.silent

If true, object isn't read by screen reader.

Description

This property controls whether an object is visible and accessible to a screen reader, and may be both set and retrieved. Setting this property to `true` will make it invisible and corresponds with deselecting the Make Object Accessible check box in the Accessibility panel. The `silent` property is available for the input and dynamic text fields, but not static.

Value(s)

Boolean—`true`, `false`

Example

```
var my_elem =
➥ fl.getDocumentDOM().getTimeline().
➥ layers[0].frames[0].elements[0];
my_elem.silent = false;
my_elem.description = "login username field";
my_elem.accName = "username";
```

tabIndex

`text.tabIndex`

Tab index value of object

Description

This property, which is only available for dynamic and input text field, corresponds with the same value found in ActionScript. `tabIndex` is used to control tab ordering on a page and determines order for a screen reader. This property may be both set and retrieved.

Value(s)

integer—The index in tab order

Example

```
// reverses tab order on a
// layer from right to left
function sorter(a, b) { return b[1]-a[1] }
var elmnts =
➥ fl.getDocumentDOM().getTimeline().
➥ layers[0].frames[0].elements;
var instncs = [];
for (var i in elmnts) {
  instncs.push([elmnts[i], elmnts[i].matrix.tx]);
}
instncs.sort(sorter);
for (var i = 0; i < instncs.length; i++) {
  instncs[i][0].tabIndex = i
}
```

textRuns

`text.textRuns`

Array of `textRun` objects

Description

An array that holds the text element's individual `textRun` objects. When different formatting is applied within a single text field, each block of consistent formatting is stored as a different `textRun` and placed in the `textRuns` array. If a text field has consistent formatting throughout, then the `textRuns` array will only hold one `textRun` object that contains all of the characters for the text field.

Value(s)

array—A collection of `textRun` objects

Example

```
fl.trace(fl.getDocumentDOM().
➥ selection[0].textRuns.length);
```

textType

`text.textType`

Type of text field

Description

The specified type of the text field—`"static"`, `"input"`, or `"dynamic"`. This property may be both set and retrieved.

Value(s)

string—`"static"`, `"input"`, or `"dynamic"`

Example

```
fl.getDocumentDOM().
➥ selection[0].textType = "dynamic";
```

useDeviceFonts

`text.useDeviceFonts`

If `true`, renders text using device font

Description

Available only for static text fields, this property determines whether the text field's fonts are rendered as device fonts from the client's computer. Although the value may be retrieved for input and dynamic text fields, attempting to set it will throw an error. For static fields the property may be set and retrieved.

Value(s)
Boolean—true, false

Example
```
if (fl.getDocumentDOM().
➥ selection[0].textType == "static") {
  fl.getDocumentDOM().
➥ selection[0].useDeviceFonts = true;
}
```

variableName

`text.variableName`

Stores the contents of text field in variable name

Description
The variable on the text element's parent timeline that will hold a reference to all of the text field's text content. If the value of the variable changes, the text in the field will change. If the text in the field changes, the variable's value will be updated. This property may be both set and retrieved, and is available only for dynamic and input text field types.

Value(s)
string—The variable to hold the text field contents

Example
```
fl.getDocumentDOM().
➥ selection[0].variableName = "userName";
```

TextAttrs

Holds common text attributes for a selection of text

Properties:

- aliasText
- alignment
- autoKern
- bold
- characterPosition
- characterSpacing
- face
- fillColor
- indent
- italic
- leftMargin
- lineSpacing
- rightMargin
- rotation
- size
- target
- url

Properties of the textAttrs Object

aliasText

`textAttrs.aliasText`

If true, text renders aliased.

Description
Text by default is antialiased (smoothed at the edges to make it appear less pixelated). Setting this property to false leaves text aliased and hard edged, which is often better when using very small fonts.

Value(s)
Boolean—true, false

Example
```
var tAttr = fl.getDocumentDOM().
➥ election[0].textRuns[0].textAttrs;
tAttr.aliasText = true;
```

alignment

`textAttrs.alignment`

Paragraph justification

Description
Specifies the paragraph alignment: "right", "left", "center", or "justify" (full justification).

Value(s)
string—"right", "left", "center", or "justify"

Example
```
var tAttr = fl.getDocumentDOM().
➥ selection[0].textRuns[0].textAttrs;
tAttr.alignment = "center";
```

autoKern

`textAttrs.autoKern`

If true, pair kerning is used.

Description

Determines whether a text field will automatically kern special letters defined in the font (true) or not (false). For example, the letters "W" and "A", when next to each other, would normally be kerned slightly closer together to accommodate the shape of the letters. This property is available only for static text fields.

Value(s)

Boolean—true, false

Example

```
var tAttr = fl.getDocumentDOM().
➥ selection[0].textRuns[0].textAttrs;
tAttr.autoKern = true;
```

bold

`textAttrs.bold`

If true, text is displayed as bold.

Description

This property, when set to true, bolds the characters in the textRun.

Value(s)

Boolean—true, false

Example

```
var tAttr = fl.getDocumentDOM().
➥ selection[0].textRuns[0].textAttrs;
tAttr.bold = true;
```

characterPosition

`textAttrs.characterPosition`

Vertical position of text

Description

Specifies whether characters in textRun are normal, superscript, or subscript. dynamic and input text will always be normal.

Value(s)

string—"normal", "superscript", or "subscript"

Example

```
var tAttr = fl.getDocumentDOM().
➥ selection[0].textRuns[2].textAttrs;
tAttr.characterPosition = "superscript";
```

characterSpacing

`textAttrs.characterSpacing`

Number representing space between characters

Description

Number defining the pixel distance between characters in textRun. An integer is expected, though a float may be passed.

Value(s)

number—Pixel distance between characters

Example

```
var tAttr = fl.getDocumentDOM().
➥ selection[0].textRuns[0].textAttrs;
tAttr.characterSpacing = 4;
```

face

`textAttrs.face`

Name of font

Description

The name of the font for the characters in the textRun.

Value(s)

string—The available font

Example

```
var tAttr = fl.getDocumentDOM().
➥ selection[0].textRuns[0].textAttrs;
tAttr.face = "Verdana";
```

fillColor

`textAttrs.fillColor`

Color of text

Description

This property specifies the color for the characters in the textRun. Values may be passed as a hexadecimal string ("#0000FF"), a base 10 number (255), or a hexadecimal number preceded by "0x" (0x0000FF).

Value(s)

number or hex string—Color value

Example

```
var my_elem =
➥ fl.getDocumentDOM().selection[0];
my_elem.textRuns[0].textAttrs.fillColor =
➥ "#FFFFFF";
my_elem.textRuns[1].textAttrs.fillColor =
➥ 10000;
my_elem.textRuns[2].textAttrs.fillColor =
➥ 0xFF0033;
```

indent

`textAttrs.indent`

Paragraph indentation

Description

This property determines the pixel amount of indentation for the first line of a paragraph within the textRun. An integer is expected, though a float may be passed.

Value(s)

number—Pixel measure of first line indent

Example

```
var tAttr = fl.getDocumentDOM().
➥ selection[0].textRuns[0].textAttrs;
tAttr.indent = 10;
```

italic

`textAttrs.italic`

If true, text is italicized.

Description

This property, when set to true, italicizes the characters in the textRun.

Value(s)

Boolean—true, false

Example

```
var tAttr = fl.getDocumentDOM().
➥ selection[0].textRuns[0].textAttrs;
tAttr.italic = true;
```

leftMargin

`textAttrs.leftMargin`

Paragraph's left margin

Description

The measure of the textRun's left margin in pixels. The acceptable range is 0 to 720 and values will automatically be limited to that range.

Value(s)

number—0 to 720 pixels

Example

```
var tAttr = fl.getDocumentDOM().
➥ selection[0].textRuns[0].textAttrs;
tAttr.leftMargin = 20;
```

lineSpacing

`textAttrs.lineSpacing`

Paragraph's line spacing

Description

The line spacing or leading for a textRun, measured in points. The acceptable range is -360 to 720 and values will automatically be limited to that range.

Value(s)

number—-360 to 720 points

Example

```
var tAttr = fl.getDocumentDOM().
➥ selection[0].textRuns[0].textAttrs;
tAttr.lineSpacing = 12;
```

rightMargin

`textAttrs.rightMargin`

Paragraph's right margin

Description

The measure of the textRun's right margin in pixels. The acceptable range is 0 to 720 and values will automatically be limited to that range.

Value(s)

number—0 to 720 pixels

Example

```
var tAttr = fl.getDocumentDOM().
➥ selection[0].textRuns[0].textAttrs;
tAttr.rightMargin = 20;
```

rotation

`textAttrs.rotation`

If `true`, characters are rotated 90 degrees.

Description

Specifies whether all characters in `textRun` will be rotated by 90 degrees (`true`) or not (`false`). This property is only valid for static text with a vertical orientation; otherwise an error is thrown

Value(s)

Boolean—`true`, `false`

Example

```
var my_elem =
➥ fl.getDocumentDOM().selection[0]
my_elem.orientation = "vertical left to right";
var tAttr = my_elem.textRuns[0].textAttrs;
tAttr.rotation = true;
```

size

`textAttrs.size`

Size of font

Description

The point size of the text. An integer is what is expected, though you may send a floating decimal number or a number within quotes as the value without error.

Value(s)

number—Point size

Example

```
var tAttr = fl.getDocumentDOM().
➥ selection[0].textRuns[0].textAttrs;
tAttr.size = 20;
```

target

`textAttrs.target`

String for target

Description

This property, which is only valid for static text, determines where the URL specified in the `url` property will load if users click the text.

Value(s)

string—`"_target"`, `"_blank"`, `"_self"`, `"_top"`, or other possible target

Example

```
var tAttr = fl.getDocumentDOM().
➥ selection[0].textRuns[0].textAttrs;
tAttr.aliasText = true;
```

url

`textAttrs.url`

String representing URL

Description

The URL for a text hyperlink. This property is only valid for static text.

Value(s)

string—A valid url

Example

```
var tAttr = fl.getDocumentDOM().
➥ selection[0].textRuns[0].textAttrs;
tAttr.url =
➥ "http://www.flashextensibility.com";
```

TextRun

Subclass of Text. Represents a string of characters.

Properties:

- `characters`
- `textAttrs`

Properties of the textRun Object

characters

textRun.characters

Text contained in textRun object

Description
The string of text within a textRun object. This may be both retrieved and set.

Value(s)
string—Characters in the string

Example
```
var t = fl.getDocumentDOM().
➥ selection[0].textRuns[0];
fl.trace(t.characters);
```

textAttrs

textRun.textAttrs

textAttrs object containing attributes of a run of text

Description
This property references the textAttrs object that holds the text attributes for the string of text in the TextRun. You may access and set individual attributes within the textAttrs object as opposed to using text.setTextAttr().

Value(s)
textAttrs object—A collection of attributes for the text

Example
```
var t = fl.getDocumentDOM().
➥ selection[0].textRuns[0];
for (var i in t.textAttrs) {
  fl.trace(i + ": " + t.textAttrs[i]);
}
t.textAttrs["size"] = 20;
```

Timeline

An object representing a single timeline (scene) of a document

Methods:

- addMotionGuide
- addNewLayer
- clearFrames
- clearKeyframes
- convertToBlankKeyframes
- convertToKeyframes
- copyFrames
- createMotionTween
- cutFrames
- deleteLayer
- expandFolder
- findLayerIndex
- getFrameProperty
- getLayerProperty
- getSelectedFrames
- getSelectedLayers
- insertBlankKeyframe
- insertFrames
- insertKeyframe
- pasteFrames
- removeFrames
- reorderLayer
- reverseFrames
- selectAllFrames
- setFrameProperty
- setLayerProperty
- setSelectedFrames
- setSelectedFrames
- setSelectedLayers
- showLayerMasking

Properties:

- currentFrame
- currentLayer
- frameCount
- layerCount
- layers
- name

Methods of the timeline Object

addMotionGuide

`timeline.addMotionGuide()`

Adds motion guide layer

Description

Adds a motion guide layer to the timeline. Creates a new layer above the current layer, sets the new layer's layerType to "guide", and the current layer's to "guided". The new layer becomes the current layer. Will only be successful on a normal layer.

Argument(s)

None

Returns

Index to the new layer if successful, otherwise returns -1—*integer*

Example

```
my_tl = fl.getDocumentDOM().getTimeline();
my_tl.addMotionGuide();
```

addNewLayer

`timeline.addNewLayer( [name]`
`➥ [, layerType] [, bAddAbove] )`

Adds new layer

Description

Creates a new layer in the current timeline

Argument(s)

name—*string*—The name to be given the new layer. If not specified, a default name will be used.

layerType—*string*—The type of layer to create. See the entry for layer.layerType. Default is "normal".

bAddAbove—*Boolean*—If true, layer will be created above the current layer. If false, it will be created below. Default is true.

Returns

Index to the new layer—*integer*

Example

```
my_tl = fl.getDocumentDOM().getTimeline();
my_tl.addNewLayer("top layer",
➥ "normal", true);
```

clearFrames

`timeline.clearFrames( [startFrame]`
`➥ [, endFrame] )`

Deletes all contents from within frame

Description

Clears a frame or a range of frames of all content. If startFrame and endFrame are both specified, content will be cleared from startFrame up to but not including endFrame. If only startFrame is specified, content will be cleared only in that frame. If neither is specified, it will clear the currently selected frame(s). If the frame or frames to be cleared are within a frame sequence, a new blank keyframe will be created at startFrame, with a blank frame sequence continuing through to the frame before endFrame.

Argument(s)

startFrame—*integer*—The first frame to clear

endFrame—*integer*—The frame after the last frame to clear

Returns

Nothing

Example

```
my_tl = fl.getDocumentDOM().getTimeline();
my_tl.clearFrames(3, 5);
```

clearKeyframes

`timeline.clearKeyframes( [startFrame]`
`➥ [, endFrame] )`

Converts keyframe to regular frame and deletes its contents

Description

Clears a keyframe or a range of keyframes of all content and converts them to regular frames. The frames content, if any, will be based on the previous keyframe in the layer. If startFrame and endFrame are both specified, content will be cleared from startFrame up to but not including endFrame. If only startFrame is specified, content will be cleared only in that frame. If neither is specified, the currently selected frame(s) will be cleared. If the frame or frames to be cleared are within a frame sequence, a new blank keyframe will be created at startFrame, with a blank frame sequence continuing through to the frame before endFrame.

Argument(s)
startFrame—*integer*—The first frame to clear

endFrame—*integer*—The frame after the last frame to clear

Returns
Nothing

Example
```
my_tl = fl.getDocumentDOM().getTimeline();
my_tl.clearKeyframes(3, 5);
```

convertToBlankKeyframes

```
timeline.convertToBlankKeyframes
➥ ( [startFrame] [, endFrame] )
```

Converts specified frame to blank keyframe

Description
Converts the specified frame to a blank keyframe. Any content in the frame will be deleted. If the frame is within a frame sequence, the remainder of that sequence will also be cleared. If startFrame and endFrame are both specified, frames from startFrame up to but not including endFrame will be converted to blank keyframes. If only startFrame is specified, only that frame will be converted. If neither is specified, this method will convert the currently selected frame(s).

Argument(s)
startFrame—*integer*—The first frame to convert

endFrame—*integer*—The frame after the last frame to convert

Returns
Nothing

Example
```
my_tl = fl.getDocumentDOM().getTimeline();
my_tl.convertToBlankKeyframes(3, 5);
```

convertToKeyframes

```
timeline.convertToKeyframes( [startFrame]
➥ [, endFrame] )
```

Converts specified frames to keyframes

Description
Converts the specified frame to a keyframe. If startFrame and endFrame are both specified, frames from startFrame up to but not including endFrame will be converted to keyframes. If only startFrame is specified, only that frame will be converted. If neither is specified, this method will convert the currently selected frame(s).

Argument(s)
startFrame—*integer*—The first frame to convert

endFrame—*integer*—The frame after the last frame to convert

Returns
Nothing

Example
```
my_tl = fl.getDocumentDOM().getTimeline();
my_tl.convertToKeyframes(3, 5);
```

copyFrames

```
timeline.copyFrames( [startFrame]
➥ [, endFrame] )
```

Copies specified frames to clipboard

Description
Copies a frame or frames to the clipboard. Copies frames starting with startFrame, up to but not including endFrame. If endFrame isn't specified, this method copies startFrame. If startFrame isn't specified, this method copies currently selected frames.

Argument(s)
startFrame—*integer*—The first frame to copy

endFrame—*integer*—The frame after the last frame to copy

Returns
Nothing

Example
```
my_tl = fl.getDocumentDOM().getTimeline();
my_tl.copyFrames(3, 5);
```

createMotionTween

```
timeline.createMotionTween( [startFrame]
➥ [, endFrame] )
```

Creates motion tween, converts frame's contents into symbol if it isn't one

Description

Creates a motion tween , converting the frame's contents into a symbol. For every keyframe specified or selected, this method sets the frame's tweenType property to "motion". Does the same for the starting frame of any frame sequence that falls within the specified or selected frames. As with other similar methods, createMotionTween operates on frames from startFrame up to but not including endFrame, or startFrame only if endFrame isn't specified. If neither are specified, this method operates on selected frames.

Argument(s)

startFrame—*integer*—The first frame of the range that will be affected

endFrame—*integer*—The frame after the last frame of the range that will be affected

Returns

Nothing

Example

```
my_tl = fl.getDocumentDOM().getTimeline();
my_tl.createMotionTween(3, 10);
```

cutFrames

```
timeline.cutFrames( [startFrame] [, endFrame] )
```

Cuts specified frames to the clipboard

Description

Cuts a frame or frames to the clipboard. cutFrames cuts frames starting with startFrame, up to but not including endFrame. If endFrame isn't specified, this method cuts startFrame. If startFrame isn't specified, this method cuts currently selected frames.

Argument(s)

startFrame—*integer*—The first frame to cut

endFrame—*integer*—The frame after the last frame to cut

Returns

Nothing

Example

```
my_tl = fl.getDocumentDOM().getTimeline();
my_tl.cutFrames(3, 5);
```

deleteLayer

```
timeline.deleteLayer( [index] )
```

Deletes layer in timeline

Description

Deletes a layer in the specified timeline. If the layer is a folder, this method will delete all layers within the folder. If there is only one layer in the timeline, it won't be deleted.

Argument(s)

index—*integer*—The index of the layers array specifying which layer to delete. If not specified, any selected layers will be deleted.

Returns

Nothing

Example

```
my_tl = fl.getDocumentDOM().getTimeline();
my_tl.deleteLayer(3);
```

expandFolder

```
timeline.expandFolder( bExpand
➥ [, bRecurseNestedParents] [, index] )
```

If true, expands layer folder; if false, collapses it.

Description

Expands or collapses folder layers

Argument(s)

bExpand—*Boolean*—true will expand folder; false will collapse it.

bRecurseNestedParents—*Boolean*—If true, all subfolders will also be expanded/collapsed.

index—*integer*—The layer number to expand/collapse. If not specified, will expand/collapse current layer. If specified or current layer isn't a folder layer, the folder layer which that layer is within will be expanded/collapsed. If -1 is specified, and bRecurseNestedParents is true, all folders will be expanded/collapsed.

Returns
Nothing

Example
```
my_tl = fl.getDocumentDOM().getTimeline();
my_tl.expandFolder(false, true, 1);
```

findLayerIndex

`timeline.findLayerIndex( name )`

Returns array of indices for layers with specified name

Description
Finds the index or indices for layer(s) with the specified name. Most layer operations require an index. If you only know the name of the layer, you can get the index of the layer with that name through this method. It is possible to have more than one layer with the same name, so results are returned in an array. Each element of the array contains an index to a layer with the specified name.

Argument(s)
name—*string*—The name of the layer to locate

Returns
indexArray—*array*—An array of indices to layers

Example
```
// delete all layers named "temp":
my_tl = fl.getDocumentDOM().getTimeline();
indexArray = my_tl.findLayerIndex("temp");
for(i=0; i<indexArray.length; i++){
  my_tl.deleteLayer(indexArray[i]);
}
```

getFrameProperty

`timeline.getFrameProperty( property )`

Returns specified frame property

Description
Returns the specified property for the selected frame or frames. If multiple frames are selected, and the specified property doesn't contain the same value in each one, returns undefined. See the entry for Frame for a list of available properties.

Argument(s)
property—*string*—The name of the property you want to retrieve

Returns
Property value—*Type depends on the type of the property selected*

Example
```
my_tl = fl.getDocumentDOM().getTimeline();
myElements =
➥ my_tl.getFrameProperty("elements");
```

getLayerProperty

`timeline.getLayerProperty( property )`

Returns specified layer property

Description
Returns the specified property for the selected layer or layers. If multiple layers are selected, and the specified property doesn't contain the same value in each one, this method returns undefined. See the entry for layer for a list of available properties.

Argument(s)
property—*string*—The name of the property you want to retrieve

Returns
Property value—*Type depends on the type of the property selected*

Example
```
my_tl = fl.getDocumentDOM().getTimeline();
myFrames =
➥ my_tl.getLayerProperty("frames");
```

getSelectedFrames

`timeline.getSelectedFrames()`

Returns array containing indices of selected frames

Description
Returns an array with information about the selected frames. It is possible to select multiple frames and multiple layers, thus the return value is store in an array with a particular structure. The array will contain sets of three integers as shown here:

```
result = [indexLayer, startFrame, endFrame,
indexLayer, startFrame, endFrame, ...]
```

Each set of three elements has the following structure: The first element is an index to a layer with selected frames.,the next element the first selected frame in that layer, and finally the next nonselected frame.

Argument(s)
None

Returns
Array (see description)—*array*

Example
```
my_tl = fl.getDocumentDOM().getTimeline();
selFrames = my_tl.getSelectedFrames();
for(n=0; n<selFrames.length; n+=3){
  layerNum = selFrames[n];
  first = selFrames[n+1];
  last = selFrames[n+2]-1;
  fl.trace("In layer " + layerNum +
➥ ", frames "+ first + " through " +
➥ last + " are selected.");
}
```

getSelectedLayers

`timeline.getSelectedLayers()`

Returns array containing indices of selected layers

Description
Returns an array of the indexes of any selected layers

Argument(s)
None

Returns
`indexArray`—*array*

Example
```
my_tl = fl.getDocumentDOM().getTimeline();
selLayers = my_tl.getSelectedLayers();
fl.trace("There are " + selLayers.length +
➥ " layers selected.";
```

insertBlankKeyframe

`timeline.insertBlankKeyframe( [`*`frameNum`*`] )`

Inserts blank keyframe

Description
Inserts a blank keyframe at the specified location or the location of the playhead

Argument(s)
`frameNum`—*integer*—The frame number at which to insert the keyframe

Returns
Nothing

Example
```
my_tl.insertBlankKeyframe(3);
```

insertFrames

`timeline.insertFrames( [`*`numFrames`*`]`
`➥ [, `*`bAllLayers`*`] [, `*`frameNum`*`] )`

Inserts specified number of frames

Description
Inserts frames into the timeline. If `numFrames` and `frameNum` are specified, will insert that many frames at that point. If not specified, this method will insert number of frames based on frame selection and location based on the start of the frame selection, for each layer that has selected frames. If no frames are selected, it will insert one frame into all layers. The location will be the current frame.

Argument(s)
`numFrames`—*integer*—How many frames to insert.

`bAllLayers`—*Boolean*—If `true`, frames will be added to all layers. If `false`, only the selected or current layer will be added.

`frameNum`—*integer*—The insertion point for the new frames.

Returns
Nothing

Example
```
my_tl = fl.getDocumentDOM().getTimeline();
my_tl.insertFrames(100, true, 50);
```

insertKeyframe

`timeline.insertKeyframe( [`*`frameNum`*`] )`

Inserts keyframe

Description
Inserts a keyframe at the specified location or the location of the playhead

Argument(s)
frameNum—*integer*—The frame number at which to insert the keyframe

Returns
Nothing

Example
```
my_tl = fl.getDocumentDOM().getTimeline();
my_tl.insertKeyframe(3);
```

pasteFrames

```
timeline.pasteFrames( [startFrame]
➥ [, endFrame] )
```

Pastes frames from clipboard into range of frames

Description
Pastes previously cut or copied frames from the clipboard into the specified timeline. This method pastes frames starting at startFrame, up to but not including endFrame. If endFrame isn't specified, this method pastes starting at startFrame. If startFrame isn't specified, it pastes into currently selected frames.

Argument(s)
startFrame—*integer*—The first frame to paste into

endFrame—*integer*—The frame after the last frame to paste into

Returns
Nothing

Example
```
my_tl = fl.getDocumentDOM().getTimeline();
my_tl.pasteFrames(3, 5);
```

removeFrames

```
timeline.removeFrames( [startFrame]
➥ [, endFrame] )
```

Deletes frame or frames

Description
Removes a frame or frames. Removes frames starting with startFrame, up to but not including endFrame. If endFrame isn't specified, this methoc removes startFrame. If startFrame isn't specified, it removes currently selected frames. If no frames are selected, it removes one frame from all layers at the current playhead position.

Argument(s)
startFrame—*integer*—The first frame to remove

endFrame—*integer*—The frame after the last frame to remove

Returns
Nothing

Example
```
my_tl = fl.getDocumentDOM().getTimeline();
my_tl.removeFrames(3, 5);
```

reorderLayer

```
timeline.reorderLayer( layerToMove,
➥ layerToPutItBy [, bAddBefore] )
```

Moves specified layer

Description
Changes the position of the specified layer

Argument(s)
layerToMove—*integer*—The index of the layer you want to reposition.

layerToPutItBy—*integer*—The index of the layer to put it next to.

bAddBefore—*Boolean*—true will put layerToMove before layerToPutItBy; false will put it after.

Returns
Nothing

Example
```
// move layer 3 to position 0:
my_tl = fl.getDocumentDOM().getTimeline();
my_tl.reorderLayer(3, 1, true);
```

reverseFrames

```
timeline.reverseFrames( [startFrame]
➥ [, endFrame] )
```

Reverses range of frames

Description
Reverses the specified or selected range of frames. If a range isn't specified in the arguments, this method reverses the selected frames.

Argument(s)
`startFrame`—*integer*—The first frame to reverse

`endFrame`—*integer*—The frame after the last frame to reverse

Returns
Nothing

Example
```
my_tl = fl.getDocumentDOM().getTimeline();
my_tl.reverseFrames(3, 5);
```

selectAllFrames

```
timeline.selectAllFrames()
```

Selects all frames in current timeline

Description
Selects all the frames in the specified timeline

Argument(s)
None

Returns
Nothing

Example
```
my_tl = fl.getDocumentDOM().getTimeline();
my_tl.selectAllFrames();
```

setFrameProperty

```
timeline.setFrameProperty( property, value
➥ [, startFrame] [, endFrame] )
```

Sets specified frame property

Description
Sets the specified property for the specified or selected frame or frames. See the entry for `Frame` for a list of available properties, excluding `duration`, `elements`, and `startFrame`, which are read-only properties.

Argument(s)
`property`—*string*—The name of the property you want to set

`value`—*Type depends on type of property*—The value you want to set it to

`startFrame`—*integer*—The first frame of which to change the property

`endFrame`—*integer*—The frame after the last frame that will be changed

Returns
Nothing

Example
```
my_tl = fl.getDocumentDOM().getTimeline();
my_tl.setFrameProperty("name",
➥ "temp", 0, 1);
```

setLayerProperty

```
timeline.setLayerProperty( property,
➥ value [, layersToChange] )
```

Sets specified layer property

Description
Sets the specified property for the specified or selected layer or layers. See the entry for `layer` for a list of available properties, excluding `duration`, `elements`, and `startFrame`, which are read-only properties.

Argument(s)
`property`—*string*—The name of the property you want to set.

`value`—*Type depends on type of property*—The value you want to set it to.

`layersToChange`—*string*—Which layers to change. Valid values are `"selected"`, `"all"`, and `"others"`. Default is `"selected"`.

Returns
Nothing

Example

```
my_tl = fl.getDocumentDOM().getTimeline();
my_tl.setLayerProperty("name",
➥ "temp", "selected");
```

setSelectedFrames

```
timeline.setSelectedFrames( startFrame,
➥ endFrame [, bReplaceCurrentSelection] )
```

Selects specified frames in current layer

Description

Selects the specified frames in the current layer. Note that there are two setSelectedFrames() methods, which differ in the number and types of arguments used.

Argument(s)

startFrame—*integer*—The first frame to select.

endFrame—*integer*—The frame after the last frame to select.

bReplaceCurrentSelection—*Boolean*—true will replace current selection; false will add to selection.

Returns

Nothing

Example

```
my_tl =
➥ fl.getDocumentDOM().getTimeline();
my_tl.setSelectedFrames(1, 10, true);
```

setSelectedFrames

```
timeline.setSelectedFrames( selectionList
➥ [, bReplaceCurrentSelection] )
```

Selects frames specified in selection array

Description

Selects the specified frames in the current timeline. Note that there are two setSelectedFrames() methods, which differ in the number and types of arguments used.

Argument(s)

selectionList—*array*—An array of layer indices and start and end frames. See the entry for timeline.getSelectedFrames for more information on the structure of this array.

bReplaceCurrentSelection—*Boolean*—true will replace current selection; false will add to selection.

Returns

Nothing

Example

```
my_tl = fl.getDocumentDOM().getTimeline();
my_tl.setSelectedFrames
➥ ([0, 1, 10, 1, 11, 20], true);
```

setSelectedLayers

```
timeline.setSelectedLayers
➥ ( index [, bReplaceCurrentSelection] )
```

Selects specified layers and all frames in those layers

Description

Selects the specified layer, makes it the current layer, and selects all the frames in it. Although "layers" is plural in the function name, you may only select one layer at a time with this method.

Argument(s)

index—*integer*—The number of the layer to select.

bReplaceCurrentSelection—*Boolean*—true will replace current selection; false will add to selection.

Returns

Nothing

Example

```
my_tl = fl.getDocumentDOM().getTimeline();
my_tl.setSelectedLayers(1, true);
```

showLayerMasking

```
timeline.showLayerMasking( [layer] )
```

If true, displays layer masking

Description

Displays or turns off display of masking by locking the masked and mask layers

Argument(s)

layer—*integer*—The index to a masked or mask layer. If omitted, will use selected layer.

Returns

Nothing

Example

```
my_tl = fl.getDocumentDOM().getTimeline();
my_tl.showLayerMasking(3);
```

Properties of the timeline Object

currentFrame

`timeline.currentFrame`

Frame index for location of playhead

Description

The number of the current frame, i.e., the location of the playhead. You can find the location of the playhead by reading this value, or move the playhead by setting this value.

Value(s)

integer—The frame number. Note that that this is merely an integer—an index to an element in the `frames` array, not a reference to the `frame` object.

Example

```
my_tl = fl.getDocumentDOM().getTimeline();
my_tl.currentFrame = 99;
```

currentLayer

`timeline.currentLayer`

Currently active layer

Description

The number of the current layer. You can find the current layer by reading this value, or cause a layer to be the `currentLayer` by setting this value.

Value(s)

integer—The layer number. Note that that this is merely an integer—an index to an element in the `layers` array, not a reference to the `layer` object.

Example

```
my_tl = fl.getDocumentDOM().getTimeline();
my_tl.currentLayer = 4;
```

frameCount

`timeline.frameCount`

Number of frames in longest layer in specified timeline

Description

The number of frames in the longest layer in the specified timeline

Value(s)

integer—The number of frames

Example

```
my_tl = fl.getDocumentDOM().getTimeline();
fl.trace("There are " + my_tl.frameCount +
➥ " frames in this timeline.");
```

layerCount

`timeline.layerCount`

Number of layers in specified timeline

Description

The number of layers in the specified timeline

Value(s)

integer—The number of layers

Example

```
my_tl = fl.getDocumentDOM().getTimeline();
fl.trace("There are " + my_tl.layerCount +
➥ " layers in this timeline.");
```

layers

`timeline.layers`

Array of layer objects

Description

An array of all the layers in the specified timeline

Value(s)

array—Each element contains a layer object.

Example

```
my_tl = fl.getDocumentDOM().getTimeline();
my_tl.layers[3].name = "temp";
```

name

`timeline.name`

Name of timeline; same as scene name.

Description
The name of the timeline. Will be seen as the name of the corresponding scene in the authoring environment.

Value(s)
string—The name of the timeline

Example
```
my_tl = fl.getDocumentDOM().getTimeline();
my_tl.name = "Dorothy";
```

Tool Functions

Flash JavaScript functions:

- activate
- configureTool
- deactivate
- keyDown
- keyUp
- mouseDoubleClick
- mouseDown
- mouseMove
- mouseUp
- notifySettingsChanged
- setCursor

Note: These functions aren't specifically part of the JSAPI Document Object Model, and aren't methods of any object. These are actually event handlers used in the JSFL script used to create custom tools. A tool JSFL file merely defines these functions, and they are called automatically in response to various events occurring in the authoring environment. See Chapter 3 for a full discussion on how to create custom tools.

activate

`Function activate()`

Called when tool becomes active

Description
The function called when a tool is selected on the toolbar and thus becomes the active tool. Used to prepare a tool for use, often by gathering parameters set in the Options dialog box of the Property Inspector. These are available as properties of the activeTool object.

Example
```
function activate(){
  the_toolObj = fl.tools.activeTool;
  width = the_toolObj.width;
}
```

configureTool

`Function configureTool()`

Called when tool is loaded at launch

Description
The function called when Flash is starting up and setting up the toolbar. Flash will read the contents of every JSFL file in the Tools directory, execute any stray code not contained in functions, and then execute the configureTool function if it exists. Used to initialize a tool, usually by specifying the tool's name, tooltip, icon, etc.

Example
```
function configureTool() {
  theTool = fl.tools.activeTool;
  theTool.setToolName("Cube 3D Tool");
  theTool.setIcon("Cube3D.png");
  theTool.setMenuString("Cube 3D Tool");
  theTool.setToolTip("Cube 3D Tool");
  theTool.setOptionsFile( "Cube3D.xml" );
}
```

deactivate

`Function deactivate()`

Called when tool becomes inactive

Description
The function called when a tool becomes inactive, usually by the user selecting another tool. Not usually necessary but exists if any cleanup is needed.

Example
```
function deactivate(){
  fl.trace("Good bye!");
}
```

keyDown

Function keyDown()

When tool is active, called if key is pressed

Description
The function called when a key is pressed while the tool is active. Can be used in conjunction with tools .getKeyDown() to find out the last key that was pressed.

Example
```
function keyDown(){
  fl.trace(fl.tools.getKeyDown());
}
```

keyUp

Function keyUp()

When tool is active, called if key is released

Description
The function called when a key is released while the tool is active. Can be used in conjunction with tools .getKeyDown() to find out the last key that was pressed.

Example
```
function keyUp(){
  fl.trace(fl.tools.getKeyUp());
}
```

mouseDoubleClick

Function mouseDoubleClick()

When tool is active, called if mouse button is double-clicked

Description
The function called when the mouse is double-clicked while the tool is active

Example
```
function mouseDoubleClick(){
  my_doc.selectAll();
}
```

mouseDown

Function mouseDown(*pt*)

When tool is active, called when mouse button is pressed

Description
The function called when the mouse button is pressed while the tool is active. Usually used to initialize a drawing mode.

Example
```
function mouseDown(){
  my_drawL.beginDraw();
  penDownPoint = fl.tools.penDownLoc;
}
```

mouseMove

Function mouseMove(*pt*)

When tool is active, called if mouse moves over stage

Description
The function called when the mouse is moved over the stage while the tool is active. Usually used to perform drawing actions on the drawing layer, if the mouse button is down.

Argument(s)
pt—*point object*—Contains x and y properties indicating the position of the mouse. This data can also be retrieved from fl.tools.penLoc.

Example
```
function mouseMove(pt){
  if(fl.tools.mouseIsDown){
    my_drawL.beginFrame();
    // drawing actions
    my_drawL.endFrame();
  }
}
```

mouseUp

Function mouseUp()

When tool is active, called if mouse button is released onstage

Description
The function called when the mouse button is released while the tool is active. Usually used to end drawing actions on the drawing layer and draw something permanent on the stage.

Example
```
function mouseUp(){
  my_drawL.endDraw();
  // draw to stage
}
```

notifySettingsChanged

Function notifySettingsChanged()

Notifies tool if user changes options in PI

Description
The function called when the user clicks OK in the Options dialog box of the Property Inspector, after changing the tool settings. Usually the actions here consist of gathering the properties that were set in the dialog box. These will be available as properties of the activeTool object. Often this function can be identical to the activate function.

Example
```
function notifySettingsChanged(){
  the_toolObj = fl.tools.activeTool;
  width = the_toolObj.width;
}
```

setCursor

Function setCursor()

Allows tool to set custom cursors

Description
The function called whenever Flash gives control back to the script to determine which cursor to use. Note, this is different from `fl.tools.setCursor()`, which is used to actually set the cursor. This function is called many times during the course of a tool being used. Flash or the operating system take control of the cursor to change it to a particular shape at various times (such as an hour glass when the system is busy, or an arrow when the cursor is positioned over menu items, etc.). When Flash and the OS aren't controlling the cursor shape, this function is called to allow you to change the cursor to the shape you want. See the entry for `fl.tools.setCursor()` for information on how to change the cursor.

Example
```
function setCursor(){
  fl.tools.setCursor(1);
}
```

ToolObj

Represents an individual tool

Methods:

- enablePIControl
- setIcon
- setMenuString
- setOptionsFile
- setPI
- setToolName
- setToolTip
- showPIControl
- showTransformHandles

Properties:

- depth
- iconID
- position

Methods of the toolObj Object

enablePIControl

toolObj.enablePIControl(*control*,
➥ *enable*)

Enables or disables control in PI

Description
Enables or disables a particular control in the Property Inspector while the tool is active

Argument(s)
control—*string*—The name of the control to enable/disable. Values depend on the mode the Property Inspector is currently in, as follows:

Shape mode: "stroke", "fill"

Text mode: "type", "font", "pointsize", "color", "bold", "italic", "direction", "alignLeft", "alignCenter", "alignRight", "alignJustify", "spacing", "position", "autoKern", "small", "rotation", "format", "lineType", "selectable", "html", "border", "deviceFonts", "varEdit", "options", "link", "maxChars", or "target"

Movie mode: "size", "publish", "background", "framerate", "player", or "profile"

enable—*Boolean*—true will enable the control; false will disable it.

Returns
Nothing

Example
```
my_toolObj.enablePIControl("stroke",
➥ false);
```

setIcon

`toolObj.setIcon( file )`

Specifies PNG file to use as tool icon

Description
Specifies which image will be used in the toolbar to represent the tool. The icon file should be a 16-by-15 pixel PNG file.

Argument(s)
file—*URI string*—Valid URI path to a PNG file

Returns
Nothing

Example
```
my_toolObj.setIcon(fl.configURI +
➥ "/Tools/myTool.png");
```

setMenuString

`toolObj.setMenuString( menuStr )`

Sets string for pop-up menu of tool

Description
Sets the string that will appear in the pop-up menu of the toolbar for this tool

Argument(s)
menuStr—*string*—The text that describes the tool

Returns
Nothing

Example
```
my_toolObj.setMenuString("Cool Tool");
```

setOptionsFile

`toolObj.setOptionsFile( xmlFIle )`

Sets options file for tool

Description
Sets the file to be used to create the Options panel for the tool

Argument(s)
xmlFile—*URI string*—Valid URI to an XML file describing the properties of the tool. See Chapter 3 for more details on how to structure this file.

Returns
Nothing

Example
```
my_toolObj.setOptionsFile(fl.configURI +
➥ "/Tools/myOptions.xml");
```

setPI

`toolObj.setPI( pi )`

Sets which PI to use with tool

Description
Puts the Property Inspector into the specified mode. If this method isn't called, the Property Inspector will be in shape mode.

Argument(s)
pi—*string*—Valid values are "shape", "text", and "movie".

Returns
Nothing

Example
```
my_toolObj.setPI("text");
```

setToolName

`toolObj.setToolName( name )`

Sets name of tool

Description
The name of the tool. This isn't displayed anywhere and is only used to configure the tool.

Argument(s)
name—*string*—The tool's name

Returns
Nothing

Example
```
my_toolObj.setToolName("coolTool");
```

setToolTip

`toolObj.setToolTip( toolTip )`

Sets tooltip for tool

Description
Sets the tool tip shown when the mouse is held over the tool icon in the toolbar.

Argument(s)
toolTip—*string*—Text to be displayed in tool tip. Generally this would be the same as the tool menu name.

Returns
Nothing

Example
```
my_toolObj.setToolTip("Cool Tool");
```

showPIControl

`toolObj.showPIControl( control, show )`

Shows or hides specified control in PI

Description
Shows or hides a particular control in the Property Inspector while the tool is active

Argument(s)
control—*string*—The name of the control to show/hide. Values depend on the mode the Property Inspector is currently in, as follows:

Shape mode: "stroke", "fill"

Text mode: "type", "font", "pointsize", "color", "bold", "italic", "direction", "alignLeft", "alignCenter", "alignRight", "alignJustify", "spacing", "position", "autoKern", "small", "rotation", "format", "lineType", "selectable", "html", "border", "deviceFonts", "varEdit", "options", "link", "maxChars", or "target"

Movie mode: "size", "publish", "background", "framerate", "player", or "profile"

enable—*Boolean*—true will show the control; false will hide it.

Returns
Nothing

Example
```
my_toolObj.showPIControl("fill", false);
```

showTransformHandles

`toolObj.showTransformHandles( show )`

If true, free transform handles are displayed when tool is active.

Description
Enables display of transform handles on the selection while the tool is active.

Argument(s)
show—*Boolean*—If true, handles will be displayed. If false, they will not.

Returns
Nothing

Example
```
my_toolObj.showTransformHandles(true);
```

Properties of the toolObj Object

depth

`toolObj.depth`

Location of tool in pop-up menu

Description
The depth of the tool in the pop-up menu. Several tools can occupy one slot in the menu bar and will appear in a pop-up menu. This property specifies which position the tool is in.

Value(s)
integer—The position in the pop-up menu

Example
```
fl.trace(my_toolObj.depth);
```

iconID

`toolObj.iconID`

Resource ID of tool

Description
An identifier for the icon of the tool

Value(s)
integer—The resource ID for the tool's icon

Example
```
fl.trace(my_toolObj.iconID);
```

position

`toolObj.position`

Location of tool in toolbar

Description
The slot of the toolbar where this tool is located.

Value(s)
integer—A number representing one of the possible positions in the toolbar

Example
```
fl.trace(my_toolObj.position);
```

Tools

Records input from keyboard and mouse

Methods:

- `constrainPoint`
- `getKeyDown`
- `setCursor`
- `snapPoint`

Properties:

- `activeTool`
- `altIsDown`
- `ctlIsDown`
- `mouseIsDown`
- `penDownLoc`
- `penLoc`
- `shiftIsDown`
- `toolObjs`

Methods of the tools Object

constrainPoint

`tools.constrainPoint(` *`startPoint,`*
➥ *`endPoint`*`)`

Allows tool's movements to be constrained

Description
If the *SHIFT* key is being held down, this method returns a point closest to the end point, but in line with the start point, either horizontally, vertically, or on a 45-degree angle. If the *SHIFT* key isn't down, it returns the end point. This method is usually used with `fl.tools.penDownLoc` and `fl.tools.penLoc` to draw straight lines or maintain the aspect ration (for drawing a perfect square or circle).

Argument(s)
`startPoint`—*point object*—An object containing x and y properties. The point to constrain endPoint to.

endPoint—*point object*—An object containing x and y properties. The point that will be constrained.

Returns
constrainedPoint, a point close to endPoint but in line with startPoint—*point object*

Example
```
pointA = fl.tools.penDownLoc;
pointB = fl.tools.penLoc;
pointB =
➥ fl.tools.constrainPoint(pointA, pointB);
```

getKeyDown

`tools.getKeyDown()`

Returns last key pressed

Description
Returns the value of the last key pressed

Argument(s)
None

Returns
keyValue—*integer*

Example
```
fl.trace(fl.tools.getKeyDown());
```

setCursor

`tools.setCursor( cursor )`

Sets which cursor tool uses

Description
Sets the current cursor to one of the predefined cursor shapes. Usually used within the setCursor Tool event handler to change the cursor when Flash and the operating system hand cursor control back to the script.

Argument(s)
cursor—*integer*—Value from 0 to 7 as follows:

0 = plus cursor

1 = black arrow

2 = white arrow

3 = 4-way arrow

4 = 2-way horizontal arrow

5 = 2-way vertical arrow

6 = X cursor

7 = hand cursor

Returns
Nothing

Example
```
my_toolObj.setCursor(3);
```

snapPoint

`tools.snapPoint( point )`

If snap setting is on, returns point that snaps

Description
If Snap to Grid is enabled, this method snaps the specified point to the nearest point on the grid. It does this by taking a point as an argument and returning the closest grid point to that given point.

Argument(s)
point—*point object*—A point that you want to snap. Usually this is fl.tools.penLoc or fl.tools.penDownLoc.

Returns
snappedPoint, the point on the grid—*point object*

Example
```
pointA =
➥ fl.tools.snapPoint(fl.tools.penDownLoc);
```

Properties of the tools Object

activeTool

`tools.activeTool`

Returns toolObj object for currently active tool

Description
Contains a reference to the currently active tool object

Value(s)
object—The reference to a tool object

Example

```
my_tool = fl.tools.activeTool;
```

altIsDown

`tools.altIsDown`

If true, ALT key is pressed.

Description

Tests whether or not the ALT key is pressed.

Value(s)

Boolean—true means ALT is pressed; false means it is not.

Example

```
if(fl.tools.altIsDown){
  // do something alternative
}
```

ctlIsDown

`tools.ctlIsDown`

If true, CTRL key is down.

Description

Tests whether or not the CTRL key is pressed

Value(s)

Boolean—true means CTRL is pressed; false means it is not.

Example

```
if(fl.tools.ctlIsDown){
  // control something
}
```

mouseIsDown

`tools.mouseIsDown`

If true, left mouse button is pressed.

Description

Tests whether or not the left mouse button is being pressed. This method is usually used within the mouseMove Tools event handler to control whether something should be drawn or not.

Value(s)

Boolean—true means the button is being pressed; false means it is not.

Example

```
function mouseMove(){
  if(fl.tools.mouseIsDown){
    // draw something
  }
}
```

penDownLoc

`tools.penDownLoc`

Position of last mouse down event

Description

The point where the mouse button was last pressed. Note that this is in local coordinates, which could be different inside a symbol than on the main stage, particularly if that symbol has been scaled, rotated, or moved. If you are going to used these coordinates with drawing layer drawing functions or document drawing functions (which use global or stage coordinates), you will have to transform between local and global coordinates. See Chapter 3 for several examples.

Value(s)

point object—An object containing an x and y property

Example

```
startPoint = fl.tools.penDownLoc;
```

penLoc

`tools.penLoc`

Current location of mouse

Description

The current point of the mouse cursor. Note that this is in local coordinates, which could be different inside a symbol than on the main stage, particularly if that symbol has been scaled, rotated, or moved. If you are going to used these coordinates with drawing layer drawing functions or document drawing functions (which use global or stage coordinates) you will have to transform between local and global coordinates. See Chapter 3 for examples.

Value(s)
point object—An object containing an x and y property

Example
```
startPoint = fl.tools.penLoc;
```

shiftIsDown

`tools.shiftIsDown`

If true, *SHIFT* key is pressed.

Description
Tests whether or not the *SHIFT* key is pressed.

Value(s)
Boolean—true means *SHIFT* is pressed; false means it is not.

Example
```
if(fl.tools.shiftIsDown){
  // do something shifty
}
```

toolObjs

`tools.toolObjs`

Array of toolObj objects

Description
An array holding all the currently configured tool objects

Value(s)
array—Each element holds a reference to a tool object.

Example
```
fl.trace("there are " +
➥ fl.tools.toolObjs.length + " tools");
```

Vertex

Contains the coordinate data of a shape

Methods:

- getHalfEdge
- setLocation

Properties:

- x
- y

Methods of the vertex Object

getHalfEdge

`vertex.getHalfEdge()`

Returns halfEdge that shares vertex

Description
Returns a reference to a halfEdge object that shares this vertex. Multiple calls to this method will return different halfEdges.

Argument(s)
None

Returns
halfEdge—*object*

Example
```
// places shape's vertices at exact pixels
var my_doc = fl.getDocumentDOM();
var my_tl = my_doc.getTimeline();
var my_layer = my_tl.layers[0];
var my_frame = my_layer.frames[0];
var my_elem = my_frame.elements[0];
var my_vertex = my_elem.vertices[0];
fl.trace(my_vertex.getHalfEdge().id);
```

setLocation

`vertex.setLocation( x, y )`

Sets location of vertex

Description
Sets the pixel coordinate position of a shape's vertex

Argument(s)
x—*float*—The x pixel position of vertex

y—*float*—The y pixel position of vertex

Returns
Nothing

Example

```
// places shape's vertices at exact pixels
var my_doc = fl.getDocumentDOM();
var my_tl = my_doc.getTimeline();
var my_layer = my_tl.layers[0];
var my_frame = my_layer.frames[0];
var my_elem = my_frame.elements[0];
var vL = my_elem.vertices.length;
my_elem.beginEdit();
for (var i = 0; i < vL; i++) {
  var x =
➥ Math.round(my_elem.vertices[i].x);
  var y =
➥ Math.round(my_elem.vertices[i].y);
  my_elem.vertices[i].setLocation(x, y);
}
my_elem.endEdit();
```

Properties of the vertex Object

x

vertex.x

x location of vertex

Description

The x pixel location of a shape's vertex on the stage. This value may be retrieved, but not set. To set a vertex position, use the vertex method `setLocation()`.

Value(s)

float—Pixel position

Example

```
// places shape's vertices at exact pixels
var my_doc = fl.getDocumentDOM();
var my_tl = my_doc.getTimeline();
var my_layer = my_tl.layers[0];
var my_frame = my_layer.frames[0];
var my_elem = my_frame.elements[0];
var vL = my_elem.vertices.length;
my_elem.beginEdit();
for (var i = 0; i < vL; i++) {
  var x =
  ➥ Math.round(my_elem.vertices[i].x);
  var y =
  ➥ Math.round(my_elem.vertices[i].y);
  my_elem.vertices[i].setLocation(x, y);
}
my_elem.endEdit();
```

y

vertex.y

y location of vertex

Description

The y pixel location of a shape's vertex on the stage. This value may be retrieved, but not set. To set a vertex position, use the vertex method `setLocation()`.

Value(s)

float—Pixel position

Example

```
// places shape's vertices at exact pixels
var my_doc = fl.getDocumentDOM();
var my_tl = my_doc.getTimeline();
var my_layer = my_tl.layers[0];
var my_frame = my_layer.frames[0];
var my_elem = my_frame.elements[0];
var vL = my_elem.vertices.length;
my_elem.beginEdit();
for (var i = 0; i < vL; i++) {
  var x =
  ➥ Math.round(my_elem.vertices[i].x);
  var y =
  ➥ Math.round(my_elem.vertices[i].y);
  my_elem.vertices[i].setLocation(x, y);
}
my_elem.endEdit();
```

VideoItem

Subclass of `Item`; a video in the Library

Refer to the entry for `Item` for properties or methods.

XMLUI

A reference to the current XML to UI dialog box

Methods:

- accept
- cancel
- get
- set

Methods of the xmlui Object

accept

`xmlui.accept()`

Exits XML toUI dialog box with accept state

Description

This method will dismiss the current XML to UI dialog box and return to where the dialog box was instantiated with an "accept" value, just as if the user had clicked the OK button within the dialog box itself. This method can be useful when additional functionality is required in the dialog box on the accept process. A developer can use a standard XML to UI button control that will call a number of JSFL commands, and then finish its sequence with this method, exiting the dialog box.

Argument(s)

None

Returns

true if dialog box exists—*Boolean*

Example

```
// on button in XML to UI file
<button id="accept_bn" label="OK"
➥ oncommand="fl.runScript(fl.configURI +
➥ 'Behaviors/script.jsfl');" />
// in script.jsfl
fl.trace("running outside script");
fl.xmlui.accept();
```

cancel

`xmlui.cancel()`

Exits XML to UI dialog box with cancel state

Description

This method will dismiss the current XML to UI dialog box and return to where the dialog box was instantiated with a "cancel" value, just as if the user had clicked the cancel button within the dialog box itself.

Argument(s)

None

Returns

true if dialog box exists—*Boolean*

Example

```
// on cancel button in XML to UI
// SWF interface
cancelListener = {};
cancelListener.click() {
MMExecute("fl.xmlui.cancel();");
}
cancel_bn.addEventListener("click",
➥ cancelListener);
```

get

`xmlui.get( name )`

Returns specified property's value in XML to UI dialog box

Description

Retrieves the named property or control value from the current XML to UI dialog box. This works for all standard controls excluding the target list, which doesn't allow its value to be set or retrieved. Once the dialog box is dismissed using accept, cancel, or the *ESC* key, values within the box aren't retrievable; therefore this method is only useful while a dialog box is open.

Argument(s)

Name of control—*string*—Determined by the id attribute for a control or property node within the XML to UI file

Returns

Value of control—*Varies depending on control*

Example

```
// in XML to UI SWF interface
var webpageURL =
➥ MMExecute("fl.xmlui.get('webpageURL');");
```

set

`xmlui.set( name , value )`

Sets specified property's value in XML to UI dialog box

Description

Retrieves the named property or control value from the current XML to UI dialog box. This works for all standard controls excluding the target list, which doesn't allow its value to be set or retrieved. Once the dialog box is dismissed using accept, cancel, or the ESCAPE button, values within the box aren't retrievable; therefore this method is only useful while a dialog box is open.

Argument(s)

Name of control—*string*—Determined by the `id` attribute for a control or property node within the XML to UI file

Value for control—*Varies depending on control*—The value to be given to control or property

Returns

`true` if control or property existed and was successfully set—*Boolean*

Example

```
// in XML to UI SWF interface
MMExecute("fl.xmlui.set('webpageURL',
➥ 'http://www.flashextensibility.com');");
```

INDEX

Symbols

A

B

C

K

L

M

N

O

P

forums.apress.com

FOR PROFESSIONALS BY PROFESSIONALS™

JOIN THE APRESS FORUMS AND BE PART OF OUR COMMUNITY. You'll find discussions that cover topics of interest to IT professionals, programmers, and enthusiasts just like you. If you post a query to one of our forums, you can expect that some of the best minds in the business—especially Apress authors, who all write with *The Expert's Voice*™—will chime in to help you. Why not aim to become one of our most valuable participants (MVPs) and win cool stuff? Here's a sampling of what you'll find:

DATABASES

Data drives everything.

Share information, exchange ideas, and discuss any database programming or administration issues.

INTERNET TECHNOLOGIES AND NETWORKING

Try living without plumbing (and eventually IPv6).

Talk about networking topics including protocols, design, administration, wireless, wired, storage, backup, certifications, trends, and new technologies.

JAVA

We've come a long way from the old Oak tree.

Hang out and discuss Java in whatever flavor you choose: J2SE, J2EE, J2ME, Jakarta, and so on.

MAC OS X

All about the Zen of OS X.

OS X is both the present and the future for Mac apps. Make suggestions, offer up ideas, or boast about your new hardware.

OPEN SOURCE

Source code is good; understanding (open) source is better.

Discuss open source technologies and related topics such as PHP, MySQL, Linux, Perl, Apache, Python, and more.

PROGRAMMING/BUSINESS

Unfortunately, it is.

Talk about the Apress line of books that cover software methodology, best practices, and how programmers interact with the "suits."

WEB DEVELOPMENT/DESIGN

Ugly doesn't cut it anymore, and CGI is absurd.

Help is in sight for your site. Find design solutions for your projects and get ideas for building an interactive Web site.

SECURITY

Lots of bad guys out there—the good guys need help.

Discuss computer and network security issues here. Just don't let anyone else know the answers!

TECHNOLOGY IN ACTION

Cool things. Fun things.

It's after hours. It's time to play. Whether you're into LEGO® MINDSTORMS™ or turning an old PC into a DVR, this is where technology turns into fun.

WINDOWS

No defenestration here.

Ask questions about all aspects of Windows programming, get help on Microsoft technologies covered in Apress books, or provide feedback on any Apress Windows book.

HOW TO PARTICIPATE:

Go to the Apress Forums site at **http://forums.apress.com/**.

Click the New User link.